Lecture Notes in Computer Science 8805

Commenced Publication in 1973
Founding and Former Series Editors:
Gerhard Goos, Juris Hartmanis, and Jan van Leeuwen

T0233814

Luís Lopes et al. (Eds.)

Euro-Par 2014: Parallel Processing Workshops

Euro-Par 2014 International Workshops
Porto, Portugal, August 25-26, 2014
Revised Selected Papers, Part I

 Springer

Volume Editor

Luís Lopes
University of Porto
CRACS/INESC-TEC and FCUP
Rua do Campo Alegre, 1021, 4169-007 Porto, Portugal
E-mail: lblopes@dcc.fc.up.pt

Workshop Editors *see next page*

ISSN 0302-9743   e-ISSN 1611-3349
ISBN 978-3-319-14324-8   e-ISBN 978-3-319-14325-5
DOI 10.1007/978-3-319-14325-5
Springer Cham Heidelberg New York Dordrecht London

Library of Congress Control Number: 2014957415

LNCS Sublibrary: SL 1 – Theoretical Computer Science and General Issues

Typesetting: Camera-ready by author, data conversion by Scientific Publishing Services, Chennai, India

Printed on acid-free paper

Springer is part of Springer Science+Business Media (www.springer.com)

Workshop Editors

APCI&E
Julius Žilinskas
Vilnius University, Lithuania
julius.zilinskas@mii.vu.lt

BigDataCloud
Alexandru Costan
Inria Rennes, France
alexandru.costan@inria.fr

DIHC
Roberto G. Cascella
Inria Rennes, France
roberto.cascella@inria.fr

FedICI
Gabor Kecskemeti
MTA SZTAKI, Budapest, Hungary
kecskemeti.gabor@sztaki.mta.hu

HeteroPar
Emmanuel Jeannot
Inria Bordeaux Sud-Ouest, France
emmanuel.jeannot@inria.fr

HiBB
Mario Cannataro
University Magna, Catanzaro, Italy
cannataro@unicz.it

LSDVE
Laura Ricci
University of Pisa, Italy
ricci@di.unipi.it

MuCoCoS
Siegfried Benkner
University of Vienna, Austria
siegfried.benkner@univie.ac.at

OHMI
Salvador Petit
University of Valencia, Spain
spetit@disca.upv.es

PADABS
Vittorio Scarano
University of Salerno, Italy
vitsca@dia.unisa.it

PROPER
José Gracia
High Performance Computing Center
Stuttgart (HLRS), Germany
gracia@hlrs.de

REPPAR
Sascha Hunold
Vienna University of Technology,
Austria
hunold@par.tuwien.ac.at

Resilience
Stephen L. Scott
Tennessee Tech University, Cookeville,
USA
sscott@tntech.edu

ROME
Stefan Lankes
RWTH Aachen, Germany
SLankes@eonerc.rwth-aachen.de

SPPEXA
Christian Lengauer
University of Passau, Germany
lengauer@fim.uni-passau.de

TASUS
Jesus Carretero
University Carlos III of Madrid, Spain
jesus.carretero@uc3m.es

UCHPC
Jens Breitbart
Technical University Munich, Germany
j.breitbart@tum.de

VHPC
Michael Alexander
Vienna University of Technology,
Austria
michael.alexander@tuwien.ac.at

Preface

Euro-Par is an annual series of international conferences dedicated to the promotion and advancement of all aspects of parallel and distributed computing. Euro-Par 2014, held in Porto, Portugal, was the 20th edition of the series. The conference covers a wide spectrum of topics from algorithms and theory to software technology and hardware-related issues, with application areas ranging from scientific to mobile and cloud computing. Euro-Par conferences host a set of technical workshops, with the goal of providing a space for communities within the field to meet and discuss more focused research topics. The coordination of the workshops was in the hands of Workshop Chairs Luc Bougé, also with the Euro-Par Steering Committee, and Luís Lopes, with the local organization. In the coordination process, we were kindly assisted by Dieter an Mey, one of the workshop chairs for the Euro-Par 2013 event at Aachen, to whom we wish to express our warm thanks for his availability, expertise, and advice. In early January 2014, a call for workshop proposals was issued, and the proposals were reviewed by the co-chairs, with 18 workshops being selected for the 2-day program:

APCI&E – First Workshop on Applications of Parallel Computation in Industry and Engineering

BigDataCloud – Third Workshop on Big Data Management in Clouds

DIHC – Second Workshop on Dependability and Interoperability in Heterogeneous Clouds

FedICI – Second Workshop on Federative and Interoperable Cloud Infrastructures

HeteroPar – 12th International Workshop on Algorithms, Models and Tools for Parallel Computing on Heterogeneous Platforms

HiBB – 5th Workshop on High-Performance Bioinformatics and Biomedicine

LSDVE – Second Workshop on Large-Scale Distributed Virtual Environments on Clouds and P2P

MuCoCoS – 7th International Workshop on Multi-/Many-Core Computing Systems

OMHI – Third Workshop on On-chip Memory Hierarchies and Interconnects: Organization, Management and Implementation

PADABS – Second Workshop on Parallel and Distributed Agent-Based Simulations

PROPER – 7th Workshop on Productivity and Performance – Tools for HPC Application Development

Resilience – 7th Workshop on Resiliency in High-Performance Computing with Clouds, Grids, and Clusters

REPPAR – First International Workshop on Reproducibility in Parallel Computing

ROME – Second Workshop on Runtime and Operating Systems for the Many-Core Era

SPPEXA – Workshop on Software for Exascale Computing - Project Workshop
TASUS – First Workshop on Techniques and Applications for Sustainable
    Ultrascale Computing Systems
UCHPC – 7th Workshop on UnConventional High-Performance Computing
VHPC – 9th Workshop on Virtualization in High-Performance Cloud
    Computing

Furthermore, collocated with this intensive workshop program, two tutorials
were also included:

Heterogeneous Memory Models – Benedict R. Gaster (Qualcomm, Inc.)
High-Performance Parallel Graph Analytics – Keshav Pingali
    (UT Austin) and Manoj Kumar (IBM)

Paper submission deadlines, notification dates, and camera-ready submission
deadlines were synchronized between all workshops. The new workshop coordination procedures, established with the 2012 edition, turned out to be very
helpful for putting together a high-quality workshop program. After the conference, the workshop organizers delivered a workshop management report on the
key performance indicators to the Workshop Advisory Board and the Steering
Committee. These reports will help to improve the procedures for, and the quality of, the workshop program of future Euro-Par conferences. Special thanks are
due to the authors of all the submitted papers, the members of the Program
Committees, the reviewers, and the workshop organizers. We had 173 paper
submissions, with 100 papers being accepted for publication in the proceedings.
Given the high number of papers, the workshops proceedings were divided into
two volumes with the following distribution:

LNCS 8805 – APCI&E, BigDataCloud, HeteroPar, HiBB, LSDVE, PADABS,
    REPPAR, Resilience
LNCS 8806 – DIHC, FedICI, MuCoCoS, OMHI, PROPER, ROME, TASUS,
    UCHPC, VHPC, SPPEXA

We are grateful to the Euro-Par general chairs and the members of the Euro-
Par Steering Committee for their support and advice regarding the coordination
of workshops. We would like to thank Springer for its continuous support in
publishing the workshop proceedings.

It was a great pleasure and honor to organize and host the Euro-Par 2014
workshops in Porto. We hope all the participants enjoyed the workshop program
and benefited from the ample opportunities for fruitful exchange of ideas.

October 2014   Luís Lopes

Organization

Euro-Par Steering Committee

Chair

Christian Lengauer   University of Passau, Germany

Vice-Chair

Luc Bougé   ENS Rennes, France

European Representatives

Marco Danelutto	University of Pisa, Italy
Emmanuel Jeannot	LaBRI-Inria, Bordeaux, France
Christos Kaklamanis	Computer Technology Institute, Greece
Paul Kelly	Imperial College, UK
Thomas Ludwig	University of Hamburg, Germany
Emilio Luque	Autonomous University of Barcelona, Spain
Tomàs Margalef	Autonomous University of Barcelona, Spain
Wolfgang Nagel	Dresden University of Technology, Germany
Rizos Sakellariou	University of Manchester, UK
Henk Sips	Delft University of Technology, The Netherlands
Domenico Talia	University of Calabria, Italy
Felix Wolf	GRS and RWTH Aachen University, Germany

Honorary Members

Ron Perrott	Oxford e-Research Centre, UK
Karl Dieter Reinartz	University of Erlangen-Nuremberg, Germany

Observers

Fernando Silva	University of Porto, Portugal
Jesper Larsson Träff	Vienna University of Technology, Austria

Euro-Par 2014 Organization

Conference Co-chairs

Fernando Silva	University of Porto, Portugal
Inês Dutra	University of Porto, Portugal
Vítor Santos Costa	University of Porto, Portugal

Local Organizing Committee

Luís Lopes	University of Porto, Portugal
Pedro Ribeiro	University of Porto, Portugal

Workshop Co-chairs

Luc Bougé	ENS Rennes, France
Luís Lopes	University of Porto, Portugal

Workshop Introduction and Organization

First Workshop on Applications of Parallel Computation in Industry and Engineering (APCI&E 2014)

Workshop Description

The APCI&E minisymposium/workshop series started in 2008 at the Workshop on State of the Art in Scientific and Parallel Computing (PARA) and continued at the International Conference on Parallel Processing and Applied Mathematics (PPAM). Since PARA was held on even years and PPAM on odd years, the APCI&E minisymposium alternated between these two conference series on parallel computing. The minisymposium was held at PARA 2008 in Trondheim (Norway), PPAM 2009 in Wroclaw (Poland), PPAM 2011 in Torun (Poland), PARA 2012 in Helsinki (Finland), and PPAM 2013 in Warsaw (Poland). This year the minisymposium was renamed as workshop and was held at the International European Conference on Parallel Processing (Euro-Par).

The Workshop APCI&E provided a forum for researchers and practitioners using parallel computations for the solution of complex industrial and engineering applied problems. Topics discussed included application of parallel numerical methods to engineering and industrial problems, scientific computation, parallel algorithms for the solution of systems of PDEs, parallel algorithms for optimization, solution of data and computation-intensive real-world problems, and others.

Organizers

Raimondas Čiegis	Vilnius Gediminas Technical University, Lithuania
Julius Žilinskas	Vilnius University, Lithuania

Program Committee

Jesus Carretero	Carlos III University of Madrid, Spain
Raimondas Čiegis	Vilnius Gediminas Technical University, Lithuania
Francisco Gaspar	University of Zaragoza, Spain
Jacek Gondzio	University of Edinburgh, UK
Mario Guarracino	CNR, Italy
Pilar Martínez Ortigosa	University of Almería, Spain
Antonio J. Plaza	University of Extremadura, Spain
Mindaugas Radziunas	Weierstrass Institute for Applied Analysis and Stochastics, Germany

Vadimas Starikovičius   Vilnius Gediminas Technical University,
                                      Lithuania
Roman Wyrzykowski   Czestochova University of Technology, Poland
Julius Žilinskas   Vilnius University, Lithuania

Additional Reviewers
Algirdas Lančinskas   Vilnius University, Lithuania
Natalija Tumanova   Vilnius Gediminas Technical University,
                                     Lithuania

Third Workshop on Big Data Management in Clouds (BigDataCloud 2014)

Workshop Description

The Workshop on Big Data Management in Clouds was created to provide a platform for the dissemination of recent research efforts that explicitly aim at addressing the challenges related to executing big data applications on the cloud. Initially designed for powerful and expensive supercomputers, such applications have seen an increasing adoption on clouds, exploiting their elasticity and economical model. While Map/Reduce covers a large fraction of the development space, there are still many applications that are better served by other models and systems. In such a context, we need to embrace new programming models, scheduling schemes, hybrid infrastructures and scale out of single data centers to geographically distributed deployments in order to cope with these new challenges effectively.

In this context, the BigDataCloud workshop aims to provide a venue for researchers to present and discuss results on all aspects of data management in clouds, as well as new development and deployment efforts in running data-intensive computing workloads. In particular, we are interested in how the use of cloud-based technologies can meet the data-intensive scientific challenges of HPC applications that are not well served by the current supercomputers or grids, and are being ported to cloud platforms. The goal of the workshop is to support the assessment of the current state, introduce future directions, and present architectures and services for future clouds supporting data-intensive computing.

BigDataCloud 2014 followed the previous editions and the successful series of BDMC / CGWS workshops held in conjunction with EuroPar since 2009. Its goal is to aggregate the data management and clouds/grids/p2p communities built around these workshops in order to complement the data-handling issues with a comprehensive system / infrastructure perspective. This year's edition was held on August 25 and gathered around 40 enthusiastic researchers from academia and industry. We received a total of ten papers, out of which four were selected for presentation. The big data theme was strongly reflected in the keynote given this year by Dr. Toni Cortes from Barcelona Supercomputing Center. The talk introduced the idea of self-contained objects and showed how third party enrichment of such objects can offer an environment where the data providers keep full control over data while service designers get the maximum flexibility.

We wish to thank all the authors, the keynote speaker, the Program Committee members and the workshop chairs of EuroPar 2014 for their contribution to the success of this edition of BigDataCloud.

Program Chairs

Alexandru Costan   IRISA/INSA Rennes, France
Frédéric Desprez   Inria ENS Lyon, France

Program Committee

Gabriel Antoniu   Inria, France
Luc Bougé   ENS Rennes, France
Toni Cortes   Barcelona Supercomputing Center, Spain
Kate Keahey   University of Chicago/ANL, USA
Dries Kimpe   Argonne National Laboratory, USA
Olivier Nano   Microsoft Research ATLE, Germany
Bogdan Nicolae   IBM Research, Ireland
Maria S. Pérez   Universidad Politecnica De Madrid, Spain
Leonardo Querzoni   University of Rome La Sapienza, Italy
Domenico Talia   University of Calabria, Italy
Osamu Tatebe   University of Tsukuba, Japan
Cristian Zamfir   EPFL, Switzerland

Second Workshop on Dependability and Interoperability in Heterogeneous Clouds (DIHC 2014)

Workshop Description

The DIHC workshop series started in 2013 with the aim of bringing together researchers from academia and industry and PhD students interested in the design, implementation, and evaluation of services and mechanisms for dependable cloud computing in a multi-cloud environment. The cloud computing market is in rapid expansion due to the opportunities to dynamically allocate a large amount of resources when needed and to pay only for their effective usage. However, many challenges, in terms of interoperability, performance guarantee, and dependability, still need to be addressed to make cloud computing the right solution for companies, research organizations, and universities.

This year's edition consisted of three sessions and focused on heterogeneous cloud platforms and aspects to make cloud computing a trustworthy environment addressing security, privacy, and high availability in clouds. The accepted papers address issues to manage complex applications and facilitate the seamless and transparent use of cloud platform services, including computing and storages services, provisioned by multiple cloud platforms. The workshop also covered HPC applications with the need of a new generation of data storage, management services and heterogeneity-agnostic programming models for a better utilization of heterogeneous cloud resources for scientific and data-intensive applications while dealing with performance and elasticity issues. Privacy and security aspects in cloud computing from theory to practical implementations were presented and discussed.

In addition to the presentation of peer-reviewed papers, the 2014 edition of the DIHC workshop includes a presentation on "Identities and Rights in e-Infrastructures" by the invited keynote speaker Jens Jensen. The keynote presented lessons from the state-of-the-art technology used to identify management in clouds and took a look into standards and the future solutions for federated identity management.

Program Chairs

Roberto G. Cascella	Inria, France
Miguel Correia	INESC-ID/IST, Portugal
Elisabetta Di Nitto	Politecnico di Milano, Italy
Christine Morin	Inria, France

Program Committee

Vasilios Andrikopoulos	University of Stuttgart, Germany
Alvaro Arenas	IE Business School, Spain
Alysson Bessani	University of Lisbon, Portugal
Lorenzo Blasi	HP, Italy
Paolo Costa	Imperial College London, UK
Beniamino Di Martino	University of Naples, Italy
Federico Facca	Create-Net, Italy
Franz Hauck	University of Ulm, Germany
Yvon Jégou	Inria, France
Jens Jensen	STFC, UK
Paolo Mori	CNR, Italy
Dana Petcu	West University of Timisoara, Romania
Paolo Romano	INESC-ID/IST, Portugal
Louis Rilling	DGA-MI, France
Michael Schöttner	University of Düsseldorf, Germany
Thorsten Schütt	ZIB Berlin, Germany
Stephen Scott	ORNL/Tennessee Technological University, USA
Gianluigi Zavattaro	University of Bologna, Italy

Additional Reviewer

Ferrol Aderholdt	Tennessee Technological University, USA

Second Workshop on Federative and Interoperable Cloud Infrastructures (FedICI 2014)

Workshop Description

Infrastructure as a service (IaaS) cloud systems allow the dynamic creation, destruction, and management of virtual machines (VM) on virtualized clusters. IaaS clouds provide a high level of abstraction to the end user that allows the creation of on-demand services through a pay-as-you-go infrastructure combined with elasticity. As a result, many academic infrastructure service providers have started transitions to add cloud resources to their previously existing campus and shared grid deployments. To complete such solutions, they should also support the unification of multiple cloud and/or cloud and grid solutions in a seamless, preferably interoperable way. Hybrid, community, or multi-clouds may utilize more than one cloud system, which are also called cloud federations. The management of such federations raises several challenges and open issues that require significant research work in this area.

The Second Workshop on Federative and Interoperable Cloud Infrastructures (FedICI 2014) aimed at bringing together scientists in the fields of high-performance computing and cloud computing to provide a dedicated forum for sharing the latest results, exchanging ideas and experiences, presenting new research, development, and management of interoperable, federated IaaS cloud systems. The goal of the workshop was to help the community define the current state, determine further goals, and present architectures and service frameworks to achieve highly interoperable federated cloud infrastructures. Priority was given to submissions that focus on presenting solutions to interoperability and efficient management challenges faced by current and future infrastructure clouds.

The call for papers for the FedICI workshop was launched early in 2014, and by the submission deadline we had received six submissions, which were of good quality and generally relevant to the theme of the workshop. The papers were swiftly and expertly reviewed by the Program Committee, each of them receiving at least three qualified reviews. The program chair thanks the whole Program Committee and the additional reviewers for the time and expertise they put into the reviewing work, and for getting it all done within the rather strict time limit. Final decision on acceptance was made by the program chair and co-chairs based on the recommendations from the Program Committee. Being half-day event, there was room for only four of the contributions, resulting in an acceptance ratio of 66%. All the accepted contributions were presented at the workshop yielding an interesting discussion on the role that federated management may play in the broad research field of cloud computing. Presentations were organized in two sessions: in the former, two papers discussed performance analysis issues of interoperating clouds, while in the later session, two papers were presented on the topic of elastic management of generic IaaS and MapReduce-based systems in interoperable and federated clouds. These proceedings include the final versions of the presented FedICI papers, taking the feedback from the reviewers and workshop audience into account.

The program chairs sincerely thank the Euro-Par organizers for providing the opportunity to arrange the FedICI workshop in conjunction with the 2014 conference. The program chairs also warmly thank MTA SZTAKI for its financial support making it possible to organize the workshop. Finally, the program chairs thank all attendees at the workshop, who contributed to a successful scientific day. Based on the mostly positive feedback, the program chairs and organizers plan to continue the FedICI workshop in conjunction with Euro-Par 2015.

Program Chairs

Gabor Kecskemeti	MTA SZTAKI, Hungary
Attila Kertesz	MTA SZTAKI, Hungary
Attila Marosi	MTA SZTAKI, Hungary
Radu Prodan	University of Innsbruck, Austria

Program Committee

Jameela Al-Jaroodi	United Arab Emirates University, UAE
Salvatore Distefano	Politecnico di Milano, Italy
Eduardo Huedo Cuesta	Universidad Complutense de Madrid, Spain
Philipp Leitner	University of Zurich, Switzerland
Daniele Lezzi	Barcelona Supercomputing Center, Spain
Nader Mohamed	United Arab Emirates University, UAE
Zsolt Nemeth	MTA SZTAKI, Hungary
Ariel Oleksiak	Poznan Supercomputer and Networking Center, Poland
Anne-Cecile Orgerie	CNRS, Myriads, IRISA, France
Simon Ostermann	University of Innsbruck, Austria
Dana Petcu	Western University of Timisoara, Romania
Ivan Rodero	Rutgers the State University of New Jersey, USA
Matthias Schmidt	1&1 Internet AG, Germany
Alan Sill	Texas Tech University, USA
Gergely Sipos	European Grid Infrastructure, The Netherlands
Massimo Villari	University of Messina, Italy

Additional Reviewers

Matthias Janetschek	University of Innsbruck, Austria
Weiwei Chen	University of Southern California, USA

12th International Workshop on Algorithms, Models and Tools for Parallel Computing on Heterogeneous Platforms (HeteroPar 2014)

Workshop Description

Heterogeneity is emerging as one of the most profound and challenging characteristics of today's parallel environments. From the macro level, where networks
of distributed computers, composed by diverse node architectures, are interconnected with potentially heterogeneous networks, to the micro level, where deeper
memory hierarchies and various accelerator architectures are increasingly common, the impact of heterogeneity on all computing tasks is increasing rapidly.
Traditional parallel algorithms, programming environments, and tools, designed
for legacy homogeneous multiprocessors, will at best achieve a small fraction of
the efficiency and the potential performance that we should expect from parallel
computing in tomorrow's highly diversified and mixed environments. New ideas,
innovative algorithms, and specialized programming environments and tools are
needed to efficiently use these new and multifarious parallel architectures. The
workshop is intended to be a forum for researchers working on algorithms, programming languages, tools, and theoretical models aimed at efficiently solving
problems on heterogeneous platforms.

Program Chair

Emmanuel Jeannot   Inria, France

Steering Committee

Domingo Giménez   University of Murcia, Spain
Alexey Kalinov   Cadence Design Systems, Russia
Alexey Lastovetsky   University College Dublin, Ireland
Yves Robert   Ecole Normale Supérieure de Lyon, France
Leonel Sousa   INESC-ID/IST, Technical University of
                                Lisbon, Portugal
Denis Trystram   LIG, Grenoble, France

Program Committee

Rosa M. Badia   BSC, Spain
Jorge Barbosa   University of Porto, Portugal
Olivier Beaumont   Inria, France
Paolo Bientinesi   RWTH Aachen, Germany
Cristina Boeres   Fluminense Federal University, Brazil
George Bosilca   University of Tennessee, USA
Louis-Claude Canon   Université de Franche-Comté, France
Alexandre Denis   Inria, France
Toshio Endo   Tokyo Institute of Technology, Japan
Edgar Gabriel   University of Houston, USA

Rafael Mayo Gual	Jaume I University, Spain
Toshihiro Hanawa	University of Tokyo, Japan
Shuichi Ichikawa	Toyohashi University of Technology, Japan
Helen Karatza	Aristotle University of Thessaloniki, Greece
Hatem Ltaief	KAUST, Saudi Arabia
Pierre Manneback	University of Mons, Belgium
Loris Marchal	CNRS, France
Ivan Milentijevič	University of Nis, Serbia
Satoshi Matsuoka	Tokyo Institute of Technology, Japan
Wahid Nasri	ESST de Tunis, Tunisia
Dana Petcu	West University of Timisoara, Romania
Antonio Plaza	University of Extremadura, Spain
Enrique S. Quintana-Ortí	Jaume I University, Spain
Thomas Rauber	University of Bayreuth, Germany
Vladimir Rychkov	University College Dublin, Ireland
Erik Saule	University of North Carolina at Charlotte, USA
H. J. Siegel	Colorado State University, USA
Pedro Tomás	INESC-ID/IST, University of Lisbon, Portugal
Jon Weissman	University of Minnesota, USA

Additional Reviewers

Jose Antonio Belloch	Jaume I University, Spain
Adrián Castelló	Jaume I University, Spain
Ali Charara	KAUST, Saudi Arabia
Vladimir Ciric	University of Nis, Serbia
Diego Fabregat-Traver	RWTH Aachen, Germany
João Guerreiro	University of Lisbon, Portugal
Francisco D. Igual	Jaume I University, Spain
Samuel Kortas	KAUST, Saudi Arabia
Lídia Kuan	University of Lisbon, Portugal
Emina Milovanovic	University of Nis, Serbia
Aline Nascimento	Fluminense Federal University, Brazil
Elmar Peise	RWTH Aachen, Germany
Alexandre Sena	Fluminense Federal University, Brazil
Paul Springer	RWTH Aachen, Germany
François Tessier	University of Bordeaux, France

5th International Workshop on High-Performance Bioinformatics and Biomedicine (HiBB 2014)

Workshop Description

The HiBB workshop series started in 2010 and its first edition was held at Ischia (Italy) in conjunction with the Euro-Par conference. Since then, the workshop has been held, always in conjunction with Euro-Par, at Bordeaux (France), Rhodes (Greece), Aachen (Germany), and Porto (Portugal), respectively, in 2011, 2012, 2013, and 2014.

Since 2010, the HiBB workshop series has included 25 regular papers, two invited talks, two panels, and one tutorial on several aspects of parallel and distributed computing applied to bioinformatics, health informatics, biomedicine, and systems biology.

The main motivation for the HiBB workshop is the increasing production of experimental and clinical data in biology and medicine, and the needs to provide efficient storage, preprocessing, and analysis of these data to support biomedical research.

In fact, the availability and large diffusion of high-throughput experimental platforms, such as next-generation sequencing, microarray, and mass spectrometry, as well as the improved resolution and coverage of clinical diagnostic tools, such as magnetic resonance imaging, are becoming the major sources of data in biomedical research, and the storage, preprocessing, and analysis of these data are becoming the main bottleneck of the biomedical analysis pipeline.

Parallel computing and high-performance infrastructures are increasingly used in all phases of life sciences research, e.g., for storing and preprocessing large experimental data, for the simulation of biological systems, for data exploration and visualization, for data integration, and for knowledge discovery.

The current bioinformatics scenario is characterized by the application of well-established techniques, such as parallel computing on multicore architectures and grid computing, as well as by the application of emerging computational models such as graphics processing and cloud computing. Large-scale infrastructures such as grids or clouds are mainly used to store in an efficient manner and to share in an easy way the huge amount of experimental data produced in life sciences, while parallel computing allows the efficient analysis of huge data. In particular, novel parallel architectures such as GPUs and emerging programming models such as MapReduce may overcome the limits posed by conventional computers to the analysis of large amounts of data.

The fifth edition of the HiBB workshop aimed to bring together scientists in the fields of high-performance computing, bioinformatics, and life sciences, to discuss the parallel implementation of bioinformatics algorithms, the deployment of biomedical applications on high-performance infrastructures, and the organization of large-scale databases in biology and medicine.

These proceedings include the final revised versions of the HiBB papers taking the feedback from the reviewers and workshop audience into account. The program chair sincerely thanks the Program Committee members and the additional reviewers, for the time and expertise they put into the reviewing work, the Euro-Par organization, for providing the opportunity to arrange the HiBB workshop in conjunction with the Euro-Par 2014 conference, and all the workshop attendees who contributed to a lively day.

Program Chair

Mario Cannataro   University Magna Græcia of Catanzaro, Italy

Program Committee

Pratul K. Agarwal   Oak Ridge National Laboratory, USA
Ignacio Blanquer   Universidad Politecnica de Valencia, Spain
Daniela Calvetti   Case Western Reserve University, USA
Werner Dubitzky   University of Ulster, UK
Ananth Y. Grama   Purdue University, USA
Concettina Guerra   Georgia Institute of Technology, USA
Pietro H. Guzzi   University Magna Græcia of Catanzaro, Italy
Vicente Hernandez   Universidad Politecnica de Valencia, Spain
Salvatore Orlando   University of Venice, Italy
Horacio Perez-Sanchez   University of Murcia, Spain
Omer F. Rana   Cardiff University, UK
Richard Sinnott   University of Melbourne, Australia
Fabrizio Silvestri   Yahoo Labs, Barcelona, Spain
Erkki Somersalo   Case Western Reserve University, USA
Paolo Trunfio   University of Calabria, Italy
Albert Zomaya   University of Sydney, Australia

Additional Reviewers

Giuseppe Agapito   University Magna Græcia of Catanzaro, Italy
Barbara Calabrese   University Magna Græcia of Catanzaro, Italy
Nicola Ielpo   University Magna Græcia of Catanzaro, Italy
Alessia Sarica   University Magna Græcia of Catanzaro, Italy

Second Workshop on Large-Scale Distributed Virtual Environments on Cloud and P2P (LSDVE 2014)

Workshop Description

The LSDVE workshop series started in August 2013, in Aachen, where the first edition of the workshop was held in conjunction with Europar 2013. LSDVE 2014, the second edition of the workshop, was held in Porto, in August 2014, again in conjunction with Europar.

The focus of this edition of the workshop was on cooperative distributed virtual environments. The recent advances in networking have determined an increasing use of information technology to support distributed cooperative applications. Several novel applications have emerged in this area, like computer-supported collaborative work (CSCW), large-scale distributed virtual worlds, collaborative recommender and learning systems. These applications involve several challenges, such as the definition of user interfaces, of coordination protocols, and of proper middle-ware and architectures supporting distributed cooperation.

Collaborative applications may benefit greatly also from the support of cloud and P2P architectures. As a matter of fact, with the emergence of readily available cloud platforms, collaborative applications developers have the opportunity of deploying their applications in the cloud, or by exploiting hybrid P2P/cloud architectures with dynamically adapting cloud support. This brings possibilities to smaller developers that were reserved for the big companies until recently. The integration of mobile/cloud platforms for collaborative applications is another challenge for the widespread use of these applications.

The LSDVE 2014 workshop aim was to provide a venue for researchers to present and discuss important aspects of P2P/cloud collaborative applications and of the platforms supporting them. The workshop's goal is to investigate open challenges for such applications, related to both the application design and to the definition of proper architectures. Some important challenges are, for instance, collaborative protocol design, latency reduction/hiding techniques for guaranteeing real-time constraints, large-scale processing of user information, privacy and security issues, state consistency/persistence. The workshop presented assessment of current state of the research in this area and introduced further directions.

LSDVE 2014 was opened by the invited talk "Decentralization: P2P and Personal Clouds" by Prof. Pedro Garcia Lopez, Universitat Rovira i Virgili. The program of the workshop included two sessions, "Cooperative Distributed Environments" and "Architectural Supports." The papers presented in the first session regard novel cooperative distributed applications, like social networks and massively multi player games, while those of the second session present architectural supports, both cloud and P2P based, for these applications.

We remark that the number of submissions to LSDVE 2014 has almost doubled over the previous edition. Finally, the extended version of selected papers accepted and presented at the workshop will be published in a special issue of the Springer journal *Peer-to-Peer Networking and Applications* (PPNA).

We wish to thank all who helped to make this second edition of the workshop a success: Prof. Pedro Garcia Lopez who accepted our invitation to present a keynote, authors submitting papers, colleagues who refereed the submitted papers and attended the sessions, and finally the Euro-Par 2014 organizers whose invaluable support greatly helped in the organization of this second edition of the workshop.

Program Chairs

Laura Ricci	University of Pisa, Italy
Alexandru Iosup	TU Delft, Delft, The Netherlands
Radu Prodan	Institute of Computer Science, Innsbruck, Austria

Program Committee

Michele Amoretti	University of Parma, Italy
Ranieri Baraglia	ISTI CNR, Pisa, Italy
Emanuele Carlini	ISTI CNR, Pisa, Italy
Massimo Coppola	ISTI CNR, Pisa, Italy
Patrizio Dazzi	ISTI CNR, Pisa, Italy
Juan J. Durillo	Institute of Computer Science, Innsbruck, Austria
Kalman Graffi	University of Düsseldorf, Germany
Alexandru Iosup	TU Delft, The Netherlands
Dana Petcu	West University of Timisoara, Romania
Andreas Petlund	Simula Research Laboratory, Norway
Radu Prodan	Institute of Computer Science, Innsbruck, Austria
Duan Rubing	Institute of High Performance Computing, Singapore
Laura Ricci	University of Pisa, Pisa, Italy
Alexey Vinel	Tampere University of Technology, Finland

7th International Workshop on Multi-/Many-Core Computing Systems (MuCoCos 2014)

Workshop Description

The pervasiveness of homogeneous and heterogeneous multi-core and many-core processors, in a large spectrum of systems from embedded and general-purpose to high-end computing systems, poses major challenges to the software industry. In general, there is no guarantee that software developed for a particular architecture will run on another architecture. Furthermore, ensuring that the software preserves some aspects of performance behavior (such as temporal or energy efficiency) across these different architectures is an open research issue.

Therefore, a traditional focus of the MuCoCos workshop is on language level, system software and architectural solutions for performance portability across different architectures and for automated performance tuning.

The topics of the MuCoCoS workshop include but are not limited to:

- Programming models, languages, libraries and compilation techniques
- Run-time systems and hardware support
- Automatic performance tuning and optimization techniques
- Patterns, algorithms and data structures for multi-/many-core systems
- Performance measurement, modeling, analysis and tuning
- Case studies highlighting performance portability and tuning.

Besides the presentation of selected technical papers, MuCoCos 2014 featured a keynote talk on "Execution Models for Energy-Efficient Computing Systems" by Philippas Tsigas, Chalmers University, Sweden.

Previous workshops in the series were: MuCoCoS 2008 (Barcelona, Spain), MuCoCoS 2009 (Fukuoka, Japan), MuCoCoS 2010 (Krakow, Poland), MuCoCoS 2011 (Seoul, Korea), MuCoCoS 2012 (Salt Lake City, USA), and MuCoCoS 2013 (Edinburgh, UK).

Program Chairs

Siegfried Benkner   University of Vienna, Austria
Sabri Pllana   Linnaeus University, Sweden

Program Committee

Beverly Bachmayer   Intel, Germany
Eduardo Cesar   Universitat Autonoma de Barcelona, Spain
Milind Chabbi   Rice University, USA
Jiri Dokulil   University of Vienna, Austria
Franz Franchetti   Carnegie Mellon University, USA
Michael Gerndt   TU Munich, Germany

Third International Workshop on On-chip Memory Hierarchies and Interconnects (OMHI 2014)

Workshop Description

The gap between processor and memory performances has been growing for more than four decades since the first commercial microprocessor was built by Intel in 1971. To avoid the memory access times caused by this gap, manufacturers implemented cache memories on-chip. Moreover, as the memory latency became larger, more cache levels were added to the on-chip memory hierarchy, and, as a consequence, on-chip networks were also integrated to interconnect the different cache structures among the different levels.

Nowadays, commercial microprocessors include up to tens of processors sharing a memory hierarchy with about three or four cache levels. In the lowest levels of the on-chip memory hierarchy, the cache structures can store hundreds of megabytes, requiring alternative memory technologies (such as eDRAM or STT-RAM) as well as new microarchitectural techniques to limit energy consumption and power dissipation. In addition, advanced on-chip networks are needed to cope with the latency and bandwidth demands of these complex memory hierarchies.

Finally, new manufacturing techniques, such as 3D integration is considered to enlarge even more the capacity and complexity of these memory hierarchies and interconnection networks.

In this context, the synergy between the research on memory organization and management, interconnection networks, as well as novel implementation technologies becomes a key strategy to foster further developments. With this aim, the International Workshop on On-chip Memory Hierarchy and Interconnects (OMHI) started in 2012 and continued with its third edition that was held in Porto, Portugal. This workshop is organized in conjunction with the Euro-Par annual series of international conferences dedicated to the promotion and advancement of all aspects of parallel computing.

The goal of the OMHI workshop is to be a forum for engineers and scientists to address the aforementioned challenges, and to present new ideas for future on-chip memory hierarchies and interconnects focusing on organization, management and implementation. The specific topics covered by the OMHI workshop have been kept up to date according to technology advances and industrial and academia interests.

The chairs of OMHI were proud to present Prof. Manuel E. Acacio as keynote speaker, who gave an interesting talk focusing on the key topics of the workshop entitled "Increased Hardware Support for Efficient Communication and Synchronization in Future Manycores," which jointly with the paper sessions finally resulted in a nice and very exciting one-day program.

The chairs would like to thank the members of the Program Committee for their reviews, the Euro-Par organizers, Manuel E. Acacio and the high number of attendees. Based on the positive feedback from all of them, we plan to continue the OMHI workshop in conjunction with Euro-Par.

Program Chairs

Julio Sahuquillo   Universitat Politècnica de València, Spain
Maria Engracia Gómez   Universitat Politècnica de València, Spain
Salvador Petit   Universitat Politècnica de València, Spain

Program Committee

Manuel Acacio   Universidad de Murcia, Spain
Sandro Bartolini   Università di Siena, Italy
João M. P. Cardoso   University of Porto, Portugal
Marcello Coppola   STMicroelectronics, France
Giorgos Dimitrakopoulos   Democritus University of Thrace, Greece
Pierfrancesco Foglia   Università di Pisa, Italy
Crispín Gómez   Universidad de Castilla-La Mancha, Spain
Kees Goossens   Eindhoven University of Technology,
                                  The Netherlands
David Kaeli   Northeastern University, USA
Sonia López   Rochester Institute of Technology, USA
Pierre Michaud   Inria, France

Iakovos Mavroidis	Foundation for Research and Technology – Hellas, Greece
Tor Skeie	Simula Research Laboratory, Norway
Rafael Ubal	Northeastern University, USA

Second Workshop on Parallel and Distributed Agent-Based Simulations (PADABS 2014)

Workshop Description

The Parallel and Distributed Agent-Based Simulations workshop series started in 2013.

Agent-based simulation models are an increasingly popular tool for research and management in many fields such as ecology, economics, sociology, etc..

In some fields, such as social sciences, these models are seen as a key instrument to the generative approach, essential for understanding complex social phenomena. But also in policy-making, biology, military simulations, control of mobile robots and economics, the relevance and effectiveness of agent-based simulation models has been recently recognized.

The computer science community has responded to the need for platforms that can help the development and testing of new models in each specific field by providing tools, libraries, and frameworks that speed up and make massive simulations.

The key objective of the workshop is to bring together researchers who are interested in getting more performances from their simulations, by using:

- Synchronized, many-core simulations (e.g., GPUs)
- Strongly coupled, parallel simulations (e.g., MPI)
- Loosely coupled, distributed simulations (distributed heterogeneous setting).

Program Chairs

Vittorio Scarano	Università di Salerno, Italy
Gennaro Cordasco	Seconda Università di Napoli, Italy
Rosario De Chiara	Poste Italiane, Italy
Ugo Erra	Università della Basilicata, Italy

Program Committee

Maria Chli	Aston University, UK
Claudio Cioffi-Revilla	George Mason University, USA
Biagio Cosenza	University of Innsbruck, Austria
Nick Collier	Argonne National Laboratory, USA
Rosaria Conte	CNR, Italy
Andrew Evans	University of Leeds, UK
Bernardino Frola	The MathWorks, Cambridge, UK
Nicola Lettieri	Università del Sannio and ISFOL, Italy

Sean Luke   George Mason University, USA
Michael North   Argonne National Laboratory, USA
Mario Paolucci   CNR, Italy
Paul Richmond   The University of Sheffield, UK
Arnold Rosenberg   Northeastern University, USA
Flaminio Squazzoni   Università di Brescia, Italy
Michela Taufer   University of Delaware, USA
Joanna Kolodziej   Cracow University of Technology and
                                 University of Science and Technology,
                                 Poland

Additional Reviewers

Carmine Spagnuolo   Università di Salerno, Italy
Luca Vicidomini   Università di Salerno, Italy

7th Workshop on Productivity and Performance – Tools for HPC Application Development (PROPER 2014)

Workshop Description

The PROPER workshop series started at Euro-Par 2008 in Gran Canarias, Spain. Since than it has been held at every Euro-Par conference. It is organized by the Virtual Institute – High Productivity Supercomputing (VI-HPS), an initiative to promote the development and integration of HPC programming tools.

Writing codes that run correctly and efficiently on HPC computing systems is extraordinarily challenging. At the same time, applications themselves are becoming more complex as well, which can be seen in emerging scale-bridging applications, the integration of fault-tolerance and uncertainty quantification, or advances in algorithms. Combined, these trends place higher and higher demands on the application development process and thus require adequate tool support for debugging and performance analysis. The PROPER workshop serves as a forum to present novel work on scalable methods and tools for high-performance computing. It covers parallel program development and analysis, debugging, correctness checking, and performance measurement and evaluation. Further topics include the integration of tools with compilers and the overall development environment, as well as success stories reporting on application performance, scalability, reliability, power and energy optimization, or productivity improvements that have been achieved using tools.

This year's keynote on "Rethinking Productivity and Performance for the Exascale Era" was given by Prof. Allen D. Malony, Department of Computer and Information Science, University of Oregon. The talk discussed directions for parallel performance research and tools that target the scalability, optimization, and programmability challenges of next-generation HPC platforms with high productivity as an essential outcome. Further, Prof. Malony stated that it is becoming more apparent that in order to address the complexity concerns unfolding in the exascale space, we must think of productivity and performance in a more connected way and the technology to support them as being more open, integrated, and intelligent.

Program Chairs

José Gracia	High-Performance Computing Center Stuttgart, Germany

Steering Committee

Andreas Knüpfer (Chair)	Technische Universität Dresden, Germany
Michael Gerndt	Technische Universität München, Germany
Shirley Moore	University of Texas at El Paso, USA
Matthias Müller	RWTH Aachen, Germany
Martin Schulz	Lawrence Livermore National Laboratory, USA
Felix Wolf	German Research School for Simulation Sciences, Germany

Program Committee

José Gracia (Chair)	HLRS, Germany
Denis Barthou	Inria, France
David Böhme	German Research School for Simulation Sciences, Germany
Karl Fürlinger	LMU München, Germany
Michael Gerndt	TU München, Germany
Kevin Huck	University of Oregon, USA
Koji Inoue	Kyushu University, Japan
Andreas Knüpfer	TU Dresden, Germany
Ignacio Laguna	Lawrence Livermore National Laboratory, USA
John Mellor-Crummey	Rice University, USA
Matthias Müller	RWTH Aachen, Germany
Shirley Moore	University of Texas at El Paso, USA
Martin Schulz	Lawrence Livermore National Laboratory, USA
Nathan Tallent	Pacific Northwest National Laboratory, USA
Jan Treibig	RRZE, Friedrich-Alexander-Universität Erlangen-Nürnberg, Germany
Felix Wolf	German Research School for Simulation Sciences, Germany
Brian Wylie	Jülich Supercomputing Centre, Germany

First International Workshop on Reproducibility in Parallel Computing (REPPAR)

Workshop Description

The workshop is concerned with experimental practices in parallel computing research. We are interested in research works that address the statistically rigorous analysis of experimental data and visualization techniques of these data. We also encourage researchers to state best practices to conduct experiments and papers that report experiences obtained when trying to reproduce or repeat experiments of others. The workshop also welcomes papers on new tools for experimental computational sciences, e.g., tools to archive large experimental data sets and the source code that generated them. This includes (1) workflow systems for defining the experimental structure of experiments and their automated execution as well as (2) experimental testbeds, which may serve as underlying framework for experimental workflows, e.g., deploying personalized operating system images on clusters.

Program Chairs

Sascha Hunold   Vienna University of Technology, Austria
Arnaud Legrand   CNRS, LIG Grenoble, France
Lucas Nussbaum   CNRS, LORIA, France
Mark Stillwell   Cranfield University, UK

Program Committee

Henri Casanova   University of Hawai'i, USA
Olivier Dalle   University of Nice - Sophia Antipolis, France
Andrew Davison   CNRS, France
Georg Hager   University of Erlangen-Nuremberg, Germany
James Hetherington   University College London, UK
Olivier Richard   LIG Grenoble, France
Lucas M. Schnorr   Universidade Federal do Rio Grande do Sul,
                       Brazil
Jesper Larsson Träff   Vienna University of Technology, Austria
Jan Vitek   Purdue University, USA

Second Workshop on Runtime and Operating Systems for the Many-core Era (ROME 2014)

Workshop Description

Since the beginning of the multicore era, parallel processing has become prevalent across the board. However, in order to continue a performance increase according to Moore's Law, a next step needs to be taken: away from common multi-cores toward innovative many-core architectures. Such systems, equipped with a significant higher amount of cores per chip than multi-cores, pose challenges in both hardware and software design. On the hardware side, complex on-chip networks, scratchpads, and memory interfaces as well as cache hierarchies, cache-coherence strategies and the building of coherency domains have to be taken into account.

However, the ROME workshop focuses on the software side because without complying system software, runtime and operating system support, all these new hardware facilities cannot be exploited. Hence, the new challenges in hardware/software co-design are to step beyond traditional approaches and to wage new programming models and OS designs in order to exploit the theoretically available performance as effectively and power-aware as possible.

This focus of the ROME workshop stands in the tradition of a successful series of events originally hosted by the Many-core Applications Research Community (MARC). Such MARC symposia took place at the Hasso Plattner Institute in Potsdam in 2011, at the ONERA Research Center in Toulouse in 2012 and at the RWTH Aachen University in 2012. This successful series was then continued by the 1st ROME workshop (*R*untime and *O*perating Systems for the *M*any-core *E*ra) at the Euro-Par 2013 conference in Aachen as a thematically related follow-up event for a broader audience.

This year, this tradition was again pursued by holding the Second ROME workshop in conjunction with the Euro-Par 2014 conference in Porto. The organizers were very happy that Prof. Norbert Eicker from Jülich Supercomputing Centre (JSC) volunteered to give an invited keynote for this workshop with the title "Running DEEP – Operating Heterogeneous Clusters in the Many-core Era."

Program Chairs

Stefan Lankes   RWTH Aachen University, Germany
Carsten Clauss   ParTec Cluster Competence Center GmbH,
                              Germany

Program Committee

Carsten Clauss   ParTec Cluster Competence Center GmbH,
                              Germany
Stefan Lankes   RWTH Aachen University, Germany
Timothy Mattson   Intel Labs, USA

Jörg Nolte	BTU Cottbus, Germany
Eric Noulard	ONERA, France
Andreas Polze	Hasso Plattner Institute, Germany
Michael Riepen	IAV GmbH, Germany
Bettina Schnor	University of Potsdam, Germany
Oliver Sinnen	University of Auckland, New Zealand
Christian Terboven	RWTH Aachen Univeristy, Germany
Carsten Trinitis	TU München, Germany
Theo Ungerer	Universität Augsburg, Germany
Josef Weidendorfer	TU München, Germany

Additional Reviewers

Christian Bradatsch	Universität Augsburg, Germany
David Büttner	TU München, Germany
Steffen Christgau	University of Potsdam, Germany
Ralf Jahr	Universität Augsburg, Germany
Tilman Küstner	TU München, Germany
Simon Pickartz	RWTH Aachen University, Germany
Randolf Rotta	BTU Cottbus, Germany
Roopak Sinha	University of Auckland, New Zealand
Vincent Vidal	ONERA, France

7th Workshop on Resiliency in High-Performance Computing in Clusters, Clouds, and Grids (Resilience 2014)

Workshop Description

Clusters, clouds, and grids are three different computational paradigms with the intent or potential to support high performance computing (HPC). Currently, they consist of hardware, management, and usage models particular to different computational regimes, e.g., high-performance cluster systems designed to support tightly coupled scientific simulation codes typically utilize high-speed interconnects and commercial cloud systems designed to support software as a service (SAS) do not. However, in order to support HPC, all must at least utilize large numbers of resources and hence effective HPC in any of these paradigms must address the issue of resiliency at large scale.

Recent trends in HPC systems have clearly indicated that future increases in performance, in excess of those resulting from improvements in single-processor performance, will be achieved through corresponding increases in system scale, i.e., using a significantly larger component count. As the raw computational performance of these HPC systems increases from today's tera- and peta-scale to next-generation multi-peta-scale capability and beyond, their number of computational, networking, and storage components will grow from the ten-to-one-hundred thousand compute nodes of today's systems to several hundreds of thousands of compute nodes and more in the foreseeable future. This substantial growth in system scale, and the resulting component count, poses a challenge for HPC system and application software with respect to fault tolerance and resilience.

Furthermore, recent experience in extreme-scale HPC systems with non-recoverable soft errors, i.e., bit flips in memory, cache, registers, and logic added another major source of concern. The probability of such errors not only grows with system size, but also with increasing architectural vulnerability caused by employing accelerators, such as FPGAs and GPUs, and by shrinking nanometer technology. Reactive fault-tolerance technologies, such as checkpoint/restart, are unable to handle high failure rates due to associated overheads, while proactive resiliency technologies, such as migration, simply fail as random soft errors cannot be predicted. Moreover, soft errors may even remain undetected resulting in silent data corruption.

The goal of this workshop is to bring together experts in the area of fault tolerance and resilience for HPC to present the latest achievements and to discuss the challenges ahead. The program of the Resilience 2014 workshop included one keynote and six high-quality papers. The keynote was given by Ives Robert from ENS Lyon with the title "Algorithms for Coping with Silent Errors."

Workshop Chairs

Stephen L. Scott   Tennessee Technological University and Oak
                                    Ridge National Laboratory, USA
Chokchai (Box) Leangsuksun   Louisiana Tech University, USA

Program Chairs

Patrick G. Bridges   University of New Mexico, USA
Christian Engelmann   Oak Ridge National Laboratory, USA

Program Committee

Ferrol Aderholdt   Tennessee Institute of Technology, USA
Vassil Alexandrov   Barcelona Supercomputer Center, Spain
Wesley Bland   Argonne National Laboratory, USA
Greg Bronevetsky   Lawrence Livermore National Laboratory, USA
Franck Cappello   Argonne National Laboratory, USA
Zizhong Chen   University of California at Riverside, USA
Nathan DeBardeleben   Los Alamos National Laboratory, USA
Kurt Ferreira   Sandia National Laboratory, USA
Cecile Germain   Université Paris-Sud, France
Larry Kaplan   Cray Inc., USA
Dieter Kranzlmueller   Ludwig Maximilians University of Munich,
                                    Germany
Sriram Krishnamoorthy   Pacific Northwest National Laboratory, USA

Scott Levy	University of New Mexico, USA
Celso Mendes	University of Illinois Urbana-Champaign, USA
Kathryn Mohror	Lawrence Livermore National Laboratory, USA
Christine Morin	Inria Rennes, France
Mihaela Paun	Louisiana Tech University, USA
Alexander Reinefeld	Zuse Institute Berlin, Germany
Rolf Riesen	Intel Corporation, USA

Workshop on Software for Exascale Computing (SPPEXA 2014)

Workshop Description

SPPEXA is a priority program of the German Research Foundation (DFG). It targets the challenges of programming for exascale performance, which have been recognized in recent years and are being addressed by national and international research initiatives around the world. Exascale computing promises performance in the range of 10^{18} floating-point operations per second. Today's fastest supercomputers are just a factor of 30 away from this mark. Software technology faces extreme challenges, mainly because of the massive on-chip parallelism necessary to reach exascale performance, and because of the expected complexity of the architectures that will be able to deliver it.

The DFG runs close to 100 priority programs at any one time, each lasting up to six years. SPPEXA started in January 2013 and will run through to the end of 2018. It consists of two three-year funding periods. In the first period, 13 projects were chosen from 67 proposals. Each project is being run by a multi-site consortium with between three and five funded research positions. The overall funding amounts to roughly 3.7 million Euro per year. Each project addresses at least two and concentrates on at most three of the following six challenges:

- Computational algorithms
- System software
- Application software
- Data management and exploration
- Programming
- Software tools

The program is more than the sum of the individual projects. There are inter-project collaborations and program-wide activities like an annual *SPPEXA Day* and an annual *Coding Week* devoted each year to a specific theme.

This workshop started with a keynote by Rosa Badia from the Barcelona Supercomputing Center and then continued with the initial results of the following six of the 13 projects:

- EXA-DUNE: Flexible PDE Solvers, Numerical Methods and Applications
- DASH: Data Structures and Algorithms with Support for Hierarchical Locality
- ExaStencils: Advanced Stencil-Code Engineering
- EXAHD: An Exa-Scalable Two-Level Sparse Grid Approach for Higher-Dimensional Problems in Plasma Physics and Beyond
- ESSEX: Equipping Sparse Solvers for Exascale
- Catwalk: A Quick Development Path for Performance Models

For more information on the program and the individual projects, please consult the website: http://www.sppexa.de.

Program Chairs

Christian Lengauer   University of Passau, Germany
Wolfgang Nagel   Technical University of Dresden, Germany

Program Committee

Christian Lengauer   University of Passau, Germany
Wolfgang Nagel   Technical University of Dresden, Germany
Christian Bischof   Technical University of Darmstadt, Germany
Alexander Reinefeld   Humboldt University of Berlin, Germany
Gerhard Wellein   Friedrich Alexander University, Germany
Ramin Yahyapour   University of Göttingen, Germany

First Workshop on Techniques and Applications for Sustainable Ultrascale Computing Systems (TASUS 2014)

Workshop Description

The TASUS workshop series started in 2014 to join researchers on ultrascale computing systems (UCS), envisioned as a large-scale complex system joining parallel and distributed computing systems, perhaps located at multiple sites, that cooperate to provide solutions to the users. As a growth of two or three orders of magnitude of today's computing systems is expected, including systems with unprecedented amounts of heterogeneous hardware, lines of source code, numbers of users, and volumes of data, sustainability is critical to ensure the feasibility of these systems. Due to these needs, currently there is an emerging cross-domain interaction between high-performance computing in clouds or the adoption of distributed programming paradigms, such as Map Reduce, in scientific applications, the cooperation between HPC and distributed system communities still poses many challenges toward building the ultrascale systems of the future. Especially in unifying the services to deploy sustainable applications portable to HPC systems, multi-clouds, data centers, and big data.

The TASUS workshop focuses specially on the software side, aiming at bringing together researchers from academia and industry interested in the design, implementation, and evaluation of services and system software mechanisms to improve sustainability in ultrascale computing systems with a holistic approach, including topics like scalability, energy barrier, data management, programmability, and reliability.

Program Chairs

Jesus Carretero	Carlos III University of Madrid, Spain
Laurent Lefevre	Inria, ENS of Lyon, France
Gudula Rünger	Technical University of Chemnitz, Germany
Domenico Talia	Universitá della Callabria, Italy

Program Committee

Francisco Almeida	Universidad de la Laguna, Spain
Angelos Bilas	ICS, FORTH, Greece
Pascal Bouvry	University of Luxembourg, Luxembourg
Harold Castro	Universidad de los Andes, Colombia
Alok Choudhary	Northwestern University, USA
Michele Colajanni	Università di Modena e Reggio Emilia, Italy
Toni Cortes	BSC, Spain
Raimondas Ciegis	Vilnius Gediminas Technical University, Lithuania
Georges DaCosta	Université Paul Sabatier, Tolouse 3, France
Jack Dongarra	University of Tennessee, USA
Skevos Evripidou	University of Cyprus, Cyprus
Thomas Fahringer	University of Innsbruck, Austria
Sonja Filiposka	University of Ss Cyril and Methodius, FYR Macedonia
Javier Garcia-Blas	University Carlos III of Madrid, Spain
Jose D. Garcia	University Carlos III of Madrid, Spain
Florin Isaila	Argonne National Labs, USA
Emmanuel Jeannot	Inria Bordeaux Sud-Ouest, France
Helen Karatza	Aristotle University of Thessaloniki, Greece
Alexey Lastovetsky	University College Dublin, Ireland
Dimitar Lukarski	Uppsala University, Sweden
Pierre Manneback	University of Mons, Belgium
Svetozar Margenov	Bulgarian Academic of Sciences, Bulgaria
Attila Marosi	Hungarian Academy of Sciences, Hungary
M. José Martín	University of Coruña, Spain
Anastas Mishev	University of Ss Cyril and Methodius, FYR Macedonia
Ricardo Morla	Universidade de Porto, Portugal
Maya Neytcheva	Uppsala University, Sweden

Ariel Oleksiak	Poznan Supercomputing Center, Poland
Dana Petcu	West University of Timisoara, Romania
Jean Marc Pierson	Université Paul Sabatier, Tolouse 3, France
Radu Prodan	University of Innsbruck, Austria
Gudula Ruenger	Technische Universität Chemnitz, Germany
Enrique S. Quintana-Orti	Universitat Jaume I, Spain
Thomas Rauber	University of Bayreuth, Germany
Karolj Skala	Ruder Boskovic Institute, Croatia
Victor J. Sosa	CINVESTAV, Mexico
Leonel Sousa	INESC, Portugal
Roman Trobec	Jozef Stefan Institute, Slovenia
Trinh Anh Tuan	Budapest University of Technology and Economics, Hungary
Eero Vainikko	University of Tartu, Estonia
Roman Wyrzykowski	Czestochowa University of Technology, Poland
Laurence T. Yang	St. Francis University, Canada
Julius Žilinskas	Vilnius University, Lithuania
Albert Zomaya	University of Sydney, Australia

7th Workshop on UnConventional High-Performance Computing (UCHPC 2014)

Workshop Description

Recent issues with the power consumption of conventional HPC hardware resulted in new interest in both accelerator hardware and low-power mass-market hardware. The most prominent examples are GPUs, yet FPGAs, DSPs, and other embedded designs may also provide higher power efficiency for HPC applications. The so-called dark silicon forecast, i.e., that not all transistors can be active at the same time, may lead to even more specialized hardware in future mass-market products. Exploiting this hardware for HPC can be a worthwhile challenge.

As the word "UnConventional" in the title suggests, the workshop focuses on usage of hardware or platforms for HPC that are not (yet) conventionally used today, and may not be designed for HPC in the first place. Reasons for its use can be raw computing power, good performance per watt, or low cost. To address this unconventional hardware, often, new programming approaches and paradigms are required to make best use of it. A second focus of the workshop is on innovative, (yet) unconventional new programming models.

To this end, UCHPC tries to capture solutions for HPC that are unconventional today, but could become conventional and significant tomorrow, and thus provide a glimpse into the future of HPC.

This year was the seventh time the UCHPC workshop took place, and it was the fifth time in a row that it was co-located with Euro-Par (each year since 2010). Before that, it was held in conjunction with the International Conference on Computational Science and Its Applications 2008 and with the ACM International Conference on Computing Frontiers 2009. However, UCHPC is a perfect addition to the scientific fields of Euro-Par, and this is confirmed by the continuous interest we see among Euro-Par attendees for this workshop.

While the general focus of the workshop is fixed, the topic is actually a moving target. For example, GPUs were quite unconventional for HPC a few years ago, but today a notable portion of the machines in the Top500 list are making use of them. Currently, the exploitation of mobile processors for HPC – including on-chip GPU and DSPs – are a hot topic, and we had a fitting invited talk on the EU Mont-Blanc project given by Axel Auweter, LRZ, Germany.

These proceedings include the final versions of the papers presented at UCHPC and accepted for publication. They take the feedback from the reviewers and workshop audience into account.

The workshop organizers want to thank the authors of the papers for joining us in Porto, the Program Committee for doing the hard work of reviewing all submissions, the conference organizers for proving such a nice venue, and last but not least the large number of attendees this year.

Program Chairs

Jens Breitbart	Technische Universität München, Germany
Dimitar Lukarski	Uppsala University, Sweden
Josef Weidendorfer	Technische Universität München, Germany

Steering Committee

Lars Bengtsson	Chalmers University of Technology, Sweden
Jens Breitbart	Technische Universität München, Germany
Anders Hast	Uppsala University, Sweden
Josef Weidendorfer	Technische Universität München, Germany
Jan-Philipp Weiss	COMSOL, Sweden
Ren Wu	Baidu, USA

Program Committee

Michael Bader	Technische Universität München, Germany
Denis Barthou	Université de Bordeaux, France
Alex Bartzas	National Technical University of Athens, Greece
Lars Bengtsson	Chalmers University of Technology, Sweden
Jens Breitbart	Technische Universität München, Germany
Giorgos Dimitrakopoulos	Democritus University of Thrace, Greece
Karl Fürlinger	LMU Munich, Germany
Dominik Goeddeke	TU Dortmund University, Germany
Frank Hannig	Friedrich-Alexander-Universität Erlangen-Nürnberg, Germany
Anders Hast	Uppsala University, Sweden
Rainer Keller	Hochschule für Technik, Stuttgart, Germany

Gaurav Khanna   University of Massachusetts Dartmouth, USA
Harald Köstler   Friedrich-Alexander-Universität
    Erlangen-Nürnberg, Germany
Dimitar Lukarski   Uppsala University, Sweden
Manfred Mücke   Sustainable Computing Research, Austria
Andy Nisbet   Manchester Metropolitan University, UK
Ioannis Papaefstathiou   Technical University of Crete, Greece
Bertil Schmidt   University of Mainz, Germany
Ioannis Sourdis   Chalmers University of Technology, Sweden
Josef Weidendorfer   Technische Universität München, Germany
Jan-Philipp Weiss   COMSOL, Sweden
Stephan Wong   Delft University of Technology,
    The Netherlands
Ren Wu   Baidu, USA
Yunquan Zhang   Chinese Academy of Sciences, Beijing, China
Peter Zinterhof Jr.   University of Salzburg, Austria

Additional Reviewers
Vlad-Mihai Sima   Delft University of Technology,
    The Netherlands

9th Workshop on Virtualization in High-Performance Cloud Computing (VHPC 2014)

Workshop Description

Virtualization technologies constitute a key enabling factor for flexible resource management in modern data centers, and particularly in cloud environments. Cloud providers need to dynamically manage complex infrastructures in a seamless fashion for varying workloads and hosted applications, independently of the customers deploying software or users submitting highly dynamic and heterogeneous workloads. Thanks to virtualization, we have the ability to manage vast computing and networking resources dynamically and close to the marginal cost of providing the services, which is unprecedented in the history of scientific and commercial computing. Various virtualization technologies contribute to the overall picture in different ways: machine virtualization, with its capability to enable consolidation of multiple underutilized servers with heterogeneous software and operating systems (OSes) and its capability to live-migrate a fully operating virtual machine (VM) with a very short downtime, enables novel and dynamic ways to manage physical servers; OS-level virtualization, with its capability to isolate multiple user-space environments and to allow for their co-existence within the same OS kernel, promises to provide many of the advantages of machine virtualization with high levels of responsiveness and performance and I/O virtualization allowing physical NICs/HBAs to take traffic from multiple VMs.

The workshop series on Virtualization in High-Performance Cloud Computing (VHPC) – originally the Workshop on Xen in High-Performance Cluster and Grid Computing Environments – started in 2006. It aims to bring together researchers and industrial practitioners facing the challenges posed by virtualization. VHPC provides a platform that fosters discussion, collaboration, mutual exchange of knowledge and experience, enabling research to ultimately provide novel solutions for virtualized computing systems of tomorrow.

VHPC 2014 was again successfully co-located with Euro-Par. We would like to thank the organizers of this year's conference and the invited speakers: Helge Meinhard, CERN, and Ron Brightwell, Sandia National Laboratories, for their very well received talks.

Program Chairs

Michael Alexander	Vienna University of Technology, Austria
Anastassios Nanos	National Technical University of Athens, Greece
Tommaso Cucinotta	Amazon, Ireland

Program Committee

Costas Bekas	IBM, Switzerland
Jakob Blomer	CERN, Switzerland
Roberto Canonico	University of Naples Federico II, Italy
Piero Castoldi	Sant'Anna School of Advanced Studies, Italy
Paolo Costa	MS Research Cambridge, UK
Jorge Ejarque Artigas	Barcelona Supercomputing Center, Spain
William Gardner	University of Guelph, Canada
Balazs Gerofi	University of Tokyo, Japan
Krishna Kant	George Mason University, USA
Romeo Kinzler	IBM, Switzerland
Nectarios Koziris	National Technical University of Athens, Greece
Giuseppe Lettieri	University of Pisa, Italy
Jean-Marc Menaud	Ecole des Mines de Nantes, France
Christine Morin	Inria, France
Dimitrios Nikolopoulos	Foundation for Research and Technology – Hellas, Greece
Herbert Poetzl	VServer, Austria
Luigi Rizzo	University of Pisa, Italy
Josh Simons	VMware, USA
Borja Sotomayor	University of Chicago, USA
Yoshio Turner	HP Labs, USA
Kurt Tutschku	Blekinge Institute of Technology, Sweden
Chao-Tung Yang	Tunghai University, Taiwan

Table of Contents – Part I

12th International Workshop on Algorithms, Models and Tools for Parallel Computing on Heterogeneous Platforms (HeteroPar 2014)

5th Workshop on High-Performance Bioinformatics and Biomedicine (HiBB 2014)

Second Workshop on Large-Scale Distributed Virtual Environments on Clouds and P2P (LSDVE 2014)

Second Workshop on Parallel and Distributed Agent-Based Simulations (PADABS 2014)

First International Workshop on Reproducibility in Parallel Computing (REPPAR 2014)

7th Workshop on Resiliency in High-Performance Computing with Clouds, Grids, and Clusters (Resilience 2014)

Table of Contents – Part II

7th International Workshop on Multi-/Many-core Computing Systems (MuCoCoS 2014)

Third Workshop on On-chip Memory Hierarchies and Interconnects (OMHI 2014)

7th Workshop on Productivity and Performance Tools for HPC Application Development (PROPER 2014)

Second Workshop on Runtime and Operating Systems for the Many-Core Era (ROME 2014)

First Workshop on Techniques and Applications for Sustainable Ultrascale Computing Systems (TASUS 2014)

7th Workshop on UnConventional High-Performance Computing (UCHPC 2014)

9th Workshop on Virtualization in High-Performance Cloud Computing (VHPC 2014)

Workshop on Software for Exascale Computing (SPPEXA 2014)

On Parallelization of the OpenFOAM-Based Solver for the Heat Transfer in Electrical Power Cables

Raimondas Čiegis, Vadimas Starikovičius, and Andrej Bugajev

Vilnius Gediminas Technical University,
Saulétekio al. 11, LT-10223, Vilnius, Lithuania
{raimondas.ciegis,vadimas.starikovicius,andrej.bugajev}@vgtu.lt

Abstract. In this work, we study the parallel performance of Open-FOAM-based solver for heat conduction in electrical power cables. The 2D benchmark problem is used for our tests. The parallelization approach used in OpenFOAM-based solver is described and a basic scalability analysis is done. Results of computational experiments on a cluster of multicore computers are presented and the parallel efficiency and scalability of the solver are analyzed.

Keywords: OpenFOAM, parallel algorithms, domain decomposition, MPI, multicore.

1 Introduction

The knowledge of heat generation and distribution in and around the high-voltage electrical cables is necessary to optimize the design and exploitation of electricity transferring infrastructure. Engineers are interested in maximum allowable current in different conditions, optimal cable parameters, cable life expectancy estimations and many other engineering factors.

Presently applicable IEC standards for the design and installation of electrical power cables are often based on the analytical and heuristic formulas.Obviously, these formulas cannot accurately account for the various conditions under which the cables are actually installed and used. They estimate the cable's current-carrying capacity (so-called *ampacity*) with significant margins to stay on the safe side [3]. The safety margins can be quite large and result in 50-70% usage of actual resources. A more accurate mathematical modelling is needed to meet the latest technical and economical requirements and to elaborate new, improved, cost-effective design rules and standards.

When we need to deal with mathematical models for the heat transfer in various media (metals, insulators, soil, water, air) and non-trivial geometries, only the means of parallel computing technologies can allow us to get results in an adequate time. To solve numerically selected models, we develop our numerical solvers using the OpenFOAM package [4]. OpenFOAM is a free, open source CFD software package. It has an extensive set of standard solvers for popular

L. Lopes et al. (Eds.): Euro-Par 2014 Workshops, Part I, LNCS 8805, pp. 1–11, 2014.

CFD applications. It also allows us to implement our own models, numerical schemes and algorithms, utilizing the rich set of OpenFOAM capabilities [5]. Adapting OpenFOAM library to specific applications still requires theoretical analysis of selected algorithms and nontrivial selection of optimal data structures for the implementation of required algorithms. Examples of such projects are described in [1, 2].

The important consequence of this software development approach is that numerical solvers can automatically exploit the parallel computing capabilities already available in the OpenFOAM package. A detailed analysis on implementation of some types of parallel algorithms for GPU processors is done in [6].

Scalability and performance of parallel OpenFOAM solvers based on MPI for various applications are investigated in [9, 10]. Computational experiments are done on homogeneous distributed parallel platforms with up to 1024 cores. It is noted in [10] that the scalability and efficiency of parallel OpenFOAM solvers is not very well understood for many applications when executed on massively parallel systems. An extensive experimental analysis of OpenFOAM selected applications is done in Prace project. A few CFD applications with different multi-physics models are approximated by FVM on mainly fully structural 3D meshes. Mesh partition is done by using Simple and Scotch tools. The presented experimental results are showing a good OpenFOAM scaling and efficiency performance on IBM Blue Gene Q and Hewlett Packard C7000 parallel systems up to 2048- 4096 cores. It is noted that such results are expected when balancing between computation, message passing and I/O work is good.

In this work, we study and analyze the parallel performance of OpenFOAM-based solver for heat conduction in electrical power cables. The main goal is to consider the scalability and efficiency of the developed parallel solver in the case when the parallel system is not big, but it consists of non homogeneous multicore nodes. The mesh is adaptive and it is partitioned by using Scotch method. Then load balancing techniques must be used in order to optimize the parallel efficiency of the solver. The second aim is to investigate the sensitivity of parallel preconditioners with respect to the number of processes.

In Section 2, we describe the benchmark problem used for all numerical tests. In Section 3, we describe our OpenFOAM-based solver and discuss the parallelization approach employed in the OpenFOAM package. The theoretical scalability analysis of the parallel algorithm is presented in Section 4 . In Section 5, we present and analyze the obtained results on parallel efficiency and scalability of the solver. Finally, some conclusions are drawn in Section 6.

2   Benchmark Problem

As a benchmark problem in this research we solve the heat conduction problem for electrical power cables directly buried in the soil. It is also assumed that the thermo-physical properties of the soil remain constant, i.e. the moisture transfer in the soil is not considered. Such a simplified problem is described by the following well-known mathematical model:

$$\begin{cases} c\rho\dfrac{\partial T}{\partial t} = \nabla \cdot (\lambda \nabla T) + q, & t \in [0, t_{max}], x \in \Omega, \\ T(x, 0) = T_b, & x \in \Omega, \\ T(x, t) = T_b, & x \in \partial\Omega, \\ T, \lambda\nabla T \ \text{are continuous}, & x \in \Omega, \end{cases} \tag{1}$$

where $T(x, t)$ is the temperature, $c(x) > 0$ is the specific heat capacity, $\rho(x) > 0$ is the mass density, $\lambda(x) > 0$ is the heat conductivity coefficient, $q(x, t, T)$ is the heat source function due to power losses, T_b is the initial and boundary temperature. Coefficients λ, c, ρ are discontinuous functions. Their values can vary between metallic conductor, insulators and soil by several orders of magnitude [3].

In this work, we have used 2D geometry for our benchmark problem. Three cables are buried in the soil as shown in Figure 1. The red area is metallic conductor, the blue area is an insulator and the gray area marks the soil.

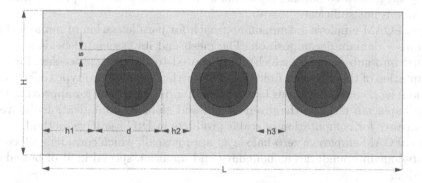

Fig. 1. 2D geometry of benchmark problem: three cables in the soil

OpenFOAM (Open source Field Operation And Manipulation) [4] is a C++ toolbox (library) for the development of customized numerical solvers for partial differential equations (PDEs). For benchmark problem (1) we obtain a numerical solver by a modification of the standard *laplacianFoam* solver, adding variable problem coefficients. OpenFOAM uses the Finite Volume Method (FVM) with co-located arrangement of unknowns [5].

Two important sub-tasks should be solved accurately for this type of approximations. First, the exact fluxes of a solution are orthogonal to the boundary of finite volumes, thus for numerical fluxes this property must be approximated accurately. In our solver this problem is solved by using a proper Delaunay triangulation of the domain. We note that OpenFOAM tool proposes iterative interpolation type orthogonalization techniques. Second, a proper interpolation should be used for definition of discontinuous coefficients λ in Laplacian term, namely *harmonic*.

Then for the 2D benchmark problem (1) by using Delaunay type triangulation we obtain FVM discretization with the four point stencil. In 3D case the uniform mesh is applied in the additional third dimension and the three-point stencil is used to approximate the fluxes in this direction. Resulting systems of linear equations with symmetric matrices are solved by preconditioned conjugate gradient method with the diagonal Incomplete-Cholesky (DIC) preconditioner.

3   Parallel OpenFOAM-Based Solver

Parallelization in OpenFOAM is robust and implemented at a low level using MPI library. Solvers are built using high level objects and, in general, don't require any parallel-specific coding. They will run in parallel automatically. Thus there is no need for users to implement standard steps of any parallel code: decomposition of the problem into subproblems, distribution of these tasks among different processes, implementation of data communication methods. A drawback of such automatic tools is that the user has very limited possibilities to modify the generated parallel algorithm if the efficiency of the OpenFOAM parallel code is not sufficient.

OpenFOAM employs a common approach for parallelization of numerical algorithms – domain decomposition. The mesh and its associated fields are partitioned into sub-domains, which are allocated to different processes. Parallel computation of the proposed finite FVM algorithm requires two types of communication: local communications between neighboring processes for approximation of the Laplacian term on the given stencil and global communications between all processes for computation of scalar products in DIC iterative method.

OpenFOAM employs a zero-halo layer approach [6], which considers cell edges on sub-domain boundaries as boundary and applies a special kind of boundary condition.

OpenFOAM supports four methods of domain decomposition, which decompose the data into non-overlapping sub-domains: simple, hierarchical, scotch and manual [4]. In all parallel tests the mesh is partitioned by using Scotch library [7]. Scotch is a library for graph and mesh partitioning, similar to well-known Metis library. It requires no geometric input from the user and attempts to minimize the number of boundary edges between sub-domains. The user can specify the weights of the sub-domains, what can be useful on heterogeneous clusters of parallel computers with different performance of processors. We will use this possibility in our computational experiments.

4   Scalability Analysis of the Parallel Algorithm

In this paper we are interested to investigate the efficiency of the parallel algorithm generated by the OpenFOAM tool with respect to load balancing and data communication costs. Thus in all numerical tests (and in the scalability analysis) we compute 10 time steps with the fixed constant number of iterations for solving systems of linear equations – 1000. In this way, we ensure that the same amount of work is done in all parallel tests, despite the possible differences in convergence due to parallel preconditioning and different roundoff errors, including data communication subroutines. The influence of mesh partitioning on parallel preconditioners is investigated in the last subsection of computational experiments.

Let us estimate the costs of the sequential algorithm to compute a solution at one time step as

$$W = (c_1 + 1000c_2)J,$$

where J is the total number of finite volumes in the mesh, c_1 estimates the costs of computation of the coefficients of the discrete system, c_2 estimates the costs of one DIC iteration.

Next let us estimate the complexity of the proposed parallel algorithm. For simplicity of theoretical scalability analysis let us assume that p homogeneous processes are used in computations. Then computation costs of the parallel algorithm can be estimated as

$$T_p^1 = (c_1 + 1000c_2)\lceil J/p\rceil.$$

Two assumptions have been used in derivation of this estimate. First, we have assumed that a perfect load balancing of sizes of partitioned mesh parts is achieved, this assumption usually is very accurately satisfied for meshes partitioned by Metis or Scotch libraries. Second, we are not taking into account that $c_1 = c_1(p)$, $c_2 = c_2(p)$ may depend on p and they can decrease for $p > 1$ due to a better cashing of smaller size discrete subproblems. In fact, such a behaviour will be illustrated by results of computational experiments. In the theoretical scalability analysis we are considering the worst case scenario.

Next we will estimate costs of communication among processors. As was stated above the implementation of the given parallel algorithm requires local send/receive of data between neighbour processes and global communication in computation of scalar products for Krylov type iterations. We assume that the largest number of data items sent between neighbour processes can be estimated as $c_3\sqrt{J}$ and let M be the largest number of neighbours for some process. Then the communication costs can be estimated as [8]

$$T_p^2 = 1000\left[r(M)(\alpha + \beta c_3\sqrt{J}) + R(p)\right].$$

Here α denotes the message startup time and β is the time required to send one element of data. Coefficients $1 \leq r(M) \leq M$ and $\log p \leq R(p) \leq p$ define the parallel efficiency of local data exchange and global reduce operations. The values of $r(M)$ and $R(p)$ depend on the implementation of MPI functions and on interconnection network of a parallel computer. For example, for a simple implementation of MPI_ALLREDUCE function, when all processors send their local values to the master processor, which accumulates results and broadcasts the sum to all processors, $R(p) = p$. On the 2D mesh network this function can be implemented with $R(p) = c\sqrt{p}$.

Thus the total complexity of the parallel algorithm is equal to

$$T_p = (c_1 + 1000c_2)\lceil J/p \rceil + 1000\big[r(M)(\alpha + \beta c_3\sqrt{J}) + R(p)\big].$$

The scalability analysis of any parallel algorithm finds the rate at which the size of the sequential algorithm W needs to grow up with respect to the number of processes p in order to maintain a fixed efficiency of the parallel algorithm $E_p = W/(pT_p)$. For a given efficiency E the isoefficiency function $W = g(p, E)$ is defined by the implicit equation [8]:

$$W = \frac{E}{1 - E} H(p, W). \tag{2}$$

The total overhead of the proposed parallel algorithm is given by

$$H(p, W) := pT_p - W$$
$$= (c_1 + 1000c_2)\big(p\lceil J/p \rceil - J\big) + 1000p\big[r(M)(\alpha + \beta c_3\sqrt{J}) + R(p)\big].$$

Let us assume that the effects of load disbalance and start-up time of communications are negligible. Then it follows from (2) that asymptotical isoefficiency functions due to local and global communications both have the same order $W = O(p^2)$.

Table 1. Analysis of the mesh decomposition algorithm: M_p denotes the largest number of neighbours, N_p denotes the maximum number of elements communicated between two processes and NT_p denotes the largest total number of elements sent by some process

	$J = 32000$	$J = 128000$	$J = 512000$	$J = 1018488$	$J = 2048000$
M_2	1	1	1	1	1
N_2	208	442	1386	3011	4854
M_4	3	2	3	3	3
N_4	148	466	1038	2383	3057
NT_4	342	826	2348	4023	6752
M_8	5	5	7	7	7
N_8	279	279	836	1224	2395
NT_8	681	681	2432	3851	5915

In Table 1 we present a basic information on the quality of the mesh decomposition algorithm. The load balancing of sizes of subproblems was very close to optimal, thus we restrict to analysis of data communicated among processes. Here M_p denotes the largest number of neighbours for some process, N_p denotes the maximum number of elements communicated between two processes and NT_p denotes the largest total number of elements sent by some process to its neighbours.

The results in Table 1 show that $O(\sqrt{J})$ is also a realistic estimate of the total number of elements sent by one process to its neighbours and the dependence of this number on p is very weak.

5   Parallel Performance Tests and Analysis

The computations were done on the Vilkas cluster at Vilnius Gediminas technical university. It consists of eight Intel Quad i7-860 processors with 4 cores (2.80 GHz) per node and eight Intel Quad Q6600 processors with 4 cores (2.4 GHz) per node. They are interconnected via Gigabit Smart Switch (http://vilkas.vgtu.lt). We also note that the sub-cluster of Intel Quad i7-860 processors is not fully homogeneous. Thus the Vilkas cluster is quite heterogeneous and therefore additional weighted load balancing is included into mesh distribution step.

In Table 2 we present CPU times of computational experiments with different nodes of the cluster. Here $i7\text{-}x$ and $q\text{-}x$ denote the x-th Intel Quad i7-860 and Intel Quad Q6600 processor, respectively. The number of iterations for solving systems of linear equations by using DIC preconditioner is fixed to 1000. In the case of Quad Q6600 nodes we have presented results only for the fastest and slowest nodes.

Table 2. CPU times of the sequential algorithm for different sizes of the problem and different processors of Vilkas cluster: $i7\text{-}x$ and $q\text{-}x$ denote the x-th Intel Quad i7-860 and Q6600 processor, respectively

	$J = 128000$	$J = 254892$	$J = 512000$	$J = 1018488$	$J = 2048000$
$i7$-0	36.7	82.7	201.9	415.9	909.2
$i7$-1	36.6	82.9	202.0	415.5	893.3
$i7$-2	36.7	82.4	198.6	413.0	887.9
$i7$-3	35.2	77.7	177.0	362.3	772.0
$i7$-4	36.8	82.4	198.3	415.8	887.6
$i7$-5	36.8	83.6	199.0	412.6	874.4
$i7$-7	36.1	81.1	190.7	390.2	839.3
$i7$-8	36.9	83.2	200.3	417.8	868.1
q-8	66.2	151.3	336.5	677.5	1441
q-13	66.3	153.9	341.3	678.2	1442

Two important conclusions follow from the presented computational results. First, due to memory cashing effects, the CPU time of the OpenFOAM solver increases over-linearly with respect to the size J of the discrete problem. On the basis of these experimental results we propose the following computation time prediction model for the parallel OpenFOAM solver

$$T_p^1(J) = \max_{x \in G} T_0(x, J/p), \qquad (3)$$

where G is set of p processors used to solve the problem of size J and $T_0(x, J/p)$ denotes the CPU time of the sequential algorithm applied for problem of size J/p on the x-th processor.

The second conclusion is that Intel Quad i7-860 processors are approximately 1.6 times faster than Q6600 processors. In addition some Intel Quad i7-860 processors are up till 1.15 times faster than the remaining processors. Thus a weighted load balancing technique can reduce the global CPU time of the parallel solver.

Next we present results of computational experiments, which confirm both conclusions. In Table 3 CPU times of the parallel OpenFOAM algorithm are given for different sizes of the discrete problem and different sets of processors.

Table 3. CPU times of the parallel OpenFOAM algorithm for different sizes of the problem and different sets of processors: $i7$-x and q-x denote the x-th Intel Quad i7-860 and Q6600 processor, respectively

	J=128000	J=254892	J=512000	J=1018488	J=2048000
$i7$-0, $i7$-1	18.8	39.3	86.7	204.9	420.2
$i7$-3, $i7$-7	18.4	38.3	86.1	193.3	394.4
q-8, q-9	30.7	73.2	162.0	337.5	689.5
$i7$-3, q-8	25.5	67.41	155.4	331.6	683.6
$i7$-0, $i7$-1	11.8	20.4	41.3	89.4	209.4
$i7$-2, $i7$-4					
$i7$-3, $i7$-5	11.4	20.4	40.9	90.0	204.3
$i7$-7, $i7$-8					
q-8, q-12	23.4	37.9	79.4	168.5	347.6
q-9, q-13					
8 $i7$ nodes	8.8	13.6	22.4	43.6	94.3
8 q nodes	22.1	28.0	44.3	86.7	179.5
16 nodes	17.3	20.5	26.2	42.7	85.4

It follows from the presented results that for two largest size discrete problems the CPU time is shorter when all 16 processors of the cluster are used.

Since Vilkas cluster is heterogeneous and consists of two types of nodes, a load balance of computational tasks can be improved by using the weighted mesh partitioning algorithm. In Table 4 CPU times of the parallel OpenFoam algorithm are given for different relative weights assigned to processors. Here $i7(w)$ and $q(w)$ denote Intel Quad i7-860 or Q6600 processors and w denotes the relative speed of this processor.

It follows from these results that adaptive mesh distribution algorithm improves the load balancing and CPU time decreases 1.3 times for the largest discrete problem.

Table 4. CPU times of the parallel OpenFoam algorithm for the adaptive mesh decomposition algorithm. Here $i7(w)$ and $q(w)$ denote Intel Quad i7-860 or Q6600 processors and w denotes the relative speed of this processor.

	$J=512000$	$J=1018488$	$J=2048000$	$J=8192000$
$i7$-$3(1)$, q-$8(1)$ q-$9(1)$	102.0	222.0	461.1	
$i7$-$3(2)$, q-$8(1)$ q-$9(1)$	89.7	189.9	381.3	
$i7$-$3(1.87)$, q-$8(1)$ q-$9(1)$	88.8	183.0	371.8	
$8\ i7(1)$, $8\ q(1)$	26.2	47.7	85.4	363.6
$8\ i7(1.5)$, $8\ q(1)$	24.3	35.5	69.4	288.2
$8\ i7(1.6)$, $8\ q(1)$	24.5	35.7	66.1	279.9

Next we have investigated the efficiency of the parallel solver when 2 and 4 cores per node are used in computations. The first conclusion is that only 2 cores are giving a reasonable speed-up of computations. Thus in Table 5 we present CPU times of the parallel OpenFoam algorithm for different numbers of processors and 2 cores per node. The size of the problem is $J = 2048000$ elements. The case 1×1 provides CPU time for the sequential algorithm.

Table 5. CPU times of the parallel OpenFoam algorithm for different numbers of processors n_d and $n_c = 2$ cores per node. The size of the problem is $J = 2048000$ elements. The case 1×1 provides CPU time for the sequential algorithm.

	1×1	1×2	2×2	4×2	8×2
$i7$-3	772.0	566.5	288.2	142.7	64.8
q-9	1441	1161	573.6	270.2	122.7

Two conclusions follow from the presented results. First, the scalability of the parallel algorithm is still good for clusters with multicore nodes. This scaling follows very similar trends as for one core per node. The second conclusion states that the retardation coefficient $\mu(n_c) > 1$ should be included into the estimate of computation costs of the parallel algorithm

$$T_p^1 = (c_1 + 1000\mu(n_c)c_2)\lceil J/p \rceil.$$

It depends on the maximum number of cores n_c per processor. This coefficient should be taken into account, since the shared-memory structure can become a bottleneck when too many cores try to access the global memory of a node simultaneously.

In the next series of computational experiments we have solved the largest problem with $J = 8192000$ elements. 16x2 processes of two types of nodes were used in computations. Since Vilkas cluster is heterogeneous, a load balancing strategy is applied in the weighted mesh partitioning algorithm. In Table 6 CPU times of the parallel OpenFoam algorithm are given for different relative weights assigned to processors.

Table 6. CPU times of the parallel OpenFoam algorithm for the adaptive mesh decomposition algorithm. Here $i7(w)$ and $q(w)$ denote Intel Quad i7-860 or Q6600 processors and w denotes the relative speed of this processor. The size of the discrete problem $J = 8192000$.

	$i7(1), q(1)$	$i7(1.4), q(1)$	$i7(1.5), q(1)$	$i7(1.6), q(1)$	$i7(1.7), q(1)$
T_{32}	279.9	229.7	216.6	206.3	202.4

Up to this point all results were obtained by fixing the number of linear solver iterations to 1000. In practice the number of iterations is calculated dynamically to fit the convergence tolerance requirement. Since we are using the conjugate gradient method with the diagonal Incomplete-Cholesky (DIC) preconditioner, the number of iterations may depend on the number of processes p. For computational tests we take $J = 2048000$. Results of computational experiments show that the time of computations is proportional to the number of iterations and the number of iterations weakly depends on the number of processes. So for different numbers of processes p we calculate the number of iterations that are performed to achieve the tolerance equal to 10^{-6}. The results in Table 7 show that the increased number of iterations lowers the efficiency, this number can occasionally also drop. But in general efficiency of parallel preconditioners is not sensitive to changes of p.

Table 7. The average number of iterations per time step for different number of processes p. The size of the discrete problem $J = 2048000$, the tolerance parameter for solver is equal to 10^{-6}.

	$p = 1$	$p = 2$	$p = 4$	$p = 8$	$p = 16$
Average number of iterations	1015.6	1140.1	1142.6	1448.2	1401.6
T_p	803.7	452	236.1	135.6	91.5

In the case of $p = 16$ processes we have used 8 nodes and 2 cores per node.

6   Conclusions

It is shown that for a developed OpenFOAM solver the scaling and efficiency performance on Vilkas cluster is good up to 32 cores when I/O effects are neglected and load balancing is used for mesh partition.

Smaller sizes of distributed discrete sub-problems enable a better caching and give a sub-linear speed-up for computational part of the parallel algorithm.

It is important to test the effects of I/O costs when balancing between computation and I/O parts of the algorithm is not good, for example when a solution should be saved every 5-10 time steps. It is well known that OpenFOAM I/O libraries are based on standard MPI I/O routines and they are introducing quite big overheads.

A hybrid MPI and OpenMP parallel model can be attractive in the case of parallel systems with a big number (12 or 16) of cores per node.

References

1. Higuera, P., Lara, J., Losada, I.: Realistic wave generation and active wave absorption for Navier–Stokes models: Application to OpenFOAM. Coastal Engineering 71(1), 102–118 (2013)
2. Petit, O., Bosioc, A., Nilsson, H., Muniean, S., Susan-Resigo, R.: Unsteady simulations of the flow in a swirl generator using OpenFOAM. International Journal of Fluid Machinery and Systems 4(1) (2011), doi:10.5293/IJFMS.2011.4.1.199
3. Makhkamova, I.: Numerical Investigations of the Thermal State of Overhead Lines and Underground Cables in Distribution Networks. Doctoral thesis, Durham University (2011)
4. OpenFOAM, http://www.openfoam.org
5. Weller, H.G., Tabor, G., Jasak, H., Fureby, C.: A Tensorial Approach to Computational Continuum Mechanics Using Object-oriented Techniques. Journal of Computational Physics 12(6), 620–631 (1998)
6. AlOnazi, A.: Design and Optimization of OpenFOAM-based CFD Applications for Modern Hybrid and Heterogeneous HPC Platforms. Master thesis, University College Dublin (2013)
7. Chevalier, C., Pellegrini, F.: PT-Scotch: A Tool for Efficient Parallel Graph Ordering. Parallel Computing 34(6-8), 318–331 (2008)
8. Kumar, V., Grama, A., Gupta, A., Karypis, G.: Introduction to parallel computing: design and analysis of algorithms. Benjamin/Cummings, Redwood City (1994)
9. Piscaglia, F., Montorfano, A., Onorati, A.: Development of fully-automatic parallel algorithms for mesh handling in the OpenFOAM-2.2.x technology. SAE Technical Paper 2013-24-0027 (2013), doi:10.4271/2013-24-0027
10. Rivera, O., Fürlinger, K., Kranzlmüller, D.: Investigating the scalability of OpenFOAM for the solution of transport equations and large eddy simulations. In: Xiang, Y., Cuzzocrea, A., Hobbs, M., Zhou, W. (eds.) ICA3PP 2011, Part II. LNCS, vol. 7017, pp. 121–130. Springer, Heidelberg (2011)

CPU and GPU Performance of Large Scale Numerical Simulations in Geophysics

Ali Dorostkar[1], Dimitar Lukarski[1], Björn Lund[2], Maya Neytcheva[1],
Yvan Notay[3], and Peter Schmidt[2]

[1] Department of Information Technology, Uppsala University, Sweden
{ali.dorostkar,dimitar.lukarski,maya.neytcheva}@it.uu.se
[2] Department of Earth Sciences, Uppsala University, Sweden
{bjorn.lund,peter.schmidt}@geo.uu.se
[3] Numerical Analysis Group Service de Métrologie Nucléaire,
Université Libre de Bruxelles, Belgium
ynotay@ulb.ac.be

Abstract. In this work we benchmark the performance of a preconditioned iterative method, used in large scale computer simulations of a geophysical application, namely, the elastic Glacial Isostatic Adjustment model. The model is discretized using the finite element method that gives raise to algebraic systems of equations with matrices that are large, sparse, nonsymmetric, indefinite and with a saddle point structure. The efficiency of solving systems of the latter type is crucial as it is to be embedded in a time-evolution procedure, where systems with matrices of similar type have to be solved repeatedly many times.

The implementation is based on available open source software packages - Deal.II, Trilinos, PARALUTION and AGMG. These packages provide toolboxes with state-of-the-art implementations of iterative solution methods and preconditioners for multicore computer platforms and GPU. We present performance results in terms of numerical and the computational efficiency, number of iterations and execution time, and compare the timing results against a sparse direct solver from a commercial finite element package, that is often used by applied scientists in their simulations.

Keywords: glacial isostatic adjustment, iterative methods, multicore, block-preconditioners, inner-outer iterations, CPU-GPU, performance.

1 Introduction

Solving realistic, large scale applied problems with advanced numerical techniques can be seen as a multidimensional optimization problem, with many levels of complexity that have to be simultaneously taken into account. We do not have anymore just one single method to be implemented and optimized on a given computer platform. The code that enables such large scale computer simulations usually requires a whole collection of algorithms, such as unstructured, adaptive or moving meshes; time-dependent processes that in turn require the

L. Lopes et al. (Eds.): Euro-Par 2014 Workshops, Part I, LNCS 8805, pp. 12–23, 2014.

repeated solution of nonlinear and/or linear systems; inner-outer solution procedures, block preconditioners that utilize internal algebraic structures, solution methods as algebraic multigrid that have a recursive nature. All this has to work efficiently on modern computer architectures. Another aspect to mention is that codes at this level of complexity can no longer be written from scratch but rather (combination of) ready toolboxes have to be used instead.

We consider as an example a large scale problem from Geophysics. We implement it using several publicly available high quality libraries and compare the performance of the underlying advanced multi-level numerical solver, the resulting scalability and performance on multicore CPU and GPU. Section 2 describes the simplified target problem and the mathematical model, used in the numerical experiments. In Section 3 we outline the solution method and the acceleration technique - a block lower-triangular preconditioner. Section 4 depicts the most important characteristics of the software packages used for the computer implementation of the numerical solution procedure. The experiments are described in Section 5. We illustrate both the numerical and computational efficiency of the numerical simulations, as well as the scalability and the parallel performance on multicore and GPU platforms. Conclusions are found in Section 6.

2   Description of the Problem – Discretization and Algebraic Formulation

The applied problem, that gives raise to the large scale linear systems of algebraic equations to be solved, is the so called glacial isostatic adjustment (GIA) model. It comprises the response of the solid Earth to redistribution of mass due to alternating glaciation and deglaciation periods. The processes that cause subsidence or uplift of the Earth surface are active today. To fully understand the interplay between the different processes, and, for example, be able to predict how coast lines will be affected and how glaciers and ice sheets will retreat, these have to be coupled also to recent global warming trend and melting of the current ice sheets and glaciers world wide. The long-term aim is to couple GIA modeling with other large scale models, such as Climate and Sea-level changes, Ice modeling etc. In this work, however, we consider only GIA models.

Mathematical Model. Although GIA model describes a very complex applied problem, here we deal with a model of modest mathematical difficulty. However, the test problem considered here appears as a building block in an extended simulation context, see [12] for more details.

The benchmark setting consists of a two-dimensional vertical cut of Earth's crust, assumed to be pre-stressed, homogeneous, visco-elastic and in a constant gravity field. The space domain is axisymmetric, 10000 km long and 4000 deep. We compute the deformations subject to the load of rectangular-shaped ice of sizes 1000 km times 2 km. The geometry of the problem is shown in Figure 1.

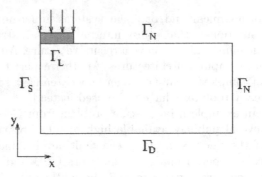

Fig. 1. The geometry of the problem

The momentum equation describing the quasi-static perturbations of such a material body is

$$-\underbrace{\nabla \cdot \sigma}_{(A)} - \underbrace{\nabla(\mathbf{u} \cdot \nabla p_0)}_{(B)} + \underbrace{(\nabla \cdot \mathbf{u})\nabla p_0}_{(C)} = \mathbf{f} \text{ in } \Omega \subset \mathbb{R}^2 \ , \tag{1}$$

where σ is the stress tensor, $\mathbf{u} = [u_i]_{i=1}^d$ is the displacement vector, p_0 is the so-called pre-stress and $\mathbf{f}$ is the body force. The boundary conditions are standard, $\sigma(\mathbf{u}) \cdot \mathbf{n} = \ell$ on Γ_L, $\sigma(\mathbf{u}) \cdot \mathbf{n} = \mathbf{0}$ on Γ_N, $\mathbf{u} = \mathbf{0}$ on Γ_D, $u_1 = 0$, $\partial_x u_2 = 0$ on Γ_S.

Term (A) describes the force due to spatial gradients in stress. Term (B) represents the so-called *advection of pre-stress* and has proven to be crucial for the successful modeling of the underlying physical processes [29]. Term (C) describes the buoyancy of the compressed material.

In addition to (1) we add appropriate constitutive relations, describing stress as a function of strain, displacements and time, namely, $\sigma(\mathbf{x}, t) = \sigma_E(\mathbf{x}) - \sigma_I(\mathbf{x}, t)$, where $\sigma_E(\mathbf{x})$ is the instantaneous stress due to elastic (reversible) response to load and $\sigma_I(\mathbf{x}, t)$ is the contribution due to inelastic response. In the target context the stress evolution is described via a heredity equation of the form

$$\sigma(\mathbf{x}, t) = C(\mathbf{x}, 0)\varepsilon_E - \int_0^t \frac{\partial C(\mathbf{x}, t - \tau)}{\partial \tau} \varepsilon(\mathbf{x}, \tau) \, d\tau \ .$$

Without describing the visco-elastic problem any further, we mention that we use the so-called Maxwell relaxation model, that simplifies the computation of the integral term. Here we consider the elastic part only, utilizing the standard relations between stress, strain and displacements, given by Hooke's law for a homogeneous, isotropic, linear, and purely elastic lithosphere, namely,

$$\sigma(\mathbf{u}) = 2\mu\varepsilon(\mathbf{u}) + \lambda(\nabla \cdot \mathbf{u})I \ , \tag{2}$$

where the coefficients μ and λ are the Lamé coefficients. We note that μ and λ are related to the Young modulus E and the Poisson ratio ν as $\mu_E = \frac{E}{2(1+\nu)}$ and $\lambda_E = \frac{2\mu\nu}{1-2\nu}$.

In order to compensate for excluding self-gravitation effects, we need to model fully incompressible materials, i.e., for which $\nu = 0.5$. However, when $\nu \to 0.5$, λ becomes unbounded. Thus, Equation (2) becomes ill-posed, and the corresponding discrete analogue of Equation (1) becomes extremely ill-conditioned. This phenomenon is known as *volumetric locking*. See, for example, [10], for further details on the locking effect.

A known remedy to the locking problem is to introduce the so-called *kinematic pressure* $p = \frac{\lambda}{\mu} \nabla \cdot \mathbf{u}$ and replacing the term $\lambda(\nabla \cdot \mathbf{u})I$ in (2), reformulate Equation (1) as a coupled system of PDEs, which yields

$$-\nabla \cdot (2\mu\varepsilon(\mathbf{u})) - \nabla(\mathbf{u} \cdot \nabla p_0) + (\nabla \cdot \mathbf{u})\nabla p_0 - \mu\nabla p = \mathbf{f} \text{ in } \Omega \qquad (3a)$$

$$\mu\nabla \cdot \mathbf{u} - \frac{\mu^2}{\lambda}p = 0 \text{ in } \Omega \qquad (3b)$$

with appropriate boundary conditions. Below we consider the solution of (3).

Space Discretization and Algebraic Formulation. We next perform a finite element space discretization of Ω, namely, consider a discretized domain Ω_h and some finite dimensional subspaces $V_h \subset V$ and $P_h \subset P$. To this end, we use mixed finite elements and the Q2-Q1 stable finite element pair of spaces for the displacements and the pressure, in order to satisfy the LBB condition (see, e.g. [11] for more details).

Remark: The handling of the visco-elastic problem and the corresponding numerical procedure are described in detail in [22]. In brief, we obtain a matrix-vector form of the problem to be solved at time t_j find the displacements $\mathbf{u}_j$ and the pressure $\mathbf{p}_j$ by solving the linear system

$$\mathcal{A}_j \begin{bmatrix} \mathbf{u}_j \\ \mathbf{p}_j \end{bmatrix} = \begin{bmatrix} \mathbf{r}_j \\ \mathbf{q}_j \end{bmatrix}, \ \mathcal{A}_j = \mathcal{A} - \frac{\Delta t_j}{2}\mathcal{A}_0, \ \mathcal{A} = \begin{bmatrix} M & B^T \\ B & -C \end{bmatrix}, \ \mathcal{A}_0 = \begin{bmatrix} M_0 & B_0^T \\ B_0 & -C_0 \end{bmatrix}.$$

The detailed forms of $\mathbf{r}_j$ and $\mathbf{q}_j$ and the matrix blocks are given in [22].

3   Numerical Solution Method and Preconditioning

To summarize, at each time t_j we have to solve a linear system with the matrix $\mathcal{A}_j$. We assume that Δt_j is small enough and from now on we investigate the solution of one representative system of equations of the type,

$$\mathcal{A}\mathbf{x} = \begin{bmatrix} M & B^T \\ B & -C \end{bmatrix} \begin{bmatrix} \mathbf{x}_1 \\ \mathbf{x}_2 \end{bmatrix} = \begin{bmatrix} \mathbf{b} \\ \mathbf{0} \end{bmatrix}, \qquad (4)$$

where $M \in \mathbb{R}^{N_u \times N_u}$ is non-symmetric, sparse and in general indefinite, and $C^{N_p \times N_p}$ is positive semi-definite. Thus, $\mathcal{A}$ is of saddle point form.

The algebraic problem in (4) is solved with an iterative solution method, preconditioned by the block lower-triangular matrix $\mathcal{D} = \begin{bmatrix} \widetilde{M} & 0 \\ B & -\widetilde{S} \end{bmatrix}$, where the block $\widetilde{M}$ approximates M, and the block $\widetilde{S}$, approximates the negative Schur complement of $\mathcal{A}$, $S = C + BM^{-1}B^T$. The block-triangular matrix $\mathcal{D}$ is one of the possible choices of a preconditioner for $\mathcal{A}$ and we refer to [9, 4] for an extensive survey on solution techniques for saddle point problems.

A matrix of the above block lower-triangular form is among the most often used preconditioners for matrices of saddle point form as in (4). For $\widetilde{M} = M$ ans $\widetilde{S} = S$, the matrix $\mathcal{D}$ is referred to as the *ideal preconditioner*, as it clusters the spectrum of $\mathcal{D}_I^{-1}\mathcal{A}$ in just two points, -1 and 1, ensuring that, for instance, GMRES (see [28]) will converge in two-three iterations, the computational cost is, however, prohibitive.

Approximating M and S by $\widetilde{M}$ and $\widetilde{S}$ respectively causes an increase in the number of iterations of the preconditioned iterative method. Eigenvalue analysis reveals that $\widetilde{M}$ must approximate M very well. In order to control the quality of this approximation, we use an inner solver for M with some suitable preconditioner. The usage of an inner solver is denoted in the sequel by $[M]$. On the other hand, approximating S by $\widetilde{S}$ has less profound effect, compared with that of $\widetilde{M}$. This is confirmed by the rigorous eigenvalue analysis provided in [25] (see in particular Corollary 4.5). For the purpose of this study we compute $\widetilde{S}$ using the so-called *element-by-element* (EBE) approach, see for instance, [16, 5, 22, 21] and the references therein. The EBE technique is very attractive as it is easily patallelizable and produces a good quality sparse approximation of the, in general, dense Schur complement.

The system $\mathcal{A}$ is solved by the flexible variant of GMRES, FGMRES, cf. [28, 27], referred to as the *outer solver*. The choice of the outer method is due to the fact that M is nonsymmetric and that the preconditioner is variable, due to the inner solvers involved. The preconditioner is thus

$$\mathcal{D} = \begin{bmatrix} [M] & 0 \\ B & -[\widetilde{S}] \end{bmatrix}. \tag{5}$$

Systems with M and $\widetilde{S}$ are solved by inner iterations using GMRES and preconditioned by an algebraic Multigrid (AMG) method.

We construct the AMG preconditioner for $[M]$ in two ways. The first option is for the block M as a whole, denoted by $[M_0]$. Alternatively, ordering the degrees of freedom (DOFs) of the displacements first in x-direction and then in y-direction reveals a block two-by-two structure of the matrix M itself. Then the block diagonal of M is a good choice to construct AMG. For an explanation, see for instance, [3]. The resulting preconditioned inner solver is denoted by $[M_1]$.

4   Implementation Details

As already pointed out, computer simulations of realistic applied problems usually result in very complex coupled models. Implementing a fully functional and flexible code for such models needs excessive coding and a substantial amount of time. Over the past decades, many libraries have been developed to ease the development process for scientific computing applications. These libraries include state-of-the-art numerical solution methods that are robust and reliable due to many years of development and rigorous testing. Using such libraries helps the researchers to concentrate on the problem itself and not on implementation technicalities.

We describe next the software used to implement the solution procedure for (4), preconditioned by (5), using $[M_0]$ for the solution of systems with M. The code is developed using $C++$ except AGMG that is available in FORTRAN. The systems $\mathcal{A}$, $[M_0]$ and $[\widetilde{S}]$ are solved with tolerance of 10^{-7} and 10^{-1} respectively. We note that solving the same system in 3D requires minor adjustment in the preconditioner and handling the boundary values. The rest is automatically taken care of through a template parameter stating the dimension of the problem.

Differential Equations Analysis Library (Deal.II) is used as the main finite element software toolbox. It is a general purpose object-oriented finite element library suitable for solving systems of partial differential equations. Deal.II is publicly available under an Open Source license. For more details on Deal.II, see [7].

Deal.II expands its functionality by providing interfaces to other packages such as Trilinos, PETSc [6], METIS [15] and others. Each package is added and used via a wrapper class in Deal.II. Data movement between Deal.II and other packages can be avoided by using the proper data structure provided by the Deal.II wrappers. For our purpose, we use the Deal.II wrapper for Trilinos.

As precondtioners for the inner solvers for M and $\widetilde{S}$ we use an AMG preconditioner, provided by Trilinos, AGMG and PARALUTION, see below.

Trilinos in its whole has a vast collection of algorithms within an object oriented framework aimed at scientific computing problems. More details about Trilinos can be found in [14]. Deal.II configures and uses the packages from Trilinos through Deal.II wrappers. In this study we use *Epetra* for sparse matrix and vector storage, *Teuchos* to provide parameters of solver and preconditioner, *ML* for multigrid preconditioning, *AZTEC* for the iterative solver (GMRES). Note that all the aforementioned packages are accessed through Deal.II wrappers.

The AMG from Trilinos is configured using Chebyshev smoother with two pre- and post-smoothing steps, uncoupled aggregation with threshold of 0.02 and one multigrid cycle. We refer to [7] for a detailed description of the settings.

PARALUTION is a sparse linear algebra library with focus on exploring fine-grained parallelism, targeting modern processors and accelerators including multi/many-core CPU and GPU platforms. The goal of this project is to provide a portable library for iterative sparse methods on state-of-the-art hardware. The library contains a solid collection of various methods for solving sparse linear systems. All solvers and preconditioners are based on matrix and vector objects.

PARALUTION separates its objects from actual hardware specification. The objects are initially allocated on the host (CPU). Then every object can be moved to a selected accelerator by a simple move-to-accelerator function. The execution is based on run-time type information (RTTI) which allows the user to select where and how to perform the operations at run time. This is in contrast to template-based libraries that need this information at compilation time.

The philosophy of the library is to abstract the hardware-specific functions and routines from the actual program which describes the algorithm. This abstraction layer of the hardware specific routines is the core of PARALUTION's design, it is built to explore fine-grained level of parallelism suited for multi/many-core devices. In this way PARALUTION differs from most of the available parallel sparse libraries which are mainly based on domain decomposition techniques. Thus, the design of the iterative solvers and the preconditioners are very different. Another cornerstone of PARALUTION is the native support of accelerators - the memory allocation, transfers and specific hardware functions are handled internally in the library. The library provides OpenMP (Host, Xeon Phi/MIC), OpenCL (NVIDIA, AMD GPUs), CUDA (NVIDIA GPUs) backends. For more details we refer to [18].

A plug-in to Deal.II is provided which is not a direct wrapper as for Trilinos, but exports and imports data from Deal.II to PARALUTION. To solve the linear problem, we use the preconditioner $[M_0]$ and own implementation of AMG. The AMG is set to have the coarsest grid size as 2000 with smooth aggregation as the coarsening method, coupling strength is set to 0.001, the smoother is of multicolored Gauss-Seidel type with relaxation parameter set to 1.3, [17]. Additionally, one pre-smoothing step, two post- smoothing steps and one multigrid cycle for preconditioning are performed. The AMG has to be constructed entirely on the CPU, while the execution can be performed on the CPU or on the GPU without any code modification.

AGMG implements an aggregation-based algebraic multigrid method [19]. It provides tools for constructing the preconditioner and to solve linear systems of equations, and is expected to be efficient for large systems arising from the discretization of scalar second order elliptic PDEs. The method is however purely algebraic. The software package provides subroutines, written in FORTRAN, which implement the method described in [23], with further improvements from [20, 24].

AGMG's parallel performance is tested on up to 370000 cores. However, currently parallel implementation is available only with MPI and, therefore, in this study we compare it's serial performance with that of Trilinos AMG.

In this study AGMG uses double pairwise aggregation for the coarsening (with quality control as in [20, 24]), performed separately on the two components of the displacement vector. Furthermore, AGMG performs one forward and one backward Gauss-Seidel sweep for pre- and post-smoothing respectively and also a K-cycle [26], i.e., two Krylov accelerated iterations at each intermediate level. The main iterative solver in AGMG is the Generalized Conjugate Residual method, [13].

ABAQUS is a general-purpose finite element analysis program, most suited for numerical modelling of structural response. It handles various stress problems, both with static and dynamic response. The program is designed to ease the solution of complex problems, and has a simple input language, with comprehensive data checking, as well as a wide range of preprocessing and post-processing

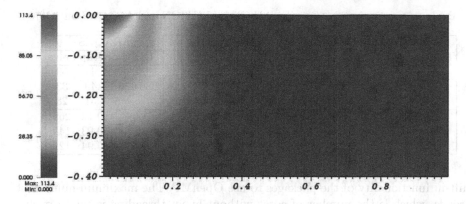

Fig. 2. GIA simulation - vertical displacements on the surface

options. However, enhanced numerical simulations of GIA problems are not straightforwardly performed with ABAQUS since important terms in the continuous model, such as prestress advection, cannot be added directly, leading to the necessity to modify the model in order to be able to use the package. These questions are described in detail in [30]. Further, ABAQUS cannot handle purely incompressible materials - ν cannot be set to 0.5 but to some closer value, such as 0.4999, for instance.

Nevertheless, ABAQUS offers highly optimized numerical solution methods. In particular, the available sparse direct solver in 2D shows nearly optimal computational complexity, see the results in [8] and the performance figures in Section 5. The direct solver can be executed in parallel and its scalability is also presented. We use here ABAQUS 6.12.

The iterative methods, included in ABAQUS can be tested only on 3D problems. For further details we refer to ABAQUS' user manual [1].

5 Performance Analysis

In this section we present the results of the numerical experiments with different software packages. The computations are performed on the following computer resources:

(C1) CPU: Intel(R) Xeon(R) 1.6GHz 12 cores
(C2) CPU: Intel(R) Core(TM) i5-3550 CPU 3.30GHz 4 cores
        GPU: NVIDIA K40, 12G, 2880 cores

In Figure 2 we illustrate the GIA simulations. We show the vertical displacements in the domain, caused by a rectangular ice load as described in the test problem.

The performance results for ABAQUS, Deal.II, Trilinos and AGMG are obtained using (C1). The solver from PARALUTION (ver 0.6.1) is tested on CPU using both resources and on the GPU using (C2). Parallelism is exploited by the

Table 1. Comparison between Deal.II, PARALUTION and ABAQUS on (C1)

No. of Threads	Deal.II + Trilinos			PARALUTION		ABAQUS		
	DOFs	Setup	Solve (2/3)	Setup	Solve (2/3)	DOFs	Setup	Solve
1		3.43	44.2 (29.4)	14.5	51.6 (34.4)		7.44	59
4	1 479 043	3.04	30.8 (20.5)	9.76	20.9 (13.9)	986 626	7.49	33
8		3.00	25.2 (16.8)	8.76	22.4 (14.9)		7.51	28
1		15.4	235 (156)	59.4	220 (147)		29.72	269
4	5 907 203	14.2	155 (103)	40.4	92.7 (61.8)	3 939 330	29.93	145
8		14.1	126 (84)	36.2	92.5 (61.7)		29.94	122

built-in functionality of the packages to use OpenMP. The maximum number of threads, which is the number of cores without hyper-threading is set to twelve on (C1) and four on (C2).

From (3) we observe that while enabling to solve the models with fully incompressible materials, we obtain a system of equation that is about 30% larger than what is solved with ABAQUS. The problem sizes are shown in Table 1.

It is evident from Table 1 that both solution techniques scale nearly exactly linearly with the problem size. However, for the two- dimensional problem at hand, the direct solver from ABAQUS is somewhat faster than the preconditioned iterative solver, implemented in Trilinos. More detailed information, including iteration counts, is given in [12], confirming experimentally the optimality of the iterative solver.

Figure 3a shows the used time of the iterative solver using Trilinos and PARALUTION on four threads. While PARALUTION is faster than Trilinos in computing the solution, it takes more CPU time in the setup phase. We note that both Trilinos and PARALUTION do not scale to more than four threads. For more details see [12]. We also note that PARALUTION performs faster than the direct solver from ABAQUS.

From experiments, not included here, performed using *valgrind*, cf. [2], one can see that the lack of scaling is due to the matrix- vector multiplications in AMG. This issue is not solvable within the shared memory programming model and using OpenMP for further developing the model and/or extending the computational domain will be a bottle neck. We expect to see better scaling by changing the programming model to MPI.

As mentioned above PARALUTION is tested on CPU using both (C1) and (C2). The results of these experiments are used as reference to compare the results of PARALUTION on the GPU with the results of ABAQUS and Trilinos. The results are presented in Figure 3b. We see that for smaller problem sizes the GPU solver from PARALUTION is slower than the CPU solver. As the problem size grows the GPU outperforms the CPU with up to four times speedup. Solving the largest problem size on the GPU leads to insufficient memory error.

We note that the discretization of the problem, corresponding to 1 479 043 degrees of freedom, on the surface of the computational domain agrees with the placement of the surface sensors that gather data from geophysical experiments. This size fits on the GPU and the performance is fastest. Trying to solve

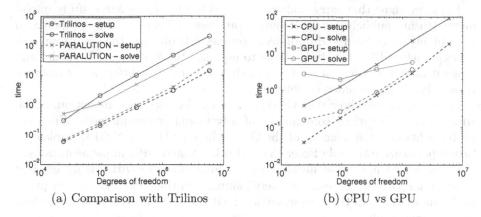

(a) Comparison with Trilinos   (b) CPU vs GPU

Fig. 3. Performance comparisons: PARALUTION

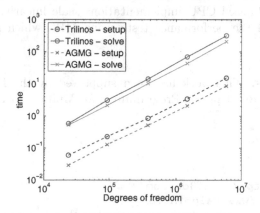

Fig. 4. Comparison between Trilinos-AMG and AGMG

problems with larger computational domain in 2D or 3D problems might fail due to insufficient memory on the currently available GPUs.

To optimize the solution process, we consider changing the AMG implementation to investigate the potential scalability of the AMG implementation itself. To this end, we replace Trilinos-AMG by AGMG. The results in Figure 4 show that AGMG has better computational efficiency. Since, we use the AGMG only serially (there is no OpenMP implementation yet) we compare the timing with the Trilinos-AMG only using one thread.

6   Conclusion

In this work we present a snapshot of the performance of a large scale computer simulation in terms of numerical efficiency, execution time and scalability on multicore platforms as well as on GPU.

First, we show that large scale coupled problems can be successfully implemented using publicly available numerical linear algebra software. Compared with highly specialized and optimized commercial software, the open source libraries, included in this study, allow to enhance the mathematical model and make it more realistic, adding features that are not straightforwardly incorporated when using commercial software.

Furthermore, we show that GPU devices can be used in complex numerical simulations with various combination of solvers and preconditioners. When the problem fits into the memory of the GPU, the PARALUTION-GPU implementation performs noticeably faster than all other tested CPU implementations.

Open source numerical libraries successfully compete with highly efficient commercial packages in terms of overall simulation time and show better price-performance ratio. In the current setting PARALUTION proves to show the best performance results.

However, due to the fact that all methods are memory bounded, none of the tested OpenMP-based CPU implementations scale linearly. This makes it necessary to extend the performance tests using MPI, which is a subject of future work.

Acknowledgments. This work has been supported by the Linnaeus center of excellence UPMARC, Uppsala Programming for Multicore Architectures Research Center.

References

1. Abaqus FEA, http://www.3ds.com/
2. Valgrind, http://www.valgrind.org
3. Axelsson, O.: On iterative solvers in structural mechanics; separate displacement orderings and mixed variable methods. Math. Comput. Simulation 50(1-4), 11–30 (1999); Modelling 1998, Prague (1998)
4. Axelsson, O.: Milestones in the development of iterative solution methods. J. Electr. Comput. Eng., Art. ID 972794, 33 (2010)
5. Axelsson, O., Blaheta, R., Neytcheva, M.: Preconditioning of boundary value problems using elementwise schur complements. SIAM J. Matrix Anal. Appl. 31(2), 767–789 (2009)
6. Balay, S., Adams, M.F., Brown, J., Brune, P., Buschelman, K., Eijkhout, V., Gropp, W.D., Kaushik, D., Knepley, M.G., McInnes, L.C., Rupp, K., Smith, B.F., Zhang, H.: PETSc Web page (2014), http://www.mcs.anl.gov/petsc
7. Bangerth, W., Kanschat, G., Hartmann, R.: deal.II differential equations analysis library, http://www.dealii.org
8. Bängtsson, E., Lund, B.: A comparison between two solution techniques to solve the equations of glacially induced deformation of an elastic earth. International Journal for Numerical Methods in Engineering 75(4), 479–502 (2008)
9. Benzi, M., Golub, G.H., Liesen, J.: Numerical solution of saddle point problems. Acta Numerica 14, 1–137 (2005)
10. Braess, D.: Finite elements, 3rd edn. Theory, fast solvers, and applications in elasticity theory. Cambridge University Press, Cambridge (2007)

11. Brezzi, F.: On the existence, uniqueness and approximation of saddle-point problems arising from Lagrangian multipliers. Rev. Française Automat. Informat. Recherche Opérationnelle Sér. Rouge 8(R-2), 129–151 (1974)
12. Dorostkar, A., Lukarski, D., Lund, B., Neytcheva, M., Notay, Y., Schmidt, P.: Parallel performance study of block-preconditioned iterative methods on multicore computer systems. Technical Report 2014-007, Department of Information Technology, Uppsala University (March 2014)
13. Eisenstat, S.C., Elman, H.C., Schultz, M.H.: Variational iterative methods for nonsymmetric systems of linear equations 20, 345–357 (1983)
14. Heroux, M.A., Willenbring, J.M.: Trilinos Users Guide. Technical Report SAND2003-2952, Sandia National Lab. (2003), http://trilinos.sandia.gov
15. Karypis, G., Kumar, V.: MeTis: Unstructured Graph Partitioning and Sparse Matrix Ordering System, Version 4.0 (2009), http://www.cs.umn.edu/~metis
16. Kraus, J.: Additive Schur complement approximation and application to multilevel preconditioning. SIAM J. Sci. Comput. 34(6), A2872–A2895 (2012)
17. Lukarski, D.: Parallel Sparse Linear Algebra for Multi-core and Many-core Platforms – Parallel Solvers and Preconditioners. PhD thesis, Karlsruhe Institute of Technology (January 2012)
18. Lurkarski, D.: Paralution project, http://www.paralution.com
19. Notay, Y.: AGMG software and documentation, http://homepages.ulb.ac.be/~ynotay/AGMG
20. Napov, A., Notay, Y.: An algebraic multigrid method with guaranteed convergence rate. SIAM J. Sci. Comput. 34(2), A1079–A1109 (2012)
21. Neytcheva, M.: On element-by-element Schur complement approximations. Linear Algebra Appl. 434(11), 2308–2324 (2011)
22. Neytcheva, M., Bängtsson, E.: Preconditioning of nonsymmetric saddle point systems as arising in modelling of viscoelastic problems. Electronic Transactions on Numerical Analysis 29, 193–211 (2008)
23. Notay, Y.: An aggregation-based algebraic multigrid method. Electron. Trans. Numer. Anal. 37, 123–146 (2010)
24. Notay, Y.: Aggregation-based algebraic multigrid for convection-diffusion equations. SIAM J. Sci. Comput. 34(4), A2288–A2316 (2012)
25. Notay, Y.: A new analysis of block preconditioners for saddle point problems. SIAM J. Matrix Anal. Appl. 35, 143–173 (2014)
26. Notay, Y., Vassilevski, P.S.: Recursive Krylov-based multigrid cycles. Numer. Lin. Alg. Appl. 15, 473–487 (2008)
27. Saad, Y.: A flexible inner-outer preconditioned GMRES algorithm. SIAM J. Sci. Comput. 14(2), 461–469 (1993)
28. Saad, Y., Schultz, M.H.: GMRES: a generalized minimal residual algorithm for solving nonsymmetric linear systems. SIAM J. Sci. Comput. 7(3), 856–869 (1986)
29. Wu, P.: Viscoelastic versus viscous deformation and the advection of pre-stress. Geophysical Journal International 108(1), 136–142 (1992)
30. Wu, P.: Using commercial finite element packages for the study of earth deformations, sea levels and the state of stress. Geophysical Journal International 158(2), 401–408 (2004)

Parallelizing a CAD Model Processing Tool from the Automotive Industry

Luis Ayuso[1], Herbert Jordan[1], Thomas Fahringer[1],
Bernhard Kornberger[2], Martin Schifko[3],
Bernhard Höckner[1], Stefan Moosbrugger[1], and Kevin Verma[3]

[1] University of Innsbruck, Institute of Computer Science, Innsbruck, Austria
{luis,herbert,tf}@dps.uibk.ac.at,
{Bernhard.Hoeckner,Stefan.Moosbrugger}@student.uibk.ac.at
[2] Geom Softwareentwicklung, Graz, Austria
bkorn@geom.at
[3] ECS, Magna Powertrain, Steyr, Austria
Martin.Schifko@ecs.steyr.com

Abstract. Large industrial applications are complex software environments with multiple objectives and strict requirements regarding standards, architecture or technology dependencies. The parallelization and optimization of industrial applications can be an intrusive modification of the source code which increases the development complexity. In this paper we describe the analysis and modifications applied to an industrial code from the automotive industry, named *Merge*, with the goal to detect and exploit parallelism in order to reduce the resulting execution time for shared memory parallel architectures. As part of this effort we tried to maximize the potential for an effective parallelization, nevertheless preserving the original algorithm and the code features as far as possible. Reasonable speedup has been achieved on a shared memory parallel architecture. Furthermore, additional potential has been located for future parallelization and optimization work.

1 Introduction

Performance-oriented development of scientific and industrial applications for parallel architectures is a time-consuming and tedious process that involves many cycles of editing, compiling, executing, and performance analysis. This paper summarizes the experience acquired during the parallelization and optimization process of the *Merge* application which is being developed in C++ by Martin Schifko (ECS, Engineering Center Steyr GmbH & Co KG) and Bernhard Kornberger (Geom e.U.). ECS develops different software solutions for the automotive industry.

The *Merge* application is a fully automatic repair-, connect-, and re-meshing-tool for triangular meshes. It fulfills the high requirements in automotive industry and is of great interest because it can significantly reduce the development cycle of automotive industry products. The process of merging and possibly repairing

L. Lopes et al. (Eds.): Euro-Par 2014 Workshops, Part I, LNCS 8805, pp. 24–35, 2014.

and remeshing triangular meshes is nowadays still often performed manually. Involving an expert is time consuming and error-prone without an analysis tool like *Merge*.

The result of a *Merge* application execution – among other uses – is utilized by electrophoretic deposition simulation (e.g., *ALSIM* software[1] developed by ECS) which requires as input a single mesh object representing an entire car. In this scenario, the *Merge* application will operate on thousands of individual car body parts to produce a unique car mesh. The execution will also enforce some characteristics of the processed meshes: e.g. non-manifold meshes will be repaired, self-intersections will be avoided while maintaining the surface shape. The geometrical details of the merge process are covered by Schifko et al.[2].

Exact evaluation of geometric predicates, vital for the robustness of the Merge application, is achieved using the 3D linear geometry kernel of the Computational Geometry Algorithms Library (*CGAL*)[3], not only at the price of execution time overhead, it also prevents from applying GPGPU techniques.

In this paper we start with a description of the *Merge* application and then describe the original parallelization and identify drawbacks. Based on this initial effort, we established clear principles for parallelization which have been applied in an improved parallelization of the *Merge* application. As a first step, we isolated code regions with potential for parallelism in the overall application which improved the modularity of the code and simplified ongoing development of *Merge*. The intended philosophy of any code modification was to interfere as little as possible with the core functionality of the program while reducing the size of code regions dedicated to parallelism management. Modifications applied to specific code regions should enable and expose parallelism without changing the original algorithmic properties.

To improve the overall parallelization and thereby reduce the computation time, we applied three optimizations comprising nested parallelism to mitigate load imbalance, reduction operations on demand to overlap map and reduce operations, and tuning OpenMP thread management to deal with the overhead of large number of threads. Experiments with several input data sets for the *Merge* application result in a speedup of up to 5.59 (when using 16 cores) compared to sequential executions.

Section 3 describes the original parallelization strategy for *Merge*. A new parallelization and optimization approach for *Merge* is explained in Section 4. Section 5 presents numerous experiments to demonstrate the effectiveness of the proposed parallelization and optimization techniques with several input data sets. Related work is discussed in Section 6 followed by Conclusion and Future Work (Section 7).

2   Architecture of the *Merge* Application

Fig. 1 shows a detail of a typical *Merge* application execution. Fig. 1a shows the superposition of different volumes, each of them defined by a different CAD file. Fig. 1b shows a single object which covers the volume corresponding to the union of Fig. 1a volumes.

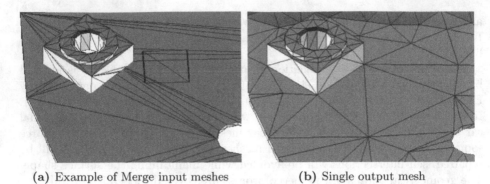

(a) Example of Merge input meshes   (b) Single output mesh

Fig. 1. Merge operation example

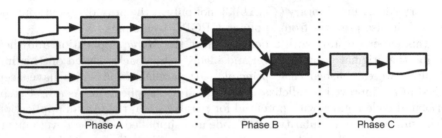

Fig. 2. *Merge*'s implicit task dependency graph

Fig. 2 shows the tree structure which intuitively describes the internal structure of the *Merge* application. This figure reveals that the internal structure fits a MapReduce pattern [4]. Each node of this tree corresponds to a certain task e.g. Repair, Offset, Merge, Export, IO. Tasks are internally organized as a sequence of algorithms, arranged and parametrized to solve a specific functionality. The term *task* refers to the execution of a sequence of algorithms on one or two data elements, and produces a single output element. Each of those data elements are loaded from a CAD file and referred to as *mesh* throughout the remainder of this paper. The *Merge* application operates on an input data set which contains a series of different CAD files. These data sets are processed by three phases:

- Phase A: Loading and preparing the input. Input meshes are read from files and then a series of algorithms is applied to each of them.
- Phase B: Merging. After the pre-process phase, meshes are pairwise merged, until a single resulting mesh is obtained. Notice that this is the actual merge operation. Although the application is called *Merge*, it actually executes several algorithms contributing additional services as part of the overall commercial solution.
- Phase C: Cleanup and export. The final resulting mesh is cleaned up such that parametrized geometrical constraints are enforced. In the end, the mesh is written into a file.

Algorithm 1. Baseline Merge Algorithm (proper synchronization implied)

Input: M ... list of meshes

---

queue $\leftarrow$ *schedule*(M)
begin parallel
  while (queue $\neq \emptyset$) **do**
    $t \leftarrow$ retrieve first runable task from queue
    process t
  end while
end parallel

As shown in Fig. 2, dependencies between tasks constrain their execution order.

3 Initial Parallel Structure

The initial *Merge* implementation, which provided the base line of our optimization and tuning efforts, has been utilizing the available parallelism on a task level, as summarized by Algorithm 1..

Algorithm 1. consists of a scheduling and an execution step. In the first step, the input data set is mapped to a list of tasks, ordered according to their dependencies, and stored in a queue. In the second step, a team of concurrently running threads retrieve tasks from the queue and executes them in parallel. When all tasks are done, the process is complete.

The basic idea of the *schedule* procedure is to instantiate the necessary tasks, determine dependencies and compute (implicitly) a topological order of the resulting task-dependency graph – as illustrated in Fig. 2. The main source of influence on the performance is to determine the order in which meshes are combined in Phase B. The corresponding operations are associative and commutative. The meshes produced by Phase A may therefore be reduced to a single mesh using an arbitrary order.

In the intention to keep the critical path length short, the scheduler of the base implementation realizes a binary reduction resembling a balanced, binary tree. Furthermore, since the computational costs of the operations in Phase B are (partially) depending on the number of triangles of the input meshes, a heuristic keeping the size of intermediate results low is utilized for its generation.

3.1 Performance Analysis

To gain insides on the behavior of the utilized algorithms and scheduling policies we traced the processing of different data sets on a parallel architecture. Fig. 3 illustrates a typical pattern that is observable when processing 6 meshes on a 4 core system. The CPU time required by tasks of Phase A are varying by up to an order of magnitude. Naturally, the longest execution of those tasks delay tasks

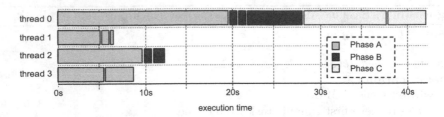

Fig. 3. Example task distribution of the baseline *Merge* implementation

of Phase B, which is made worse by the balanced nature of the reduction tree. Finally, the tasks of Phase C, whose constraints demand a sequential execution, are responsible for roughly a fifth of the sequential execution time. The best experimentally observed speedups have been ∼ 2.5 for a large number of input files on an 8 core system.

3.2   Improvement Potential

The information gained from the initial analysis lead us to focus on two approaches for increasing *Merge*'s performance:

- *Nested Parallelism* – the low resource utilization due to the high load imbalance in Phase A and the sequential Phase C could be improved by unveiling and utilizing nested parallelism within the individual tasks
- *Dynamic Reduction* – the constraint imposed of a balanced binary reduction tree could be dropped by merging temporary results according to the (dynamic) order they are completed, thereby reducing the time threads are stalled due to unfinished temporary results

The implementation and application of corresponding techniques is the topic of the following section.

4   New Parallelization and Optimization Strategy

To improve the performance of the code by increasing its resource utilization we applied a series of steps as covered in the following subsections.

4.1   Step 1: Nested Parallelism

Nested parallelism can effectively help reducing the load imbalance by lowering the granularity of the workload to be distributed among the available resources. Unfortunately, to benefit from this, parallelism within the individual tasks has to be identified and utilized.

Essentially there are two potential approaches for speeding up a single task being applied on a single input mesh. Either the operations to be applied themselves are distributed among parallel resources or the input mesh is partitioned into smaller meshes, which then are processed concurrently. However, due to the nature of the applied algorithms, the integrity of the processed meshes is essential. Consequently, only the first approach could be pursued.

Fortunately, meshes themselves are essentially just collections of triangles. Hence, many of the applied procedures within the involved tasks offer good opportunities for data parallelism. The profile of the execution helped to identify loops dominating the execution time to obtain worthwhile candidates for parallelization. Each of those were inspected for dependencies preventing their iterations to be processed concurrently and if present, the alternatives were studied. In general, three types of loops were found:

- *embarrassing parallel loops* – where each iteration is working fully independently of any other iteration. For instance, frequently an operation has to be applied on all triangles of a mesh or all the edges or points referenced by those. An extended, yet almost equally simple to handle, variant is a reduction loop aggregating values computed by iterations into an overall result utilizing a commutative and associative operator. The parallelization of this kind of loops is straightforward.
- *parallel loops with false dependencies* – where each iteration is conducting operations on a shared data structure, e.g. the processed mesh, while those operations have no effect in the operations of the remaining iterations. The dependency between loop iterations is only introduced by the utilized containers and index structures. Those dependencies are not essential for the algorithm, yet prohibit a parallel execution. Typically, adding fine grained locking and atomic operations to those data structures would help resolving the problem, yet a modification of elements producing this dependencies, and implemented on third-party codes was not feasible.
  For the loops fitting in this category, the parallelization was implemented by separating the identification of manipulations to be conducted on the shared data structure from the actual application. The first step can so be conducted in parallel and results in a list of closures encapsulating manipulation operations. Those operations are then applied in a second step sequentially. Occasionally, identified update operations where sorted such that parts of them could be applied concurrently.
- *inherently sequential loops* – where each iteration is depending on the results of the immediate previous iteration. In those cases no parallelization could be done and other code sections dominating the execution time were considered.

The scheduling policies to be utilized for the parallelized loops were also studied. In general, the identified loops exhibit a rather irregular workload distribution among its iterations and even for regular loops a *dynamic loop scheduling scheme* proved to be most profitable due to the fact that their computation happens in a nested context including threads of other tasks competing for resources.

Algorithm 2. Improved Merge Algorithm (proper synchronization implied)

Input: M ... list of meshes

---

stack $\leftarrow \epsilon$
for all $m \in M$ **do**
   $r \leftarrow$ phaseA(m)
   while (stack $\neq \epsilon$) **do**
      $r \leftarrow$ phaseB(r, pop(stack))
   end while
   push(stack, r)
end for
return phaseC(pop(stack))

In general, those parallelization steps have been rather straightforward. The biggest lesson that could be drawn from this process is the fact that OpenMP and C++ idioms are sometimes in conflict. In particular OpenMP's restriction on the structure of for loops, including the requirement of *random access iterators* not provided by all types of collections and the (current) exclusion of the C++11[5] for-each loop are minor, yet cumbersome restrictions. More severe issues, however, are implied by object oriented design patterns and the associated principle of *information hiding* making it difficult to identify dependencies and potential race conditions in manipulated code.

Those issues are not unknown in general, yet our experience provides further evidence for those and a motivation to provide improved tool support and/or increased flexibility in the future.

4.2   Step 2: Reduction on Demand

This section focuses on the top-level structure of the parallel implementation which has been summarized in Algorithm 1.. The separation of the scheduling step and the execution is prohibiting the consideration of dynamically obtained information into the organization of the reduction operation of Phase B. Furthermore, load management responsibilities have been explicitly included in the application code by the utilization of the included (global) *queue* and the imposed work-fetching scheme. Both activities could and should be delegated to the runtime system.

The baseline implementation was utilizing *boost threads* for the top level parallelism, resulting in a mixture of runtime systems when combined with the nested OpenMP based parallel codes. Hence, in a first step the top level parallelism has been restructured to utilize OpenMP as well – thereby providing the OpenMP runtime system the full control on thread spawning and management decisions.

In a second step *schedule* function and the *queue* were replaced by an eager reduction scheme summarized by Algorithm 2. based on a parallel for-all loop. In this approach meshes that are ready for being included in the reduction step of Phase B are put on a *stack*. Whenever a mesh r is yield by Phase A, the current result r is combined with all available meshes stored in the stack. Thus constituting a dynamic reduction scheme combining meshes as soon as they are available.

Unfortunately, like the baseline implementation, our approach encodes an explicit scheduling policy for the reduction operations. Ideally, this responsibility would also be delegated to the runtime system by utilizing an *OpenMP custom reduction* incorporated in version 4.0. However, since the *Merge* application is targeted to be compiled by the *Microsoft* C++ compiler and this version is not yet supported an ad hoc implementation was required.

On the other hand, explicit scheduling policies do provide the opportunity to integrate heuristics to manage the reduction process. The base implementation aimed for minimizing the size of temporary results while our approach is an eager reduction not considering any algorithm specific traits and hence risking and increasing the computational complexity of the overall process. Yet, as will be demonstrated in the experimental section, the latter approach resulted in faster execution times for the investigated scenarios.

Table 1. Experiment inputs

	orbit	cubes	carPart	cylParts
Number of input files	8	44	32	4
Total # triangles	3.1MB	9MB	37.24MB	0.24MB
Sequential time	75.8	780.99	1354.53	21.22

Table 2. Original MapReduce (seconds)

Cores	Original				Step 1			
	Orbit	Cubes	carPart	CylParts	Orbit	Cubes	carPart	CylParts
2	56.00	456.97	1191.92	19.00	43.3	469.0	780.1	13.5
4	48.84	342.05	1021.23	18.54	28.7	318.5	610.5	11.9
8	46.51	310.96	860.11	18.48	20.1	243.9	374.9	6.7
16	46.90	315.35	992.96	18.61	18.6	535.7	361.6	11.6

Table 3. Reduction on demand (seconds)

Cores	Step 2				Step 3			
	Orbit	Cubes	carPart	CylParts	Orbit	Cubes	carPart	CylParts
2	35.19	431.64	671.32	10.32	34.0	450.1	741.4	9.2
4	26.49	271.29	479.19	9.11	26.1	308.3	397.1	6.8
8	25.50	263.07	454.28	8.35	15.4	217.6	269.7	5.0
16	25.78	269.24	456.99	9.1	16.8	289.3	238.2	6.8

4.3   Step 3: Tuning OpenMP Thread Management

For the code version exploiting nested parallelism, the analysis of the experiments conducted on a variety of configurations – exhibiting a different number of cores – shown diminishing results for larger scale systems (see Section 5). An investigation of those results revealed that this effect could not only be attributed to higher synchronization overhead caused by increased lock contention. Instead the nested parallel code led to an increase in the number of concurrently active threads competing for CPU time – a number that grows exponentially with the nesting level. The default policy of OpenMP[6] – to create thread groups consisting of the same number of threads as physical cores available on the system – amplifies this effect on larger scale systems. As an example, a 3-level nested parallel code section leads to the creation of up to 64 threads on a 4-core system, 512 threads on an 8 core system, and up to 4096 threads on a 16 core system. Despite having a large number of threads is beneficial for overcoming load-balancing issues, a too large number of threads leads to congestion and hence overhead introduced by the OS-level scheduler.

Consequently, a fine-tuning of the thread spawning policy was required. One widely utilized possibility is to integrate the thread spawning control into the application code in order to determine the number of threads – during runtime – to be utilized to execute concurrent regions [7]. Yet this would have led to dependencies between otherwise unrelated parts of the code, solely introduced for the thread management. Also, it would require the integration of an internal mechanism to monitor the parallel execution of the application.

Fortunately, an alternative is provided by OpenMP by offering parameters for tuning thread-spawning policies. While limiting the maximum number of nested parallel levels is less applicable, since the required nesting level is depending on the current state of the execution, parameters limiting the maximum number of simultaneously active threads have turned out to be most beneficial. Preliminary investigations resulted in acceptable performance improvements for larger systems when fixing this value to twice the number of available cores. This threshold value corresponds to the best speedup for most of the tests inputs. Yet, we suspect that smarter policies may lead to even higher performance. This particular problem, regarding on how to manage thread spawning policies in highly unbalanced, irregular codes is the topic of future investigations.

5   Evaluating Results

The experiments described in this section have been executed on a two socket Intel Xeon Processor E5-4650 Sandy Bridge EP. A fill-socket-first affinity policy was adopted. The source code was compiled with GCC 4.8.2 with optimization level -O3 and executed on Fedora 19 with Linux Kernel 3.12.11.

The experiments were conduced using 4 different data sets (Table 1), each of them covers a different number of inputs. The data sets were designed to stress certain regions of the code during development and to expose different behaviors regarding performance.

Table 2 shows runtime measurements for two configurations of the original MapReduce. The columns named *Original* correspond to the original parallel implementation. Step 1 stands for the *OpenMP* implementation of the approach using nested parallelism. Step 1 column exhibits lower execution times up to 8 cores, while for a higher number of cores, competition between threads deteriorate performance (as detailed in Section 4.3). E.g. the *Cubes* data set shows a longer execution time for Step 1 (16 cores) than the original approach.

Execution time measurements for the described reduction on demand approach are shown in Table 3. Step 2 column presents the measurements for the nested parallel implementation using dynamic reduction. The column Step 3 presents data corresponding to executions of the same implementation as in Step 2 with a different configuration: the maximum number of spawned threads was bounded to two times the amount of cores used. Step 3 implementation excels at scenarios with bigger input file sizes (like *carPart* data set), those executions can benefit of a less congested system where long time executing tasks do not need to compete with others. Fine grained scenarios (like *Cubes* data set) consist of short time running tasks which are less vulnerable to congestion, therefore – for these data sets – step 3 technique will present a non-monotonic behavior, leading to poor results on larger systems.

Fig. 4 illustrates the achieved speedup of each approach by comparing it to a sequential execution, derived from execution times shown in Tables 2 and 3. The speedup measurements show that the thread limited execution of the dynamic reduction approach (step 3) excels for most of the input data sets. A different behavior is shown for the *cubes* data set: a large number of uniformly sized small meshes (compared to the other data sets) benefits the original implementation. As described in Section 3, the original implementation of Phase A can benefit of a balanced workload when utilizing equally distributed mesh sizes. This feature of the *cubes* data set leaves little room for improvement, although speedup was achieved for all configurations with the nested parallel approach that uses a dynamic reduction (step 2).

6   Related Work

The MapReduce pattern provides the foundation for the *Hadoop* framework. The porting procedure of a C++ development into *Hadoop* is analyzed in Gudmundsson et al.[8]. C++ codes needed to be wrapped into the *Hadoop* Java framework loosing the opportunity to expose finer granularity parallelism. Distributed MapReduce developments lack of the capability of exploiting nested parallelism[9] which is our main contribution.

C++11 [7] provides of native mechanisms to exploit concurrency which on the one hand can lead to efficient and portable parallel implementations. On the other hand, managing parallelism and concurrent tasks synchronization needs to be addressed by the programmer. The solutions provided along this paper (specially nested parallelism) require a global management of concurrent tasks, which according to the C++11 model would require an ad hoc implementation.

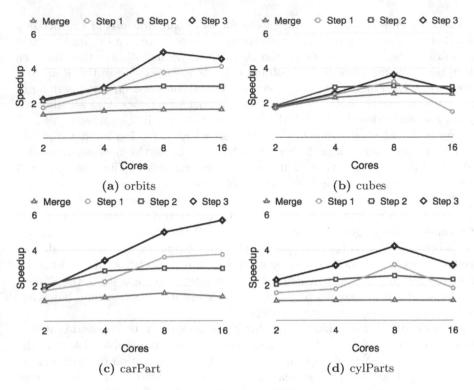

Fig. 4. Speedup: comparison of different approaches

Regarding congestion experienced with nested parallelism, Tanaka et al.[10] substitute the standard implementation of *OpenMP* by a *lightweight process* model which mitigates the impact of thread competition. The *Insieme* compiler [11] benefits of nested recursive parallel regions – generating multiple versions of the nested tasks – and maximizes the utilization of cores.

7   Conclusion and Future Work

This paper discussed the incremental process of improving the performance of an industrial application from the automotive industry that intersects and repairs meshes generated by a CAD application. Starting from the original code version that was already parallelized, we identified the requirement of unveiling, exposing and utilizing nested parallelism to provide enough parallel workload to overcome initial load-balancing issues. Moreover, a statically scheduled binary reduction operation has been re-factored to a dynamically orchestrated reduction schema whose structure depends on the actual execution time of the described steps to mitigate additional load balancing issues. Finally, tuning runtime parameters influencing the management of nested parallelism provided an additional performance increase, improving the speedup from 2.9 – when executing the nested parallel approach with reduction on demand – to a total of 5.69 for the best scenario.

Future work will address a more sophisticated API for exploiting parallelism of C++ codes.

Acknowledgements. This research has been funded by the Austrian Research Promotion Agency under contract 834307 (AutoCore).

References

[1] Engineering Center Steyr: ALSIM, a simulation tool for the dynamical dip painting process (June 2014), http://alsim.ecs.steyr.com

[2] Schifko, M., Jüttler, B., Kornberger, B.: Industrial application of exact boolean operations for meshes. In: Proceedings of the 26th Spring Conference on Computer Graphics, SCCG 2010, pp. 165–172. ACM, New York (2010)

[3] Wein, R., Fogel, E., Zukerman, B., Halperin, D.: Advanced programming techniques applied to cgal's arrangement package. Computational Geometry 38(1-2), 37–63 (2007); Special Issue on CGAL

[4] Dean, J., Ghemawat, S.: Mapreduce: Simplified data processing on large clusters. Commun. ACM 51(1), 107–113 (2008)

[5] ISO: ISO/IEC 14882:2011 Information technology — Programming languages — C++. International Organization for Standardization, Geneva, Switzerland (February 2012)

[6] OpenMP Architecture Review Board: OpenMP application program interface version 3.0 (May 2008)

[7] Williams, A.: C++ Concurrency in Action. Manning, Pearson Education (2012)

[8] Gumundsson, G.Ó., Amsaleg, L., Jónsson, B.Ó.: Distributed High-Dimensional Index Creation using Hadoop, HDFS and C++. In: CBMI - 10th Workshop on Content-Based Multimedia Indexing, Annecy, France (2012); Quaero

[9] Hindman, B., Konwinski, A., Zaharia, M., Stoica, I.: A common substrate for cluster computing. In: Proceedings of the 2009 Conference on Hot Topics in Cloud Computing, HotCloud 2009. USENIX Association, Berkeley (2009)

[10] Tanaka, Y., Taura, K., Sato, M.: Performance evaluation of openmp applications with nested parallelism. In: Dwarkadas, S. (ed.) LCR 2000. LNCS, vol. 1915, pp. 100–112. Springer, Heidelberg (2000)

[11] Thoman, P., Jordan, H., Fahringer, T.: Compiler multiversioning for automatic task granularity control. Concurrency and Computation: Practice and Experience (2014)

Parallelization of a Tridimensional Finite Element Program for Structural Behaviour Analysis

João Coelho, António Silva, and J. Piteira Gomes

LNEC - Laboratório Nacional de Engenharia Civil
Av. do Brasil 101 1700-066 Lisbon, Portugal
{jpcoelho,ai,pgomes}@lnec.pt

Abstract. We develop a parallelization method using the PETSc toolkit and apply it to a time-varying structural analysis program based on the finite element method in order to reduce its total computation time. This is a common problem in engineering as the spatial discretization of large structures frequently originates meshes of sizeable dimensions and large linear systems which must be solved over time. As a practical example we consider the analysis of the Peti concrete dam through 66 years of operation, using a finite element mesh of about 13 thousand nodes each with 3 degrees of freedom. Preliminary results are obtained using a local, distributed memory cluster and show that a significant decrease in the program's total running time is achieved.

Keywords: structural analysis, parallelization, finite element, cluster computing.

1 Introduction

Over the past few years parallel computing models have been growing in relevance and acceptance, both in research and industry fields, as traditional sequential programming performance improvement is slowing down as a result of physical limitations imposed upon transistor enhancement and failing to properly respond to new challenges [1]. However, solutions to many of these challenges rely on specific, sequentially designed processes which must be adapted to this new paradigm in order to remain useful and capable of solving modern problems.

In this article we develop a parallel version of such an existing solution, a sequential finite element (FE) method program used for time-varying structural analysis within the domain of civil engineering. This program is particularly suited for the analysis of thermal, hygrometric and mechanical behaviour of structures over long periods of time (≥ 50 years), and its main core resides in iteratively solving a large-sized system of linear equations.

As required spatial and temporal resolutions increase, meaning larger meshes and more time iterations, so does the computational workload and thus the total running time of the program. This has urged us to develop a new version of the program that would be able to exploit parallelism using the Message-Passing Interface (MPI) and suit a distributed hardware architecture, with the

L. Lopes et al. (Eds.): Euro-Par 2014 Workshops, Part I, LNCS 8805, pp. 36–47, 2014.

purposes of i) reducing the simulation's total running time, ii) allowing for better-resolution meshes to be explored within a reasonable amount of time, and iii) improving code maintainability.

As an application case study we analyse the behaviour of the Peti dam, located in Brazil, considering viscoelastic behaviour on a mesh with 13,135 nodes, 3 degrees of freedom per node, through 66 years of operation. For the computational effort the LNEC cluster Medusa is used.

2 Problem Formulation

Before proceeding any further we should describe the general problem being solved and the theoretical background for the proposed solution. A brief description of the working use case is also presented.

2.1 Theoretical Framework

In order to study the behaviour of concrete dams over time, a viscoelastic model has been developed, which makes it possible to analyse the structural behaviour of concrete dams or other plain concrete structures subject to swelling, by considering the different load histories during their lifetime. The model is based on an incremental technique making use of the finite element method[1].

The discretisation of load histories allows to consider: i) the action of the dead weight of concrete; ii) the actions corresponding to variations in the reservoir water level (hydrostatic pressures and uplifts); iii) the thermal actions corresponding to seasonal air and water temperatures, by taking into account the influence of solar radiation; and iv) the free swelling of concrete.

In order to model the concrete time behaviour, considering the concrete maturing process, the incremental constitutive relation corresponding to a Kelvin chain is used[4]. By assuming material isotropy time-invariant Poisson ratio, the constitutive relation for 3D equilibrium is derived; then, discretizing the analysis period in time intervals $\Delta t_r = t_r - t_{r-1}$, applying the equilibrium equation to the extremes of interval Δt_r and assuming the time intervals to be small, so as to have the elastic modules $E(t)$ and $E^i(t)$ approximately constant and equal to their values in the mean instant of the interval Δt_r, the constitutive viscoelastic equation in incremental form can be obtained:

$$\Delta \underline{\sigma} = E_r^* \underline{C}^{-1} (\Delta \underline{\epsilon}_r + \Delta \underline{\epsilon}_r^0 + \Delta \underline{\epsilon}_r^*) \tag{1}$$

On the basis of the constitutive viscoelastic incremental relation (1) and using the principle of virtual works, the following equilibrium equation is obtained for each finite element:

$$\underline{K}^e(t)\underline{\dot{\sigma}}_e = (\underline{\dot{f}}^a)_e + (\underline{\dot{f}}^0)_e + (\underline{\dot{f}}^*)_e \tag{2}$$

---

[1] Here we present only a summary of the complete formulation, which can be found in [3].

where $\underline{K}^e(t)$ is the elementary stiffness matrix and the vectors $(\underline{\dot{f}}^a)_e$, $(\underline{\dot{f}}^0)_e$ and $(\underline{\dot{f}}^*)_e$ correspond, in each finite element, to the time derivatives of nodal forces equivalent to applied loads, to prescribed strains and to the effect of the load history, respectively.

For small time intervals Δt_r the time derivatives can be approached by incremental relations $\dot{\sigma} \cong \Delta\sigma_r/\Delta t_r$ and $\dot{f} \cong \Delta f_r/\Delta t_r$. Therefore, by properly superposing (2) for all the structural elements, the following equilibrium equation can be written for the entire structure, in the incremental form

$$\underline{K}(t)\Delta\underline{u} = \Delta\underline{f}^a + \Delta\underline{f}^0 + \Delta\underline{f}^* \tag{3}$$

This equation must be solved for all time steps, while updating of the stiffness matrix $\underline{K}$ in each one of them.

2.2   Peti Case Study

As a case study example we will consider the brazilian Peti concrete dam. It began operating in 1945 and we must study its behaviour for 66 years up to 2011. For that we have built a finite element mesh of nelem = 2366 elements and nnos = 13135 nodes, each with 3 degrees of freedom, which satisfactorily approximates the dam's structure, and have also periodic experimental data for determining other relevant data structures, such as the derivatives of nodal forces vectors. The resulting stiffness matrix $\underline{K}$ is symmetric and positive-definite, and since this is a very rigid structure interactions occur only among contiguous neighbour (and foundational) nodes, hence $\underline{K}$ is also a sparse matrix. Figures 1 and 2 show the actual dam and the finite element mesh used in calculations.

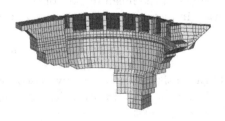

Fig. 1. Peti dam   **Fig. 2.** Peti dam finite element mesh

3 Serial Approach

Our current approach for solving problems of this kind relies on a serial algorithm implemented with a Fortran 77 code first developed in 2001 and since then only sporadically adapted or reviewed, usually to fit new specific situations or requirements; hence its maintenance, along with its performance, also presents a challenge which we will try to address in Section 4. A necessary first step before delving into parallelization is to understand how the serial solution works and what its limitations are.

The core of the computation is solving 3, which is done by establishing a separation between instantaneous and delayed responses (the *phase* of the computation), and considering that the increments due to loads, Δf^a and Δf^0, occuring at an interval $\Delta t_r = t_r - t_{r-1}$ are applied at instant t_{r-1} and remain constant in the interval.

Subsequently, the system is solved for the increment in displacements $\Delta u_r^{(inst)}$, $\Delta K(E_{r-1/2})\Delta u_r^{(inst)} = \Delta f^a + \Delta f^0$, and then both the stress increments $\Delta \sigma_s^{(inst)}$ and the corresponding strain increments $\Delta \epsilon_s^{(inst)}$ are computed. Then, the nodal forces due to swelling actions are computed again until the variations in the stress field are sufficiently small so as to fulfil the convergence conditions and by ensuring the equilibrium and compatibility conditions.

The analysis of the delayed behaviour begins with the computation of the global stiffness matrix ΔK for $E = E_r^*$. Then, the vector of nodal forces equivalent to the effect of the load history $\Delta f_r^*(\Delta \epsilon^*)$ is calculated and subsequently the equation system $\Delta K(E_r^*)\Delta u_r^{(del)} = \Delta f^*$ is solved, thus obtaining $\Delta u_r^{(del)}$ and, with that, the increment in displacements corresponding to the interval Δt. This allows computing the stress and strain increments corresponding to the viscoelastic behaviour of concrete.

Under the serial approach global stiffness matrix assembly is accomplished through the usual process, thoroughly described in literature (*e.g.* in [7]). A key feature of this process is that each finite element contributes to the global stiffness matrix independently of any other element, which an open door to parallelization as it suggests performing the global assembly separately for every element and then merging everything together in the end.

As a first attempt at parallelization, we have tried to preserve this structure and focus on parallelizing the main structures' assembly process as well as the actual linear system computation.

4 Parallelization Process

Our work focused on building a parallel solution to this problem that would i) reproduce the original serial results, ii) run within a reasonable amount of time, and iii) allow for easier code maintenance.

As a first step we looked for computational load hotspots in the serial implementation, two of which were readily identified: the global stiffness matrix K assembly and the linear system $Kx = f$ solve. These steps are carried out twice for every timestep, thus representing a large portion of the calculation; this led us to search for an appropriate tool for numerically solving large linear systems of equations in parallel.

4.1   Finding Suitable Tools

Among several available tools addressing numerical solution of linear systems, the PETSc library [2] was selected as the best fit to our purposes, as it allows for developing our solution within a framework that permits further adapting and enhancing, thus not limiting its applicability to any fixed set of problems and enabling its iterative improvement.

PETSc uses the MPI standard for communications between parallel processors; since this standard fits the distributed memory model most suited to the cluster architecture, we adopted it as well.

We also meant to address the issue of poor code maintainability, which arises mostly from the way the code was developed — by several engineers rather than programmers, with each iteration attempting to solve a particular problem —, from the general lack of programming background among the developers and from the absence of solid documentation. As a first step towards improving code readibility and usability for present and future users, we decided to migrate the original program from Fortran 77 to C, which in fact meant thoroughly rewriting the code in C while also adapting its structure to fit the parallel, distributed memory model.

4.2   Implementing Parallelization

We now attempt to describe the main steps of the parallelization process, which was driven primarily by the need to address the two identified hotspots, solving the linear equations system and assembling the global stiffness matrix, and compassed both adapting the Code structure to be fit for parallellization and rewriting it in C.

As a first approach we focused on minimizing communications ahead of memory usage, since the main goal was to minimize running times and no severe limitations of memory availability were imposed; this led to creating local copies in each processor for most input scalar values and data arrays — those used by an *a priori* undetermined set of processors in calculations.

This approach allows us to avoid communication overhead, and despite the need for most data strucutres to be globally available, some are also only used locally in their own processor; this locality arises from the introduction of domain partitions, an essential step for dividing the workload among processors.

Domain Partitioning. A suitable data partition must be defined in order to enable splitting the computational workload as evenly as possible between all available nodes. In our study we face two main types of operations: node-oriented (such as the interaction between global stiffness matrix K or characteristic forces vector f) and element-oriented (mainly finite-element techniques); hence we must create two separate partitions, one that is node-oriented and another element-oriented.

The node-oriented partition is naturally assumed by PETSc and implemented via `GetNodeRanges` using the standard PETSc routine `PetscSplitOwnershipBlock`. By specifying the total number of nodes nnos and the number of processors world this routine returns the local number of nodes lnnos in each processor; we then obtain the lower and upper bounds lbound and ubound by adding lnnos cumulatively over all processors, as shown in Table 1's example.

Table 1. Example of nodal partition for world = 4 and nnos = 309

Rank	lnnos	lbound	ubound
0	77	0	77
1	77	77	154
2	77	154	231
3	78	231	309

On the element level, we create a manual domain partition rather than using an intrinsic PETSc method. In order to minimize communications, we assign an element to the processor who has the most nodes it is connected with, so that when looping through all nodes linked to an element most of them will be stored in the same processor. By implementing this process we created an array `elemproc` of `nelem` entries which has, for each element, the rank of the processor it belongs to. Henceforth each iteration of all element-oriented loops must verify the condition `elemproc[ el] == rank`, which guarantees it is only run in its home processor.

We further create a *ghost region* for each processor comprising all nodes which are not local but are connected to at least one local element, so that all nodes of all local elements are also locally stored — either as a local node or a ghost node. This allows for the removal of communications in element-oriented operations by duplicating *foreign* node information in each processor.

Matrix Assembly. Building the stiffness matrix K contributes heavily to the program's total running time since the entire routine must be repeated for every time-phase iteration throughout every mesh element; it was therefore a main focus of our parallelization process. The method for assembling K sequentially can be roughly described by the following pseudo-code:

```
for every time iteration nit
 for every phase iteration iid
  for every element el
   for every element node il
    for every other element node jl
     val = kelem[ el, il, jl] * El nit, iid]
     assign val to proper position in K
```

A similar process must be undertaken to account for foundation nodes, the difference being that by considering the whole foundational structure as a single, 1304-node element, the element loop is removed and the node loops are run through 1304 iterations instead of 20.

Having already defined both element- and node-oriented domain partitions, we had to define which one to use to parallelize this particular process. Although the element partition is the most immediate assumption — we could simply split the element loop among the processors, — this would require introducing a different process to account for foundation nodes; by applying node-oriented parallelism, on the other hand, we address both assembly phases without the need for a second loop.

```
for (nit=0; nit<nint; nit++){
 for (iid=0; iid<2; iid++){
  MatZeroEntries( K );
  for (int i=lbound; i<ubound; i++){
   MatAssembleDiag( i, nit, iid );
   if(fund==1) MatAssembleInser(i, nit, iid);
  }
  MatAssemblyBegin( K );
  MatAssemblyEnd( K );
```

Here parallelism is achieved by limiting the assembly loop to the interval [lbound, ubound[, and the treatment of foundation nodes is neatly carried out by the `MatAssembleInser` routine. This assembly method, in turn, requires the creation of a node-element table by which we should be able to find, for a given node, all elements it belongs to (the inverse of the `incid` array), thereby limiting the assembly element loop only to connected elements. For this purpose we create three separate arrays, described in Table 2.

Table 2. Node-element association arrays

Array	Size	Description
celems	$nnos$	# of elements connected to each node
selems	$nnos + 1$	index of 1st node element in aelems
aelems	$\sum_{i=0}^{nnos-1} \text{celems}[i]$	node elements global indexes in sequence

With these arrays we can easily define the algorithm for the node-oriented assembly, which essentially amounts to adapting the initial algorithm to loop through node elements instead of all elements. Actual value assignment is only performed for the upper triangular part of the matrix and matrix symmetry is exploited by using the matrix object K created earlier with PETSc routine `MatCreateSBAIJ`[2]. The block structure of K also allows for the use of

---

[2] This creates a symmetric block matrix; block size (`bsize` = 3).

`MatSetValuesBlocked` to assign values to a 3x3 matrix block rather than individually, further enhancing runtime performance. Assembling the foundation part follows an identical procedure, again with the exception of the node elements loop.

Linear System Solve. Solving the linear system $Kx = f$ constitutes the core operation of this program, as it must be repeated for every time-phase iteration and claims, along with K matrix assembly, the greatest share of computation resources; hence, it is another major focus of our parallelization approach.

Working with PETSc, solving this system is simply a matter of creating and properly setting up the stiffness matrix K, the right-hand side (RHS) vector f and the solution vector x, and afterwards calling a solver operator to compute x. An early decision on whether this solver should use direct or iterative methods had to be made; even though both methods could be used, there was no opportunity to explore both of them so we decided to rely on iterative methods based on the assumption that those were most suited for solving systems of large sparse matrixes.

We build the RHS vector f by adding up contributions from various sources such as hydrostatic pressure, thermal expansions of imposed deformations, as specified in the input data file. The actual construction of f is also parallelized by using PETSc data structures and the domain partitions already specified to divide the workload among processors.

Solving the system then simply amount to calling the chosen iterative solver with K, f and x as inputs. Section 5.3 presents a detailed analysis of available methods and explains our choice of solver.

5 Case-Study Results

Building a preliminary parallel version of the program allowed us to use it to obtain partial results and compare them to the output from the original serial version. In order to generate these results, the program was run on the Medusa cluster, a LNEC-based infrastructure for high-performance computing (HPC); we then evaluated parallel results for accuracy and conducted a performance analysis as a way of determining the actual benefits of implementing parallelism and using the HPC infrastructure to run the simulation.

5.1 Medusa Cluster

Numerical results for the program were obtained on the Medusa cluster, the LNEC HPC infrastructure which comprises a set of 67 Fujitsu Siemens PRIMERGY RX220 servers each with 2 dual-core CPUs of 2GB each, linked by a 1 GBit/s Ethernet connection and running a Scientific Linux 6 operating system. A NFS filesystem was used to store the results.

5.2   Results Validation

In order to evaluate the results of parallelization, we should first guarantee that actual simulation results are consistent with the serial version's, so as to ensure the preservation of the original behaviour. However the delayed response modulus is not yet completed, which prevents a full comparison; we therefore ran a test to verify all the stages of the program except for the delayed response, including building data structures, assembling the stiffness matrix and solving the linear system.

In order to carry out this test we ran the simulation through the entire time period (all 66 years) considering a constant elastic module and varying the dam water level (and thus the hydrostatic pressure on its structure). We expected to obtain a linear response of the total displacements as a function of the water level; in fact, Figure 3 shows that the behaviour observed in control node 5062, located in the top-center region of the dam (subject to the greatest displacements), matches these expectations.

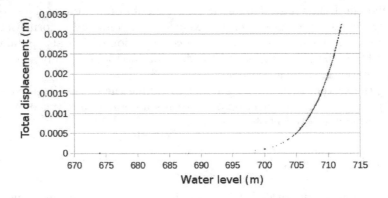

Fig. 3. Displacements in node 5062 with instantaneous response

Despite this test's limited scope, it is reasonable to assume that adjusting the delayed response shouldn't significantly affect the total running time of the simulation, which allows us to proceed with the performance analysis for the parallelized version despite the exactness of the delayed response remaining to be checked.

5.3   Performance Analysis

The primary goal of this work was to reproduce the results of the original serial simulation in the least possible amount of time. Having established the consistency of the parallel results in Section 5.2, we then focused our research in minimizing the program's running time. Two major factors determine the program's running time: first of all the time spent solving the matrix equation $Kx = b$, and secondly the amount of calculations assigned to each core. Therefore, a natural assumption is that the choice of both the Krylov subspace (KSP) method employed and the number of cores in which to run the simulation weight the most on the application's overall running time.

KSP Solver. Given the iterative structure of the program, choosing a suitable solver is a crucial issue, so we must find which KSP method — solver and preconditioner — suits our problem best; as a first approach we chose to focus only in choosing an appropriate solver, for simplicity, using the default Block-Jacobi preconditioner and leaving its optimization to a later stage of the work. Table 3 shows benchmark results for a selection of available methods suitable for solving a sparse, symmetric and positive definite matrix. The values presented refer to the elapsed real time obtained with the `time` command when running the parallel program in 4 cores for only 10 iterations. Based on these results the conjugate gradient method was selected as the best-performing KSP solver, while both preconditioned conjugate residuals and pipeline conjugate gradient methods present suitable alternatives.

Table 3. Benchmark analysis of KSP solvers

Solver	cg	pcr	pipecg	lgmres	symmlq
Elapsed time (s)	708.77	716.65	728.48	786.87	825.87

Number of Cores. Certainly the number of cores the program is run in also contributes decisively to the simulation's total running time. We use the most common definitions of speedup, $S_N = \frac{t_1}{t_N}$, and efficiency, $E_N = \frac{S_N}{N}$, with t_N being the total running time for N processors and t_1 the time taken by the parallel simulation to run in a single core; ideally we should rather use the running time of the serial implementation [5], however this data is unavailable to us for the current state of development of the program, and merely resorting to the time used by the complete serial program would not result in a meaningful comparison since the parallel version would be performing only a fraction of the serial's workload.

In a fully parallelizable context a speedup of $S_N = N$ would be expected, however the existence of limiting factors such as uneven load distirbution and communication overhead leads us to expect running time to decay as a function of the number of cores until a minimum threshold is reached. We tested this behaviour by running the simulation (using the *cg* solver) in a varying number of cores, as shown in Table 4.

Table 4 shows the expected decay pattern with an apparent lower limit of about 9 hours. We have managed to achieve a maximum speedup of 4.08 with an efficiency of 12.8%, which stands as a good result for the parallelization method employed. The decline in efficiency, although natural, is steeper than anticipated

Table 4. Performance indicators for varying number of cores

Cores	1	2	3	4	6	8	12	16	24	32
Running time (h)	39.70	27.32	21.84	24.23	19.38	13.87	12.88	10.47	10.25	9.72
Speedup	-	1.45	1.82	1.64	2.05	2.86	3.08	3.80	3.87	4.08
Efficiency	-	0.727	0.606	0.410	0.341	0.358	0.257	0.237	0.161	0.128

and might indicate flaws in the parallel implementation — some of which were to be expected since, at this stage, little attention was paid to optimization and the main focus was to achieve a working implementation. It may also be a result of the limited size of the mesh, in which case we would expect a larger mesh to exhibit a slower efficiency decay; however we have thus far not been able to consistently test this hypothesis.

Similar works (*e.g.* [6]) have obtained parallel speedups of only about 1.3 running in 8 processors with $E_8 \approx 40\%$, whilst our simulation manages $S_8 = 2.86$ and $E_8 = 35.8\%$; this supports the parallelization approach chosen, despite the limitations imposed on such comparisons[3].

In our case, since our goal is to run the simulation as quickly as possible, we should use as many processors as there are available; we should note, however, that if only greatly limited resources were available, running in more than 16 cores would probably not have been worthwhile, since the efficiency in that case drops well below 25%. In general, a decision model weighting both these parameters should be constructed and used to decide on the optimal number of running cores.

It remains to be seen how these results would change for larger, finer-grained meshes; our expectation is that the bottom limit would rise only slightly (given that most of the program's computational load is distributed) and that it would therefore be possible to run this larger mesh in approximately the same amount of time by using more processors. This is as issue that we will address in future work.

6   Concluding Remarks

We have developed a parallelization method for a finite element structural analysis application and used it to obtain a parallel program which solves a real engineering problem, fundamentally allowing us to obtain the results of the original simulation at least four times faster.

Results coherence with original application has not yet been thoroughly tested due to this work's early stage of development, however these initial results are encouraging and match our expectations.

---

[3] Comparing speedup and efficiency results presents a difficult task since final results depend on many factors other than the number of cores used, hence this comparison is useful mostly to check the results' order of magnitude.

LNEC's cluster infrastructure Medusa was fundamental in obtaining these results, however the size of our case study prevented us from obtaining significant performance gains for more than 16 processors; in order to fully explore Medusa's potencial, finer-grained meshes will need to be considered.

Future work will necessarily lean upon extending the current application to fully reproduce previous results and to feature the inclusion of a damage model as a means of simulating cracking processes in the dam; this will introduce a nonlinear dimension to the computation which is likely to slow down the simulation. We expect future development of this work to ultimately allow for the solution of previously impossible or over-simplified structural analysis problems.

Acknowledgments. Part of this work is funded by the TIMBUS project, co-funded by the European Commissions 7th Framework Programme (FP7/2007-2013) under grant agreement No 269940.

References

1. Asanovic, K., Bodik, R., Demmel, J., Keaveny, T., Keutzer, K., Kubiatowicz, J., Morgan, N., Patterson, D., Sen, K., Wawrzynek, J., Wessel, D., Yelick, K.: A view of the parallel computing landscape. Commun. ACM 52(10), 56–67 (2009), http://doi.acm.org/10.1145/1562764.1562783
2. Balay, S., Adams, M.F., Brown, J., Brune, P., Buschelman, K., Eijkhout, V., Gropp, W.D., Kaushik, D., Knepley, M.G., McInnes, L.C., Rupp, K., Smith, B.F., Zhang, H.: PETSc users manual. Tech. Rep. ANL-95/11 - Revision 3.4, Argonne National Laboratory (2013), http://www.mcs.anl.gov/petsc
3. Batista, A.: Análise do comportamento ao longo do tempo de baragens abbada. Ph.D. thesis, Technical University of Lisbon (1998)
4. Bazant, Z., Wu, S.: Dirichlet series creep function for aging concrete. Journal of the Engineering Mechanics Division (ASCE) 99 EM2 (1993)
5. Coelho, J., Silva, A.: Computação paralela no lnec - guia introdutório e estudo de caso. Tech. rep., LNEC - Laboratório Nacional de Engenharia Civil (2013)
6. Fu, C.: Parallel computing for finite element structural analysis on workstation cluster. In: 2008 International Conference on Computer Science and Software Engineering, vol. 3, pp. 291–294. IEEE (2008)
7. Zienkiewicz, O.C., Taylor, R.: The finite element method for solid and structural mechanics. Elsevier Butterworth-Heinemann, Amsterdam (2005)

A Comprehensive Empirical Comparison
of Parallel ListSieve and GaussSieve

Artur Mariano[1], Özgür Dagdelen[2], and Christian Bischof[1]

[1] Institute for Scientific Computing, Technische Universität Darmstadt
[2] Cryptography and Computer Algebra, Technische Universität Darmstadt
`artur.mariano@sc.tu-darmstadt.de`, `oezguer.dagdelen@cased.de`,
`christian.bischof@sc.tu-darmstadt.de`

Abstract. The security of lattice-based cryptosystems is determined by the performance of practical implementations of, among others, algorithms for the Shortest Vector Problem (SVP).

In this paper, we conduct a comprehensive, empirical comparison of two SVP-solvers: ListSieve and GaussSieve. We also propose a practical parallel implementation of ListSieve, which achieves super-linear speedups on multi-core CPUs, with efficiency levels as high as 183%. By comparing our implementation with a parallel implementation of GaussSieve, we show that ListSieve can, in fact, outperform GaussSieve for a large number of threads, thus answering a question that was still open to this day.

Keywords: sieving, superlinear speedup, shortest vector, parallel.

1 Introduction

Cryptography aims mostly at protecting information sent over an insecure channel. The implementation of cryptosystems is usually a three-phase engineering process. First, a cryptosystem with a certain underlying mathematical problem is specified. Second, an implementation of an algorithm that solves the underlying mathematical problem is used to identify hard instances of the problem. Third, these instances are used to define parameters for the implementation of the cryptosystem. Therefore, practical implementations of these algorithms are required for the implementation of secure, real-world cryptosystems.

In 1996, Ajtai found out that the mathematical properties of some lattice problems have interesting properties for cryptography, such as average-case to worst-case hardness [1]. Since Ajtai's discoveries, a significant amount of work has been done in this field, commonly referred to as *lattice-based cryptography*.

A lattice Λ is a discrete additive subgroup of $\mathbb{R}^m$. The *dimension* $n \leq m$ of a lattice Λ is the maximum number of mutually linearly independent vectors in Λ. Any such n linearly independent vectors form a *basis*, which represents the lattice. We denote a basis in a column matrix $\mathbf{B} = [\mathbf{b}_1, \ldots, \mathbf{b}_n]$. The lattice $\Lambda(\mathbf{B})$ is defined by the linear integer span of the basis vectors $\mathbf{b}_1, \ldots, \mathbf{b}_n$, namely

$$\Lambda(\mathbf{B}) = \left\{ \sum_{i=1}^{n} a_i \mathbf{b}_i \ : \ a_i \in \mathbb{Z} \right\} .$$

L. Lopes et al. (Eds.): Euro-Par 2014 Workshops, Part I, LNCS 8805, pp. 48–59, 2014.

For $n > 2$ there are infinitely many possible bases of a lattice.

Lattice-based cryptography is particularly attractive since it is believed to be resistant against attacks operated with quantum computers, in contrast to problems from number theory, such as factorization of large composite numbers or the computation of discrete logarithms [15]. The security of lattice-based cryptosystems is based on the hardness of specific lattice problems. One of these problems is the Shortest Vector Problem (SVP). The SVP can be formally defined as the computation of a vector $\mathbf{v} \in \Lambda \setminus \{0\}$ where $\|\mathbf{v}\| = \min_{\mathbf{x} \in \Lambda \setminus \{0\}} \|\mathbf{x}\|$. The norm of the shortest vector is denoted by λ_1. This problem can be stated for every norm; in this work, we address the Euclidean norm, the most common in this context. Algorithms that solve this problem are called *SVP-solvers*.

The SVP is known to be NP-hard under randomized reductions [2], and therefore, no polynomial-time algorithms for this problem are expected to be found. In fact, only algorithms that find an approximation to the solution of the SVP, such as the LLL [9] and the Block Korkine Zolotarev (BKZ) [14], are known to run in feasible time for high lattice dimensions. However, the returned vector, while somewhat short, might not be short enough to break a cryptosystem. In fact, LLL and BKZ are lattice basis reduction algorithms, i.e., given a lattice basis, they find another basis with short, nearly orthogonal vectors. BKZ uses an SVP-solver as a sub-routine, which finds the shortest vector of small lattice dimensions, called blocksize [14].

There are two main families of SVP-solvers: enumeration and sieving algorithms. Currently, the fastest SVP-solver is enumeration with extreme pruning [6], which consists in a depth-first traversal of a pruned tree. While enumeration algorithms were extensively studied and implemented in several computer architectures [5,4,8], sieving algorithms attracted lesser attention in this regard.

Published in 2010 [11], ListSieve and GaussSieve are currently the most relevant sieving algorithms. While ListSieve was considered impractical and important mainly for theoretical purposes, GaussSieve was presented as a practical, efficient heuristic of ListSieve. Some work has been done on sieving algorithms since [10,3], but there are still some open questions. For instance, although ListSieve is considered impractical, there are neither assessments of ListSieve in practice nor empirical comparisons of both algorithms. Moreover, only one study [13] (cf. Section 2) focused on the practical behaviour of the original GaussSieve algorithm.

The parallelization of GaussSieve was investigated on multi-core CPUs. Very recently, it was shown that GaussSieve can scale linearly, using scalable lock-free lists [10]. However, the first steps in the parallelization of GaussSieve date back to 2010, when Milde et al. implemented GaussSieve in parallel, with a ring structure of several instances of GaussSieve [12]. As the scalability of the implementation was limited, Milde et al. suggested that ListSieve could possibly outperform GaussSieve for a large number of threads, a question that remains open to this day and we answer in this paper.

The contribution of this paper is twofold. First, we present the first empirical analysis of the workflow of ListSieve and of how it compares to GaussSieve.

Second, we propose the first parallel implementation of ListSieve, which relaxes its properties, thus lowering the workload in comparison to the original algorithm. As a direct result, it achieves super-linear speedups on multi-core CPUs, up to 32 threads, and it outperforms the parallel GaussSieve implementation presented in [12] for a big number of threads, while returning the same vector.

Notation. Vectors and matrices are written in bold face, vectors are written in lower-case, and matrices in upper-case, as in vector $\mathbf{v}$ and matrix $\mathbf{M}$. The ith coordinate of a vector $\mathbf{v}$ is denoted by $\mathbf{v}_i$. $\langle \mathbf{v}, \mathbf{p} \rangle$ denotes the inner product of two vectors $\mathbf{v}$ and $\mathbf{p}$. The Euclidean norm of $\mathbf{v}$ is given by $||\mathbf{v}||$. $\mathbf{v}$ is called a *zero vector* if $||\mathbf{v}|| = 0$.

Roadmap. Section 2 provides some background of sieving algorithms and discusses a previous study of their properties. Section 3 presents the results of our experiments with ListSieve and GaussSieve and Section 4 presents the first parallel implementation of ListSieve. Section 5 concludes the paper.

2   The ListSieve and GaussSieve Algorithms

All sieving algorithms follow an identical structure. They build a list L of somewhat random vectors, referred to as *samples*, typically generated with Klein's algorithm [7], remove the zero vectors from L and apply a sieving technique on it. The sieving process is iteratively executed until a certain stopping criterion, $K \geq c$, where K is the number of collisions, is met. c is usually set in the form $c = \alpha \times mls + \beta$, where mls is the maximum size of L up to that point. When the sieving process finishes, the shortest vector of the lattice is expected to be in the list L, with a certain, yet high probability. The generation of vectors and the sieving process go hand in hand in practical implementations, since the number of samples that are necessary for the algorithm to converge is not known upfront.

In ListSieve's original form (see [11]), samples are generated with perturbations, a technique useful to infer the asymptotic complexity of the algorithms. The pseudo-codes presented in Algorithm 1 and Algorithm 2, on the other hand, are practical implementations of ListSieve and GaussSieve, wherein randomly generated vectors are not perturbed.

ListSieve samples vectors with Klein's algorithm and reduces them as much as possible against the vectors stored in L, where the freshly reduced vector is inserted in L once the reduction process is finished. When the sample is reduced to the zero vector, a collision takes place and the whole iteration is wasted. Once in L, vectors are never removed or modified. According to the original description of the algorithms, the reduction process can pick the vectors in L in any order. However, it is known that keeping L ordered by increasing norm is more efficient in practice, since the process can be aborted when a vector bigger than the sample is found.

In contrast to ListSieve, GaussSieve also reduces the elements already in L against one another. As a result, the elements in L will be pairwise reduced, which means that the inequality $\min(||\mathbf{p} \pm \mathbf{v}||) \geq \max(||\mathbf{p}||, ||\mathbf{v}||)$ holds for all $\mathbf{v}, \mathbf{p} \in L$. This is precisely the property that governs the Gauss/Lagrange basis reduction algorithm for two dimensional lattices, hence the name of the algorithm. We note that the asymptotic time complexity of the algorithm is not known.

Another difference between the algorithms lies in the data structures that they use. GaussSieve uses a list L that, in contrast to ListSieve, can both grow and shrink, and a stack S that temporarily keeps vectors that are removed from L. The use of the stack eases the handling of the vectors that no longer verify the aforementioned inequality. This happens because when a vector $\mathbf{v}$ is generated and reduced against an element in L, there might be elements in L that are no longer pairwise reduced with $\mathbf{v}$. Reverting this is not as simple as reducing such vectors by $\mathbf{v}$, because it might happen that they become no longer Gauss-reduced with other elements in L thereafter. These elements are therefore brought to stack S (and reduced against $\mathbf{v}$) and picked in the subsequent iteration, as if they were freshly generated vectors, thus becoming pairwise-reduced with the whole list L.

Previous studies. The original paper of ListSieve and GaussSieve does not show tests pertaining to the workflow of the algorithm, since it only aimed at proving that GaussSieve outperformed another SVP-solver known at that time, NVSieve [11]. The authors showed (1) the number of samples that GaussSieve requires to converge, in comparison to NVSieve, which fell into disuse ever since, and (2) the execution runtime of GaussSieve in comparison to NVSieve and Schnorr-Euchner enumeration in NTL[1], when solving the SVP on lattices in various dimensions.

Since ListSieve and GaussSieve were published, only one study about the practical behaviour of GaussSieve was presented, by Schneider [13], and no studies were published on ListSieve. In particular, Schneider investigated the following parameters of GaussSieve:

- its performance, on various types of lattices, namely ideal, cyclic and random lattices. GaussSieve's performance, in terms of runtime, iterations, list size and collisions, was not affected by the type of the underlying lattice.

Algorithm 1: ListSieve

Input: Basis $\mathbf{B}$, stopping criterion c;	**function** ListReduce($\mathbf{p}$,L)
Init.: $L \leftarrow \{\}$	**while** $\exists \mathbf{v}_i \in L : ||\mathbf{p} - \mathbf{v}_i|| \leq ||\mathbf{p}||$
	$\wedge\ ||\mathbf{p}|| \geq ||\mathbf{v}_i||$ **do**
while $K < c$ **do**	$\quad \mathbf{p} \leftarrow \mathbf{p} - \mathbf{v}_i$;
$\quad \mathbf{p} \leftarrow$ SampleKlein($\mathbf{B}$);	**return** $\mathbf{p}$;
$\quad \mathbf{v} \leftarrow$ ListReduce($\mathbf{p}$,L);	**end function**
$\quad$ **if** $||\mathbf{v}|| = 0$ **then**	
$\quad\quad K \leftarrow K + 1$;	**function** BestVector(L)
$\quad$ **else**	**return** $\mathbf{p} : \forall \mathbf{v} \in L,\ ||\mathbf{p}|| < ||\mathbf{v}||$;
$\quad\quad L \leftarrow L \cup \{\mathbf{v}\}$;	**end function**
return BestVector(L);	

---

[1] http://www.shoup.net/ntl/

Algorithm 2: GaussSieve

Input: Basis $\mathbf{B}$, stopping criterion c;
Init.: $L \leftarrow \{\}, S \leftarrow \{\}, K \leftarrow 0$

while $K < c$ **do**
  | **if** S.size()!=0 **then**
  | | $\mathbf{v} \leftarrow$ S.pop();
  | **else**
  | | $\mathbf{v} \leftarrow$ SampleKlein($\mathbf{B}$);
  | $\mathbf{v} \leftarrow$ GaussReduce($\mathbf{v}, L, S$);
  | **if** $\|\mathbf{v}\| = 0$ **then**
  | | $K \leftarrow K + 1$;
  | **else**
  | | $L \leftarrow L \cup \{\mathbf{v}\}$;
return BestVector(L)

function GaussReduce($\mathbf{p}, L, S$)
while $\exists \mathbf{v}_i \in L : \|\mathbf{v}_i\| \leq \|\mathbf{p}\| \wedge \|\mathbf{p} - \mathbf{v}_i\| \leq \|\mathbf{p}\|$ **do**
  | $\mathbf{p} \leftarrow \mathbf{p} - \mathbf{v}_i$;
while $\exists \mathbf{v}_i \in L : \|\mathbf{v}_i\| > \|\mathbf{p}\| \wedge \|\mathbf{v}_i - \mathbf{p}\| \leq \|\mathbf{v}_i\|$ **do**
  | $L \leftarrow L \setminus \{\mathbf{v}_i\}$;
  | S.push($\mathbf{v}_i - \mathbf{p}$);
return $\mathbf{p}$;
end function

- (1) the number of vectors removed from the list and pushed to the stack and (2) the reductions, i.e., the number of vectors used to reduce a vector generated with Klein's algorithm. Schneider concluded that both are approximately ten times the list size. This means that, on average, ten points are used to reduce each vector, and the same number reduced and removed from the list. Considering an exponential list size, this amount is negligible.
- the quality of the best vector in GaussSieve over time. The norm of this vector decreases only a few times during the execution of the algorithm.

Additionally, Schneider found out that collisions happen only once the shortest vector of the lattice is found, growing exponentially from then on. When the norm of the shortest vector is known, it has been shown that the algorithm can be greatly accelerated. Last but not least, it has been shown that lattice reduction affects GaussSieve in a positive manner, but to a much lesser degree than it affects enumeration algorithms.

While these experiments provide important insight about the practical behaviour of GaussSieve, they neither show how GaussSieve and ListSieve compare regarding the selected parameters nor they cover the whole spectrum of parameters of interest. The trials reported in this paper cover the following relevant additional parameters, in ListSieve (**LS**) or both algorithms (**LS-GS**):

- (**LS-GS**) The over-time progression of the *best* vector (the shortest vector in L at every instant). This analysis was previously done for GaussSieve only.
- (**LS-GS**) Comparison of the algorithms in terms of runtime.
- (**LS**) The maximum number of vectors used in a sample reduction, and the position of the latest used vector among all iterations.
- (**LS**) The performance of ListSieve in parallel and its scalability on CPUs.

3 Analysis of ListSieve and GaussSieve

This section presents the results of our study on ListSieve and GaussSieve. For GaussSieve, we used a publicly available version[2], referred to as the *gsieve* library, from which we also generated ListSieve, by removing specific operations. For the sake of fairness, both implementations use dynamic data structures and have no optimizations but the ones provided by gcc -O2.

Section 3.1 shows the progression of the best vector on two different Goldstein-Mayer lattices, in dimensions 50 and 60, available from the svp-challenge website[3]. For determining the function that governs the runtime of the algorithms, detailed in Section 3.2, we used a broader spectrum of lattices (dimensions 50 to 66, in steps of 2). We investigate further properties of ListSieve and GaussSieve, on lattices in dimensions 40, 50 and 60, in Section 3.3. The experiments were conducted on a server equipped with 2 Intel E5-2670 CPU-chips, each with eight 64-bit instruction set cores equipped with Simultaneous Multi-Threading (SMT), running at 2.60 GHz, and with 128 GB of RAM. The machine runs Ubuntu 11.10, and no other user-level processes were running during the trials.

3.1 Quality of the Best Vector over Time

From here on, let the term *best vector* be the shortest vector that an algorithm knows at a given point in time. Once the algorithm ends, this vector will coincide with a shortest vector of the lattice, unless the shortest vector is not found. The interest of studying its progression over time is twofold. First, it provides insight about the smoothness of the algorithm, and identifies possible discontinuities in its progression. Second, it is essential to determine the progression of the quality of its solution, since very short vectors can suffice to break cryptosystems.

In these experiments, ListSieve and GaussSieve ran on lattices that were BKZ-reduced with blocksize 10. Bigger blocksizes rend the assessment of the progression of the algorithm over time useless, since BKZ almost finds the shortest vector per se. We depict the norm of the first vector in L (the current *best vector*), at the end of each iteration, i.e., after the generation of the random vector as well as its reduction (pairwise-reduction in GaussSieve). Figure 1 shows the evolution of the quality of the *best vector* in ListSieve and GaussSieve, over time, for lattices in dimensions 50 and 60, respectively. Not surprisingly, GaussSieve converges faster than ListSieve. Nonetheless, the total number of changes of the *best vector* during a run is of the same order. Although the smoothness of the algorithms are somewhat alike, GaussSieve finds new *best vectors* faster.

As shown in Figure 1, no new vectors are found until roughly half of the total running time, for both algorithms. The total running time for ListSieve (resp. GaussSieve) in dimension 50 is 52 (resp. 9.8) seconds. However, a shortest vector is already found after 30.16 (resp. 7.94) seconds. The reason why both algorithms do not terminate at that point is because the norm of the shortest vector (i.e.,

---

[2] http://cseweb.ucsd.edu/~pvoulgar/impl.html
[3] http://www.latticechallenge.org/svp-challenge/

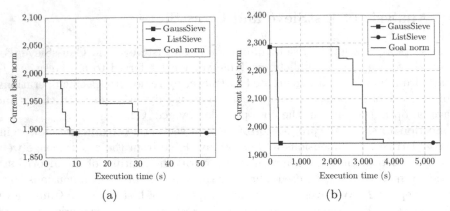

Fig. 1. Best vector's quality over time in ListSieve and GaussSieve, for lattices in dimension 50 in (a) and 60 in (b)

λ_1) is not known upfront for a given lattice. In fact, the algorithms terminate if a given number of collisions take place (cf. Section 2). If λ_1 was known upfront, ListSieve (resp. GaussSieve) could be sped up by a factor of 1.72 (resp 1.23). In dimension 60, the results are very similar.

3.2   Runtime Complexity

We conducted a sequence of trials to empirically determine the growth of List-Sieve's runtime, in comparison to GaussSieve. Prior to these trials, it had been shown that the empirical growth of GaussSieve was governed by $2^{0.57n-23.5}$, for a lattice in dimension n, on a given architecture [13], but no comparison with ListSieve was provided.

Our trials show that the execution time of ListSieve grows according to $2^{0.58n-22.33}$, whereas GaussSieve's grows according to $2^{0.568n-25.46}$. To arrive at this model, we ran the algorithms with several lattices, in dimensions 50-66, in steps of 2. Figure 2 shows both the runtime of ListSieve and GaussSieve and the total number of iterations required for convergence. The execution time of both algorithms differs by an (almost) constant factor. The same holds for the total number of iterations.

3.3   Used Vectors, List Size and Iterations

In both algorithms, L is consulted in every iteration to reduce the sampled vector. The longer this list, the longer the runtime, unless the algorithm only accesses the vectors ultimately selected for reduction, regardless of L's size.

To partially overcome this problem, these algorithms stop accessing vector $\mathbf{v}_{i+1}$ and subsequent ones when vector $\mathbf{v}_i$ is not suitable for the reduction process due to its norm. To this end, the vectors in L must remain ordered by increasing norm, and it is additionally assumed that a vector $\mathbf{p}$ is not reduced against a

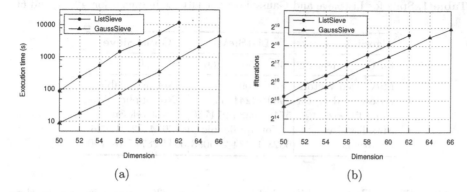

(a)   (b)

Fig. 2. Runtime, in (a), and number of iterations, in (b), for ListSieve and GaussSieve, for lattices in dimensions spanning from 50 to 66, in steps of 2

vector $\mathbf{v}$ in the list, if $\mathbf{v}$'s norm is larger than $\mathbf{p}$'s. While checking L for suitable vectors becomes less of a problem with this optimization, both the complexity and time of adding vectors to L are increased. As both lookups and insertions in L occur at every iteration, except for collisions, this does not represent an improvement in terms of complexity. In short, this only shifts the problem, it does not solve it.

Ideally, L would only keep vectors that are ultimately selected for the reduction process. While maintaining the benefits of an ordered list, it would also avoid (expensive) insertions of worthless vectors in L. To this end, one could set a norm bound, after which vectors would be discarded. However, the selection of a bound is not a simple task. First, no good bound is known upfront and experiments should be conducted to empirically determine one. Second, the precise impact of not using all the possible vectors in the reduction process is yet to be determined, although this greatly affected GaussSieve in a negative way [12].

To this end, we verified how many vectors are actually used during an execution of ListSieve and what is the latest element in L that sampled vectors are reduced against. This is very difficult to determine in GaussSieve because vectors might fluctuate between the list and the stack, and their reduction process is not concluded at the end of each iteration. Table 1 shows the final and max list size, the iterations of each algorithm, and two additional parameters that we analyzed for ListSieve and GaussSieve:

- *Max. used vectors*, which indicates the maximum number of vectors in L used to reduce a sampled vector, among all the iterations of the algorithm.
- *Latest used vector*, which indicates the latest position in the list that the randomly generated vector was reduced against.

As explained in Section 2, the size of L in GaussSieve changes during its execution. Table 1 shows the maximum list size in GaussSieve's execution. The number of iterations for convergence grows slightly faster for ListSieve than

Table 1. Stats for ListSieve and GaussSieve, for lattices in dimension 40, 50 and 60

Algorithm	ListSieve			GaussSieve		
Lattice dimension	40	50	60	40	50	60
Max. used vectors	83	109	153	Not applicable		
Latest used vector	2969	14241	77125	Not applicable		
Final list size	5748	39385	271766	Not relevant		
Max list size	Not applicable			1130	4182	17826
Iterations	6523	43474	299083	5044	28777	184790

for GaussSieve. That is, while ListSieve requires ≈30% more iterations than GaussSieve for dimension 40, that factor is ≈50% (resp. ≈60%) in dimension 50 (resp. 60). Moreover, only a small number of vectors are used for the reduction process in ListSieve. For instance, only at most 83 vectors are used in the reduction process of the lattice in dimension 40, while the list contains 5748 vectors at the end of the execution. Interestingly, the number of used vectors merely doubles from dimension 40 to 60, whereas the list size becomes 47 times bigger.

Another important observation is that ListSieve does not use any vector for reduction after a certain position. The latest used vector was only roughly at the middle of the list for dimension 40, and seems to be smaller for higher dimensions. As a result, it might be possible to set a limit of vectors that L holds, without impairing performance, an issue which we will investigate in the future.

4 Parallel Implementation of ListSieve

In contrast to GaussSieve, which has been parallelized on multi-core CPU-platforms [10,12], there are no studies concerning the parallelization of ListSieve. We think that the main reason for the lack of studies addressing the parallelization of ListSieve is the (unverified) belief in its impracticality. There are essentially three reasons for studying the parallelization of ListSieve. First, as we show in this paper, the performance variations between ListSieve and GaussSieve are not as big as thought. Second, it was previously suggested that parallel versions of ListSieve could possibly outperform parallel versions of GaussSieve [12], a claim that we address first-hand. Third, ListSieve is much easier to port to parallel architectures, such as GPUs.

We implemented and assessed the performance of a parallel version of List-Sieve, written in C, which makes use of OpenMP to manage the execution of threads. The list L was implemented as a singly linked list, where each element points to its successor. Each thread follows the workflow of the original algorithm: they sample a vector **p**, reduce it against every element **v** in L, thereby generating **p'**, and insert **p'** in the list L. To avoid the use of synchronization, each thread inserts an element **p'**, between two vectors $\mathbf{v}_1$ and $\mathbf{v}_2$, in the list L, by setting **p'**'s next pointer pointing to $\mathbf{v}_2$ and then setting $\mathbf{v}_1$'s next pointer pointing to **p'**.

This relaxes the properties of the algorithm, which results in a smaller reduction process. There are two relaxations that *might* occur. First, (1) a given thread t_1 might be reducing its sample $\mathbf{p}_1$ in position k_1 of the list L while another thread t_2 inserts a vector $\mathbf{p}_2$ in position k_2, with $k_2 < k_1$. As a result, the reduction of $\mathbf{p}_1$, by thread t_1, will not take the vector $\mathbf{p}_2$ into account in that iteration, which we refer to as a *missed reduction*. Note that the vector will be visible in the following iteration. Second, (2) a sample is lost if two threads try to insert their samples at contiguous positions of L.

We found out that this synchronization-avoiding relaxation of the properties of ListSieve did not change the quality of the output, since the output of every run of our parallel ListSieve implementation was identical to the output of the *gsieve* library. This is not completely surprising, as (1), i.e. missing reductions, does not seem problematic because reductions will only be missed in a specific iteration (if missed at all), and the reduction could actually be unsuccessful in first place and (2), i.e. losing vectors, is very unlikely to happen, due to the length of the list, and the fact that threads are not likely to insert vectors in L at the same time.

The stopping criterion of the implementations is as defined in Section 2, set up with $\alpha = 0.1$ and $\beta = 200$. The code was compiled with g++ 4.6.1 (since NTL, used for BKZ, is written in C++) with the optimization flag -O2, which showed to be slightly better than -O3. Lattices were reduced with BKZ, with blocksize 20. Every experiment was repeated three times and the best sample was chosen. The elapsed time of lattice reduction is not included.

Figure 2 shows the execution time of our parallel version of ListSieve, for lattices in dimensions 40, 50 and 60, with 1-32 threads, on the test platform described in Section 3. As shown in Table 2, the speedup and efficiency are quite modest for dimension 40, because there is not enough work to compensate for the parallel execution overhead. For bigger lattices, the speedup is super-linear for all cases except for 32 threads in dimension 50, which concerns the use of SMT. In fact, with SMT, the efficiency drops for the three lattices. For dimension 60, the speedup and efficiency seem to grow with the number of threads, which means that the more threads are used, the more the properties of ListSieve are relaxed. As a result, it might happen that, for a very high number of threads, the number of missed reductions becomes problematic and more iterations are required for convergence, which will impair scalability.

Table 2. Runtime (R) in seconds, Speedup (S) and Efficiency (E) of our implementation on three lattices. The grayed out row, for 32 threads, concerns the use of SMT.

Threads	Dimension 40			Dimension 50			Dimension 60		
	R	S	E	R	S	E	R	S	E
1	1.1228	1.00	100%	33.7169	1.00	100%	2210.7188	1x	100%
2	0.4861	2.31x	116%	13.8189	2.44x	122%	770.3057	2.87x	144%
4	0.2587	4.34x	109%	6.1101	5.52x	138%	326.5866	6.77x	169%
8	0.2384	4.70x	59%	3.0440	11.08x	139%	150.8266	14.66x	183%
16	0.2657	4.23x	26%	1.9017	17.73x	111%	75.8777	29.14x	182%
32	0.2414	4.65x	15%	1.7373	19.41x	61%	49.1252	45.00x	141%

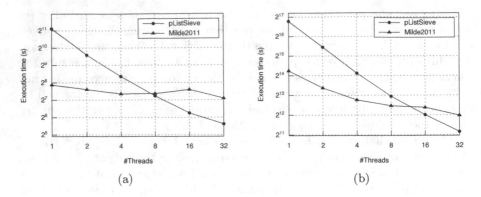

Fig. 3. Comparison of our ListSieve implementation (*pListSieve*) and *Milde2011* for a BKZ-reduced lattice with blocksize 20 in dimension 60 (a) and 70 in (b)

We also compared our implementation with the parallel GaussSieve implementation described in [12], from here on referred to as *Milde2011*. The code was provided by the authors. The implementation makes use of a ring structure connecting several instances of GaussSieve, each containing a local list, and a private stack S. Each thread samples a new vector **p** and reduces it against the elements in its local list. Afterwards, **p'** is handed over to the next thread which itself reduces the vector further against the elements in its local list. When the vector returns to the thread that released it, it is added to the local list of that thread.

Figures 3(a) and 3(b) compare the performance of our implementation and *Milde2011*, on lattices in dimensions 60 and 70, respectively. For the sake of convenience, the lattice in dimension 70 was BKZ-reduced with blocksize 32, for both implementations. For the lattice in dimension 60, *Milde2011* scales only up to 4 threads, and with 32 threads, at a limited rate. As our implementation scales super-linearly, it beats GaussSieve for 8 and more threads. For the lattice in dimension 70, *Milde2011* scales better, but also at a much lesser degree than our implementation. As a result, our implementation outperforms *Milde2011* for more than 8 threads. Note that GaussSieve is clearly faster for 1 thread, in both cases. This result indicates that ListSieve is indeed a practical SVP-solver and might take more advantage of massively parallel architectures than GaussSieve.

5   Conclusions

In this paper, we presented the results of a comprehensive empirical comparison of ListSieve and GaussSieve, two sieving algorithms that are very relevant in lattice-based cryptography. Although ListSieve has been considered impractical, we show that it can indeed be practical, especially on parallel platforms.

Another surprising discovery is that ListSieve only uses a small number of the stored vectors, a ratio that decreases with the dimension of the used lattice. This is very important because it might be used to reduce the memory usage of the algorithm, a critical problem of sieving algorithms.

Our parallel implementation of ListSieve relaxes the properties of the algorithm, allowing (1) some vector reductions to be missed and (2) some vectors to be lost, for the sake of reduced synchronization overhead. It achieves superlinear speedups on a multicore CPU-chip for up to 32 threads. In particular, an efficiency level of 182% is achieved for 16 threads on a lattice in dimension 60. As a result, it outperforms the parallel *Milde2011* GaussSieve implementation for a large number of threads, a question posed in [12] that was open to this day. Among other factors, this result is particularly relevant because the algorithm is a better candidate than GaussSieve to run on massively parallel architectures, such as GPUs, since it has fewer dependencies, especially if the properties of ListSieve are relaxed as we propose in this paper.

References

1. Ajtai, M.: Generating hard instances of lattice problems (extended abstract). In: STOC 1996, pp. 99–108. ACM (1996)
2. Ajtai, M.: The Shortest Vector Problem in L2 is NP-hard for Randomized Reductions (Extended Abstract). In: STOC 1998, pp. 10–19. ACM, NY (1998)
3. Fitzpatrick, R., et al.: Tuning GaussSieve for Speed. In: LATINCRYPT 2014, Florianópolis, Brazil (September 2014)
4. Dagdelen, Ö., Schneider, M.: Parallel enumeration of shortest lattice vectors. In: D'Ambra, P., Guarracino, M., Talia, D. (eds.) Euro-Par 2010, Part II. LNCS, vol. 6272, pp. 211–222. Springer, Heidelberg (2010)
5. Detrey, J., Hanrot, G., Pujol, X., Stehlé, D.: Accelerating Lattice Reduction with FPGAs. In: Abdalla, M., Barreto, P.S.L.M. (eds.) LATINCRYPT 2010. LNCS, vol. 6212, pp. 124–143. Springer, Heidelberg (2010)
6. Gama, N., Nguyen, P.Q., Regev, O.: Lattice enumeration using extreme pruning. In: Gilbert, H. (ed.) EUROCRYPT 2010. LNCS, vol. 6110, pp. 257–278. Springer, Heidelberg (2010)
7. Klein, P.: Finding the closest lattice vector when it's unusually close. In: SODA 2000, pp. 937–941 (2000)
8. Kuo, P.-C., Schneider, M., Dagdelen, Ö., Reichelt, J., Buchmann, J., Cheng, C.-M., Yang, B.-Y.: Extreme Enumeration on GPU and in Clouds. In: Preneel, B., Takagi, T. (eds.) CHES 2011. LNCS, vol. 6917, pp. 176–191. Springer, Heidelberg (2011)
9. Lenstra, A., et al.: Factoring polynomials with rational coefficients. Mathematische Annalen 261(4), 515–534 (1982)
10. Mariano, A., et al.: Lock-free GaussSieve for Linear Speedups in Parallel High Performance SVP Calculation. In: SBAC-PAD 2014, Paris, France (2014)
11. Micciancio, D., Voulgaris, P.: Faster exponential time algorithms for the shortest vector problem. In: SODA 2010, PA, USA, pp. 1468–1480 (2010)
12. Milde, B., Schneider, M.: A parallel implementation of GaussSieve for the shortest vector problem in lattices. In: Malyshkin, V. (ed.) PaCT 2011. LNCS, vol. 6873, pp. 452–458. Springer, Heidelberg (2011)
13. Schneider, M.: Analysis of Gauss-Sieve for Solving the Shortest Vector Problem in Lattices. In: Katoh, N., Kumar, A. (eds.) WALCOM 2011. LNCS, vol. 6552, pp. 89–97. Springer, Heidelberg (2011)
14. Schnorr, C., Euchner, M.: Lattice basis reduction: Improved practical algorithms and solving subset sum problems. Math. Programming 66(1-3), 181–199 (1994)
15. Shor, P.W.: Polynomial-time algorithms for prime factorization and discrete logarithms on a quantum computer. SIAM J. Comput. 26(5), 1484–1509 (1997)

Data Parallelism in Traffic Control Tables with Arrival Information

Juan F.R. Herrera[1], Eligius M.T. Hendrix[2],
Leocadio G. Casado[1], and René Haijema[3]

[1] University of Almeria (ceiA3), Spain
{juanfrh,leo}@ual.es
[2] Universidad de Málaga, Spain
Eligius.Hendrix@wur.nl
[3] Wageningen University, The Netherlands
Rene.Haijema@wur.nl

Abstract. Traffic lights can be controlled dynamically through rules reacting on the number of waiting vehicles at each light. A rule can be captured by a so-called Traffic Control Table (TCT). The Value Iteration method from Stochastic Dynamic Programming has been used for simple networks to derive a TCT. This work studies the generation of a TCT-based rule that takes the arrival information of new vehicles into account. The question is how to generate such a table for simple intersections (or a network of these). The generation is particularly difficult due to the computational work involved in the Value Iteration process.

The problem is formulated as a Markov Decision Process and the parallelization of the Value Iteration method for this problem is discussed. We are specifically interested in exploiting the structure of the problem for simple infrastructures, with only a few traffic lanes, using a parallel algorithm.

Keywords: Markov Decision Process, Stochastic Dynamic Programming, Value Iteration, Traffic Control.

1 Introduction

Dynamic decision making represents a wide area in real life, where the main goal is taking a decision from a certain state, i.e., decide the action x being in state s and time t. Here, we consider the problem of minimizing the waiting time at traffic lights.

Traffic lights were introduced in the early twentieth century to make traffic safer in places where traffic from different directions intersects at what is called a junction or intersection. To give priority to several traffic flows, the vehicles approaching from other flows must wait before getting right of way. The overall waiting time can be reduced if there exists a conveniently controlled sequence in the traffic lights network. This problem has been considered by theorists as well as engineers [2, 6–8].

L. Lopes et al. (Eds.): Euro-Par 2014 Workshops, Part I, LNCS 8805, pp. 60–70, 2014.

The optimal control traffic in a traffic junction is based in what we call a Traffic Control Table (TCT). This table determines which flow combination has priority given the current traffic state (number of waiting vehicles in each queue) in the traffic junction. To find a TCT which minimizes the vehicle waiting time, one can model the problem as a Markov Decision Process (MDP) and apply a Value Iteration algorithm, based on backward induction [3–5]. The idea of backward induction was introduced by Bellman in 1953 to solve (stochastic) dynamic programming [1]. Backward induction can be applied in dynamic optimization problems where time is discrete, for solving stationary systems without a time horizon.

Dynamic programming usually deals with a considerable number of states. Executing the Value Iteration algorithm requires to store all this information in main memory. An efficient access to these values can facilitate the cache location and therefore save computational time. In this work, the study of parallelizing the Value Iteration algorithm is tackled taking the data management into account.

The paper is structured as follows. In Section 2, a MDP model is described for the decisions captured in a TCT. Section 3 provides the algorithm of Value Iteration for the described problem. Section 4 applies the method to a simple infrastructure. The parallel algorithm as well as the experimental results will be shown in Sections 5 and 6 respectively. Conclusions and future work are presented in Section 7.

2   Model Description

The main goal is to calculate a TCT that determines how to manage the traffic lights considering the traffic density, so that overall waiting time is minimized in the long run. The table should capture which flows should get green light given the current state of the traffic. The problem is formulated as a MDP.

2.1   Goal

The waiting time of a vehicle is defined as the time from the moment a vehicle joins the queue until it crosses the stopping line. The practical objective is to find a control that minimizes the Expected Waiting (EW) time in the long run. Little's law formalizes the relationship between the arrival rate λ, EW time, and the number of waiting vehicles in a queue (EQ) as follows:

$$EQ = \lambda \times EW.$$

If the number of vehicles waiting in the queues is minimized, the waiting time is also minimized. The MDP algorithm does not need to keep track of the time a particular vehicle is waiting, but it does so for the number of queued vehicles.

2.2   Model Assumptions

The optimization problem of determining the traffic lights control is modelled as a stochastic and discrete-time control process. Given the state s of the traffic and the lights, an action x must be chosen from the available ones. The optimal choice $x(s)$ is then derived via the process of Value Iteration.

The model is based on the following ingredients:

- Time is divided into slots.
- A slot is the time required for a vehicle to leave a queue and cross an intersection. It also determines the safety distance between two vehicles.
- Traffic lights can be changed only at the end of a slot.
- The change from green to red light requires two slots of yellow: $Y1$ and $Y2$.
- The decision of changing the traffic light state is implemented instantly.
- While the light is green or yellow, at most one vehicle can cross the intersection in a slot.
- Vehicles move at a constant speed. The queued vehicles do not move, except for the first queued vehicle when the light allows it.
- To facilitate the analysis, the vehicle length is neglected. Therefore, a traffic junction is never stuck due to traffic.

2.3 Summary of Notations

The notation used throughout this paper is defined below. A crossing or intersection consists of F traffic flows or lanes, where each flow f consists of a lane and an associated queue. Vector $q = (q_1, \ldots, q_F)$ stores the number of vehicles waiting in each queue. Although in reality queues may contain Q or more vehicles, queues are truncated at Q vehicles to facility numerical computation of an optimal policy. We will also consider the possibility of having arrival information in a vector $a^{(f)}$ as will be specified in the next section. The traffic lane set $\mathcal{F} = \{1, \ldots, F\}$ can be partitioned in C disjoint subsets called combinations. Conflicting traffic flows do not get green simultaneously. The various combinations are given beforehand and determine the instance of the problem. All the lanes within a combination simultaneously receive green, red or yellow light. If a combination receives green or yellow light, the remaining ones receive red light.

2.4 Formulation as a Markov Decision Process

To model the problem, the following parameters are used:

- $\mathcal{S}$: a finite set of states. A state is defined by the light and the number of vehicles waiting in the queues that define the intersection. The number of states is countable because the number of intersections as well as the queue length are limited. The queues associated to each intersection are artificially truncated at some maximal queue length. Arrival information of new vehicles is also considered in state s.
- $c(s)$: cost of state s, defined by the number of vehicles waiting in the queues that describe the state s.

- λ_f: the probability that a new vehicle joins traffic flow f in a slot and therefore $(1 - \lambda_f)$ is the probability that no vehicle joins the traffic flow.
- $\mathcal{E}$: a finite set of possible events. Each event represents the arrival or not of a new vehicle at a lane f. Notice that the event does not depend on the state.
- $\mathcal{X}(s)$: a finite set of possible actions to control the lights. The set of possible actions depends on the state s.

State s: For the dynamic traffic control, the state of the MDP is the current light situation and state of traffic flows. The possible light states are denoted by index $l \in \mathcal{L} = \{1, \ldots, L\}$, where $L = 1 + 3^C$ as either all lights are red or only one of each of the C combinations has green, $Y1$ or $Y2$. The state of traffic flows for this model is:

- q : The number of vehicles waiting in each lane.
- $a^{(f)} = (a_1, \ldots, a_M)^{(f)}$: M arrival information slots are available for lane f, where $a_i^{(f)} \in \{0, 1\}$ determines whether a car arrives at queue f in i time slots from now.

Both the maximum number of vehicles in a single queue Q and the number of arrival information slots M may be flow specific.

Therefore, a state s is defined by $s = (l, q, a)$. The number of possible states is given by

$$|\mathcal{S}| = |\mathcal{L}| \cdot (Q + 1)^F \cdot 2^{M \cdot F}. \tag{1}$$

Control Action x: Given a state s, the action $x \in \mathcal{X}(s) \subseteq \mathcal{L}$ immediately adjusts the lights.

State Transition: During a slot, one vehicle arrives at traffic flow f with probability λ_f. The stochastic event e is defined as a vector of F elements $e = (e_1, \ldots, e_F)$, where $e_f \in \{0, 1\}$ denotes the number of vehicles that enter the infrastructure at lane f, within the coming time slot. Let function $\Delta_f(x)$ denote whether lane f has right of way ($\Delta_f(x) = 1$) or not ($\Delta_f(x) = 0$) when the lights are changed due to action x. As a result of decision x, state (l, q, a) changes into state

$$T(x, s_j, e_i) = (x, (q_1 + a_1^{(1)} - \Delta_1)^+, (a_2^{(1)}, \ldots, a_M^{(1)}, e_1), \ldots, (a_2^{(F)}, \ldots, a_M^{(F)}, e_F)).$$

Objective Function: The objective function is to minimize the number of vehicles waiting at the queues. The contribution to the objective function over a single time slot is $c(s) = \sum_f q_f$. The associated cost in a general MDP usually depends on the state s as well as the decision x. In the model we are interested in, it depends on the state only, so we have the cost function $c(s)$.

Bellman's Principle of Optimality: The strategy $x(s)$ is optimal [1] if there exists a function $v(s)$ and a scalar d such that $\forall s \in \mathcal{S}$

$$v(s) - d = c(s) + \min_{x \in \mathcal{X}(s)} [E\{v(T(x, s, e))\}], \qquad (2)$$

where E symbolizes the expected value with respect to the stochastic event e. The transition function $T(x, s, e)$ describes the next state to be reached after taking the decision x in the state s on event e.

Essential in the described model is that the number of events is finite, such that they can be numbered as e_i with probability of occurrence p_i. In addition, we also consider that the countable state space is finite, such that the states are indexed $j = 1, \ldots, |\mathcal{S}|$. This implies that the value function v can be captured by a vector V with elements $V_j = v(s_j)$. The Bellman equation (2) implies to find a valuation vector V and a constant d such that

$$V_j - d = c(s_j) + \min_{x \in \mathcal{X}(s_j)} \sum_i p_i V_k, \qquad (3)$$

where k is the state index value related to state $T(x, s_j, e_i)$. Notice that the index values of the reachable states from state s_j are a subset

$$\mathcal{K}_j = \{k : s_k = T(x, s_j, e_i) \ \forall i, \forall x \in \mathcal{X}(s_j)\}$$

of all states $\mathcal{S}$. If one has a valuation V, also the optimum control value can be derived from

$$X_j = x(s_j) = \arg \min_{x \in \mathcal{X}(s_j)} \sum_i p_i V_k, \qquad (4)$$

where again $V_k = T(x, s_j, e_i)$.

3 Value Iteration through Backward Induction

Bellman introduced the term "backward induction" and also indicated the way to solve (3) using fixed point theory, where (3) is repeated iteratively. The latter process is called Value Iteration [9]. One way to deal with that (see Algorithm 1) is to copy a current valuation vector V into a vector W and determine a new valuation V according to

$$V_j = c(s_j) + \min_{x \in \mathcal{X}(s_j)} \sum_i p_i W_k, \ j = 1, \ldots, |\mathcal{S}|, \qquad (5)$$

where k is the state index related to state $T(x, s_j, e_i)$.

The Value Iteration should lead to convergence towards $d = V_j - W_j$, for all $j = 1, \ldots, |\mathcal{S}|$. Convergence to the scalar d is measured by the so-called

$$\text{span}(V, W) = \max_j (V_j - W_j) - \min_j (V_j - W_j).$$

The iterative procedure of Algorithm 1 stops whenever $\text{span}(V, W)$ is smaller than a pre-specified value ϵ, which indicate the accuracy in estimating d.

Algorithm 1. Value iteration

1: Set vector V to zero
2: **repeat**
3:    Copy vector V into vector W
4:    **for** $j = 1, \ldots, |S|$ **do**
5:       $V_j = c(s_j) + \min_{x \in \mathcal{X}(s_j)} \sum_i p_i W_k$
6:    **end for**
7: **until** $\max_j(V_j - W_j) - \min_j(V_j - W_j) < \epsilon$

How is this property translated into the TCT model? In the first place, notice that the strategy $x(s)$ represents the idea of a TCT. In the model, the set of states S is countable as it is based on the light colours and the number of waiting vehicles. In addition, a maximum number of vehicles in a queue is defined, such that the total number of states becomes finite. The value of states beyond the limit Q are obtained by extrapolation. The function $v(s)$ is represented by vector V and $x(s)$ is the final TCT given by (4). The computational challenge is that $|S|$ is usually high. An important observation for the defined model is that the computation of V_j requires a small index subset $\mathcal{K}_j$ for values W_k of the index set $\mathcal{S}_j$.

The research question is how to handle the retrieval of W_k values from memory in the computational process, such that the loop over j in Algorithm 1 can be done in an efficient way.

4 Studied Case of the TCT Model

In [3], a code is introduced to denote a specific infrastructure. For instance, I1F2C2 stands for a single intersection with $F = 2$ traffic flows (or lanes) and $C = 2$ combinations. Figure 1 shows the simple infrastructure that will be elaborated:

I1F2C2 is a single T-shape intersection (T-junction) with two traffic flows, $\mathcal{F} = \{1, 2\}$. Vehicles in lane 1 drive from west to east, while vehicles in lane 2 drive from north to east, i.e., they turn left. Each direction has a single lane with its corresponding queue at the stopping line. Additionally, lane 1 has arrival information slots, represented by the vector a.

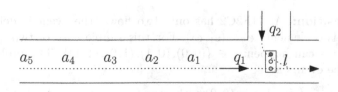

Fig. 1. I1F2C2 infrastructure

The preliminary results focus on this infrastructure. The specific features of the I1F2C2 case are as follows.

State s: A state s is defined by $s = (l, q, a)$, see Section 2. The traffic light states are

$$\mathcal{L} = \{0, 1, 2, 3, 4, 5, 6\} = \{Red, GF1, GF2, Y1F1, Y2F1, Y1F2, Y2F2\},$$

where:

0. *Red:* Red light for all the flows.
1. *GF1:* Green light for flow 1.
2. *GF2:* Green light for flow 2.
3. *Y1F1:* Yellow light for flow 1 (slot 1).
4. *Y2F1:* Yellow light for flow 1 (slot 2).
5. *Y1F2:* Yellow light for flow 2 (slot 1).
6. *Y2F2:* Yellow light for flow 2 (slot 2).

The state of traffic flows for this case is:

- $q = (q_1, q_2)$. The number of vehicles waiting in each lane.
- $a = (a_1, \ldots, a_M)$. As only flow 1 has arrival information, the flow index is omitted. The element $a_t \in \{0, 1\}$ determines the presence or absence of a vehicle in slot t. For example, if $a_t = 1$, a vehicle arrives to the queue in t time slots.

The number of possible states for the I1F2C2 case is given by

$$|\mathcal{S}| = |\mathcal{L}| \cdot (Q + 1)^2 \cdot 2^M.$$

Control Action x: The possible subsets $\mathcal{X}(s) \subset \mathcal{L}$ are enumerated as follows.

$$\mathcal{X} = \begin{cases} \{1, 2\} = \{GF1, GF2\} & \text{if } l = 0 = Red \\ \{1, 3\} = \{GF1, Y1F1\} & \text{if } l = 1 = GF1 \\ \{4\} = \{Y2F1\} & \text{if } l = 3 = Y1F1 \\ \{0\} = \{Red\} & \text{if } l = 4 = Y2F1 \\ \{2, 5\} = \{GF2, Y1F2\} & \text{if } l = 2 = GF2 \\ \{6\} = \{Y2F2\} & \text{if } l = 5 = Y1F2 \\ \{0\} = \{Red\} & \text{if } l = 6 = Y2F2 \end{cases}$$

State Transition: As I1F2C2 has only two flows, the event is defined as a vector e of two elements $e = (e_1, e_2)$. For this simple case of two lanes, four possible events can happen: $e \in \{(0, 0), (0, 1), (1, 0), (1, 1)\}$. The probability p_i related to the events is:

$$\begin{cases} i = 1, e = (0, 0) \text{ with } p_1 = (1 - \lambda_1)(1 - \lambda_2) \\ i = 2, e = (0, 1) \text{ with } p_2 = (1 - \lambda_1)\lambda_2 \\ i = 3, e = (1, 0) \text{ with } p_3 = \lambda_1(1 - \lambda_2) \\ i = 4, e = (1, 1) \text{ with } p_4 = \lambda_1\lambda_2 \end{cases}$$

For instance, let $M = 5$. During a slot, the arrival information denoted by $a = (a_1, a_2, a_3, a_4, a_5)$ shifts towards $a \leftarrow (a_2, a_3, a_4, a_5, e_1)$, i.e., the arriving vehicles at the lane are approaching and a_1 represents the vehicle that is added to the queue.

Depending on the traffic light state, the queue length will increase or not. Suppose that flow 1 has red light ($l \in \{0, 2, 5, 6\}$, so $\Delta_f(x) = 0$). A vehicle which is one slot upstream away from queue f, increases the number of vehicles in queue 1. When x sets the colour to green or yellow for lane 1 ($l \in \{1, 3, 4\}$, so $\Delta_f(x) = 1$) and the queue 1 is not empty ($q_1 > 0$), the vehicle is added to the queue. If the queue is empty ($q_1 = 0$), the vehicle crosses the stop line of flow 1 without delay. The transition of queue 1 is given by $q_1 \leftarrow q_1 + a_1 - \Delta_1(x)$.

For lane 2, there exists no information about the arrival of new vehicles to the queue, therefore the next state of queue 2 depends on e_2 and action x. The transition of queue 2 is given by $q_2 \leftarrow (q_2 + e_2 - \Delta_2(x))^+$ vehicles.

Objective Function: Having two queues, the objective function is

$$c(s) = q_1 + q_2 .$$

5   Parallel Approach

The sequential Algorithm 1 is an iterative process where the vector V of size $|\mathcal{S}|$ is updated based on previous values of V_j stored in vector W until a termination condition holds. The natural way to tackle the parallelization of Algorithm 1 is to distribute the evaluation of V between processors. The set of state values V can be partitioned in different ways depending on $|\mathcal{S}|$ and on the characteristics of the final architecture. When message passing is used, the number of messages should be as small as possible. For shared-memory architectures, the access to values in W should be done in such a way that the probability they are available in cache level 1 is increased.

Both methods need a synchronization point at the end of the update of V to check the termination condition and to have the data W available for the next iteration. This is an additional challenge for the parallelization of the process.

Taking these considerations into account, an option is to store the values of V and W as a matrix, where the columns are the values of lights and the rows are the different combinations of queue states and arrival information. In a shared-memory architecture, the matrix can be computed row wise, where each thread is in charge of a chunk of the matrix. In a distributed-memory architecture, a reasonable solution is a partition of the matrix into columns. In this way, the number of messages is not high, although the message size may easily be big.

5.1   Computational Complexity

The workload is related to the number of flows (F), the maximum size of a queue (Q) and the number of states (M) that describes the arrival information. The

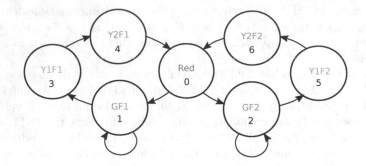

Fig. 2. Message passing in lights distribution for MPI approach

limit imposed on the queue length makes the state space finite. Higher values of queue lengths introduce state situations with an extremely low probability of occurrence. This hinders the convergence of Value Iteration. Therefore, for each iteration the complexity of the algorithm is given by $|\mathcal{S}|$ as specified by (1).

5.2   MPI Approach

The MPI approach is mainly used for distributed-memory systems. Figure 2 shows the message passing for the parallelization using MPI, where each MPI process is in charge of the evaluation of the values of V associated to one value of the light state $l \in \mathcal{L} = \{0, 1, 2, 3, 4, 5, 6\}$. A greater parallel degree can be achieved by parallelizing each MPI process.

The main drawback of the described MPI approach is the imbalance between processes. For instance, a process in charge of $l \in \{Red, GF1, GF2\}$ requires more data from vector W to update V_j values than processes in charge of yellow lights. In addition, the maximum number of processes in I1F2C2 is seven according to the developed strategy.

5.3   Threaded Approach

This approach is used in shared-memory architectures. Having V as a matrix, where each thread is in charge of the evaluation of a set of rows facilitates the use of an arbitrary number of threads. Matrix V is partitioned into chunks of rows, each to be dealt with by one thread. A drawback is that usually the effective number of threads is bounded by the number of cores in the shared-memory architecture.

6   Preliminary Results

Experiments have been carried out in a node of *BullX-UAL* cluster, with two Intel® Xeon® E5-2650 processors and 64 GB of main memory. Algorithms have

Table 1. Numerical results using threads

N. of threads	Q50M10		Q100M5	
	Time (s)	Speedup	Time (s)	Speedup
1	240	–	511	–
2	119	2	260	2
4	56	4	133	3.8
8	31	7.7	68	7.5
16	17	14	36	14.2

been coded in C and compiled using gcc with MVAPICH and POSIX threads API.

The arrival ratio is $\lambda_f = 0.2$ for each incoming flow $f = 1, 2$. The accuracy is set to $\epsilon = 0.01$. TCTs are generated for I1F2C2 with two different settings:

Q50M10: Queue length $Q_1 = Q_2 = 50$. Arrival information slots $M = 10$.
Q100M5: Queue length $Q_1 = Q_2 = 100$. Arrival information slots $M = 5$.

6.1   MPI Approach

Results for the MPI approach using seven processes shows a poor performance with a speedup of less than 3 due to the imbalance of the workload among processes and the cost of message passing.

6.2   Threaded Approach

Table 1 shows the experimental results for the threaded version varying the number of threads. The achieved speedup is near linear. As future work we plan to perform a reordering of the rows of value functions V and W assigned to each thread to improve the cache locality of the needed data.

7   Conclusion and Ongoing Work

Solving dynamic optimization problems by the Value Iteration algorithm is a challenge from the point of view of running the process in parallel. Each iteration of the algorithm requires a synchronization. This paper studied the algorithm for generating the best traffic control table. The difficulty of these problems increases with the number of traffic flows and intersections, and the inclusion of arrival information. A near linear speedup has been obtained with a threaded version for a basic instance of the problem. Future investigation will focus on parallel computation of traffic control tables for more complicated infrastructures that imply a larger number of traffic states. To do so, a parallelization in two levels (MPI for inter-node and threads for intra-node) is convenient to achieve a good performance in a cluster of shared-memory nodes.

Acknowledgments. This work has been funded by grants from the Spanish Ministry (TIN2008-01117 and TIN2012-37483) and Junta de Andalucía (P11-TIC-7176 and P12-TIC-301), in part financed by the European Regional Development Fund (ERDF). J.F.R. Herrera is a fellow of the Spanish FPU program.

References

1. Bellman, R.: A Markovian Decision Process. Journal of Mathematics and Mechanics 6(5) (1957)
2. van den Broek, M.S., van Leeuwaarden, J.S.H., Boxma, I.J.B.F.A., Bounds, O.J.: Approximations for the fixed-cycle traffic-light queue. Transportation Science 40(4), 484–496 (2006)
3. Haijema, R.: Solving large structured Markov Decision Problems for perishable inventory management and traffic control. Ph.D. thesis, Universiteit van Amsterdam (2008)
4. Haijema, R., Hendrix, E.M.T.: Traffic responsive control of intersections with predicted arrival times: A Markovian approach. Computer-Aided Civil and Infrastructure Engineering 29(2), 123–139 (2014)
5. Haijema, R., van der Wal, J.: An MDP Decomposition Approach for Traffic Control at Isolated Signalized Intersections. Probability in the Engineering and Informational Sciences 22, 587–602 (2008)
6. van Leeuwaarden, J.S.H.: Delay analysis for the fixed-cycle traffic-light queue. Transportation Science 40(2), 189–199 (2006)
7. Newell, G.F.: Approximation methods for queues with application to the fixed-cycle traffic light. SIAM Review 7(2), 223–240 (1965)
8. Papageorgiou, M., Diakaki, C., Dinopoulou, V., Kotsialos, A., Wang, Y.: Review of road traffic control strategies. Proceedings of the IEEE 91(12), 2043–2067 (2003)
9. Puterman, M.L.: Markov Decision Processes: Discrete Stochastic Dynamic Programming, 1st edn. John Wiley & Sons, Inc., New York (1994)

Parallel Shared-Memory
Multi-Objective Stochastic Search
for Competitive Facility Location

Algirdas Lančinskas[1], Pilar Martínez Ortigosa[2], and Julius Žilinskas[1]

[1] Institute of Mathematics and Informatics, Vilnius University,
Akademijos 4, 08663 Vilnius, Lithuania
{algirdas.lancinskas,julius.zilinskas}@mii.vu.lt
http://www.mii.lt
[2] Universidad de Almería, ceiA3
Ctra. Sacramento s/n, La Cañada de San Urbano 04120, Almería, Spain
ortigosa@ual.es
http://www.ual.es

Abstract. A stochastic search algorithm for local multi-objective optimization is developed and applied to solve a multi-objective competitive facility problem for firm expansion using shared-memory parallel computing systems. The performance of the developed algorithm is experimentally investigated by solving competitive facility location problems, using up to 16 shared-memory processing units. It is shown that the developed algorithm has advantages against its precursor in the sense of the precision of optimization and that it has almost linear speed-up on 16 shared-memory processing units, when solving competitive facility location problems of different scope reasonable for practical applications.

Keywords: Facility Location, Multi-Objective Optimization, Stochastic Search, Shared Memory Parallel Computing.

1 Introduction

The location of facilities deals with the determination of the optimal location for a facility (or a set of facilities) which is important for the firms providing services to customers in a certain geographical region. It is believed that facility location as a science has originated from Pierre de Fermat, Evangelistica Torricelli, and Battista Cavallieri as these people independently proposed the basic Euclidean spatial median problem early in the seventeenth century [2]. But formally, the Alfred Weber's book [16] is assumed to be the most important starting point in the history of location science. Nowadays there are a lot of models of facility location proposed in literature, e.g. [3,5,12,14], which differ on their properties such as location space, describing possible locations for the facilities being located, attractiveness of facilities, or behavior of customers when choosing the facility to buy a service.

L. Lopes et al. (Eds.): Euro-Par 2014 Workshops, Part I, LNCS 8805, pp. 71–82, 2014.

1.1 Competitive Facility Location for Firm Expansion

Important characteristic of the models of facility location is the market environment. Consider a company is planning an establishment of several facilities in a region where other companies are already providing a service. The new facilities must be located with respect to the competition with the preexisting ones for the market share. Such a kind of facility location models are known as Competitive Facility Location (CFL) models.

If the company planing establishment of new facilities is already in the market, then it is encountered with the Competitive Facility Location for Firm Expansion, where the impact of the new facilities on the preexisting facilities of the same company should be taken into account.

In this research we are interested in the bi-objective (of two objectives) CFL problem for firm expansion, which has been proposed by Fernández et al. in [4].

Consider two firms A and B, providing a service to a set I of demand points. The firm A has a set F_A of n_A facilities and the firm B has a set F_B of n_B facilities, providing service for customers in a given geographical region and competing for the market.

The firm A wants to open a set F_X of n_X facilities in order to increase the market share. On one hand the new facilities can attract new customers from the rival firm B thus increasing the total market share of the company A. On the other hand the new facilities can attract customers who are already served by own facilities from F_A, thus giving raise of the effect of cannibalism. Therefore the firm A faces a multi-objective optimization problem to find the optimal locations for the new facilities with respect to maximization of the market share captured by the new facilities and simultaneous minimization of the effect of the cannibalism.

1.2 Multi-Objective Optimization

In general a problem of facility location as well as the CFL problem for firm expansion can be formulated as a mathematical optimization problem to find a *decision vector* $\mathbf{x}^* = (x_1^*, x_2^*, \ldots, x_d^*)$, describing the locations of the facilities expected to be established, so that the value of the *objective function* $f(\mathbf{x}^*)$, describing the fitness of the selected locations, would be the minimal

$$f(\mathbf{x}^*) = \min_{\mathbf{x} \in \mathbb{D}} f(\mathbf{x}), \qquad (1)$$

where $\mathbb{D}$ is a set of all possible decision vectors, called *search space*. The objective function usually is based on a relevant criterion, such as maximization of the market share of the company, minimization of costs of establishment or further maintaining of the prospective facilities, minimization of costs of communication between a facility and the customers, etc.

Like most of real-world optimization problems, location of the facilities usually requires simultaneous consideration of more than one criterion. For example, maximization of the market share of the new facilities and minimization of communication costs, minimization of communication cost while maximizing the distance from a residential area, or all of them: maximization of the market share and distance to a residential area, while minimization of communication costs. Thus a decision maker faces a *multi-objective optimization problem*.

Without reducing the generality further we will consider the CFL problem for firm expansion, described in Section 1.1. The problem consists of two objectives; one is subject to maximization (the market share of the new facilities) whereas another one is subject to minimization (the effect of cannibalism). Due to conflicting objectives, comparison of two decision vectors by the value of a single objective is meaningless as a better decision vector for one objective can be worse, or even the worst for another one. However, the fitness of two different decision vectors can be compared by the *dominance relation*. In terms of multi-objective optimization two different decision vectors x and y can be related with each other in three different ways: x *dominates* y and vice versa, as well as none of them are dominated by the other.

In general it is said that the decision vector x dominates the decision vector y if x is strictly better than y by at least one objective, but not worse by any other objective. The dominance relation is denoted by $x \succ y$, and the decision vector x is called a *dominator* of y. If none of two decision vectors can be distinguished as a dominator of the other, it is said that these decision vectors are *indifferent* in the sense of dominance relation.

A decision vector x which has no dominators in the whole search space $\mathbb{D}$ is called *non-dominated*, or *Pareto-optimal*, and a set of non-dominated vectors is called the *Pareto set*. The corresponding set of the values of the objective functions is called the *Pareto front*.

Determination of the exact Pareto front of a multi-objective optimization problem is usually a hard and time consuming task, which can be even intractable within an acceptable time. On the other hand solution of practical problems usually does not require to find the exact Pareto front, but rather its approximation. Therefore multi-objective optimization methods approximating the Pareto front as well as parallel computing techniques are usually used to tackle practical problems.

1.3   Related Works

A great amount of work devoted to an approximation of the Pareto front can be found in the literature with reference to facility location. A well known class of such algorithms are Evolutionary Algorithms (EAs), which require little knowledge about the problem being solved. For example, Redondo et al. [13] proposed a general multi-objective optimization heuristic algorithm, suitable to continuous multi-objective optimization problems; Zitzler et al. [17] proposed the Strength Pareto Evolutionary Algorithm (SPEA2) and Huapu and Jifeng [6] utilized it to solve a bi-level programming model to optimize the location problem of distribution centers; Deb et al. [1] proposed the Non-dominated Sorting Genetic Algorithm (NSGA-II) and Villegas et al. [15] utilized it to solve a bi-objective facility location problem by minimizing operational cost of Colombian Coffee supply network and maximizing the demand.

Although EAs are popular due to applicability to various practical problems, their performance can be notably improved by incorporating a local search thus deriving so called memetic algorithms. For example, Medaglia et al. [11] utilized hybrid NSGA-II and mixed-integer programming approach to solve bi-objective obnoxious facility location problem related to the hospital waste management network; Lančinskas et al. [7] proposed a Multi-objective Single Agent Stochastic Search (MOSASS) and incorporated it in the NSGA-II, thus developing a memetic multi-objective optimization algorithm called NSGA/LSP.

The NSGA-II as well as most of EAs are quite fast, however it can be time consuming if the evaluation of the objective functions are expensive in the sense of computational resources. In order to reduce the computational time, parallel variants of NSGA-II have been proposed in [8], some of which have been applied to solve the competitive facility location problems using the large scale computing system in [9]. Consequently the parallel version of memetic algorithm NSGA/LSP, suitable for hybrid distributed-shared memory architecture of parallel computing system, has been proposed and applied to solve the CFL problems in [10]. The main disadvantage of the parallel memetic algorithm appears to be a sequential local optimization of a single solution, which leads to an idle time of some processing units during the local optimization procedure.

In this paper we will focus on development and investigation of the parallel multi-objective local search algorithm, by modifying previously proposed MOSASS, as well as its application to solve CFL problems using shared-memory parallel computing system.

The reminder of the paper is organized as follows: Sections 2 and 3 consist of the descriptions of the MOSS and its parallel version proposed, respectively; the experimental investigation of the developed algorithms and discussion of the obtained results are presented in Section 4, and conclusions of the research are formulated in Section 5.

2   Multi-Objective Stochastic Search

The Multi-Objective Stochastic Search (MOSS) algorithm is based on Multi-Objective Single Agent Stochastic Search (MOSASS), previously proposed in [7]. In MOSASS a new decision vector is generated in the neighborhood of a single initial decision vector, which is updated only if its dominator is found. MOSS uses a multi-agent concept, where new decision vectors are generated in a neighborhood of a certain decision vector that has been randomly selected from the set of all non-dominated decision vectors found so far.

The MOSS algorithm begins with an initial set A of non-dominated decision vectors, which can be generated at random over the search space $\mathbb{D}$, or obtained by other multi-objective optimization algorithm, e.g. NSGA-II, SPEA2, etc. The set A can also consist of a single decision vector that can be interesting to a decision maker and which neighborhood should be locally explored.

A decision vector $\mathbf{x}$ is randomly selected from the set A to represent a reference decision vector in generation of the new decision vector $\mathbf{x}' = \mathbf{x} + \xi$, where $\xi = (\xi_1, \xi_2, \ldots, \xi_d)$ is a vector of random values. Each ξ_i is generated by

$$\xi_i = \begin{cases} \mathcal{N}(b, \sigma), & \text{if } r_i \leq 1/d, \\ 0, & \text{if } r_i > 1/d, \end{cases} \tag{2}$$

where $\mathcal{N}(b, \sigma)$ stands for a random number, generated following the Gaussian distribution with the bias b and the standard deviation σ, r is a random number uniformly generated over $[0, 1]$, and d is the number of variables. Such a probabilistic method for generation of a neighbor decision vector leads to the change of a single coordinate in average when generating a new decision vector; see [7] for details and advantages of the method.

If the generated decision vector is non-dominated in the set A then the set is updated by including $\mathbf{x}'$ and removing all decision vectors dominated by it:

$$A \leftarrow (A \cup \{\mathbf{x}'\}) \setminus \{\mathbf{x} \in A : \mathbf{x}' \succ \mathbf{x}\}. \tag{3}$$

The iteration is then assumed to be successful and the algorithm proceeds to the next iteration. If the new decision vector is dominated by any one from the set A, then the opposite decision vector $\mathbf{x}'' = \mathbf{x} - \xi$ is considered. If $\mathbf{x}''$ is non-dominated in the set A, then the set A is updated by including $\mathbf{x}''$ and removing all dominated decision vectors similarly to (3). The iteration is then assumed to be successful and the algorithm proceeds to the next iteration.

If the opposite decision vector $\mathbf{x}''$ is dominated in A then the iteration is assumed to be failed.

In the case of success, the number of repetitive successful iterations is increased by one, and the number of repetitive failures is reset to zero. In the case of failure, the number of repetitive failures is increased by one and the number of repetitive successes is reset to zero.

The values of b and σ are dynamically adjusted with respect to the repetitive success or failures in generation of a neighbor decision vector. For the detailed description of adjustment of the parameters' values we refer to [7].

3 Parallel Multi-Objective Stochastic Search

The MOSS algorithm can be briefly separated into three main parts: (i) the initialization of the algorithm, where loading of initial data and assignment of initial values of the parameters take place, (ii) the main loop, where iterative process of approximation of the Pareto front takes place, and (iii) the finalization, where processing and output of the obtained result take place.

The first and third parts are much less time-consuming, comparing with the second one, and their consideration as sequential parts should not make a significant impact on the performance of the parallel algorithm. The most time-consuming part of the algorithm is the second one, where the main computational effort is on the evaluation of the values of the objective functions. Assuming that the evaluations of the fitness of different decision vectors can be considered as independent tasks, they can be assigned to different processing units. In such a distribution of tasks the consistent access to the values of all algorithm parameters and to the whole set A of the non-dominated decision vectors found so far must be guaranteed for all processing units. Moreover if one of the processing units is updating a parameter, access of any other processing unit to that parameter is blocked in order to keep memory or data consistency.

Taking these considerations into account, the parallel version of MOSS, called ParMOSS, has been developed using shared-memory parallel programming libraries. ParMOSS begins with initialization of the parameters of the algorithm as well as the data and parameters of the optimization problem to be solved. This part of the algorithm is insignificant in the sense of computational effort, and, therefore, is performed by a single processing unit – the master.

Further the computational effort is distributed among all the processing units being used for the computations. Each of the units randomly selects a decision vector $\mathbf{x}$ from the set A, generates its neighbor $\mathbf{x}'$, and evaluates its values of the objective functions. Since the values of the objectives are evaluated, the dominance relation of the generated decision vector with those in the set A is checked. During this procedure the access for updating the set A is blocked for other processing units due to consistency memory requirements.

If $\mathbf{x}'$ is non-dominated regarding the set A, then the set is updated by including $\mathbf{x}'$ and removing all dominated decision vectors (see (3) and its description). The access to the set A is also denied for other processing units till the update is complete, as well as the accesses to the bias b and the counter of the repetitive success iterations are denied while their values are being updated.

If $\mathbf{x}'$ is dominated by any of decision vectors from A, then the opposite decision vector $\mathbf{x}''$ is considered, using the same strategy and policies to access the memory, as it is when considering $\mathbf{x}'$.

Principal scheme of the ParMOSS algorithm is given in Fig. 1. The scheme is based on the standard scheme for EA, but the parallel part of the algorithm with critical operations are highlighted. The dashed lines in the scheme mark the boundaries of the region where operations are performed by all processing units (the parallel region), and the hatched figures mark critical operations, which can be performed by a single processing unit at one time; i.e. if one processing unit performs operation enabling limited access to the set, any access to the set is denied for all other processing units.

4   Computational Experiments

The developed parallel algorithm ParMOSS has been applied to solve CFL problems, described in Section 1.1, using real geographical coordinates and populations of 5000 cities and towns in Lithuania, considered as demand points.

It was assumed that the firms A and B have $n_A = n_B = 3$ preexisting facilities and that the firm A wants to extend its market share by establishing a set F_X of $n_X = 3$ facilities. The simplest model of the behavior of customers when

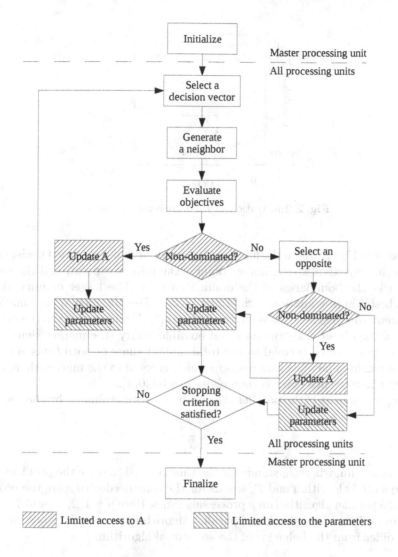

Fig. 1. Principal scheme of the ParMOSS algorithm

choosing the most attractive facility has been used, assuming that all customers from a single demand point choose the nearest facility.

Ten thousands function evaluations have been devoted for approximation of the Pareto front. Due to stochastic nature of the algorithm, each experiment has been performed 100 times, using different randomly generated initial decision vector, and the average results have been computed.

The precision of the approximation of the Pareto front has been evaluated by the Hyper-Volume (HV) metric, proposed by Zitzler and Thiele in [18]. The HV measures the area captured by the points in the obtained Pareto front approximation and the given reference point r. The concept of the HV metric is

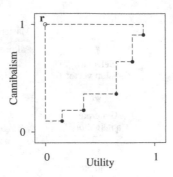

Fig. 2. Illustration of the hyper-volume metric

illustrated in Fig. 2, where the filled points stand for non-dominated decision vectors in the objectives space, hollow point – the reference point, and the dashed line marks the boundaries of the dominated area. The larger dominated area means better approximation of the Pareto front. The obtained approximation of the Pareto front has been scaled to the interval $[0, 1]^2$ with respect to the extreme values of the objectives – the maximal possible utility (the market share of the new facilities), which is equal to the total market share of both firms A and B, and the maximal possible cannibalism, which is equal to the market share of the firm A. The reference point is then chosen to be $[0, 1]$.

The performance of the parallel algorithm has been evaluated by the speed-up

$$S_p = \frac{T_0}{T_p} \tag{4}$$

of the algorithm, where T_0 stands for the time needed to solve the problem using the sequential algorithm and T_p stands for the time needed to solve the problem using the parallel algorithm on p processing units. Here $p = 1, 2, \ldots$ and T_1 might differ from T_0 as the behavior of parallel algorithm on a single processing unit might differ from the behavior of the sequential algorithm.

4.1   Impact on the Precision

Since MOSS has been derived from MOSASS by changing the strategy for selection of the decision vector from the set of non-dominated ones, the impact of the modification on the quality of the approximation must be investigated.

The quality of the approximation has been investigated by solving the CFL problem with 5000 demand points. The problems have been solved by sequential versions of MOSASS and MOSS.

The obtained results are presented in Fig. 3, where the vertical axis stands for the number of function evaluations, the horizontal one – for the average values of HV, and different curves stand for the different algorithms.

One can see from the figure, the proposed MOSS algorithm notably outperforms its precursor MOSASS independent on the number of function evaluations devoted for the approximation.

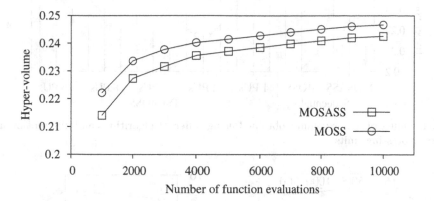

Fig. 3. Values of hyper-volume, obtained using different algorithms and different numbers of function evaluations

The parallel version of MOSS does not have exactly the same behavior as the sequential one, therefore it must be verified if the quality of the approximation has not been reduced when parallelizing.

The verification has been done by solving the CFL problem of different scope: 1000 and 5000 demand points. The problems have been solved by the parallel algorithm ParMOSS using different numbers of processing units: 1, 2, 4, 8, and 16. The obtained results have been additionally compared with the results obtained by sequential version of the algorithms.

The results are illustrated in Fig. 4, where two first couples of columns show average HV, obtained by sequential versions of MOSASS and MOSS, respectively, whereas the following ones – show average HV, obtained by ParMOSS using different numbers of processing units; different columns in a couple represent different number of demand points, and interval segment on the top of the column illustrates the confidence interval of the mean with the confidence level 0.05.

One can see from the figure that the variation of values of HV, obtained using ParMOSS on different numbers of processing units is very slight and can be considered as insignificant. This leads to the conclusion that the parallelization of MOSS does not negatively effect the precision of the approximation.

4.2   Speed-Up of the Algorithm

The efficiency of the parallel algorithm ParMOSS has been evaluated by solving the CFL problem using four different numbers of demand points: 5000, 1000, 500, and 100. The time required for computations using 5000 demand points is around 100 seconds. The problem of the smaller scope – 1000 demand points

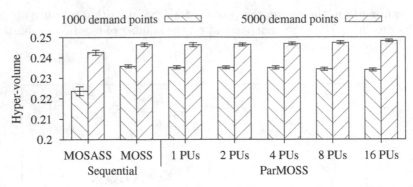

Fig. 4. Values of hyper-volume, obtained using different algorithms and different number of processing units

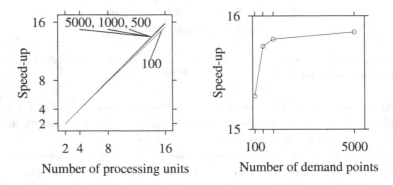

Fig. 5. The speed-up of ParMOSS, obtained using different numbers of demand points, versus the number of processing units (on the left) and the speed-up, obtained using 16 processing units, versus the number of demand points (on the right)

requires around 20 seconds, 500 demand points – 10 seconds, and 100 demand points – 2 seconds. The main effort of the computational resources (more than 99%) has been devoted to the function evaluation in all the cases, except the smallest one – 100 demand points, when function evaluations require a little bit less than 99% of all computational resources.

The time needed to solve a problem using MOSS was 0.3–0.4% larger comparing with its precursor MOSASS, as well as the ParMOSS on one processing unit requires 0.3–0.4% more time than sequential MOSS.

The speed-up of ParMOSS, obtained using 2, 4, 8, and 16 processing units is given in the left image of Fig. 5, where the horizontal axis corresponds to the number of processing units, and the vertical one – to the speed-up. One can see from the figure, the speed-up of the algorithm is almost linear for all experiments except for the case of using 16 processing units to solve the smallest problem with 100 demand points.

The dependence of the speed-up of the algorithm, obtained using 16 processing units, on the number of demand points is illustrated in the right image of Fig. 5, where the horizontal axis corresponds to the number of demand points, and the vertical axis – to the speed-up from the range from 15 to 16.

The obtained results show that ParMOSS has almost linear speed-up, since the further reduction of the demand points is not reasonable in practical CFL problems, and vice versa – further increment of the scope of the problem cannot reduce the speed-up, but rather increase, as the time required for function evaluations will be increased, thus increasing the fully parallel part of the algorithm.

5   Conclusions

The parallel algorithm for multi-objective optimization, based on stochastic search, has been developed and experimentally investigated by solving the competitive facility location problem for firm expansion using up to 16 shared-memory processing units.

The results of the investigation showed that the modifications, made to the sequential algorithm, improve the precision of the optimization, measured by the hyper-volume metrics, as well as make the algorithm more suitable for parallel computing.

The performance results of the parallel algorithm showed that the algorithm has almost linear speed-up using up to 16 processing units, solving competitive facility location problem for firm expansion of different scope, reasonable in practical applications.

Acknowledgments. This work has been supported by the project "Theoretical and engineering aspects of e-service technology development and application in high-performance computing platforms" (No. VP1-3.1-ŠMM-08-K-01-010) funded by the European Social Fund.

References

1. Deb, K., Pratap, A., Agarwal, S., Meyarivan, T.: A fast and elitist multiobjective genetic algorithm: NSGA-II. IEEE Transactions on Evolutionary Computation 6, 182–197 (2002)
2. Drezner, Z., Klamroth, K., Schobel, A., Wesolowsky, G.O.: The Weber problem. In: Drezner, Z., Hamacher, H. (eds.) Facility Location: Applications and Theory, pp. 1–36. Springer, Berlin (2002)
3. Farahani, R.Z., Rezapour, S., Drezner, T., Fallah, S.: Competitive supply chain network design: An overview of classifications, models, solution techniques and applications. Omega 45(0), 92–118 (2014)
4. Fernández, J., Pelegrín, B., Plastria, F., Tóth, B.: Planar location and design of a new facility with inner and outer competition: An interval lexicographical-like solution procedure. Networks and Spatial Economics 7(1), 19–44 (2007)
5. Friesz, T., Miller, T., Tobin, R.: Competitive networks facility location models: a survey. Papers in Regional Science 65, 47–57 (1998)

6. Huapu, L., Jifeng, W.: Study on the location of distribution centers: A bi-level multi-objective approach. In: Logistics, pp. 3038–3043. American Society of Civil Engineers (2009)
7. Lančinskas, A., Ortigosa, P.M., Žilinskas, J.: Multi-objective single agent stochastic search in non-dominated sorting genetic algorithm. Nonlinear Analysis: Modelling and Control 18(3), 293–313 (2013)
8. Lančinskas, A., Žilinskas, J.: Approaches to parallelize pareto ranking in NSGA-II algorithm. In: Wyrzykowski, R., Dongarra, J., Karczewski, K., Waśniewski, J. (eds.) PPAM 2011, Part II. LNCS, vol. 7204, pp. 371–380. Springer, Heidelberg (2012)
9. Lančinskas, A., Žilinskas, J.: Solution of multi-objective competitive facility location problems using parallel NSGA-II on large scale computing systems. In: Manninen, P., Öster, P. (eds.) PARA. LNCS, vol. 7782, pp. 422–433. Springer, Heidelberg (2013)
10. Lančinskas, A., Žilinskas, J.: Parallel multi-objective memetic algorithm for competitive facility location. In: Wyrzykowski, R., Dongarra, J., Karczewski, K., Waśniewski, J. (eds.) PPAM 2013, Part II. LNCS, vol. 8385, pp. 354–363. Springer, Heidelberg (2014)
11. Medaglia, A.L., Villegas, J.G., Rodrguez-Coca, D.M.: Hybrid biobjective evolutionary algorithms for the design of a hospital waste management network. Journal of Heuristics 15(2), 153–176 (2009)
12. Plastria, F.: Static competitive facility location: An overview of optimisation approaches. European Journal of Operational Research 129(3), 461–470 (2001)
13. Redondo, J.L., Fernández, J., Álvarez, J.D., Arrondoa, A.G., Ortigosa, P.M.: Approximating the Pareto-front of continuous bi-objective problems: Application to a competitive facility location problem. In: Casillas, J., Martínez-López, F.J., Corchado, J.M. (eds.) Management of Intelligent Systems. AISC, vol. 171, pp. 207–216. Springer, Heidelberg (2012)
14. ReVelle, C., Eiselt, H., Daskin, M.: A bibliography for some fundamental problem categories in discrete location science. European Journal of Operational Research 184(3), 817–848 (2008)
15. Villegas, J., Palacios, F., Medaglia, A.: Solution methods for the bi-objective (cost-coverage) unconstrained facility location problem with an illustrative example. Annals of Operations Research 147, 109–141 (2006)
16. Weber, A.: Theory of the Location of Industries. University of Chicago Press (1929)
17. Zitzler, E., Laumanns, M., Thiele, L.: SPEA2: Improving the strength Pareto evolutionary algorithm for multiobjective optimization. In: Giannakoglou, K.C., Tsahalis, D.T., Périaux, J., Papailiou, K.D., Fogarty, T. (eds.) Evolutionary Methods for Design Optimization and Control with Applications to Industrial Problems, pp. 95–100 (2001)
18. Zitzler, E., Thiele, L.: Multiobjective optimization using evolutionary algorithms – a comparative case study. In: Eiben, A.E., Bäck, T., Schoenauer, M., Schwefel, H.-P. (eds.) PPSN 1998. LNCS, vol. 1498, pp. 292–301. Springer, Heidelberg (1998)

Web Services Based Platform for the Cell Counting Problem

Juan Carlos Castillo[1], Francisco Almeida[1],
Vicente Blanco[1], and M. Carmen Ramírez[2]

[1] Departamento de Ingeniería Informática y de Sistemas, Universidad de la Laguna,
España
[2] Labotario de Biología Celular y Molecular de C.M., Universidad de Castilla la
Mancha, España
{jcastill,falmeida,vblanco}@ull.es, Carmen.Ramirez@uclm.es

Abstract. Cell image processing and analysis is a crucial task in any
health science laboratory. Cell counting is a common task usually made
by technicians with the support of a custom software tuned with experiment requirements. In this work we present a web services based platform
focused on the cell counting problem. Using OpenCF, a web services development framework, we integrate in a single platform services oriented
to image processing and classifying, cell counting based on a set of parameters, and data post-processing (plot generation, datasheets, etc.). A
GUI added to the platform helps to launch jobs with image sets, and the
execution of different tasks from a web service based client.

1   Introduction

Image pattern search and matching is a common problem in different research
fields. This problem has been widely studied but it is still under research. In
health sciences, pattern matching and cell or other microorganism in a sample
is one of the most common tasks we can find daily in laboratories. This work is
mainly developed by qualified technicians using different tools like microscopes
or other analysis equipment. This process uses to be costly in terms of time and
resources, and is one of the difficulties to obtain medical research results.

The method to identify and compute a number of cells in health science uses
to follow a similar pattern in most of the situations. Only the different tools used
in each experiment vary. In general, the method follows a set of steps. First, a
target sample is obtained. Then, a set of procedures are applied in order to stand
out the factors under study. And finally, the sample is processed under a visual
media by a technician or a custom instrument. This last step is critical since
the availability of resources implies that results can't be obtained immediately.
Actually, sample processing are delegated to laboratory equipment while the
technicians use to obtain the sample and supervise the process. The sample
analysis process usually generates digital images with data. Image analysis uses
to be hard (and sometimes impossible) to do only by research staff without using
computing facilities. Some kind of software will be needed to obtain the relevant
information. This software uses to be very specialized and expensive.

L. Lopes et al. (Eds.): Euro-Par 2014 Workshops, Part I, LNCS 8805, pp. 83–92, 2014.

In this work, we propose to implement the image processing which is done in laboratories in a remote platform using web services. The use of web services can accelerate the analysis procedure and reduce time in the obtaining of results, as has been exposed in [1]. The novelty of web services based approach in this field is the high capacity to process images in computing facilities outside the laboratories. These can lead to minimize delay in processing queues of results (with parallel HPC systems). Resources can be decentralized, dedicated laboratory equipment can be minimized, and the costs in space and maintenance can be lowered. Other advantage in this approach is the increase of different types of processing that can be done. There is a widespread types of specialized servers in image processing that could be accessible through web services.

The proposed solution to process data remotely is based in the integration of LLCECO [2], a cell image processing software, in a web services platform. LLCECO is a cell counting and classifying software developed by the High Performance Computing Group at La Laguna University in collaboration with the Biology Cellular and Molecular Laboratory at Castilla La Mancha University. The web services platform where this software was integrated is OpenCF [3]. LLCECO has been developed from scratch for this project. The LLCECO base design has been conceived as a tool to be used in the context of remote computing services.

The paper is structured as follows. Section 2 describes the state of the art in the technologies used. The software for auto-guided cell counting is described in Section 3. Section 4 presents OpenCF, the web services framework used in this project, and Section 5 describes the integration of LLCECO in the OpenCF web services framework. As an example, an use case of this platform is presented in Section 6. Finally, Section 7 shows conclusions and expressions of interests in the field of cell counting problem as well as some future work remarks.

2 Related Work

It has been growing interest in the use of web services based platforms [4]. Big software companies like Rackspace, Microsoft, Google or Amazon are promoting these kind of platforms as a technology solution for its products. Research labs and science groups are also interested [5]. Image processing is one of the most required web services by users. It can be found in facial recognition in social networks or in more complex algorithms on astronomical images [6]. Any web services platform of the companies cited above use a large amount of services related with this field [7].

In the field of medicine and biology fields we can found web services based tools like Inbiomed [8], a platform for processing image biomedical information with methods, data, and image analysis integrated in a single tool using web services, or caGrid [9]. Both are general purpose platforms, with a large set of web services supporting enterprises procedures involved in this projects. One drawback of these approaches is that the tools are designed to adapt to the specific research labs where they are used. Their integration in other research environments seems to be complex.

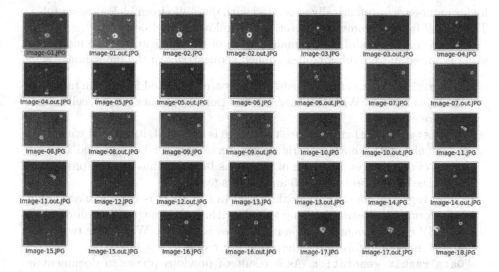

Fig. 1. Folder with original and resulting images

Other important aspect in biomedical image processing is the software used in labs and research centers where privative software attached to specific instruments (citrometers, microscopes, etc) can be usually found. There are other lightweight and portable alternatives like CellC Cell Counter [10], Pixcavator [11] or GSA Image Analyser [12], usually cheaper and of general purpose. This applications implements the base image processing and counting algorithms, but restricted to one image with a fixed set of parameters given by the user. The main drawback against web service platforms is the limit imposed by the computing resources at laboratories. If there is an increase in the number of images processed by this systems, the cost of analytics process also increase in terms of time and qualified staff resources.

3   LLCECO

LLCECO (La Laguna Cell Counter) is a desktop software tool developed to identify and count different type of cells. This software is the result of a joint effort from the High Performance Computing Group at La Laguna University and the Biology Cellular and Molecular Lab at Castilla La Mancha University. LLCECO was developed in Python and C languages. It allows to process a set of input images, classify them, get optimal processing parameters automatically, identify and count patterns of cells, and generate customized documents with the resulting data. The LLCECO architecture is designed in three independent modules: preprocessing, processing and post-processing modules (see Figure 2).

The preprocessing module has the responsibility to perform tasks like getting the images to be processed, get configuration parameters for processing and post-processing modules, or manage a folder tree to save and compress images. The folder names are automatically generated with date info from biological samples. The rest of input parameters are set to the following modules.

The processing module is the main engine of the application. The module is also organized in four sub-modules applied sequentially to the input image set:

- Image classification. A mean of pixels are computed for certain ranges in the RGB schema. With this task, information about background, cell colors, etc. are obtained.
- Parameter calculation. Once the image is classified, its aligned with a set of samples with known generic parameters. This set is composed by four types of cell images, and each of them has been obtained by the processing and classifying of sets from 25 and 50 images.
- Counting. The counting algorithm used in LLCECO is the Circular Hough transform [13]. Before applying the algorithm, the image is transformed to an HSV color scheme and a Gaussian filter is applied. With these two operations, noise and false circle detection are reduced.
- Data result generation. As a result of previous phases, a document is generated with all image data (number of cells, statistics data, etc) and original images with a mark overlay for each identified cell.

The post-processing module is the most versatile and configurable one. It manages a set of templates to generate resulting data files. It is composed by three steps: plot generation, template application and resulting data files compression. Plots are generated with the data obtained during the processing phase, aligning samples with the number of cells per image and per sets of images. To obtain the resulting data files, a set of spreadsheets templates are used, applying statistical operations, formulas, etc. The operation specified in spreadsheet templates depends on the input parameters of the preprocessing phase. Finally, a compressed file is generated with all this information.

LLCECO is a light, portable application with new features in development. It is really easy to add new templates to this software. This provides a high degree of freedom useful to adapt LLCECO to any other laboratory. We have considered the possibility to process the image set in high performance parallel computers to accelerate the results generation.

It's worth to mention that the software has a modular design, which allows to interact with each module independently. Other modules or services with new functionalities can be added, and then can also be offered as services. This features facilitate platform extensibility to other input/output devices or to other image processing algorithms.

4   OpenCF Web Services Platform

OpenCF is a web services based framework for computing that has been developed at La Laguna University. It design provides a portable framework, easy to install, with a fast setup, and smooth use. OpenCF has a modular software architecture composed by a server module and a client module (see Figure 3).

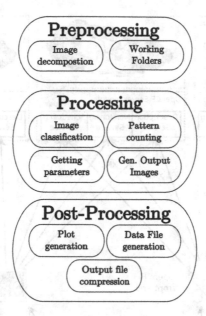

Fig. 2. LLCECO modules

Both modules can be extended independently or even substituted by other components to provide new functionalyties without modifying the remaining system components. OpenCF is oriented to HPC systems and its queue systems. The access, execution and load scheduling on HPC systems are supported by this framework.

The client module (front–end) and the server module (back–end) implement the three lower layers of the web services stack: Service Description, XML messaging, and Transport. The fourth level, Service Discovering, has not been implemented for the sake of security. The user access to web portal is implemented on the client side. Communication between client and server modules is verified by traditional authentications techniques.

The server module manages jobs executions on HPC system, offering them as web services and taking care of excution status. Each HTTP request received by server module from OpenCF client is assigned to an independent execution thread with an independent instance of the server module.

The client module provides an user interface and traslates user request to server requests. The server module receives this requests from authenticated clients and translate them to jobs for the batch system. These modules are also decomposed in smaller parts: Control Access modules, Request Manager, and Collector are in both server and client sides. The client module acts as a front–end and manages a database with information generated by the system. The server, as a back–end, includes modules for batch script generation and job submission to batch system.

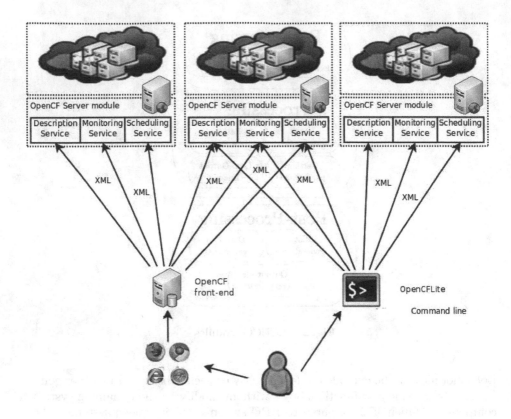

Fig. 3. OpenCF software architecture

The OpenCF server allows the easy add of services from available applications or libraries. Only requires a XML file describing tasks (name, description and arguments) for each application/routine we wish to add as a web service. The new services are offered to OpenCF clients configured at the server automatically. The client receives the service information showing users the service name, arguments, short description, and the OpenCF server offering the service.

OpenCF also implements monitoring and scheduling services [14]. The client shows common services to different servers grouped as a single service. Using an scheduling policy (for example, sorting servers by a metric like "normalized computational power"), the system will send a request to the best candidate server.

5   LLCECO Integration in OpenCF

The framework we have developed integrates the OpenCF web service platform with the LLCECO application. The synergy generated by this effort provides a set of advantages. With LLCECO offered as a web service in OpenCF, we can

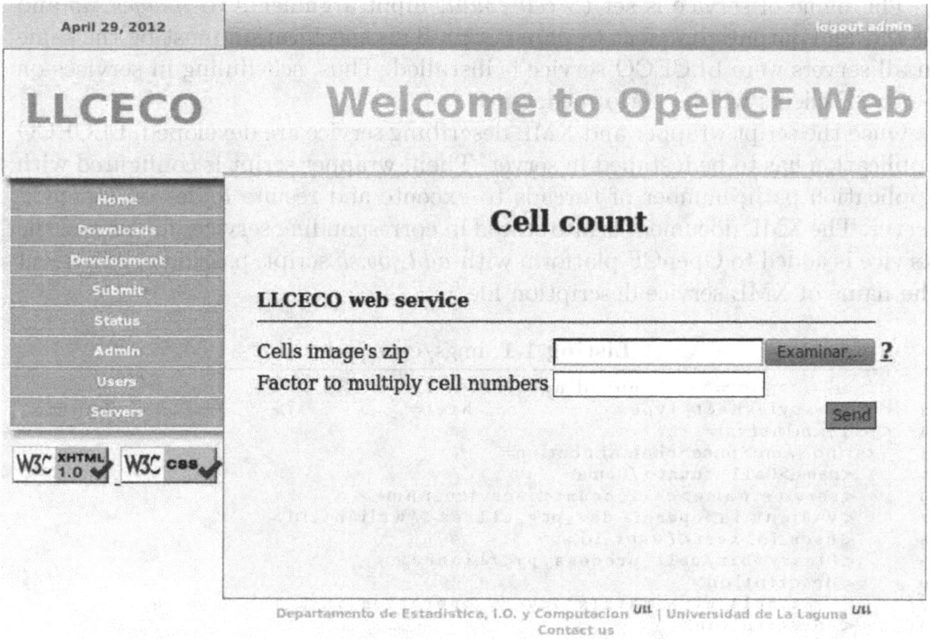

Fig. 4. LLCECO Web service in OpenCF

process images remotely and efficiently with a simple interface. We have used the OpenCF platform over other similar tools (like OpenNebula or Eucalyptus [15]) because of its easy integration of external modules (LLCECO) and it's support for parallel systems. The integration has been developed in two steps: first, an application wrapper for LLCECO is developed and then we describe it as a service in OpenCF.

Communication between OpenCF and LLCECO is carried out through a wrapper layer. The wrapper translates server requests to application commands for both input arguments passing and data results collecting. This layer is implemented as a Python script that reads arguments from command line and talks with LLCECO application. OpenCF platform gathers input parameters through its web interface front-end (Fig. 4). A request to LLCECO service is sent to OpenCF server. After processing the service, a call to the LLCECO wrapper is made, passing input parameters as arguments. Once LLCECO application has ended, the wrapper gathers results and compress all the information in a file. The file is assigned to the results in web service with the ID task, allowing the user to download it through OpenCF client interface. The service also sends an email to final user once the taks is completed.

We have described LLCECO service in OpenCF as usual with an XML file. We have set service name, a short description, and the set of input and output parameters (name, type of argument and description, etc. See Listing 1.1).

The name of service is set to *cell_count*, input arguments to *images_zip* and *factor*, and output argument to *output_zip*). This specification must be the same in all servers were LLCECO service is installed. Thus, scheduling in services on OpenCF clients will be performed.

Once the script wrapper and XML describing service are developed, LLCECO application has to be installed in server. Then, wrapper script is configured with application path, number of threads to execute and results folder on OpenCF server. The XML document is also stored in corresponding services folder and the service is added to OpenCF platform with *add_job.sh* script, passing as argument the name of XML service description file.

Listing 1.1. imgs/code.xml

```
1   <?xml version="1.0" encoding="UTF-8"?>
2   <?xml-stylesheet type="text/xsl" href="job.xsl"?>
3   <job xmlns:xsi="http://www.w3.org/2001/XMLSchema-instance"
4      xsi:noNameSpaceSchemaLocation="job.xsd">
5      <name>Cell count</name>
6      <service_name>cell_count</service_name>
7      <wclient_id>opencf-dev_pcg_ull_es</wclient_id>
8      <user_id>test</user_id>
9      <binary>bin/cell_process.py</binary>
10     <description>
11        Example of a matrix invert operation in R
12     </description>
13     <argument type="base64Binary">
14        <name>images_zip</name>
15        <sdesc>Zip file with cells image</sdesc>
16        <ldesc>
17           Zip containing a directory with images of cells
18        </ldesc>
19        <fname_in_server>images.zip</fname_in_server>
20     </argument>
21     <argument type="integer">
22        <name>factor</name>
23        <sdesc>Factor to multiply cell numbers</sdesc>
24     </argument>
25     <output_file>
26        <name>output_zip</name>
27        <description>
28           All the input and results files of the execution
29           of the service.
30        </description>
31     </output_file>
32   </job>
```

6   Use Case

To show the usefulness of this platform, we have processed a set of samples from Cellular and Molecular Biology Lab at CRIB, Castilla La Mancha University. The data are stored in two folders with images from two cell cultures with 25 and 40 images respectively. Only one request is registered on the platform where both folders are included in a compressed file (approximately 6Mb, with an upload time around a couple of seconds in a local research network and less than a minute from a home adsl line). The system returns a compressed file with a folder including processed images and a datasheet with resulting data and plots.

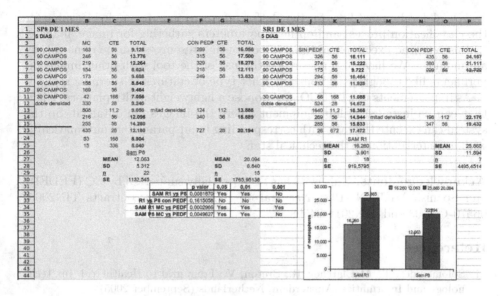

Fig. 5. Results spreadsheet with data, statistical analysis, and plots

The whole image processing and computed data takes only a few seconds. The bottleneck in the applications is located in sending and receiving data (with bigger archive sizes, files can be split to optimize the process).

If the number of requests to the platform increases, we can use an HPC cluster to keep the execution times in this range. The service could scale to a high number of requests easily. Figure 1 shows the output corresponding to one of the image folders. Figure 5 shows the spreadsheet resulting for an experiment with an ANOVA statistical analysis.

7   Conclusions and Future Work

In this work we present a general web services based computing platform for the cell counting problem on biomedical images. This tool is composed by the integration of a web services framework (OpenCF) with an application to process and count cells (LLCECO). The platform offers a web interface where the user can process the cell counting on a set of images. The user must provide a compressed file with target images stored in folders. A set of input parameters will also be provided to specify process configuration. As a result, a set of files with data analysis and output images is provided. Our goal with this platform is to improve the working pace in labs and research centers than needs the analysis and counting of cells in their experiments, reducing costs and time to obtain results.

This platform differs from others in flexibility, portability, general services and computing power. By using web services we can access to a cloud of servers to process images without intervention by the user and the computing power is higher than those systems we can find in laboratories.

Actual development lines for the platform focuses on auto–guided learning for the classification process and optimal parameters gathering for image analysis. In this way, the execution of tasks in computing resources can be done totally autonomous. We have also researched the use of the tool with other image experiments like topographical images, other type of cultures or spermiograms.

As improvements to LLCECO, we propose a lightweight multi–platform client that can be installed in lab equipment where the images are obtained. So the system can execute the task with corresponding input parameters automatically, without intervention of the technical staff.

Acknowledgements. This work has been partially supported by EC (FEDER) and Spanish MICINN (Plan Nacional de I+D+I) under contracts TIN2008-06570-C04-03 and TIN2011-24598.

References

1. Solomonides, T., McClatchey, R., Breton, V.: From grid to HealthGrid. In: Technology and Informatics, Amsterdam, Netherlands (September 2005)
2. Castillo, J.: Llceco: La laguna cell counter (2012), http://opencf.pcg.ull.es/redmine/projects/opencfcc
3. Santos, A., Almeida, F., Blanco, V.: Lightweight web services for high performace computing. In: Oquendo, F. (ed.) ECSA 2007. LNCS, vol. 4758, pp. 225–236. Springer, Heidelberg (2007)
4. Darrow, B.: Amazon is no.1 who's next in cloud computing (2012)
5. Evangelinos, C.H.C.: Cloud computing for parallel scientific hpc applications: Feasibility of running coupled atmosphere-ocean climate models on amazons ec2. In: First Workshop on Cloud Computing and its Applications, Chicago, USA (2008)
6. Almeida, F., Blanco, V., Delgado, C., de Sande, F., Santos, A.: Idewep: Web service for astronomical parallel image deconvolution. J. Netw. Comput. Appl. 32(1), 293–313 (2009)
7. Fronckowiak, J.: Processing images with amazon web services (2008)
8. Perez, D., Crespo, J., Biomedical, A.A.: image processing integration through inbiomed: A web services-based platform. Biological and Medical Data Analysis, 34–43 (2005)
9. Zhang, J., Madduri, R., Tan, W., Deichl, K., Alexander, J., Foster, I.: Toward semantics empowered biomedical web services. In: 2011 IEEE International Conference on Web Services (ICWS), pp. 371–378 (July 2011)
10. Selinummi, J., Jenni Seppälä, O.Y.H., Puhakka, J.A.: Software for quantification of labeled bacteria from digital microscope images by automated image analysis. BioTechniques 39(6), 859–863 (2005)
11. Saveliev, P.: Pixcavator (2011), http://inperc.com/wiki/index.php?title=Cellcounting
12. GSA: Gsa image analyser (2012), http://image.analyser.gsa-online.de/
13. OpenCV: Hough circle transform (2012), http://opencv.itseez.com/doc/tutorials/imgproc/imgtrans/hough_circle/hough_circle.html.
14. Santos, A., Almeida, F., Blanco, V., Castillo, J.C.: Web services based scheduling in opencf. Journal of SuperComputing, 88–114 (2010)
15. Sempolinski, P., Thain, D.: A comparison and critique of eucalyptus, opennebula and nimbus. Critique, 417–426 (November 2010)

Automata-Based Dynamic Data Processing for Clouds

Reginald Cushing[1], Adam Belloum[1], Marian Bubak[1,2], and Cees de Laat[1]

[1] Informatics Institute, Universiteit van Amsterdam, Amsterdam, The Netherlands
[2] Department of Computer Science, AGH University of Science and Technology,
Krakow, Poland
{R.S.Cushing,A.S.Z.Belloum,C.T.A.M.deLaat}@uva.nl,
Bubak@agh.edu.pl

Abstract. Big Data is a challenge in many dimensions one of which is its processing. The often complicated and lengthy processing requires specialized programming paradigms to distribute and scale the computing power. Such paradigms often focus on ordering tasks to fit an underlying architecture. In this paper, we propose a new and complementary way of reasoning about data processing by describing complex data processing as set of state transitions, specifically, a non-deterministic finite automata which captures the essence of complex data processing. Through a P2P implementation of this model we demonstrate the dynamism, intrinsic scalability and adeptness to Cloud architectures.

Keywords: Automata-based modeling, Dynamic Cloud Computing, Data Defined Networking, Big Data, Distributed Data Processing, AaaS.

1 Introduction

The growing emphasis on data processing capabilities due to the increasing volumes of data leads us to rethink the relationship between process and data [1]. Too often, the processing model and the data model are left as two disjoint areas; for example, workflow and MapReduce systems focus mainly on ordering tasks and do not intrinsically describe data transformations. Data often flows through these systems in a *pinball* fashion where it percolates through processes until it reaches the end process. Data provenance is the main approach to collecting data state as a means of its flow through the system but this is a *post-mortem* approach whereby we build a data flow graph after execution. Processes are often ordered to exploit the underlying infrastructure thus the same data processing workflow might look different for using grids, clouds or services. It is just to say that every data-centric workflow has an implicit data transition map which can be used to aid data processing, querying and data provenance. For example, coupling data with a state map in a workflow will provide a wider context for the data object as at any point in time you can deduce the current state of the data from the previous states and the possible future states i.e. what to expect from such data.

L. Lopes et al. (Eds.): Euro-Par 2014 Workshops, Part I, LNCS 8805, pp. 93–104, 2014.
© Springer International Publishing Switzerland 2014

The proliferation of cloud-based processing means that data processing is increasingly becoming service oriented, specifically each single task is an Application-as-a-Service (AaaS). The potential scale of inter-cloud systems coupled with the dynamism of the infrastructure makes it increasingly difficult to coordinate a cohort of applications in a traditional central scientific workflow systems.

Asking "what do we want out of this data?" combined with the increased variety and velocity of data production means we need to be able treat data objects as distinct entities where each data object can take different processing paths inside a workflow just by changing states. For example, a typical parametric study workflow would setup a several process stages. The state of the data is usually the progress within the workflow itself which is not always indicative of the actual data state. Extracting features from data, the extracted features represent the new state and not so much the process that extracted them. A string that has been decided to be English by some function is said to be in an *English* state rather then in the state *outputOfFucntion*. This new level of information allows us to reason about data in terms of its state rather than just the processes.

In this paper we propose a data processing paradigm using Non-deterministic Finite Automata (NFA) where data transits from state to state as being processed. This enables us to construct data processing networks which capture the essence of data processing without knowledge of the underlying infrastructure. We prove this paradigm with an implementation, Pumpkin, which implements a data processing virtual network for cloud systems. The rest of the paper is structured as follows: Sec. 2 covers background material related to our contribution, Sec. 3 introduces the automata-based data process model and proof architecture description, Sec. 4 evaluates the applicability of the model to various use-case scenarios and finally, Sec. 5 discusses future work and concludes.

2   Related Work

In eScience, coordinating multiple tasks for running *in-silico* experiments is often the realm of Scientific Workflow Management Systems (SWMS). SWMS come in many forms and shapes and can vary in the computational model, types of processes used, and types of resources used. Many base their model on process flow [2] and also include a form of control flow [3], others implement data flow models [4] and some propose eccentric models such as based on chemical reactions [5]. A common denominator in most workflow systems is that the unit of reason is the process i.e. the abstract workflow describes a topology of tasks configured in a certain way. MapReduce [6] can be considered as a restricted workflow with two abstract tasks, *map()* and *reduce()*, aimed at exploiting data parallelism on locally distributed infrastructures such as data warehouses. In our approach we add a data layer on top of common workflow topologies. This approach allows us to model data processing as a sequence of state transitions and reason about data itself by reducing complex data processing to a set of atomic data transformations which can, inherently, be distributed.

Recently an initiative to provide a mechanism for content aggregation, called Research Object[1] has been proposed and is aiming at providing a way to annotate objects composing and a systems, making their type and relationships explicit.

Automata and state machines have been used in computing since its conception and have wide applications in most areas of computing. Of interest to us is its applicability to event stream processing [7] whereby automata is used to model queries in a distributed environment that queries streams of events such as stock events. The model used is an extension of the traditional NFA where instead of a finite input alphabet they read relational streams whereby state transitions are controlled by predicates. In our case predicates are dynamically generated by functions that process the data.

This work is inspired by the actor model proposed for concurrent computing, the actor model keep intern the mutable state and communicate using asynchronous messages [8]. Actors perform a certain task in response to a message, actors are autonomous and are able to create new actors creating a hierarchy of actors. In our approach, we build on top of the actor model whereby actors consume and produce state tags and do not send messages directly to each other but through a state tag routing system.

Coordination languages and more precisely the data flow-oriented category of coordination languages which focus on managing the communication among distributed collaborative applications as described in [9] and [10], are based on a similar approach where the coordination is not centralized in a specific component, but rather model as part of the network as in REO, an exogenous coordination model for constructing application using a calculus of channels and connectors [9]. Our approach is considerably simpler since it does not impose any constraints on the communication channels, the communication is always assumed to be asynchronous and the channels are not typed. We do not model communication *per se* but communication is a byproduct of a data state transition.

3   Automata-Based Data Transformation Paradigm

We employ the formal definitions of NFA for describing data processing as an automaton. A NFA is defined as a 5 tuple $(Q, \Sigma, \delta, q_0, F)$ where Q is a finite set of state, Σ is the input alphabet, δ is the transition function, $q_0 \in Q$ is a start state, $F \subseteq Q$ is the set of final states. We extend the standard model so that we do not have a finite alphabet but a set of selection functions of the sort $\sigma(d, q)$ where q is the input state, $d \in D$ is the input data object to be processed. A selection function performs data processing, selects the next data state and returns a tuple (D', T), D' is a set of data objects produced by the processing of d and $T \subset Q$ is the set of new state tags generated non-deterministically by the selection function. A state tag is identical to a state but we distinguish between a state identifier as a tag and the actual state as state. The state tag generated by the selection function controls the transition function. The transition and selection function can be considered as nested functions as in Fig. 1.

---

[1] http://www.researchobject.org/ontologies/

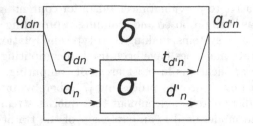

Fig. 1. Nested transition, δ, and selection, $\sigma \in \Sigma$, functions over $d_n \in D$. The transition is controlled by the output of the selection function.

In our model every data object has an associated NFA which describes the possible final state the data object it can transit to. The current state shows the progress of the data object. The transition function, $\delta(q, \sigma(d, q))$ defines the set of states that are reachable from state q with selection function σ. Given a data object at state q, only a subset of selection functions in Σ can act on the data and produce state transitions. We define this set of functions as $H_q \subseteq \Sigma$. The transition function can then be extended to multiple functions such that $\delta(q, H_q)$ defines all the states that are reachable from state q and functions H_q.

Figures 2 and 3 illustrate simple data automata. Figure 2 shows an automata which, when attached to a string data object, will filter the string as being English and having and *isa* and/or *hasa* relation. The initial state of the string is RAW since nothing is yet known about the string. $f(d)$ is the only function in H_{RAW} thus the transition $\delta(RAW, f(d, RAW))$ is taken. The functionality of $f(d, RAW)$ will determine the next state. The selection function $f(d, RAW)$ returns processed data and a state tag $ENG|NENG$ meaning the string is either English or not. If the string results in state ENG it can take further transitions. At state ENG, $(h(d), g(d)) \in H_{ENG}$ this means that both transitions $\delta(q_{ENG}, g(d, ENG))$ and $\delta(q_{ENG}, h(d, ENG))$ are taken simultaneously. This allows for string d to be concurrently filtered on multiple criteria.

Another NFA pattern is shown in Fig. 3. Here a data object is iteratively looped until a condition is met. The data object alternates between $READY$ and $UNSAT$ until a satisfiable condition such as a converged state is met at which point the data object transits to a SAT state.

3.1 Transformation Rules

Transformation rules are the set of production rules that define each transition function. These rules define mappings between state tags in the form:

- $(q_1, q_2, ...) \xrightarrow{A} (j_1, j_2, ...)$
- $(j_1, j_2, ...) \xrightarrow{B} (k_1, k_2, ...)$

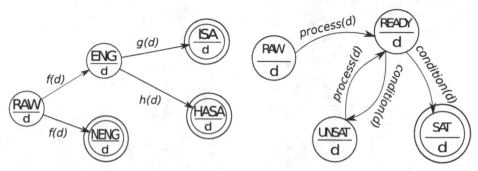

Fig. 2. A simple automaton showing the filtering of English language strings with an *isa* and *hasa* relation

Fig. 3. An iterative pattern which processes data d until a final state *SAT* is reached

Where q_n, j_n and k_n are members of Q and A, B are functions and members of σ. The global state tag graph is constructed from following state production rules. This allows for the state tag graph to grow dynamically by adding new rules to the database whereby the inference engine will automatically extend the mappings. As with other production rule based systems, querying the inference engine can reveal important information about possible processing of the data by forward chaining the rules. Thus, in a collaborative environment, one can discover new possibilities for data processing. On the other hand, using backward chaining, one can query the provenance of the data by showing what transitions a particular data object took to be in the current state. Another possibility is learning of possible gaps in a network where new functions are needed to fill the gaps.

3.2 Transition Operations

In our model selection functions are not simple one-to-one state tag transition. State tags can be combined using binary logic. This means that a selection function, $\sigma(d, q)$, can map an arbitrary number of state tags under these binary operations to other state tag statements. Figure 4 depicts some simple examples of these transition operations. The default transition operation is *or* thus if not explicitly states a function with multiple output state tags will either output one state tag or the other. Multiple input state tag means that a certain function accepts any data object in any of the defined states. The *and* operator acts as logic split and merge. A function simultaneously output multiple data objects with different state tags. Also, a function can accept **only** a number of data objects in a particular state thus multiple different transitions as needed to transform a data object into a new data object with different state. The latter is an example of correlating 2 datasets and producing a new, processed dataset.

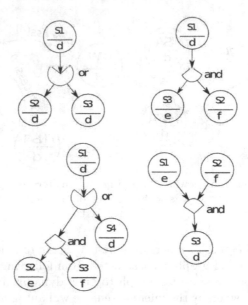

Fig. 4. Transition operations: Data in a state can transit to different simultaneous states. Two or more data objects can merge into a single state.

3.3   Architecture of Pumpkin Framework

The described model above is implemented as the Pumpkin framework[2]. The architecture implements a P2P distributed system for routing and processing data based on state tags. This overlay network between nodes is what we dub a Data Defined Network (DDF) as routes are setup based on the need for data transitions. The distributed characteristic of the system removes control centrality and the P2P characteristic allows for data being processed to pass directly between nodes thus minimizing third party data stores for intermediate data. The architecture is designed with the emerging cloud computing paradigm and virtual infrastructures in mind therefore one of the goals of Pumpkin is the coordination of bags of VMs to produce collective work.

The architecture of a single Pumpkin node in the network is illustrated in Fig. 5. The architecture builds around the concept of dynamically loading functions as is done in many web service containers. In addition to dynamically loading functions, a Pumpkin node implements a stack of control functionality to achieve the P2P capabilities. Most notable is the data routing based on state tags. Each Pumpkin node exposes a set of interfaces for accessibility. The interfaces can be categorized into control, data, and messages. Control and monitoring are user for user interaction and these include HTTP and FTP. Each node implements a TFTP server and client for file transfers between nodes. Messages in the form of data packets are the main mechanisms for communication between nodes.

---

[2] https://github.com/recap/pumpkin

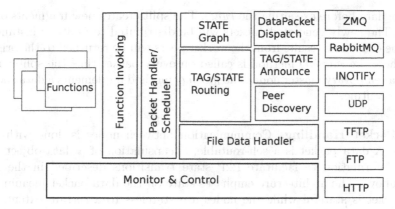

Fig. 5. Anatomy of a Pumpkin node. Connectivity is provided by a set of handlers (right), the core components (center) provide data packet handling and routing while the functions are the selection functions described in Sec. 3.

Node discovery is done in two main ways. Nodes on the same local network will discover each other through UDP broadcasts. Pumpkin nodes on public facing interfaces can act as supernodes by disseminating peer information amongst nodes. Through broadcasts each peer learns other peers' publish endpoints where information regarding state tags and functions is announced. This information is used by every node to build a view of the global state machine and a state tag routing table. The routing table is the crux of the Pumpkin network as it allows data state transitions over networks or shared memory for local functions. Pumpkin uses ZeroMQ[3] as its main messaging library. RabbitMQ[4] messaging is used as a proxy when Cloud instances are unable to open P2P connections.

Functions. Functions implement the selection function in the NFA model described above. These are loaded dynamically at startup of every node or deployed during runtime. A function is essentially an implementation of an interface class that overrides a *run()*, and optionally *split()*, *merge()*, *on_load()*, *on_unload()* methods. Each function can accept multiple state tags and also produce multiple state tags. The numbers of possible transitions of a function is defined by the cross product between the input state tags and output tags.

A function is invoked as follows: upon reception of a data packet, Pumpkin extracts the relevant information from the packet and locate the appropriate class. After a staging sequence where data files might be downloaded from the previous node, the *run()* method is called. This step is bypassed if the received packet is part of a merge function in which case the *merge()* method is called on the packet. Each class can optionally define a *split()* and *merge()* methods. This scenario is useful when processing data packets in parallel would improve execution time. As an example, if a data packet containing a CSV file where each record is an input to a Monte-Carlo simulation then it would be advantageous to

---

[3] http://zeromq.org/
[4] http://www.rabbitmq.com/

split the data before executing the *run()*. The split creates new fragments of the packet. The newly generated packets will be distributed to multiple instance of the same class. The results from the worker peers will be returned to the original peer where the *merge()* method is called on every packet thus the spliter node acts as a temporary master node. The *merge()* method implements a data specific merging routine.

Data Packet Handling. Communication between nodes is done with data packets. A data packet is a self-routable, encapsulation of a data object with header information to facilitate P2P state transitions described in the NFA model above. The architecture emphases state on the data packet meaning the data packet is stateful while the nodes are stateless to a certain extent. The data packet is modeled as a container into which arbitrary data can be placed, extracted, modified, and replaced. The container header describes the identification and processing status of the container. Identification is based on four fields; ship, container, box, and fragment. The analogy here is with cargo ships where a ship is a collection of containers and a container is a collection of boxes, i.e. a ship is the set of data D and a container is $d \in D$. A fragment ID is assigned when a box is split during processing into smaller chunks as would be the case to distribute data processing. The ship ID represents the execution context of the data; e.x. all data pertaining to an experiment would carry the same ship ID. Container and box ID are used to identify parts and sub-parts of the data. Together these fields represent the unique ID of data packet as it is being routed between nodes.

A mechanism for reliability can be enabled, albeit with a performance penalty. With reliability enabled nodes share responsibility of a data packet. The mechanism works as follows: Upon sending a data packet a node A retains the packet in a buffer until the peer node B sends back a Processed ACKnowledgment (PACK) back to A. A PACK is only sent after node B finished processing the packet and has dispatched it forward at which stage B becomes responsible for the packet. Upon reception of a PACK at A, the latter is relieved of its responsibility. If a PACK is not received in a timely fashion, node A will activate the TTL field in the data packet and resend the packet upon time expiration. Each node is equipped to detect duplicates, thus if B where to receive the duplicate packet it will reject it immediately. The TTL field can be tuned for different packets so that process hungry packets can have higher TTLs. As can be imagined this mechanism will put extra pressure on the system especially on packet buffers which are awaiting acknowledgments and thus the whole mechanism can be disabled in scenarios where it is not needed e.z. a streaming application.

4   Evaluation

As a proofing application we implemented a Tweeter filter engine based on the proposed model, and furthermore we evaluated the applicability to two real world scientific workflows.

Tweeter Filter Engine. A Tweeter workflow is used as a proofing application for the distributed architecture. As Pumpkin is intended for virtual infrastructures and cloud computing it follows that testing is done on such an infrastructure. Our testbed is a private cloud infrastructure using OpenNebula on a 48-core AMD machine. Each VM is set to 0.1 CPU and 256 MB memory thus creating a relatively resource-lite VM. All VMs are configured to share a network bridge therefore all VMs appear to be on a LAN. Each VM is setup with a Pumpkin installation and deployed with different functions so as to create the test scenarios.

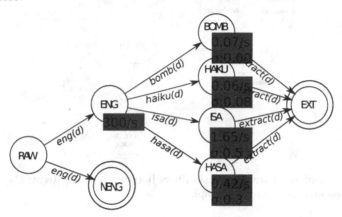

Fig. 6. A NFA describing data transitions. This NFA is mapped to 11 nodes where the functions *eng()*, *isa()* and *haiku()* where replicated on different VMs. The transition rates show the average rate tweets made a new transition; in this figure σ means standard deviation.

The Tweeter test scenario is setting up a state machine as a filter network for Tweeter feeds[5]. In this scenario every Tweet is packaged as a data packet and given the initial state of *RAW*. These packets are injected into the network and traverse the appropriate nodes to end in a final state. Each state transition acts as a filter thus tagging the data along the way with a state tag. The first filter *eng()* will tag the tweets with state *ENG* or state *NENG*. The *ENG* tagged data packets will move forward into the network while the other packets are dumped since a final state was reached. The last final state in Fig. 6 is an extraction state where we can monitor what packets are being generated. The results in Fig. 6 illustrates the rate at which data packets are transitioned into the 4 given filters i.e. accepted by the filter. Notable is that these state transitions are done in parallel due to the intrinsic parallelism defined in the state automaton in Fig. 6. Another level of parallelism is achieved from the replica functions hosted on different nodes. For this experiment there where *2 × eng()*, *2 × isa()*, *1 × hasa()*, *1 × bomb()*, *3 × haiku()* functions hosted. The dynamism implemented in Pumpkin means that state transitions (in this case filters) can be added dynamically. Such an example is the function to state *BOMB* where

---

[5] http://snap.stanford.edu/data/twitter7.html

its VM startup was purposely retarded to demonstrate the dynamic addition of functions and the new flow of data. Along with these illustrated functions two instances of the *ENG* transition function where running in parallel to each other and also in parallel to the other functions.

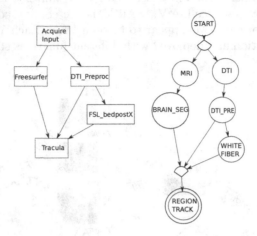

Fig. 7. Left: workflow for tracking brain fibers between regions. Right: Data transformations represented as a state tag graph.

Tracking Brain Regions. Figure 7 shows a medical workflow for analyzing brain regions[6] using MRI and DTI. The characteristics of this workflow are that is it is a long running workflow (approximately 48 hours on commodity hardware) and it needs to run on multiple patients. In this case having a data processing structure represented as a data transition graph aids tracking patient processing data by knowing, at any time, in which state the data is. The main functions in the workflow (Left in Figure 7) are distributed on different virtual machines. The patient scans are then transformed using the data transformation graph (Right in Figure 7). Every patient's data will have an associated data transition graph while indicating the state and progress of the processing. These graphs are all processed on the same workflow. The architecture implicitly allows for scaling up by adding more virtual machines hosting certain functions of the workflow. This replication of tasks allows multiple patient data graphs to be processed simultaneously.

Blood Flow Simulation. The blood flow simulation [11] and sensitivity analyses workflow is a computational intensive workflow with intricate data transition stages. The data transition graph aids in capturing the data flow as data enters different states. The characteristics of the workflow are that multiple models (in *Sepran* stage) can exist. The data transition graph can then easily capture data from different models since the output data would be in different states. The parallelism in this scenario is achieved two-fold; from distributing functions

---

[6] http://www.bioinformaticslaboratory.nl/twiki/bin/
   view/EBioScience/TraculaDoc

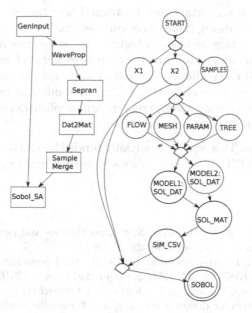

Fig. 8. Left: workflow for sensitivity analyses on blood flow simulations. Right: Data transformations represented as a state tag graph.

on different virtual machines and using split/merge functionality on seeds to split the sample input into separate data packets which can then be processed simultaneously on different nodes hosting the same function.

5   Conclusion and Future Work

In this paper we described an innovative model for data processing based on NFA. The model takes a data centric approach to describe abstract data processing as a sequence of state transitions. The state of the data gives it context, we extended this context down to the processing and network levels where a distributed implementation, Pumpkin, exploits this information to process and route data to appropriate peer nodes for further processing. The results demonstrated how the model and the implementation work well in virtual environments and can be used to achieve distributed collaborative computing on cloud resources due to its P2P nature. We showed that the processing network can adapt quickly to new functionality through the discovery and dynamic loading. This means that the network can adapt quickly to varying data by injecting new functions. The P2P nature removes centralized bottlenecks in the network and therefore can scale well.

The usage of data packets as data processing parcels allows us to investigate added data routing attributes. The presented model data is routed based solely on its state. One can envision a data routing table with attributes such as energy and security thus a data packet can be routed and processed through greener or secure nodes.

In our implementation, data states are tags. These tags give limited context to the data while processing. Since tags can essentially be URLs to ontologies then we can think of tags as links to higher level semantics and therefore can explore this rich semantic level directly at processing and network layers. In Supercomputing 2013[7] we showed our initial approach to extending the data defined networking to Internet Factories [12] while ongoing research is looking into further symbioses between infrastructure and application such as congestion healing by self optimizing the infrastructure.

Acknowledgments. This work was partially funded by COMMIT (http://www. commit-nl.nl) and VPH-Share (http://www.vph-share.eu) projects.

References

1. Michael, K., Miller, K.W.: Big data: New opportunities and new challenges (guest editors' introduction). Computer 46, 22–24 (2013)
2. Missier, P., et al.: Taverna, reloaded. In: Gertz, M., Ludäscher, B. (eds.) SSDBM 2010. LNCS, vol. 6187, pp. 471–481. Springer, Heidelberg (2010)
3. Altintas, I., Berkley, C., Jaeger, E., Jones, M., Ludascher, B., Mock, S.: Kepler: an extensible system for design and execution of scientific workflows. In: Proceedings of the 16th International Conference on Scientific and Statistical Database Management 2004, pp. 423–424 (2004)
4. Cushing, R., Koulouzis, S., Belloum, A., Bubak, M.: Applying workflow as a service paradigm to application farming. In: Concurrency and Computation: Practice and Experience, pp. n/a–n/a (2013)
5. Fernandez, H., Tedeschi, C., Priol, T.: A chemistry-inspired workflow management system for scientific applications in clouds. In: Escience, pp. 39–46. IEEE Computer Society (2011)
6. Dean, J., Ghemawat, S.: Mapreduce: Simplified data processing on large clusters. Commun. ACM 51, 107–113 (2008)
7. Brenna, L., Gehrke, J., Hong, M., Johansen, D.: Distributed event stream processing with non-deterministic finite automata. In: Proceedings of the Third ACM International Conference on Distributed Event-Based Systems, DEBS 2009, pp. 3:1–3:12. ACM, New York (2009)
8. Haller, P., Odersky, M.: Scala actors: Unifying thread-based and event-based programming. Theoretical Computer Science 410, 202–220 (2009), Distributed Computing Techniques
9. Arbab, F.: Composition of interacting computations. In: Goldin, D., Smolka, S., Wegner, P. (eds.) Interactive Computation, pp. 277–321. Springer, Heidelberg (2006)
10. Cortes, M.: A coordination language for building collaborative applications. Computer Supported Cooperative Work (CSCW) 9, 5–31 (2000)
11. Huberts, W., et al.: A pulse wave propagation model to support decision-making in vascular access planning in the clinic. Medical Engineering and Physics 34 (2012)
12. Strijkers, R., Makkes, M.X., de Laat, C., Meijer, M.: Internet factories: Creating application-specific networks on-demand. In: To appear in Journal of Computer Networks (2014)

---

[7] http://youtu.be/DP5TLgW1hW4

Scientific Workflow Partitioning
in Multisite Cloud*

Ji Liu[1,2,3,5], Vítor Silva[4], Esther Pacitti[2,3,5],
Patrick Valduriez[1,2,5], and Marta Mattoso[4]

[1] Microsoft-Inria Joint Centre, Paris, France
[2] LIRMM, Montpellier, France
[3] University Montpellier 2, France
[4] COPPE/UFRJ, Rio de Janeiro, Brazil
[5] Inria, Montpellier, France
{ji.liu,patrick.valduriez}inria.fr,
{silva,marta}@cos.ufrj.br,
{esther.pacitti}@lirmm.fr

Abstract. Scientific workflows allow scientists to conduct experiments
that manipulate data with multiple computational activities using Scientific Workflow Management Systems (SWfMSs). As the scale of the
data increases, SWfMSs need to support workflow execution in High
Performance Computing (HPC) environments. Because of various benefits, cloud emerges as an appropriate infrastructure for workflow execution. However, it is difficult to execute some scientific workflows in
one cloud site because of geographical distribution of scientists, data
and computing resources. Therefore, a scientific workflow often needs to
be partitioned and executed in a multisite environment. Also, SWfMSs
generally execute a scientific workflow in parallel within one site. This
paper proposes a non-intrusive approach to execute scientific workflows
in a multisite cloud with three workflow partitioning techniques. We describe an experimental validation using an adaptation of Chiron SWfMS
for Microsoft Azure multisite cloud. The experiment results reveal the
efficiency of our partitioning techniques, and their superiority in different
environments.

Keywords: scientific workflow, scientific workflow management system,
workflow partitioning, parallel execution, multisite cloud.

1 Introduction

Scientific experiments generally contain multiple computational activities to
process experimental data and these activities are related by data or control

---

* Work partially funded by CNPq, CAPES, FAPERJ, INRIA (Hoscar and Music
projects) and Microsoft (Zcloudflow project), and performed in the context of the
Institut de Biologie Computationnelle (www.ibc-montpellier.fr).

L. Lopes et al. (Eds.): Euro-Par 2014 Workshops, Part I, LNCS 8805, pp. 105–116, 2014.

dependencies. Scientific Workflows (SWfs) enable scientists to model these data processing activities together to be automatically executed. A SWf is the assembly of scientific data processing activities and data dependencies between them [9]. An activity is a description of a piece of work that forms one logical step within a scientific workflow representation. A data dependency is a relationship that represents the fact that one activity (output activity) consumes the output data of another activity (input activity). One activity may consist of several executable tasks for different parts of experimental data during SWf execution. A task is the representation of an activity within a one-time execution of this activity, which processes a part of its input data. As the amount of experimental data becomes huge, data-intensive scientific workflows become an important issue.

A Scientific Workflow Management System (SWfMS) is a tool to manage SWf representation, execution and data sets in various computing environments. SWfMSs may exploit High Performance Computing (HPC) to execute SWfs within reasonable time. The HPC environment may be provided by a cluster, grid or cloud. Cloud computing, which promises virtually infinite resources, scalable services, stable service quality and flexible payment policies, has recently become a viable solution for workflow execution.

In general, one cloud site is sufficient for executing one user application. However, in the case of SWfs, some important restrictions may force their execution in a multisite cloud, i.e. a cloud with multiple distributed data centers, each being explicitly accessible to cloud users. For instance, some activities need to be executed at a cloud site trusted by the scientists for workflow monitoring without malicious attack, i.e. scientist security restriction; some activities need to be moved to another cloud site because of stored big input data at that site and the cost of transferring this big data to another site is very high, i.e. data transfer restriction; some activities have to be executed at a site where more computing resources are available, i.e. computing capacity restriction; some other activities may invoke special programs (instruction data), which are located at a specific cloud site and cannot be moved to another site because of proprietary reasons, i.e. proprietary restriction. The configuration data, which includes workflow representation files or workflow parameters, can be located at one site or distributed at different sites. In this situation, multisite cloud is appealing for data-intensive scientific workflows.

For a given application, a multisite cloud configuration, which is the configuration of Virtual Machines (VMs) at each site, can be homogeneous, with homogeneous computing capacity at each site, e.g. 8 VMs at sites 1 and 2, or heterogeneous, e.g. 8 VMs at site 1 and 2 VMs at site 2. The homogeneous configuration is obviously easier to deal with in terms of workflow partitioning and execution. However, even the homogeneous configuration makes it difficult to reproduce experiments as the allocation of VMs to real resources is typically controlled at runtime by the cloud provider. For instance, at time t_1, one VM may be allocated to a processor that is already very busy (e.g. running 16 other VMs) while at time t_2, the same VM may be allocated to an underloaded processor (e.g. running 2 other VMs).

In order to execute SWfs in a multisite cloud environment, a SWfMS can generate a Workflow Execution Plan (WEP) for workflow execution. Similar to the concept of Query Execution Plan (QEP) in distributed database systems [16], the WEP is a program that captures optimization decisions and execution directives, typically the result of compiling and optimizing a workflow. Since the multiple sites are interconnected but share nothing, the WEP includes a workflow partitioning result, which is the decision of partitioning a workflow into workflow fragments for independent execution. A workflow fragment (or fragment for short) can be defined as a subset of activities and data dependencies of the original workflow (see [14] for a formal definition). In order to execute a fragment within reasonable time at one site, the WEP generally contains a workflow parallelization plan, which parallelizes the workflow execution.

We formulate the problems addressed in this paper as follows. A SWf $W = \{V,E\}$ consists of a set of activities V and a set of dependencies E. A multisite cloud $MS = \{S_1, S_2, ..., S_n\}$ is composed of multiple cloud sites, each of which has multiple computing nodes and stores its own data (input data, instruction data or configuration data of W). The workflow execution time is the entire time to execute a SWf at a given execution environment. Given a SWf W and a multisite cloud MS, the multisite cloud execution problem is how to execute W in MS in a way that reduces execution time while respecting restrictions.

We propose a non-intrusive approach to execute a SWf in a multisite cloud. We propose three partitioning techniques with consideration of restrictions and present the existing parallel execution techniques for the execution within one site. Note that workflow pre-partitioning technique does not mean we cannot explore the elasticity within one cloud site. We validate our approach with a data-intensive SWf using Chiron [15] SWfMS in Microsoft Azure [2] cloud. The experiment results reveal that our approach can reduce execution time. Since the occupied computing resources do not change, the reduction of execution time may lead to less lease time, which corresponds to less monetary cost.

This paper is organized as follows. Section 2 discusses worflow parallelism and related work on workflow parallel execution. Section 3 introduces our system model based on an adaptation of Chiron for multisite cloud. Section 4 presents the SWf we use for experimentation. Section 5 details our three workflow partitioning techniques. Section 6 presents our experimental validation with Microsoft Azure. Section 7 concludes.

2   Related Work

Workflow partitioning and execution in a multisite cloud remains a challenge and little work has been done. Deng *et al.* [10] adopt a clustering method based on data-data, data-activity and activity-activity dependencies. This method is adapted for workflow structures, but it may have big amount of data to be transferred between workflow fragments. Chen *et al.* [7] present workflow partitioning based on storage constraints. Since a cloud environment can offer big storage capacity and the VMs can be mounted additional storage resources before or during workflow exeuciton, the storage capacity limitation is not general in a cloud environment. In addition, this method do not take data transfer cost and different computing capacity at each site into consideration. Tanaka and Tatebe [17] use a Multi-Constraint Graph Partitioning (MCGP) algorithm [12] to partition a workflow. This approach partitions a workflow by minimizing the removed dependency and balancing the activities in each fragment. However, this approach is appropriate only for homogeneous execution sites. In this paper, we propose several partitioning techniques to address data transfer restriction and computing capacity restriction in the multisite cloud. Because of workflow partitioning, distributed provenance data is supported in the multisite cloud. In addition, data compression and file archiving is proposed to accelerate the data transfer between different cloud sites.

3   System Model

In this section, we present our workflow parallelization and scheduling methods, system model based on Chiron SWfMS, its adaptation for multisite cloud and a SWf partitioner.

A SWfMS exploits workflow parallelization and scheduling methods to enable parallel execution within one cloud site. Through parallelization, the WEP can achieve activity parallelism or data parallelism. Activity parallelism parallelizes the execution of different activities. It has two types: independent parallelism and pipeline parallelism. Independent parallelism is achieved when independent activities are executed in different computing nodes. When the execution of one activity does not dependent on the result of another activity, these two activity are independent activities. Otherwise, these two activities are dependent activities. Pipeline parallelism is obtained when dependent activities are executed in parallel. Data parallelism is realized by having the execution of the same activity on different parts of data in different computing nodes. Moreover, hybrid parallelism combines two or more types of parallelism to achieve better performance.

After parallelizing workflow execution, a SWfMS should schedule executable tasks to available computing nodes. A SWfMS can generate a static Scheduling Plan (SP) to schedule the tasks before workflow execution. Since the static SPs are generated before workflow execution, the workflow execution time is reduced. There are some existing static scheduling algorithms presented in [6,19]. However, since it is difficult to precisely predict the variation of execution environment or the workload of the executable tasks, static SPs do not achieve good performance on load balancing for dynamic changing execution. A SWfMS can also exploit dynamic scheduling method according to runtime environment features. Some dynamic scheduling methods are detailed in [5,13]. Although it takes time to generate SPs during workflow execution, the dynamic scheduling method can achieve better load balancing performance for a dynamic changing environment. Moreover, SWfMSs can use hybrid scheduling methods, i.e. the combination of static and dynamic scheduling method to reduce execution time and achieve load balance at the same time.

Chiron implements an algebraic approach for data-intensive scientific workflows proposed by Ogasawara *et al.* [15], to perform workflow parallelization and scheduling. This approach associates each activity with an operator, which has a semantic meaning for parallel execution. Since it models workflow data as relations similar to relational database management systems, this approach can optimize the entire workflow parallel execution based on well-founded relational algebra query optimization models [14].

The algebraic approach also allows online provenance data to be managed (and stored in a database by Chiron) for workflow activity monitoring [8]. Provenance data is the metadata that captures the derivation history of a dataset, including the original data sources, intermediate datasets, and the workflow computational steps that were applied to produce this dataset [8].

Chiron was initially developed for a one site execution environment as shown in Fig. 1-*A*. In a one site environment, a database is installed in a master node and all the computing nodes share storage resources through Network File System. Chiron achieves activity parallelism, data parallelism and dynamic scheduling for workflow parallelization as explained in Section 2. Chiron was modified to gather necessary produced data at the end of SWf execution at one site.

In a multisite cloud environment (see Fig. 1-*B*), all the sites have the same configuration as one site environment, i.e. a database installed in a master node and shared storage resources, while each site can have different numbers of slave computing nodes. We developped a SWf partitioner to automatically partition a processed SWf representation file into workflow fragment representation files when the first activity in each fragment is given. All the activities in a fragment are placed together in the processed SWf representation file. The SWf partitioner removes the dependencies in the original SWf and generates corresponding configuration files for each fragment. The execution of the generated fragments should respect the dependencies removed from the original SWf. Let us suppose that, in a SWf, activity A_2 consumes the output data produced by activity A_1. If these two activities are allocated to different fragments, their data dependencies will be removed from the explicit data dependencies. In this case, the fragment that contains activity A_2 should be executed after the execution of the fragment that contains activity A_1.

In order to reduce data transfer volume between different sites, we can use data compression and file archiving techniques. Data compression can just reduce the volume of transferred data to reduce transmission time. Through file archiving, we can also transfer the data at a relatively high speed to reduce transmission time. When transferring one file between two sites and the default transfer speed is less than the highest transfer speed between two sites, the file transfer is accelerated (accelerating phase) at the beginning and decreased (decreasing phase) at the end. The data transfer rate remains high in the middle (high speed transfer phase). If we transfer several small files, there will be many accelerating and decreasing phases. But if we transfer a big file of the same data volume, there will be an accelerating phase and a decreasing phase while the high speed transfer phase will be longer. Therefore, the transmission speed of a big file is higher than that of several small files of the same data volume. In the remainder of the paper, we note data refining as the combination of file archiving and data compression.

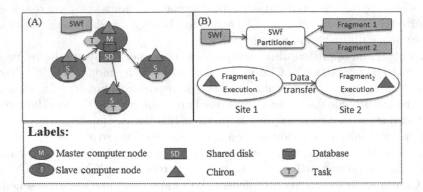

Fig. 1. The architecture of Workflow Execution in Chiron. Fig. *A* presents workflow execution in one site using Chiron before modification. Fig. *B* shows the multisite workflow execution using SWf partitioner and modified Chiron.

4   Use Case: Buzz Workflow

This section presents Buzz workflow [11], a data-intensive scientific workflow, as a use case to illustrate our partitioning techniques. Buzz workflow is modeled and executed using Chiron. Buzz workflow searches for trends and measures correlations in published papers from scientific publications. This scientific workflow uses data collected from bibliography databases such as the DBLP Computer Science Bibliography (DBLP) [1] or the U.S. National Institutes of Health's National Library of Medicine (PubMed). We used a DBLP 2013 XML file of $1,29GB$ as input for Buzz workflow in our experiments.

Buzz workflow has thirteen activities (Fig. 2(a)). Each activity has a specific operator according to the algebraic approach. Boxes in the figure represent workflow activities together with the involved algebraic operators. *FileSplit* activity is responsible for gathering all scientific publications from bibliography databases. *Buzz* activity uses these publications to identify buzzwords (a word or phrase that can become popular for a specific period of time). *WordReduce* activity organizes these publications according to buzzword and publication year, and it also computes occurrences of identified words. Furthermore, *YearFilter* activity selects buzzwords that appeared in the publications after 1991, while *BuzzHistory* activity and *FrequencySort* activity create a history for each word and compute its frequency. With this information, *HistogramCreator* activity generates some histograms with word frequency varying the year. On the other hand, *Top*10 activity selects ten of the most frequent words in recent years, whilst *ZipfFilter* activity selects terms according to a Zipf curve that is specified by word frequency values [18]. Moreover, *CrossJoin* activity merges results from *Top*10 activity and *ZipfFilter* activity. *Correlate* activity computes correlations between the words from *Top*10 activity and buzzwords from *ZipfFilter* activity. Using these correlations, *TopCorrelations* activity takes the terms that have a correlation greater than a threshold and *GatherResults* activity presents these selected words with the histograms.

In the remainder of the paper, we assume that there are two cloud sites (S_1 and S_2) to execute Buzz workflow. A fixed activity is located at a specific site and cannot be moved to another site because of additional restrictions, i.e. scientist security, data transfer, computing capacity and proprietary issues. We also assume that the first activity (*FileSplit*) is a fixed activity at S_1 since the input data located at S_1 is very big. In addition, we assume that the last activity (*GatherResults*) is a fixed activity at S_2 because of proprietary issues. Finally, scientists at S_2 need to monitor the execution of activity *HistogramCreator* without malicious attack and thus, *HistogramCreator* becomes a fixed activity at S_2, which is trusted by scientists.

5   Workflow Partitioning Techniques

We propose three techniques for workflow partitioning, i.e. scientist privacy, data transfer minimizing and computing capacity adaptation.

The first technique, Scientist Privacy (SPr), is for better supporting workflow activity monitoring under scientist security restriction. When a SWf contains an activity that needs to be monitored by scientists, this activity is defined as a locking activity to be executed at a trusted cloud site to avoid malicious attack during workflow execution. A locking activity implies that this activity and all the following activities should be assigned to a same workflow fragment, in order to provide further workflow activity monitoring. The following activities represent the activities that process the output data or the data produced from the output data of the locking activity. In order to partition a workflow based on scientist privacy technique, a SWfMS identifies the locking activity. Then it can partition the workflow by putting the locking activity and its available following activities (the following activities that are not fixed activities) into a fragment. According to this technique, Buzz workflow is partitioned into two fragments as shown in Fig. 2(b). As scientists need to analyze some histogram files produced by *HistogramCreator* activity at runtime at S_2 (trusted by scientists), *HistogramCreator* activity is handled as a locking activity. This activity and the following activities (*ZipfFilter, CrossJoin, Correlate, TopCorrelations* and *GatherResults*) are assigned to the same fragment while the other activities stay in another fragment.

The second technique is Data Transfer Minimizing (DTM), which minimizes the volume of data to be transferred between different workflow fragments. It is based on the fact that it takes much time to transfer certain amount of data from one site to another site. If the amount of data to be transferred between

112   J. Liu et al.

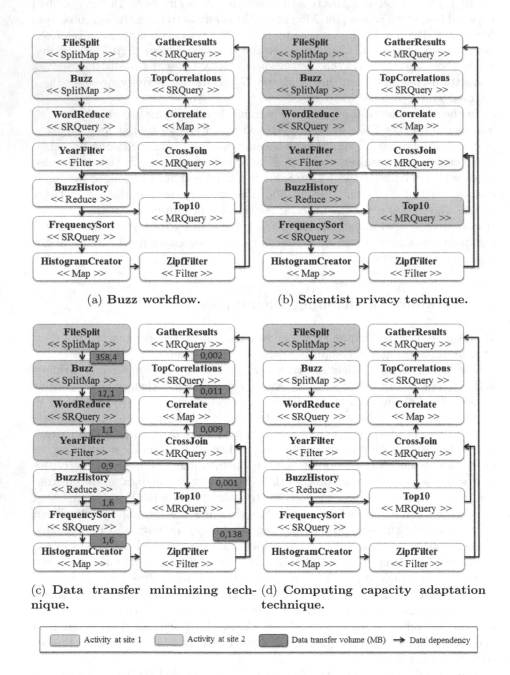

(a) Buzz workflow.

(b) Scientist privacy technique.

(c) Data transfer minimizing technique.

(d) Computing capacity adaptation technique.

Fig. 2. Buzz workflow partitioning

fragments is minimized, the time to transfer data between different sites can be reduced so as to reduce the entire execution time. During workflow design, the ratio between the volume of input data and output data can be offered. The scientists can estimate the data transfer for each data dependency based on the volume of input data of the SWf. There are five steps to partition a workflow based on this technique. The first step is to remove the dependencies that connect two activities at the same site in each route. The second step is to identify all the possible routes to connect the fixed activities at any two different sites. A route is a combination of a pipeline of activities and the dependencies between activities. The third step is to chose selected dependencies. The dependency that has the least data transfer volume in each route is put in the Selected Dependencies (SD). The dependencies that share the same input activity with the dependencies in SD are also put in SD. Fourth, we delete the dependencies from SD while ensuring that SD is enough to partition a SWf. The deletion begins from the dependency of the biggest data transfer volume to that of the smallest. Finally, the workflow can be partitioned to fragments by removing all the dependencies in SD from the original workflow. With this technique, Buzz workflow is partitioned as shown in Fig. 2(c). The dark gray boxes represent the data transfer volume for the corresponding dependencies. The data dependencies of each possible route between *FileSplit* and *HistogramCreator* is analyzed. The dependencies (*YearFilter* to *BuzzHistory* and *YearFilter* to *Top10*) are put in SD. Since it is necessary to remove the two dependencies to partition Buzz workflow, we do not delete any dependency from SD. Finally, Buzz workflow is partitioned by removing the selected dependencies (*YearFilter* to *BuzzHistory* and *YearFilter* to *Top10*).

The third technique is Computing Capacity Adaptation (CCA), which adapts SWfs partitioning to the computing capacity at different cloud sites. This technique is for the heterogeneous multisite cloud configurations, which may be incurred by the different configurations of different groups of scientists. If a scientific workflow is partitioned into two workflow fragments that are sequentially executed, i.e. one fragment begins execution after the execution of another one, a SWfMS can put all the possible activities to one fragment while leaving fixed activities in another fragment. As an example, Buzz workflow is partitioned into two fragments (WF_1 and WF_2) as shown in Fig. 2(d) . Since the input data of activity *FileSplit* is relatively big and located at a specific site, we keep this activity in the gray fragment, which is done by combining the computing capacity adaptation technique and the data transfer minimizing technique. Then, the white fragments can be scheduled to a cloud site that has more computing capacity.

6   Validation

In this section, we present experiments to validate our approach, by executing Buzz workflow using our partitioning techniques in Microsoft Azure cloud. The virtual machines (VMs) are distributed at two cloud sites: Western Europe (Amsterdam, Netherlands) and Eastern US (North Virginia). In the first experiment, we use a homogeneous configuration by creating two A4 VMs at both of Western Europe site and Eastern US site. In the second experiment, we use a heterogeneous configuration by creating two A4 VMs at the Western Europe site and eight A4 VMs at the Eastern US site. Each A4 VM has 8 CPU cores, 14 GB of RAM memory, 127 GB of instance storage and a network of 800 Mbps [4,3].

We executed Buzz workflow with Chiron and the SWf partitioner. We used Linux tar command and Linux scp command for data refining and data transfer. We launched the workflow fragment execution by hand at each cloud site, which resembles to the cooperation between two scientist group. In our execution, Chiron exploits data parallelism and the dynamic scheduling method for workflow parallel execution within one site. Table 1 shows the experimental results. Elapsed time 1 represents the execution time without considering data transfer time. Elapsed time 2 shows the execution time plus the data transfer time. Elapsed time 3 is the execution time plus data transfer time with data refining. Data transfer 1 reveals the data transfer time without data refining. Data transfer 2 presents the data refining and data transfer time. The three techniques correspond to the three partitioning techniques as explained in Section 5.

Table 1. Experimental Results

Approach (Time in minutes)	Execution time 1	Transmission time 1	Execution time 2	Transmission time 2	Execution time 3
1st experiment	2*A4 VM (EU) + 2*A4 VM (US)				
SPr technique	199	38	237	0	199
DTM technique	186	0	186	0	186
CCA technique	209	35	245	0.5	209
1st experiment	2*A4 VM (EU) + 8*A4 VM (US)				
SPr technique	198	38	236	0	198
DTM technique	182	0	182	0	182
CCA technique	169	35	201	0.5	169

In the first experiment, the workflow execution time of the three techniques without considering data transfer time is different because there is a different amount of data loaded into RAM memory for the white workflow fragment execution. Since the DTM technique minimizes the data transfer between two fragments, it also reduces the data to be transferred from disk to RAM at the beginning of the second fragment (white fragment) execution. When the data is transferred without data refining, the execution time of the DTM technique is 21.5% and 24.1% less than the SPr and the CCA technique. When the data is transferred with data refining, the DTM technique saves 6.5% and 11.0% of the execution time compared to the SPr and the CCA technique. As the two sites have the same computing capacity and it incurs big data transfer volume, the CCA is the least efficient technique. In this experiment, the workflow execution with the best partitioning technique (DTM with data refining) takes 24.1% less time than the least efficient technique (CCA without data refining). In the second experiment, because of the difference of computing capacity at two cloud sites, the execution of the CCA technique takes the least amount of time without considering data transfer. When the data is transferred without data refining, the DTM technique is still the best performance because of the minimized data transfer cost. This technique yields a gain of 22.9% and 10.4% of the execution time compared to the SPr and CCA technique. However, when we use data refining techniques, the third technique yields the best performance because of the adaptation of workflow partitioning to the computing capacity at each cloud site. In this case, the workflow execution of the CCA technique takes 14.6% and 7.1% less time compared to the SPr and DTM technique. In this experiment, the best partitioning technique (CCA with data refining) saves 28.4% time compared to the least efficient technique (SPr without data refining).

The experiments reveal that the DTM technique with data refining is the best for a homogeneous configuration and that the CCA technique with data refining has better performance for a heterogeneous configuration.

7 Conclusion

The cloud is emerging as an appropriate infrastructure for workflow execution. However, because of different restrictions, a scientific workflow often needs to be partitioned and executed in parallel in a multisite environment. In this paper, we proposed a non-intrusive approach to execute scientific workflows in a multisite cloud with three workflow partitioning techniques. We proposed a system model based on Chiron SWfMS and its adaptation to multisite cloud and a SWf partitioner. We presented the scheduling of workflow fragment execution by respecting all the data dependencies in the original SWf. We described an experimental validation using an adaptation of Chiron SWfMS for Microsoft Azure multisite cloud. The experiments experiments reveal the efficiency of our partitioning techniques, and their superiority in different environments. The experiment results show that data transfer minimizing technique with data refining, i.e. file archiving and data compression, has better performance (24.1% of time saved compared to computing capacity adaptation technique without data refining) for homogeneous configurations while computing capacity adaptation technique with data refining (28.4% of time saved compared to scientist privacy technique without data refining) is appropriate to heterogeneous configurations.

References

1. DBLP Computer Science Bibliography, http://dblp.uni-trier.de/
2. Microsoft Azure, http://azure.microsoft.com
3. VM bandwidth in Azure, http://windowsazureguide.net/tag/auzre-virtual-machines-sizes-bandwidth/
4. VM parameters in Azure, http://msdn.microsoft.com/en-us/library/azure/dn197896.aspx

5. Anglano, C., Canonico, M.: Scheduling algorithms for multiple bag-of-task applications on desktop grids: A knowledge-free approach. In: 22nd IEEE Int. Symposium on Parallel and Distributed Processing (IPDPS), pp. 1–8 (2008)
6. Blythe, J., Jain, S., Deelman, E., Gil, Y., Vahi, K., Mandal, A., Kennedy, K.: Task scheduling strategies for workflow-based applications in grids. In: 5th IEEE Int. Symposium on Cluster Computing and the Grid (CCGrid), pp. 759–767 (2005)
7. Chen, W., Deelman, E.: Partitioning and scheduling workflows across multiple sites with storage constraints. In: Wyrzykowski, R., Dongarra, J., Karczewski, K., Waśniewski, J. (eds.) PPAM 2011, Part II. LNCS, vol. 7204, pp. 11–20. Springer, Heidelberg (2012)
8. Costa, F., Silva, V., de Oliveira, D., Ocaña, K.A.C.S., Ogasawara, E.S., Dias, J., Mattoso, M.: Capturing and querying workflow runtime provenance with prov: a practical approach. In: EDBT/ICDT Workshops, pp. 282–289 (2013)
9. Deelman, E., Gannon, D., Shields, M., Taylor, I.: Workflows and e-science: An overview of workflow system features and capabilities. Future Generation Computer Systems 25(5), 528–540 (2009)
10. Deng, K., Kong, L., Song, J., Ren, K., Yuan, D.: A weighted k-means clustering based co-scheduling strategy towards efficient execution of scientific workflows in collaborative cloud environments. In: IEEE 9th Int. Conf. on Dependable, Autonomic and Secure Computing (DASC), pp. 547–554 (2011)
11. Dias, J., Ogasawara, E.S., de Oliveira, D., Porto, F., Valduriez, P., Mattoso, M.: Algebraic dataflows for big data analysis. In: IEEE Int. Conf. on Big Data, pp. 150–155 (2013)
12. Karypis, G., Kumar, V.: Multilevel algorithms for multi-constraint graph partitioning. In: ACM/IEEE Conf. on Supercomputing, pp. 1–13 (1998)
13. Maheswaran, M., Ali, S., Siegel, H.J., Hensgen, D., Freund, R.F.: Dynamic matching and scheduling of a class of independent tasks onto heterogeneous computing systems. In: 8th Heterogeneous Computing Workshop, p. 30 (1999)
14. Ogasawara, E., Oliveira, D., Valduriez, P., Dias, J., Porto, F., Mattoso, M.: An algebraic approach for data-centric scientific workflows. Proceedings of the VLDB Endowment (PVLDB) 4(12), 1328–1339 (2011)
15. Ogasawara, E.S., Dias, J., Silva, V., Chirigati, F.S., de Oliveira, D., Porto, F., Valduriez, P., Mattoso, M.: Chiron: a parallel engine for algebraic scientific workflows. Concurrency and Computation: Practice and Experience 25(16), 2327–2341 (2013)
16. Özsu, M.T., Valduriez, P.: Principles of Distributed Database Systems. Springer (2011)
17. Tanaka, M., Tatebe, O.: Workflow scheduling to minimize data movement using multi-constraint graph partitioning. In: 12th IEEE/ACM Int. Symposium on Cluster, Cloud and Grid Computing (Ccgrid), pp. 65–72 (2012)
18. Tarapanoff, K., Quoniam, L., Henrique, R., de Araújo, J., Alvares, L.: Intelligence obtained by applying data mining to a database of french theses on the subject of brazil. Information Research 7(1) (2001)
19. Topcuouglu, H., Hariri, S., Wu, M.: Performance-effective and low-complexity task scheduling for heterogeneous computing. IEEE Trans. on Parallel and Distributed Systems 13(3), 260–274 (2002)

Dynamic Scheduling of MapReduce Shuffle under Bandwidth Constraints

Sylvain Gault and Christian Perez

Avalon Research Team
Inria / LIP, ENS Lyon, France
{sylvain.gault,christian.perez}@inria.fr

Abstract. Whether it is for e-science or business, the amount of data produced every year is growing at a high rate. Managing and processing those data raises new challenges. MapReduce is one answer to the need for scalable tools able to handle the amount of data. It imposes a general structure of computation and let the implementation perform its optimizations. During the computation, there is a phase called *shuffle* where every node sends a possibly large amount of data to every other node. This paper proposes and evaluates two algorithms to improve data transfers during the *shuffle* phase under bandwidth constraints.

Keywords: Big Data, MapReduce, shuffle, scheduling, network, contention, bandwidth, regulation.

1 Introduction

In the past decades, the amount of data produced by scientific applications has never stopped growing. Several solutions have been proposed to handle these new order of magnitude in data production. Among them Google proposed to use MapReduce [5] in order to handle the web indexing problems in its own data-centers. This paradigm, inspired by functional programming, distributes the computation on many nodes that can access the whole data through a distributed file system. MapReduce users usually implement an application by only providing a *map* and a *reduce* function.

The global process of a MapReduce application mainly consists in 3 steps, *map*, *shuffle* and *reduce* as shown in Fig. 1. During the *map* phase, every *mapper* process reads a chunk of data and applies the *map* function on every record of that chunk to produce a number of key-value pairs. All those key-value pairs

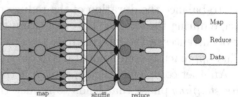

Fig. 1. Typical structure of a MapReduce application

make up what is called the *intermediate data*. Within every *mapper* process, the intermediate data is split into *partitions*. A partition represents the set of data to send to a given *reducer* process. Then during the *shuffle* phase, all the pairs

L. Lopes et al. (Eds.): Euro-Par 2014 Workshops, Part I, LNCS 8805, pp. 117–128, 2014.

with an equal key are gathered into a single *reducer* to build pairs made of a key and a list of values. The *reducer* process can thus run the *reduce* function on every pair and produce one result per intermediate key. Every *mapper* may send some data to every *reducer*.

Most work that try to optimize MapReduce have mainly focused on the *map* phase [4,9,14,13]; the *shuffle* has been largely forgotten despite it might take a non-negligible amount of time.

To optimize the performance / cost ratio, most MapReduce platforms run on moderately high-end commodity hardware. Nowadays, a classical HDD can produce a throughput of more than 1 Gbps, and even more with RAID configurations, while the network remain bound to 1 Gbps. The time taken by the *map* phase is expected to be equivalent to that of the *shuffle*. Some works [11] show that when contention occurs in a LAN, the overall throughput drops because of the delay needed by TCP to detect and retransmit the lost packets.

Problem statement. In a MapReduce application, it is quite common that the *mappers* do not process the same amount of data and that the *map* processes do not terminate at the same time. Thus, sharing the bandwidth equally among the mappers (as would do the network stack by default) may lead to a suboptimal bandwidth usage due to the mappers that finished later and those with more intermediate data. How to improve the *shuffle* phase? This work proposes and compares several scheduling algorithms to optimize the *shuffle* phase.

This paper is structured as follow: Section 2 reviews some related works that optimize the *shuffle* phase. Section 3 describes the proposed algorithms while a few important implementation details are presented in Sect. 4. Experimental results are discussed in Sect. 5. Section 6 concludes the paper.

2   Related Work

Some works have investigated the problem of the transfer cost during the *shuffle* phase of a MapReduce application. Most of them focus on optimizing the task and data placement during or just after the *map* phase.

The LEEN [8] (locality-aware and fairness-aware key partitioning) algorithm try to balance the duration of the reduce tasks while minimizing the bandwidth usage during the *shuffle*. This algorithm relies on statistics about the frequency of occurrences of the intermediate keys to get to create balanced data partitions. This approach is complementary to ours.

Another complementary approach is the HPMR [10] algorithm. It proposes a *pre-shuffling* phase that leads to reduce the amount of transferred data as well as the overall number of transfers. To achieve this, it tries to predict in which partition the data will go into after the *map* phase and tries to place this *map* task on the node that will run the *reduce* task for this partition.

Conversely, the Ussop [12] runtime, targeting heterogeneous computing grids, adapts the amount of data to be processed by a node with respect to its processing power. Moreover it tends to reduce the intermediate amount of intermediate data to transfer by running the *reduce* task on the node that hold most of the data to be reduced. This method can also be used together with our algorithms.

A MapReduce application can be seen as a set of divisible tasks since the data to be processed can be distributed indifferently on the *map* tasks. It is then possible to apply the results from the divisible load theory [2]. This is the approach followed by Berlińska and Drozdowski [1]. They consider a runtime environment in which the bandwidth of the network switch is less than the maximum bandwidth that could be used during the *shuffle* phase, thus inducing contention. To avoid this contention, they propose to model the execution of a MapReduce application as a linear program that generates a static partitioning and a static schedule of the communications based on a set of communication steps. While interesting, we showed in a previous work [6] that this approach is hardly scalable and that the chosen communication pattern is clearly suboptimal.

3 Shuffle Optimization

3.1 Platform and Application Models

We consider as a platform model a cluster connected by a single switch, thus forming a star-shaped network. Every link connecting a node to the switch has a capacity of C byte/s and the switch have a bandwidth of σ byte/s. σ is supposed to be an integer multiple of the link bandwidth. Thus $\sigma = l \times C$. Above l concurrent transfers, communications will suffer from contention.

A MapReduce application is represented here by the number of *mapper* processes m, and the number of *reducer* processes r. There are more *reducers* than what the switch can support, meaning that $r \geq l$. A *map* task i will transfer $\alpha_{i,j}$ bytes to the *reduce* task j. We call $\alpha_i = \sum \alpha_{i,j}$ the amount of data a *mapper* process i will have to send. Let $V = \sum \alpha_i$ be the size of all intermediate data.

We also assume that a *mapper* cannot send its data before its computations are finished. A *mapper* i finishes its computation S_i seconds after the first *mapper*. For the sake of simplicity, the *mappers* are numbered by the date of termination of the computation. Thus, $S_i < S_{i+1}$ and $S_1 = 0$. Figure 2 show the Gantt chart of a possible execution of a MapReduce application following this model. The computation time is green (or dark gray), the transfer time is light gray and in red (or black) is the idle time.

As we mainly focus on the throughput, the model ignores any latency as well as any mechanism of the network stack that could make the actual bandwidth lower than expected for a short amount of time, such as the TCP slow-start.

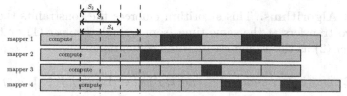

Fig. 2. Gantt of a possible execution following the application model

The transfer time of a chunk is proportional to its data size. This network model also ignores any acknowledgment mechanism of the underlying network protocols that can consume bandwidth and any interaction between CPU usage and bandwidth usage. Therefore, in order to make these assumptions realistic, we choose to map one *mapper* or *reducer* process per physical node.

3.2 Sufficient Conditions of Optimality and Lower Bound

We aim at optimizing the time between the start of the first transfer and the end of the last transfer. Indeed, in the general case, a *reduce* task cannot start before all input data are available. Thus, all the *reduce* tasks will start almost at the same time, which corresponds to the end of the *shuffle* phase.

Sufficient condition. From the above models, we can derive a few properties of an optimal algorithm. It would be trivial to prove that an algorithm that uses all the available bandwidth from the beginning to the end of the *shuffle* phase would be optimal. One way to achieve this, is by making all the transfers end at the exact same time. This is not a necessary condition for an algorithm to be optimal since, in some cases, these requirement cannot be met.

Lower bound. From this sufficient condition, a lower bound of the *shuffle* duration t that will be used in the analysis of the experiments can be computed [7] as

$$t = S_l + \frac{V - C \sum_{i=1}^{l-1}(S_l - S_i)}{\sigma}$$

3.3 Algorithms

To maximize the use of the bandwidth during the *shuffle* phase, we design and evaluate three algorithms. The first one is the simplest and probably the one implemented in every framework. The second algorithm is based on two ordered lists. The thrid algorithm is based on bandwidth regulation. Let describe them.

Start-ASAP Algorithm. As a reference algorithm, we consider the simplest algorithm which consist in starting every transfer as soon as the intermediate data are available. It thus relies on the operating system and on the network equipment to share the bandwidth between multiple transfers.

List-Based Algorithms. This algorithm enforces the constraints there must never be two transfers at the same time from a single *mapper* (1) or toward a single *reducer* (2) as this would create some contentions.

$$start(i,j) \geq end(i,j') \vee end(i,j) \leq end(i,j') \ \forall i \in [1..m], j, j' \in [1..r], j \neq j' \ (1)$$
$$start(i,j) \geq end(i',j) \vee end(i,j) \leq end(i',j) \ \forall i, i' \in [1..m], j \in [1..r], i \neq i' \ (2)$$

Algorithm. To fulfill the constraints (1) and (2), the list-based algorithm handles the *mappers* and *reducers* in a list from which a *reducer* is taken and associated to a *mapper* to form a couple that represents a transfer. When at least one *mapper* is ready to start a transfer, the first ready *mapper* is taken from the list of *mappers*. Then, the algorithm iterates through the list of *reducers* to take the first that the current *mapper* has not transferred its data to yet. Once found, the *reducer* and the *mapper* are removed from their lists. When the transfer is done, the *reducer* is put back at the end of the list of reducers thus keeping it ordered by date of last finished transfer. The *mapper* is inserted back into the list keeping the list ordered by the increasing number of remaining transfers. It may happen that for a given *mapper* there is no *reducer* it has not already transferred its data. In that case, the next entry in the list of *mappers* is considered.

More formally, that means that there are two lists named *ml* and *rl*. *ml* is empty in the beginning and it will contain only the id of the *mappers* that have finished their *map* computation and still have some intermediate data to transfer. *ml* is assumed to be automatically ordered by the number of remaining transfers, like a priority queue. *rl* contains the id of every *reducer* in the beginning, and it is ordered by the fact that the *reducer* id will be always be queued at the end.

The transfer to start is chosen as follow. While no *mapper* $i \in ml$ has been chosen, take the next *mapper* i from *ml*. Iterate through *rl* until a *reducer* j is found that i has some data to send to. Once this is found, break every loop, (i, j) is the transfer to start. As a last step, i is removed from *ml* and j is removed from *rl*. The full algorithm is described in [7].

Limitations. Although we expect this algorithm to perform better than the reference algorithm, some corner cases may still remain. Indeed, it may happen a *mapper* has some transfers left to do but cannot start them because all the reducers are already busy transferring. We can expect that this situation is more common when l is almost as large as r. Moreover, the scalability of this algorithm seems limited since the centralized scheduler has to be queried for every transfer, and their number grows with the number of nodes.

Two Phase Per-Transfer Regulation. The idea of this algorithm is based on the sufficient condition of an optimal algorithm that uses all the bandwidth of the switch and that terminates all the transfers at the same moment. For this, we assume that for a given data transfer, a given bandwidth can be maintained. We also assume that the bandwidth can be modified dynamically. The way we achieved this is explained in [7].

This algorithm computes the bandwidth to be allocated to every sending *mapper* process with respect to the amount of data to send. This bandwidth is then distributed among the transfers *mapper* $\rightarrow$ *reducer* inside the *mapper* process. This algorithm is expected to never allocate too much bandwidth to a given *mapper* process and to finish all the transfers at the same time.

Model addition. For this algorithm we name $ready(t)$ the set of *mapper* processes that have finished their computation but not the transfer of their intermediate data. $\beta_{i,j}(t)$ is the bandwidth allocated to the transfer from *mapper i* to *reducer j* at a date t, and $\beta_i(t) = \sum \beta_{i,j}(t)$ the bandwidth allocated to a given *mapper* process i. $\alpha_i(t)$ is also the amount of intermediate data a ready mapper i still has to transfer to the reducers at date t. And $\alpha_{i,j}(t)$ the amount of data still to be transferred from *mapper i* to *reducer j*.

Algorithm. The first phase computes the values for $\beta_i(t)$, the bandwidth allocated to *mapper i*. The second phase applies a very similar algorithm for every process in order to distribute the bandwidth among the transfers.

The first phase is done by computing $\beta_i(t) \leftarrow \sigma \frac{\alpha_i(t)}{V(t)}$ for every *mapper i*. If one value for $\beta_i(t)$ is larger than C, then it is set to C, and the remaining bandwidth is redistributed among the other *mappers*. It should be noted that when the bandwidth of a *mapper i* is reduced to C, it means that this process will not be able to complete its transfers at the same time of the others. In this case, this algorithm may not be optimal. The second phase is done by computing $\beta_{i,j} \leftarrow \beta_i(t) \frac{\alpha_{i,j}(t)}{\alpha_i(t)}$ for every transfer (i,j). The full algorithm is presented in [7].

The complexity of one iteration of the first phase is $\mathcal{O}(m)$ because it has to compute $\beta_i(t)$ for every *mapper i*. This computation could be repeated a maximum of m times. Thus this first phase run in $\mathcal{O}(m^2)$ in the worst case. The complexity of the second phase is $\mathcal{O}(m \times r)$ because $\beta_{i,j}(t)$ has to be computed for every *mapper i* and every *reducer j*. The complexity of the algorithm is then $\mathcal{O}(m^2 + m \times r)$. This may sound large, but, the second phase can be distributed and every *mapper i* can share its allocated bandwidth itself and it can compute $\beta_{i,j}(t)$ from $\beta_i(t)$ on its own. Thus reducing the worst-case complexity of the whole algorithm to $\mathcal{O}(m^2 + r)$.

Limitations. Although this algorithm prevents any contention on the switch or on the private links of the *mappers*, contention may happen on the *reducers* side. However, since $r \geq l$, this case should not occur very often.

4   Implementation Details

To evaluate these algorithms, we have implemented them in our own MapReduce framework HoMR (HOmemade MapReduce) which has been developed in the context of the French ANR MapReduce project. It is based on HLCM/L²C [3], a software component model. HoMR is written in C++ and it relies on CORBA for inter-process communications.

The two phase algorithm recomputes the allocated bandwidths every time a transfer terminates, or every 5 seconds if nothing happened. This enables to avoid a slight imprecision in the bandwidth control to be compensated. The value of 5 seconds has been chosen arbitrarily. However, experiments have shown that the computed bandwidth for every *mapper* is always slightly different.

To reach the maximal bandwidth of a single link, every *mapper* uses 4 threads to send data per transfer. This value has been suggested by the experiment with tc presented in Sect. 5.2. It has been further confirmed by tests with HoMR.

5   Experiments

To evaluate these algorithms, we have performed some experiments on the GRID'5000 experimental testbed. First we ensure the environment behaves as expected, and we compare the 3 algorithms presented in this document.

5.1   Platform Setup

The model assumes that the platform is a switched star-shaped network with a limited bandwidth on the switch. The central point of our algorithms is to control the bandwidth used during the *shuffle* phase. Thus, to evaluate our algorithms in the case of several switch bandwidth limit configurations, we simulated a switch by the mean of a node dedicated to routing packets.

This may not be an optimal simulation of a switched network since the routing mechanism implies a *store-and-forward* method of forwarding the packets, instead of a *cut-through* as most switches do. However, we believe that this does not has a large effect on the measured throughputs and this enables to easily control the overall bandwidth available on that routing node.

As all the packets will have to traverse twice the network interface of the router node, we need a fast network to simulate a switch with a throughput greater than 1 Gbps. Thus, we used *InfiniBand 40G* interfaces with an *IP over InfiniBand* driver for the ease of use. The bandwidth of the router is controlled with the Linux tc tool. The performance behavior of this setup is tested in Sect. 5.2. As the network is based on fast network interface controllers (NIC), the bandwidth of the private links is configured to 1 Gbps. The tc rules used are based on the htb algorithm to limit the outgoing bandwidth and on the default algorithm to limit the incoming bandwidth. The operating system of the nodes is Debian wheezy with Linux 2.6.32 as a kernel.

Experiments have been done on the Edel cluster of Grid'5000. Each node has 2 quad-core CPUs Intel Xeon E5520 @2.27 GHz, and it equipped with 24 GB of memory, 1 Gigabit Ethernet and 1 InfiniBand 40G cards.

5.2   Preliminary Tests

tc Regulation on Router. To test whether we can limit correctly the bandwidth on the router we used 2 nodes and a router node. Only the router node has a limited bandwidth. The limit is varied by steps of 100 Mbps up to 12 Gbps. The actual bandwidth is measured with iperf with 4 parallel clients threads on the client side. Every measure is run 5 times.

Figure 3(a) shows the results of this experiment. Globally, we observe that the measured bandwidth stay roughly between 90% and 95% of the target bandwidth until the maximal bandwidth of the system is reached. Also, the measures are quite stable as the difference between the maximal and minimal measured bandwidth never exceed 0.28 Gbps or 8% of the average bandwidth.

However, some steps are clearly distinguishable around 5 Gbps and 7 Gbps. Similar results have been obtained on another cluster with *InfiniBand 20G* network adapters. We have no real explanation for that. The results on a newer

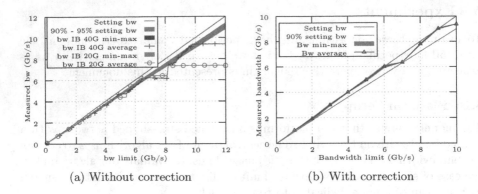

(a) Without correction

(b) With correction

Fig. 3. Bandwidth limitation on Linux + `tc` on InfiniBand

version of Linux (not shown here) are completely different. Thus, we think that this is a performance bug in Linux.

To still get the targeted bandwidth, we built a lookup table to set the bandwidth limit that would produce the bandwidth actually targeted. Figure 3(b) show the measured bandwidth with respect to the corrected setting bandwidth. It can be noted that the larger step from Fig. 3(a) could not be completely corrected and that the bandwidth of 10 Gbps cannot be reached. Except from those outliers, the measured bandwidth is always between 96% and 103% of the target bandwidth. However, the lookup table has been tested only when one node emit the data and one node receive them. It is not impossible that when several nodes send data at the same time the bandwidth drift shown in Fig. 3(a) is not the same. This would make the correction applied inaccurate.

Bandwidth Regulation. The two phase algorithm relies on the ability to regulate the bandwidth. The method we used for this is described in [7]. To check whether it performs correctly, we set up an experiment with only two nodes interconnected by an *InfiniBand 40G* network. We then vary the size of the messages from 4 bytes to 64 MB and the target bandwidth from 1 KB/s to 1 GB/s and measure the overall average bandwidth. Each measure is repeated 10 times.

Figure 4 shows a 3D plot of the results this experiment. It shows the actual bandwidth with respect to the message size and to the targeted bandwidth. Some points are missing in the results because the execution time required for them would have been too long. The colors (or gray scale) represent the percentage of variability.

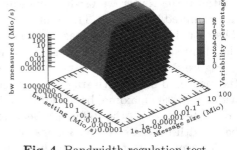

Fig. 4. Bandwidth regulation test

This figure shows 3 distinct areas. A black plan for small targeted bandwidth and large enough message size, a purple (or gray) plan for small message size and high targeted bandwidth, and a *roof* for large message size and large targeted bandwidth. The black plan is the area where the regulation algorithm works perfectly. The purple plan is the area where the system is CPU-bound. And the *roof* is the area where the system is bound by the network bandwidth.

5.3 Synchronous Transfer Start

The first experiment with our algorithms is simple and all other experiments are only variations of this one. The MapReduce job is a word count application. However, for the sake of simplicity and control, the data are not read from a file, they are generated by a component *WordGenerator*. This enables to control the amount of intermediate data produced. In order to control the time at which the *map* computations end, an artificial synchronization barrier is added. In the next experiment, an imbalance is simulated by adding a sleep after this barrier. This enables to evaluate the behavior of the *shuffle* phase.

For this first experiment all the *map* computations finish at the exact same time and every *mapper* have the same amount of intermediate data. Every *mapper* process generates 2.56 GB of intermediate data. The same amount of data has to be sent to every *reducer*. The router's bandwidth is varied from 1 Gb/s to 10 Gb/s. The time taken from the start of the first transfer to the end of the last transfer is measured and compared to the lower bound. This experiment is run with 10 *mappers* and 10 *reducers*. Every configuration is run 5 times.

Figure 5 displays the results of this experiment in terms of percentage with respect to the lower bound. As every measure has been made 5 times, the median time is represented on this figure.

The results for the list-based algorithm are close to what was expected. The lists-based algorithm has a behavior close to the optimal. Performance degradations occur for a switch bandwidth of 7 Gb/s and 10 Gb/s. Those configurations, as shown in Fig. 3(b), are known not to offer the actual bandwidth targeted.

The two phase regulation algorithm

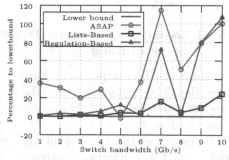

Fig. 5. Median time taken by all the 3 algorithms under various bandwidth restriction with same amount of data and synchronous start of transfers

rithm shows a good behavior for a switch bandwidth less or equal to 8 Gb/s. Above that limit it creates contentions and it exhibits a behavior as bad as the reference algorithm. Also, for 7 Gb/s, this algorithm produces a peak of bad performance. This can be interpreted as a high sensitivity to overestimation of the switch bandwidth.

Regarding the variability of the performance, the list-based algorithm has a good stability. The standard deviation of the time of the shuffle phase is no more than 3%. The two other algorithms have a variability between 0% and 17%.

5.4   1 Second Steps between Computation End

The second experiment is very similar to the previous one. Only a one-second delay between the end of every *map* computation has been added, thus creating a slight imbalance among the *mapper* process.

Figure 6 displays the results of this experiments in terms of percentage with respect to the lower bound.

The list-based algorithm has a similar behavior as in the previous experiment. The reference algorithm also has a better performance. This is due to the fact that in the beginning and in the end, not all the *mappers* are transferring data, thus there is less contention and less performance degradation. The global behavior of the list-based and two phase algorithms remain the same. However the two phase algorithm appears to be super-optimal by up to 5% for some

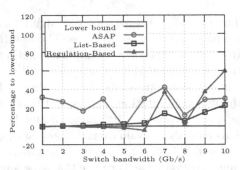

Fig. 6. Median time taken by all the 3 algorithms under various bandwidth restriction with same amount of data and 1 second step between transfer start

configurations. The cause is not very clear. It is supposed that raising the limit bandwidth as done in Fig. 3(b) is only valid for a single source and single destination network.

5.5   1 Second Step between Transfer Start with Heterogeneous Amount of Data

The third and final experiment combines the delay before starting the transfers and imbalance of the amount of intermediate data.

The results of this experiment are displayed in Fig. 7 in terms of percentage with respect to the lower bound.

The results shows that the list-based algorithm has a more regular behavior. It produces a performance variability of less than 2%. As previously, the reference algorithm has poor performance for small bandwidth as it generates some contentions. It also has a variability

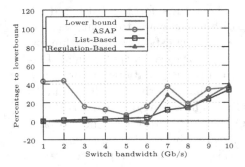

Fig. 7. Median time taken by the 3 algorithms under various bandwidth restriction, with an imbalanced amount of intermediate data and non-synchronous transfer start

between 2% and 14%. Its performance is equivalent to that of two phase and lists-based algorithms for a router bandwidth which is large enough. Globally, the reference algorithm has a bowl-shaped performance curve centered around 5 Gb/s. The left part seems to be due to the decrease of the contention ratio, leading to an increase of the performance; the right part seems to be due to the imbalance among the amount of intermediate data to transfer that makes the increase of the bandwidth of the router has only a slight impact in the actual performance. Except for a bandwidth limit of 7 Gbps, the two phase algorithm achieves performance close or better than the list-based algorithm. It also has a variability usually less than 3%, except for a bandwidth limit of 7 and 10 Gbps where some contentions occur.

6   Conclusion and Future Work

The two phase algorithm performs equally or better than the list-based one when the switch bandwidth is precisely known, but it is quite sensitive to an over-estimation of this parameter. The impact of contention on the *reducers'* side has been ignored here and should be investigated. Taking the bandwidth regulation from the *reducers*'s side may be beneficial. The list-based may hardly scale and it requires the switch bandwidth to be an integer multiple of the link bandwidth.

Several assumptions have been made in this work, and removing them would be a step forward. On the experiment part, the most important assumption is that Linux + tc mimic the behavior of a real switch, which could be investigated further.

On the model part, some simplifications have been made which may not always be realistic. This is, however, a crucial step towards a more general solution. Forcing the *mappers* and *reducers* to be located on distinct nodes each is a strong requirement that could be addressed by allowing the list-based algorithm to pick only one of the collocated process, and by adding an intermediate phase to the two phase algorithm that would distribute the bandwidth allocated to a node among the processes.

Assuming a single-switch network is also a strong constraint. However, it could be mitigated by discriminating the same-switch transfers from the others and tweaking the algorithm parameters accordingly.

Automatically determining the parameters of the algorithms, such as link and switch bandwidths, would remove this burden from the user. Making the estimated bandwidth dynamic would also make those algorithms more robust against the disturbances that may be caused by the other users of a cloud infrastructure. Also, network topology discovery would be very important to ease their usage.

In the end, the *shuffle* phase has been largely ignored by the academic work despite being a potentially important bottleneck. This has showed that a no-op algorithm lead to bad performance in case of network contention and smarter algorithms are proven to be more efficient.

Acknowledgment. This work is supported by the French National Research Agency (Agence Nationale de la Recherche) in the framework of the MapReduce project under Contract ANR-10-SEGI-001. The experiments referenced in this paper were carried out using the Grid'5000/ALADDIN-G5K experimental testbed, an initiative from the French Ministry of Research through the ACI GRID incentive action, INRIA, CNRS and RENATER and other contributing partners.

References

1. Berlinska, J., Drozdowski, M.: Scheduling Divisible MapReduce Computations. Journal of Parallel and Distributed Computing 71(3), 450–459 (2010)
2. Bharadwaj, V., Robertazzi, T.G., Ghose, D.: Scheduling Divisible Loads in Parallel and Distributed Systems. IEEE Computer Society Press (1996)
3. Bigot, J., Pérez, C.: On High Performance Composition Operators in Component Models. In: High Performance Scientific Computing with special emphasis on Current Capabilities and Future Perspectives, Advances in Parallel Computing, vol. 20, pp. 182–201. IOS Press (2011)
4. Chen, Q., Zhang, D., Guo, M., Deng, Q., Guo, S.: Samr: A self-adaptive mapreduce scheduling algorithm in heterogeneous environment. In: 2010 IEEE 10th Int. Conf. on. Computer and Information Technology (CIT), pp. 2736–2743 (June 2010)
5. Dean, J., Ghemawat, S.: Mapreduce: Simplified data processing on large clusters. In: Proc. of the 6th Conf. on Symposium on Opearting Systems Design & Implementation, OSDI 2004, vol. 6, p. 10. USENIX Association (2004)
6. Gault, S.: Ordonnancement dynamique des transferts dans MapReduce sous contrainte de bande passante. In: ComPAS 2013 / RenPar'21 - 21eme Rencontres Francophones du Parallélisme (January 2013)
7. Gault, S., Desprez, F.: Dynamic Scheduling of MapReduce Shuffle Under Bandwidth Constraints. Tech. Rep. Inria/RR-8574
8. Ibrahim, S., Jin, H., Lu, L., Wu, S., He, B., Qi, L.: LEEN: Locality/fairness-aware key partitioning for mapreduce in the cloud. In: 2010 IEEE Second Int. Conf. on Cloud Computing Technology and Science (CloudCom), pp. 17–24 (November 2010)
9. Kwon, Y., Balazinska, M., Howe, B., Rolia, J.: Skewtune: Mitigating skew in mapreduce applications. In: Proc. of the 2012 ACM SIGMOD Int. Conf. on Management of Data, SIGMOD 2012, pp. 25–36. ACM (2012)
10. Seo, S., Jang, I., Woo, K., Kim, I., Kim, J.S., Maeng, S.: HPMR: Prefetching and pre-shuffling in shared mapreduce computation environment. In: IEEE Int. Conf. on Cluster Computing and Workshops, CLUSTER 2009, pp. 1–8 (August 2009)
11. Steffenel, L.: Modeling network contention effects on all-to-all operations. In: 2006 IEEE Int. Conf. on Cluster Computing, pp. 1–10 (September 2006)
12. Su, Y.L., Chen, P.C., Chang, J.B., Shieh, C.K.: Variable-sized map and locality-aware reduce on public-resource grids. Future Generation Computer Systems 27(6), 843–849 (2011)
13. Zaharia, M., Borthakur, D., Sen Sarma, J., Elmeleegy, K., Shenker, S., Stoica, I.: Job scheduling for multi-user mapreduce clusters. Tech. Rep. UCB/EECS-2009-55, EECS Department, University of California, Berkeley (April 2009)
14. Zaharia, M., Borthakur, D., Sen Sarma, J., Elmeleegy, K., Shenker, S., Stoica, I.: Delay scheduling: A simple technique for achieving locality and fairness in cluster scheduling. In: Proc. of the 5th European Conf. on Computer Systems, EuroSys 2010, pp. 265–278. ACM (2010)

Balanced Graph Partitioning with Apache Spark

Emanuele Carlini[1], Patrizio Dazzi[1],
Andrea Esposito[2], Alessandro Lulli[2], and Laura Ricci[2]

[1] Istituto di Scienza e Tecnologie dell'Informazione (ISTI)
Consiglio Nazionale delle Ricerche (CNR)
{name.surname}@isti.cnr.it
[2] Dipartimento di Informatica
Università di Pisa
{surname}@di.unipi.it

Abstract. A significant part of the data produced every day by on-line services is structured as a graph. Therefore, there is the need for efficient processing and analysis solutions for large scale graphs. Among the others, the *balanced graph partitioning* is a well known NP-complete problem with a wide range of applications. Several solutions have been proposed so far, however most of the existing state-of-the-art algorithms are not directly applicable in very large-scale distributed scenarios. A recently proposed promising alternative exploits a vertex-center heuristics to solve the balance graph partitioning problem. Their algorithm is massively parallel: there is no central coordination, and each node is processed independently. Unfortunately, we found such algorithm to be not directly exploitable in current BSP-like distributed programming frameworks. In this paper we present the adaptations we applied to the original algorithm while implementing it on Spark, a state-of-the-art distributed framework for data processing.

Keywords: graph partitioning, distributed algorithm, approximated algorithm.

1   Introduction

In the recent years we experienced an exponential growth and availability of structured and unstructured data. Every day, large amounts of data is produced by on-line services like social networking, social media, fora, newsletters, mailing-lists, etc. Normally, this data needs deep analysis, in order to exploit its intrinsic value. However, due to the data size, efficient analysis cannot be performed with the computational capabilities of a single machine. Instead, it is a common practice to rely on efficient approaches and scalable solutions able to conduct these computations by orchestrating the work of a vast, distributed, set of computational resources.

A significant part of the aforementioned data is modelled as a graph (sometimes as an hyper-graph), in which vertices represent entities and (hyper-) edges represent the relationship between them. Usually, computation on graph relies

L. Lopes et al. (Eds.): Euro-Par 2014 Workshops, Part I, LNCS 8805, pp. 129–140, 2014.

heavily on locality, in the sense that the computation for a vertex is done considering its neighbours in the graph. Hence, when going distributed an important issue is data partitioning: extremely large scale graphs must be distributed to hosts in such a way that, for each vertex, most of the adjacent edges are stored on the same host [11].

The identification of good partitions is a well-known and well-studied problem in graph theory [6]. The aim of graph partitioning, sometimes referred to as the solution of the min-cut problem, is to divide a graph into a defined amount of components, such that to minimize the number of edges connecting the components. A variant of the min-cut problem is the balanced (or uniform) graph partitioning problem. In this case it is also important that the components present a balanced amount of nodes.

A balanced graph partitioning has many relevant applications, including biological networks, parallel programming, and on-line social network analysis and it can be used to minimise communication cost and to balance workload. As suggested by this considerable amount of potential applications the problem is not new and there are many proposed solutions. In the last years, a large amount of algorithms have been conceived, implemented and optimised for achieving good graph partitioning [1], [10], [9], [14], [15], [19]. Some of these solutions are parallel, and most of them implicitly assume to have a not expensive, random access to the entire graph. In contrast to this vision, current large scale graphs are composed by billions of nodes and hundreds of billions of edges, e.g., user relationships and interaction graphs from online social networking services such as Facebook or Twitter. Clearly, these graphs do not fit into the main memory of a single computer but are distributed, with only a small fraction of the nodes hosted on a single computer.

Despite the interest on the problem, only recently distributed approaches for efficient balanced partitioning have been proposed. Among the others, JA-BE-JA [17] is a recent promising approach that employs a fully distributed, vertex-center heuristics. In JA-BE-JA each node of the graph is a virtual processing unit, having only the information about its neighbourhood. The nodes also acquire knowledge about a small subset of random nodes in the graph by using purely local interactions. Initially, every node selects a random partition, and over time nodes swap their partitions with each other in a way that increases the number of neighbours in the same partition as themselves.

JA-BE-JA aims at dealing with extremely large distributed graphs. To this end the algorithm exploits its locality, simplicity and lack of synchronisation requirements. JA-BE-JA was evaluated using different datasets. Some of them were synthetically generated graphs that are well-known in the graph partitioning community. They are part of a publicly downloadable archive made available by Chris Walshaw [21]. The authors of JA-BE-JA also tested their approach with real datasets, a set of sampled graphs extracted by Facebook [20] and Twitter [2]. For comparison they used METIS [8], showing that their distributed solution can in some cases outperform the results achieved by METIS. Most of their experiments have been conducted by implementing the JA-BE-JA algorithm on the PeerSim [16] simulator. Further, the authors of JA-BE-JA claims that due to its flexibility, it can be adapted easily to the currently available graph processing frameworks such as Pregel [12], GraphLab [11] or Spark [24] by means of the Bulk Synchronous Parallel (BSP) abstraction.

Starting from JA-BE-JA (detailed in Section 2), our main contribution is the implementation and analysis of JA-BE-JA in Apache Spark. Before porting JA-BE-JA to Spark, we implemented a BSP-like version of JA-BE-JA over PeerSim. Our version adds a BSP barrier on the PeerSim communications, so to simulate the execution on a Spark-like environment. From the analysis of the BSP-PeerSim we noticed a sensible reduction of the performance with respect to the original formulation and that gave us an idea of the performance we could expect on Spark. When porting on Spark, we implemented our own BSP abstraction, as the current available technologies (e.g. Bagel and GraphX) have been not suitable to accommodate easily the execution of JA-BE-JA. The whole description of the porting work is detailed in Section 3.1.

Further, to reduce random access to the nodes of the graph when applying the heuristics of JA-BE-JA, we relaxed the consistency constraint on the knowledge of the nodes about their neighborhood (Section 3.2). Finally, we validate our solution by extensive experiments and we found that the relaxed version of JA-BE-JA retains the same performance in terms of the quality of the min-cut, but it reduces considerably the amount of memory used (Section 4).

2   JA-BE-JA and the Balanced Min-Cut Problem

The balanced k-way graph partitioning is a well-know problem in graph theory and often it is referred as the k-way min-cut problem. Here, we give a formal formulation of this problem, derived from the one defined by the JA-BE-JA authors.

Consider an undirected graph $G = (V, E)$, with V representing the set of vertices and E the set of edges. A k-way partitioning divides the set V into k subsets. The fewer edges cross the boundaries of each subgraph (or component), the higher is the quality of the achieved partitioning. The *balanced* version of the problem consists in having the components of approximately the same size.

A formal description of k-way partitioning can be given with the help of a partition function $\pi : V \rightarrow \{1, \ldots, k\}$ that assigns a color to each vertex of the graph. Thus, π_p indicates the color of node p. The vertices of the same color belongs to the same partition. Let N_p indicate the neighbourhood of vertex p and $N_p(c)$ the set of neighbours of p having color c. The number of neighbours of node p is denoted by d_p, and $d_p(c) = |N_p(c)|$ is the number of neighbours of p with color c.

Now consider the *energy* of the system as the number of existing edges connecting nodes with different colours. Accordingly, the energy of a node is the number of its neighbours with a different color, and the energy of the graph is the sum of the energy of the nodes.

$$E\left(G, \pi\right) = \frac{1}{2} \sum_{p \in V} \left(d_p - d_p(\pi_p)\right) \tag{1}$$

where the sum is divided by two to avoid to sum each edge twice. Given this formal description, the balanced optimisation problem can be expressed as the problem of finding the optimal partitioning π^*.

$$\pi^* = argmin E(G, \pi) \tag{2}$$

$$s.t. \quad |V(c_1)| = |V(c_2)| \quad \forall c_1, c_2 \in \{1, \ldots, k\} \tag{3}$$

where $V(c)$ is the set of nodes with color c.

2.1   JA-BE-JA

JA-BE-JA is a distributed algorithm for resolving the balanced k-way problem. Given a "colored" graph as defined above, the idea behind JA-BE-JA is to apply a local heuristic to drive the system into a lower energy state.

The local heuristics is executed by all the nodes in parallel. Each node attempts to swap the color to the most dominant color among its neighbors, by: (i) selecting another node from either its neighbors or from a random sample, and (ii) considering the utility of the color swapping. If the color swapping decreases the energy, then the two nodes swap their colors; otherwise, they keep their colors. To avoid remaining in a local optimum solution, JA-BE-JA employs a simulated annealing technique.

Since node just exchange colors, the distribution of colors (i.e. the number of partition) is maintained during the whole process. Therefore, if the color at the start is assigned uniform, the final result it is expected to have balanced partitions.

3   Our Distributed Implementation

In this section we present our distributed implementation and the adaptations that have been required in order to efficiently exploit JA-BE-JA into a BSP-like environment.

JA-BE-JA is designed to fit two models: one host-one node and one host-multiple nodes (respectively also called "one-to-one" and "one-to-many"). The "one-to-one" node case represents a fully distributed P2P computation, the "one-to-many" model, instead, exploits a shared-memory support to short-cut the communications performed between the vertices located on the same machine. This latter solution is not Pregel-like because introduces the concept of sub-supersteps (involving intra-superstep communications) and different user-defined functions are executed for each vertex, depending on the exploitation of the shared-memory. If on the one hand this approach may speed-up the computation, on the other hand it does not fit most of the current Pregel-like frameworks. Therefore our focus is on the "one-to-one" model.

According to the original authors, JA-BE-JA can be ported in Pregel-like environment if those assumptions hold:

- the nodes of the graph are processed periodically and asynchronously;
- each node only has access to the state of its immediate neighbours and a small set of random nodes in the graph: no shared memory is required;
- nodes could be placed either on an independent host each, or processed in separate threads in a distributed framework;
- nodes communicate only through messages over edges of the graph;

To evaluate the suitability of JA-BE-JA in a Pregel-like environment, we first implemented it (starting from the original code of the authors) in a modified version of PeerSim that emulates the synchronisation barrier of the BSP (we refer to it as bsp-simulation). To comply with the assumptions above the algorithm has been modified in the following aspects:

- **access-to-neighbours**; An assumption at the basis of JA-BE-JA is the availability to access the neighbours and a small random sample of the graph. However, the local search operator requires also the knowledge about the neighbourhood of the neighbours. To overcome this limitation our BSP-friendly version of JA-BE-JA implements an additional message to retrieve the neighbourhood of any node. Although this gives us the ability to operate according to the assumptions, it slows down the performance. In terms of number of supersteps, as periodically one superstep is used to obtain information from the neighbours, and in term of number of messages as $2 \cdot |E|$ messages are injected in the system at each superstep;
- **threads**; The active and passive threads of JA-BE-JA have been collapsed in a single workflow. This let us to adhere to the BSP specification, where computations are kind of monolithic sequences between two supersteps.

As a consequence of this adaptation the performances of the graph partitioning decreased significantly, showing that JA-BE-JA can not be realised by adopting the BSP abstraction without a payback. To validate our findings we also implemented JA-BE-JA in Apache Spark (referred to as bsp-spark). These two points are discussed in more details in the next section.

3.1   Spark, Bagel, GraphX and Our BSP Abstraction

Apache Spark is an efficient and scalable data processor. In the last years many heterogeneous enterprises have chosen Spark [13, 22] because of the different operations available to be performed over data. Machine learning, Data Mining and Computational Science are just a bunch of viable areas where Spark is employed in. Also graph processing is aimed. Spark is bundled with Bagel and GraphX. Bagel is a plain Spark implementation of the Pregel-like APIs. GraphX is a young custom framework that aims to efficient graph processing, by exploiting its statical topology.

The *Resilient Distributed Dataset* [23] abstraction is the key concept underlying the Spark computations. A RDD is an immutable data structure distributed over several different machines. The distributed computation is achieved by the derivation of a RDD directly from a previous one or from stable storage. The chain of transformations, is called *lineage*. Fault-tolerance is faced by recomputing the lineages starting from the stable storage or a checkpoint if present.

In spite of the existing out of the box abstractions provided by Spark, we develop our own custom implementation of the BSP abstraction over Spark. In fact, both Bagel and GraphX were inadequate to satisfy the requirements as a P2P-like algorithm such as JA-BE-JA. More precisely JA-BE-JA relies on the access of a random sample of the graph for each node, whereas a GraphX's computation involves only neighbours i.e. no random sample is available. Beside, Bagel performs the computation without exposing to the developers the hooks required to calculate the total energy i.e. the edge-cut computation requires to be performed before or after a BSP-superstep in order to be stable. Our BSP-like implementation suspends the computation accordingly in order to perform the execution of the hooks.

Our BSP-like implementation also addressed several technical issues that have arisen when implementing iterative algorithms in Spark. In fact, in our case the computation is *massively* iterative, thus the RDD's lineage could eventually be so long to deplete the stack space reserved by the Java Virtual Machine. To address this issue we forced a periodic check-pointing of the RDDs on disk, to prevent the accumulation of long lineage chains. This solutions increased the amount of disk swapping and the total time of computation, but accomplished in avoiding stack overflows even for large graphs. RDD transformations could also throw "Out-of-Memory" exceptions if intermediate data (e.g. data referring to previous supersteps) were not dropped along the super-steps. Bagel does not take into account this aspect, therefore to limit this problem, we careful deallocated any intermediate data accordingly.

3.2   A Faster Implementation

To further improve our JA-BE-JA implementation, we focused on the optimization of the completion time. We notice that most part of the computation time was taken by the mechanism introduced to resolve the access-to-neighbour issue explained above. This mechanism forced us to reserve some supersteps for acquiring the information about the neighbourhood of neighbours, increasing the computation time significantly.

To avoid this problem, we implemented a mechanism in which nodes piggyback theirs neighbourhood information in the original messages. This mechanism guarantee a certain degree of consistency, but still cause the the nodes to run the local heuristic on possibly stale data.

In other words, we relaxed the assumption of the original JA-BE-JA on the consistency of the nodes knowledge about their neighbours. Although this introduced a certain degree of approximations, we greatly reduced the processing time. Section 4 supports these claims with experimental evidence.

4 Experimental Results

To evaluate the performances of our proposed solution we compared the different implementation of JA-BE-JA described in the paper:

- **original-simulation**: the original implementation provided by the authors of the JA-BE-JA paper;
- **bsp-simulation**: our implementation over PeerSim that emulates the BSP abstraction;
- **bsp-spark**: our implementation over Spark, which includes also our own BSP abstraction implementation. This implementation has also an approximated version.

The analysis of the performances relied on a set of metrics to estimate the viability of our customised version of the JA-BE-JA algorithm with the current BSP-based distributed programming frameworks. The selected metrics are:

- **edge-cut**, the number of edges that cross the boundaries of each subgraph. It corresponds to the *energy* definition given by Formula 1 in Section 2. These metrics gives an estimation about the quality of the cut, with lower value corresponding to a better cut.
- **convergence**, the number of cycles or supersteps required to achieve a substantially definitive edge-cut result. The performances are inherently dependent by the actual iterations needed;
- **speed-up**, a simple comparative value between two or more solutions that investigates the relative performances, i.e. speedup $= \frac{p_1}{p_2}$ where p_1, p_2 are two execution times of different solutions.

All the experiments have been conducted by using as input three datasets freely available online. Two datasets were taken from the Walshaw archives[1] (4elt and vibrobox) and one of the Facebook social network[2].

4.1 Bsp-Simulation vs Original-Simulation

The first set of experiments estimates the impact derived from implementing JA-BE-JA in a BSP-like environment. Every experiment has been conducted varying the number of partitions (2, 4, 8, 16, 32, 64) and manually terminated after 1000 supersteps.

Figure 1 depicts the edge-cut value obtained by original-simulation and the bsp-simulation version. The results shown are computed averaging the results of 10 runs. As it can be noticed the original-simulation provides better values than the bsp-simulation, according to the edge-cut metric.

---

[1] http://staffweb.cms.gre.ac.uk/~wc06/partition/
[2] http://socialnetworks.mpi-sws.org/

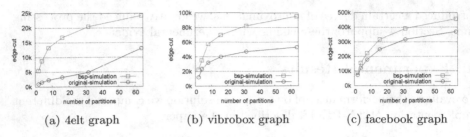

(a) 4elt graph   (b) vibrobox graph   (c) facebook graph

Fig. 1. original-simulation vs. bsp-simulation edge-cut as function of partitions number (1000 supersteps)

4.2   Bsp-Peersim vs bsp-Spark

This experiment has been conducted varying the number of partitions (2, 4, 8, 16, 32, 64) and manually terminated after 1000 supersteps.

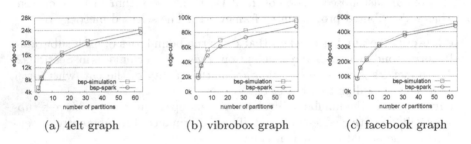

(a) 4elt graph   (b) vibrobox graph   (c) facebook graph

Fig. 2. Bsp-simulation vs. bsp-spark edge-cut as function of partitions number (1000 supersteps)

Figure 2 depicts the edge-cut value obtained by the bsp-spark and bsp-simulation. The results shown are computed averaging the results of 10 runs. In this case the edge-cut values achieved by bsp-simulation and bsp-spark are very close, indicating that bsp-simulation is able to provide a good approximation of the computations performed against a real Pregel-like distributed framework.

4.3   Comparison of Original-Simulation, bsp-Simulation and bsp-Spark

We conducted this set of experiments to evaluate the values of edge-cut obtained by the original-simulation, bsp-simulation, and bsp-spark versions of JA-BE-JA. The evaluation focuses on the amount of cycles/supersteps required by the different versions of the algorithm to converge towards a stable value in terms of edge-cut. The experiment is manually terminated after 1000 supersteps. The results shown are computed averaging the results of 10 runs. It can be observed that both the bsp-spark and bsp-simulation versions provide similar values, whereas the original-simulation offers results that are significantly better. As a consequence it can be stated that the original-simulation either underestimates the edge-cut value that can obtained by a distributed implementation or underestimates the amount of supersteps required to achieve such a value.

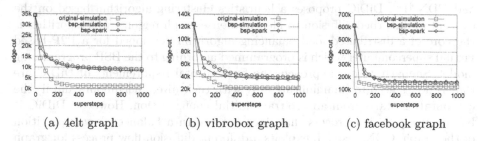

(a) 4elt graph   (b) vibrobox graph   (c) facebook graph

Fig. 3. Edge-cut of original-simulation, bsp-simulation, and bsp-spark over 1000 supersteps

4.4 Evaluation of the Approximation

This experiment measured the speed-up that we achieve by introducing a degree of approximation on the information that each vertex owns about its neighbours. Every experiment has been conducted varying the number of partitions (2, 8, 32) and averaging the results achieved by 10 distinct runs. It is easy to notice that the speed-up decreases when the number of partitions increases. Intuitively, this is due to the increased amount of "colours" that each vertex can assume. Greater is the set of possible colours, higher is the probability to have a wrong information about the colour of a vertex.

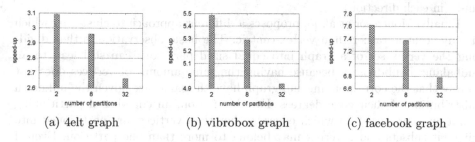

(a) 4elt graph   (b) vibrobox graph   (c) facebook graph

Fig. 4. SpeedUp of the approximated bsp-spark version compared to bsp-spark as function of the partition number

5 Discussion and Related Work

Over the years several graph clustering algorithms [8] have been proposed in the research area of parallel processing. However, almost all these algorithms require to have random access to the entire graph. This makes such solutions poor suitable for the analysis of very large graphs that cannot fit into the memory of a single machine.

On the other way, algorithms suitable for the analysis of such large graphs require only a partial knowledge on the graph. Apart from JA-BE-JA which has been extensively described in Section 2, other proposals in this area are DiDiC [3] and CDN [18]. DiDiC proposes a heuristics clustering algorithm based on the concept of disturbed diffusion to identify dense graph regions. The algorithm is the core of a distributed load balancing algorithm developed for a P2P-based virtual supercomputer which is programmed according to the BSP programming model. Similarly to our approach, the fundamental requirements of DiDiC are that i) nodes need to communicate only with their direct neighbours and ii) the computation starts from an arbitrary initial configuration. However, DiDiC is based on a diffusion process that does not return a balanced k-way partition of the graph. CDN, instead, exploits a different diffusion-flow process for graph clustering.

An alternative approach is based on a randomised computation of min-cut. Several proposals extends the randomised global min-cut algorithm edge contraction algorithm proposed by Karger [7]. The basic idea of Karger's algorithm is to pick uniformly at random an edge of the graph and merge its endpoints into a single "supernode". If you pick a random edge, likely it comes from parts of the graph that contain more edges in the first place, and this is the heuristics the algorithm is based on. The procedure is repeated until the graph includes a single pair of "supernodes" and the final graph is exploited to return the guessed min-cut. The definition of a distributed algorithm based on Karger's approach is not straightforward. A recent proposal from Ghaffari et al. [4] defines a new technique, the random layering technique, to support the distributed randomised min-cut. The algorithm is defined according to a synchronous message passing model where in each time unit, a given amount of bits can be sent over every link (in each direction).

Finally, Montresor et al. [5] proposes a different approach to clustering which is edge-centric rather than vertex-centric. The basic observation is that dividing the vertex set of a graph into equal sized partitions can still lead to an unbalanced subdivision because having the same amount of vertices does not imply that the corresponding sub-graph have the same size, given the unknown distribution of their edge degrees. For this reason, an edge-based partitioning solution is proposed, in which edges, rather than vertices, are partitioned into disjoint subsets and a vertex may belong to more than one partition. Even if this solution presents several advantages, it cannot benefit from current graph processing frameworks which are intrinsically vertex-centred.

6   Conclusions

In this paper we presented an adaptation to the JA-BE-JA algorithm to make it suitable to be efficiently computed by a BSP-like distributed computing framework. We firstly implemented JA-BE-JA over a modified version of PeerSim, which forces the simulator to comply with the BSP model. Then, we implement a second version of it in Apache Spark. To this end we first developed a BSP-like abstraction on top of it. The development of this layer was required because the existing BSP abstractions resulted inadequate to match our requirements. On top of this BSP-like abstraction we implemented a Spark version of our BSP-friendly version of JA-BE-JA. This version supports two different consistency models for data. The simpler version corresponds to a stricter consistency model which requires each vertex to have an up-to-date knowledge about its neighbourhood. The other consistency model accepts a certain degree of approximation on the information about neighbours.

Our findings show that the experiments conducted on the BSP version of Peer-Sim are much more similar to the ones effectively achievable using a distributed framework like Spark. The experiments also show that the Spark version adopting the relaxed consistency model runs significantly faster than the former one, still providing good performances in terms of edge-cut.

Acknowledgement. We greatly thank the authors of the JA-BE-JA original paper for providing the source code of their implementation, and Marco Distefano for the support in setting the machines for the tests.

References

[1] Enright, A.J., Van Dongen, S., Ouzounis, C.A.: An efficient algorithm for large-scale detection of protein families. Nucleic Acids Research 30(7), 1575–1584 (2002)

[2] Galuba, W., Aberer, K., Chakraborty, D., Despotovic, Z., Kellerer, W.: Outtweeting the twitterers - predicting information cascades in microblogs. In: Proceedings of the 3rd Wonference on Online Social Networks, WOSN 2010, p. 3. USENIX Association, Berkeley (2010)

[3] Gehweiler, J., Meyerhenke, H.: A distributed diffusive heuristic for clustering a virtual p2p supercomputer. In: IPDPS Workshops, pp. 1–8 (2010)

[4] Ghaffari, M., Kuhn, F.: Distributed minimum cut approximation. In: Afek, Y. (ed.) DISC 2013. LNCS, vol. 8205, pp. 1–15. Springer, Heidelberg (2013)

[5] Guerrieri, A., Montresor, A.: Distributed edge partitioning for graph processing. CoRR abs/1403.6270 (2014)

[6] Hendrickson, B., Leland, R.: A multi-level algorithm for partitioning graphs. In: Proceedings of the IEEE/ACM SC95 Conference on Supercomputing 1995, p. 28 (1995)

[7] Karger, D.R.: Global min-cuts in rnc, and other ramifications of a simple min-out algorithm. In: Proc. of the Fourth Annual ACM-SIAM Symposium on Discrete Algorithms, pp. 21–30. Society for Industrial and Applied Mathematics (1993)

[8] Karypis, G., Kumar, V.: Parallel multilevel k-way partitioning scheme for irregular graphs. In: Proceedings of the 1996 ACM/IEEE Conference on Supercomputing. Supercomputing 1996, IEEE Computer Society, Washington, DC (1996)

[9] Karypis, G., Kumar, V.: A fast and high quality multilevel scheme for partitioning irregular graphs. SIAM Journal on scientific Computing 20(1), 359–392 (1998)

[10] Karypis, G., Kumar, V.: Parallel multilevel series k-way partitioning scheme for irregular graphs. Siam Review 41(2), 278–300 (1999)

[11] Low, Y., Bickson, D., Gonzalez, J., Guestrin, C., Kyrola, A., Hellerstein, J.M.: Distributed graphlab: a framework for machine learning and data mining in the cloud. Proceedings of the VLDB Endowment 5(8), 716–727 (2012)

[12] Malewicz, G., Austern, M.H., Bik, A.J., Dehnert, J.C., Horn, I., Leiser, N., Czajkowski, G.: Pregel: a system for large-scale graph processing. In: Proceedings of the 2010 ACM SIGMOD International Conference on Management of Data, pp. 135–146. ACM (2010)

[13] Metz, C.: Spark: Open source superstar rewrites future of big data (June 2013), http://www.wired.com/2013/06/yahoo-amazon-amplab-spark/all/

[14] Meyerhenke, H., Monien, B., Sauerwald, T.: A new diffusion-based multilevel algorithm for computing graph partitions of very high quality. In: IEEE International Symposium on Parallel and Distributed Processing, IPDPS 2008, pp. 1–13. IEEE (2008)

[15] Meyerhenke, H., Monien, B., Schamberger, S.: Graph partitioning and disturbed diffusion. Parallel Computing 35(10), 544–569 (2009)

[16] Montresor, A., Jelasity, M.: Peersim: A scalable p2p simulator. In: Ninth International Conference on Peer-to-Peer Computing 2009, pp. 99–100. IEEE (2009)

[17] Rahimian, F., Payberah, A., Girdzijauskas, S., Jelasity, M., Haridi, S.: Ja-beja: A distributed algorithm for balanced graph partitioning. In: 2013 IEEE 7th International Conference on Self-Adaptive and Self-Organizing Systems (SASO), pp. 51–60 (September 2013)

[18] Ramaswamy, L., Gedik, B., Liu, L.: A distributed approach to node clustering in decentralized peer-to-peer networks. IEEE Trans. Parallel Distrib. Syst. 16(9), 814–829 (2005)

[19] Sanders, P., Schulz, C.: Engineering multilevel graph partitioning algorithms. In: Demetrescu, C., Halldórsson, M.M. (eds.) ESA 2011. LNCS, vol. 6942, pp. 469–480. Springer, Heidelberg (2011)

[20] Viswanath, B., Mislove, A., Cha, M., Gummadi, K.P.: On the evolution of user interaction in facebook. In: Proceedings of the 2nd ACM Workshop on Online Social Networks, WOSN 2009, pp. 37–42. ACM, New York (2009), http://doi.acm.org/10.1145/1592665.1592675

[21] Walshaw, C.: The graph partitioning archive (June 2012), http://staffweb.cms.gre.ac.uk/~wc06/partition/

[22] Zaharia, M.: The growing spark community (October 2013), http://databricks.com/blog/2013/10/27/the-growing-spark-community.html

[23] Zaharia, M., Chowdhury, M., Das, T., Dave, A., Ma, J., McCauley, M., Franklin, M.J., Shenker, S., Stoica, I.: Resilient distributed datasets: A fault-tolerant abstraction for in-memory cluster computing. In: Proceedings of the 9th USENIX Conference on Networked Systems Design and Implementation, p. 2. USENIX Association (2012)

[24] Zaharia, M., Chowdhury, M., Franklin, M.J., Shenker, S., Stoica, I.: Spark: Cluster computing with working sets. In: Proceedings of the 2nd USENIX Conference on Hot Topics in Cloud Computing, HotCloud 2010, p. 10. USENIX Association, Berkeley (2010), http://dl.acm.org/citation.cfm?id=1863103.1863113

A Visual Programming Model to Implement Coarse-Grained DSP Applications on Parallel and Heterogeneous Clusters

Farouk Mansouri, Sylvain Huet, and Dominique Houzet

GIPSA-LAB, 11 rue des Mathmatiques
Grenoble Campus BP46, France
firstname.lastname@gipsa-lab.grenoble-inp.fr

Abstract. The digital signal processing (DSP) applications are one of the biggest consumers of computing. They process a big data volume which is represented with a high accuracy. They use complex algorithms, and must satisfy a time constraints in most of cases. In the other hand, it's necessary today to use parallel and heterogeneous architectures in order to speedup the processing, where the best examples are the supercomputers "Tianhe-2" and "Titan" from the top500 ranking. These architectures could contain several connected nodes, where each node includes a number of generalist processor (multi-core) and a number of accelerators (many-core) to finally allows several levels of parallelism. However, for DSP programmers, it's still complicated to exploit all these parallelism levels to reach good performance for their applications. They have to design their implementation to take advantage of all heterogeneous computing units, taking into account the architecture specificities of each of them: communication model, memory management, data management, jobs scheduling and synchronization ... etc. In the present work, we characterize DSP applications, and based on their distinctiveness, we propose a high level visual programming model and an execution model in order to drop down their implementations and in the same time make desirable performances.

1 Introduction

The DSP applications require a high computing power. They process increased data volume (data length) which reach ten or so of Go. Also, data units are represented more and more precisely (data floating point encoding), from single precision (32 digits) to quadruple precision (128 digits). They use complex algorithms (time complexity) in linear, quadratic or exponential time, and are usually constrained in execution time (latency or throughput).

To satisfy this need, it's possible today to get a Tera-flop computing power with a thousand dollars price by using parallel and heterogeneous hardware architectures, which include generalist multi-core processors (Intel Xeon or AMD Opteron), supported by many-core accelerators (GPU, Xeon phi, Cell) and structured in the form of a cluster of connected nodes with a high bandwidth network.

L. Lopes et al. (Eds.): Euro-Par 2014 Workshops, Part I, LNCS 8805, pp. 141–152, 2014.

Certainly, these architectures can be the best response for computing power requirements of DSP applications. However, they present some difficulties of use. In fact, to produce performance with that last, the programmer has to deal with heterogeneous computing units using different languages or API. He has to manage synchronization, memory allocation, data transfer and the load balance between the processes. Consequently, programming models are necessary to hide all this hardware specifications, and produce easily and efficiently the desired performance.

In the present work, we propose a visual programming model based on data flow graph (DFG) model which allows to users to easily express their applications. It includes an execution model (Runtime) based on StarPU, and adapted for DSP implementing on heterogeneous platform (CPU, GPU, Cell) and dynamically scheduling of tasks on computational units. First, we present in section 2 the DSP applications and highlight their characteristics and distinctiveness. In the section 3, we give the features to efficiently implement them and discuss the existing programming models to do that. In the section 4, we describe our programming model and explain its conception parts. Finely, in the section 5, we present experimentations and results of applying our model of programming (MoP) on a real world application.

2   Distinctiveness of DSP Applications

DSP applications are in form of repetitive (iterative) processing of data set of input digital signals, which produce an output signals or a results (Fig.1). In the classic algorithmic aspect as shown in the example Algorithm 1, it represents the main loop which iteratively process all data units using several functions.

Fig. 1. Illustration of DSP applications

Theses functions, also called operators or kernels, fire each data unit of input signal, where each of them represents an independent processing with some input and output arguments. So, in almost cases of DSP applications, it's possible to model them in form of DFG [9,2], where nodes of the graph represent the kernels and the edges represent the data trading between operators as a flow. The figure (Fig.2) illustrates this DFG model representing the given example in Algorithm 1. That model emphasizes the movement of data and models programs as a series of connections. Explicitly defined input and output arguments synchronize operations. Where an operation runs as soon as all of its inputs become valid. Thus, that model are inherently parallel and allows to user to easily express task parallelism on his application. In addition, in DSP applications, all input data units are processed using the same actors (kernels), for example in video processing, each input image is processed in the same manner using the same

---

Algorithm 1. Synthetic DSP application

Input: Number of iterations (Nbr). Input data set ($Data_{in}$).
Output: Output data set ($Data_{out}$).
1: **for each** $Data_{unit}$ in $Data_{in}$ **do**
2:     $Var_1 \leftarrow Producer()$
3:     $Var_2 \leftarrow kernel_1(Var_1)$
4:     $Var_{3_1} \leftarrow Kernel_2(Var_2)$
5:     $Var_{3_2} \leftarrow Kernel_3(Var_2)$
6:     $Var_4 \leftarrow Kernel_4(Var_{3_1}, Var_{3_2})$
7:     $Var_5 \leftarrow Kernel_5(Var_4, Var'_4)$
8:     $Var'_4 \leftarrow Var_4$
9:     $Consumer(Var_5)$
10: **end for**

---

algorithm. So, the idea is to overlap the execution of multiple DFG, where each DFG processes one date unit. Also, according to the data kind and the algorithm of each kernel, it's interesting in most of cases to offload the execution of certain of kernels on a massively parallel computation unit (accelerators) like GPU, Xeon Phi or Cell.

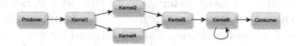

Fig. 2. Data flow graph (DFG) model of DSP application (the example)

Taking into account these characteristics, we set up some rules to apply in implementation and execution of DSP applications on parallel and heterogeneous architectures: First, express task parallelism using the DFG modeling. It allows to highlight the dependencies between the tasks and detect the tasks able to be executed in parallel. Second, optimize data parallelism. Identify the tasks according to their Flynn taxonomy [6]. The MISD (Memory bounds) tasks are oriented to generalist processors and the SIMD tasks (Compute bounds) towards the accelerators. Third, implement graph parallelism. In fact, in order to optimize the occupancy of computing units composing the cluster, deal with several graphs to process several input data unit in the same time.

In the next section (Section 3), based on extracted distinctiveness and the rules cited above, we focus on the implementation side of the DSP applications, and we discuss on which programming model is more suitable for programmers to easily and efficiently porting these applications on parallel and heterogeneous architectures.

3   Implementing DSP Applications on Clusters

As presented in the preceding section (Section 2), the DSP applications have some characteristics that programmers must exploit in order to take advantage of targeted heterogeneous and parallel architectures. First: To highlight the kernels able to be executed in parallel (task parallelism), they have to express their algorithm in the form of a set of tasks using threads or process technologies. They have to manage these threads for communicating between them or to be synchronized, according to the application's dependencies on the both shared and distributed memory architectures. In addition, to profit from the accelerator's capacity to speedup the SIMD processing (data parallelism), the user has to offload a part of their task towards these compute units. To do this, he has to deal with memory allocation on accelerators, copy-in the input data, launch the execution, copy-out the results and finally freedom the used memory zone. Also, the DSP applications are mostly iterative, so it's a good idea to unroll the main loop of the application and therefore process a number of data units in the same time (graph parallelism) in order to increase the occupancy of computing units. To do that, the code writers must duplicate the process (thread) in charge of executing the main loop taking care to guarantee the data coherence by restricting some variables or sharing others. All this implementation features are necessary for porting DSP applications on heterogeneous clusters but not enough to optimize productivity of the hardware. In fact, the programmer must cope with others difficulties like communication cost which must be masked by overlap it with the computation time, or the load balancing between the computational units which must be assumed by a good scheduling of tasks.

Applying all these implementation rules is very hard. The programmer has to combine the handling of some API, language or extension of language which are low level for certain or restricted to specific hardware for others. For example, the programmer has to use Pthread , TBB [13] or OpenMP [4] to generate threads and express task parallelism on each node of the cluster (shared memory architecture), but also the MPI [11] or PGAS [5] model to manage them by creating processes onto many nodes (distributed memory architectures). He has to use CUDA [14] or OpenCL [10] to address accelerators like the GPU, Cell or Xeon-Phi and offload a part of a SIMD work on it. In the other case, the higher level tools like OpenACC [8], OmpSS [3] or StarPU [1] which are based on the low level tools, must be the solution. They offer more abstraction of the hardware and can target the complete cluster. But some of them are restricted to a particular MoP, for example OpenAcc express only the data parallelism. Others of them like OmpSS are rather oriented to decorating an existing sequential code by inserting some PRAGMA directive and transforming it at compilation time into a parallel code. The rest, based on API like StarPU is, in our opinion, the most adapted programming models to implement high level applications on heterogeneous cluster. It offers an interface based on a large routines and structures which the programmers can use to design their applications, and in addition proposes a runtime which manages the tasks, their dependencies and dynamically schedule their executions on the architecture. However, it's not adapted (specified) to DSP applications as characterized in the section 2 with their iterative and repetitive form, and also it's still complicated to handle because of the number of routines and data structures proposed to the user as interface to implement their applications. Because of these reasons, we propose in the next section, a programming model based on a DFG model to make easier the application modelling and automatize the generation of the directional acyclic graph (DAG) of tasks in order to adapt StarPU to the implementing of DSP applications on heterogeneous cluster.

4   Proposed Programming Model

We propose, in this section, a visual programming model as an extension of StarPU programming model [1] which we enrich by giving some functionalities specified to DSP applications, in order to allow for programmers to implement easily and efficiently their programs on parallel and heterogeneous clusters. Our MoP is a high level abstraction concept. The programmers don't have to worry about several architecture specificities, like memory management, task creation and synchronization, load balancing etc... They can implicitly express task, data and graph parallelisms in their implementations to optimally take advantage of hardware. Also, because it's based on StarPU, our MoP take in charge shared and distributed memory architectures, and deal with many-node cluster using the messages passing interface (MPI [11]).

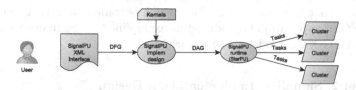

Fig. 3. SignalPU design: Three levels of processing

Bellow, we present our proposed MoP in form of 3 levels of processing as shown in the figure (Fig.3). First, the user can easily express his application, by using an XML interface, in the form of DFG. Thus, he is saved to manipulate the StarPU's API for creating tasks, for managing the buffers between each couple of tasks, or for submitting jobs onto the corresponding computation unit. Second, the implementation of application is designed by using some functionalities like: graphs unfolding techniques [12], pipelining of tasks, buffers re-use, initialization saving ... etc. The aim is to produce a DAG of independent tasks. Also here, the user doesn't have to deal with the API to unroll the main loop or to manage necessary memory buffers for that.Finally, in the third level, the StarPU runtime is used to physically manage the set of tasks and execute it on the cluster according to a dynamic scheduling to balance the load and favour the locality.

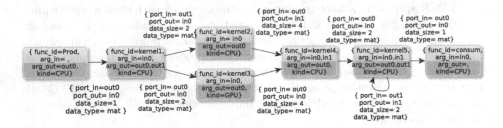

Fig. 4. The DFG-XML of the synthetic DSP application

Next, we describe all these steps of our proposed MoP with more details through a synthetic example of DSP application:

4.1 Level 1: SignalPU DFG-XML Interface

In this step, programmer has to express his application using the DFG-XML interface. First, he has to describe each kernel (operator) of his algorithm in the form of a node (vertex) using an XML structure. He has to put the name of functions which will be called in the code, the number of input and output arguments of these functions, and the architecture kind corresponding to each of them (CPU, GPU, Cell, Xeon Phi ...). Second, he has to describe in the same manner all data flows in the form of graph edges with a structure including information about type and size of data which is traded between kernels. After that, a DFG of application is produced as exemplified in the figure Fig.4, which represents DFG-XML modelling of Algorithm 1.

4.2 Level 2: SignalPU Implementation Design

In this step, illustrated in the figure Fig.5, a DAG of tasks is iteratively produced from the result of the previous processing level (the DFG-XML interface) using some functionalities adapted to DSP applications. This DAG represents a set of independent tasks linked by several kinds of data dependencies (Fork-join, producer-consumer, inter-graph producer-consumer), witch are ready to be concurrently executed on the cluster. The aim of this step is to design the execution in order to optimally take advantage of all levels of parallelism (task, data, graph parallelism) by overcoming overheads due to the execution management, like memory management (Allocation, affectation and free of buffers), data management (Copy-in, copy-out), tasks management (Creation, dependencies management, scheduling, status updating, destruction) ... etc. Next, we describe used functionalities to do that:

First, from the DFG-XML model of application, we create a set of "codlet" which is a StarPU structure and represents a mould of tasks. So, for each node in the DFG we match a "codlet" which contains all informations about the corresponding kernel (Number of input arguments, the number of output arguments,

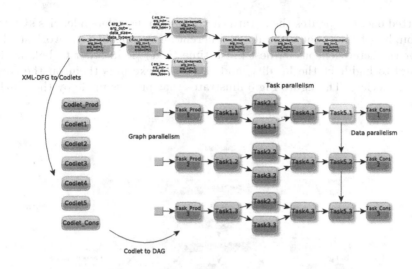

Fig. 5. The creation process of DAG of tasks of synthetic DSP application

function identifiers, architecture kinds ...), which will characterise his tasks children. After that, based on unfolding techniques [12] which allow to unroll the main loop of the application to unravel hidden concurrency, we iteratively create tasks corresponding to all codlets, and progressively we connect them according to the dependency informations contained in the DFG-XML structure (Data type, data size, input argument, output argument, input node, output node). Also, during that process, we affect in turn to tasks the corresponding buffers according to a "First available-First affected" rule. So a buffer is affected to a new task, if and only if it's not still used by the old "sister" task. So, by using that technique named "Buffers re-use", we reduce the overhead due to memory management by the allocation and the freeing. In addition, in order to reduce overhead due to tasks management, we limit the number of submitted tasks by using pipelining functionality. So, at runtime, only a fixed levels of task is managed (Dependencies, scheduling, task status updating, ... etc), where each pipeline level corresponds to a graph level in the DAG. Finally, we use a functionality which we call "Initialisation saving" to preserve the initialisation part of each task. So, each task leaves his initialisation data to his sister task on each device. Thus, the production or the copy of that initialisation data is made only one time per kernel per device.

4.3   Level 3: SignalPU Runtime (StarPU)

In this step, the submitted DAG of tasks generated in the previous level is physically processed by StarPU runtime. So, he manages tasks by creating the submitted one, he updates their status according to data dependencies synchronization, he schedules them thanks to different algorithms like the work stealing (ws) or the heterogeneous earliest finish time (heft) [1] in order to balance the load and to highlight the locality, and finally, he executes them on the corresponding devices. The figure Fig.6 illustrates that process made by the StarPU runtime.

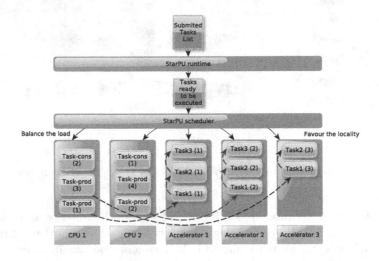

Fig. 6. StarPU runtime's levels

Thus, according to these three steps of our proposed MoP, the programmer can easily implement his DSP applications in high abstraction level, and efficiently take advantage of the optimizations: Task parallelism (TP) by extracting tasks in the DFG which are able to be executed in the same time. Data parallelism (DP) by off-loading some tasks on (SIMD) accelerators. Graph parallelism (GP) by overlapping the processing of some graphs. And the optimally scheduling tanks to load balance versus data locality using StarPU runtime.

5   Validation

In this section we present a real world experimentation in order to validate our approach and demonstrate the interest of its usage. We use the saliency application to process a set of images on the heterogeneous CPU-GPU architecture. First, we describe the saliency application and give its algorithm. Then, we explain its implementation using our programming model. And finally, we give the results and discuss their impacts.

5.1   The Saliency Application

Based on the primate's retina, the visual saliency model is used to locate regions of interest, i.e. the capability of human vision to focus on particular places in a visual scene. The implementation that we use is the one proposed by [7]. His algorithm (Algorithm 2) is: First, the input image (r-im) is filtered by a Hanning function to reduce intensity at the edges. In the frequency domain,(cf-fim) is processed with a 2-D Gabor filter bank using six orientations and four frequency bands. The 24 partial maps (cf-$maps[i; j]$) are moved in the spatial domain (c-$maps[i; j]$). Short interactions inhibit or excite the pixels, depending on the orientation and frequency band of partial maps. The resulting values are normalized between a dynamic range before applying Itti's method for normalization, and suppressing values lower than a certain threshold. Finally, all the partial maps are accumulated into a single map that is the saliency map of the static pathway.

Algorithm 2. Static pathway of visual model

Input: An image r_im of size $w \cdot l$
Output: The saliency map
1: $r\_fim \leftarrow Hanning filter(r\_im)$
2: $cf\_fim \leftarrow FFT(r\_fim)$
3: **for** $i \leftarrow 1$ **to** orientations **do**
4:     **for** $j \leftarrow 1$ **to** frequencies **do**
5:         $cf\_maps[i, j] \leftarrow GaborFilter(cf\_fim, i, j)$
6:         $c\_maps[i, j] \leftarrow IFFT(cf\_maps[i, j])$
7:         $r\_maps[i, j] \leftarrow Interactions(c\_maps[i, j])$
8:         $r\_normaps[i, j] \leftarrow Normalizations(r\_maps[i, j])$
9:     **end for**
10: **end for**
11: $saliency\_map \leftarrow Summation(r\_normaps[i, j])$

5.2   The SignalPU Implementation

To implement the application with our programming model, the first step is to model its algorithm (Algorithm 2) given before in the form of DFG-XML using the SignalPU interface. For this, we represent each of all functions ($Hanning filter()$, $FFT()$, $GaborFilter()$, $IFFT()$, $Interactions()$, $Normalizations()$, $Summation()$) with a node in the graph including the characteristics of each of them (architecture kind, input arguments, output arguments). Then, we represent the data flow between each twice kernels with an edge in the graph including its characteristics (data type, data size). In the figure (Fig.7) we present the DFG result of this step.

   At runtime, the DFG-XML description of the saliency application is analyzed and DAG of independent tasks is iteratively generated, where each task represents the execution of each kernel's code (function's code) for each image on

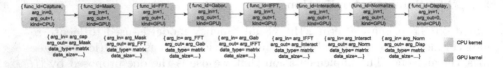

Fig. 7. The DFG-XML model of the visual saliency application

the corresponding computation unit (CPU,GPU). Thus, we haven't to use the StarPU's API for describing the application's tasks. Also, we have not to manage the buffer's allocating and freeing. We haven't written the main loop which processes the set of input images, and don't have to unroll it. The StarPU's API is almost entirely masked.

5.3 The Results

In this subsection, we present the results of experimentations where we show the performance provided by the implementation based on our programming model using the proposed optimizations (Graph unfolding, Dynamic scheduling, Buffers reuse, Tasks pipelining, Initialization saving). The aim is to highlight the performance gain by using these optimizations to take advantage of parallelism and heterogeneity of clusters. The architecture used for the experimentations is a CPU-GPU node composed of a 4 cores CPU (intel-i7 core) and 3 GPU (NVIDIA Quadro 400, NVIDIA Quadro 400, NVIDIA GeForce GTX TITAN).

In the figure Fig.8, we present the total time necessary to process 1000 images (512x512 pixels) of 3 executions using different processing units. This total time is composed of the effective execution time on the processing units, plus the sleeping time which represents the time went without doing anything on the device, plus the overhead time which represents additional time consumed by managing the work (Tasks management, Scheduling, Buffer management, ...). For the first execution, we use 1 CPU core and 1 GPU (Quadro) to process images. In the GPU bar chart, we can show that execution time is higher compared to overhead time and sleeping time thanks to graph unfolding optimization which reduce waiting time. In the CPU bar chart, execution time is lower because the application is more GPU need. In the second experimentation, we use 1 CPU core and 2 GPU (Quadro). Here, we can show that total time necessary decreases compared to the first execution, so we note a speedup equal to 1.7 x. Also, thanks to dynamic scheduling, we can see the result of load balance between the 2 GPUs processing unit, thus the execution time is the same in the both GPU bar chart. In the third execution, we use 1 CPU core and 3 GPUs to enhance performance. And, we obtain a speedup equal to 2.2x compared to the first execution. Also here, we can note the advantage of using dynamic scheduling to reduce execution time and balance the load, and the graph unfolding to reduce sleeping time. But also the advantage of using the buffers reuse technique, the pipelining of tasks and the initialization data saving to stabilize overhead time.

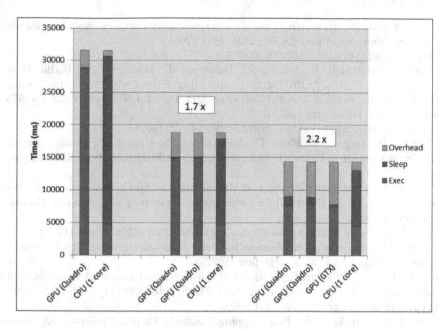

Fig. 8. Processing time of 1000 images using different processing units

6   Conclusion

In this paper we presented our proposed programming model used to implement DSP applications, allowing a high level abstraction from the hardware specificities thanks to its visual data-flow programming capabilities, and in the same time, producing a good performance of application's implementation through exploiting task parallelism, data parallelism, graph parallelism (graph unfolding), and dynamic scheduling. First, we described DSP applications and specified their characteristics in order to implement them in an optimal way. Then, we proposed an XML interface to easily describe DSP applications in the form of a DFG model. In addition, we proposed an execution model based on StarPU runtime and exploiting some techniques. We used unfolding techniques to construct DAG of independent tasks, which we submit in pipeline mode and configured to reuse a static buffers and to save the initializations data on devices in order to reduce overhead time, after that we dynamically schedule and process them on heterogeneous and parallel architecture. Finally, we experimented our MoP on the real-world saliency application and shown that's easier to use our programming model to design it, but at the same time, it's possible to efficiently take advantage of architecture's power to speed up the execution.

References

1. Augonnet, C., Thibault, S., Namyst, R.: StarPU: a Runtime System for Scheduling Tasks over Accelerator-Based Multicore Machines. Research Report RR-7240. INRIA (2010)

2. Bhattacharya, B., Bhattacharyya, S.: Parameterized dataflow modeling for dsp systems. Trans. Sig. Proc. 49(10), 2408–2421 (2001),
   http://dx.doi.org/10.1109/78.950795
3. Bueno, J., Martinell, L., Duran, A., Farreras, M., Martorell, X., Badia, R.M., Ayguade, E., Labarta, J.: Productive cluster programming with ompss. In: Jeannot, E., Namyst, R., Roman, J. (eds.) Euro-Par 2011, Part I. LNCS, vol. 6852, pp. 555–566. Springer, Heidelberg (2011),
   http://dl.acm.org/citation.cfm?id=2033345.2033405
4. Chandra, R., Dagum, L., Kohr, D., Maydan, D., McDonald, J., Menon, R.: Parallel Programming in OpenMP. Morgan Kaufmann Publishers Inc., San Francisco (2001)
5. Chen, W.Y.: Optimizing Partitioned Global Address Space Programs for Cluster Architectures. Ph.D. thesis, EECS Department, University of California, Berkeley (December 2007),
   http://www.eecs.berkeley.edu/Pubs/TechRpts/2007/EECS-2007-140.html
6. Flynn, M.: Some computer organizations and their effectiveness. IEEE Transactions on Computers C-21(9), 948–960 (1972)
7. Itti, L., Koch, C., Niebur, E.: A model of saliency-based visual attention for rapid scene analysis. IEEE Trans. Pattern Anal. Mach. Intell. 20(11), 1254–1259 (1998),
   http://dx.doi.org/10.1109/34.730558
8. Kirk, D.B., Hwu, W.M.W.: Programming Massively Parallel Processors: A Hands-on Approach, 1st edn. Morgan Kaufmann Publishers Inc., San Francisco (2010)
9. Lee, E., Messerschmitt, D.: Static scheduling of synchronous data flow programs for digital signal processing. IEEE Transactions on Computers C-36(1), 24–35 (1987)
10. Munshi, A., Gaster, B., Mattson, T., Ginsburg, D.: OpenCL Programming Guide. OpenGL, Pearson Education (2011),
    http://books.google.fr/books?id=M-Sve_KItQwC
11. Pacheco, P.S.: Parallel Programming with MPI. Morgan Kaufmann Publishers Inc., San Francisco (1996)
12. Parhi, K., Messerschmitt, D.: Static rate-optimal scheduling of iterative data-flow programs via optimum unfolding. IEEE Transactions on Computers 40(2), 178–195 (1991)
13. Reinders, J.: Intel threading building blocks - outfitting C++ for multi-core processor parallelism. O'Reilly (2007)
14. Sanders, J., Kandrot, E.: CUDA by Example: An Introduction to General-Purpose GPU Programming, 1st edn. Addison-Wesley Professional (2010)

Fast Parallel Connected Components Algorithms on GPUs

Guojing Cong[1] and Paul Muzio[2]

[1] IBM TJ Watson research center, Yorktown Heights, NY 10598, USA
gcong@us.ibm.com
[2] CUNY High Performance Computing Center, Staten Island, New York, 10324
p.muzio@csi.cuny.edu

Abstract. We study parallel connected components algorithms on GPUs in comparison with CPUs. Although straightforward implementation of PRAM algorithms performs relatively better on GPUs than on CPUs, the GPU memory subsystem performance is poor due to non-coalesced random accesses.

We argue that generic sort-based access coalescing is too costly on GPUs. We propose a new coalescing technique and a new meta algorithm to improve locality and performance. Our optimization achieves up to 2.7 times speedup over the straightforward implementation. Interestingly, our optimization also works well on CPUs.

Comparing the best-performing algorithms on GPUs and CPUs, we find our new algorithm is the fastest on GPUs and the second fastest on CPUs, while the parallel Rem's algorithm is the fastest on CPUs but does not perform well on GPUs due to path divergence.

Keywords: Multi-core, GPU, CPU, Connected Components.

1 Introduction

GPUs have become alternative platforms to traditional CPUs for algorithms with substantial data parallelism. We study connected components (CC) algorithms with large, sparse inputs on GPUs in comparison with CPUs. CC is representative of graph problems with fast theoretic parallel algorithms that oftentimes perform poorly on cache-based machines due to irregular memory accesses.

Prior studies show that several parallel graph algorithms perform better on GPUs than on CPUs (e.g., see [12,10,15]). Our experiments with CC confirm the performance advantage of GPUs for the straightforward implementation of PRAM algorithms. The memory subsystem performance is nonetheless still poor due to non-coalesced random accesses. We argue that generic sort based coalescing is ineffective for improving performance on GPUs unless the hardware coalescing width is increased.

Several architectural features (see Section 2 for details) make it challenging for locality optimization on GPUs. The amount of GPU device memory is limited, and the overhead to improve locality is large while the performance gain

L. Lopes et al. (Eds.): Euro-Par 2014 Workshops, Part I, LNCS 8805, pp. 153–164, 2014.

is modest. Large asymptotic overhead in most cache-friendly and I/O-efficient algorithms makes it unlikely for them to perform well on GPUs.

We propose a low-cost technique to improve coalescing for CC on GPUs. We aslo present a new meta algorithm motivated by evolution random graph theory that further improves locality for graft-and-shortcut based algorithms. Our implementation achieves up to 2.7 times speedup over the straightforward implementation. Interestingly, the same optimizations apply on our target CPU, and our implementation beats the best prior cache-friendly implementation.

We rank the performance of the optimized algorithms on GPUs and CPUs. Our new algorithm is the fastest on the target GPU and the second fastest on the target CPU, while parallel Rem's algorithm is the fastest on the CPU but does not perform very well on the GPU. On average the best algorithms on the two platforms have comparable performance over a range of input graphs.

Our study focuses primarily on random graphs and scale-free graphs [11]. Both have small diameters. They are the most challenging inputs in terms of memory performance. The input graph is represented as $G = (V, E)$, with $|V| = n$ and $|E| = m = O(n)$. We create a random graph with n vertices and m edges by randomly adding m unique edges to the vertex set. Scale-free graphs are generated using the R-MAT model [6] with a=0.45, b=0.15, c=0.15, d=0.25. In ranking the best implementations on the two platforms, we also include a large-diameter graph and a real-life twitter graph. We defer the introduction of these graphs to Section 6.

The rest of the paper is organized as follows. Section 2 introduces the target platforms and the baseline algorithm. Section 3 evaluates prior techniques for improving locality on GPUs. Section 4 presents an optimization for the graft-and-shortcut approach, and section 5 introduces the meta algorithm that further improves coalescing for CC. Section 6 ranks the best implementations on the two platforms. In section 7 we give our conclusion and future work.

2   The Platforms and the Base-Line Algorithm

GPUs and CPUs are markedly different. CPU cores typically run at higher frequency than GPU cores, and exploit instruction level parallelism through out-of-order execution. Large caches, sophisticated prefetching, and branch prediction are common in mainstream CPUs. In contrast, the streaming multiprocessor (SM) in GPUs is relatively simple. Each SM has a single fetch unit and multiple scalar units. An instruction is fetched and executed in parallel on all scalar units for a group of data elements (a warp). *Path divergence* occurs on a conditional branch where threads take different paths. The threads on diverging paths are serialized. While each hardware thread is relatively light-weight and weak, GPU employs a large number of them to hide memory latency.

We use NVIDIA Tesla S2050 and IBM P755 as our GPU based platform and CPU based platform, respectively. These machines were introduced to the market at approximately the same time. P755 has 4 Power7 chips. Each chip has 8 cores running at 3.61 GHz, and each core is capable of four-way simultaneous multithreading (SMT). P755 supports up to 128 threads. Each Power7 core has 32KB L1, 256KB L2, and 4MB on-chip L3 caches. The Tesla S2050 has four Fermi GPUs running at 1.15GHz. We use one GPU as we study only shared-memory algorithms. Each GPU has 14 SMs, 448 cores, and 2GB global memory. Fermi has 64 KB configurable shared memory and L1 cache. The shared L2 is 768K.

We use a variant of the classic Shiloach-Vishkin algorithm (SV) [19] as our baseline algorithm on GPUs. We denote this algorithm CC when in no danger of confusion with the problem it solves. CC was shown to run faster than SV on CPUs [4].

CC uses m processors. It starts with n isolated vertices. Each processor inspects an edge, and tries to graft the larger endpoint (by index) to the smaller one. Grafting creates $k \geq 1$ connected components, and each component is then shortcut to a single super-vertex. Grafting and shortcutting continue on the reduced graph $G' = (V', E')$ with V' being the set of super-vertices and E' being the set of edges among super-vertices until no grafting is possible. The formal description of one graft-and-shortcut iteration in CC is shown in Algorithm 1.[1].

Algorithm 1. $CC(El, D)$, El is the input edge list, $D[i]$ is the current component vertex i belongs to

1: **for** $1 \leq i \leq m$ parallel **do** {graft}
2:     **if** $D[El[i].u] < D[El[i].v]$ **then**
3:         $D[D[El[i].v]] \leftarrow D[El[i].u]$
4:     **end if**
5: **end for**
6: **for** $1 \leq i \leq n$ parallel **do** {shortcut}
7:     **while** $D[i] \neq D[D[i]]$ **do**
8:         $D[i] \leftarrow D[D[i]]$
9:     **end while**
10: **end for**

Figure 1 shows the best performance of CC, with up to 128 threads on P755 and 14 SMs, 448 cores on S2050, on three inputs – a random graph with 50M vertices, 200M edges, a random graph with 100M vertices, 200M edges, and a scale-free graph with 20M vertices, 200M edges. For these inputs, CC is about 2.5 to 4 times faster on S2050 than on P755.

In our experiments, unless noted otherwise, we use maximum input sizes that fit in the GPU global memory. In Figure 1 the performance on P755 peaked with 32 threads instead of 128 threads. The performance on S2050 peaked at 12 SMs instead of 14 SMs. Our experiments confirm that straightforward implementation of PRAM algorithms tends to run faster on GPUs than on CPUs.

The memory subsystem on neither platform delivers data fast enough to keep all processors busy. This is largely due to the indirect, random accesses in CC. As profiling shows that *graft* dominates the execution time (on both platforms

---

[1] For simplicity and following the tradition of SV, Algorithm 1. assumes that each edge (u,v) appears twice in the edge list as $< u, v >$ and $< v, u >$. In our implementation each edge appears once to limit memory consumption.

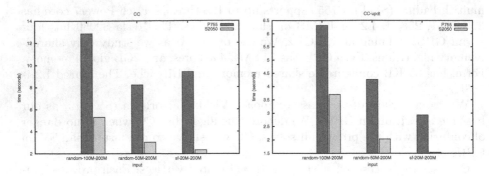

Fig. 1. Straightforward implementation　　　　**Fig. 2.** With coalescing

between 90 and 95 percent of time is spent on *graft*), in our study we focus our optimization effort on *graft*.

3　Locality Optimization on GPUs

Coalescing, that is, merging multiple accesses to memory locations within a short range into one transaction, is critical to performance on GPUs. We consider improving locality to facilitate coalescing (improved locality also results in better cache performance).

Cache-friendly sequential algorithms on CPUs abound in literature (e.g., see [1,13]). Cache-friendly *parallel* algorithms are proposed for modern multicore systems (e.g., see [5,2,8,3]). In practice these parallel algorithms are oftentimes too complex to implement, and have very large algorithmic overhead. Cong and Makarychev proposed *coordinated scheduling* of parallel irregular accesses to improve locality [9]. On cache-based platforms their implementation (*Schd*) achieved superior performance over the straightforward implementation for CC and other graph problems. Unfortunately, in our experiments even Schd incurs too much overhead relative to its performance gain on GPUs.

Chiang *et al.* proposed a sort-based PRAM simulation approach for designing graph algorithms with good locality [7]. A generic sort based approach to order memory accesses for coalescing works as follows for *graft*. Each edge $(u, v) \in El$ is augmented as an edge $(u, v, u', v') \in El'$. Here u' and v' store the component that u and v belong to, respectively. El' is first sorted with u as key, and all $El[i].u' = D[El[i].u]$ $(1 \leq i \leq m)$ are retrieved. Then El' is sorted again with v as key, and all $El[i].v' = D[El[i].v]$ $(1 \leq i \leq m)$ are retrieved. After two rounds of sorting, $u' = D[u]$ and $v' = D[v]$ for each edge $(u, v, u', v') \in El'$. Note that the retrievals of $D[u]$ and $D[v]$ corresponding to line 2 in Algorithm 1. are coalesced. Random accesses at line 3 can be handled similarly.

We analyze the overhead and performance gain of sorting relative to line 2 in Algorithm 1.. We argue that even the fastest integer sort on current GPUs (i.e., radix sort [18]) is too costly for improving coalescing.

Assume on a GPU $w > 1$ is the coalescing width, that is, random accesses to a range of w words are coalesced. Let T_{orig} be the memory access time for retrieving Ds on line 2 of Algorithm 1., and T_{sort} be the memory access time used in the sort based approach, respectively.

Theorem 1. *For a graph of n vertices and $m = O(n)$ edges, it is necessary that $w > 2^{8/41 \log n}$ for $T_{sort} < T_{orig}$.*

Proof. Let S and R be the time of sequentially accessing $2m$ words and the time of randomly accessing $2m$ words, respectively. $T_{orig} \geq R$.

In the sort-based approach, as $w > 1$, a linear ordering on the accesses is not necessary for coalescing. The n vertices are partitioned into blocks of size w. El' is sorted with the block *ids* of the endpoints as keys. First $El[i].u/w$ is used as key for the retrieval of $D[El[i].u]$, then $El[i].v/w$ is used ask key for the retrieval of $D[El[i].v]$. Each pass of radix sort works with b key bits. It takes $\frac{\log(n/w)}{b}$ passes to sort m keys ranging between 1 and n/w. Computing the histogram in each pass requires one round of sequential accesses to $4m$ words (u' and v' are carried along) that costs $2S$. Copying to the target locations takes $\lceil 2^b/w \rceil S$ time. Thus T_{sort} is at least

$$2 \left(\frac{\log \frac{n}{w}}{b} \right) \left(1 + \left\lceil \frac{2^b}{w} \right\rceil \right) 2S = 4(\log n - \log w) \frac{(1 + \lceil \frac{2^b}{w} \rceil)}{b} S$$

For any given n and w, T_{sort} is minimized at $b = \log w$ with the value $8(\log n - \log w)S/\log w$. In order that $T_{sort} < T_{orig}$, we need $8(\log n - \log w)S/\log w < R < wS$, and we have $w > 2^{8/41 \log n}$.

For a sparse graph with $n = 200M$ vertices and $m = 400M$ edges that fits in memory, we need $w > 73.01$ for the sort-based approach to beat the straightforward implementation. On most GPUs $w \leq 32$. Unless the coalescing width is increased, sort-based techniques that have been shown to work on CPUs do not improve performance on GPUs.

Software prefetching is another technique to improve the memory performance of parallel graph algorithms on CPUs [9]. In our experiments we did not observe any performance improvement on S2050 with software prefetching. Inter-thread prefetching shows modest performance improvement (e.g., 16%) on simulators (e.g., see[14]). In practice, as thread and thread block scheduling is not deterministic, no studies on actual hardware as we know have shown any significant performance improvement for graph algorithms.

4   Optimizing Graft-and-Shortcut

We have argued that generic sort-based approaches are too costly on current GPUs. We now explore optimizations specific to the graft-and-shortcut pattern in CC.

Accesses to D at lines 2-3 in Algorithm 1. are irregular and not coalesced. Line 2 compares the current components that u and v are in, and line 3 makes a union of the two components by grafting the tree rooted at the larger endpoint to the one rooted at the smaller endpoint. While accesses to $D[u]$s and $D[v]$s determined by edges $(u,v) \in E$ are random, the D values evolve in a pattern that can be exploited for coalescing. First, $D[i]$ is non-increasing for each vertex i ($1 \leq i \leq n$) from one iteration to the next. In fact, for most vertices their D values steadily decrease, and the number of unique D values (hence the number of unique super-vertices) also decreases. Instead of retrieving the current components using u and v as indices, we introduce an *update* step after *shortcut* that replaces each edge (u, v) with $(D[u], D[v])$. The revised algorithm CC-updt is shown in Algorithm 2.. The *update* step is done at lines 11-13.

Algorithm 2. CC-updt(El, D), $|El| = m$, $|D| = n$

1: **for** $1 \leq i \leq m$ parallel **do** {graft}
2:   **if** $El[i].u < El[i].v$ **then**
3:     $D[El[i].v] \leftarrow El[i].u$
4:   **end if**
5: **end for**
6: **for** $1 \leq i \leq n$ parallel **do** {shortcut}
7:   **while** $D[i] \neq D[D[i]]$ **do**

8:     $D[i] \leftarrow D[D[i]]$
9:   **end while**
10: **end for**
11: **for** $1 \leq i \leq m$ parallel **do** {update}
12:   $El[i].u \leftarrow D[El[i].u]$, $El[i].v \leftarrow D[El[i].v]$
13: **end for**

In comparison with CC (Algorithm 1.), at first glance CC-updt simply shifts the random accesses from line 2 to line 12. Assuming in each iteration the same grafting choices are made in CC and CC-updt (races among processors may result in different drafting patterns), the same amount of random memory accesses appear to occur in both algorithms. However, as D values become more and more regular, we show accesses to D become increasingly more likely to be coalesced.

Theorem 2. *On average in each iteration CC-updt issues at least $n/2$ fewer random accesses than CC.*

Proof. In the first iteration both algorithms have the same number of random accesses. The number of unique active super-vertices (where grafting can happen) is reduced at least by half by each iteration in CC-updt. After the first iteration, at least $n/2$ edges have two endpoints within the same super-vetex, and for them the accesses to D are coalesced in the second iteration. The number of random accesses is thus reduced by at least $n/2$. The reduction is at least $n/2 + n/4$ in the third iteration, and at least $n/2 + n/4 + \cdots + n/2^{i-1}$ in the i-th ($1 \leq i \leq \log n$) iteration. In the last iteration where no grafting is possible, the reduction is $m \geq n = 2(n/2)$. Thus on average each iteration issues at least $n/2$ fewer random accesses.

We evaluate the performance of CC-updt on S2050. The results with a scale-free graph of 20M vertices and 200M edges are shown in Figure 2. Speedups between 1.75 and 1.83 are achieved. The observed performance improvement is due to better coalescing and possibly better cache performance. Performance study of CC-updt in comparison to CC is also done on P755. The speedups are between 1.66 and 3.0, as shown in Figure 2. Comparing Figures 1 and 2, we notice that the performance gap between P755 and S2050 is reduced for CC-updt.

5 A Meta Algorithm for Further Improvement

We propose a new meta algorithm motivated by the following result from evolution random graph theory [16] that further improves coalescing.

Theorem 3. *Under the Erdös-Rényi model there is a unique giant component of order $f(c)n$ in the graph when $m \sim cn$ with $c > 1/2$.*

Function $f(c)$ approaches 1 as c increases[2]. We exploit the giant component for coalescing. The algorithm, *Stages*, is shown in Algorithm 3..

Stages first permutes the edges in El, and then divides them into groups, $El_1, El_2, \cdots, El_g$, with $|El_i| > n/2$ ($1 \leq i \leq g - 1$) except possibly for El_g. Next for each group El_i ($1 \leq i \leq g$) Stages invokes a connected components algorithm, say, CC, with El_i and D, and updates the endpoints of each edge in El_{i+1} with the current components they belong to. When Stages terminates, $D[i]$ ($1 \leq i \leq n$) is the connected component for vertex i.

Algorithm 3. Stages(El, D), $|El| = m$, $|D| = n$, $1/2 < q < m/n$

1: randomly permute El
2: divide El into groups $El_1, El_2, \cdots, El_g$, with $|El_i| = qn$, $1 \leq i < g$, $1/2 < q \leq m/n$, and $|El_g| = m - (g-1)qn$
3: **for** $1 \leq i \leq g$ **do**
4:     Call CC (El_i,D)
5:     **if** $i < g$ **then** {update}
6:         **for** $1 \leq j \leq |El_{i+1}|$ parallel **do**
7:             $El_{i+1}[j].u \leftarrow D[El_{i+1}[j].u]$, $El_{i+1}[j].v \leftarrow D[El_{i+1}[j].v]$
8:         **end for**
9:     **end if**
10: **end for**

Theorem 4. *Algorithm 3. computes connected components.*

Proof. By induction. By the correctness of CC, the connected components of the induced graph with El_1 are computed and contracted. Each vertex i ($1 \leq i \leq n$) belongs to a component represented by $D[i]$. Assume after processing k groups $El_1, El_2, \cdots, El_k$ of edges ($1 \leq k < g$), the connected components of the induced

---

[2] $f(c) = 1 - \frac{1}{2c} \sum_{k=1}^{\infty} \frac{k^{k-1}}{k!} (2ce^{-2c})^k$.

graph are computed and contracted, and $D[i]$ is the connected component for vertex i ($1 \leq i \leq n$). The *update* step in Algorithm 3. transforms the edges in E_{k+1} of the original graph into edges of the current contracted graph. Subsequent computation in CC is with edges in E_{k+1} on super-vertices with $i = D[i]$ ($1 \leq i \leq n$). All other vertices have $D[i] < i$, that is, each of them shoots a pointer to its super-vertex. The components for these vertices are updated in the *shortcut* step in CC when it sets $D[i] \leftarrow D[D[i]]$ for all vertices. After CC, connected components on edges induced by $El_1, El_2, \cdots, El_{k+1}$ are computed with $D[i]$ representing the current component for each vertex i ($1 \leq i \leq n$).

CC takes $O(\log^2 n)$ time with $O(m + n)$ processors under CRCW PRAM. With p processors CC takes $O\left(\frac{m+n}{p} \log^2 n\right)$ time. Graft-and-shortcut in Stages takes $O\left(\frac{m}{pqn}(qn + n) \log^2 n\right)$ time, while *update* takes $O\left(\frac{m}{p} \log n\right)$ time. CC and Stages have the same asymptotic complexity when $qn = \Theta(m)$. Stages degenerates into CC when $qn = m$.

Let T_{cc} and T_{stgs} be the (worst-case) number of non-coalesced random accesses in *graft* for CC and Stages, respectively.

Lemma 1. $T_{cc} - T_{stgs} > \left(2m - 2qn - \frac{m}{qn}(1 - f^2(q))\right) \log n$

Proof. As CC takes at most $\log n$ arounds of *graft* with $2m$ random accesses each, $T_{cc} = 2m \log n$. Similarly, in Stages the first group of qn edges incur at most $2qn \log n$ random accesses. A component of size $f(q)n$ forms after the first group of edges are processed. For the second group the probability that an edge is contained in the giant component is $f^2(q)$. The expected number of random accesses is at most $2(1 - f^2(q))qn \log((1 - f(q))n + 1)$. Before the jth ($1 < j \leq g$) group of qn edges, the giant component is of size $f((j - 1)q)n$, and the number of random accesses in processing the jth group is at most $2(1 - f^2((j - 1)q))qn \log((1 - f((j - 1)q))n + 1)$. Let $f(0) = 0$, we have

$$
\begin{aligned}
T_{stgs} &\leq \quad \sum_{k=0}^{\frac{m}{qn}-1}(1 - f^2(kq))2qn \log((1 - f(kq))n + 1) \\
&\leq \; 2qn\left(\log n + \sum_{k=1}^{\frac{m}{qn}-1}(1 - f^2(q)) \log((1 - f(q))n + 1)\right) \\
&= 2qn\left(\log n + \left(\frac{m}{qn} - 1\right)(1 - f^2(q)) \log((1 - f(q))n + 1)\right)
\end{aligned}
$$

$$
\begin{aligned}
T_{cc} - T_{stgs} &\geq 2m \log n - 2qn\left(\log n + \left(\frac{m}{qn} - 1\right)(1 - f^2(q)) \log((1 - f(q))n + 1)\right) \\
&> \qquad\qquad \left(2m - 2qn - \frac{m}{qn}(1 - f^2(q))\right) \log n
\end{aligned}
$$

The extra cost of random memory accesses in *update* is at most $2m - 2qn$. $T_s > T_{cc} - T_{stgs}$ when n is large enough and $m = O(n)$.

Our results are derived for random graphs. The experiments below show the technique is effective for other graphs.

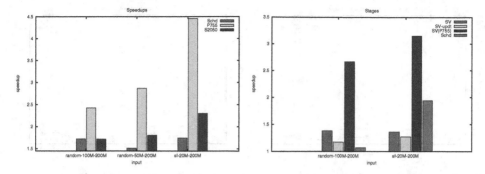

Fig. 3. CC-updt speedups   **Fig. 4.** Stages speedups

Figure 3 shows the speedups of Stages over CC for three different inputs on
P755 and S2050. We use 128 hardware threads on P755 and 14 SMs on S2050.
In our implementation $q = 1$. The speedups achieved on S2050 are between 1.7
to 2.3. Stages is much faster than CC on P755. The speedups are between 2.4
and 4.5. In the figure *Schd* shows the speedup of coordinated scheduling over
CC on P755. Schd is the best prior locality optimized implementation of CC.
On P755 Stages clearly outperforms Schd.

As a meta algorithm, Stages can be used to optimize other parallel connected
components algorithms. Figure 4 shows for a random graph and a scale-free
graph the speedup of stages over various connected components algorithms. SV,
SV-updt (with an additional *update* step), and Schd are called at line 4 of Algorithm 3. instead of CC. For each input, the two bars on the left are the speedups
of Stages over SV and SV-updt on S2050, and the two bars on the right are
the speedups over SV and Schd on P755. We use 14 SMs on S2050 and 128
threads on P755. Stages improves the performance of all algorithms studied.
The speedups on S2050 are between 1.07 to 2.6, and the speedups on P755 are
between 1.3 and 3.1.

6   Ranking the Algorithms

We now rank the performance of the algorithms on S2050. Due to their similarity to CC and CC-updt, we do not include SV and SV-updt in our rankings.
We include parallel Rem's algorithm (Rem) by Patwary *et al.* [17] in our study.
In comparison to CC and SV, Rem is not based on the PRAM model. It does
not shortcut the trees, and uses union-find structures to determine whether two
vertices are in the same component. Rem is largely asynchronous and resolves
data races through a verification algorithm. Rem is efficient for a moderate number of threads. One drawback of Rem is that increasing the available parallelism
can result in many rounds of verification and thus degrades performance. Rem
is faster than CC on current CPUs [17]. Our optimizations do not apply to Rem
as it does not shortcut the trees.

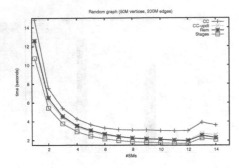 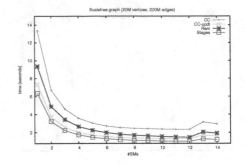

Fig. 5. Performance of four implementations on a random graph

Fig. 6. Performance of four implementations on a scale-free graph

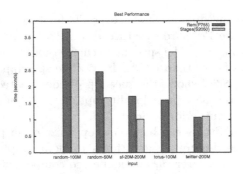

Fig. 7. Performance comparison on P755 and S2050

Figures 5 and 6 show on S2050 the performance of CC, CC-updt, Stages, and Rem with the same inputs, that is, a random graph with 50M vertices, 200M edges, and a scale-free graph with 20M vertices, 200M edges, respectively. CC-updt is always faster than CC, and Stages is always faster than CC-updt. Rem is slower than CC-updt for the scale-free graph.

Our new algorithm, Stages, is the fastest on S2050, while Rem (with software prefetching) is the fastest on P755 (due to limited space, we do not show the performance plots for CC, CC-updt, Stages, Schd, and Rem on P755). The relative poor performance of Rem on S2050 is largely due to path divergence resulted from its complex control flow in union-find.

We compare the performance of Stages on S2050 and Rem on P755. In addition to random graphs and scale-free graphs, we include a 2D torus and a sample of the twitter network in our test. Torus represents graphs (such as VLSI circuits) of regular topology with long diameters, and the twitter network is an example of real life social networks. The torus has about 100M vertices. The twitter sample has 35M vertices and 200M edges.

Figure 7 shows the performance of the fastest implementations on the two platforms. We use 128 threads on P755 and 14 SMs on S2050. The two algorithms have roughly comparable performance for small-world graphs. Stages on S2050 is faster than Rem on P755 with the random graphs and the scale-free graph. Rem on P755 is faster than Stages on S2050 with the torus. They have similar performance with the twitter graph.

7   Conclusion and Future Work

We present our study of optimizing connected components algorithms on GPUs in comparison with CPUs. We show that straightforward implementation of PRAM algorithms performs relatively better on GPUs than on CPUs. However, the memory subsystem of GPUs does not deliver data fast enough keep all SMs busy.

We argue that generic techniques to improve locality for better performance are too costly on GPUs. We propose a low-cost coalescing optimization for CC. We further present a meta algorithm that improves coalescing for several connected components algorithms. Interestingly, these optimizations also improve performance on CPUs. In fact, our implementation beats the best prior locality-optimized implementation on P755.

We find that Stages is consistently the fastest algorithm on S2050. Rem is fast on P755, but its performance suffers from path divergence on S2050. Rem has similar performance as CC-updt on S2050. Stages on S2050 and Rem on P755 on average have similar performance over a range of inputs.

In future work we will study graph algorithms on multi-GPUs and a cluster of GPUs. We will also study architectural support for efficient execution of graph algorithms on emerging architectures.

References

1. Arge, L., Bender, M.A., Demaine, E.D., Holland-Minkley, B., Munro, J.I.: Cache-oblivious priority queue and graph algorithm applications. In: Proceedings of the 34th Annual ACM Symposium on Theory of Computing, Montreal, Canada, pp. 268–276 (2002)
2. Arge, L., Goodrich, M.T., Nelson, M., Sitchinava, N.: Fundamental parallel algorithms for private-cache chip multiprocessors. In: Proceedings of the Twentieth Annual Symposium on Parallelism in Algorithms and Architectures, SPAA 2008, pp. 197–206. ACM, New York (2008)
3. Arge, L., Goodrich, M.T., Sitchinava, N.: Parallel external memory graph algorithms. In: 24th IEEE International Parallel & Distributed Processing Symposium, Atlanta, Georgia, USA (2010)
4. Bader, D.A., Cong, G.: A fast, parallel spanning tree algorithm for symmetric multiprocessors (SMPs). In: Proceedings of the 18th International Parallel and Distributed Processing Symposium (IPDPS 2004), Santa Fe, New Mexico (April 2004)
5. Blelloch, G.E., Chowdhury, R.A., Gibbons, P.B., Ramachandran, V., Chen, S., Kozuch, M.: Provably good multicore cache performance for divide-and-conquer algorithms. In: In Proc. 19th ACM-SIAM Sympos. Discrete Algorithms, pp. 501–510 (2008)

6. Chakrabarti, D., Zhan, Y., Faloutsos, C.: R-MAT: A recursive model for graph mining. In: Proc. 4th SIAM Intl. Conf. on Data Mining (April 2004)
7. Chiang, Y.-J., Goodrich, M.T., Grove, E.F., Tamassia, R., Vengroff, D.E., Vitter, J.S.: External-memory graph algorithms. In: Proceedings of the 1995 Symposium on Discrete Algorithms, pp. 139–149 (1995)
8. Chowdhury, R., Silvestri, F., Blakeley, B., Ramachandran, V.: Oblivious algorithms for multicores and network of processors. In: 24th IEEE International Parallel & Distributed Processing Symposium, Atlanta, Georgia, USA (2010)
9. Cong, G., Makarychev, K.: Optimizing large-scale graph analysis on multi-threaded, multi-core platforms. In: Proceedings of the 2012 IEEE International Parallel & Distributed Processing Symposium, IPDPS 2012, pp. 414–425. IEEE Computer Society, Washington, DC (2012)
10. Dehne, F., Yogaratnam, K.: Exploring the limits of GPUs with parallel graph algorithms. CoRR, abs/1002.4482 (2010)
11. Goh, K.-I., Oh, E., Jeong, H., Kahng, B., Kim, D.: Classification of scale-free networks. Proc. Natl. Acad. Sci. 99, 12583–12588 (2002)
12. Hong, S., Oguntebi, T., Olukotun, K.: Efficient parallel graph exploration on multi-core cpu and gpu. In: 2011 Int'l Conf. on Parallel Architectures and Compilation Techniques (PACT), pp. 78–88 (October 2011)
13. Ladner, R., Fix, J.D., LaMarca, A.: The cache performance of traversals and random accesses. In: Proc. 10th Ann. Symp. Discrete Algorithms (SODA-1999), pp. 613–622. ACM-SIAM, Baltimore (1999)
14. Lee, J., Lakshminarayanaand, N.B., Hyesoon, K., Vuduc, R.: Many-thread aware prefetching mechanisms for GPGPU applications. In: 43rd Annual IEEE/ACM Int'l Symp on Microarchitecture (MICRO), pp. 213–224 (December 2010)
15. Luo, L., Wong, M., Hwu, W.: An effective gpu implementation of breadth-first search. In: 2010 47th ACM/IEEE Design Automation Conference (DAC), pp. 52–55 (June 2010)
16. Palmer, E.M.: Graphical evolution. Wiley-Interscience Series in Discrete Mathematics. Wiley (1985)
17. Patwary, M.A., Ref, P., Manne, F.: Multi-core spanning forest algorithms using the disjoint-set data structure. In: Proceedings of the 2012 IEEE International Parallel & Distributed Processing Symposium, IPDPS 2012, pp. 827–835. IEEE Computer Society Press, Washington, DC (2012)
18. Satish, N., Harris, M., Garland, M.: Designing efficient sorting algorithms for many-core GPUs. In: Proceedings of the 2009 IEEE Int'l Symp. on Parallel&Distributed Processing, IPDPS 2009, pp. 1–10. IEEE Computer Society, Washington, DC (2009)
19. Shiloach, Y., Vishkin, U.: An $O(\log n)$ parallel connectivity algorithm. J. Algs 3(1), 57–67 (1982)

An Empirical Evaluation of GPGPU Performance Models

Souley Madougou[1], Ana Lucia Varbanescu[1],
Cees de Laat[1], and Rob van Nieuwpoort[2]

[1] University of Amsterdam, Amsterdam, The Netherlands
[2] Netherlands eScience Center, Amsterdam, The Netherlands

Abstract. Computing systems today rely on massively parallel and heterogeneous architectures to promise very high peak performance. Yet most applications only achieve small fractions of this performance. While both programmers and architects have clear opinions about the causes of this performance gap, finding and quantifying the real problems remains a topic for performance modeling tools. In this paper, we sketch the landscape of modern GPUs' performance limiters and optimization opportunities, and dive into details on modeling attempts for GPU-based systems. We highlight the specific features of the relevant contributions in this field, along with the optimization and design spaces they explore. We further use a typical kernel example (tiled dense matrix multiplication) to assess the efficacy and usability of a set of promising approaches. We conclude that the available GPU performance modeling solutions are very sensitive to applications and platform changes, and require significant efforts for tuning and calibration when new analyses are required.

Keywords: performance modeling, performance analysis and prediction, GPU architectures.

1 Introduction

Today's computing landscape is dominated by parallel, heterogeneous systems. This evolution has been triggered by the significant performance gains that many-core architectures can offer (e.g., over 1 TFLOP for a Xeon Phi CPU [1] or a regular, consumer GPU card [2,3]).

Attaining the best possible performance on such platforms for real-world applications is very challenging because it requires a lot of manual tuning: the algorithms require tailored implementations for specific hardware, and a large design and optimization space must be (manually) explored. In this trial-and-error process, both design and program tuning are based on a mix of designers' and programmers' expertise. As a result, the optimization space is only partially explored and most applications run far below their own peak performance of the given hardware system [4,5].

We believe this practice of searching for performance needs to change. Instead of using word-of-mouth and primitive, in-house performance models and empirical program tuning, we advocate a systematic approach through and beyond

L. Lopes et al. (Eds.): Euro-Par 2014 Workshops, Part I, LNCS 8805, pp. 165–176, 2014.

existing performance modeling and engineering tools, which have been found very useful for traditional parallel systems. However, heterogeneous computing still focuses much more on application case-studies [6] and programming systems [7,8] than on developing and using performance modeling techniques. Yet, the "affordability" of high performance promised by the ubiquity of heterogeneous computing can only be enjoyed with the support of the appropriate performance modeling tools and approaches.

The first step in this direction is to provide a clear picture of the tools we have available now. Thus, the contribution of this work is twofold. First, we sketch the performance modeling landscape for heterogeneous systems by focusing on representative and promising methods. Second, for our empirical evaluation, we select seven different approaches to performance modeling specific to GPUs. For each one of them, we highlight the methodology and the specific features, the design and/or optimization space it explores, its possible shortcomings; we further apply it to a tiled dense matrix multiplication kernel from the CUDA SDK on four platforms from two generations of NVIDIA GPUs (GTX480, Tesla C2050, GTX-Titan, and/or K20) and report our results.

2   GPU Execution Model and Performance Factors

In this section, we briefly describe the execution model and some architectural features of modern GPUs that either contribute to or limit the performance of GPGPU applications. We believe that any performance modeling approach for the latter should capture some or all of those features; moreover, when analyzing a set of selected GPGPU performance models in Section 3, we rely on those features to assess the adequacy of the model to current GPUs. Without loosing generality, we will use NVIDIA's Compute Unified Device Architecture (CUDA) terminology for concepts pertaining to GPUs and their programming.

2.1   Execution Model

The processing power of GPUs resides in their array of Streaming Multiprocessors (SMs). When a GPGPU program invokes a kernel grid, the multiple thread blocks (TBs) of the grid are distributed to the SMs that have the necessary computing resources. Threads in a TB execute concurrently, and multiple TBs will execute concurrently. As TBs terminate, new blocks are launched on vacated SMs. Instructions are pipelined to harness instruction-level parallelism (ILP) inside a thread, and thread-level parallelism (TLP) is achieved in hardware.

SMs execute threads in groups of 32 (NVIDIA GPUs) parallel threads called *warps*. Each warp is scheduled for execution by a warp scheduler which issues the same instruction for all the warp's threads (Single Instruction Multiple Threads, SIMT, execution model). When threads diverge due to control flow, all divergent paths are executed serially with inactive threads in a path disabled.

2.2 Performance Factors and Optimization Space

At a very coarse level, performance on current GPUs is achieved by following a few basic optimization principles: *1)* maximize parallel execution, *2)* optimize memory usage in order to achieve maximum memory bandwidth and *3)* optimize instruction usage in order to achieve maximum instruction throughput. We detail each of these principles in the remainder of the section.

GPU kernels must expose *sufficient parallelism* to "fill" the platform. Specifically, for arithmetic operations, there should be sufficient independent instructions to accommodate multi-issue and hide latency. For memory operations, enough requests must be in flight in order to saturate the bandwidth. This is achieved by either having more independent work within a thread (ILP or independent memory accesses) or more concurrent threads or, equivalently, more concurrent warps (TLP). While ILP may be inherent to the code or deduced by the compiler, TLP and load-balance are decided by the execution configuration and the actual available resources. The ratio between the active warps on an SM and the maximum number of warps per SM is called *occupancy* in CUDA jargon, and it is a measure of utilization. Occupancy is limited by the number of registers and the amount of shared memory used by each thread block, and the thread count per block. Low occupancy always corresponds to performance degradation. The required occupancy depends on the kernel: a kernel exhibiting good ILP may need less occupancy, while a memory-bound kernel needs more to hide the high latency affecting memory accesses.

Global memory, the largest memory space with the greatest latency, is accessed at warp granularity via memory transactions of certain sizes (32, 64 or 128 bytes on current GPUs). When a warp executes a memory instruction, it attempts to *coalesce* the memory accesses of its composing threads into as few as possible such transactions, depending on the memory access patterns. The more transactions are necessary, the more unused data are transferred, limiting the achieved memory throughput. The number of necessary transactions varies among device generations (i.e., the compute capability). Access patterns along with the number of concurrent memory accesses in flight heavily impact the memory subsystem performance, leading to significant degradation when coalescing conditions are not met. Following Little's law, there should be $Latency \times Bandwidth$ bytes in transit in order to totally hide the memory latency. It is therefore crucial that a model is capable of evaluating the memory-level parallelism (MLP) available in a kernel.

Shared memory has higher ($\sim 10\times$) bandwidth and lower latency ($20 - 30\times$) than global memory. It is divided into equally-sized memory modules, called *banks*, which can be accessed simultaneously to increase performance. For example, N memory requests from N distinct banks can be serviced simultaneously; however, memory requests for two or more different words in the same bank lead to *bank conflicts* serialization, decreasing the achieved throughput significantly.

Additionally, most recent GPUs ship with L1 and L2 caches, which, if not game changers, at least disrupt the way shared memory and global memory are accessed. As L1 and the shared memory use the same region of on-chip memory and their respective sizes are program configurable, their respective sizing has an impact on performance with regard to, for instance, register spilling and occupancy. Global memory operations now only reach the device DRAM on cache misses.

To summarize, we expect GPU performance models and their adjacent tools to capture and/or analyze parallelism and concurrency, occupancy, memory access patterns and their impact on global and local memory, as well as caching.

3   An Empirical Evaluation of GPU Performance Models

Our empirical evaluation starts from the assumption that performance modeling is based on a smart combination of application and architecture models. A performance modeling tool must be (1) *accurate*, (2) *fast* or *tunable* for accuracy versus speed and (3) *easy to use*, to favor adoption from the user community. We further favor performance modeling tools based on *reusable application and hardware models*. Application models should consider performance factors such as available parallelism and memory accesses and be hardware-agnostic. Likewise, hardware models must capture salient performance features such as the number of SMs, the SIMD width, amount of shared memory or of cache levels. Finally, an ideal modeling tool should not be limited to only predicting runtime. Instead, it should also highlight *performance bottlenecks* both from the application and the hardware, and eventually provide hints to fix them.

Guided by these requirements, the remainder of this section describes several GPU performance models, discussing their approaches, and results in analyzing a benchmark kernel. Given its popularity among such performance tools, we selected a tiled dense matrix multiplication (MM) kernel from the CUDA SDK as benchmark. To compute the product C of two square matrices A, and B, the kernel uses $t \times t$ block matrices (or tiles), with t divisible by both A and B size. A grid of $width_C/t \times height_C/t$ TBs is launched where each TB computes the elements of a different tile of C from a tile of A and a tile of B. The kernel is optimized by loading both tiles of A and B into shared memory to avoid redundant transfers from global memory.

3.1   PMAC Framework [9]

A relatively old framework for distributed systems analysis, PMAC is extended with diverse tools [10,11,12] for handling heterogeneity and evaluating the performance benefits of porting a kernel to a given accelerator. In a typical scenario, the PMAC Idiom Recognizer (PIR) can be used to automatically collect a set of well-known compute and memory access patterns (so-called idioms) present in a given source code [12]. After PIR has discovered idioms, their performance on a given accelerator is evaluated using micro-benchmarks. To this aim, the data footprint for each idiom needs to be captured using the PEBIL binary instrumentation tool [11]. Gather/Scatter and stream idioms have been tested on 2 types of accelerators, GPUs and an FPGA, showing 82% - 99% accuracy.

Evaluation. MM is only composed of the stream idiom, so we do not have to use PIR for this simple case. Predicting the performance of stream on an accelerator boils down to evaluating the time taken by memory operations as the framework assumes these are dominant in the execution time. Equation (1) estimates this time over all basic blocks pertaining to the idiom, with $MemRef_{i,j}$ being the number of references of basic block i of type j, $RefSize$ the reference size in bytes and $MemBW_{\text{stream}}$ the bandwidth of the stream idiom on the target accelerator.

$$MemTime = \sum_{i}^{allBB} \frac{\#MemRef_{i,j} \times RefSize}{MemBW_{\text{stream}}} . \tag{1}$$

We run PEBIL on the MM binary to get all the basic blocks along with the memory references and their sizes. Using the CUDA version of MM, several runs with different matrix sizes must be performed to collect run-times. A model for $MemBW_{\text{stream}}$ is built from these data via regression, as shown in Fig. 01. The model itself is given by the following equation, with s being the data size:

$$MemBW_{\text{stream}}(s) = -0.0020 \times \max(0, 3072-s) + 0.0003 \times \max(0, s-3072) + 7.0709 \tag{2}$$

According to the framework, the value from (1) and the actual GPU time from running MM on the GPU should be similar. However, we found the outputs can differ significantly, as shown in Fig. 02. Additionally, some tools are not readily available (PIR), others are difficult to use and with no proper documentation (PEBIL). Finally, the framework provides only limited support for heterogeneity (idioms) and, in general, says nothing about bottlenecks and how to overcome them.

Summary. PMAC seems too complex and tedious to use, and only characterizes an application by idioms. The observed accuracy is low. Finally, (1) only works for memory-bound kernels.

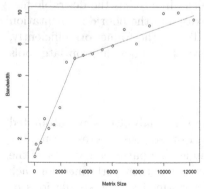
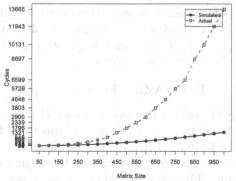

Fig. 1. Piecewise linear regression of the memory throughput versus matrix size data of MM kernel on NVIDIA Tesla C2050

Fig. 2. Elapsed clock cycles for different matrix sizes for MM on NVIDIA Tesla C2050, as predicted by (1) and calibrated from actual run times

3.2   Eiger Framework [13]

Eiger is an automated statistical methodology for modeling program behavior on different architectures. To discover and synthesize performance models, the methodology goes trough 4 steps: *1*) experimental data acquisition and database construction, *2*) a series of data analysis passes over the database, *3*) model selection and, finally, *4*) model construction. For the training phase (step 1), the application is executed on the target processor, facilitating the measurement of execution time and the collection of multiple parameter values (characterizing both processors and applications, 47 in total). In step 2, principal component analysis (PCA) is performed on the collected data. The generated principal components are post-processed so they have either strong or weak relationships with the initial metrics. Finally, an analytical performance model is constructed using parametric regression analysis. The approach is validated on 12 applications from different GPU benchmark suites and the CUDA SDK.

Evaluation. Eiger is a promising approach with support for GPUs and desirable features such as independent application and hardware characterization, allowing one to generically include major performance features from both the application and the hardware into the modeling. The first column in Table 11 shows some of the metrics used in a GPGPU use case. Besides static code analysis and instrumentation, the experimental data collection stage leverages Ocelot [14], a PTX simulator, for features necessitating code emulation. A software package[1] for interacting with Ocelot is provided to ease the modeling process, but this requires significant improvements on documentation and usability, especially on using Ocelot to extract relevant metric values. Therefore, we ended up using the NVIDIA profiler to build the database based on the correspondences shown in Table 11. We have trained the model on a Tesla C2050 and predicted the runtime on a Geforce GTX580. Even though both GPUs correspond to Fermi architecture, the predictions accuracy shown in Fig. 13 is not ideal. Observe that the more accurate the model, the closer the data points to the $y = x$ line.

Summary. Eiger is a promising approach which already has the desirable features for a usable system. However, its complexity and the poor documentation of the provided software make it hard to use. To use the framework efficiently, one must have good knowledge of many statistical methods, appropriate tools for those, and C++ programming.

3.3   STARGAZER Framework [15]

The STAtistical Regression-based GPU Architecture analyZER is an automated GPU performance exploration framework based on stepwise regression modeling. STARGAZER sparsely and randomly samples the parameter values of the full GPU design space. Simulation or measurement is then performed for each sample. Finally, stepwise linear regression is performed on the simulations or measurements to find the most influential (architectural) parameters to the performance of the application. The linear regression basis is enhanced with spline

---

[1] https://bitbucket.org/eanger/eiger

Table 1. Metric correspondence. For performance counter definition, see http://docs.nvidia.com/cuda/profiler-users-

Eiger metric	Counter
memory efficiency	(gld_efficiency+gst_efficiency)/:
memory intensity	ldst_executed / inst_executed
memory sharing	code analysis
activity factor	CUDA occupancy
SIMD/MIMD	execution configuration
DMA size	code analysis

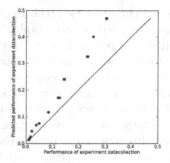

Fig. 3. Prediction accuracy

functions to allow nonlinearity between independent variables of the regression as interactions between architectural parameters usually affect performance in a nonlinear manner. Analysis of the relationships between the application runtime and the most influential architectural parameters allows the discovery of performance bottlenecks. Several CUDA applications from benchmark suites are used to test the system with good average accuracy (around 99%).

Evaluation. STARGAZER aims at GPU design space pruning and, as such, only considers hardware characteristics. It captures parallel execution behavior through metrics like block concurrency and SIMD width. There are also metrics to capture intra- and inter-warp memory coalescing. However, there are no metrics for estimating shared memory bank conflicts or control flow divergence. As a statistical framework, STARGAZER needs to collect data for all considered hardware characteristics. Python and R scripts are provided to perform this task by using the GPGPU-Sim [5] simulator. Depending on the space to explore and the dataset (e.g., the matrix size for MM), it can take days to generate training data. One alternative is to use actual measurements, but extracting all design space parameter values may not be straightforward or even possible. We ran our MM kernel in GPGPU-Sim with Tesla C2050 GPU settings to collect data and build a model which predicts the run time as measured by GPGPU-Sim reasonably well. However, run times obtained by GPGPU-Sim are orders of magnitude higher than those of the actual hardware for the same matrix size.

Summary. STARGAZER is usable for design space exploration, but the proposed metrics do not cover all the current GPU performance features, leading in turn to low accuracy for some applications. We believe that adding more relevant hardware features and application characteristics, and especially providing a faster way of acquiring experimental data, would make STARGAZER one of the few tools actually usable in practice.

3.4 WFG Modeling Tool [16]

A GPU analytical performance modeling tool is defined by abstracting a GPU kernel as a Work Flow Graph (WFG), based on which the kernel execution time is estimated. The kernel is represented by its dependence graph (both control flow and data dependence graph). The nodes of the WFG are instructions which are either computation or memory (global or shared) operations, the edges are either transition arcs from the control flow or data dependence arcs. Transition arcs are labeled by the average number of cycles required to execute the source node, while data dependence arcs are labeled with the portion of GPU load latency that is not covered by interleaving execution of different warps. The tool aims to accurately identify performance bottlenecks in the kernel. Symbolic evaluation of certain fragments of code is used to determine loop bounds, data access patterns and other program characteristics. The effects of SIMD pipeline latency, memory bank conflicts, and uncoalesced memory accesses are highlighted in the WFG. The tool is validated on 4 kernels and shows reasonable accuracy.

Evaluation. The model considers major performance factors such as TLP and MLP, memory access patterns and different latencies. However, as an analytical performance modeling tool, WFG lacks runtime information such as achieved occupancy or memory and instruction efficiency, which limits its potential prediction accuracy. The crux of the model is the program dependence graph representation of the kernel, generated by a compiler front-end - which is not publicly available, making it impossible for us to directly evaluate this model for our MM application. However, we managed to build an approximate WFG in a different way. Equation 4 in [16], $Latency_{BW} = \max(0, \frac{CYC_{mem} - CYC_{compute}}{NUM_{mem}}) + \frac{SIMD_{work}}{SIMD_{engine}}$, estimates memory stalls due to lack of available bandwidth per warp. $CYC_{compute}$, CYC_{mem}, and NUM_{mem} represent the average number of compute cycles, global memory cycles, and operations per warp, respectively. $SIMD_{work}$ is the warp size and $SIMD_{engine}$ the number of SPs in a SM. For a memory-bound kernel like MM, this will significantly contribute to the total runtime. Using code analysis and the profiler, we can determine the values of the relevant metrics to evaluate the equation. Assuming correspondences between metrics in Equation 4 and combinations of hardware performance counters measured by the CUDA profiler, as shown in Table 13, we plot the values of LatencyBW from both the profiler and the model in Fig. 14. We observe that global memory latency as seen by the application (thus Equation 4) and by the hardware do not always agree.

Summary. WFG captures most of the major performance factors on GPUs, except caching. However, it is complex and aimed at consumption by optimizing compilers. We have struggled to build WFG for the MM kernel, and found it inaccurate for the cases, where matrices are small, and, probably fit in caches.

3.5   The MWP-CWP Analytical Model [17]

In this model, the characteristics of a CUDA application are captured in two different metrics: MWP (memory warp parallelism), the amount of memory requests that can be serviced in parallel, and CWP (computation warp parallelism) or how much computation can be done while a warp is waiting for the memory. Using only these two metrics, the application performance can be assessed. The

Table 3. The correspondence between WFG metrics and combinations of performance counters and hardware specification. WordSize is determined from the application; Cycles per instruction (CPI) and BWPerSM are determined from the hardware specifications; all the other metrics are extracted from the CUDA profiler.

WFG metric	Counter
$Latency_{BW}$	1-sm_efficiency / warps x stall_data_request x elapsed_cycles_sm
$CYC_{compute}$	inst_per_warp x CPI
NUM_{mem}	gld_request + gst_request
CYC_{mem}	NUM_{mem} / warps x WordSize x BWPerSM

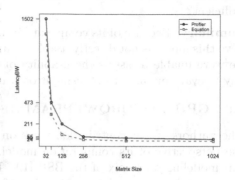

Fig. 4. Comparison of LatencyBW from the profiler (measurement) and from the model (predicted) for different matrix sizes

metrics computations require 17 hardware and application parameters obtained from either hardware specification or micro-benchmarking for the former and extracted from either the source or the PTX code for the latter. Furthermore, the model is static, so no run of the application is necessary. Instead, parameters of the application are estimated and fed into the model, which calculates the expected execution time. The model is validated using two NVIDIA GPUs and shows good results.

Evaluation. We have attempted to predict the performance of the MM kernel (also used in the paper) on a newer GPU, a GTX480. While we were able to preserve 12 parameters from the original paper [17], the rest of 5 parameters required micro-benchmarking. However, the authors have decided to deprecate the benchmarking suite as it *became obsolete for the new generation of GPUs*[2]. Our attempts of approximating the results of these benchmarks using platform similarities have failed: the predicted performance was far off from the observed performance on the GTX480. We conclude from this that the recalibration of this model for new generations of GPUs is very time consuming, if at all possible. We add to this the perceived difficulty of modeling new applications, which require very detailed inspection of the code (be it CUDA or PTX) to determine, at instruction level, the characteristics of operations and memory accesses, and that is cumbersome even for relatively experienced CUDA programmers. Finally, we argue that the model does capture the inner workings of a GPU, but requires too much effort for the provided result: it only predicts the execution time, without really pointing out what the problems of the implementation are. This questions its usability for real applications: modeling requires a PTX version of the running code and a calibration of the model for the specific GPU. As

---

[2] This statement was made in a direct discussion with one of the authors.

both these elements must be available, why isn't a simple run on the GPU not sufficient?

Summary. Because of its complexity in both modeling and calibration, we believe this model is not directly usable for application design and tuning. Further, we were unable to assess the usability of this model, and we could not obtain any relevant predictions by using it on a new GPU platform.

3.6   GPU *a la* (QRQW) PRAM [18]

The authors of this contribution focus on a high level model of the GPU from the perspective of its computation model. Specifically, they base their analytical modeling on a mix of the BSP [19], PRAM [20], and QRQW PRAM [21] models and get a good approximation of the execution times. Compared with the MWP-CWP model (see Section 3.5), this is a much more lightweight modeling approach, in which only 7 platform parameters are used (5 from the specifications and 2 from the occupancy calculator). The other 6 parameters are approximating the application behavior: the geometry of the kernel execution, the computational load of a thread, and the data size. The model computes a predicted execution time by "mapping" the dataset on the threads and approximating a cumulated number of cycles of the execution. In the case of this model, the difficulty lies in assessing the cycles per thread, *i.e.* characterizing the application. This is an approximation step that can be done by either calibration (e.g., micro-benchmarking) or source code analysis, but should be portable between different platforms. Thus, a model of the application can be reused for performance prediction on multiple platforms.

Evaluation. To assess the usability of this model, we have attempted to predict the runtime of the matrix multiplication (as implemented in the original paper [18]) on the GTX480 and GTX-Titan, with mixed results. For the GTX480 (the Fermi architecture), we were able to predict the execution time for multiple execution scenarios with accuracies ranging between 3% and 10% (in the order of milliseconds). However, for the GTX-Titan (the Kepler architecture) we were unable to get any good predictions: the measurements were consistently pessimistic, with errors ranging from 30% up to 70%. This indicates that the model might not capture some of the new features of the Kepler architecture.

Summary. We believe this model is promising for high-level approximations of the execution times, and it is probably very useful, once calibrated, to assess different geometries and/or application parameters (e.g., the tile sizes in the matrix multiplication). However, the calibration of the model for a given application remains challenging, and we are skeptical if the model can analyze applications where the mapping of data-items to threads is non-trivial.

3.7   Quantitative Analysis [22]

The authors of this model have an ingenious solution for analyzing the performance of a GPU application: they first measure "everything" about the target GPU, express an application model in terms of consumption of these resources, and finally detect the application bottlenecks by checking which of these resources is dominating the application runtime. Once the bottleneck is found, the execution time is estimated using the tabulated benchmarking results which are the achievable numbers for (1) instruction throughput (per class of instructions), (2) shared memory bandwidth, and (3) global memory bandwidth in conditions of variable occupancy of the platform (i.e., when varying the number of blocks and threads). The application model is a detailed breakdown of the instructions in the code - computation and memory accesses alike. The observed accuracy of this model is within 15%.

Evaluation. In order to evaluate this model for a new GPU, the micro-benchmarking needs to be reapplied. As the suite is not available, we were unable to model another GPU, hence the lack of prediction for the GTX480 and GTX-Titan. Moreover, the analysis of the shared and global memory, as presented in the original paper, was performed on non-cache architectures. It is unclear whether the code instrumentation can detect caching operations and treat them separately. If that is not possible, architectures such as Fermi or Kepler will get very inaccurate predictions for memory-intensive applications.

Summary. The model is interesting because it provides more insight into the causes of the performance behavior of applications. However, the micro-benchmarking suite is necessary for calibration, and we are not convinced that the approach will work when caches play a significant role. We were unable to perform any predictions on the GTX480 or GTX-Titan because we did not have access to the benchmarking suite.

4   Conclusion

In this work, we presented an overview of existing performance analysis and prediction tools dedicated to GPGPU computing. We further selected, based on citations and usage according to our own literature survey, a set of seven popular and/or interesting tools discussed in literature. We evaluated these seven GPU performance modeling tools with slightly disappointing results: only two approaches were able to predict, with a reasonable accuracy, the runtime of a well-known kernel on newer hardware. Three of the seven models were able to provide hints into the performance bottlenecks which could help programmers and designers improve their current solutions.

We believe our study is a good starting point for a much needed, thorough investigation of the stat-of-the-art in performance modeling for GPUs. Our future work aims at transforming this study into a comprehensive survey of the performance modeling for heterogeneous architectures with highlight on what is working and what needs to be improved.

References

1. Saule, E., Kaya, K., Çatalyürek, Ü.V.: Performance evaluation of sparse matrix multiplication kernels on intel xeon phi. CoRR abs/1302.1078 (2013)
2. NVIDIA Corporation: Press release: Nvidia tesla gpu computing processor ushers in the era of personal supercomputing (June 2007)

3. Advanced Micro Devices (AMD) Inc. Press release: Amd delivers enthusiast performance leadership with the introduction of the ati radeon 3870 x2 (January 2008)
4. Asanovic, K., et al.: A view of the parallel computing landscape. Commun. ACM 52(10), 56–67 (2009)
5. Bakhoda, A., Yuan, G.L., Fung, W.W.L., Wong, H., Aamodt, T.M.: Analyzing cuda workloads using a detailed gpu simulator. In: ISPASS, pp. 163–174. IEEE (2009)
6. Mudalige, G.R., Vernon, M.K., Jarvis, S.A.: A plug-and-play model for evaluating wavefront computations on parallel architectures. In: IPDPS, pp. 1–14. IEEE (2008)
7. Diamos, G.F., Yalamanchili, S.: Harmony: An execution model and runtime for heterogeneous many core systems. In: Proceedings of HPDC 2008, pp. 197–200. ACM, New York (2008)
8. Linderman, M.D., Collins, J.D., Wang, H., Meng, T.H.: Merge: A programming model for heterogeneous multi-core systems. SIGPLAN Not. 43(3) (March 2008)
9. Snavely, A., Carrington, L., Wolter, N., Labarta, J., Badia, R., Purkayastha, A.: A framework for performance modeling and prediction. In: Proceedings of SC 2002, pp. 1–17. IEEE Computer Society Press, Los Alamitos (2002)
10. Tikir, M.M., Laurenzano, M.A., Carrington, L., Snavely, A.: PSINS: An open source event tracer and execution simulator for MPI applications. In: Sips, H., Epema, D., Lin, H.-X. (eds.) Euro-Par 2009. LNCS, vol. 5704, pp. 135–148. Springer, Heidelberg (2009)
11. Laurenzano, M., Tikir, M., Carrington, L., Snavely, A.: Pebil: Efficient static binary instrumentation for linux. In: ISPASS 2010, pp. 175–183 (March 2010)
12. Carrington, L., Tikir, M.M., Olschanowsky, C., Laurenzano, M., Peraza, J., Snavely, A., Poole, S.: An idiom-finding tool for increasing productivity of accelerators. In: Proceedings of ICS 2011, pp. 202–212. ACM, New York (2011)
13. Kerr, A., Anger, E., Hendry, G., Yalamanchili, S.: Eiger: A framework for the automated synthesis of statistical performance models. In: Proceedings of WPEA 2012 (2012)
14. Kerr, A., Diamos, G., Yalamanchili, S.: A characterization and analysis of ptx kernels. In: Proceedings of IISWC 2009, Washington, DC, USA, pp. 3–12 (2009)
15. Jia, W., Shaw, K., Martonosi, M.: Stargazer: Automated regression-based gpu design space exploration. In: ISPASS 2012, pp. 2–13 (April 2012)
16. Baghsorkhi, S.S., Delahaye, M., Patel, S.J., Gropp, W.D., Hwu, W.M.W.: An adaptive performance modeling tool for gpu architectures. SIGPLAN Not. 45(5), 105–114 (2010)
17. Hong, S., Kim, H.: An analytical model for a gpu architecture with memory-level and thread-level parallelism awareness. SIGARCH Comput. Archit. News 37(3), 152–163 (2009)
18. Kothapalli, K., Mukherjee, R., Rehman, M., Patidar, S., Narayanan, P.J., Srinathan, K.: A performance prediction model for the cuda gpgpu platform. In: HiPC 2009, pp. 463–472 (December 2009)
19. Valiant, L.G.: A bridging model for parallel computation. Commun. ACM 33(8), 103–111 (1990)
20. Fortune, S., Wyllie, J.: Parallelism in random access machines. In: Proceedings of STOC 1978, pp. 114–118. ACM, New York (1978)
21. Gibbons, P.B., Matias, Y., Ramachandran, V.: The queue-read queue-write asynchronous pram model. In: Euro-Par 1996. LNCS, vol. 1124, pp. 279–292. Springer, Heidelberg (1996)
22. Zhang, Y., Owens, J.: A quantitative performance analysis model for gpu architectures. In: HPCA 2011, pp. 382–393 (February 2011)

Towards the Transparent Execution of Compound OpenCL Computations in Multi-CPU/Multi-GPU Environments*

Fábio Soldado, Fernando Alexandre, and Hervé Paulino

NOVA-LINCS / Departamento de Informática, Faculdade de Ciências e Tecnologia,
Universidade Nova de Lisboa, 2829-516 Caparica, Portugal
herve.paulino@fct.unl.pt

Abstract. Current computational systems are heterogeneous by nature, featuring a combination of CPUs and GPUs. As the latter are becoming an established platform for high-performance computing, the focus is shifting towards the seamless programming of the heterogeneous systems as a whole. The distinct nature of the architectural and execution models in place raise several challenges, as the best hardware configuration is behavior and data-set dependent. In this paper, we focus the execution of compound computations in multi-CPU/multi-GPU environments, in the scope of Marrow algorithmic skeleton framework, the only, to the best of our knowledge, to support skeleton nesting in GPU computing. We address how these computations may be efficiently scheduled onto the target hardware, and how the system may adapt itself to changes in the CPU's load and in the input data-set.

1 Introduction

Most of the current computational systems are intrinsically heterogeneous, featuring a combination of multi-core CPUs and GPUs. However, the discrepancies of the programming and execution models in place make the programming of these hybrid systems a complex chore. Consequently, only experts with deep knowledge of parallel programming, and even computer architecture, are able to fully harness the available computing power.

The OpenCL specification has been designed with the purpose of enabling code portability across a wide range of architectures. However, the portability of performance is not guaranteed. In fact, it depends greatly on device-specific optimizations, which are cumbersome to implement, due to the low level nature of the programming model. Moreover, when targeting multiple devices, it is still up to the programmer to assume the parallel decomposition of the problem. Accordingly, the definition of high level programming constructs for heterogeneous computing has been the driver of a considerable amount of recent research both

---

* This work was partially funded by FCT-MEC in the framework of the PEst-OE/EEI/UI0527/2014 and PTDC/EIA-EIA/111518/2009 projects.

L. Lopes et al. (Eds.): Euro-Par 2014 Workshops, Part I, LNCS 8805, pp. 177–188, 2014.

at library and language level. A growing tendency is to build upon the notion of algorithmic skeleton [1–7].

We share this vision. Algorithmic skeletons render a template-based programming model that abstracts the complexity inherent to parallel computing by factorizing known solutions in the field into high level parameterizable structures. We claim that these characteristics can be used to, on one hand, hide the heterogeneity of the underlying hardware and, on the other, provide tools to cope with such heterogeneity, enabling device-specific parallel decompositions and optimizations. To that extent, we have been developing an algorithmic skeleton framework, entitled Marrow [8,9], for the orchestration of OpenCL kernels. Marrow offers both data and task-parallel skeletons, and is the first on the GPU computing field to support skeleton composition, through nesting.

In this paper, we grow the Marrow framework to provide a skeletal programming model for the transparent programming of computational systems comprising multiple CPUs and GPUs. Our proposal distinguishes itself from the current state of the art by supporting the execution of compound computations, having in mind data locality requirements. Most of the current frameworks either expose the heterogeneity to the programmer [5] (and [10] when considering performance) or selectively direct the computations exclusively to one of their CPU and GPU back-ends [1–4, 10, 11]. In turn, the proposals that tackle the transparent conjoint use of both CPUs and GPUs either restrict their scope to the execution of single kernels [12,13] or require previous knowledge on the computation to run [14]. The contributions of this paper are thus on the definition of strategies to distribute the load of a Marrow compound computation across multiple CPUs and GPUs, and to adapt this distribution to different input data-sets and to the CPUs' load fluctuations.

2   The Marrow Framework

Marrow is a C++ algorithmic skeleton framework for the orchestration of OpenCL computations. It provides a set of data and task-parallel skeletons that can be combined, through nesting, to build compound computations. A Marrow computation may be interpreted as a tree of skeleton constructions that apply a particular behavior to their sub-tree, down to the leaf nodes, which represent the actual OpenCL kernels. The framework takes upon itself the entire host-side orchestration required to correctly execute these computational trees (CTs), including the proper ordering of the data-transfer and execution requests, and the communication between the tree nodes. The following skeletons are currently supported:

Pipeline - a pipeline of data-dependent CTs; **Loop** - *while* and *for* loops over a CT; **Map** - application of a CT upon independent partitions of a data-set; **MapReduce** - extension of *Map* with a subsequent reduction stage.

The Marrow programming model comprises two main stages: the construction of the CTs and the subsequent issuing of execution requests. The framework allows for the composition of arbitrary OpenCL kernels. Accordingly, for the sake of correctness and efficiency, setting up a CT leaf requires the specification of the interface of the wrapped computational kernel, namely in what concerns its input and output parameters. For that purpose, the framework supplies a set of data-types to classify these parameters as vector or scalar values; mutable or immutable, and global or local. Moreover, the programmer may specify a kernel-specific local work-group size, for computations that are bound to particular sizes, and upon how many elements of the multi-dimensional range each computing thread (aka OpenCL work-unit) operates on. For instance, a thread may work upon multiple pixels of an image. This information will be used by the framework to compute the number of threads (OpenCL workspace) required to run the kernel.

```
1   vector<shared_ptr<IWorkData>> inData(2);
2   vector<shared_ptr<IWorkData>> outData(1);
3   // Gaussian noise kernel wrapper
4   outData[0] = inData[0] = shared_ptr<IWorkData> (new BufferData<cl_uchar4>());
5   inData[1] = shared_ptr<IWorkData> (new FinalData<int>(factor));
6   unique_ptr<IExecutable> gaussKernel (new KernelWrapper(gaussNoiseKernelFile, gaussNoiseFunction, inData, outData
        , 2)); // 2 is the number of elementary units computed per thread
7   // Solarise kernel wrapper
8   inData[1] = shared_ptr<IWorkData> (new FinalData<int>(threshold));
9   unique_ptr<IExecutable> solariseKernel (new KernelWrapper(solariseKernelFile, solariseFunction, inData, outData)
        );
10  // Mirror kernel wrapper
11  ...
12  // 3-stage pipeline
13  unique_ptr<IExecutable> pipeline (new Pipeline(gaussKernel, solariseKernel, mirrorKernel));
```

Listing 1. Image filter pipeline

Listing 1 presents a snippet of the construction of a pipeline with three stages. The setting up of the computation tree is a bottom-up process. It grows from the leafs, that take the form of KernelWrapper objects (line 8 and 11), which enclose a kernel's logic and domain in a single computational unit. The specification of the kernels' interface is expressed via the parameters of the associated wrapper. In this particular case, all kernels receive and output a single buffer (representing an image) and a final scalar value.

3   Cooperative Multi-CPU/Multi-GPU Execution

The main contribution of this paper is on the execution of Marrow CTs in hybrid multi-CPU/multi-GPU environments. To accomplish such enterprise we must address three key challenges: 1) how to efficiently decompose a CT among the multiple CPU and GPU devices; 2) how to efficiently distribute the work load among the available hardware resources, and; 3) how to adapt this distribution to different input data-sets and to the CPUs' load fluctuations. Due to space restrictions we will focus mainly on challenges 2 and 3, addressing the first lightly. For more details we refer the reader to a companion technical report [15].

Computational Tree Decomposition: To address this challenge we apply the same locality-aware approach that we devised for multi-GPU computing. We leverage the work-group based organization of OpenCL executions, namely the fact that work-groups (groups of threads) execute asynchronously and independently over data. Consequently, we opt to decompose the computation's data-set into partitions that can be adjusted to the best possible work-group size

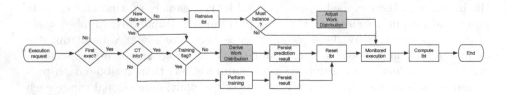

Fig. 1. The top-level work-distribution decision process

for each device. In that sense, we extend the scope of OpenCL's SPMD (Single Operation Multiple Data) based execution model to multiple devices, where each OpenCL work-group computes the CT over a partition of the input data-set.

The decomposition of the input data-set must be subjected to user-defined restrictions imposed in the CT's kernel specifications, but also be driven by the characteristics of the underlying hardware, such as the size of AMD wave-fronts or NVIDIA warps. Furthermore, in order to really leverage the aforementioned locality properties, the data communicated between two consecutive kernel executions must be partitioned in such a way that, each of such partitions may be communicated between the kernels simply by persisting in the device's memory across their execution. As a result, two kernel executions that communicate data-sets must expect an identical partitioning of such sets, with respect to their number and size(s), regardless the individual work-group size restrictions of either kernel. This approach induces a partitioning process with global vision of the computation, defining what we call a CT's *locality-aware domain decomposition*.

Work-Load Distribution: To efficiently execute computations composed by multiple (arbitrary) OpenCL kernels in hybrid multi-CPU/multi-GPU environments, we must engender a solution that is able to deliver good performances without requiring previous knowledge on the CT to execute.

In [9] we addressed this issue for heterogeneous multi-GPU environments. The workload is statically distributed among the devices, according to their relative performance. This static approach, although simple, delivers good performance results for GPU-accelerated executions, due to the specialized nature of the underlying execution model: one kernel execution at a time, with no preemption and no input/output operations. These premises are not valid for CPU executions. The execution time of a CPU computation is highly conditioned by the load of the processor, which is time-shared by multiple threads, and by hardware optimizations that cannot be fully controlled by the programmer, such as cache memory management. Therefore, to adequately balance the load of arbitrary computations between CPU and GPU of devices is still a challenge.

In this paper we are particularly interested in recurrent applications of CTs upon possibly different data-sets with different sizes. Therefore, we want to have a lightweight mechanism that is able to infer a suitable configuration for a CT's execution, given a particular parameterization. We address this challenge via profile-based self-adaptation. We still rely on static scheduling: the workload is distributed in advance between the available devices. However, this distribution resorts to a CT-specific profile built from past runs. Furthermore, we refine this information for subsequent executions, so that the distribution may be adapted to alterations of the CPUs' load and/or of the input data-set's size. The first execution of a CT upon a particular workload is preceded by the inference of the best configuration (of the ones known to the system) to run such computation. From that point on, subsequent executions are monitored by a controlling process that identifies, and corrects, load unbalances, so that the ensuing executions may be better adapted to the system's current load.

The top-level work-flow of the work-distribution process is depicted in Fig. 1. The entire decision process builds on the availability of historic data about the target CT's execution. This knowledge-base (KB) stores information about the best configuration for a given input data-set. The primary source is a training process that is triggered whenever there is no information about the target CT, or the user explicitly demands it through the framework's configuration settings. If none of these conditions hold, the framework will try to determine a suitable workload distribution from the KB. Such enterprise is trivial if the necessary information is already available, otherwise it will have to be derived from the existing knowledge. Both the training and the derivation branches terminate with the persisting of the attained result, qualified with the process employed. As a result, the derivation process also contributes to populate the KB, serving as a cache for following executions.

Once a work-distribution configuration has been derived, the execution proceeds under the monitoring of the controller process. This process simply calculates the deviation (dev) between the execution times of each concurrent application of the CT over a partition of the original data-set, and computes a load balancing threshold $lbt(n) = isUnbalanced(dev) \times w + lbt(n-1) \times (1-w)$, for the given execution number n – $isUnbalanced(x)$ indicates if the deviation falls out of the allowed interval, and w denotes the weight assigned to the last execution relatively to the historic data. The use of a weighted historic data factor makes lbt less sensitive to sporadic unbalanced executions.

When a CT is applied recurrently, but over data-sets with different characteristics, the work-distribution process may configured to revert to (a) the training process or to (b) the derivation of a new workload distribution from the KB. Option (a) is tailored for applications that operate over the same type of data-sets for long periods of time. In such cases, it compensates to have the best possible configuration, even if it takes some time to obtain it. Option (b) is more directed to applications that operate over indiscriminate types of data-sets, and want to build on previous knowledge to adjust the framework to the particularities of each of such types.

Dimensions to consider in the training process: The Marrow framework is modular and extensible, in the sense that it allows for multiple OpenCL back-ends, each one specialized for a given type of device. These back-ends are exposed as *execution platforms* that abstract the OpenCL communication details to the remainder modules and encapsulate all the device-specific optimizations. They are also responsible for supplying an iterator over which of their configuration parameters must be included in the training process. The current Marrow implementation features two execution platforms: CPU and GPU. The first supplies an iterator over the affinity fission configurations the device supports, a subset of: $(\bigcup_{i=1}^{4}\{L_i\_CACHE\})\cup\{NUMA\}\cup\{NO\_FISSION\}$, while the second offers an iterator over the number of overlapped executions to be performed in the GPU.

The training process: The process searches for the best parameterization of the existing execution platforms for the computation at hand. The algorithm performs an uniform search over the search space, spanning all possible combinations. This strategy is viable for the dimension of our current space. Nonetheless, in the future, scalability requirements may lead to the use of other techniques.

The algorithm requires a stoppage criterion, in the form of a `precision` value, a quality factor, in the form of the number of executions to be performed in each possible configuration, and the `task` to execute. It also assumes the existence of the CPU and GPU execution platforms, as well as of the `scheduler` module responsible for performing the static distribution of the work among the available devices. Given these premises, for each CPU_fission/GPU_overlap configuration the algorithm behaves as follows: 1) reconfigure the existing execution platforms; 2) activate the `scheduler`'s profiling mode, providing it the precision value and the quality factor; 3) perform the loop to obtain the best workload distribution for the current configuration - the *scheduler* internally determines the next configuration to test and computes the average execution time for the `nTrainingExecutions`; 4) store the work distribution that yielded the best performance and the associated execution time; 5) select the best performing configuration and reconfigure the execution platforms accordingly, and; 6) decompose the input data-set in conformance to the current parallelism level.

Concerning the CPU/GPU work-distribution internally determined by the `scheduler`, we have formulated two strategies: **50/50 split** evens, as much as possible, the time that each device type (CPU or GPU) takes to carry out the computation. For that purpose, it continuously transfers increasingly smaller parts of the load from the worst to the better performing device type. The relative execution times are expected to converge after a small number of iterations, being the algorithm bound to the `precision` value passed to the scheduler. **CPU assisted GPU execution** lessens the CPUs' role to a mere assistant of the GPUs, contributing only to lighten the latter's load. To that end, the strategy incrementally assigns work to the CPU so that the CT's overall execution time is minimized, independently of the devices' relative execution times.

Configuration Derivation: The configuration derivation process is twofold, represented by the two darker boxes in Fig. 1. Box "*Derive work distribution*" represents the derivation required to kickoff the execution of a CT, whenever the training flag in not active. For that purpose, we infer, by the means of interpolation, a workload distribution for the given input data-set from the information currently stored in the KB. The function to interpolate may be multidimensional, bound to the CT's number of input arguments. Our current approach employs the *nearest-neighbor* method sustained by the Euclidean distance over a multidimensional space, with as many dimensions as number of input arguments. The framework allows for the simple integration of new interpolation methods, and in the future other approaches may be implemented.

The second box "*Adjust work distribution*" is triggered whenever the value of $lbt \approx 1$. In order for the load balancing process to be as little intrusive as possible to the application's global execution, we employ a two-level approach, where the first level is considerable lighter, computationally, than the second. This **first** level tries to re-balance the load by simply transferring a percentage of the workload from the slowest performing device type to the other. The work transference is iteratively applied in the following executions of the CT, until the execution time of the parallel executions converge below the $maxDev$ upper bound. The **second** level reverts to a partial execution of the training process that only considers the current fission/overlap configuration.

4   Experimental Results

The purpose of this study is to quantify the performance gains that the conjoint use of the CPU and GPU may deliver relatively to GPU-only executions, and to assess the efficiency of the proposed work distribution and balancing strategies.

For the experiments, we resorted to five benchmarks that make use of the different skeletons available in Marrow. The first two make use of the *Pipeline* skeleton. **Filter Pipeline** composes three image filters: Gaussian Noise, Solarize and Mirror. All of them may be independently applied to distinct lines of the image to be processed. Accordingly, the line is the partition's elementary unit. **FFT** is a set of Fast-Fourier Transformations (FFTs) where FFT is pipelined with its inversion. The decomposition elementary unit is the size of each FFT which is 512 kBytes. Ergo, each device is assigned with a set of such FFTs. The third benchmark is the iterative **N-Body** simulation supported by the *Loop* skeleton. The kernel implements the direct-sum algorithm that, for each single body, computes its interaction with all the remainder. Therefore, there is a dependency on the whole data-set, requiring replication to all the data-set to all devices. The distribution is hence performed at body level, entailing a synchronization point in-between each iteration. The final two benchmarks are simple *Map* applications. The BLAS **Saxpy** routine computes a single-precision multiplication of a constant with a vector added to another vector. The computation is embarrassingly parallel and does not require any partitioning restrictions. **Segmentation** performs a transformation over a gray-scale three dimensional image. Although there is no algorithmic dependencies between pixel elements, the elementary size is set to the size of the first two dimensions so the partitioning is performed only over the last one.

All experiments were conducted on a system featuring one hyper-threaded six-core Intel(R) Core(TM) i7-3930K CPU @ 3.20GHz, with 6 L1 and L2 caches (one per core) and a single L3 cache, shared by all cores; two AMD HD 7950 GPU devices attached to two dedicated PCIe x16 lanes; and 32 GBytes of RAM.

For each benchmark we have established three parameterization classes and two baselines, that report the time for the GPU-only accelerated execution of the

Table 1. Benchmark characterization

Benchmark	Input type	Input argument	1 GPU Baseline execution time	50/50 Training Configuration (fission/overlap)	Level of parallelism	Distribution (GPU/CPU)	CPU assisted GPU Training Configuration (fission/overlap)	Level of parallelism	Distribution (GPU/CPU)	2 GPUs Baseline execution time	50/50 Training Configuration (fission/overlap)	Level of parallelism	Distribution (GPU/CPU)	CPU assisted GPU Training Configuration (fission/overlap)	Level of parallelism	Distribution (GPU/CPU)
Filter pipeline	Image (pixels)	1024x1024	1.97	L2/3	9	91.8/8.2	L1/3	9	92.5/7.5	1.12	L3/2	5	94.6/5.4	L1/3	12	96.8/1.2
		2048x2048	5.10	L3/4	8	92.9/7.1	none/4	8	93.8/6.3	3.84	L3/4	9	90.1/3.9	none/3	7	96.8/1.2
		4096x4096	16.80	none/4	5	93.8/6.3	none/4	5	93.8/6.3	11.76	none/4	9	96.9/3.1	none/4	9	97.5/2.5
FFT	Size of data-set	128MB	35.28	L2/3	9	32.8/67.2	L2/4	10	37.5/62.5	23.76	L1/4	14	59.8/40.2	L2/3	12	52.5/47.5
		256MB	67.83	L2/4	10	31.3/68.7	L1/4	10	30.0/70.0	43.12	L1/4	14	58.6/41.4	L2/4	14	55.0/45.0
		512MB	88.93	L1/3	9	37.1/62.9	L2/1	7	15.0/85.0	77.21	L1/4	14	56.3/43.8	L1/4	14	57.5/42.5
NBody	Number of bodies	16384	37.17	-	-	-	L1/1	7	95.0/5.0	29.87	-	-	-	L3/1	3	98.8/1.2
		32768	101.56	-	-	-	L2/1	7	97.5/2.5	69.63	-	-	-	L2/1	8	98.8/1.2
		65538	356.85	-	-	-	L2/1	7	98.8/1.2	200.76	-	-	-	L2/1	8	98.8/1.2
Saxpy	Number of elements	1×10^8	2.56	L1/2	8	41.4/58.6	L2/2	8	37.5/62.5	1.59	none/2	5	75.0/25.0	L1/2	10	67.5/32.5
		10×10^8	14.91	L1/2	8	45.3/54.7	none/4	8	67.5/32.5	10.97	L3/4	9	87.5/12.5	none/4	9	88.8/11.2
		50×10^8	72.86	L1/3	9	43.8/56.3	L1/3	9	47.5/52.5	46.84	L3/4	9	85.2/14.8	L1/4	14	77.5/22.5
Segmentation	Number of elements	1MB	0.79	none/2	3	59.3/40.1	none/1	2	55.0/45.0	0.72	none/1	3	69.5/30.5	none/2	5	85.6/14.4
		8MB	2.88	none/4	5	81.3/18.7	L3/4	5	78.8/21.2	1.87	none/3	7	86.3/11.7	none/2	5	88.8/11.2
		60MB	16.70	none/4	5	82.6/17.4	L1/4	10	78.8/21.2	10.75	none/4	9	93.0/7.0	L1/4	14	88.8/11.2

benchmarks using just one or the two available GPUs. Table 1 presents, for each of the determined parameterization classes, the baseline execution times and the results of applying the two training strategies to both the single and dual GPU setups. We do not present the result of the 50/50 split training for the NBody benchmark because the results are not usable. From this table we may observe that the best fission/overlap configuration depends on several factors: the actual computation, the input data-set's size, the number of devices, and the training strategy. Nonetheless, there is an aspect that spans most of the results: the correlation between the data-set's size and the level of fission and overlap. The advantages of the overlap tendentiously increase with the size of the data-set, leveraging the scalability lend by the two PCIe buses. In turn, the advantages of fission seem to decrease, implying that the fission support in the AMD OpenCL implementation (version 1348.5) is particularly beneficial when a data-set's partition fits the fission cache level.

Speedup Results: Figures 2 and 3 present the speedups obtained by the CPU+ GPU ensemble when compared to the GPU-only baselines. The results show that the use of the hybrid infrastructure is beneficial in almost every conducted experiments - the NBody benchmark is the exception. The impact is, naturally, more visible in the single GPU configuration, where the gains range from 1.3 to 3, whilst in the 2 GPU configuration they range from 1.4 to 2.6. The speedups are particularly noticeable in the communication-bound computations. Paradigmatic examples are the smaller parameterization classes of Saxpy and Segmentation, where the CPU boosts the overall performance more than twice for both the 1 and 2 GPUs configurations. In both these benchmarks, as the data-set's size increases so does the computational weight, mitigating the benefits of the CPU. This behavior may also be observed in the FFT benchmark. The FFT kernels are computationally heavy but also operate upon large data-sets: 128 to 512 MBytes. It is the ever-present trade-off between the overhead of data-transfers and the computational complexity of the computation.

Filter Pipeline is more computation bound. Three different computations are applied over a single image transferred to the GPU. Nonetheless, the CPU's utility is still more visible with smaller images, where less parallelism is required. In NBody the advantages of using the CPU are minimum due to the large amount of work assigned to the GPU. Loop's execution model is more complex than the remainder skeletons, using the GPU for executing the loop's body,

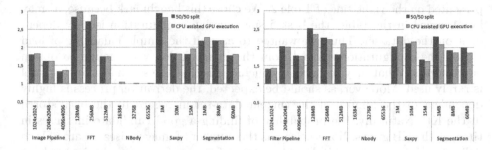

Fig. 2. Speedup: CPU+1GPU vs 1GPU   **Fig. 3.** Speedup: CPU+2GPUs vs 2GPUs

Table 2. Filter Pipeline: training's results versus interpolation from past executions

Image id	Image size	Training result				Derivation	Balancing		Resulting distribution		Exec.	Relative
		Fission	Overlap	GPU (%)	CPU (%)	Exec. time	Nearest neighbour	Level 1	Level 2	GPU (%)	CPU (%)	time	perf.
Image 1	1024x1024	L3	3	90.8	9.2	1.10							
Image 2	512x512	L3	2	87.5	12.5	0.54	Image 1	6	1	81.0	19.0	0.64	84%
Image 3	1024x2048	L1	4	91.5	8.5	1.74	Image 1	2	0	90.7	9.3	1.87	93%
Image 4	2048x512	L2	3	89.8	10.2	1.06	Image 1	4	0	90.6	9.4	1.07	100%
Image 5	2048x2048	none	4	92.9	7.1	3.17	Image 3	1	0	90.6	9.4	3.48	91%
Image 6	4096x4096	L3	4	93.8	6.3	12.59	Image 5	0	0	91.8	8.2	13.41	94%

and the CPU for iteration synchronization and evaluating the loop's condition. Our current profiling process is not able to differentiate the work performed on each type of processor, an issue that opens the door to more fine-grained profiling approaches. Nonetheless, in this particular benchmark, delegating the execution almost entirely to the GPUs is the best option. We artificially forced other distributions with worse results.

Regarding the two training strategies, the 50/50 split seems to be more reliable, as it tries to balance the load among the device types, while also taking into consideration the overall execution time. However, the results are quite close and even converge when the precision is very high.

Efficiency of the Work Distribution and Load Balancing Strategies: We selected the Filter Image benchmark to evaluate how does our configuration derivation behaves in the presence of different input data-sets. We begin with an empty KB, and populate it as the benchmark is successively applied to images *Image 1* to *Image 6*. Thus, when *Image i* is executed the KB contains knowledge about images *Image 1* to *Image i − 1*.

To establish individual baselines, we independently ran the training process for each image. The left-side of Table 2 presents such results. Then, beginning with the empty KB, we resorted to our nearest neighbor interpolation to successively apply the benchmark to images *1* to *6*. The benchmark was configured to run 500 times, so that we could count how many times the load balancing process was triggered, and its level — the framework was configured to considered balanced all runs whose partial execution times stay within 88% of each other. We also measured the final workload distribution, and the performance loss relatively to the one obtained from the training process. All these values are presented on the right-side of Table 2. We chose this benchmark because, as may be observed in the table, the best fission/overlap configuration is very dependent on the data-set. Thus, we wanted to asses if the simple balancing of load within the configuration derived from the interpolation was enough to obtain good results. What may be initially concluded is that the second balancing level is rarely used. Moreover, as should be expected, the derivation process is highly dependent of the affinity of the current data-set in regard to the ones stored in the KB. Naturally, the probability of finding a good candidate increases in time, as the KB grows. Nonetheless, as the number of images rises we are able to deliver performances within less than 10% of the performance obtainable from the training process.

For our last experiment, we selected the 50 million parameterization class of the Saxpy benchmark to study how the framework adapts to load fluctuations in the CPU. From Table 1 we have that the initial workload distribution is GPU ← 49.61% and CPU ← 50.39%. To introduce the load fluctuation on the CPU we implemented an application that spawns as many software threads as available

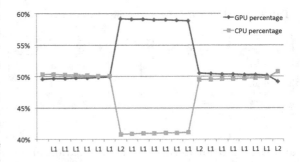

Fig. 4. Saxpy subjected to load fluctuations

hardware threads, each running a computationally heavy algebraic problem. Fig. 4 depicts the framework's adaptation to the sudden increase in the CPU's load. The process begins with the successive application of the level 1 load balancing strategy (L1 in the chart). However, the solution is not sufficiently aggressive to quickly shift the work to the GPU and, thus, the second level (L2 in the chart) is forced to kick in. The distribution stabilizes at GPU ← 58.18% and CPU ← 40.82%. As we terminate the load inducing application, the system becomes unbalanced once again. The balancing process restarts and, upon a first level 2 execution, the system is mostly balanced. Yet, in order for it to stay within the pre-determined 88% mark for balanced executions, a second burst of load balancing operations is required. The final distribution is GPU ← 49.22% and CPU ← 50.78%.

5   Related Work

There are several skeleton/template frameworks that address GPU computing. However, their focus in solely on data-parallel skeletons and none of them support skeleton nesting, thus no compound behaviors can be offloaded to the GPU. Heterogeneity support in such frameworks comes in two flavors. The first approach is to include, at language level, constructions to determine where the computation must take place, such is the case of Muesli [5]. The second approach obliges the programmer to direct the compilation at either CPUs or GPUs. This category includes SkePU [1] and Thrust [4], which feature multiple mutual exclusive backends, for either GPGPU or shared-memory parallel programming. SkePU can be combined with the StarPU scheduler to provide computation locality abstraction. Although StarPU has the capability to schedule tasks on both multi-core CPUs and GPUs simultaneously, when a task is submitted to SkePU, only the best performing device for the given input size is selected.

In [12], the authors propose a run-time infrastructure for executing MapReduce computations on hybrid CPU/GPU systems. They propose different methods for work distribution, from the scheduling of map tasks across the devices, to the placing of the map stage on a device and of the reduction stage on the other, much like what we allow in our MapReduce skeleton. The dynamic work distribution tries to adjust the task block sizes for subsequent executions of tasks in the same application.

Dandelion [10] offers a LINQ-based programming model for heterogeneous systems, extended with other constructions, such as loops. A specialized compiler generates code for both CPU and GPU from the source code, while the run-time system transparently offloads computations to the GPU, when the workload so justifies. Good performance requires the programmer to convey some GPU-related information, and no CPU+GPU support is provided.

The works presented in [11] and [16] address the paralellization of nested loops in heterogeneous environments. They both resort to polyhedral optimization techniques which restrict their scope to loops with affine expressions. The first selects the best device to run the computation but never resorts to CPU+GPU wide computations. The second generates OpenCL code for CPU, GPU and CPU+GPU environments, selecting the best hardware depending on the data flow requirements. Very few results are given for CPU+GPU environments.

Finally, in [14], the presented solution allows for work-partitioning among devices based on a performance model updated at run-time. This solution, however, requires the existence of multiple versions of the program, one for each different device present in the system.

6   Concluding Remarks

In this paper we have presented a systematic approach for the cooperative multi-CPU/multi-GPU execution of Marrow computations. We have proposed a locality-aware domain decomposition of Marrow skeleton trees that promotes data-locality but, simultaneously, allows for the multiple OpenCL kernels to be executed under different work-group configurations, as long as communication compatibility is assured. We have also proposed profile-based workload distribution and load balancing strategies, that build from past runs of a given computational tree to derive suitable configurations for subsequent executions. The experimental results show that our approach brings speedups up to 300% over GPU-only executions. Moreover, they also provide some insight on the framework's ability to adapt to data-sets of different sizes and to fluctuations on the

CPU's load. Regarding future work, the focus is on the improvement of our configuration derivation. We want to refine our profile-based approach with more sophisticated interpolation techniques, and combine these with static analysis of the kernel's code, in order to reduce the weight of the training stage.

References

1. Dastgeer, U., Li, L., Kessler, C.: Adaptive implementation selection in the skePU skeleton programming library. In: Wu, C., Cohen, A. (eds.) APPT 2013. LNCS, vol. 8299, pp. 170–183. Springer, Heidelberg (2013)
2. Steuwer, M., Gorlatch, S.: SkelCL: Enhancing openCL for high-level programming of multi-GPU systems. In: Malyshkin, V. (ed.) PaCT 2013. LNCS, vol. 7979, pp. 258–272. Springer, Heidelberg (2013)
3. AMD Corporation: Bolt C++ Template Library,
   http://developer.amd.com/tools/heterogeneous-computing/
4. Hoberock, J., Bell, N.: Thrust: A parallel template library,
   http://thrust.github.io/
5. Ernsting, S., Kuchen, H.: Algorithmic skeletons for multi-core, multi-GPU systems and clusters. Int. J. High Perform. Comput. Netw. 7(2), 129–138 (2012)
6. Huynh, H.P., et al.: Scalable framework for mapping streaming applications onto multi-GPU systems. In: PPoPP 2012, pp. 1–10. ACM (2012)
7. Dubach, C., others: Compiling a high-level language for GPUs (via language support for architectures and compilers). In: PLDI 2012, pp. 1–12. ACM (2012)
8. Marques, R., Paulino, H., Alexandre, F., Medeiros, P.D.: Algorithmic Skeleton Framework for the Orchestration of GPU Computations. In: Wolf, F., Mohr, B., an Mey, D. (eds.) Euro-Par 2013. LNCS, vol. 8097, pp. 874–885. Springer, Heidelberg (2013)
9. Alexandre, F., Marques, R., Paulino, H.: On the support of task-parallel algorithmic skeletons for multi-GPU computing. In: SAC 2014, pp. 880–885. ACM (2014)
10. Rossbach, C.J., Yu, Y., Currey, J., Martin, J.-P., Fetterly, D.: Dandelion: a compiler and runtime for heterogeneous systems. In: SOSP 2013, pp. 49–68. ACM (2013)
11. Dollinger, J.F., Loechner, V.: Adaptive runtime selection for GPU. In: ICPP 2013, pp. 70–79. IEEE Computer Society Press (2013)
12. Chen, L., Huo, X., Agrawal, G.: Accelerating MapReduce on a coupled CPU-GPU architecture. In: SC 2012, pp. 25:1–25:11. IEEE Computer Society Press (2012)
13. Lee, J., et al.: Transparent CPU-GPU collaboration for data-parallel kernels on heterogeneous systems. In: PaCT 2013, pp. 245–255. IEEE (2013)
14. Colaço, J., Matoga, A., Ilic, A., Roma, N., Tomás, P., Chaves, R.: Transparent application acceleration by intelligent scheduling of shared library calls on heterogeneous systems. In: Wyrzykowski, R., Dongarra, J., Karczewski, K., Waśniewski, J. (eds.) PPAM 2013, Part I. LNCS, vol. 8384, pp. 693–703. Springer, Heidelberg (2014)
15. Soldado, F., Alexandre, F., Paulino, H.: Transparent execution of compound OpenCL computations in multi-CPU/multi-GPU environments. Technical report, CITI/DI, Universidade NOVA de Lisboa (2014)
16. Dathathri, R., et al.: Generating efficient data movement code for heterogeneous architectures with distributed-memory. In: PaCT 2013, pp. 375–386. IEEE (2013)

Concurrent Data Structures in Architectures with Limited Shared Memory Support

Ivan Walulya, Yiannis Nikolakopoulos,
Marina Papatriantafilou, and Philippas Tsigas

Computer Science and Engineering
Chalmers University of Technology, Sweden
{ivanw,ioaniko,ptrianta,tsigas}@chalmers.se

Abstract. The Single-chip Cloud Computer (SCC) is an experimental multicore processor created by Intel Labs for the many-core research community, to study many-core processors, their programmability and scalability in connection to communication models. It is based on a distributed memory architecture that combines fast-access, small on-chip memory with large off-chip private and shared memory. Additionally, its design is meant to favour message-passing over the traditional shared-memory programming. To this effect, the platform deliberately does not provide hardware supported cache-coherence or atomic memory read/write operations across cores. Because of these limitations of the hardware support, algorithmic designs of concurrent data structures in the literature are not suitable.

In this paper, we delve into the problem of designing concurrent data structures on such systems. By utilising their very efficient message-passing together with the limited shared memory available, we provide two techniques that use the concept of a coordinator and one that combines local locks with message passing. All three achieve high concurrency and resiliency. These techniques allow us to design three efficient algorithms for concurrent FIFO queues. Our techniques are general and can be used to implement other concurrent abstract data types. We also provide an experimental study of the proposed queues on the SCC platform, analysing the behaviour of the throughput of our algorithms based on different memory placement policies.

1 Introduction

Shared concurrent data structures are necessary tools for inter-thread communication and synchronization. They provide multiple threads with access to shared data, guaranteeing the integrity of the latter. The commonly assumed model for providing algorithmic constructions of such data structures is the shared memory programming model, with a uniform address space and all threads having a uniform view of memory. In the literature there is a plethora of data structure implementations that guarantee high concurrency and resiliency (commonly through non-blocking guarantees, that avoid the use of locks [1, 2]). However, hardware that supports shared memory models does not scale very well with

L. Lopes et al. (Eds.): Euro-Par 2014 Workshops, Part I, LNCS 8805, pp. 189–200, 2014.

highly increasing numbers of cores. Furthermore, traditionally assumed cache-coherence is hard to achieve on many-core architectures. Consequently, from a hardware perspective, it is preferable to have a message-passing model, despite shared-memory programming being more desirable at the software level. Hence the high motivation for studying algorithmic implementations of concurrent shared data structures in alternative architectures and system models.

The Single-chip Cloud Computer (SCC) is a 48-core homogeneous experimental processor created by Intel Labs for the many-core research community [3]. The SCC is a hybrid system providing both shared and private memory, but favors message-passing over shared-memory programming, as the cores communicate using a low latency message passing architecture through the on-die mesh network. Neither hardware supported cache-coherence, nor atomic memory read/write operations across cores are provided. Shared memory access is manually instrumented while each of the 48 P54C cores is strongly memory ordered. Message-passing is ideal for transfer of small amounts of data due to the limited size of the message passing buffers, but not very efficient for large data transfers. In addition, replicating all datasets and exchanging them as messages is less efficient and more wasteful than using the data directly in shared memory.

Challenges in providing algorithmic data structure implementations in such a system model are summarized as follows: (i) the absence of universal atomic primitives (e.g. Compare&Swap) makes it hard or impossible to have fully non-blocking implementations [4] (ii) we need to construct an abstraction to the application layer that guarantees safety and provides liveness properties achievable within the bounds of the architecture.

We study the possibilities enabled by the configurable SCC architecture and propose a set of methods that address the above challenges for architectures that combine message-passing with shared-memory We propose that the message-passing operations not only can provide data-transfer, but also can be exploited for coordinating shared-memory access and synchronization of concurrent operations. We provide two techniques that build on this; one that uses the concept of a coordinator and one that combines spin locks with message passing. Our methods are inspired by ideas from shared-memory programming and distributed data structures; all three achieve high concurrency and resiliency properties. These techniques allow us to design three efficient algorithms for concurrent FIFO queues, while they can be also used to implement other concurrent abstract data types. The first, based on the blocking two-lock queue by Michael and Scott [2], provides fine-grained synchronization by using a distinct lock for the head and tail pointers of the queue, while uses the message passing to coordinate access to the data. Two more queue implementations are presented, that are based on leader based coordination by using the message passing communication.

The structure of the paper is the following. In section 2 we describe the model of the system and the studied problem. Section 3 presents the proposed implementations, while in section 4 correctness and progress guarantees are discussed. Section 5 presents an experimental evaluation and related work is discussed in section 6. Section 7 concludes the paper.

2   System Model and Problem Description

The SCC consists of a 6x4 mesh of dual-core tiles. The die has four on-chip memory controllers, making it capable of addressing up to a maximum of 64GB off-chip memory, in addition to 16Kb SRAM located on each tile. The off-chip memory is divided into segments private to each core and segments accessible to all cores. Non-uniform memory access (NUMA) applies to both on and off-chip memory. The chip features a 2D mesh network used to carry inter-tile communications by memory read/write operations. Packet routing on the mesh employs Virtual Cut-Throughswitching with X-Y routing [5]. Processing threads executing on the platform communicate by reading and writing to the on-chip shared SRAM, commonly referred to as the *message passing buffers (MPB)*. Data read from these buffers is only cached in L1 cache and tagged as MPB type (MPBT). MPBT cache lines can be explicitly invalidated. The platform deliberately provides neither hardware supported cache-coherence, thus shared memory accesses are manually instrumented while each of the cores is strongly memory ordered. Each core on the chip is assigned a Test&Set register, which can be used to build spin locks instrumental in constructing synchronization primitives or communication protocols. We refer the reader to [6] for more details on the platform.

The problem studied in this work is how to develop linearizable concurrent data structures for many-core systems that combine the shared memory and message-passing model, as the one in the SCC architecture outlined above — i.e. without universal atomic primitives — and provide to as high extent as possible liveness properties, throughput and scalability. The access methods to the shared data structures are invoked by units of execution (processes/threads). Implementations of such methods need to rely on the system's communication methods described above. The correctness of such data structures is commonly evaluated with safety properties that are provided by their method specifications. Linearizability [1] is a commonly used and desirable target: an implementation of a concurrent object is *linearizable* if every concurrent execution can be mapped to a sequential equivalent that respects the real time ordering of operations. Liveness properties of concurrent data structure implementations, such as non-blocking properties, are also desirable since they ensure system-wide progress as long as there are non-halted processes. In the stystem model under consideration, the absence of universal atomic primitives (e.g. Compare&Swap) makes it hard or impossible to have fully non-blocking implementations [4].

More specifically in the paper we present linearizable concurrent implementations of FIFO queues that also achieve liveness properties to the extent possible. Besides throughput, fairness is an important property of concurrent implementations. We follow the definition in [7], i.e. to study each core's i number of operations ops in relation to the total operations achieved. More formally, $fairness = \min\left\{\frac{\min(ops_i)}{average_i(ops_i)}, \frac{average_i(ops_i)}{max(ops_i)}\right\}$. Values close to 1 indicate fair behavior, while lower values imply the existence of a set of cores being treated differently from the rest.

3   New Methods and Implied FIFO Queues with Limited Shared Memory

The main ideas in the methods we propose are the following: Our approach in ensuring mutual exclusion and thread coordination starts with implementing fine-grain locking mechanisms by exploiting local per core Test&Set primitives along with message passing based communication. The latter is used in order to enable the concurrent copying or accessing of data to the off-chip memory. We then present a client server model that further exploits the low latency communication and reduces blocking conditions. Moving towards a non-blocking algorithmic construction, we improve the last design by using acknowledgments that help reducing dependencies within concurrent operations.

3.1   Critical Sections over Local Spin Locks

We start by proposing the utilization of the local per core Test&Set in order to derive a method for spin locking over a mesh network and its use for an implementation of a concurrent queue. The queue design is based on the two-lock queue by Michael & Scott [2], implemented as a static memory array in shared off-chip memory. The two locks utilized, one for each of the head and tail pointers, allow an enqueue operation to proceed in parallel with a dequeue one. These pointers are stored in the fast access message-passing buffer (MPB).

Due to the NUMA architecture of the SCC, cores experience different latencies while accessing MPB or off-chip memory. With this in mind, we sought to increase parallelism by limiting the work inside the critical sections to updating the head or tail pointer; i.e. a thread holds a lock *only* for the duration of updating the respective pointer. This is achievable because the data structure is stored in statically allocated memory.

The general procedure for the two-lock queue methods is as described below. To enqueue an item to the list:

1. A core acquires the *enqueue_lock* or *tail_lock* and reads the current tail pointer. The pointer holds the offset to the next empty index in the array and not the last added item; thus it refers to a place holder in the queue.
2. The enqueuer increments the tail pointer and writes back the new value of the pointer to the MPB.
3. Then it releases the lock, allowing other processes to proceed and acquire the enqueue_lock, while enqueuer proceeds to add the data item to the address location read to the shared off-chip memory .

An item is logically added to the list as soon as the tail pointer position is incremented and written back, albeit the data item not having been added to the shared off-chip memory. There is a possibility of a dequeuer reading an item that is yet to be added to the queue. To prevent a dequeuer from reading a null item value, a flag bit is added to the data item to indicate that the latter has absolutely been enqueued to the list. To dequeue a data item:

1. A process acquires the *dequeue_lock*, reads the queue_t pointer, and checks if the head_offset is equal to the tail_offset.
2. If true, the queue is momentarily empty and the dequeuer releases the lock returning an appropriate value to the caller indicating an empty queue.
3. If the queue is not empty, the dequeuer reads the current queue's head offset. Then increments the head offset pointer, writes the new value back to MPB and releases the *dequeue_lock*.
4. After releasing the lock, it proceeds to check the node's dirty flag to confirm that the dequeued data item has been enqueued previously. If the flag is not set, the dequeueing processes spins on the flag until it is set. When this happens, the dequeuer can proceed and return the value of the node.

The enqueue/dequeue thread releases the lock before writing/reading data to the high latency off-chip memory. Early release of the lock implies that the critical section is reduced to incrementing the head or tail pointer indexes, however physically adding an item to the data structure is not included in the critical section.

Despite the blocking nature of the algorithm, we allow for multiple concurrent memory reads/writes to the off-chip shared memory, resulting in an optimized implementation that suits the SCC NUMA architecture. We also observe that since the platform does not support cache coherence, every request for the lock takes a cache miss thus generating network traffic. Network congestion has a significant impact on system performance, therefore as a result of the X-Y routing used , lock placement on the mesh is very imperative.

3.2   Critical Sections over Message Passing and Hybrid Memory

Memory contention and network congestion when many cores simultaneously try to acquire a lock are bound to degrade system performance and increase execution time within critical sections. To overcome problems associated with lock synchronization, we created a shared queue to which concurrent access is synchronized by message-passing. In this abstraction, one node (the server) owns the data structure, and all other nodes (the clients) request exclusive ownership to elements of the data structure at a given time.

Hybrid Memory Queue. The queue data structure resides in off-chip shared-memory, with the server holding pointers to the head and tail of the queue in its private memory. For a core to add an item to the queue, it must request for the position of the tail from the server. A node removing an item from the list also acquires the head position in a similar procedure. All this communication takes place in the MPB. The server handles enqueue/dequeue requests in a round-robin fashion polling over dedicated communication slots. The server process loops over the slots, reading requests, writing responses to the response buffers, and correspondingly exclusively updates the queue pointers. The clients spin over receive slots in their local MPB buffers until a response is received from the server.

We implement the message-passing mechanism utilizing receiver side placement i.e. the sender writes the data to the receiver's local MPBs. This way, both the server and the clients spin on local memory while polling for incoming messages, thus reducing network traffic. To manage the message-passing buffers, the server allocates slots in its local MPB memory, one for each of the participating cores. Each client core can have only one outstanding request at a time. The server also requires a slot on the client core's local MPB memory for writing responses for the requesting core. After each client request is made, the client core spins on this receive buffer for a response from the server.

Particularly for an *enqueue*, the client sends a request for the queue tail-offset to the server and spins on a slot in its local MPB afterwards, waiting for a response. On receiving the enqueue request message, the server updates the queue tail pointer and responds with the previous offset to the requesting core. The enqueueing client then proceeds to add the data to the shared memory location pointed to by the offset and completes the operation by setting the flag on the memory slot to true. Similarly a *dequeue* operation starts with a request for the head offset to the server. The latter handles the request returning an appropriate offset. The client spins until the dirty flag on the memory slot is true before removing the data from the list, so that it does not try to dequeue an item from a stalled operation.

Hybrid Memory Queue with Acknowledgments. In the previous solution, the use of flags to indicate completion of an enqueue process may result in blocking of the dequeue method. This blocking could be indefinite if the enqueueing process fails before adding a node to the allocated memory location. To eliminate this and improve the concurrency and liveness properties of the method, we add an acknowledgement step to the enqueue procedure, where the enqueuer notifies the server after writing the data item to shared memory.

The server maintains a private queue of pointers to locations in the shared memory where data nodes have been enqueued successfully and the server has been acknowledged. Similarly to the previous design, the client requests for a pointer in the shared memory from the server via the MPB. The server replies as before and when acknowledged it adds the appropriate memory offset to its private queue of memory locations. Respectively a dequeuer is assigned with pointers only from this private queue, thus making sure it can proceed and dequeue the data item from shared memory without blocking. This implementation adds an extra message-exchange phase, nevertheless it solves problems arising from failed client processes during an enqueue method call.

Memory Management. The algorithms presented in this paper utilize statically allocated arrays in off-chip shared memory. Queues built with underlying arrays are bounded by the size of the array and algorithms have to address memory reclamation/reuse. One popular way of addressing the memory reuse problem is to deploy the array as a circular buffer. However, naive implementations of circular buffers run into an issue of array indices growing indefinitely. In our algorithms we use the approach of a linked list of arrays. In this approach, when the head pointer gets to the end of the current array, a new block of memory is allocated, and a pointer to this new block is added to the current block [8].

In our designs, head and tail pointers hold references to memory addresses and not indices, therefore we do not have to deal with indefinitely increasing array indices. On the grounds that shared memory is managed by the application and not the operating system, we can combine both mechanisms, that is circular buffer and linked list of arrays re-use the allocated static memory and resize the data structure respectively.

4 Correctness and Progress Guarantees

Followingly, limited to space constraints, we sketch the steps for proving the correctness of the implemented algorithms and also study their liveness properties.

Claim. All the three algorithms can be proved to maintain the following safety properties, by using induction, similar to the proof sketch of [2]. (i) The queue is a list of nodes that are always connected. (ii) New items are only added to the end of the list. (iii) Items are only removed from the beginning of the list (iv) Tail always points to the next empty slot in the list. (v) Head always points to the first element in the list.

Based on these properties now the following lemmas can be proved:

Lemma 1. *If a dequeue method call returns an item x, then it was previously enqueued, thus Enqueue(x) precedes Dequeue(x).*

Lemma 2. *If an item x is enqueued at a node, then there is only one dequeue method call that returns x and removes the node from the queue.*

The latter lemmas, along with the fact that all the data structure operations are serialized either by locks or by the server's request handling, imply the following:

Theorem 1. *The presented FIFO queues are linearizable to a sequential implementation.*

Moving to the liveness properties of the proposed implementations, the lock based queue is a blocking but deadlock and livelock-free implementation, since there exists no dependency when owning shared resources and the locks used are livelock-free. The message-passing based queue algorithms utilize a *Server-Client* model of interaction, in which all clients' progress depends on the server due to the request-response interactions to ascertain the values of the head and tail pointers. This dependence of all clients on the server forces us to present liveness properties assuming a fault-free server. Under this assumption and considering that the server handles requests in a round-robin fashion we can see that:

Lemma 3. *The server responds to every client request in bounded time.*

Message-passing based algorithm. Lemma 3 guarantees that an enqueue method's poll for memory allocation will be arbitrated eventually. Similarly for the dequeue operation's polling for the position of the head. However, the dequeue method loops again, after receiving the pointer to the queue head and before reading the nodes value, in order to check that an item was successfully enqueued to the assigned slot. It fails to terminate this loop, only if the enqueue fails to successfully add data items to the allocated slot. Consequently, the dequeue operation would be blocked with respect to the corresponding enqueue operation. Other operations in the system will succeed though, despite this blocked dequeue operation. Thus this blocking is only at an enqueue-dequeue pair level and does not deter progress of other processes i.e. system progress. We propose the term "pairwise-blocking" to describe this behavior.

Definition 1 (Pairwise-blocking). *Pairwise blocking is the condition under which the progress failure of a process affects at most one other process in the system (its pair).*

In the context of the latter queue data structure, a dequeue operation can be pairwise-blocked to the respective enqueue operation. Consequently we can show:

Theorem 2. *Message-passing based algorithm is pairwise-blocking.*

Message-passing based algorithm with acknowledgments. To eliminate the possibility of blocked operations, the enqueue method call notifies the server when successfully adding a node to the data structure, which is the point when the node is logically added. In this way, the server maintains record of added nodes, and only allocates successfully enqueued memory slots to a dequeuer. The above along with lemma 3 assist in showing that the restrictions of pairwise-blocking have been eliminated.

5   Experimental Study

In this section, we comprehensively evaluate the throughput, fairness and scalability of the algorithms described in sections 3.1 and 3.2. We begin by giving a detailed description of our experimental setup. Then we present experimental results and an evaluation of the different concurrent queue implementations.

Setup and Methodolody. We implemented the algorithms on the Intel SCC platform running cores at 533MHz, mesh routers at 800MHz and 800MHz DDR3 memory. All algorithms and testing code are written in C and compiled with *icc* targeted for the P54C architecture. The version of icc used was only validated for GCC version 3.4.0, and an experimental Linux version 3.1.4scc Image loaded on each core. In the experiments, we treat each core as a single unit of execution and assume only one application thread/process running per core. We run the algorithms for 600ms per execution, with each core choosing randomly an enqueue or a dequeue operation with equal probability. We varied contention levels by adding "other work" or "dummy executions" to the experiments. The dummy executions consist of 1000 or 2000 integer increment operations. We also randomized the execution and duration of the dummy work on the different cores, as we compared the algorithms under different contention levels. *High* *contention* is the execution in which no dummy work is done in between queue method calls, while as under *low contention* conditions we execute dummy work every after calling a queue method. We measured system throughput as the number of successful enqueue and dequeue operations per millisecond. Fairness, as introduced in Sec. 2, is used to analyze how well each core performs in relation to the other cores.

5.1   Experimental Results

Figure 1 presents the results of the study, showing the system throughput and the fairness of our algorithms. In this experiment, the locks were located on tile (x=5,y=0) and we used the core 0 on tile (x=0,y=0) as the server for the message-passing algorithms. Using one core as a dedicated server, we only run experiments up to 47 contending cores in the message-passing algorithms.

To evaluate the benefit of latency hiding in the two-lock data structure, we examined the performance of the data structure without the early release of the lock (henceforth MSW-Queue). From Fig. 1(a), we observe that the optimized implementation of the two-lock concurrent data structure with early release of the lock achieves higher system throughput than the MSW-Queue implementation under high contention. The figure also shows that message-passing based algorithms achieve less system throughput, however, with very high level of fairness to all participating cores.

Figure 1(b) shows that the fairness of the lock-based algorithms drops as we increase the number of cores due to increasing contention for the head and tail pointers. Because of the NUMA architecture and mesh network, this observation led us to investigate the throughput and fairness of the system as we vary the placement of the locks on the chip. We present the results of this experimentation later in this section. Under low contention system configuration, all algorithms give a linear improvement in system throughput with increasing number cores. One key observation was that the lock-based algorithms give almost identical throughput and fairness values.

Performance in Relation to Lock Location. In this experiment, we selected 5 cores scattered around the chip and measured the throughput of these cores as we increased the number of participating cores. The additional cores were also scattered uniformly around the chip so as to spread the traffic almost evenly on the mesh network. When running the experiments, we activated a single core on each tile until all the tiles hosted an active core, after which, we started activating the second core on every tile.

Additionally, we changed the positions of the lock and repeated the experiment, so as to investigate how the performance of the system varies with lock placement in the grid. XY routing [5] used on the SCC motivated the decision to perform these experiments because it does not evenly spread traffic over the whole network, resulting in a highest load in the center of the chip. This creates the need to find an optimal location for the locks so that the system performance does not degrade tremendously as we increase the number of executing cores.

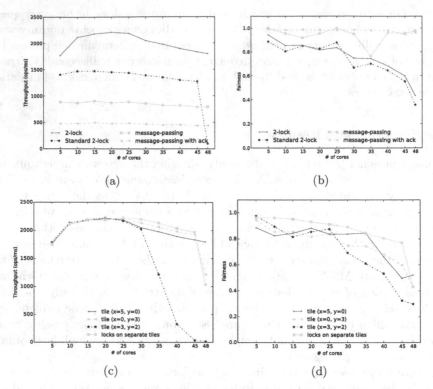

Fig. 1. Throughput and fairness at high contention of the different queue implementations (a, b) and the different lock positions for the lock based implementation (c, d)

We plot the results in Fig. 1(c) and 1(d). The degradation of performance varies with the location of the locks, with the highest performance degradation experienced when we place the lock at tile (x=3,y=2).

When the lock is placed in the middle of the chip, tile (x=3,y=2), the high contention for the lock creates very high traffic load in the middle of the chip, which degrades performance to almost a halt. With the network overloaded due to contention for the lock, the core holding the lock delays to release the lock. Contending cores cannot acquire it, continuing to spin. This creates a situation where the lock is not used, and thus no progress is achieved by the system. This deterioration in system throughput is evident in Fig. 1(c). Figure 1(d) presents the fairness values for the different lock positions, generally fairness decreases as we increase contention, but it is more paramount when the locks are positioned in the middle of the mesh.

We also performed the experiments under low contention configuration. In this case, congestion does not impact lock acquisition and release and there is a linear throughput improvement with the increase in participating cores. We further observed that placing the locks in the middle of the chip, we achieved very good throughput figures. This confirms the earlier intuition that network congestion delays release of the lock thus deteriorating system performance. We further analyzed the throughput of each core relative to its distance from the

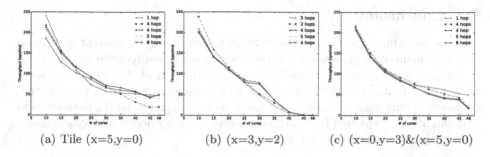

(a) Tile (x=5,y=0)   (b) (x=3,y=2)   (c) (x=0,y=3)&(x=5,y=0)

Fig. 2. Core throughput with changes in lock location and an increasing number of executing cores at high contention

locks. For this analysis, we plot the throughput of each core against the number of executing cores. This allows us to observe how increasing contention affects the core's throughput with regards to its location and distance from the locks. Figure 2 shows the results from 5 cores and different lock placements as discussed previously. The performance of each core degrades with an increasing number of executing cores. It is also clear that for a low number of executing cores, the cores closer to the locks have a higher throughput. However, as we increase the core count, the throughput of these cores deteriorates, and in some cases (Fig 2(a)), it is worse than for cores further from the locks. To reduce the congestion on a single area of the chip for the 2-lock algorithm, we placed the two locks in different locations on the chip. In this case, the cores achieved almost identical performance as no single core has a much better latency advantage with regards to the distance from both enqueue and dequeue locks (Fig. 2(c)).

6   Related Work

Petrovic et al. [9] provide an implementation that takes advantage of hardware message-passing and cache-coherent shared memory on hybrid processors. They propose HYBCOMB, a combining algorithm in which threads elect a combiner that handles requests from other threads for operations to be executed in mutual exclusion. The identity of the combiner is managed using a shared variable that is updated using a CAS, thus not viable without atomic read/write instructions;

Delegation of critical sections to a dedicated server has also been considered in the design of a NUMA friendly stack [10]. Similarly migration of critical-sections was used to implement remote core locking [11]. In this work, a thread that wants to execute a critical section, migrates the critical section to a dedicated server thread. The general idea is to replace lock acquisitions with software remote procedure calls. All the above solutions require a shared memory model and cache-coherent hardware architecture. The emergence of non-uniform memory access many-core architectures with or without cache coherence is limiting the portability of concurrent data structures based on a shared memory model. Our algorithms can be implemented on new multi-core platforms without support for cache coherent shared memory model or universal atomic primitives.

7   Conclusion

The proposed implementations illustrate that constructing concurrent data structures on many-core processors without atomic read-modify-write primitives or
uniform address space is a possible but non-trivial task. We further make a
proposition that, for architectures that combine message-passing with shared-
memory, the message-passing is not necessarily only essential for data-transfer
but can also be exploited to coordinate shared-memory access and synchronization of operations on the different cores.

Acknowledgements. We extend our gratitude to Intel for access to the SCC.
The research leading to these results has received funding from the European
Union Seventh Framework Programme (FP7/2007-2013) under grant agreement
No: 611183, EXCESS Project, www.excess-project.eu.

References

[1] Herlihy, M., Shavit, N.: The Art of Multiprocessor Programming. Morgan Kaufmann Publishers Inc., San Francisco (2008)

[2] Michael, M.M., Scott, M.L.: Simple, fast, and practical non-blocking and blocking
concurrent queue algorithms. In: Proceedings of the fifteenth annual ACM symposium on Principles of distributed computing, PODC 1996, pp. 267–275. ACM
(1996)

[3] J., Dighe, Howard, o.: A 48-core ia-32 message-passing processor with dvfs in
45nm cmos. In: 2010 IEEE International Solid-State Circuits Conference Digest
of Technical Papers (ISSCC), pp. 108–109 (2010)

[4] Herlihy, M.P.: Impossibility and universality results for wait-free synchronization.
In: Proceedings of the Seventh Annual ACM Symposium on Principles of Distributed Computing, PODC 1988, pp. 276–290. ACM, New York (1988)

[5] Zhang, W., Hou, L., others: Comparison research between xy and odd-even routing
algorithm of a 2-dimension 3x3 mesh topology network-on-chip. In: WRI Global
Congress on Intelligent Systems, GCIS 2009, vol. 3, pp. 329–333 (2009)

[6] Intel Cooporation: SCC External Architecture Specification (November 2010)

[7] Cederman, D., Chatterjee, B., et al.: et al.: A study of the behavior of synchronization methods in commonly used languages and systems. In: Proceedings of the
27th IEEE International Parallel & Distributed Processing Symposium (2013)

[8] Gidenstam, A., Sundell, H., Tsigas, P.: Cache-aware lock-free queues for multi-
ple producers/Consumers and weak memory consistency. In: Lu, C., Masuzawa,
T., Mosbah, M. (eds.) OPODIS 2010. LNCS, vol. 6490, pp. 302–317. Springer,
Heidelberg (2010)

[9] Petrovic, D., André, Schiper, o.: Leveraging hardware message passing for efficient
thread synchronization. In: 19th ACM SIGPLAN Symposium on Principles and
Practice of Parallel Programming. Number EPFL-CONF-190495 (2014)

[10] Calciu, I., Gottschlich, J.E., Herlihy, M.: Using elimination and delegation to implement a scalable numa-friendly stack. In: Proc. Usenix Workshop on Hot Topics
in Parallelism, HotPar (2013)

[11] Ozi, J.P., David, F., et al.: Remote core locking: migrating critical-section execution to improve the performance of multithreaded applications. In: Proc. Usenix
Annual Technical Conf., pp. 65–76 (2012)

Optimal Data Partitioning Shape for Matrix Multiplication on Three Fully Connected Heterogeneous Processors

Ashley DeFlumere and Alexey Lastovetsky

School of Computer Science and Informatics
University College Dublin
Belfield, Dublin 4, Ireland

Abstract. Parallel Matrix Matrix Multiplication (MMM) is used in scientific codes across many disciplines. While it has been widely studied how to optimally divide MMM among homogenous compute nodes, the optimal solution for heterogeneous systems remains an open problem. Dividing MMM across multiple processors or clusters requires consideration of the performance characteristics of both the computation and the communication subsystems. The degree to which each of these affects execution time depends on the system and the algorithm used to divide, communicate, and compute the MMM data. Our previous work has determined the optimum shape must be, for all ratios of processing power, communication bandwidth and matrix size, one of six well-defined shapes for each of the five MMM algorithms studied. This paper further reduces the number of potentially optimal candidate shapes to three defined shapes known as Square Corner, Square Rectangle, and Block Rectangle. We then find, for each algorithm and all ratios of computational power among processors, ratios of overall computational power and communication speed, and problem size, the optimum shape. The Block Rectangle, a traditional 2D rectangular partition shape, is predictably optimal when using relatively homogeneous processors, and is also optimal for heterogeneous systems with a fast, medium and slow processor. However, the Square Corner shape is the optimum for heterogeneous environments with a powerful processor and two slower processors, and the Square Rectangle is optimal for heterogeneous environments composed of a two fast processors and a single less powerful processor. These theoretical results are confirmed using a series of experiments conducted on Grid'5000, which show both that the predicted optimum shape is indeed optimal, and that the remaining two partition shapes perform in their predicted order.

1 Introduction

The problem of partitioning Parallel Matrix Matrix Multiplication (MMM) optimally over an arbitrary number of processors has been the subject of extensive study. While this problem, when approached using homogeneous processors, presents a challenge, it is significantly more substantive when considering

L. Lopes et al. (Eds.): Euro-Par 2014 Workshops, Part I, LNCS 8805, pp. 201–214, 2014.

heterogeneous systems. High performance scientific computing platforms are increasingly heterogeneous, so it is necessary to find the optimum heterogeneous MMM data partition shape[1]. While a system may be heterogeneous in its computational power, its communication interconnect, or some combination of both, this paper will focus on heterogeneity in computational power.

The bulk of the previous study of MMM partitioning on heterogeneous platforms has been concerned with finding the optimal *rectangular* partitioning[2][3][4]. Even when restricting the optimality problem to only rectangular shapes, it is complex and NP-complete for an arbitrary number of heterogeneous processors[5]. The underlying assumption that the optimal shape should be rectangular has only recently been questioned.

Our previous work challenged this traditional assumption, and explored both rectangular and non-rectangular data partition shapes[6][7]. These papers, encompassing work with both two and three processor systems, show optimal, and potentially optimal, partition shapes that have both expected and unexpected shapes. The two processor case, for instance, has an optimal data partition shape which is non-rectangular for highly heterogeneous systems, *i.e.*, when the ratio of computational power between the two processors is greater than three.

The complexity of the optimal shape problem necessitates beginning with a small number of processors in order to establish an extensible method for identifying potentially optimal partition shapes. This novel method, called the Push Technique, incrementally improves a partition shape by decreasing its volume of communication. The Push Technique has previously been applied to the case of three heterogeneous processors, and identified six potentially optimal partition shapes, called candidates. These are seen in Fig. 1.

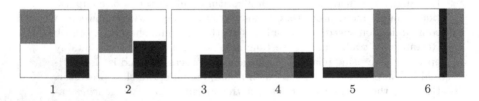

Fig. 1. The candidate partition shapes previously identified as potentially optimal three processor shapes. Processors P, R, and S are in white, grey, and black, respectively. (1) Square Corner (2) Rectangle Corner (3) Square Rectangle (4) Block 2D Rectangular (5) L Rectangular (6) Traditional 1D Rectangular.

These cases, with small numbers of processors, are also practically significant. Consider a GPU-CPU hybrid system. The concept of abstract processors may be used to model this type of system[8]. Each logical processor represents an independent group of tightly coupled devices such as cores on the same socket, or a GPU and its host core. In this way, a modern hybrid compute node is modelled by a small number of abstract heterogeneous processors.

This paper proves that the optimal candidates may be further reduced to just three optimal partition shapes, the Square Corner, the Square Rectangle, and the

Block Rectangle. For each MMM algorithm, each of these shapes is optimal for a subset of the possible ranges of computational power ratios and communication bandwidths. Together, they describe the optimal shape for all possible ranges of these values. These theoretical results are further verified using experiments on GRID'5000.

2   Problem Description

Throughout, we will make several assumptions, as follows:

1. Matrices A, B and C are square, of size $N \times N$, and identically partitioned among Processors P, R, and S, represented in figures as white, grey and black, respectively.
2. Processor P computes faster than Processors R and S by ratio, $P_r : R_r : S_r$, where $S_r = 1$.
3. All Processors may communicate with all other Processors, with no constraints on network topology.

For all algorithms, we use the Hockney Model[9] of communication $T_{comm} = \alpha \times \beta M$. For simplicity, we will set $\alpha = 0$. The total volume of communication is calculated as $M = \sum_{i=1}^{N} N(p_i - 1) + \sum_{j=1}^{N} N(p_j - 1)$, where p_i is the number of processors assigned elements in row i, and p_j is the number of processors assigned elements in column j. The method of computation in all algorithms is assumed to be SUMMA[10].

3   Theoretical Results

3.1   Methodology

Partition shapes have defined metrics that are used to determine the optimality of a given shape in a particular problem space. Some of these metrics quantify the volume of communication of a particular shape. The volume of communication is, in turn, used to create the model of communication time, T_{comm}, within the constraints of the MMM algorithm. The volume of elements assigned to each processor for computation, and the relative computational power of each processor, is used to create the model of computation time, T_{comp}. These two fundamental parts of the MMM, T_{comm} and T_{comp}, are combined according to the MMM algorithm to create a total execution time, T_{exe}, for the particular partition shape.

The partition shape which minimises the execution time for a specific MMM algorithm is said to the be the optimum shape. However, no single shape is the global optimum for an entire MMM algorithm. Each shape has unique characteristics which allow for increased performance under certain conditions, such as varied processor computational ratios, and the ratio between overall computation and communication speeds.

The sections below describe the process of forming the T_{exe} model for each shape using each MMM algorithm and analysing those models to find the minimum, and thereby the optimum. The proofs for all theorems found throughout this paper may be examined in [11].

3.2 Pruning Candidates

Upon further inspection of the six potentially optimal candidate shapes found in [7], it is possible to analytically reduce this to three candidate shapes.

Theorem 1 (Three Candidates). *The three partition shapes known as Rectangle Corner, L Rectangle and Traditional Rectangle, have a higher theoretical volume of communication than the Block Rectangle shape. The optimal shape must be among the remaining three candidate shapes, Block Rectangle, Square Rectangle and Square Corner.*

From here, we will analyse only the remaining three candidate partition shapes: Square Corner, Square Rectangle, and Block Rectangle.

3.3 Serial Communication with Barrier (SCB)

Serial Communication with Barrier (SCB) is a simple MMM algorithm in which all data is sent by each processor *serially*, and only once communication completes among all processors does the computation proceed in *parallel* on each processor.

The execution time is given by,

$$T_{exe} = V\beta + \max(c_P, c_R, c_S)$$

where V is the volume of communication, β is the bandwidth of the communication links and c_X is the time taken to compute the assigned portion of the matrix on Processor X.

Each processor is assigned data in proportion to the computational power. Processors P, R and S, with ratios $P_r : R_r : 1$ will be assigned $\frac{P_r N^2}{T}, \frac{R_r N^2}{T}$ and $\frac{N^2}{T}$ elements to compute, respectively. For all shapes, the computation time is identical for barrier algorithms, so communication time is the focus.

Square Corner. The Square Corner shape is composed of a matrix partitioned into two small squares for Processors R and S, while Processor P is assigned the non-rectangular remainder of the matrix. This shape type is only valid for computational power ratios such that non-overlapping squares for Processors R and S may be formed, which is possible when $P_r \geq 2\sqrt{R_r}$.

$$T_{comm(SC)} = 2N\left(\sqrt{\frac{R_r N^2}{T}} + \sqrt{\frac{N^2}{T}}\right) \times \beta \tag{1}$$

Square Rectangle. The Square Rectangle shape is composed of an N height rectangle, R, and a square, S, while Processor P is assigned the non-rectangular remainder of the matrix. The communication time is given by,

$$T_{comm(SR)} = \left(N^2 + 2N\sqrt{\frac{N^2}{T}} \right) \times \beta \qquad (2)$$

Block Rectangle. The Block Rectangle partition shape is composed of two h height rectangles of combined width N. Processor P is assigned the rectangular remainder of the matrix.

$$T_{comm(BR)} = \left(2N^2 - \frac{P_r N^2}{T} \right) \times \beta \qquad (3)$$

Optimum SCB Shape. The optimum data partitioning shape minimises T_{comm}. A graphical representation of these three functions can be seen in Fig. 2.

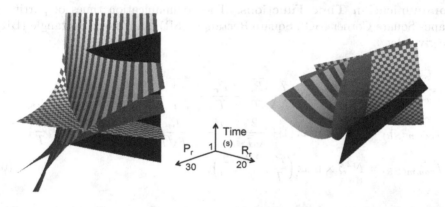

Fig. 2. The SCB T_{comm} functions for the three candidate shapes, Square Corner (white and grey stripes), Block Rectangle (solid grey), and Square Rectangle (white and grey checkerboard). The x-axis is the relative computational power of P, P_r, from 1 to 30. The y-axis is the relative computational power of R, R_r, from 1 to 20. The z-axis is the communication time in seconds. The vertical black surface is the equation $x = y$, and represents the problem constraint $P_r \geq R_r$. On the left, viewed from the front, on the right, viewed from underneath (the lowest function is optimal).

Theorem 2 (SCB Square Corner). *The Square Corner partition shape minimises execution time, i.e. is the optimum, using the SCB MMM algorithm for all processor computational power ratios such that $P_r < 2T - 2\sqrt{R_r T} - 2\sqrt{T}$.*

Theorem 3 (SCB Square Rectangle). *The Square Rectangle partition shape minimises execution time, i.e. is the optimum, using the SCB MMM algorithm for all processor computational power ratios such that $P_r < T - 2\sqrt{T}$.*

Corollary 4 (SCB Block Rectangle) *The Block Rectangle partition shape minimises execution time, i.e. is the optimum, for all processor computational power ratios except those specified in Theorems 2 and 3.*

3.4 Parallel Communication with Barrier (PCB)

In the Parallel Communication with Barrier (PCB) algorithm, all data is sent among processors in *parallel*, and only once communication completes does the computation processed in *parallel* on each processor. The execution time of this algorithm is given by,

$$T_{exe} = \max(v_P, v_R, v_S) \times \beta + \max(c_P, c_R, c_S)$$

where v_X is the volume of data elements which must be sent by Processor X. As with SCB, the focus in this algorithm is on communication time because computation time is not dependent on the data partition shape.

Communication Time Functions. The communication times of partition shapes Square Corner (SC), Square Rectangle (SR), and Block Rectangle (BR) are given by,

$$T_{comm(SC)} = 2N^2\beta \times \max\left(\sqrt{\frac{R_r}{T}} - \frac{R_r}{T} + \sqrt{\frac{1}{T}} - \frac{1}{T}, \frac{R_r}{T}, \frac{1}{T}\right) \tag{4}$$

$$T_{comm(SR)} = N^2\beta \times \max\left(1 + \frac{2}{\sqrt{T}} - \frac{R_r}{T} - \frac{R_r}{T\sqrt{T}} - \frac{3}{T}, \frac{R_r}{T} + \frac{R_r}{T\sqrt{T}}, \frac{3}{T}\right) \tag{5}$$

$$T_{comm(BR)} = N^2\beta \times \max\left(\frac{P_r}{T}, \frac{2R_r}{T}, \frac{2}{T}\right) \tag{6}$$

PCB Optimal Shape. The optimum partition shape minimises T_{comm}. The graph of these three functions is found in Fig. 3.

Theorem 5 (PCB Square Corner). *The Square Corner partitioning shape minimizes execution time, i.e. is the optimum shape, when using the PCB MMM algorithm and the computational power ratios are such that $P_r > 2(\sqrt{R_rT} - R_r + \sqrt{T} - 1)$.*

Theorem 6 (PCB Square Rectangle). *The Square Rectangle partitioning shape minimizes execution time, i.e. is the optimum shape, when using the PCB MMM algorithm and the computational power ratios are such that $P_r < 2R_r + \frac{R_r}{\sqrt{T}} - 2\sqrt{T} - 1$ and $P_r > 5 + \frac{R_r - 2}{\sqrt{T}}$.*

Corollary 7 (PCB Block Rectangle) *The Block Rectangle partition shape minimises execution time, i.e. is the optimum, for all processor computational power ratios except those specified in Theorems 5 and 6.*

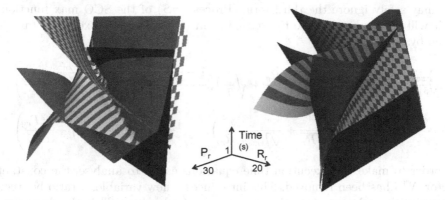

Fig. 3. The PCB T_{comm} functions for the three candidate shapes, Square Corner (white and grey stripes), Block Rectangle (solid grey), and Square Rectangle (white and grey checkerboard). The vertical black surface is the equation $x = y$, and represents the problem constraint $P_r \geq R_r$. On the left, viewed from the front, on the right, view from underneath (the lowest function is optimal).

3.5   Serial Communication with Bulk Overlap (SCO)

In the Serial Communication with Bulk Overlap (SCO) algorithm, all data is sent by each processor *serially*, while in *parallel* any elements that can be computed without communication are computed. Only once both communication and over-lapped computation are complete does the remainder of the computation begin. The execution time is given by,

$$T_{exe} = \max\left(\max(T_{comm}, o_P) + c_P, \max(T_{comm}, o_R) + c_R, \max(T_{comm}, o_S) + c_S\right)$$

where T_{comm} is the same as that of the SCB algorithm, o_X is the number of seconds taken by Processor X to compute any elements not requiring communication, and c_X is the number of seconds taken to compute the remainder of the elements assigned to Processor X.

Square Corner Of the three candidate partitions, only the Square Corner has an o_X term which is not equal to zero, *i.e.* it contains elements which may be computed without any communication amongst processors. The overlap-able area may be seen Fig. 4. The addition of the non-zero o_P term implies that c_P will no longer be equal to c_R and c_S if we continue to naively assign the volume of elements as $\frac{N^2 P_r}{T}$. As Processor P should be assigned a larger portion of the matrix to compute than suggested by P_r.

To determine this optimal size, we first assume that the volumes (and thereby the size of the squares) assigned to Processors R and S should decrease in proportion to each other, so their computation times remain equal ($c_R = c_S$). The size of a side of the square R, r, and a side of the square S, s, is set at $s = \sqrt{\frac{r^2}{R_r}}$.

We may safely ignore the third term (Processor S) of the SCO max function, as it will always be equal to the second term (Processor R). Execution time is given by,

$$
\frac{T_{exe}}{N^3\beta} = \max\left(\max\left(\frac{2}{N}\left(\sqrt{\frac{R_r}{T}} + \sqrt{\frac{1}{T}}\right), \frac{1 - \frac{r}{\sqrt{R_r}} - 2r + \frac{r^2}{R_r} + \frac{2r^2}{\sqrt{R_r}} + r^2}{c}\right.\right.
$$
$$
\left.\left. +\frac{2}{c}\left(r - r^2 - \frac{r^2}{\sqrt{R_r}} + \frac{r}{\sqrt{R_r}} - \frac{r^2}{R_r}\right), \quad \frac{2}{N}\left(\sqrt{\frac{R_r}{T}} + \sqrt{\frac{1}{T}}\right) + \frac{r^2 P_r}{cR_r}\right)\right.
$$

In order to make the execution time equations easier to analyse, the constant factor $N^3\beta$ has been removed. This introduces a new variable, a ratio between computation and communication speeds, $c = Sp\beta$, where $\frac{Sp}{N}$ is the number of elements computed per second by Processor P. The size of N and r have been normalised, so that $\frac{r}{N}$ becomes r, and r is understood to be $0 \leq r < 1$.

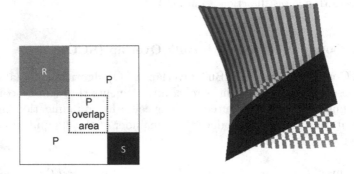

Fig. 4. On the left, the area of Processor P which does not require communication in the Square Corner partition shape is enclosed in dotted lines. On the right, the graph of execution time functions for the SCO algorithm. Axes as are in previous graphs, and $N = 3000$ and $c = 50$.

Optimal Size of R and S. The optimal size of r is given by,

$$
r = \frac{\sqrt{-\left(\frac{P_r}{R_r} + 1 + \frac{1}{R_r}\right)\left(\frac{2c}{N}\sqrt{\frac{R_r}{T}} + \frac{2c}{N}\sqrt{\frac{1}{T}} - 1\right)}}{\left(\frac{P_r}{R_r} + 1 + \frac{1}{R_r}\right)} \tag{7}
$$

The full derivation of this value may be found in [11].

Square Rectangle and Block Rectangle. The computation of no portion of matrix C may be overlapped with communication. The execution time function is equivalent to that for the SCB algorithm. Total execution time is given by,

$$\frac{T_{exe(SR)}}{N^3\beta} = \frac{1}{N} + \frac{2}{N}\sqrt{\frac{1}{T}} + \max\left(\frac{P_r}{Tc}, \frac{P_r}{Tc}, \frac{P_r}{Tc}\right)$$

$$\frac{T_{exe(BR)}}{N^3\beta} = \frac{2}{N} - \frac{P_r}{TN} + \max\left(\frac{P_r}{Tc}, \frac{P_r}{Tc}, \frac{P_r}{Tc}\right)$$

SCO Optimal Shape

Theorem 8 (SCO Square Corner). *The Square Corner partition shape minimizes execution time, i.e. is the optimum shape, when using the SCO MMM algorithm for computational ratios such that*
$P_r > \frac{\frac{2}{N}(\sqrt{\frac{R_r}{T}}+\sqrt{\frac{1}{T}})+\frac{2}{c}(r-r^2-\frac{r^2}{\sqrt{R_r}}+\frac{r}{\sqrt{R_r}}-\frac{r^2}{R_r})-\frac{2}{N}}{\frac{1}{Tc}-\frac{1}{TN}}$ *and* $P_r > \frac{2c}{N}(\sqrt{R_rT}+\sqrt{T})+$
$2T(r-r^2-\frac{r^2}{\sqrt{R_r}}+\frac{r}{\sqrt{R_r}}-\frac{r^2}{R_r})-\frac{Tc}{N}-\frac{2c}{N}\sqrt{T}$, *where r is the optimal size of the square R, given in (7).*

Theorem 9 (SCO Square Rectangle). *The Square Rectangle partition shape minimizes execution time, i.e. is the optimum shape, when using the SCO MMM algorithm for computational ratios such that* $P_r < T-2\sqrt{T}$ *and* $P_r < \frac{2c}{N}(\sqrt{R_rT}+\sqrt{T})+2T(r-r^2-\frac{r^2}{\sqrt{R_r}}+\frac{r}{\sqrt{R_r}}-\frac{r^2}{R_r})-\frac{Tc}{N}-\frac{2c}{N}\sqrt{T}$

Corollary 10 (SCO Block Rectangle) *The Block Rectangle partition shape minimizes execution time, i.e. is the optimum shape, for all processor computational power ratios except those specified in Theorems 8 and 9.*

3.6   Parallel Communication with Bulk Overlap (PCO)

In the Parallel Communication with Bulk Overlap (PCO) algorithm all data is sent among processors in *parallel*, while in *parallel* any elements that can be computed without communication are computed. Once both communication and overlapped computation are complete, the remainder of the computation begins. The execution time for this algorithm is given by,

$$T_{exe} = \max\left(\max(T_{comm}, o_P)+c_P, \max(T_{comm}, o_R)+c_R, \max(T_{comm}, o_S)+c_S\right)$$

where T_{comm} is the same as that of the PCB algorithm. As with the SCO algorithm, we simplify the equations by removing constant $N^3\beta$, normalising N, and making the size of s dependent on the size of r. The optimal size of r is derived in [11].

Square Corner

$$\frac{T_{exe}}{N^3\beta} = \max\left(\max\left(\frac{2}{N}\max\left(r - r^2 + \frac{r}{\sqrt{R_r}} - \frac{r^2}{R_r}, r^2\right), \frac{1 - \frac{r}{\sqrt{R_r}} - 2r + \frac{r^2}{R_r} + \frac{2r^2}{\sqrt{R_r}} + r^2}{c}\right.$$

$$\left.+2\frac{r - r^2 + \frac{r}{\sqrt{R_r}} - \frac{r^2}{\sqrt{R_r}} - \frac{r^2}{R_r}}{c}, \quad \frac{2}{N}\max\left(r - r^2 + \frac{r}{\sqrt{R_r}} - \frac{r^2}{R_r}, r^2\right) + \frac{r^2 P_r}{cR_r}\right)$$

(8)

Square Rectangle and Block Rectangle. As with the SCO algorithm, the Square Rectangle and Block Rectangle shapes do not have a portion which may be overlapped with communication. The time of execution, as with PCB model, is given by,

$$\frac{T_{exe(SR)}}{N^3\beta} = \max\left(\frac{1}{N} + \frac{2}{N\sqrt{T}} - \frac{R_r}{NT} - \frac{R_r}{NT\sqrt{T}} - \frac{3}{NT}, \frac{R_r}{NT} + \frac{R_r}{NT\sqrt{T}}, \frac{3}{NT}\right) + \frac{P_r}{Tc} \quad (9)$$

$$\frac{T_{exe(BR)}}{N^3\beta} = \max\left(\frac{P_r}{NT}, \frac{2R_r}{NT}, \frac{2}{NT}\right) + \frac{P_r}{Tc} \quad (10)$$

PCO Optimal Shape. As with the PCB algorithm, the Block Rectangle shape is superior to the Square Rectangle shape when $P_r > 2R_r + \frac{R_r}{\sqrt{T}} - 2\sqrt{T} + 2$. When examining all three shapes to determine the optimal, we see that as c decreases, all three equations converge. However, for larger values of c, the clear winner for all computational power ratios is the Square Corner shape as seen in Fig. 5. The full proof of this is found in [11].

Fig. 5. The PCO execution time functions for Square Corner (white and grey stripes), Block Rectangle (solid grey), and Square Rectangle (white and grey checkerboard). The x-axis, P_r, is 1 to 30, and the y-axis, R_r displays values 1 to 20. The vertical black surface is $x = y$. The Square Corner shape is increasingly superior as c increases. Shown here is $N = 3000$ and $c = 300$.

3.7   Parallel Interleaving Overlap (PIO)

The Parallel Interleaving Overlap (PIO) algorithm, unlike the previous algorithms described, does not use bulk communication. At each step data is sent, a row and a column (or k rows and columns) at a time, by the relevant processor(s) to all processor(s) requiring those elements, while, in *parallel*, all processors compute using the data sent in the previous step. The execution time for this algorithm is given by,

$$T_{exe} = \text{Send } k + (N-1) \times \max\Big(\beta(V_k), \max\big(k_P, k_R, k_S\big)\Big) + \text{Compute } (k+1)$$

where V_k is the number of elements sent at step k, and k_X is the number of seconds to compute step k on Processor X.

In the case of the PIO algorithm, the processors compute at the same time, meaning the optimal distribution will be in proportion to their computational power. The optimal size of the r and s is therefore $\sqrt{\frac{R_r N^2}{T}}$ and $\sqrt{\frac{N^2}{T}}$, respectively. In order to analyse the equations, we remove the constant factor $N^4 \beta$ and focus on the dominant middle term which is multiplied by $(N-1)$.

Execution Time. The execution time for each partition shape, Square Corner (SC), Square Rectangle (SR), and Block Rectangle (BR), is given by,

$$\frac{T_{exe(SC)}}{N^4 \beta} = \max\left(\frac{2}{N^2}\left(\sqrt{\frac{R_r}{T}} + \sqrt{\frac{1}{T}}\right), \frac{P_r}{Tc}\right) \tag{11}$$

$$\frac{T_{exe(SR)}}{N^4 \beta} = \max\left(\frac{2}{N^2}\left(1 + 2\sqrt{\frac{1}{T}}\right), \frac{P_r}{Tc}\right) \tag{12}$$

$$\frac{T_{exe(BR)}}{N^4 \beta} = \max\left(\frac{P_r}{N^2 T}, \frac{P_r}{Tc}\right) \tag{13}$$

PIO Optimal Shape. When computation time dominates, all three partition shapes are equivalent. However, when communication time dominates, they differ.

Theorem 11 (PIO Block Rectangle). *The Block Rectangle partition shape minimises execution time when using the PIO algorithm for computational power ratios such that* $P_r < 4\sqrt{T}$.

Corollary 12 (PIO Square Corner) *The Square Corner partition shape minimises execution time, i.e. is the optimum shape, for all processor computational power ratios except those specified in Theorem 11 when using the PIO algorithm.*

4   Experimental Results

To validate the theoretical results of this paper we present experiments undertaken on Grid'5000 in France using the Edel cluster at the Grenoble site. Each algorithm was tested using three nodes, comprised of 2 Intel Xeon E5520 2.2 GHz CPUs per node, with 4 cores per CPU. The communication interconnect is MPI over gigabit ethernet, and the computations use ATLAS. Heterogeneity in processing power was achieved using the cpulimit program, an open source code that limits the number of cycles a process may be active on the CPU to a percentage of the total. For space considerations, we present only results from SCB and PCB here.

4.1   Serial Communication with Barrier

The experimental results, for communication time, with the SCB algorithm can be found in Fig. 6. Note it is not possible to form a Square Corner shape at ratio 1 : 1 : 1. These experiments show that the theoretical optimum does indeed outperform the other possible shapes, which also perform in the expected order. We did find, that while the Square Corner and Square Rectangle shapes are theoretically identical at the 14 : 5 : 1 ratio, the Square Rectangle performed slightly better experimentally.

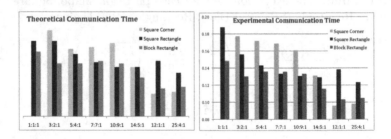

Fig. 6. On the left is the theoretical relative communication time for Square Corner, Square Rectangle and Block Rectangle when using the SCB algorithm. On the right is the experimental communication time (in seconds) for given ratios of $P_r : R_r : 1$. The value of N is 5000.

4.2   Parallel Communication with Barrier

The experimental results, for communication time, with the PCB algorithm can be found in Fig. 7. Note it is not possible to form a Square Corner shape at ratio 1 : 1 : 1. The results conform to the theoretical predictions with the optimum shape performing best, and the other two shapes performing in their predicted order.

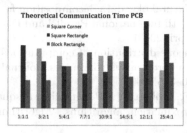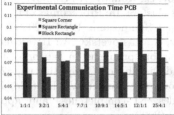

Fig. 7. On the left is the theoretical relative communication time for Square Corner, Square Rectangle and Block Rectangle partition shapes when using the PCB algorithm. On the right is the experimental communication time (in seconds) for given ratios of $P_r : R_r : 1$. The value of N is 5000.

5   Conclusions

On three fully connected heterogeneous processors, the optimal data partition shape depends on the relative computational power of each processor and the ratio between computational power and communication speed and is one of just three well-defined shapes. In general, the Square Corner shape is optimal for systems with a single fast processor, and two slower processors, the Square Rectangle shape is optimal for systems with two fast processors and a less powerful processor, and the Block Rectangle shape is optimal for relatively homogeneous systems and systems with a faster, medium and slower processor.

These results show that the optimal data partition is not exclusively rectangular. Of the three optimal shapes, two are non-rectangular. One of these, the Square Rectangle, has never before been considered. Without the Push technique, this non-symmetrical and unconventional shape would not be known to be the optimum.

Acknowledgement. Experiments presented in this paper were carried out using the Grid'5000 experimental testbed, being developed under the INRIA ALADDIN development action with support from CNRS, RENATER and several Universities as well as other funding bodies (see https://www.grid5000.fr). This research was conducted with the financial support of Science Foundation Ireland under Grant Number 08/IN./I2054.

References

1. Dongarra, J.J., Meuer, H.W., Simon, H.D., Strohmaier, E.: Top500 supercomputer sites, http://www.top500.org/
2. Clarke, D., Lastovetsky, A., Rychkov, V.: Column-based matrix partitioning for parallel matrix multiplication on heterogeneous processors based on functional performance models. In: Alexander, M., et al. (eds.) Euro-Par 2011, Part I. LNCS, vol. 7155, pp. 450–459. Springer, Heidelberg (2012)

3. Dovolnov, E., Kalinov, A., Kilmov, S.: Natural bloc data decomposition for heterogeneous clusters. In: Proceedings of the 17th International Parallel and Distributed Processing Symposium, IPDPS 2003 (April 2003)
4. Kalinov, A., Lastovetsky, A.: Heterogeneous distribution of computations solving linear algebra problems on networks of heterogeneous computers. Journal of Parallel and Distributed Computing 61, 520–535 (2001)
5. Beaumont, O., Boudet, V., Rastello, F., Robert, Y.: Partitioning a square into rectangles: NP-completeness and approximation algorithms. Algorithmica 34, 217–239 (2002)
6. DeFlumere, A., Lastovetsky, A., Becker, B.A.: Partitioning for parallel matrix-matrix multiplication with heterogeneous processors: The optimal solution. In: Parallel and Distributed Processing Symposium Workshops (IPDPSW), pp. 125–139 (2012)
7. DeFlumere, A., Lastovetsky, A.: Searching for the optimal data partitioning shape for parallel matrix matrix multiplication on 3 heterogeneous processors. In: Parallel and Distributed Processing Symposium Workshops, IPDPSW (2014)
8. Zhong, Z., Rychkov, V., Lastovetsky, A.: Data partitioning on heterogeneous multicore and multi-GPU systems using functional performance models of data-parallel applications. In: IEEE International Conference on Cluster Computing (CLUSTER), pp. 191–199. IEEE (2012)
9. Hockney, R.: The communication challenge for mpp: Intel paragon and meiko cs-2. Parallel Computing 20(3), 389–398 (1994)
10. Van De Geijn, R., Watts, J.: SUMMA: Scalable universal matrix multiplication algorithm. Concurrency-Practice and Experience 9(4), 255–274 (1997)
11. DeFlumere, A., Lastovetsky, A.: Theoretical results on optimal partitioning for matrix matrix multiplication on three fully connected heterogeneous processors. School of Computer Science and Informatics, University College Dublin, Tech. Rep. UCD-CSI-2014-01 (2014)

Scalable SIFT with Scala on NUMA

Frank Feinbube, Lena Herscheid, Christoph Neijenhuis, and Peter Tröger

Hasso Plattner Institute
University of Potsdam, Germany
{frank.feinbube,lena.herscheid,peter.troeger}@hpi.uni-potsdam.de,
christoph.neijenhuis@appetico.com

Abstract. *Scale-invariant feature transform* (SIFT) is an algorithm to identify and track objects in a series of digital images. The algorithm can handle objects that change their location, scale, rotation or illumination in subsequent images. This makes SIFT an ideal candidate for *object tracking* – typically denoted as *feature detection* – problems in computer imaging applications.

The complexity of the SIFT approach often forces developers and system architects to rely on less efficient heuristic approaches for object detection when streaming video data. This makes the algorithm a promising candidate for new parallelization strategies in heterogeneous parallel environments.

With this article, we describe our thorough performance analysis of various SIFT implementation strategies in the Scala programming language. Scala supports the development of mixed-paradigm parallel code that targets shared memory systems as well as distributed environments. Our proposed SIFT implementation strategy takes both caching and *non-uniform memory architecture* (NUMA) into account, and therefore achieves a higher speedup factor than existing work. We also discuss how scalability for larger video workloads can be achieved by leveraging the actor programming model as part of a distributed SIFT implementation in Scala.

1 Introduction

The research field of *computer vision* focusses on the automated extraction of numerical or semantic information from real world image data. It steadily gains importance due to the rising amount of image and video data in daily processing tasks. Application domains include robotics, medical systems, autonomous vehicles, satellite picture processing and semi-automated manufacturing.

The problem domain of visual data processing can be separated into the batch processing of large very images, and the online processing of a steady stream of small images. Most of this data is not recorded in a controlled studio environment, but comes from an *uncontrolled environment*. The camera, or target objects in the video data, may constantly change their position and lightning conditions.

One of the most challenging tasks in image data processing is the identification and tracking of interesting objects, typically denoted as *feature detection*.

L. Lopes et al. (Eds.): Euro-Par 2014 Workshops, Part I, LNCS 8805, pp. 215–226, 2014.

Application examples are robots or vehicles automatically following given paths or objects, the continous tracking of players on a soccer field, the alignment of machine activities to human hands in medical environments, the detection of logos in TV streams, or any kind of face recognition approach. The algorithm known to be most accurate in this field is SIFT, originally proposed by Lowe [6]. The multi-stage algorithm is known to be computationally intense, which makes it hardly applicable in soft-realtime applications such as online video analysis.

With the given hard computational problem, the question arises if and how modern parallel execution environments can be leveraged efficiently for a SIFT implementation. Modern many-core systems not only provide parallel processing capabilities, but also implement a *non-uniform memory architecture* (NUMA), were data locality becomes a crucial aspect of performance optimization. When the amount of data to be processed becomes to large for a single system, an implementation must also be able to scale out the computation to multiple machines.

Discussions of an efficient SIFT implementation mostly either solely focus on single systems, single GPU accelerators, or distributed systems only. For this reason, we discuss how SIFT can be realized in heterogeneous parallel environments with NUMA characteristics. We rely on the *Scala programming language* in our approach, which has proven to be suitable for large-scale data processing tasks in both shared memory and shared-nothing environments. Productivity-focused programming languages have proven suitable even for some areas of high performance computing [2]. Scala is designed to allow for a high degree of parallelization and scalability.

Our article contributes a thorough performance analysis of various strategies for the Scala programming language. Our approach is cache- and NUMA-aware and therefore achieves a higher speedup factor than existing work. It allows supports the scale-out of the processing to multiple compute nodes, which is to the best of our knowledge not considered for SIFT so far.

2   Basics and Related Work

SIFT was first invented and described by Lowe in 1999 [6]. He refined and patented the algorithm in 2004 [7]. Since then, it has been widely used for automatic features detection in images.

SIFT determines a set of characteristic *features* or *keypoints* for an input image and represents it as a set of descriptors. An outline of the SIFT algorithm is depicted in Figure 1. The algorithm works on monochrome images, extracted from the video stream, in order to keep the impact of lighting changes low. Different *Gaussian blur filters* are applied to the monochrome image at different scales, in order to blur away all but the most characteristic structures. Subsequently, extrema of the so-called *difference of gaussians* (DoG) are detected as features. The DoG is the difference between two versions of the image which have been blurred with different Gaussian filters.

Figure 2 illustrates how the DoG maintains the most characteristic structures in the image, while abstracting away from small, potentially instable, details.

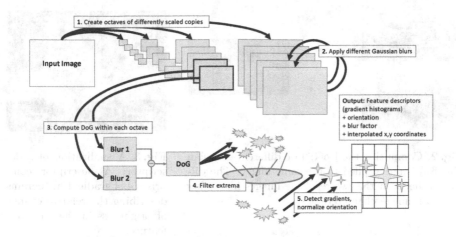

Fig. 1. Illustration of the SIFT algorithm: **1.** A *scale space*, consisting of differently scaled images is constructed. For each scale, a group of identical images is created: an *octave*. In our example, there are four scales of octaves with a size of five. **2.** For each octave, a differently configured Gaussian blur filter is applied to each of the images. **3.** The DoG of all two subsequent images within an octave is computed. This yields extreme values in areas with characteristic image features. **4.** Only extrema that lie above certain thresholds and exist across different scales are filtered out. **5.** Finally, the resulting *feature descriptors* contain information about the brightness gradient, the orientation and position of features. These are the outputs of the SIFT algorithm.

Formally, a *feature* describes the relative change of brightness in a certain area. Figure 3 depicts a feature descriptor. In the final phase of SIFT, the dominant *orientation* found in these histograms is saved as a descriptor property.

Features are invariant to scaling and rotation. Due to their flexible nature, SIFT behaves robustly against noise, changes in the lighting conditions and affine distortions. This stability makes it an attractive algorithm in all sorts of uncontrolled computer vision scenarios.

Table 1 summarizes related work on parallelizations of the SIFT algorithms for CPUs. Since our focus lies on NUMA scalability rather than single image performance, we describe the related work with a *speedup factor*, in order to express how efficiently additional compute resources are used. Because the speedup factor takes the number of used physical cores into consideration, it allows us to compare different implementations running on different test systems from related work.

Feng et al. [3] studied a number of performance optimizations and their impact on parallel SIFT on a 4-socket quadcore HP ProLiant DL580 G5 server. They observe that the use of SIMD optimizations can halve the runtime. In their experiments, a combination of thread affinity, false sharing removal and synchronization reduction yields a 25% performance improvement. The OpenMP-based implementation achieves speedup factors of 9.7 for large pictures and 11 for small

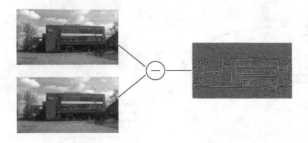
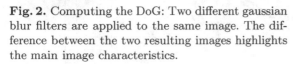

Fig. 2. Computing the DoG: Two different gaussian blur filters are applied to the same image. The difference between the two resulting images highlights the main image characteristics.

Fig. 3. Visualization of a descriptor: A descriptor comprises 4x4 gradient histograms describing the relative change of brightness in the area of a feature.

pictures. Further, Feng et al. investigate the scalability of their implementation in a CMP simulator with 64 cores (each equipped with its own L1 cache, but sharing the L2 cache). In this environment, a speedup of 52 for large pictures and 39 for small pictures is achieved.

Zhang et al. [13] presented another OpenMP-based SIFT implementation. On an 2-socket quadcore HP ProLiant DL380 G5 server test system, they achieve a speedup of 5.9-6.7 depending on the feature density of the test images. For 640x480 images, their speedup factor is slightly higher than that of Feng et al.'s implementation.

Warn et al. [11] proposed a straight-forward parallelization approach: The three most expensive loops of the serial SIFT++ implementation [10] were parallelized with OpenMP. This implementation works best with large satellite pictures and achieves a speedup of factor 2 on the eight core test system.

Several related SIFT implementations improve the processing performance by utilizing GPU acceleration hardware [5,9,11,12]. Since the analyzed data first must be moved to accelerator card memory, the above named approaches suffer from significant data copying overhead. Warn et al. [11] show that it is feasible to execute only a part of SIFT, namely the Gaussian blurring algorithm, on the GPU. In this case, even with a copying overhead that eats up 90% of the execution time, the GPU version is 13 times faster than the CPU version.

Since absolute performance over various hardware architectures is not well comparable, we benchmarked our implementation against the state-of-the-art OpenCV implementation [4] on our test system. We executed the Scala code in a serial version, in order to be comparable to the serial OpenCV implementation. Our implementation is 1.29 times faster for a resolution of 1980x1080 and 1.18 times faster for 800x600.

Table 1. Overview of related work on SIFT parallelization. Speedups are expressed as factors relative to the execution on one core. The speedup factor denotes the ratio *speedup/physical cores*. Our implementation achieves superlinear speedup, since it is optimized for cache and NUMA locality on our target server system.

	Image Size	Features	Processors	Cores / Processor	Cores	Speedup	Speedup Factor
Feng et al. [3]	HDTV	1038	4	4	16	9.7	0.61
	720x576	700	4	4	16	11	0.69
	HDTV	1038	1	64	64	52	0.81
	720x576	700	1	64	64	39	0.61
Zhang et al. [13]	640x480	200-1000	2	4	8	5.9-6.7	0.73-0.84
Warn et al. [11]	4136x1424	40000	2	4	8	2-3	0.25-0.38
Our	854x480	1400-2700	1	6	6	7.15	**1.19**
Approach	854x480	1400-2700	2	6	12	13.21	**1.10**
(150 video frames)	854x480	1400-2700	4	6	24	24.23	**1.01**

3 Approach

Our example application of SIFT is the detection of company logos in high definition video streams, mainly for the purpose of advertising management and copyright control. In such a scenario, the feature detection needs to provide high accuracy even if the tracked image part is partially occluded or distorted. Since the processing works on large data amounts, it must be also fast and scalable at the same time. We focus on single-image performance and on overall scalability by combining single-node optimization (see Section 4) with multi-node optimizations (see Section 5).

To achieve good single-node performance on modern architectures, the implementation strategy must be NUMA-aware. This includes the consideration of memory hierarchies and the parallel utilization of multiple cores / processors in the system. Scalability is realized by supporting a distributed execution style, where parallel parts of the program run on different cluster / cloud machines. The requirement of scalability implies that the inter-node communication in the SIFT implementation must be limited to a neccessary minimum.

Our choice for Scala allows us to rely on the *actor programming paradigm* for the concurrent operation, as implemented in the *Akka* [1] framework. Each concurrent actor is parallelized in itself, in order to achieve the best possible utilization of node-local parallelism. We follow the common *farmer-worker* paradigm, were a central "master" actor is responsible for distributing image workload to other actors. Each of these "worker" actors receives an image, performs SIFT on it and sends the resulting descriptors and features back to the master. The functional programming model supported in Scala is well suited for parallelization, since it outlines algorithmic dependencies and allows the runtime to manage the actual execution. Scala includes both imperative and functional features.

Since the computation of the Gaussian pyramid, descriptor orientation, and filtering steps in SIFT can overlap, we defined additionally dedicated actors for these stages. They may be distributed across different cores or processors, accessing the image (or intermediate) data on this node. Due to the transparency of distribution in the Scala actor model, these computational units can be placed on resources in a flexible manner. This allows to switch between local and distributed execution without additional coding effort. The programming paradigm for all steps and sub-steps in the SIFT algorithm remains the same. Any mentioning of the term *node* in the following explanations therefore relates both to NUMA nodes in a single system (meaning processor sockets), or machine nodes in a parallel distributed system.

3.1   Test System and SIFT Configuration

All measurements mentioned in the subsequent sections were carried out on a Fujitsu RX600 S5 server. It contains four Intel Xeon E7530 CPUs with 1.86 Ghz and 6 physical cores and runs a Debian operating system (Version 6.0). Our *Java virtual machines* (JVMs) has the version 1.6.0_24. We used the Scala programming language (version 2.9.1) and the Akka framework (version 2.0).

SIFT was configured as described in [7]. The initial image size was doubled. We computed five octaves of six scaled images each. During filtering, a threshold of 5% of the maximum contrast was used.

We used two test datasets. The first is a single HDTV image, which contains 9697 features (an average number for photographs). The image contains regions with both high feature densities (e.g., trees) and low feature densities (e.g., sky).

The second test dataset is a movie with a resolution of 854x480, showing a bicycling robot[1]. Images in the test film contain an average of 1400 to 2700 features.

Since *just-in-time compilation* (JIT) optimizations occur adaptively during runtime, all of our measurements are preceded by a warm-up phase of several seconds.

4   Single-Node Performance Optimizations

Before we discuss distribution techniques for SIFT stages across NUMA nodes, we show how to maximize the performance on single processors with multiple cores.

---

[1] https://www.youtube.com/watch?v=wH8KzseCW58, November 25, 2014.

4.1   Two-dimensional Data Structure for Images

The pixels of a two-dimensional image can either be saved as a two-dimensional array (represented as an array of arrays), or as a one-dimensional array. The two-dimensional array uses slightly more memory to store the references from the outer array to the inner arrays.

Allocation has a large influence on the overall runtime of the SIFT algorithm, since it creates many intermediate results. The HotSpot JVM, being the execution environment for Scala code, is optimized for the allocation of small objects; they can be allocated out of a buffer within ten native CPU cycles [8]. However, for large image sizes (e.g. HDTV), the resulting one-dimensional array is bigger than the buffer allows. We therefore used a two-dimensional array, where each inner array is created by the thread that is going to fill it with values. This leads to a more fine-grained allocation scheme that fits to the execution environment optimizations. The HotSpot JVM now creates one allocation buffer per thread, and each of them can use it without further synchronization. The two-dimensional array with thread-local allocation of the inner arrays is faster than the one-dimensional array when both are parallelized. Without thread-local allocation or parallelization, it is slower. For HDTV images, the JVM allocates the one-dimensional array slowly because of it size. The two-dimensional array uses up to 60% less time than the one-dimensional array when parallelized. With smaller image sizes, the parallelization overhead grows: For image sizes of $240x135$ pixels, parallel and serial execution take roughly the same amount time.

We conclude that using a nested two-dimensional array for image representation increases performance, because it leads to more JVM-friendly allocation patterns.

4.2   Optimization of the Gaussian blur

For a two-dimensional image, the Gaussian blur filter is applied in two phases: First, the image is blurred in the horizontal dimension. This intermediate result is then blurred in the vertical dimension. This is visualized in the left column in Figure 4.

A widely used optimization technique is to save the intermediate result with flipped dimensions. This approach is visualized in the second column. For the final result, we flip the dimensions again, bringing it back to the original layout.

Flipping the dimensions ensures that the pixels are read along the cache line. It is worthwhile to optimize for reading, because more pixels are read than written[2]. However, writing is not cache line aware. When used with the proposed two-dimensional data structure, the inner array cannot be tied to a single thread - multiple threads need to write into it. It is therefore not possible to use the thread local allocation buffer. Due to false sharing, additional synchronization overhead may occur.

---

[2] Depending on the scale, the blurring needs to read between 11 and 27 pixels for one written pixel.

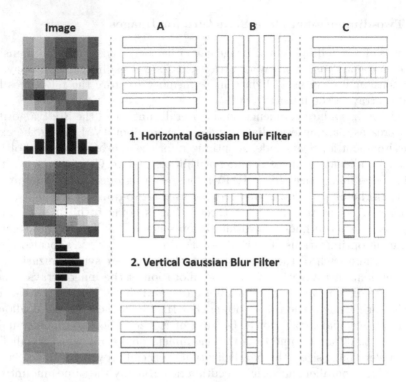

Fig. 4. Illustration of the two phases of the Gaussian blur: the first phase (red) blurs horizontally, the second phase (blue) vertically. *A (read-optimized)*: Pixels are read along the cache line. *B (write-optimized)*: Pixels are written into one inner array, but read from multiple arrays. *C (combined approach)*: The second phase does not flip the image, allowing both read- and write-optimization. The resulting image is mirrored.

Neither cache misses during writing, nor false sharing impose a problem when we optimize for writes. Threads read pixels from multiple arrays, and not along cache lines, but write into a single one. This write-optimized approach is visualized in the third column. It yields better scalability, but worse serial performance. For multi-core processors, it performs worse than the read-optimization.

We applied an optimization that exploits the fact that the blurred images are further processed in subsequent SIFT stages. The intermediate result of the blurring remains flipped. Thus, during the second phase, the algorithm can read and write into inner arrays simultaneously, accessing the cache lines when reading and the thread local allocation buffers when writing. This approach is visualized in the fourth column. Subsequent stages of SIFT have to be aware of the flipped images. Features, coordinates and orientation have to be adjusted before exporting the result image. The options for Gaussian blur are read-optimized for using cache lines (option 1), write-optimized for using thread-local allocation (option 2), or option 1 with a second phase that does not flip the image and is both optimized for using cache lines and thread-local allocation (option 3).

Our experiment show that option 1 and 3 perform similarly when executed serially, but option 2 is 67% slower. With six threads, option 2 is still 35% slower than option 1, while option 3 is 16% faster and turns out to be the best approach.

4.3 Optimization of the Order of SIFT Stages

Each octave of the Gaussian pyramid is created by blurring five images and subtracting them from their predecessor. The blurring creates one intermediate image. For the original image to still be inside the last-level cache after blurring, the cache needs to hold at least three images. The subtraction reads two images and writes a new one. For the next subtraction, one of the two images is read again, which is still in the cache if it holds more than three images.

The subtraction can be done directly after one image has been blurred, which will be present in the last-level cache because it has just been written. The other image will only be present if the cache holds more than six images. In this case, the image used for the next blurring is also still in the cache. Another possibility is to first blur all five images, then subtract them. If the subtraction is done backwards, for the first subtraction the last-level cache will hold the image that has just been blurred, and, if the cache holds more than four images, the other image as well. If the cache can hold at least 16 images the order does not matter, since all final and intermediate images fit into it. Similarly, if the cache can hold less than three images the order does not matter, because images have to be constantly loaded from main memory.

In our evaluated configuration with an L3 cache, it can hold about four images in the largest octave, and more than 16 images in the next octave (because the image size is quartered). We therefore first blur all five images of one octave and then subtract them, starting in reverse order with the image last blurred.

After the Gaussian pyramid has been created, extrema need to be detected and interpolated before the orientations and descriptors can be computed. Lowe [7] originally proposed extrema detection and interpolation as two separate steps. However, the interpolation stage accesses the same data as the extrema detection. To exploit the L2 cache more efficiently, we propose to interpolate immediately after each extremum has been detected.

The computation of the orientation and the descriptor works on the same image area and the steps share some intermediary data. We propose to execute both steps immediately after each other to optimize the use of the L2 cache.

The number of features per image is not predictable, but generally decreases with increasing blur. Images may even contain fewer features than cores available. If feature computation is done per image, significant parallelization overhead may arise. We propose to collect extremas from all octaves first and compute the features for all octaves together.

In our experimental evaluation of the described approach, we first create the Gaussian pyramid for all octaves, detect extrema, and then compute the features for all octaves together in a second step, which includes orientation and descriptor computation. As described in [3], the creation of features scales better. As Table 2 shows, the runtime of Gaussian pyramid creation rises from 43% of the combined runtime to 48% with 6 threads and to 50% with activated hyperthreading. For both stages, activated hyperthreading, and using 12 threads instead of 6, increases the speedup significantly. During feature computation, hyperthreading raises the speedup from 4.86 to 7.23. Because the pyramid creation constantly loads image data from the main memory into the cache, the main memory connection becomes a bottleneck sooner than during feature creation, which works on the same image area for a longer time.

Table 2. Scalability of the main SIFT stages

	1 Core		6 Cores (6 Threads)			6 Cores with HT (12 Threads)		
	Runtime	%	Runtime	%	Speedup	Runtime	%	Speedup
Pyramid	10258 ms ± 126	43%	2635 ms ± 96	48%	3.89	1890 ms ± 36	50%	5.43
Features	13814 ms ± 193	57%	840 ms ± 399	52%	4.86	1909 ms ± 159	50%	7.23

5   Scaling with Multiple Nodes

Our Scala implementation achieves scalability by distributing the workload across different nodes following the actor paradigm. As explained before, these nodes may either be part of a single machine (NUMA processor nodes) or a distributed environment.

While modern JVMs are NUMA-aware in themselves, the official Java API does not allow NUMA-aware application programming and provides no interface to control the distribution of threads on processors. If a single JVM is used in such a NUMA environment, uncontrollable latency can occur when accessing memory allocated by a remote thread. This problem even arises when the threads work on seperate data items, since runtime and object management is still centralized in one JVM instance. To avoid such problems, we apply a typical approach were each NUMA node in the system runs a dedicated JVM instance. We used the `numactl` program to bind the JVM instances to specific processors, and launch a single actor per NUMA node. The actors themselves are parallelized and cache aware (see Section 4).

As discussed in Section 3, our architecture comprises a master who decodes the video stream and distributes frames to worker actors. The workers perform stages of SIFT and reply with messages containing the features they found.

Varying numbers of features in different video frames can lead to an unbalanced distribution of workload. Therefore, we initially fill the messaging mailbox of each SIFT-actor with two images. When the actor finishes the computation on one image, the mailbox is filled up again by the master. This simple approach leaves enough work left per actor to hide potential memory latency effects.

The performance penalty for using one JVM for the whole system instead of using a seperate JVM per NUMA node is severe. In our test system, using two

JVMs on two NUMA nodes instead of one leads to a performance improvement of 54%. With four JVMs on four NUMA nodes the improvement is 79% as compared to using a single JVM.

For simple codecs, the image decoding speed on the master node is dominated by the speed of reading from disk. Thus, the maximum achievable throughput in batch processing scenarios is determined by disk access speed. With faster disk access, it is possible to scale out to more worker actors.

5.1   Execution on Multiple Machines

An expected, but still somehow impressive, outcome of the experimental evaluation is the fact that no additional modifications were needed to get a fully distributed SIFT implementation. The actor-based programming model makes the transition from a single NUMA system to a distributed system painless and straightforward – it basically boils down to the coordinated startup of multiple JVM's on different machines, running the same code as described above.

The additional amount of machines induces the typical increase in communication and synchronization overhead, but adds scalability to the given solution. Distributing SIFT over multiple machines increases the image throughput, which makes the overall analysis truly scalable. Widely known I/O optimizations for cluster computing, such as fast interconnects or parallel file systems, can help to decrease the latency impact from the networking part of distribution. From our point of view, the main advantage is that the proposed actor-based implementation can remain unchanged. Performance optimization now becomes an operational aspect, and no longer is a dedicated task for the developer. This allows for effortless re-use of such an implementation in different execution environments. When distributed across 5 machines, we achieved a speedup 3.74.

6   Conclusion

In this article, we presented several insights into how a scalable implementation of SIFT can be realized using the actor paradigm. As shown in Table 1, our implementation achieves superlinear speedup due to its cache-aware and NUMA-aware optimizations. We optimize for single node performance by fine-tuning the different SIFT stages for optimal exploitation of the L2 and L3 caches. As discussed in Section 4, this includes flipping the image twice during Gaussian blurring, saving it in a allocator-friendly two-dimensional data structure, and re-ordering the extrema detection and interpolation for better L2 cache efficiency.

Our Scala code is furthermore optimized for scalability in NUMA environments. Each NUMA node runs a dedicated actor, ensuring data locality and allowing distributed processing.

Since Gaussian blurring accounts for two thirds of the runtime, future work should invest additional effort into parallelizing this part of the algorithm. GPUs, due to their massively data parallel processing powers, are well suited for image filtering tasks, when the data transfer overhead problem is finally solved.

To allow fast and scalable support for live video recognition, the current video frame needs to be subdivided into multiple image parts and processed in parallel. Due to the nature of the SIFT algorithm, this leads to significant overhead, since the additional image margins – needed by both the Gaussian blurring and the extrema detection – have to be copied. This overhead grows with the number of actors and hinders seamless scalability. We are aware of this problem already and plan to further investigate optimizations for the live processing scenario.

References

1. Akka, http://akka.io/ (Online; accessed May 28 2014)
2. Amedro, B., Bodnartchouk, V., Caromel, D., Delbe, C., Huet, F., Guillermo, L.T.: Current State of Java for HPC. Technical Report RT-0353, INRIA (2008)
3. Feng, H., Li, E., Chen, Y., Zhang, Y.: Parallelization and characterization of SIFT on multi-core systems. In: IEEE International Symposium on Workload Characterization, IISWC 2008, pp. 14–23. IEEE (2008)
4. Hess, R.: An open-source siftlibrary. In: Proceedings of the international conference on Multimedia, pp. 1493–1496. ACM (2010)
5. Heymann, S., Muller, K., Smolic, A., Frohlich, B., Wiegand, T.: SIFT implementation and optimization for general-purpose GPU. In: Proceedings of the international conference in Central Europe on computer graphics, visualization and computer vision, vol. 144 (2007)
6. Lowe, D.G.: Object recognition from local scale-invariant features. In: The Proceedings of the Seventh IEEE International Conference on Computer Vision, vol. 2, pp. 1150–1157. IEEE (1999)
7. Lowe, D.G.: Distinctive image features from scale-invariant keypoints. International Journal of Computer Vision 60(2), 91–110 (2004)
8. Sun Microsystems. Memory management in the Java HotSpot virtual machine (2006)
9. Sinha, S.N., Frahm, J.-M., Pollefeys, M., Genc, Y.: GPU-based video feature tracking and matching. In: EDGE, Workshop on Edge Computing Using New Commodity Architectures, vol. 278, p. 4321 (2006)
10. Andrea Vedaldi Sift++, http://www.robots.ox.ac.uk/~vedaldi/code/siftpp.html (Online; accessed May 28, 2014)
11. Warn, S., Emeneker, W., Cothren, J., Apon, A.W.: Accelerating SIFT on parallel architectures. In: CLUSTER, pp. 1–4 (2009)
12. Wu, C.: SiftGPU, http://cs.unc.edu/~ccwu/siftgpu/ (Online; accessed May 28, 2014)
13. Zhang, Q., Chen, Y., Zhang, Y., Xu, Y.: SIFT implementation and optimization for multi-core systems. In: IEEE International Symposium on Parallel and Distributed Processing, IPDPS 2008, pp. 1–8. IEEE (2008)

Non-linear Iterative Optimization Method
for Locating Particles Using HPC Techniques

Gloria Ortega[1], Julia Lobera[2], Inmaculada García[3], María del Pilar Arroyo[4],
and Gracia Ester Martín Garzón[1]

[1] Informatics Dpt., Univ. of Almería, Agrifood Campus of Int. Excell., ceiA3, 04120
Almería, Spain
{gloriaortega,gmartin}@ual.es
[2] Centro Universitario de la Defensa de Zaragoza, 50090 Zaragoza, Spain
jlobera@unizar.es
[3] Computer Architecture Dpt., Univ. of Málaga, 29080 Málaga, Spain
igarciaf@uma.es
[4] Aragón Institute of Engineering Research (I3A), Univ. of Zaragoza, 50009,
Zaragoza, Spain
arroyo@unizar.es

Abstract. Tomography has been recently introduced in fluid velocimetry to provide three dimensional information of the location of particles. In particular, author's previous works have proven the potential of
Optical Diffraction Tomography for biological and microfluidic devices.
In general, image reconstruction methods at visible wavelengths have
to account for diffraction. First Born Approximation has been used for
three dimensional image reconstruction, but a non-linear reconstruction
method is required when multiple scattering is not negligible. Therefore,
to improve the spatial resolution of the fluid velocimetry techniques, a
non-linear iterative optimization should be used to locate the seeding
particles and compute afterward the flow velocity field. This inversion
method requires the solution of the Helmholtz equation, computationally highly demanding due to the size of the problem. Therefore, High
Performance Computing is required to find the particle locations. This
work shows the results of accelerating this task using GPU computing
and a customized storing format.

Keywords: ODT, Helmholtz equation, GPU-based application, High
Performance Computing.

1 Introduction

Holographic Particle Image Velocimetry (HPIV) provides simultaneous three
components, three-dimensional (3C-3D) measurements of a seeded fluid flow
[2,6]. Classical analysis of HPIV recordings assumes that the particle illuminating and the scattered beam do not suffer multiple scattering. In practice,
however, multiple scattering effects increase background noise, decreasing the

L. Lopes et al. (Eds.): Euro-Par 2014 Workshops, Part I, LNCS 8805, pp. 227–238, 2014.

number of velocity vectors that can be retrieved from a given flow field [11]. Tomographic methods using several recordings from different observation directions have been proposed in the last years to mitigate this problem [19,20]. In Tomographic Particle Image Velocimetry the particles within the entire volume need to be imaged in focus, which is obtained by setting proper numerical aperture (NA). The application of Optical Diffraction Tomography (ODT) in HPIV [13], and more specifically the non-linear ODT, would improve the spatial resolution. ODT is a non-damaging radiation technique that provides a 3D map of the object refractive index from holographic recordings of scattered fields with different illumination or observation directions. If the linear approximation is assumed, the spectral components of the field scattered by the object are directly related to the spectral components of the object refractive index field [5,22]. Some impressive advances have been done recently in coherent microscopy [10,14], even though these measurements are incomplete and the assumption of weak scattering is severely restrictive.

For the non-linear ODT approach, image reconstruction is considered the solution that better explains the scattered far field but it requires large and powerful computational resources. In the implementation of the optimization method, the Helmholtz equation [7] needs to be solved for a known refractive index distribution and illuminating field - the forward problem. Appropriate sampling is roughly a tenth of the wavelength, and due to the size of volume of interest in biological flows the computational requirements are very demanding. Thus, the performance of the non-linear Optical Diffraction Tomography in HPIV is determined by the selected computing strategy, and this is particularly true for its implementation for 3D problems. The use of a priori information concerning the object can reduce instability in optimization and computation time [4,13]. In fluid velocimetry we usually have additional information about the object, such as the diameter and the optical properties of the seeding particles, effectively reducing the particle imaging reconstruction problem to a particle location problem [21].

In this context, High Performance Computing (HPC) is required to implement and validate the aforementioned model. HPC allows the scientific community to extend their models and accelerate their simulations by the exploitation of a wide variety of computing resources. However, the selection of HPC architectures and programming interfaces for the models to be developed require an important effort. Earlier works have shown the parallel computation capability of GPUs in performing ODT models [10,16]. In this paper, we discuss an implementation of a Non-Linear ODT model at a source-level MATLAB compiler calling MEX-files for using GPU routines, which is also experimentally evaluated. Moreover, this work shows the feasibility of this approach and the outstanding imaging capability of non-linear ODT compared to linear tomographic approaches.

2   Description of NLODT-P Model

In fluid velocimetry the studied flow is seeded by small particles with a refractive index different from the background. Typically, a coherent source is used to illuminate the flow, and this illuminating beam is scattered by the seeding particles, which allows to determine their location at one instant of time. To determine the velocity field of the flow, two consecutive recordings are required. In particular, we will focus our attention on the combination of several simultaneous recordings to recover the position of each particle on a certain volume of interest at one time.

The proposed method consists in a minimization of the cost function defined by the square root difference between the measured and the computed scattering field by the seeding particles. This is a non-linear optimization problem that would be addressed by a modified Conjugated Gradient Optimization Method (CGM) [13]. The search direction at the first iteration is the negative gradient of the cost function. Although the gradient can be expressed by an analytical equation, it still requires the resolution of the forward problem twice. This forward problem consists of computing the scattered field $E_s(r)$ by a known object and an illuminating beam $E_r(r)$. According to scalar diffraction theory the (complex) amplitude of a monochromatic electric field, $E(r) = E_s(r) + E_r(r)$, propagating in a medium of (complex) refractive index, $n(r)$, obeys the Helmholtz equation [18] which can be rewritten in the following inhomogeneous form using the appropriate transformation described in [13]:

$$(\nabla^2 + k_0^2 n^2(r))E_s(r) = f(r)E_r(r) \tag{1}$$

where $f(r)$ is the scattering potential, defined by:

$$f(r) = -k_0^2(n^2(r) - 1) \tag{2}$$

Our objective is to find the particle field position that minimizes the square difference between the measured $E_m(r)$ and the computed field that should be measured, $cost(f)$, according to the available estimation of the refractive index, $E_c(f, r)$:

$$cost(f) = \sum_i |E_m^i(r) - E_c^i(f, r)|^2 \tag{3}$$

where for any hologram there is a separate contribution (i) to the cost function.

CGM has been chosen to minimize this cost function. Thus, given a scattering potential, the gradient of the cost function can be taken as an image of the difference between the real $n(r)$ and its available estimation. This image is typically a smooth distribution with several local maxima, even when some sharp refractive index changes are expected, as for our case of particles on a flow. Furthermore, in general the object in fluid velocimetry applications is a sparse distribution of particles of known refractive index and shape. Subsequently a relatively small matrix PL that stores the location of the particles could describe the 3D refractive index field.

Bearing in mind the previous considerations, the developed model referred as NLODT-P is detailed below. A procedure presenting the most important steps involved in the NLODT-P model are shown in Algorithm 1.

This model is composed by a first procedure (step), where the location of the first particle is determined and an iterative process, where the remaining

Algorithm 1. Algorithm of the NLODT-P model.

```
1:  #Step 1. Location of the 1st particle (line 2)
2:  Compute PL(1)
3:  It = 2
4:  while It < iterMax and Value < threshold do
5:      for i = 1, 2, ... until i < Number of holograms do
6:          #Step 2. Update the refractive index field (line 7)
7:          Update n(r)
8:          #Step 3. Compute the updated gradient, g(r) (lines 9 - 14)
9:          E_s^i(r) = Forward(E_r^i(r), n(r))
10:         E_{r,n}^i(r) = E_s^i(r) + E_r^i(r)
11:         E_c^i(r) = Filter(E_s^i(r), k_0^i, NA)
12:         E_{m,n}^i(r) = Forward((E_c^i(r) - E_m^i(r))^*, n(r))
13:         E_{m,n}^i(r) = E_{m,n}^i(r) + (E_c^i(r) - E_m^i(r))^*
14:         g(r)^* = g(r)^* + (E_{m,n}^i(r), E_{r,n}^i(r))
15:     end for
16:     #Step 4. Locate next particle (lines 17 and 18)
17:     g_{MF}(r) = Matched_Filtering(g(r), sample)
18:     [PL(It), Value] = max(abs(g_{MF}))
19:     It = It + 1
20: end while
```

particles are located. The initial step does contain computations similar to the subsequent iterations, but no special computing resources are required, therefore it is considered separately. Next, the main details for every NLODT-P step are described.

Step 1. Location of the 1st particle

In [12] it has been shown that the gradient of the cost function can be expressed as the sum of the simulated Bragg holograms between the illuminating field and the back propagated measured field. In particular, for the initial iteration, the illuminating field $E_r^i(r)$ and the back propagation of the measured field $E_m^i(r)$ are considered undisturbed. Thus the gradient is essentially the First Born Approximation of the scattering potential:

$$f(r)^* \approx \sum_i E_m^i(r)^* E_c^i(r) \tag{4}$$

where * represents the conjugate value. So, the particle location could be obtained from the location of the absolute value of the maximum of $f(r)^*$. Although a better performance of the model can be obtained if a matched-filtering is previously applied. This matched-filter can be obtained considering the (linear) ODT image from an isolated particle.

Step 2. Update the refractive index field, $n(r)$

From the a priori knowledge of the object in fluid velocimetry, we assume that the refractive index field can only take: (1) the refractive index of the seeding particles within a spherical region around any located particle; and (2) the fluid refractive index in the remaining voxels of the volume of interest. So, if a new particle is located the refractive index around its position is updated.

Step 3. Compute the updated gradient, g(r)

The gradient $g(r)$ of the cost function provides the distribution that should be added to the estimated scattering potential $f(r)$ to minimize the cost function according to the classical Conjugated Gradient Optimization Method. However, our model does not need to solve the full image problem neither to update the scattering potential. Once an estimation of the scattering potential is available, a similar expression to Equation 4 can be obtained for the new gradient $g(r)$. However, the meanings of both interfering fields and its computational strategy have changed:

- Update illuminating field: $E_{r,n}^i(r)$. We need to take into account the presence of the particles already located. The forward solver computes the scattered field $E_s^i(r)$ due to the object described by $n(r)$ and the original illuminating field $E_r^i(r)$. The updated illuminating beam, $E_{r,n}^i(r)$ will be the sum of both fields $E_r^i(r) + E_s^i(r)$.
- Update measured field: $E_{m,n}^i(r)$. The back propagation of the measured field is computed in two stages: Firstly, the expected or computed measured field: $E_c^i(r)$ can be obtained by filtering the $E_s^i(r)$ to take into account the numerical aperture and the far field situation of the recording devices. Secondly, the difference between the measured field and the computed measured field $(E_m^i(r) - E_c^i(r))$ is back-propagated taking into account the diffraction introduced by the estimated refractive index $n(r)$. Let us remark that the role of the illuminating beam in this case will be the conjugated remaining field: $(E_m^i(r) - E_c^i(r))^*$.

As in the initial iteration, a separate contribution to the gradient $g(r)$ should be obtained for each hologram.

Step 4. Locate next particle and exit

As for the initial iteration, the most probable position of next particle is the absolute maximum of the matched-filtered gradient $(g_{MF}(r))$. The position is stored in the output variable PL, and the peak value $(Value)$, can be used to decide the end of the iterations. Experience shows that value will decrease in each iteration and a convenient value of *threshold* ensures the process stop. However, the criterion to select an appropriate value of the threshold is not addressed in this work. Thus, a maximum number of iteration is imposed $(iterMax)$.

In each iteration of the optimization problem, the Helmholtz equation (Forward solver in Algorithm 1) has to be solved. The Helmholtz equation is an example of a linear elliptic Partial Differential Equation (PDE), which has been extensively studied [18]. It can be numerically solved by means of an appropriate transformation based on Green's functions and a spatial discretization [7,18], for example, Finite Element Method (FEM) [8,9]. FEM discretizes the region of interest in small elements, assuming the function $E(r)$ can be approximated to a constant value in each of these elements. A regular mesh of elements is usually considered when the object shape is the unknown (inverse problems). So, the spatial derivatives of the Laplace operator can be discretized with a seven-point stencil in 3D.

Thus, when the discretization process is based on FEM and a spatial regular 3D mesh, the linear system of equations resulting from Equation 1 is described by a matrix with only seven non-zero diagonals. Therefore, FEM transforms the 3D Helmholtz equation into the linear system $(Ax = b)$, where the independent term, b, depends on the illumination field (E_r), the unknown vector, x, identifies the scattered field and the matrix A, related to the refractive index $(n(r))$, is sparse and exhibits a strong regularity in both the pattern and the values of its non-zero elements and has a very large size which depends on the number of spatial discretization points or voxels into the volume (Vol) [17]. It means that the Forward solver actually consists on the resolution of a large size linear system of equation composed by complex number.

3   Experimental Validation of the Model

In order to validate our model we have chosen an apparently simple particle distribution consisting on four $2\mu m$ particles recorded with three inline holograms. The illumination (and observation) direction for each hologram is chosen along x, y and z axis, respectively. We consider a typical coherent illumination provided by a He-Ne laser, with $\lambda = 0.633\mu m$ and that the holograms are recorded at far field with a $NA = 0.55$ microscope objective.

The volume of interest has been divided in $160 \times 160 \times 160$ voxels of one tenth of the wavelength. Multiple scattering presences will be due to two main reasons: (1) the particle cannot be considered as point source and (2) the scattering field diffracted by one particle will modify the illuminating beam that reaches the others.

One of the most difficult particle distributions to recover is shown in Figure 1, as for any of the holograms there is always one particle obscured by the others. The minimum distance between particles is $3\mu m$.

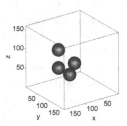

Fig. 1. 3D view of the particle distribution problem

The particle distribution of solving a linear ODT image problem is shown in Figure 2. The scattering potential obtained from Equation 4, which coincides with the first gradient, is shown on the left, and the filtered gradient with the matched filter obtained from Figure 1 on the right.

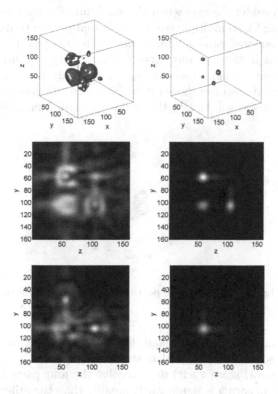

Fig. 2. Gradient (left) and filtered gradient (right) computed at the initial iteration: 3D view of the surface at 0.6 the maximum value (top) and 2D views at $z = 57$ pixels (middle) and at $z = 104$ pixels (bottom)

Top row pictures in Figure 2 show the shape of the voxels with higher values (above 0.6 the maximum value). To better illustrate the blurred image, the modulus of the gradient at the planes centered on the particle positions are shown below: plane $z = 57$ pixels (middle row) and plane 104 pixels (bottom row).

Although the expected resolution of the system should be $\lambda/(2NA) = 9$ pixels. The position of the particles cannot be recovered from the linear ODT image (left row). However, taking into account that particles cannot be considered point sourced and computing the matched-filtered gradient, we can clearly identify the position of four peaks. The error of the particle positions are below 2.5 pixels, that means $0.16\mu m$. As expected, NLODT-P can also solve this particle distribution problem with similar error results. For this case, the use of a matched-filter was enough to unravel the linear ODT image.

However, for real fluid velocimetry application, the number of particles will increase to the order of one thousand particles. In that case, the effect of the multiple scattering between particles will be more significant. In addition, a limited optical access can make compulsory the iterative optimization. To illustrate the problem let consider the case when the minimum distance between particles is $2\mu m$ (close enough), so multiple scattering is mainly due to its proximity (see Figure 3). We considered two configurations: (1) a full-optical access with three in-line hologram as in the previous experiment and (2) a slightly more realistic set-up, in which we illuminate as before, but we only have one camera. The observation direction has been chosen pointing along the direction $\widetilde{k}_{obs} = 1, 1, 1$. That means the camera will look to the particle distribution of Figure 3 roughly as the reader.

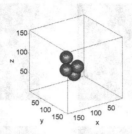

Fig. 3. 3D view of the particle distribution problem

As expected, the linear ODT image does not solve the four particles. The matched-filtered scattering potential is shown in Figure 4. For the full optical access configuration (Figure 4 left) does resolve the four particles. The particle image at the bottom corner is significantly smaller than the others. That particle image cannot be recovered from the one-camera configuration (Figure 4 right). Only the other three particles can be envisaged, even for any other selection of the iso-valued surface.

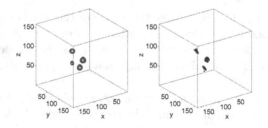

Fig. 4. Linear ODT image after computing the corresponding Match-filter of the particle distribution of Figure 3 for a three-in-line hologram configuration (left) and three illumination and one observation direction configuration (right)

Meanwhile NLODT-P finds the particle position for both configurations, with a position error roughly of 4.6 pixels ($0.3\mu m$). Further work using more realistic problems with larger number of particles, is needed. It has also to be considered the non-linear ODT performance when there is a particle size distribution and some background noise is present. From these small numerical experiments, it can be derived that the performance of NLODT-P is clearly advantageous compared to the linear approach. In the next section it will be shown that the combination of MATLAB with GPUs for solving the Forward problem makes feasible the study of such kind problems and, subsequently, the NLODT-P for fluid velocimetry applications.

4 GPU-Based Implementation of the Model

The computational cost of the advanced numerical model described in this paper is very high. So, it is essential to apply High Performance Computing techniques to its implementation. The implementation of the NLODT-P model is based on the exploitation of both, the MATLAB framework and GPU computing by means of MEX-files routines. As aforementioned, our starting point has been a MATLAB implementation of NLODT-P, for which the procedure with the highest computational cost (Forward solver) has been accelerated using a GPU device.

The Forward solver is in charge of obtaining a solution for the 3D Helmholtz PDE. The large system of equations obtained from the discretization of the 3D Helmholtz PDE can be solved using different solvers. In this paper, a Krylov subspace method, the Biconjugate Gradient method (BCG) is used for solving the Helmholtz equation [3]. Moreover, the regularities of the sparse matrix A have been exploited on a GPU device. From a computational point of view, BCG has a high memory requirement because of the storage of a large sparse matrix (A) [15]. It is necessary to use strategies for the reduction of memory resources runtime because the ODT model has double precision complex numbers. Bearing in mind that the sparse matrix exhibits several regularities, a specific storage format, which stores the minimal information to define the sparse matrix, is considered. In this way, both, memory requirements and BCG runtime are considerably reduced since this new format requires less memory accesses to read sparse matrix elements. The format which takes advantage of the regularities of A was called "Regular Format (RF)" and was defined in [16]. RF optimally minimizes the amount of data needed to store the sparse matrix. RF significantly reduces the memory requirements with respect to the coordinate list format (COO) in a factor of 10.

5 Computational Experiments

This section analyses the computational performance of our NLODT-P model with different dimensions of the volume. In order to show the evolution of the runtime of our NLODT-P model, several tests (with different dimensions of Vol) have been carried out. Four particles of 0.5μ diameter have been located in the tested volumes. The remaining parameters of the example are: Number of holograms= 3, $iterMax = 4$ and the values of Vol range from 200^3 to 280^3 voxels. For the evaluation, a CPU ($2\times$ 4 Intel Xeon E5620 cores, 48 GB RAM,

2.4 GHz clock speed and under Linux) and a GPU device NVIDIA Tesla M2090 have been considered. The NVIDIA GPU, which is CUDA enabled [1], is used in parallelizing the Forward solver. The main characteristics of the GPU device are shown in Table 1.

As it is well known, there can still be significant differences in performance between a program written in MATLAB and one written in a lower-level language, say C. In this work, the model has been developed and tested for several examples using (1) MATLAB framework; and (2) MATLAB framework and CUDA programming. It means that one GPU device is called from MATLAB for accelerating the two Forward solvers involved for each iteration. Figure 5 shows the runtime (in seconds) of the execution of NLODT-P using both approaches (only MATLAB framework and CUDA-MATLAB combination). For the GPU implementation of NLODT-P, the runtime is approximately reduced by a factor of $\approx 40\times$ with respect to the initial MATLAB version.

Table 1. Characteristics of the GPU for the evaluation of NLODT-P

	Tesla M2090
Peak GFlops (single precision)	1331
Peak GFlops (double precision)	665
Memory Bandwidth (GB/s)	177
Clock rate (GHz)	1.3
Device memory (GB)	6
CUDA Cores	512

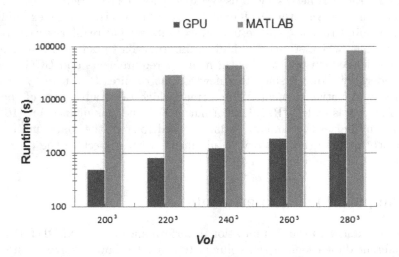

Fig. 5. Evolution of the runtime of NLODT-P using different values for Vol (from 200^3 to 280^3). The remaining parameters of the example are: Number of holograms = 3 and $iterMax = 4$.

6 Conclusions

In this paper we have detailed a three dimensional non-linear ODT model to locate particles, as part of a fluid velocimetry technique. We have presented some numerical experiments to illustrate the accuracy, reliability and effectiveness of the Non-Linear ODT model compared to the Linear ODT one. In particular, we have considered some circumstances when an image post-processing, such as a matched filter, could be enough to unravel the linear ODT image, and when an iterative optimization such as NLODT-P will be compulsory. We have implemented the model using MATLAB combined with GPU computing by means of MEX-files. Acceleration factors $\approx 40\times$ with respect to the approach that only uses MATLAB framework have been obtained. Additionally, the use of a specific format to store the large sparse matrix (A), involved in the BCG method, has reduced the memory requirements until $\approx 10\times$ with respect to the traditional format for specifying sparse matrices in MATLAB (coordinate list (COO)).

As consequence of this work we can say the NLODT-P is able to improve the accuracy of linear ODT methods to locate particles into a fluid and the High Performance Computing is essential to develop and apply this approach. Our future work will be focused on the extension of the NLODT-P model to experimental data of practical interest, it means that larger volumes will have to be computed. For this purpose, an additional effort based on the integration of the distributed resolution of the Helmholtz equation in combination with MATLAB will be carried out. Thus, the resolution of larger problem sizes of practical interest will be possible.

Acknowledgments. G. Ortega is a fellow of the Spanish FPU programme. Work partially supported by the Spanish Ministry of Science (TIN2008-01117, TIN2012-37483-C03-03) and J. Andalucía (P10-TIC-6002, P11-TIC7176), partially financed by the European Reg. Dev. Fund (ERDF).

References

1. Nvidia Cuda Toolkit V5.5 (RN-06722-001_v5.5.) (accessed April 21, 2014)
2. Arroyo, M.P., Hinsch, K.D.: Recent Developments of PIV towards 3D Measurements. In: Topics in Applied Physics, Particle Image Velocimetry, vol. 112, pp. 127–154. Springer, Heidelberg (2008)
3. Axelsson, O., Kucherov, A.: Real valued iterative methods for solving complex symmetric linear systems. Numerical Linear Algebra with Applications 7(4), 197–218 (2000)
4. Ayasso, H., Duchêne, B., Mohammad-Djafari, A.: Bayesian inversion for optical diffraction tomography. J. Mod. Opt. 57(9), 765–776 (2010)
5. Belkebir, K., Sentenac, A.: High-resolution optical diffraction microscopy. J. Opt. Soc. Am. A 20(7), 1223–1229 (2003)
6. Coupland, J.M., Halliwell, N.A.: Particle image velocimetry: Three-dimensional fluid velocity measurements using holographic recording and optical correlation.. Applied Optics 31(8), 1005–1007 (1992)

7. Gumerov, N.A., Duraiswami, R.: Fast Multipole Methods For The Helmholtz Equation In Three Dimensions. Electronics & Electrical. Elsevier Science & Technology Books (2004)
8. Banerjee, U., Babuska, I., Osborn, J.E.: Generalized Finite Element Methods- Main ideas, Results and Perspective. Journal of Computational Methods 1(01), 765–776
9. Ihlenburg, F., Babuška, I.: Finite element solution of the Helmholtz equation with high wave number Part I: The h-version of the FEM. Computers & Mathematics with Applications 30(9), 9–37 (1995)
10. Kim, K., Kim, K.S., Park, H., Ye, J.C., Park, Y.: Real-time visualization of 3-D dynamic microscopic objects using optical diffraction tomography. Opt. Express 21(26), 32269–32278 (2013)
11. Koek, W.D., Bhattacharya, N., Braat, J.J.M.: Influence of virtual images on the signal-to-noise ratio in digital in-line particle holography. Opt. Express (13), 2578–2589 (2005)
12. Lobera, J., Coupland, J.M.: Multiple Scattering in HPIV: Use of ODT Analysis Techniques. Photon (2006)
13. Lobera, J., Coupland, J.M.: Optical diffraction tomography in fluid velocimetry: the use of a priori information. Measurement Science and Technology 19(7), 74013 (2008)
14. Maire, G., et al.: Experimental Demonstration of Quantitative Imaging beyond Abbe's Limit with Optical Diffraction Tomography. Phys. Rev. Lett. 102, 213905 (2009)
15. Ortega, G., Garzón, E.M., Vázquez, F., García, I.: Exploiting the regularity of differential operators to accelerate solutions of PDEs on GPUs. In: Proc. of CMMSE, Benidorm. Spain, June 26–30, pp. 908–917 (2011)
16. Ortega, G., Lobera, J., Arroyo, M.P., García, I., Garzón, E.M.: High Performance Computing for Optical Diffraction Tomography. In: Proc. of HPCS, pp. 195–201. IEEE Computer Society, Madrid (2012)
17. Ortega, G., Lobera, J., Arroyo, M.P., García, I., Garzón, E.M.: Parallel resolution of the 3D Helmholtz Equation based on multi-GPU clusters. Concurrency Computat. Pract. Exper. (2014), doi:10.1002/cpe.3212
18. Sadiku, M.N.O.: Numerical Techniques in Electromagnetics. Second Edition. CRC Press, Boca Raton (2001)
19. Sheng, J., Malkiel, E., Katz, J.: Single Beam Two-Views Holographic Particle Image Velocimetry. Appl. Opt. 42(2), 235–250 (2003)
20. Soria, J., Atkinson, C.: Towards 3C-3D digital holographic fluid velocity vector field measurement-tomographic digital holographic PIV (Tomo-HPIV). Meas. Sci. Technol. 19(7), 74002 (2008)
21. Soulez, F., Denis, L., Thiébaut, É., Fournier, C., Goepfert, C.: Inverse problem approach in particle digital holography: out-of-field particle detection made possible. J. Opt. Soc. Am. A 24(12), 3708–3716 (2007)
22. Wolf, E.: Three-Dimensional structure determination of semi-transparent objects from holographic data. Opt. Commun. 1(4), 153–156 (1969)

GPU Accelerated Stochastic Inversion of Deep Water Seismic Data

Tomás Ferreirinha[1], Rúben Nunes[2],
Amílcar Soares[2], Frederico Pratas[1], Pedro Tomás[1], and Nuno Roma[1]

[1] INESC-ID / IST, Universidade de Lisboa, Portugal
[2] CERENA / IST, Universidade de Lisboa, Portugal

Abstract. Seismic inversion algorithms have been playing a key role in the characterization of oil and gas reservoirs, where a high accuracy is often required to support the decision about the optimal well locations. Since these algorithms usually rely on computer simulations that generate, process and store significant amounts of data, their usage is often limited by their long execution times. In fact, the acceleration of these algorithms allows not only a faster execution, but also the development of larger and more accurate models of the subsurface. This paper proposes a novel parallelization approach of a state of art Stochastic Seismic Amplitude versus Offset Inversion algorithm, by using heterogeneous computing platforms based on a unified OpenCL programming framework. To take full advantage of the computational power made available by systems composed by multiple (and possibly different) accelerators, a spatial division of the simulation space is performed, enabling the parallel simulation of multiple regions of the geological model. This allows achieving a performance speed-up of 22.8× using two distinct GPUs without compromising the accuracy of the obtained models.

Keywords: Stochastic Inversion of Seismic Data, Heterogeneous computing, Graphics Processing Unit (GPU), OpenCL.

1 Introduction

In the last few years, High Performance Computing (HPC) platforms have been playing a key role in the Oil and Gas prospecting industry. As a result of the increased computing capabilities that have been offered to this industry, complex computational models of the subsurface can now be applied to estimate reserves and to diagnose and improve the performance of oil and gas producing fields. However, such applications are characterized by huge execution times (up to months), limiting their usefulness in most cases.

Stochastic algorithms have an important role in the characterization of oil and gas reservoirs, where accurate predictions are essential and the available information is often scarce and expensive. To compensate this issue, complex geological interpretations are made by using approximate computational models that simulate the oil reservoirs. Some related stochastic algorithms have

L. Lopes et al. (Eds.): Euro-Par 2014 Workshops, Part I, LNCS 8805, pp. 239–250, 2014.

already been optimized and parallelized in multi-core General Purpose Processors (GPPs) [1–3]. Some promising results were also obtained by using Graphics Processing Units (GPUs), such as the parallel implementation of the Stochastic Simulation with Patterns (SIMPAT) algorithm [4].

However, typical approximations result in models with a high level of uncertainty, leading to a faulty understanding of the geological structure and consequently to drilling errors. The recently proposed stochastic seismic Amplitude Versus Offset (AVO) inversion algorithm [5] using the Direct Sequential Simulation (DSS) [6] approach represents a promising methodology to solve geophysical inversion problems. It improves the generated models at a cost of a significantly more complex processing of the gathered data, with strict non deterministic dependencies among the several operations.

To the best of the authors' knowledge, only one parallel implementation of the DSS algorithm was proposed [3], where a multi-core approach was implemented by considering a straightforward functional decomposition of the algorithm, presenting considerable limitations in terms of scalability.

This paper proposes a parallelization approach of the stochastic seismic AVO inversion algorithm by considering heterogeneous platforms, composed by several devices with different computational capabilities. To achieve such a flexible solution, the proposed implementation uses the OpenCL API, allowing each part of the algorithm to be easily migrated among the several coexisting GPPs and GPUs. After a careful analysis of the characteristics of the algorithm, it was verified that the most significant part of the algorithm is composed by millions of dependent iterations that individually are not computationally demanding. Due to the lack of data parallelism opportunities presented, a relaxation of the algorithm was considered in order to efficiently exploit the highly parallel architecture of such platforms, significantly reducing the algorithm execution time without compromising the quality of the obtained models.

2   Stochastic Seismic AVO Inversion

The main goal of seismic inversion problems is to estimate a set of models that characterize the physical properties of the Earth subsurface, given a limited set of observed measurements. The reservoir models that are generated via stochastic inversion algorithms can be significantly improved with the integration of different kinds of information [7], *e.g.* well log and seismic reflection data. The most common methodology to incorporate this seismic information, in stochastic fine grid models, is known as geostatistical inversion [8]. Here, a state of art Stochastic Seismic AVO Inversion algorithm [5] is considered, which is an iterative method, based on the Global Stochastic Inversion [7,9] approach. This method directly inverts the density (ρ), P-wave velocity (Vp) and S-wave velocity (Vs) models, allowing the use of AVO analysis, which can not be done with the more common acoustic inversion methods. The stochastic seismic AVO inversion method can be summarized in the following steps, which are also illustrated in Figure 1:

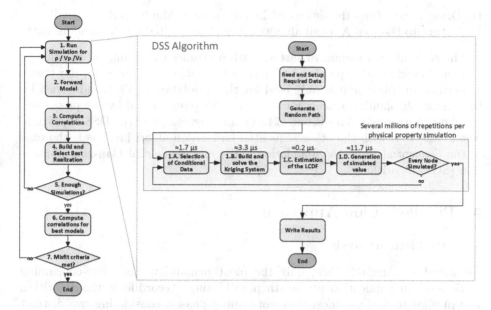

Fig. 1. Stochastic seismic AVO inversion algorithm flowchart. The highlighted procedure corresponds to the most computational demanding part of the whole algorithm.

1. Stochastic simulation of the ρ, Vp and Vs models, by using the DSS with joint probability distributions algorithm;
2. Calculation of the synthetic pre-stack seismic cube with the simulated ρ, Vp and Vs models, by using Shuey's approximation [5];
3. Comparison between the synthetic seismic cube and the real seismic data, creating a correlation cube that evaluates multiple regions of the model;
4. Definition of the best ρ, Vp and Vs models, using a genetic based algorithm;
5. Repeat steps 1 to 4 until no more realizations are desired;
6. Creation of the correlation cubes regarding the best ρ, Vp and Vs models;
7. Repeat of the whole procedure, using the best models and respective correlation cubes to condition the next generation of simulations.

The stochastic simulation (step 1) adopts a Direct Sequential Simulation and Cosimulation [6] approach, which starts by defining a random path through a grid of nodes, to be considered during the simulation process. The stochastic nature of the algorithm depends on this random path in order to find multiple equiprobable models, and consequently to converge. Afterwards, each node is simulated at a time, conditioned by the real data and all the previously simulated values. The simulation procedure can be summarized in the following steps:

A. Randomly select a node from a regular grid;
B. Construct and solve a kriging system for the selected node;
C. Estimate a Local Cumulative Distribution Function (LCDF) at the selected node, by linear interpolating both the real and the experimental data available in the neighbourhood (kriging estimate);

D. Draw a value from the estimated LCDF, using a Monte Carlo method;

E. Return to the step A, until all nodes have been visited by the random path.

The cosimulation variant of this algorithm enables the simulated variable to be conditioned to other previously simulated variables, without any prior transformation. In this case it is only used for the simulation of Vp (conditioned by the previously simulated density model) and Vs (conditioned by the previously simulated Vp model). This is one of the main advantages of the DSS algorithm, when compared with the other sequential simulation algorithms, as is the case of the Sequential Indicator Simulation (SIS) and Sequential Gaussian Simulation (SGS) algorithms.

3 Parallelization Approach

3.1 Problem Analysis

As stated by Amdahl's law, only the most demanding and time-consuming sections of an application are worth parallelizing. Accordingly, the algorithm was profiled to find the most time consuming phases, considering two distinct datasets: a smaller one composed of a grid of 101x101x90 nodes, and a larger and more realistic one with 237x197x350 nodes. For such purpose, the execution time of the different parts of the algorithm was accurately measured using the Performance Application Programming Interface (PAPI) [10] to interface with the hardware performance counters. From the obtained profiling results, it was verified that more than 90% of the algorithm execution time is spent in the generation of the ρ/Vp/Vs models. Consequently, this part of the algorithm was chosen as the prime focus for acceleration. In addition, other performance counters were used in order to evaluate the limiting factor of the algorithm performance. It was verified that the application has a significant amount of memory instructions per floating point operation, which indicates that the application is mainly memory bounded. The same conclusion can be drawn by using Sched-Mon [11] to analyse the Cache-Aware Roofline model [12], where it is clearly observed that the execution samples are located in the memory bounded region of the model (see Figure 2).

The subsequent study considered a comprehensive analysis of the several existing data dependencies in the generation of the ρ/Vp/Vs models. In particular, as represented in Figure 3(a), nodes from a not strictly defined neighbourhood of the node being simulated are selected as conditioning data. As represented in Figure 3(b), the estimation of the local conditional distribution function (step C) requires the values of the previously simulated nodes (step D). As a consequence, although steps A and B can be parallelized, the algorithm execution path is limited by the sequential random path through every node, composed by steps C and D, which still represents approximately 85% of the execution time. Thus, by only performing the first two steps in parallel, it will be hard to significantly accelerate the execution. Finally, individually accelerating each step of the algorithm would also be difficult, since the complexity of the algorithm

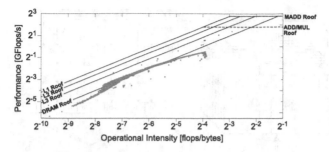

Fig. 2. Roofline model of the sequential execution of the DSS algorithm. Each point in the chart represents a 10ms sample of the program execution.

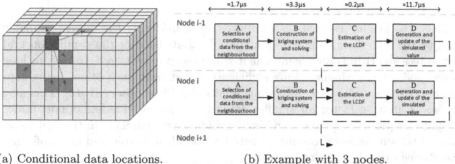

(a) Conditional data locations.   (b) Example with 3 nodes.

Fig. 3. Data dependencies on the stochastic simulation of the ρ, Vp and Vs models

lies in the number of nodes that are required to be simulated (usually several millions) and not in the simulation of a single node, that not only presents few parallelization opportunities but also does not take enough time to be worth the overhead of transferring data to other devices.

3.2 Parallelization Approach

To circumvent the limitation imposed by the described data dependencies, the proposed approach is based on a relaxation of this problem by dividing the simulation grid in multiple tri-dimensional sub-grids, and then randomly selecting a node per sub-grid. Therefore, at each step of the simulation procedure, a set of nodes are simulated and updated at once, conditioning the subsequent nodes to be simulated (see Figure 4). Along the simulation, every sub-grid will select the nodes to be simulated through the same relative sub-path, thus granting a constant distance between the nodes being simulated in parallel. Note that the considered sub-divisions of the simulation grid are not required to be cubic. In fact, the anisotropic nature of the seismic data being processed indicates that there are significantly less dependencies in the vertical direction, which allows for a greater vertical division of the simulation grid.

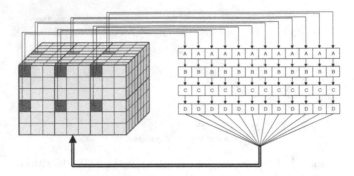

Fig. 4. Parallelization approach based on a spatial division of the original grid

Since the kriging estimate is computed by considering the closest available data to the node being simulated, a spatial sub-division of the simulation grid guarantees algorithm convergence, as it will be seen in section 4. In fact, as long as the nodes being simulated are sufficiently apart from each other, being kept outside of the search range, no data conflicts should be observed [13]. This may become a limiting factor for smaller datasets, which provide less opportunities to split the grid in many pieces without avoiding such conflicts in the first iterations of the simulation procedure, where few data is available and not uniformly distributed over the simulation grid.

Considering the GPU architecture and the adopted OpenCL programming framework, there are at least two different ways to map the proposed approach: each sub-grid is simulated by a distinct OpenCL work-group, being the inherent parallelism of the algorithm explored by the OpenCL work-items within each work-group; each sub-grid is simulated by a distinct work-item. The main difference regarding both approaches is concerned with the number of nodes being simulated at the same time, since in the former approach more resources are being assigned to the simulation of a single node, thus limiting the number of nodes that can actually be simulated at the same time. However, those resources are only completely used when the code itself is parallelizable by a multiple of the warp/wavefront size, which is not the case for a significant part of the algorithm, where only a single work-item in the work-group would effectively be performing useful computations. Although the second approach allows for a greater amount of nodes to be simulated in parallel, it is more memory demanding (intermediate buffers need to be replicated for every node under simulation), and performance losses may occur due to warp divergence and non-coalesced memory accesses, since each thread is simulating its own node, which may lead to different execution paths or accesses to different regions of the memory. In case that the device memory available is not enough, the simulation procedure is performed by simulating the grid layer by layer, keeping a complete copy of the grid being simulated only in the host device. This layers must contemplate not only the blocks that will be simulated but also the neighbour blocks that will condition the simulation.

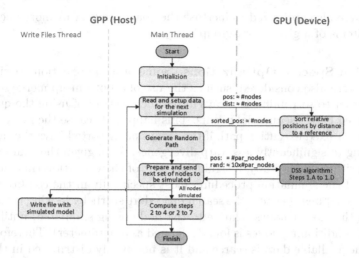

Fig. 5. Execution flowchart of the algorithm. The DSS Algorithm being executed in the GPU is the most computational demanding part.

Accordingly, as illustrated in Figure 5, only tasks related with the simulation procedure are effectively being performed by the GPU devices, being the host device responsible not only by the generation and sending of the data required in every step of the simulation procedure (overlapped with the computations), such as the nodes to be simulated in parallel in the following step or the random values required during the procedure, but also by performing all the other not so significant parts of the algorithm.

3.3   Considered Optimizations

Optimization of the DSS Algorithm Kernels. Several optimizations were considered in order to optimize the performance of the proposed implementation. A significant improvement comes with the efficient usage of local memory in order to optimize not only parallel reductions, which are required to compute the mean and variance of the previously simulated nodes in order to compute the probability distribution functions, but also to improve the access times to global memory buffers that are frequently used. Another aspect that in some cases may be significant is the overhead related with the OpenCL calls. In fact, considering the current AMD GPU drivers, those overheads are in the order of hundreds of microseconds, which may become significant if there are a considerable number of kernel calls or memory transfers per iteration. At this respect, the data transfers were performed using the minimum number of OpenCL enqueue buffer calls possible, and a balance was achieved between the size of the kernels, which influences the number of registers being used and consequently limits the occupation of the device, and the number of kernel calls, which is related not only with the number of different kernels but also with the number of divisions that are performed to the simulation grid. The used data structures and its indexing were also optimized to increase the coalescence of memory accesses by the work-items of a given work-group.

Application Specific Optimizations. Some other application specific optimizations were also considered, such as the use of a bottom-up merge sort algorithm in order to sort multiple arrays in parallel, instead of using the quick-sort that provided better sequential results. This happens because the merge sort algorithm has a fixed execution path if the arrays being sorted have the same size, thus leading to significantly less warp divergence. Also, given the characteristics of the algorithm under study, a significant part of the execution time lies in the first steps of the simulation procedure, most specifically in the conditional data search. This happens because the search procedure starts by looking for available data from the closest nodes relative to the node being simulated, until a given number of conditioning nodes is found (defined as a parameter). Therefore, since initially the available data is scarce and it is not evenly distributed in the simulation grid, the simulation of nodes in regions with few available data results in significantly larger execution times. This problem was minimized by postponing the simulation of nodes from blocks in which there is not enough available data both in the block itself and in the neighbour blocks. This optimization can be performed during the definition of the random path, since it is only required to know the number of available data per block in each iteration. As a result, the execution time of the first steps is significantly reduced at the cost of some extra steps in the end of the simulation algorithm, when there is already a large amount of available data, thus reducing the global execution time.

Optimizations to the Rest of the Algorithm. Finally, some optimizations outside of the simulation procedure were also performed, such as the use of the bitonic sort algorithm in order optimize the sorting of the array that stores the nearest relative positions to a given reference, according to the non-euclidean distances between nodes (related with the anisotropy of the data). Moreover, the output files that have to be written during the execution of the algorithm are also written in parallel by a different GPP thread, thus becoming overlapped with the computations, in order to avoid as much overhead as possible.

3.4   Multi-device Approach

Another important aspect that should also be considered is concerned with the possibility of using multiple devices, in order to ensure another level of scalability. A scalable approach was thus devised to decrease the execution time when multiple GPU and GPP devices are available. Under such condition, the proposed approach starts by first dividing the complete grid between the OpenCL enabled accelerators, and then by sub-partitioning the sub-grids into smaller blocks which are computed in parallel in each device. Also, to efficiently exploit different computational capabilities delivered by different devices, the load is balanced by distributing the nodes to be simulated between the multiple devices

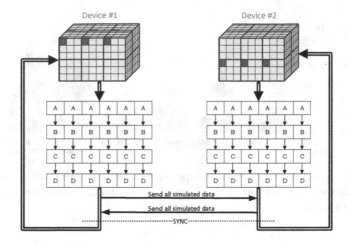

Fig. 6. Multi-device parallelization approach

according to real-time performance measurements. Nevertheless, since the simulation grid is stored in the device memory, it must be updated after the parallel simulation of every bundle of nodes with the information being computed in the other devices. This implies an all-to-all communication scheme and consequently a synchronization point. In the end of the simulation procedure, the resulting model must be read from any device, since every device has an updated copy of the simulation grid (see Figure 6).

4 Experimental Results

The experimental setup considered the execution of 5 iterations of the algorithm, composed by 8 sets of simulations each, over two real datasets: one with 101x101x90 and other with 237x197x350 nodes. Performance was measured by comparing the execution times obtained using multiple heterogeneous environments with the sequential execution of the algorithm in an Intel i7-3820 processor, using the -O3 compiler optimization flag.

Figure 7 shows the obtained performance results when considering several distinct mappings (programmed with the same OpenCL source code). It must be noted that the simulation of the different physical properties (ρ, Vp and Vs) uses different data along the simulation procedure, which naturally introduces some variations in the resulting execution times (18%, 17% and 65% of the simulation execution time respectively). Also, only the time during the simulation procedure itself (effectively being accelerated) was considered for those speed-up measurements, without considering the time required to setup the simulation data (5% of the sequential simulation execution time).

From the obtained results, it can be observed that the execution time was significantly reduced in all the considered mappings. Namely, a speed-up of 15.8× was obtained, considering the execution of the whole algorithm using a single

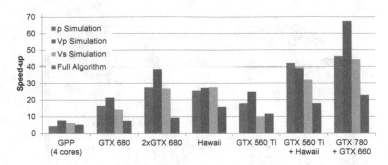

Fig. 7. Execution speed-up results compared to the sequential GPP implementation, when considering different heterogeneous environments, using the dataset with 237x197x350 nodes

GPU, and performance improvement of 5.3× when the algorithm was mapped into the GPP. In the latter case, the obtained speed-up is bigger than 4 (number of cores) due to the use of the hyper-threading technology. The observed performance improvements are coherent with previously mentioned limitations of the sequential implementation. In fact, by comparing the effective bandwidth of the sequential implementation (using the L1/L2/L3 cache hit rates), with the Hawaii GPU theoretical bandwidth, a speed-up of 15× was expected. The speed-ups observed experimentally were greater than this theoretical value because the algorithm was optimized in order to efficiently use the shared memory, and the computational parts of the algorithm are also being parallelized (e.g. parallel reductions), further improving the algorithm performance.

Regarding the multi-device approach, when considering two GTX 680 GPUs, higher improvements were verified in the simulation procedures (up to ≃1.8× when comparing with a single device execution). However, only a global speed-up of 1.24× was obtained because, as the performance is being improved, this procedure becomes less significant in the overall execution time (see Figure 8(a)). Significant improvements were also verified when considering the cooperative execution with multiple different devices, which demonstrates the scalability of the considered implementation in heterogeneous environments. Namely, by using devices from different manufacturers with different computational capabilities, a global speed-up of 18× was obtained.

It must be noted that a slightly worse scalability was verified in the less computational demanding simulations (ρ and Vp), because the non-coalesced memory accesses of the conditional data search procedure, due to the parallel access to different regions of the grid, becomes a significant limiting factor. Also, the machine using GTX 680 GPUs uses a different host device (Xeon E5-2609), which justifies the observed full algorithm speed-up differences. Nevertheless, although the obtained multiple device speed-up is slightly below the theoretical limit (mainly due to the communication overhead), the load-balancer successfully managed to divide the work-load between the available devices, maximizing the achieved performance.

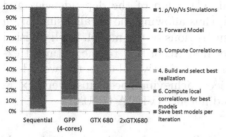 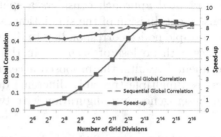

(a) Functional workload distribution, using the 237x197x350 dataset.

(b) Convergence and speed-up analysis, using the 101x101x90 dataset.

Fig. 8. Graphical analysis of the obtained results comparing with the sequential implementation of the algorithm

Despite being memory demanding, this implementation occupied approximately 580 MB of the device memory which, considering modern devices, still leaves room for a significant scaling of the problem size until a layer by layer simulation approach is required (that implies a slightly increased communication overhead).

Finally, Figure 8(b) presents the evolution of both the speed-up and the global correlation coefficient with the number of grid-divisions (which corresponds to the nodes being simulated in parallel). The results were obtained by performing several independent runs of 10 iterations, using the Hawaii GPU and considering the dataset composed by 101x101x90 nodes. As it can be observed, when comparing the simulated models with real data, the convergence is still verified, since the obtained global correlation coefficients are similar both for the parallel and sequential implementations of the algorithm. This demonstrates that the applied relaxations, toward an efficient parallelization, do not affect the quality of the results. In fact, it can be verified that, even when a very significant amount of sub-grids was considered (resulting in a simulation composed only by 15 steps), the convergence of the algorithm was still verified. This is mainly due to the postponing optimization that avoids simulating nodes that have few or no conditional data in the neighbour blocks. As a result, when the block size becomes smaller (i.e., the number of grid divisions increases), a consistent spatial distribution of the physical property being simulated is granted, which improves the algorithm convergence.

5   Conclusions

This paper proposes a parallelization of a state of the art stochastic seismic AVO inversion algorithm in heterogeneous platforms. The acceleration of such algorithms not only allows for faster reservoir modeling, but also to make it possible to develop larger and more accurate computational models of the Earth's subsurface. To circumvent the strict data dependencies presented by this algorithm, the adopted approach considers a spatial relaxation of the dependencies and consequent division of the simulation grid, thus allowing the parallel simulation of multiple nodes corresponding to different regions of the model. Such division comes with no loss of accuracy in the results. According to the obtained experimental results, the proposed acceleration efficiently balances the work-load between multiple (possibly different) devices, achieving speed-ups over 22× in the heterogeneous configuration with two different NVIDIA GPUs.

Acknowledgment. This work was partially supported by national funds through Fundação para a Ciência e a Tecnologia (FCT), under projects: Threads (PTDC/EEA-ELC/117329/2010), P2HCS (PTDC/EEI-ELC/3152/2012) and project PEst-OE/EEI/LA0021/2013.

References

1. Stinessen, B.O.: Profiling, Optimization and Parallelization of a Seismic Inversion Code. PhD thesis, Norwegian University of Science and Technology (2011)
2. Hysing, A.D.: Parallel Seismic Inversion for Shared Memory Systems. PhD thesis, Norwegian University of Science and Technology (2010)
3. Nunes, R., Almeida, J.A.: Parallelization of sequential gaussian, indicator and direct simulation algorithms. Computers & Geosciences 36(8), 1042–1052 (2010)
4. Tahmasebi, P., Sahimi, M., Mariethoz, G., Hezarkhani, A.: Accelerating geostatistical simulations using graphics processing units (GPU). Computers & Geosciences 46, 51–59 (2012)
5. Azevedo, L., Nunes, R., Soares, A., Neto, G.: Stochastic seismic AVO inversion. In: 75th EAGE Conference & Exhibition Incorporating SPE EUROPEC 2013 (2013)
6. Soares, A.: Direct sequential simulation and cosimulation. Mathematical Geology 33(8), 911–926 (2001)
7. Caetano, H.M.V.: Integration of seismic information in reservoir models: Global Stochastic Inversion. PhD thesis, Universidade Técnica de Lisboa (2009)
8. Haas, A., Dubrule, O.: Geostatistical inversion-a sequential method of stochastic reservoir modelling constrained by seismic data. First Break 12(11) (1994)
9. Soares, A., Diet, J., Guerreiro, L.: Stochastic inversion with a global perturbation method. In: EAGE Petroleum Geostatistics (2007)
10. Browne, S., Dongarra, J., Garner, N., Ho, G., Mucci, P.: A portable programming interface for performance evaluation on modern processors. International Journal of High Performance Computing Applications 14(3), 189–204 (2000)
11. Taniça, L., Ilic, A., Toms, P., Sousa, L.: Schedmon: A performance and energy monitoring tool for modern multi-cores. In: 7th International Workshop on Multi/many-Core Computing Systems, MuCoCus 2014 (2014)
12. Ilic, A., Pratas, F., Sousa, L.: Cache-aware roofline model: Upgrading the loft. IEEE Computer Architecture Letters (2013)
13. Vargas, H., Caetano, H., Filipe, M.: Parallelization of sequential simulation procedures. In: EAGE Petroleum Geostatistics (2007)

QCD Library for GPU Cluster with Proprietary Interconnect for GPU Direct Communication

Norihisa Fujita[1], Hisafumi Fujii[1], Toshihiro Hanawa[2], Yuetsu Kodama[3], Taisuke Boku[1,3], Yoshinobu Kuramashi[3], and Mike Clark[4]

[1] Graduate School of Systems and Information Engineering, University of Tsukuba, Tsukuba, Japan
[2] Information Technology Center, The University of Tokyo
[3] Center for Computational Sciences, University of Tsukuba, Tsukuba, Japan
[4] NVIDIA Corporation

Abstract. QUDA is a Lattice QCD library that can use NVIDIA's Graphics Processing Unit (GPU) accelerators, and is widely used as a framework for Lattice QCD applications. In this paper, we apply our novel proprietary interconnect network called the Tightly Coupled Accelerators (TCA) architecture, to inter-node GPU communication in QUDA. The TCA architecture was developed for low-latency inter-node communication among accelerators connected through the PCI Express (PCIe) bus on PC clusters. It enables direct memory copy between accelerators, such as GPUs, over nodes in the same manner as an intra-node PCIe transaction. We assess the performance of TCA on QUDA by a high-density GPU cluster HA-PACS/TCA, which is a proof-of-concept testbed for TCA architecture. The results show that our interconnection network system, which effects a stronger scaling than ordinary InfiniBand solutions on PC clusters with GPUs, significantly reduces communication latency. The execution time for Conjugate Gradient (CG) iteration shows that the TCA implementation is 2.14 times faster than peer-to-peer MPI implementation and 1.96 times faster than MPI remote-memory access (RMA) implementation, where InfiniBand QDRx2 rail network is used in both cases.

1 Introduction

In recent years, research related to General-Purpose computing on Graphics Processing Units (GPGPU) has focused on High Performance Computing (HPC). Many GPGPU clusters are in the TOP500 list of the most powerful computer systems [1]. In general, GPUs use Peripheral Component Interconnect Express (PCIe) [2] buses in order to communicate with CPUs and other GPUs in the same computation node. However, the transfer bandwidth of a PCIe bus is at most several tens part of the memory bandwidth of a GPU. Thus, the bandwidth of PCIe buses becomes a bottleneck for parallel GPU applications. Moreover, since GPUs cannot communicate directly with GPUs in other nodes, the CPU has to assist data exchange between GPUs from different nodes. As the data is thus relayed through the CPU, inter-node GPU communication latency becomes larger than inter-node CPU communication latency.

L. Lopes et al. (Eds.): Euro-Par 2014 Workshops, Part I, LNCS 8805, pp. 251–262, 2014.

In past research, we developed an interconnection network system based on the Tightly Coupled Accelerator (TCA) architecture that enables inter-node GPU communication. The TCA architecture is based on the concept of expanding the PCIe link to inter-node communication between accelerators over the multiple nodes. In this network system, all devices connected through PCIe can theoretically communicate directly across nodes. In this paper, we apply our TCA technology to QUDA which is widely used as a framework for Lattice QCD applications with NVIDIA GPU accelerators.

2   QUDA

QUDA is an open-source Lattice Quantum Chrono-Dynamics (LQCD) framework library developed by Mike Clark et al. that supports NVIDIA GPU accelerators [3,4]. Roughly speaking, there are two kinds of computations in QUDA: stencil computations in the Dirac operator, and computations to solve linear equations using Krylov solvers. QUDA supports multiple Krylov solvers, such as the Conjugate Gradient (CG) method and the BiConjugate Gradient Stabilized (BiCGSTAB) method, which are chosen according to the matrix type that needs to be solved.

QUDA supports a single GPU environment as well as a multi-node and multi-GPU environment [5]. It can use the MPI [6] and Lattice QCD Message Passing (QMP) [7] as a communication API. We will add TCA support to QUDA as an extension of the MPI. As we detail in the next section, the TCA architecture is currently not self-contained. Because of this, we employ MPI for the general preparation phase of the computation, which does not affect overall performance, and TCA for critical communication in the body of the main loop of the code.

3   Tightly Coupled Accelerators (TCA) Architecture and PEACH2

Tightly Coupled Accelerator (TCA) architecture enables inter-node GPU communication using PCIe technology as a communication link. The PCI Express Adaptive Communication Hub ver. 2 (PEACH2) is a proof-of-concept implementation of the TCA architecture developed at the Center for Computational Sciences in the University of Tsukuba [8][9]. It is an interface board for low-latency inter-node communication among accelerators.

3.1   Overview of TCA Architecture

TCA uses PCIe as an inter-node communication channel. PCIe is a serial bus interface that is widely used to connect most peripheral devices, including extension boards such as GPUs, Ethernet boards, and InfiniBand HCAs in PCs. While PCIe is commonly used for intra-node interconnection, it is possible to extend it to inter-node interconnection using PCIe external cables [10] under

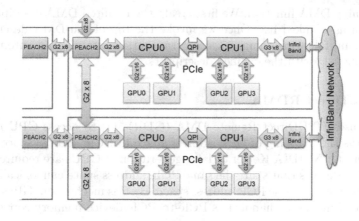

Fig. 1. TCA connection in the HA-PACS/TCA cluster

the following condition. PCIe is a packet-based network that consists of one root complex (RC) and a few end points (EPs) in a single-address space of the network. RC is usually a CPU and EPs are extension boards. Since only one RC is allowed in a PCIe network, we cannot assign multiple nodes to a PCIe network without special routing mechanisms. The PEACH2 chip acts as a router to effect inter-node communication, hence solving this problem to allow multiple RCs in a network system.

Figure 1 shows a typical computation node with the PEACH2 board and multiple GPUs. An Intel Xeon E5 (SandyBridge-EP or IvyBridge-EP architecture) processor is assumed to be the host CPU because it supports the local switching of PCIe on the chip in order to handle multiple PCIe devices that are directly attached to the CPU. We implement this configuration on the Highly Accelerated Parallel Advanced system for Computational Sciences with the TCA feature (HA-PACS/TCA) GPU cluster, which is a proof-of-concept testbed for the TCA architecture. The PEACH2 board is connected to CPU0 and the Infini-Band HCA is connected to CPU1, where both network interfaces require eight lanes of PCIe respectively. Since all CPUs and GPUs share the same PCIe address space, PEACH2 can access all of their memory. However, we assume to use only two GPUs (GPU0 and GPU1) connected to the same CPU with the PEACH2 board because PCIe communication throughput degrades drastically over Intel's QuickPath Interconnect (QPI). This problem of PCIe communication over QPI is a well-known fact and does not limit the use of the TCA concept in general. For example, we can connect four or more GPUs to PEACH2 without creating a bottleneck if an appropriate PCIe switch, such as PLX, is used instead of the internal PCIe switch on an Intel Xeon E5 CPU.

PEACH2 has a DMA Controller (DMAC) with four DMA channels. *DMA descriptors* are prepared to invoke PEACH2's DMAC. We can prepare multiple DMA descriptors for various communication patterns. It contains information regarding the source memory region and the destination region. PEACH2's DMAC has a chaining DMA function. We first create the required DMA descriptors and chain them as a linked list. Once we invoke the top of the DMA descriptor in a DMA chain, following communication transactions are invoked automatically and continuously with the chained descriptors.

3.2 GPUDirect RDMA

PEACH2 uses GPUDirect Remote DMA (GDR) [11] to access GPU memory, which allows the mapping of GPU address space to PCIe address space. CUDA 5.0 or later and NVIDIA Kepler or later generation of GPUs are required to use GDR. Other devices that share the same PCIe address space can logically access GPU memory in the same PCIe address space. By this mechanism, GPU-to-GPU memory copying can be handled as PCIe-to-PCIe device memory copying.

4   Implementation of QUDA on TCA Architecture

We focus on accelerating communication during stencil computations in QUDA by using the TCA architecture. The original QUDA uses send-receive semantics, i.e., a point-to-point protocol, in both the MPI and Lattice QCD Message Passing (QMP) communication schemes. On the other hand, since TCA supports Remote Memory Access (RMA) Write and Read (emulated by Proxy Write) in one-sided communication, we need to change the communication structure of QUDA from its original point-to-point protocol.

4.1   MPI-3 Remote Memory Access

TCA supports only one-sided write operations, such as the MPI_Put function. Therefore, we first rewrite QUDA's communication protocol using MPI-3 Remote Memory Access (RMA) before rewriting it using TCA. We consider that two-phase porting (MPI point-to-point → MPI RMA → TCA) is more reasonable than direct porting from MPI point-to-point to TCA because new RMA-version of code can be applied for any MPI-3 ready GPU clusters, which is expected to enhance the performance even without TCA. In the performance comparison, we compare the original point-to-point MPI, MPI-RMA and TCA implementations.

We implement MPI RMA support and TCA support based on the method of the QUDA communicator, which consists of multiple communicators in its abstraction layer. We call our extended method the "QUDA RMA method." Figure 2 shows the basic code flow of the RMA method. We describe the details of these functions in the following subsections.

4.2   Message Handle

QUDA has a MsgHandle object that represents a communication entity. In its implementation, the MPI point-to-point protocol contains an MPI_Request created

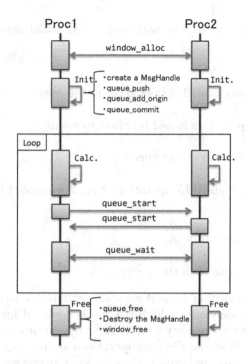

Fig. 2. Basic code flow of the RMA method

by persistent APIs, such as the `MPI_Send_init` function, to preserve communication properties. `MPI_Request` contains all information required by `MPI_Send` and `MPI_Recv` such as pointers, data types, data lengths, etc. We extend `MsgHandle` to support RMA communication for MPI RMA and TCA. We describe the details of the extension for the two implementations in Section 5.

4.3   Memory Window Object

We introduce an `RmaWindow` object that represents a memory region for RMA. Since QUDA uses only GPU memory for RMA communication, an `RmaWindow` does not contain CPU memory. The source and destination memory regions specified using the RMA method must belong to an `RmaWindow`.

4.4   RMA Operation Queue

We introduce an `RmaQueue` object used for RMA operation management. An `RmaQueue` object has two kinds of information: that associated with `MsgHandle`, and the origin rank of the communication process.

We can use the following functions in the method:

Alloc

creates a new queue associated with a specified `RmaWindow`.

Free

destroys a queue.

Start

starts RMA operations with `MsgHandles` in the queue.

Wait

waits for RMA operations issued by Start to complete.

Push

adds an RMA operation to the queue.

Commit

tells the queue that all RMA operations have been added (Pushed) and the relevant queue is ready.

Add Origin

adds an origin process to wait.

Clear

removes all operations from the queue.

The *Add Origin* operation is used to wait until RMA write operations on remote processes are completed. The RMA method should know which rank of process would write to its memory to wait these operations before the next calculation begins. The *Push* and *Commit* operations are too expensive to perform one after the other. Thus, we have to reuse the same queue as much as possible. Since the *Start* and the *Wait* operations do not modify the contents of the queue, we can reuse the same `RmaQueue` if we do not need to modify the communication pattern. This condition is satisfied by typical scientific computations, including QUDA's communication protocol.

4.5   Rewriting Point-to-Point Communication

We rewrite point-to-point communication to RMA communication in QUDA. We only use RMA write operations, replacing send operations with write operations and removing receive operations. This is required to attain high performance in TCA implementation, where RMA Write is the fundamental communication operation.

In order to hide communication latency in MPI point-to-point implementation, MPI communications and subsequent calculations are pipelined and overlapped using the `MPI_Isend` and `MPI_Irecv` functions. To implement overlapping, we need a fine-grained synchronization method. However, since MPI RMA synchronization methods are not fine grained, the *Wait* queue operation waits until all RMA operations are completed. We intend to improve the performance of RMA synchronization area in future research.

QUDA supports domain decomposition in the dimensions x, y, z, and t. The communication pattern (message address, length and communicating partners) of each dimension is not changed over the loop iteration. Therefore, we can apply the DMA chaining mechanism of PEACH2 to this communications repeatedly.

5   RMA Implementation

5.1   MPI RMA Implementation

In MPI point-to-point implementation, a `MsgHandle` object contains an `MPI_Request` and `MPI_Datatype` attributes, and the `RmaWindow` object contains an `MPI_Win` object. Since MPI does not provide a persistent API for RMA APIs, such as the `MPI_Send_init` function, a `MsgHandle` contains all parameters that will be passed to the `MPI_Put` function in MPI RMA implementation. We can create an `MPI_Request` through the `MPI_Rput` function. However, we cannot use the `MPI_Rput` function because the request begins automatically. In MPI RMA implementation, the `Commit` queue operation does nothing. There is no space for optimization in this phase.

The *Wait* queue operation uses the `MPI_Win_post`, `MPI_Win_start`, `MPI_Win_complete`, and `MPI_Win_wait` functions to wait for RMA operations. The `MPI_Win_post` function starts an exposure RMA epoch and the `MPI_Win_complete` function closes the epoch. These functions control RMA access from specified processes. We only wait to complete the RMA operations that are related to a process, namely RMA write operations initiated by the process and operations that will write to the process. The `Add Origin` operation creates an `MPI_Group` to be passed to the first argument of the `MPI_Win_post` function.

5.2   TCA Implementation

The TCA environment is developed on the CUDA Toolkit [12] provided by NVIDIA. Therefore, GPU manipulations, such as memory management, data transfer, and kernel launch, are conducted in the same manner as when TCA is not used. TCA uses the PCIe address space to specify memory location. However, pointers from the PCIe address space are generally not the same as CPU/GPU pointers used in applications. Thus, we use the *memory handle* model API to avoid using the inconvenient PCIe address space. We create a handle of GPU memory allocated through the CUDA API (e.g., `cudaMalloc`). It is called a `tcaHandle` and contains the PCIe address of the memory region and the node id.

In TCA implementation, a `MsgHandle` object contains all parameters to pass to the TCA APIs, as in the MPI RMA implementation. In the MPI RMA implementation, we can use `MPI_Win` to communicate with all processes in an MPI version of communicator. However, since a `tcaHandle` object can be used with a node determined at its time of creation, we have 16 handles for all nodes in it.

In contrast to MPI implementation, the `Commit` queue operation is important for TCA implementation. We create DMA descriptors and a DMA chain in the operation. To achieve the best performance on TCA, all communication should be in the form of a series of DMA chains. Transactions in a DMA chain are begun using the `tcaStartDMADesc` function in the stencil communication phase.

We wait for RMA operations in the queue to be completed in the `Wait` queue operation. In addition to waiting for these, the RMA method knows the ranks

Table 1. The node specifications of HA-PACS/TCA

CPU	Intel(R) Xeon(R) CPU E5-2680 v2 2.80 GHz × 2
CPU Memory	64 GB / CPU
GPU	NVIDIA Tesla K20X × 4
GPU Memory	6 GB / GPU
IB HBA	Mellanox Connect-X3 Dual-port QDR
PEACH2	1 board / node
OS	CentOS 6.4
CUDA Toolkit	version 6.0
GPU Driver	version 311.67
MPI	MVAPICH2-GDR 2.0b built for CUDA 6.0

of processes that will write to the target process using the `Add Origin` queue operation, so that we wait for all RMA operations issued to the process by other processes in the `Wait` queue operation.

6   Performance Evaluation

In this section, we compare the performance of three implementations: MPI point-to-point (the original QUDA implementation), MPI RMA, and TCA.

6.1   Machine Environment

For performance evaluation, We use the HA-PACS/TCA GPU cluster, which was developed in the Center for Computational Sciences at the University of Tsukuba. The node specifications are listed in Table 1 and the node construction is shown in Figure 1. There are two CPUs in a node; a PEACH2 board is attached to CPU0 and an InfiniBand HCA is attached to CPU1. We use CUDA Toolkit 6.0 and MVAPICH2-GDR 2.0b as an MPI implementation.

PEACH2 and InfiniBand do not access GPU memory over QPI because of performance degradation. Therefore, PEACH2 only directly accesses the memories of GPU0 and GPU1, whereas InfiniBand only directly accesses the memories of GPU2 and GPU3, as shown in Figure 1. Since QUDA supports only one GPU per process, we measured and compared single-GPU performances in this study. We use GPU0 to measure the performance of TCA and GPU2 for that of Infini-Band.

6.2   Performance Measurement

We use the `invert_test` test program provided by QUDA for performance measurement. It solves a linear equation using a CG solver and shows its performance in terms of GFLOPS and the number of iterations.

X, Y, Z, and T denote the mesh size in each dimension x, y, z, and t, respectively, on each process. n_X, n_Y, n_Z, and n_T denote the number of processes of each dimension. N_X, N_Y, N_Z, and N_T denote the mesh size of each dimension in total, where $(N_X, N_Y, N_Z, N_T) = (X \times n_X, Y \times n_y, Z \times n_Z, T \times n_T)$.

We measured two kinds of mesh size parameters, $(N_X, N_Y, N_Z, N_T) = (8, 8, 8, 8)$ named "Small Model" and $(N_X, N_Y, N_Z, N_T) = (16, 16, 16, 16)$ named "Large Model", and various node sizes to assess the strong scaling. Since current PEACH2 implementation supports up to 16 nodes in a network, we made our measurement using 16 nodes at most. Figure 3 shows the performance using MPI point-to-point, MPI-RMA, and TCA for the Small Model, whereas Figure 4 shows the performance of each of the three networks for the Large Model. These performance are measured on Rank 0. With the same number of computation nodes (processes), the process granularity of the $(8, 8, 8, 8)$ problem is $\frac{1}{16}$ of the $(16, 16, 16, 16)$ problem because it is a four-dimensional domain decomposition problem. Since the number of iterations of the CG solver may differ for each configuration, the time magnitudes in Figures 3 and 4 are normalized by the number of iteration. The message size in the Small Model is $2 \times \frac{24\text{KB}}{n}$, where n is the number of nodes in a dimension. The message size in the Large Model is $2 \times \frac{192\text{KB}}{n}$. Since there are two neighboring processes in each dimension, two messages are issued for each dimension if the dimension is divided into processes.

In case of the Small Model, the TCA implementation is faster than both MPI implementations in all configurations. In the case of $(n_x, n_y) = (2, 2)$, the TCA implementation is 2.14 times faster than the MPI point-to-point implementation and approximately 1.96 times faster than the MPI RMA implementation. The calculation times do not scale well in this problem because the mesh size is too small and the high cost of launching CUDA kernels renders them a bottleneck. The MPI RMA implementation is slightly faster than the MPI point-to-point implementation in all configurations.

For the Large Model, since the peak bandwidth of TCA is lower than that of InfiniBand [1], TCA is slower than the MPI implementations for some configurations. The TCA implementation is slower than both MPI implementations in cases involving two nodes, is almost eve with the MPI peer-to-peer implementation in cases involving four nodes, and is faster than the MPI peer-to-peer implementation in cases involving eight and 16 nodes. In the case of $(n_x, n_y) = (4, 4)$, the TCA implementation is 1.14 times faster than the MPI peer-to-peer implementation. Since the MPI RMA implementation does not support overlapping between calculation and communication at present, as described in the previous section, the MPI RMA implementation is slower than the MPI peer-to-peer implementation in some configurations. In contrast to cases involving large numbers of nodes, the MPI point-to-point implementation and the MPI RMA implementation exhibit almost identical performance in cases involving small numbers of nodes.

---

[1] Due to FPGA technology used in PEACH2, all PCIe ports are limited as PCIe gen.2 x8 lanes while InfiniBand dual port QDA HCA can use PCIe gen.3 x8 lanes. Therefore, TCA achieves much shorter latency than InfiniBand but the bandwidth becomes lower beyond certain message size.

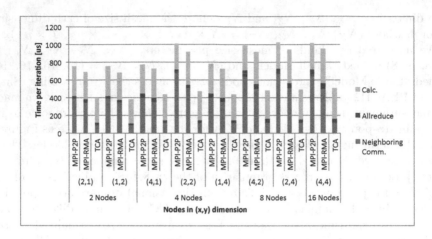

Fig. 3. Performance in the case of the Small Model

The Small Model where $(n_x, n_y) = (2, 2)$ is the configuration most improved by TCA in both measurements. In communication time comparisons in particular, the TCA implementation is 5.90 times faster than the MPI peer-to-peer implementation in the Small Model when $(n_x, n_y) = (2, 4)$, and is 4.54 times faster than the MPI RMA implementation in the Small Model when $(n_x, n_y) = (2, 4)$.

In the comparison between communication times in Figure 3 and Figure 4, and between the message sizes of the two problem sizes, we see that TCA is useful for communication involving small messages. A message in the Small Model is less than or equal to 24 KB in all configurations. The message size in the Large Model when $(n_x, n_y) = (4, 4)$, which is the configuration most improved in the Large Model by TCA, is 48 KB for the x and y dimensions. However, since the bandwidth of the TCA for large messages is lower than that of InfiniBand [8], TCA performance in the Large Model with two nodes is unsatisfactory. We think that the application can be accelerated by adopting a hybrid approach by switching the channel of a message depending on the message size and its destination GPU. We plan to continue work on improving the performance of TCA application. In general, in a strong configuration, it is important for applications to transfer small messages quickly because the message size in applications decreases as the number of nodes increases.

7   Related Work

APEnet+[13] is a field-programmable gate array (FPGA)-based 3D torus network architecture that, like TCA, supports direct GPU communication [14] but uses their original protocol.

Mellanox's InfiniBand Host Bus Adapter (HBA) supports GPUDirect RDMA for direct GPU memory access [15]. We can use GPU pointers with the Verbs

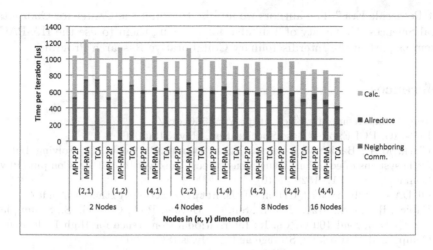

Fig. 4. Performance in the case of the Large Model

API if the environment supports RDMA. Some MPI implementations [16,17] support the use of InfiniBand HBA with GPUDirect RDMA. By using a GDR-supported MPI, we can pass GPU pointers to a few MPI APIs. For example, we can pass a GPU pointer to the first argument of the MPI_Send function.

These technologies are similar to TCA but do not use the PCIe protocol. Since TCA does not need to convert PCIe into another protocol, it has an advantage over rival technologies in terms of communication latency.

8   Conclusion

In this paper, we ported the open-source Lattice QCD framework library QUDA, which supports NVIDIA GPU accelerators, to our novel interconnection TCA. TCA is an interconnection concept to expand the PCIe channel to inter-node communication. It enables us to access GPU memory across the network.

TCA only supports one-sided write operations, such as the MPI_Put function. Therefore, we first extended QUDA's communication abstraction layer to support RMA, and then implemented TCA API support and MPI RMA support on it.

In the performance comparison among the MPI point-to-point implementation, the MPI RMA implementation, and the TCA implementations, the execution time of CG iteration shows that the TCA implementation is 2.14 times faster than the MPI peer-to-peer implementation and 1.96 times faster than the MPI RMA implementation in case of the Small Model, where $(n_x, n_y) = (2, 2)$.

Acknowledgments. This research was partially supported by the Japan Science and Technology Agency's (JST) CREST program "Research and Development of Unified Environment on Accelerated Computing and Interconnection for

Post-Petascale Era." The authors would like to thank the Center for Computational Sciences, University of Tsukuba, for allowing them to use the HA-PACS system as part of the Interdisciplinary Collaborative Research Program.

References

1. Top500 Supercomputer Sites, http://top500.org/
2. PGI-SIG. PCI Express Base Specification, Rev. 3.0 (2010)
3. Clark, M.A., Babich, R., Barros, K., Brower, R.C., Rebbi, C.: Solving Lattice QCD systems of equations using mixed precision solvers on GPUs. Comput. Phys. Commun. 181, 1517–1528 (2010)
4. QUDA - A Library for QCD on GPUs, http://lattice.github.io/quda/
5. Babich, R., Clark, M.A., Joo, B., Shi, G., Brower, R.C., Gottlieb, S.: Scaling lattice QCD beyond 100 GPUs. In: International Conference for High Performance Computing, Networking, Storage and Analysis (SC) (2011)
6. Message Passing Interface (MPI) Forum Home Page, http://www.mpi-forum.org/
7. Lattice QCD Message Passing (QMP), http://usqcd.jlab.org/usqcd-docs/qmp/
8. Hanawa, T., Kodama, Y., Boku, T., Sato, M.: Interconnect for Tightly Coupled Accelerators Architecture. In: IEEE 21st Annual Symposium on High-Performance Interconnects (HOT Interconnects 21), pp. 79–82 (2013)
9. Hanawa, T., Kodama, Y., Boku, T., Sato, M.: Tightly Coupled Accelerators Architecture for Minimizing Communication Latency among Accelerators. In: The Third International Workshop on Accelerators and Hybrid Exascale Systems, AsHES (2013)
10. PGI-SIG. PCI Express External Cabling Specification, Rev. 1.0 (2007)
11. NVIDIA GPUDirect — NVIDIA Developer Zone, https://developer.nvidia.com/gpudirect.
12. CUDA Toolkit, https://developer.nvidia.com/cuda-toolkit
13. Ammendola, R., Biagioni, A., Frezza, O., Lo, F.: APEnet+: high bandwidth 3D torus direct network for petaflops scale commodity clusters. J. Phys. Conf (2011)
14. Ammendola, R., Biagioni, A., Frezza, O., Lo, F.: APEnet+: a 3D Torus network optimized for GPU-based HPC Systems. J. Phys. Conf. (2012)
15. Mellanox Products: Mellanox OFED GPUDirect RDMA Beta, http://www.mellanox.com/page/products_dyn?product_family=116.
16. MVAPICH2, http://mvapich.cse.ohio-state.edu/overview/mvapich2/.
17. OpenMPI, http://www.open-mpi.org/.

Mario: Interactive Tuning of Biological Analysis Pipelines Using Iterative Processing

Martin Ernstsen[1,*], Erik Kjærner-Semb[2,**], Nils Peder Willassen[2],
and Lars Ailo Bongo[1]

[1] Dept. of Computer Science and Center for Bioinformatics, University of Tromsø, Norway
[2] Dept. of Chemistry and Center for Bioinformatics, University of Tromsø, Norway
martin.ernstsen@ksat.no, erikkj@imr.no,
nils-peder.willassen@uit.no, larsab@cs.uit.no

Abstract. Biological data analysis relies on complex pipelines for cleaning, integrating, and summarizing data before presenting the results to a user. Specifically, biological data analysis is usually implemented as a pipeline that combines many independent tools. During development, it is necessary to tune the pipeline to find the tools and parameters that work well with a particular dataset. However, as the dataset size increases, the pipeline execution time also increases and parameter tuning becomes impractical. No current biological data analysis frameworks enable analysts to interactively tune the parameters of a biological analysis pipelines for large-scale datasets. We present Mario, a system that quickly updates pipeline output data when pipeline parameters are changed. It combines reservoir sampling, fine-grained caching of derived datasets, and an iterative data-parallel processing model. We demonstrate the usability of our approach through a biological use case, and experimentally evaluate the latency, throughput, and resource usage of the Mario system. Mario is open-sourced at bdps.cs.uit.no/code/Mario.

Keywords: Iterative processing, interactive processing, biological data analysis, parameter tuning, provenance.

1 Introduction

Recent technological advances in instrument, computation and storage technologies have resulted in large amounts of biological data [1]. To realize the full potential for novel scientific insight in the data, it is necessary to transform it to knowledge through analysis. A computer system for analyzing biological data typically consist of three main components: the input data, a set of tools in a pipeline, and finally a data exploration tool (Fig. 1). Biotechnology instruments such as short-read sequencing machines produce the input data. The datasets can range in size from megabytes to many terabytes. A series of tools process the data in a pipeline where the output of one tool is the input to the next tool (Fig. 1). A specific biological data analysis

---

* Now at Kongsberg Satellite Services AS, Tromsø, Norway.
** Now at Institute of Marine Research, Bergen, Norway

In Proc. of 5th International Workshop on High Performance Bioinformatics and Biomedicine (HiBB'14)

L. Lopes et al. (Eds.): Euro-Par 2014 Workshops, Part I, LNCS 8805, pp. 263–274, 2014.
© Springer International Publishing Switzerland 2014

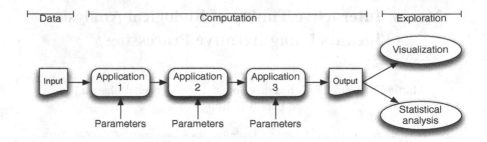

Fig. 1. A biological data analysis pipeline

project often requires a unique combination of tools. There are hundreds of available tools, ranging from small mall, user-created scripts to large, complex applications. Finally, the pipeline results are exported to a data exploration tool for interpretation by biomedical researchers. An important and time-consuming part of bioinformatics analysis is pipeline setup and configuration. This includes selecting tools, and the best parameters for each tool. The parameters used may have a big impact on the quality and hence usability of the pipeline output, but the long processing time of existing biological analysis pipelines makes such parameter tuning impractical and time consuming.

We believe a system for interactive parameter tuning of biological data analysis pipelines should satisfy the following requirements: (i) the data processing should scale to the upcoming peta-scale datasets; (ii) when pipeline parameters are changed, the pipeline data processing should provide low end-to-end latency to enable quick updates of the pipeline output; (iii) the system should support unmodified pipelines and tools, since it is not practical to make and maintain changes to the source code of the many tools used in pipelines. The system should also handle input and output from each stage regardless of the tool data format; and (iv) the systems should manage provenance information [2] to ease parameter tuning and ensure result reproducibility.

To our knowledge, no existing system fulfills all these requirements. Pipeline managers such as Galaxy [3] do not scale to peta-scale datasets. Data-intensive computing systems such as MapReduce [4], [5] scale to peta-scale datasets, but are not suited for low-latency processing. Systems for iterative and interactive processing of large-scale data, such as Spark [6], Dremel [7], HaLoop [8], Naiad [9], and Nectar [10] require changes to the pipeline tool's source code.

We propose the Mario system. It fulfills all four requirements. Mario has a parallel shared-nothing architecture for computations and scalable storage. It combines reservoir sampling, fine-grained caching of derived datasets [10], and an iterative data-parallel processing model with low end-to-end latency. Mario provides transparent iterative processing and a storage model that is agnostic to the data types used by the tools [11]. It enables data provenance by storing detailed pipeline configurations associated with pipeline input-, intermediate-, and output data.

We contribute by providing a requirements analysis for biological analysis pipeline parameter tuning, and describing the design and implementation of Mario. We also contribute with an experimental evaluation of the performance and resource usage of Mario. In addition, we describe how we used HBase as storage backend for biological data, and we demonstrate the usability of Mario through a metagenomics case study.

2   Architecture and Design

We make the following assumptions that form the basis for the architecture and design of Mario: (i) input data can be split into parts with fine granularity; (ii) no intermediate pipeline stage requires access to the complete input data; and (iii) there is enough storage to hold all intermediate data.

The first two assumptions allow iterative processing of the dataset with inspection of output as the computation proceeds. This is our approach for achieving low end-to-end latency during pipeline tuning. The third assumption allows caching of intermediate data to avoid recomputing the full dataset after configuration changes.

The first assumption usually holds, since many genomic analysis tools either base the analysis on fine-grained parts such as sequences of nucleotides or gene expression values, or they use a summarization or machine learning algorithms on fine-grained parts. The second assumption is true for most algorithms that scale to large datasets. These typically split the data to independent parts, and distribute and process these independently on many nodes. In addition, tools that aggregate data from the full dataset can often easily be replaced by incremental versions that maintains a summary of the full dataset between iterations. The third assumption usually holds for clusters designed for data-intensive computing.

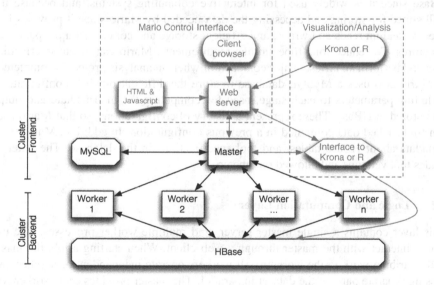

Fig. 2. Mario architecture. Greyed out parts are not implemented in current prototype.

The Mario architecture (Fig. 2) consists of four tiers: storage, logic/computation, the web server and the client/UI. The system runs on a cluster of computers, with the master process at the cluster frontend, and the workers at the compute nodes of the cluster. These are co-located with an HBase [12], [13] installation that has the HBase master at the frontend and the HBase region servers at the compute nodes. The web server and the MySQL server can be located on the cluster frontend, or on separate computers. The user runs the Mario controller and the data exploration tools on her computer.

To analyze a dataset using Mario, a user would first load the input data into HBase. She would then use a web interface such as Galaxy [3] to define the pipeline by specifying, for each pipeline stage: the tool to execute, the tool version, and the tool parameters. The configuration can specify that a dataset should be sampled with a given sample size. Mario uses a file-based approach for incremental processing [11], so it is not necessary to modify tool code. The user then starts the initial computation. As the computation proceeds, the user can change the parameters or tool used in a stage by sending an updated configuration to the master, which will start scheduling work with the new configuration. If the new configuration does not produce satisfactory results, Mario can restore a previous configuration by reading data for a previous configuration from the storage layer.

2.1 Storage Layer

The primary component of the storage layer is HBase, where Mario stores input-, intermediate-, and output data. Intermediate and output data can be stored in multiple versions resulting from the use of different parameters to pipeline stages. The HBase storage architecture is demonstrated to scale to peta-scale datasets [13]. We chose HBase since it is widely used for interactive computing systems, and because it is well suited for storing and accessing the data needed by Mario since it provides low-latency random reads and writes, and efficient storage and compression of sparse data structures. To reduce long-time storage requirements, Mario can delete intermediate data and perform an HBase major compaction when an analysis project is completed.

Mario also uses a MySQL database to store the different pipeline configurations, including parameters to each stage, used for computing the intermediate and output data stored in HBase. These represent a history of configurations, so that Mario users can find cached data computed in a previous configuration. In addition, Mario stores metadata about HBase tables, and tool specifications in the database. The latter includes tool versions and allowed parameters.

2.2 Logic and Computation Layer

This layer contains a single master server, and multiple worker processes. The user would interact with the master through a web client. When starting a job, the master will distribute work to the workers. All workers operate independent of another, processing separate parts of the dataset in parallel. The master provides each worker with the current configuration of the pipeline and the HBase row key of the data to be processed. The master can also query HBase for the location of the HBase region server responsible for a row, and assign the row to a Mario worker located on the same server. This will improve data locality and therefore reduce network traffic.

The master retrieves the row keys from HBase, but does not retrieve the data stored under each key or perform any processing. The reservoir sample is stored in memory as a list of row keys. This sample is the main source of memory usage in the master. However, assuming 20-byte key length, a large sample of four million keys will only consume 80MB of memory.

The worker processes wait for messages from the master server. When receiving a message, the worker reads the data associated with the keys in the message from HBase. The pipeline stages process the data, and write intermediate and final output into HBase. When a worker has completed its work, it sends a message to the master. This enables the master to adjust work distribution to the capacity of the workers, and to notify visualization tools that new results are available. The worker processes may be CPU and memory intensive depending on the computation done in each tool.

2.3   Web Server, and the Visualization and Analysis Interface

The web server hosts the Mario control application and forwards requests from this application to the master server. The web server also forwards data generated by a *visualization and analysis (VA) interface* to data exploration tools.

A data exploration tool uses Mario's VA interface to retrieve results from HBase, either periodically or when notified of the presence of new results by the Mario master. To integrate Mario with a visualization system such as Krona [14] or METAREP [15], an interface must be implemented that updates the data structures used by the exploration tool. For Krona, this involves generating an XML-file of the organism hierarchies found in the data. For METAREP, a search engine data structure must be updated (refer to [16] for details). For integration with end-user statistical analysis, the interface can be implemented in for example R.

3   Implementation

In this section, we describe the implementation of data storage in HBase, and the reservoir sampling algorithm. Additional implementation details are in [16].

3.1   HBase Tables

Mario stores data in HBase tables. A table consists of rows that are identified by row keys. Each row contains cells that store data. The cells are uniquely identified by a key consisting of column family, column, and timestamp. The key is stored, together with each cell, in a byte array within an immutable file that is lexicographically ordered by row key. HBase allows adding columns dynamically. Mario uses column names generated at runtime to provide a mapping between the data in the column and the pipeline configuration used to generate that data.

The HBase table for an analysis pipeline has two column families: *in* and *out*. The unique row key is dataset dependent, and can for example be the line number in the input file that contains the data value, or a sequence ID in a FASTA file. The input data is stored in the *in* column family before the pipeline is executed. Output from pipeline stages are stored in the *out* column family. HBase column names are pipeline execution version numbers that combine a unique ID for each tool, the version of the stage tool configuration, and the version of the tool that produced the input data. Since only a small subset of rows are processed to test each configuration, most columns will be empty for most of the rows. HBase is ideally suited for storage of such sparse data.

Fig. 3 shows a version tree for an example three-tool pipeline where the user has modified tool parameters three times. The top row shows the column names for the initial versions of each stage of the pipeline. The second branch is the result of changing the parameters of the first tool of the pipeline, but leaving the other two tools unchanged. Even if only the first stage is changed, the version numbers of the downstream stages are incremented to create columns for storing the data based on the output from the new first stage. In the same way, the lower branch in Fig. 3 is the result of changing the second stage of the pipeline. The resulting HBase table will have eight columns in the *out* family.

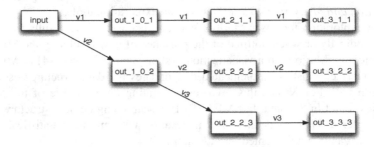

Fig. 3. Data version with HBase column names

3.2 Reservoir Sampling

The Mario master server uses the reservoir sampling algorithm described in [17] to produce a random sample of elements from an HBase table. The algorithm does one pass through the table keys, and requires the generation of one random number per key. It guarantees that each element in the table has equal probability of being in the sample. The single-pass property of reservoir sampling make this technique well suited for sampling large datasets where performance is I/O limited. If weighted sampling is required other single pass algorithms such as [18] could be implemented without a significant I/O performance overhead.

4   Evaluation

The goal of the experimental evaluation is to: (i) demonstrate the usefulness of Mario for biological analysis pipeline tuning; (ii) validate the suitability of HBase as a storage backend for an iterative, interactive system; and (iii) validate the architecture and the design choices made for the Mario prototype.

4.1 Methodology

We used a nine-node cluster, where each compute node has an 8 core Intel Xeon 3.6GHz CPU, 32GB DRAM, and 2 x 2TB disks. The network was 1Gbps Ethernet using a single switch. The operating system was CentOS 6.31. We used the Cloudera Hadoop CDH4.3.0, with HBase v0.94.6 and Hadoop v2.0.0. We used ZeroMQ v3.2.4 for communication. The HBase master server had a JVM with 4GB of memory. HBase regionservers allocated 12GB of memory. Unless otherwise noted, we measured the elapsed wall time. We repeated all experiment five times, and report average time and sample standard deviation.

4.2   Use Case: Taxonomic Classification of Metagenomics Samples

To demonstrate the usefulness of Mario for biological analysis pipeline tuning, we analyze the results of a taxonomic classification in metagenomics samples (details are in [19]). The rarefaction curve in Fig. 4 shows that most of the phyla are identified with only 6-8 million reads and that most of the classes and orders are found with 10-12 million reads. However, even with 2 million reads 75% of the orders are discovered. This shows that processing a small subset of the data provides initial biological insight.

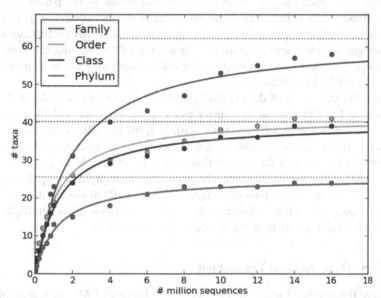

Fig. 4. Rarefaction curves for analyzing species richness and sample completeness of different taxonomic ranks. Figure is from [19], which provides additional experiment details.

4.3   HBase as Storage Backend for Biological Data

We first evaluate HBase read and write performance for biological datasets. Since Mario relies on HBase for storage, these results provide a lower bound for the end-to-end latency and throughput of Mario data processing.

Mario will execute jobs that access both large and small amounts of data. Earlier evaluations of the Google BigTable/ HBase design [13] have demonstrated its scalability for datasets with millions of rows. We therefore focus on the latencies of reading and writing small amounts of data to and from HBase. We generated a synthetic dataset representative of FASTA files, and BLAST [20] tabular output. The FASTA files have random nucleotide sequences, ranging in length between 100 and 5000 bases. IDs were random 15 character strings. The BLAST output is similar to the output generated using the −m 8 option.

To evaluate the performance of tables stored on a single region server, versus regions on multiple servers, we use a table with only 200KB of data, and a table with approximately 500GB of data. The latter is large enough to fill the aggregated DRAM on the cluster (288GB). It is generally recommended to compress HBase tables [13]. We use the Snappy compression algorithm since it offers the highest encoding and decoding rate of the HBase compression algorithms. HBase also uses Bloom filters to avoid having to scan files for keys that are not in the file [13]. For all experiments, we enable the client scanner cache to reduce the number of RPC requests to HBase region servers. Disabling it significantly decreases performance. In addition, we use deferred log flushing. Mario accepts data loss since the data can easily be recomputed. The default write ahead logger gives orders of magnitude worse performance. We flush the HBase cache between each measurement to get the worst-case performance results. Informal experiments show that a warm cache improves performance by an order of magnitude. We spent a considerable amount of time tuning these and other parameters [16]. Others have reported similar efforts required even by experts to performance tune HBase installations [21].

Reading 200 000 rows of data (22MB) from an almost empty table, and a table larger than the DRAM size on the cluster takes respectively 11 and 13 seconds, regardless of compression and Bloom filter settings ([16] has additional details). Since we flush the HBase caches between each experiment, these represents worst-case results, but still we consider the read performance sufficient for Mario.

Writing 200 000 rows (22MB) into respectively an empty and populated HBase takes 10 and 7 seconds, regardless of compression setting ([16] has additional details). Writing to a populated table is faster since writes are distributed on multiple region servers. We consider the write performance sufficient for Mario.

4.4   Mario Overhead and Throughput

We measure the overhead added to the end-to-end latency of Mario. We define end-to-end latency as the time from a computation is started, until the first results are ready to be visualized. In addition, we measure the throughput of Mario, which we define as the amount of data that can be processed per time unit. We use a dummy four-stage pipeline using the Linux *cat* tool in each stage. Since cat has no computation, it represents an I/O intensive application. For more computation intensive applications, Mario overhead will contribute less to the wall clock execution time, and the throughput will be reduced.

To emulate a user tuning pipeline parameters, each experiment consists of three executions of the dummy pipeline with the same input data (FASTA-type generated as described above). Before the second execution, the last two stages are marked as modified. Before the third execution, the modifications are reverted.

Table 1. Time top process one row (one nucleiotode sequence)

	Avg (ms)	SD
Execution 1	68	6.4
Execution 2	7	1.4
Execution 3	6	1.1

Table 2. Time to process 200 000 rows (500MB)

	2 Workers		4 Workers		8 Workers	
	Avg (ms)	SD	Avg (ms)	SD	Avg (ms)	SD
Execution 1	11699	766	11784	1871	10817	1224
Execution 2	7432	288	8279	2497	8302	1377
Execution 3	7689	483	8406	2334	8563	2096

Table 3. Time to process 10 000 row sample of 200 000 rows using eight workers

	Avg (ms)	SD
Execution 1	10777	242
Execution 2	55	6
Execution 3	38	13

The Mario overhead is 68ms for the first stage, and 7 and 6 ms for the second and third execution (Table 1). The reduced latencies in executions 2 and 3 are due to the data being cached in HBase after the first execution. In the second execution, the worker detect that data exists for the first two stages, and only executes cat for the last two pipeline stages. In the third execution, the pipeline result are read directly from the cache without executing any pipeline tools. However, there is no significant performance difference between these executions. The results demonstrate that the end-to-end latency added by Mario is very small.

To measure the throughput of Mario, we use a 200 000 row (500MB) dataset, which is approximately the size of a two million short read dataset, and which is large enough to provide initial biological insight (section 4.2). The throughput is limited by task distribution, and does not improve with more workers (Table 2). The 500MB dataset will fit in the cache of a single HBase region server. The Mario master will therefore read row keys from an in-memory cache, but still be limited by the time it takes to iterate over the sequence of keys and transmit task messages to workers. For a pipeline with more computationally intensive jobs, additional workers will improve throughput. The results demonstrate that Mario provides high throughput data processing.

4.5 Sampling

To measure the overhead of sampling, we use the experiment setup described in the previous section. The Mario master creates a sample size of 10 000 keys from the 200 000 row dataset, and distributes the samples to eight workers. Our results show that the execution time with sampling (Table 3) is similar to the time without sampling

(Table 2). This shows that the sampling algorithm has very low overhead, since it in addition to executing the sampling algorithm must put the samples in a local in-memory array, and transmit the keys in the array to the workers. The results for executions 2 and 3 (Table 3), demonstrate that transmitting the samples to the workers is also cheap. To conclude, Mario provides efficient reservoir sampling of datasets.

4.6   Mario Resource Usage

Mario servers are co-located on cluster work nodes with the bioinformatics applications doing the analysis. It is therefore important that Mario does not perturb these by using excessive CPU, memory, or network bandwidth. We use Ganglia to measure the aggregated resource usage of the Mario, HBase and HDFS servers. We initialized an HBase table with one million FASTA rows (2.5GB), and executed the dummy pipeline described in section 4.4 on eight Mario workers.

Our results show a peak load of 1.3 (of 8.0) for CPU load. This CPU usage is for processing I/O, and may be overlapped with tool I/O waiting time. The peak network usage is 30MB/s and aggregated usage of 900Mbps, both well within the capacity of our Gigabit Ethernet. In addition, most bioinformatics analysis tools are not communication intensive. The Mario servers have a small memory footprint. However, Mario relies on HBase region servers for which we had to allocate 12GB JVM heap space to get good performance. We believe the memory usage is acceptable since current compute cluster nodes typically have at least 32GB of DRAM.

5   Related Work

Frameworks such as Hadoop MapReduce [4], [5] have widely been adopted for large-scale data-intensive computing, including genomics data processing [22]. However, these frameworks are not well suited for low-latency data processing.

Our approach for tuning a data analysis pipeline was inspired by the Pig Pen debugging environment for Pig programs [23]. Pig Pen provides developers with a small dataset created by sampling from the real dataset, and by generating data that is similar to the real data. However, Pig is typically not used for biological data analysis.

The Galaxy [3] pipeline managers is similar to Mario in that the user can compose a pipeline from existing applications, but Galaxy supports the creation of more general execution graphs, as opposed to Mario's linear pipeline model. A linear model makes it easier to implement iterative data processing. In addition, Mario provides automatic parallelization.

Distributed systems for iterative, incremental, and interactive processing of large-scale datasets include systems designed for a specific application domain (such as Mahout [24] for machine learning), or programming model (such as HaLoop [8] for Hadoop MapReduce, and Dremel [7] for SQL queries). These are not suitable for Mario's data processing model. Instead general approaches and systems such as Spark [6], or Naiad [9] could be used to implement Mario processing. We also believe Mario should be integrated with a cluster resource management systems such as Mesos [25] to facilitate sharing of a cluster with other interactive and batch processing jobs.

6 Conclusion and Future Work

We have presented Mario, a system for iterative and interactive processing of large-scale biological data. Our approach allows users to interactively tune biological analysis pipelines, which is vital to find the tools and parameters that give insight to a particular biological dataset and problem. By quickly computing a result for a subset of the data that still gives meaningful biological insight, the user can overcome the limitation of the long-processing time of existing large-scale data analysis pipelines. Low-latency updates to pipeline results allows pipeline developers to make more parameter changes in order to improve the quality of the analysis results.

Our approach uses reservoir sampling to reduce the amount of data processed to achieve biological meaningful results. We enable interactive tuning by combining fine-grained caching of derived datasets, and an iterative, data-parallel processing model. This allows low-latency calculation of the first results, and in addition high-throughput incremental computation of the remaining results. Mario also offers integrated data provenance by storing detailed pipeline configurations associated with pipeline input, intermediate, and output data.

Although we applied Mario for a dummy pipeline, we believe it can be integrated with pipeline managers such as Galaxy [3], and visualization systems such as Krona [14] or METAREP [15]. Mario has an interface that allows writing a module that can aggregate and present data in the format required by visualization tools. Mario uses the GeStore [11] approach for adding transparent updates to pipelines implemented in for example Galaxy. We plan to improve the performance of Mario by implementing locality-aware scheduling by handling stragglers. We believe the Spark system [6] is well suited to solve these problems. We also plan to implement the Mario controller interface, and to add support for management of datasets for multiple pipelines.

Interactive tuning of biological analysis pipelines is vital for the development of solutions to future large-scale data analysis problems in the biological community. We have demonstrated the usability of our approach for pipeline parameter tuning, and we have experimentally evaluated the latency, throughput, and resource usage of the Mario system. We believe the Mario approach and system are useful not only for biological analyses, but potentially also for other data analysis disciplines.

Acknowledgements. Thanks to Jon Ivar Kristiansen for help setting up HBase, and to Bjørn Fjukstad, Giacomo Tartari, and Einar Holsbø for comments to the paper.

References

1. Kahn, S.D.: On the Future of Genomic Data. Science 331(6018), 728–729 (2011)
2. Bose, R., Frew, J.: Lineage retrieval for scientific data processing: a survey. ACM Comput. Surv. 37(1), 1–28 (2005)
3. Goecks, J., Nekrutenko, A., Taylor, J.: Galaxy: a comprehensive approach for supporting accessible, reproducible, and transparent computational research in the life sciences. Genome Biol. 11(8) (2010)
4. Hadoop homepage (2014), http://hadoop.apache.org/

5. Dean, J., Ghemawat, S.: MapReduce: a flexible data processing tool. Commun. ACM 53(1) (2010)
6. Zaharia, M., Chowdhury, M., Das, T., Dave, A., Ma, J., McCauley, M., Franklin, M.J., Shenker, S., Stoica, I.: Resilient distributed datasets: a fault-tolerant abstraction for in-memory cluster computing. In: Proc. of NSDI 2012. Usenix (2012)
7. Melnik, S., Gubarev, A., Long, J.J., Romer, G., Shivakumar, S., Tolton, M., Vassilakis, T.: Dremel: interactive analysis of web-scale datasets. In: Proc. VLDB Endow. 2010, vol. 3(1–2) (2013)
8. Bu, Y., Howe, B., Balazinska, M., Ernst, M.D.: The HaLoop approach to large-scale iterative data analysis. VLDB J. 21(2), 169–190 (2012)
9. Murray, D.G., McSherry, F., Isaacs, R., Isard, M., Barham, P., Abadi, M.: Naiad: a timely dataflow system. In: Proceedings of the Twenty-Fourth ACM Symposium on Operating Systems Principles - SOSP 2013, pp. 439–455 (2013)
10. Gunda, P.K., Ravindranath, L., Thekkath, C.A., Yu, Y., Zhuang, L.: Nectar: automatic management of data and computation in datacenters. In: Proc. of OSDI 2010. Useinx (2010)
11. Pedersen, E., Willassen, N.P., Bongo, L.A.: Fseries Transparent Incremental Updates for Genomics Data Analysis Pipelines. In: an Mey, D., et al. (eds.) Euro-Par 2013. LNCS, vol. 8374, pp. 311–320. Springer, Heidelberg (2014)
12. Apache HBase, http://hbase.apache.org/
13. Chang, F., Dean, J., Ghemawat, S., Hsieh, W.C., Wallach, D.A., Burrows, M., Chandra, T., Fikes, A., Gruber, R.E.: BigTable: A Distributed Storage System for Structured Data. ACM TOCS 26(2), 1–26 (2008)
14. Ondov, B.D., Bergman, N.H., Phillippy, A.M.: Interactive metagenomic visualization in a Web browser. BMC Bioinformatics 12(1), 385 (2011)
15. Goll, J., Rusch, D., Tanenbaum, D.M., Thiagarajan, M., Li, K., Methé, B.A., Yooseph, S.: METAREP: JCVI Metagenomics Reports - an open source tool for high-performance comparative metagenomics. Bioinformatics 26(20), 2631–2632 (2010)
16. Ernstsen, M.: Mario - A system for iterative and interactive processing of biological data, Master's thesis, University of Tromsø (2013)
17. Sidirourgos, L., Kersten, M., Boncz, P.: Scientific discovery through weighted sampling. In: 2013 IEEE International Conference on Big Data, pp. 300–306 (2013)
18. Efraimidis, P.S., Spirakis, P.G.: Weighted random sampling with a reservoir. Inf. Process. Lett. 97(5), 181–185 (2006)
19. Kjærner-Semb, E.: Exploring Bioinformatic Software for Taxonomic Classification of Metagenomes, Master thesis, University of Tromsø (2013)
20. Altschul, S.F., Gish, W., Miller, W., Myers, E.W., Lipman, D.J.: Basic local alignment search tool. J. Mol. Biol. 215(3), 403–410 (1990)
21. Stonebraker, M., Abadi, D., DeWitt, D.J., Madden, S., Paulson, E., Pavlo, A., Rasin, A.: MapReduce and parallel DBMSs: friends or foes? CACM 53(1), 64 (2010)
22. Taylor, R.C.: An overview of the Hadoop/MapReduce/HBase framework and its current applications in bioinformatics. BMC Bioinformatics (11 Suppl.1), S1 (2010)
23. Gates, A.F., Natkovich, O., Chopra, S., Kamath, P., Narayanamurthy, S.M., Olston, C., Reed, B., Srinivasan, S., Srivastava, U.: Building a high-level dataflow system on top of Map-Reduce: the Pig experience. In: Proc. of VLDB Endowment, vol. 2(2) (2009)
24. Mahout homepage (2014), https://mahout.apache.org/
25. Hindman, B., Konwinski, A., Zaharia, M., Ghodsi, A., Joseph, A.D., Katz, R., Shenker, S., Stoica, I.: Mesos: a platform for fine-grained resource sharing in the data center. In: Proc. of NSDI 2011. Usenix (2011)

Biochemical Application Porting by Interoperating Personal and IaaS Clouds

Tibor Barat[1] and Attila Kertesz[2,1]

[1] University of Szeged, Department of Software Engineering
H-6720 Szeged, Dugonics ter 13, Hungary
Barat.Tibor@stud.u-szeged.hu
[2] MTA SZTAKI Computer and Automation Research Institute
H-1518 Budapest, P.O. Box 63, Hungary
kertesz.attila@sztaki.mta.hu

Abstract. Researchers of various disciplines ranging from Life Sciences and Astronomy to Computational Chemistry, create and use scientific applications producing large amount of complex data relying heavily on compute-intensive modelling, simulation and analysis. Cloud Computing has reached a maturity state and high level of popularity that various Cloud services have become a part of our lives. The goal of this research is to apply this new technology to support and ease the execution of scientific applications and manage the produced user data in a convenient way, accessible from different places and devices. In this paper a biochemical application is examined as a use case for exemplifying our approach. We provide a general way for porting this biochemical application to an interoperable, heterogeneous environment consisting of Infrastructure and Personal (i.e. storage) Clouds. Our approach stores the application data in Personal Clouds and produce this data in Infrastructure Clouds in an autonomous way. Finally, we evaluate the ported application by using Ubuntu One, Dropbox, OpenNebula and Amazon. Our results show that users can benefit from this approach, and utilize data and infrastructure Cloud services in a transparent and efficient way.

1 Introduction

Researchers of various disciplines ranging from Life Sciences and Astronomy to Computational Chemistry, create and use scientific applications producing large amount of complex data relying heavily on compute-intensive modelling, simulation and analysis. Nowadays Cloud Computing has reached a maturity state and high level of popularity that various Cloud services have become a part of our lives. These services are offered at different Cloud deployment models ranging from the lowest infrastructure level to the highest software or application level. Within Infrastructure as a Service (IaaS) solutions we can differentiate public, private, hybrid and community Clouds according to recent reports of standardization bodies [5]. The previous two types may utilize more than one

L. Lopes et al. (Eds.): Euro-Par 2014 Workshops, Part I, LNCS 8805, pp. 275–286, 2014.

Cloud system, which is also called as a Cloud federation [7]. One of the open issues of such federations is the interoperable management of data among the participating systems. Another popular family of Cloud services is called Cloud storage services or Personal Clouds. With the help of such solutions, user data can be stored in a remote location, in the Cloud, and can be accessed from anywhere. Mobile devices can also benefit from these Cloud services: the enormous data users produce with these devices are continuously posted to online services. The aim of our research is to propose an approach that interoperates Infrastructure and Personal (i.e. storage) Clouds, and to develop a solution that manages application data in Personal Clouds and process it in Virtual Machines (VM) of Infrastructure Clouds in an autonomous way.

In this paper we examine a biochemical application that generates conformers of flexible molecules, here a tetrapeptide (Tyr-Pro-Phe-Phe-NM2), by unconstrained molecular dynamics at high temperature to overcome conformational bias then finishes each conformer by simulated annealing and energy minimization to obtain reliable structures. The main contributions of this paper are: (i) to provide a way for porting biomedical applications into a heterogeneous environment consisting of Infrastructure and Personal Clouds, and executing them in an interoperable and autonomous way, (ii) to propose a solution based an a biochemical use case of a real-world application that manages Ubuntu One, Dropbox, OpenNebula and Amazon, and (iii) to evaluate this application to determine the performance of the proposed solution.

Regarding related works in the area of application porting to Grids and Clouds, Valverde in [9] has already shown, how to execute TINKER binaries [11] in EGEE Grids [10], but this solution used only a low-level, command line interface. On the contrary, we propose a general, high-level solution using a portal framework to provide an easily accessible graphical user interface for non-Grid expert users. In our previous work [6] we have shown how to port a biochemical application to Grids, Supercomputers and Infrastructure Clouds. In this work we take a step forward, and incorporate Personal Clouds to the execution environment to store application data, and to provide a solution more convenient and transparent for users.

The remainder of this paper is as follows: Section 2 presents the considered biochemical application; Section 3 describes our approach for autonomous application execution with interoperating Infrastructure and Personal Clouds. Finally, Section 4 discusses the performed evaluations, and the contributions are summarized in Section 5.

2   The TINKER Conformer Generator Application

The application (shown in Figure 1) generates conformers by unconstrained molecular dynamics at high temperature to overcome conformational bias (T) then finishes each conformer by simulated annealing and/or energy minimization to obtain reliable structures. The parameter files contain reference for the molecular force field (in the present case Amber99), vacuum/implicit water (here

GBSA) environment, target temperatures, etc. The aim is to obtain conformation ensembles to be evaluated by multivariate statistical modeling. It uses the TINKER library [11] for molecular modeling for QSAR studies for drug development. The target end users are biologists or chemists, who need to examine molecule conformers with the TINKER package.

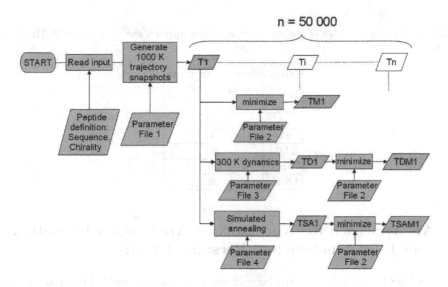

Fig. 1. TINKER Conformer Generator application

The conformer generation algorithm in its present form comprises five different conformer finishing methods:

1. minimizing the initial conformational states generated at high temperature (TM),
2. performing a short low temperature (e.g. 300 K) dynamics with the high temperature conformations to simulate a low temperature thermodynamical ensemble (TD),
3. minimizing the above low temperature states (TDM),
4. cooling the high temperature states by simulated annealing, e.g. to 50 K, or completely to 0 K (TSA),
5. minimizing the annealed states (TSAM).

The reason why to generate the conformational states or conformers (which are conformational states at some local energy minima) is to investigate which of them suits better for the subsequent multivariate statistical modeling (namely quantitative structure-activity relationships studies, QSAR), then the algorithm may be simplified. Our most recent successful QSAR modeling makes use of the TSAM structures which is the most computationally costly method, but may serve as a reference method to obtain the most reliable thermodynamical ensembles. Regarding execution times, Table 1 shows the average run times of the various methods in the vacuum environment used in the application on a single 2GHz CPU machine (the abbreviations discussed in this paragraph correspond to the ones shown in Figure 1). If we use the implicit water (GBSA) environment, the execution of the different steps takes 1,5 times longer. This means that the execution of the whole application takes around 5-8 days.

Table 1. Execution times of the main steps of the application on a single 2GHz CPU machine

Step	Execution time (hours)
T	13
TM	28
TD	3
TDM	28
TSA	26
TSAM	28

3   An Approach for Autonomous Application Execution over Infrastructure and Personal Clouds

Besides IaaS Cloud solutions the largest amount of user provided data are stored at Cloud storage services also called as Personal Clouds [5,3]. Their popularity is accounted for easy access and sharing through various interfaces and devices, synchronization, version control and backup functionalities. The freemium nature [17] of these services maintain a growing user community, and their high number of users also implies the development of other higher level services that make use of their cloud functionalities. To overcome the limits of freely granted storage, users may sign up to services of different providers, and distribute their data manually among them.

In this work, we have chosen Ubuntu One [13] as a Personal Cloud to design our proof-of-concept implementation. This Cloud service is available primary for Ubuntu users, and makes able to store, synchronize and share user data in the Cloud. It is operated by Canonical [14], and a newly registered user can use 5 GBs free storage. It also provides a web-based graphical interface called Ubuntu One Dashboard (see Figure 2), accessible by a Launchpad account.

In order to access files stored in Ubuntu One from an API, we used REST API [15] and the Oauth standard [21]. In this way we can refrain from sending user names and passwords with each request, instead we can authenticate ourselves by so called tokens, consisting of a single string. The main steps for acquiring and using these tokens is depicted in Figure 3.

By issuing an API call we can get information for a user account on the following data: username, maximum capacity of the usable storage, root path and paths of user created folders. Uploaded files are called as *nodes*. Once a

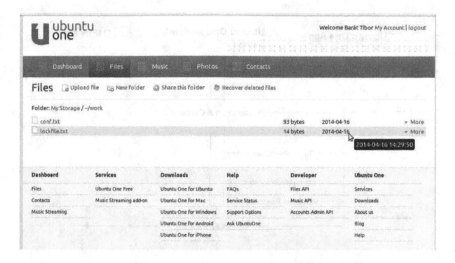

Fig. 2. Ubuntu One Dashboard

node is queried by providing its path, we can get additional information on its availability (private/public), its parent directory, node unique id, creation and latest modification date and a generation number (useful for version control). The *GET* command provides a list of public files, in a JSON format. We used the U1FileAPI library [16] for implementing the communication between the Infrastructure and Personal Clouds. In this way we applied methods as single asynchronous threads.

Our proposed solution shown in Figure 4. By using this approach, users only need to make available his/her data in a Personal Cloud, and to specify with a configuration file the order of data processing (by linking VM methods to data). Once this configuration file is available and at least one VM (executing the necessary service for processing user data) is running in an IaaS Cloud, the autonomous data processing starts and goes on till all data is processed. Steps 1 to 5 (in Figure 4) denote communication between an Infrastructure and a Personal Cloud:

- In Step 1, the configuration file is downloaded to a VM, and the first yet not reserved task is selected.
- In Step 2, the modified configuration file is uploaded back to the storage containing the new reservation.
- In Step 3, the VM downloads the data to be processed in the selected task.
- In Step 4, once the data processing is finished, the results are uploaded to the storage.
- And finally in Step 5, the configuration file is refreshed denoting the successful execution of the selected task.

In the followings we describe our proof-of-concept implementation using the TINKER Conformer Generator (TCG – introduced in Section 2) application

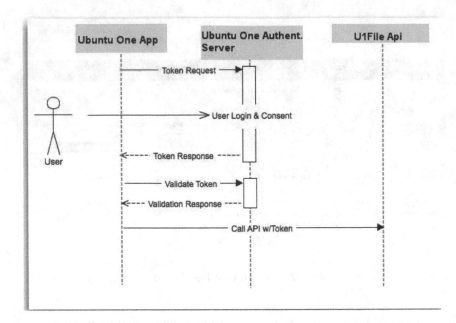

Fig. 3. OAuth usage steps

as a use case. We used three scripts managed by a Java web application to execute TCG in a VM: the master script (*master.sh*) to perform the initial conformer generation (task T in Figure 1), the worker script (*worker.sh*) to perform additional conformer finishing methods for 1000 conformers at a time (including TM, TD, TDM, TSA and TSAM tasks, selection is based on the input data), and the uploading script (*upload.sh*) to compress the sub-results to a single result file. In this way the execution of the ported TCG consists the execution of a master task in the first phase, followed by running 50 worker tasks for processing the 50000 conformers (possibly in parallel) in the second phase, finally calling the uploading script to create the final result in the third phase.

The greatest challenge in porting TCG to this environment was to manage the configuration file properly for the maximum 50 competing parallel workers. A synchronization problem occurs when more than one VM try to modify properties of our configuration file (typically for reserving a task). This problem is exemplified in Table 2 for two competing threads A and B that both try to increment the value of a variable. Thread A reads the value of the variable in Step 2, while Thread B in Step 3. In Steps 4 and 5 they increment the read value in parallel, and write it back in Steps 6 and 7. After two incrementation the value of the variable should be 2 instead of 1.

To solve this issue, first we used the (*listDelta*) method provided by Ubuntu One to track file changes denoted by incremental generation numbers (instead of time stamps) – this is a unique capability of Ubuntu One. In this way we could synchronize VM access to the configuration file by locking it for Steps 1, 2 and

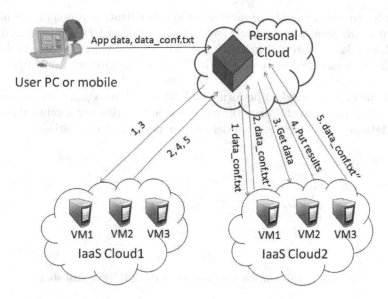

Fig. 4. The proposed solution for interoperating IaaS and Personal Cloud services

Table 2. Synchronization problem

Time	Thread A	Thread B	Value
1	-	-	0
2	read	-	0
3	-	read	0
4	increment	-	0
5	-	increment	0
6	write	-	1
7	-	write	1

5 (to avoid the selection of the same task by multiple VMs). Unfortunately this solution gave a poor performance according to our evaluations (caused by unexpected delays of the *readLine* method of the U1FileAPI library [16]), therefore we have chosen a different solution that can be used by any Personal Clouds, not only by Ubuntu One.

In order to find a better solution for synchronization we turned our attention to Amazon SimpleDB [18]. It provides access to a non-relational database running in the Amazon Cloud. We used its free service providing up to 1 GB data transfer over 25 hours of usage. With this solution we could easily manage concurrent access to our configuration file now moved to this Cloud service. The value of a variable stored in SimpleDB can be incremented in three steps:

1. Get the value of the variable from SimpleDB,
2. increment this value,
3. and finally put the new value instead of the old one in the database.

In order to avoid the above mentioned synchronization problem, we use the so called conditional put or conditional update of SimpleDB in the third step. With this update before writing back the incremented value we can check if the value has been modified since we read it. If this is the case, we won't update the value, otherwise we do write it back. Of course, if the value has been changed by someone else, we need to perform the first two steps again (reading out and incrementing the correct value) till we are able to write our modification back to the database. The next section details our performed evaluations.

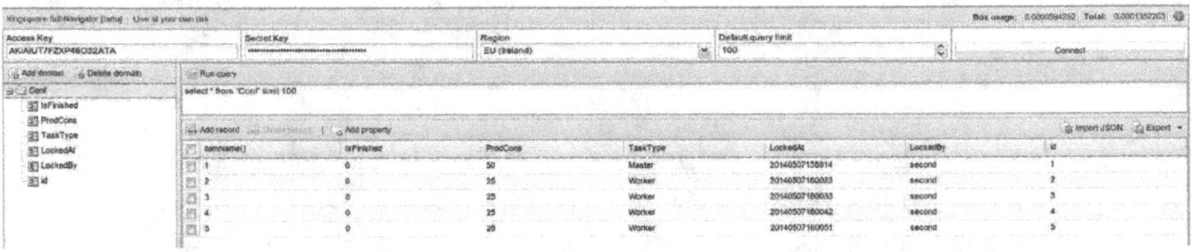

Fig. 5. Configuration parameters in the SdbNavigator tool

4   Evaluation

We have performed our evaluations by using a private IaaS Cloud based on OpenNebula [20]. It has been developed by a national project called SZTAKI Cloud [12], which was initiated in 2012 to perform research in Clouds, and to create an institutional Cloud infrastructure for the Computer and Automation Research Institute of the Hungarian Academy of Sciences. Since 2013 it operates in experimental state, and since 2014 it is in production state available for all researchers associated with the institute. It runs OpenNebula 4.4 with KVM, and controls over 440 CPU cores, 1790 GBs of RAM, 66 TBs shared and 35 TBs local storage for serving an average of 250 Virtual Machines (VM) per day for the last month.

The ported TCG application has been deployed in VMs started at SZTAKI Cloud by a desktop application using the Amazon AWS API [19]. With this tool we can deploy a certain number of VMs in the SZTAKI Cloud that start the TCG application in a web service. First these TCG instances (capable of behaving as masters, workers or uploaders) connect to Ubuntu One and to the Amazon SimpleDB service and query the configuration parameters stored there in a loop till there is any task to perform.

We can also follow the changes of the configuration parameters of the ported TCG application with the SdbNavigator interface tool, which is a free and open source Amazon SimpleDB Administration Interface [22]. A screenshot taken during our evaluation is shown in Figure 5.

To reserve a task, an instance writes its VM identifier and the time of reservation to SimpleDB (to the *LockedBy* and *LockedAt* fields respectively – shown in Figure 5). After reservation, depending on the type of the actual task (*TaskType*)

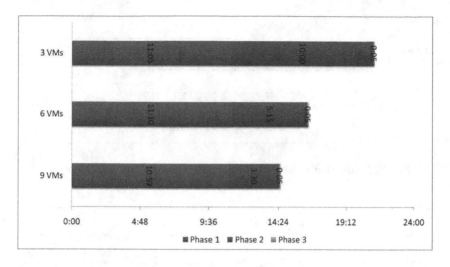

Fig. 6. Evaluation results with Ubuntu One and OpenNebula

the instance downloads the input files from Ubuntu One, and runs the corresponding script.

We have performed the evaluations in three rounds by deploying 3, 6 and 9 VMs at SZTAKI Cloud each having 4 virtual CPUs and 4 GBs of memory. In the first phase, a master task is executed by one VM (the rest of the VMs are waiting for worker tasks), then worker tasks are started in parallel in the second phase, finally an upload task is performed in the third phase to create the final result file. The evaluation results are shown in Figure 6. From these results we can clearly see that by increasing the number of deployed VMs the total execution time is decreasing.

To increase heterogeneity, and to show a scenario when academic and commercial IaaS Clouds are interoperated through a Personal Cloud, we created another evaluation by using Dropbox, OpenNebula and Amazon. We used the same template configuration for OpenNebula (denoted by ONe in the figure) to start 3 VMs in SZTAKI Cloud, and for Amazon (denoted by AM) we also started 3 VMs with Linux Micro instances. It took around 10 minutes to perform the initial input data transfers and to deploy the IaaS VMs to start with Phase 1. We measured nearly the same performance as in the previous round with 6 OpenNebula VMs. The result is shown in Figure 7. Detailed measurement results for Phase 2 of this experiment is depicted in Figure 8. In these diagrams we can see how the VMs of different IaaS systems competed for tasks, and how long it took them to compute these tasks in total (the curve marks the start time of task computations by VMs – except for the first task, which started at 0:00). In both evaluations, the data transfer time between the Personal and the IaaS Clouds were negligible (up to 1 or 2 minutes).

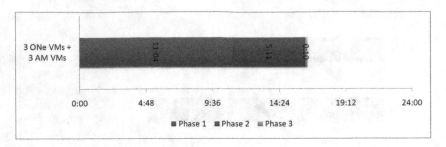

Fig. 7. Evaluation results with Dropbox, OpenNebula and Amazon

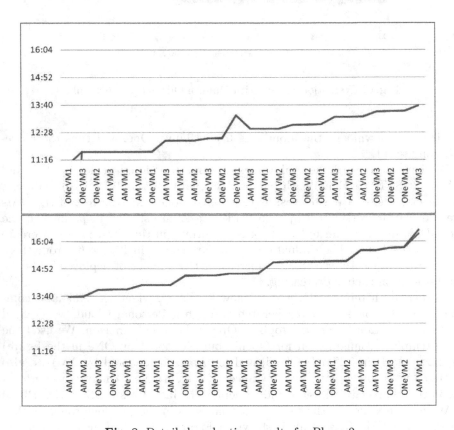

Fig. 8. Detailed evaluation results for Phase 2

5   Conclusion

Cloud Computing has reached a maturity state and high level of popularity that various Cloud services have become a part of our lives. By using mobile devices, users produce enormous data that need to be processed. The aim of our research was to develop a solution that manages user application data in Personal Clouds and process it in VMs of IaaS Clouds in an autonomous way.

In this paper we exemplified our approach by porting a biochemical application into a heterogeneous environment consisting of infrastructure and Personal Clouds, and executing it in an interoperable and autonomous way. With the evaluation of this real-world application by interoperating Ubuntu One, Dropbox, OpenNebula and Amazon, we have shown that users can benefit from our proposed approach and utilize Personal and IaaS Cloud services in a transparent and efficient way. Our future work aims at investigating the applicability of the proposed solution in a hybrid Cloud-Desktop Grid environment, and generalizing the proposed porting solution and developing mobile clients to further ease the management of application executions.

Acknowledgment. The research leading to these results has received funding from the EU FP7 IDGF-SP project under grant agreement 312297.

References

1. Bozman, J.: Cloud Computing: The Need for Portability and Interoperability. IDC Executive Insights (August 2010)
2. Dillon, T., Wu, C., Chang, E.: Cloud Computing: Issues and Challenges. In: Proc. of the 24th IEEE International Conference on Advanced Information Networking and Applications, pp. 27–33 (2010)
3. Fraunhofer Institute for Secure Information Technology. On THE Security of Cloud Storage Services, SIT Technical reports (March 2012),
   http://www.sit.fraunhofer.de/content/dam/sit/en/documents/
   Cloud-Storage-Security_a4.pdf
4. Gagliardi, F., Muscella, S.: Cloud Computing – Data Confidentiality and Interoperability Challenges. In: Book: Cloud Computing, Computer Communications and Networks, pp. 257–270. Springer, London (2010)
5. Jeffery, K., Neidecker-Lutz, B.: The Future of Cloud Computing, Opportunities for European Cloud Computing beyond 2010. Expert Group Report (January 2010)
6. Kertesz, A., Otvos, F., Kacsuk, P.: A Case Study for Biochemical Application Porting in European Grids and Clouds. Special Issue on Distributed, Parallel, and GPU-Accelerated Approaches to Computational Biology, Concurrency and Computation: Practice and Experience, Early View (August 2013)
7. Kertesz, A.: Characterizing Cloud Federation Approaches. In book: Cloud Computing - Challenges. In: Mahmood, Z. (ed.) Limitations and R&D Solutions. Springer Series on Computer Communications and Networks (accepted in 2014)
8. Kertesz, A.: Legal Aspects of Data Protection in Cloud Federations. In: Nepal, S., Pathan, M. (eds.) Book: Security, Privacy and Trust in Cloud Systems, Signals & Communication, pp. 433–455 (2014)
9. Valverde, J.: Simplifying job management on the Grid. EMBnet. News 14(2), 25–32 (2008)
10. Enabling Grids for E-sciencE (EGEE) project (June 2011),
    http://public.eu-ogoo.org/
11. Tinker molecular modelling package (May 2011),
    http://dasher.wustl.edu/tinker/

12. The SZTAKI Cloud project website (May 2014),
    http://cloud.sztaki.hu/en/home
13. Ubuntu One (May 2014), https://one.ubuntu.com/dashboard/
14. Canonical Ubuntu website (June 2013), http://www.canonical.com/products
15. REST API (May 2014),
    https://one.ubuntu.com/developer/files/store_files/cloud
16. Ubuntu One Files Java library (U1FileAPI) (May 2014),
    https://one.ubuntu.com/developer/files/store_files/android
17. Wikipedia – Freemium utilization (April 2014),
    http://en.wikipedia.org/wiki/Freemium
18. Amazon SimpleDB (March 2014), https://aws.amazon.com/simpledb/
19. Amazon AWS documentation (March 2014),
    https://aws.amazon.com/documentation/
20. OpenNebula website (March 2014), http://opennebula.org/documentation
21. Oauth standard documentation (March 2014),
    http://oauth.net/documentation/
22. SdbNavigator interface (May 2014), http://www.kingsquare.nl/sdbnavigator

The Role of Trusted Relationships on Content Spread in Distributed Online Social Networks

Valerio Arnaboldi, Massimiliano La Gala, Andrea Passarella, and Marco Conti

IIT-CNR, Via G. Moruzzi 1, 56017, Pisa, Italy
{v.arnaboldi,m.lagala,a.passarella,m.conti}@iit.cnr.it

Abstract. In Distributed Online Social Networks (DOSN) content spread will largely depend upon trust relationships between users, who are likely to allocate resources only to help spreading content coming from peers with whom they have a strong enough relationship. This could lead to the formation of isolated groups of intimates in the network, and to the lack of a big enough connected component, essential for the diffusion of information. In this paper we simulate the outcome of such restrictions by using a large-scale Facebook data set, from which we estimate the trust level between friends. We then simulate content spread on the same network assuming that no central control exists, and that social friendship links exist only above certain levels of trust. The results show that limiting the network to "active social contacts" of the users leads to a high node coverage. On the other hand, the coverage drops for more restrictive assumptions. Nevertheless, selecting a single excluded social link for each user and adding the respective node in the network is sufficient to obtain good coverage (i.e. always higher than 40%) also in case of strong restrictions.

Keywords: Distributed online social networks, Trust based communications, Information diffusion.

1 Introduction

Online Social Networks (hereinafter OSN) like Facebook and Twitter are becoming essential everyday tools useful in many different situations, from the management of personal social relationships to advertisement and professional networking. This makes them one of the most important cases nowadays of large-scale virtual environments. Despite this, the fast pace at which OSN are growing rises some fundamental questions regarding the sustainability of their architectures. In fact, OSN are generally based on centralised solutions, that guarantee more control upon user's data and consequently generate more value for the service providers. Nevertheless, the large amount of communication data generated by OSN requires huge storage capacity and complex solutions for providing instant access to the users. In addition, from a more ethical point of view, OSN often use the personal data of their users for commercial purposes, contralising, together with the data, also wealth, possibly resulting in power law economies [12].

L. Lopes et al. (Eds.): Euro-Par 2014 Workshops, Part I, LNCS 8805, pp. 287–298, 2014.

Several distributed alternatives to OSN have been proposed in the last years, broadly identified by the term Distributed Online Social Networks (DOSN). DOSN (e.g. diaspora* or PeerSon [6]) replicate OSN features in a fully decentralised way. Specifically, DOSN permit to manage a *digital personal space* for each user, where the latter can leave or receive asynchronous messages or post other kind of personal information. Moreover, DOSN support the creation of *social links* between users, giving different access policies to digital personal spaces for friends compared to strangers. DOSN also provide instant messaging functionality in the form of private communications.

In DOSN, each user maintains her personal data locally or on intermediate servers, and interactions between users occur through peer-to-peer (P2P) communications. Compared to OSN, DOSN provide the user with much more control over her personal data, and data decentralisation guarantees privacy and low complexity. Since in DOSN data are completely decentralised and rely upon the personal devices of the users the circulation of information cannot be controlled via a centralised server. For this reason, content can only be disseminated in the network through chains of social links between users. Clearly, users are inclined to favour the dissemination of content coming from trusted social contacts (i.e. with a strong enough relationship), which generally share similar interests with the users due to the effect of homophily, for which people tend to bond with similar alters [7]. In addition, the restriction of information diffusion to trusted peers lowers the amount of content coming from all possible social links without discrimination that could waste local resources contributed by users' devices to support DOSN functionality. Therefore, it is reasonable to assume that DOSN users will be willing to help replicating and disseminating content coming only from a set of users they trust most, and discarding the rest. This is clearly a double-edge sword, because it also limits the spread of information to possible interested users, and may potentially reduce data availability. It is therefore important to understand the effect of this type of filtering on content dissemination in DOSN.

In this paper we simulate the impact of the restriction of communication to trusted contacts in DOSN on information diffusion in the network. To do this, we study the topology of the graph induced by the restriction of social links to trusted relationships only. In particular, we look at the size and the number of components containing connected nodes in the graph. Each component represents a portion of the original network through which information can reach all the connected nodes. Clearly, different network components (and thus different information dissemination patterns) emerge depending on whether more or less strict trust restrictions are considered. Since the collection of network graphs representing DOSN is difficult, for the distributed nature of the system, we take a larger scale Facebook graph as starting point. We estimate the trust level between connected users through the frequency of interactions between them (which is well backed-up by results in sociology [11,4]), and simulate content diffusion on this network considering different thresholds for defining trusted links. We assume that no central control exists on this network and we select the set of trusted contacts for its users according to their contact frequency, then studying the properties of the resulting graph. Specifically, if a social relationship is not trusted (i.e. it does not have a sufficiently high contact frequency), the respective social link is not included in the graph we used in simulation. To assess the impact of the selection of trusted links, we define the minimum level of trust by setting a threshold on the contact frequency of the links to be included in the graph. We take values of this threshold equal to the frequencies of contact that have been used in the literature for defining different levels of social relationships [11]. In particular, we consider the well known ego network model [14], whereby social relationships of a user (ego) can be divided in concentric layers of increasing size and decreasing social intimacy (i.e. corresponding to decreasing tie strength and fewer interactions) In this way we obtain different social graphs with different minimum levels of trust, that coincide with a natural categorisation of social relationships in humans. Note that this way of estimating trust lends itself to automatic systems to decide on which social links to accept content, just by monitoring the frequency of interactions on them.

The results of the analysis indicate that limiting content spread to social contacts that coincide with the definition of "active social contacts" of the users, which corresponds to the most external layer in the ego network model, leads to a network graph with a sufficiently large component of connected nodes, which covers more than 96% of the original Facebook network. Restricting content spread to the next layer of the ego networks, or further, makes the relative size of the biggest connected component (and therefore coverage) drop below 30%. Since the remaining components are very small compared to the largest one for all the used thresholds, diffusing information in the network could be problematic when the largest component does not cover a sufficiently high number of nodes. As a possible solution to increase node coverage in case of very restrictive thresholds we investigate the effect of adding to the graph only one social contact for each user, selected with different possible strategies (e.g. select the link with highest/lowest contact frequency with the user, select a random acquaintance, etc.). The results indicate that this solution considerably increases the number of covered nodes, even in case of very strong trust. Noticeably, the best strategy is a probabilistic selection of a social contact based on their contact frequency with the considered user, whereas taking always the contact with highest/lowest contact frequency (below the minimum contact frequency imposed by the restriction) leads to worse results in terms of number of nodes covered. Clearly, adding a contact to the list of trusted nodes represents a cost for the users in terms of additional unwanted content, but limiting the choice to a single node should be a reasonable solution for them since they would receive a global return in terms of quality and quantity of information circulating in the network.

The paper is organised as follows: in Sect. 2 we describe the Facebook data set we have used for the analysis. Hence, in Sect. 3 we introduce the methodology we use, in particular how we define the values of the threshold we use in the analysis. Then, in Sect. 4 we report the results of the analysis. In Sect. 5 we

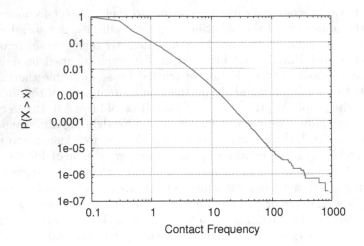

Fig. 1. CCDF of the contact frequency for the links

describe the related work in the literature, especially the most relevant DOSN solutions already existing. Last, in Sect. 6 we draw the conclusions of our work.

2 Data Set Description

To perform our analysis, we use a large-scale Facebook data set containing information about social interactions between users. The data set represents a large Facebook regional network, with more than 3 million users and more than 23 million social links between them, which has been downloaded in 2008, when the default privacy policy allowed users within a regional network (a feature removed by Facebook in 2009) to see all the personal data of other users in the same network. The data set is publicly available for research[1] and it has been largely used for other analyses since it shows typical social network characteristics [15,3,1].

The data set contains information about the existence of social links between users, that are represented by a *social graph*, where nodes represent Facebook users and links Facebook friendships between them. On the other hand, social interactions recorded in the data set are represented by a series of *interaction graphs*, each of which contains the number of interactions occurred on the social links within temporal windows of increasing duration. The interaction graphs identify communications occurred respectively *one month*, *six months*, *one year* before the download, and for the *all* the duration of the relationships. By combining these graphs, we have been able to estimate the contact frequency between users, following the procedure described in [3], obtaining a unique graph where the links are weighted by the contact frequency between the involved users.

---

[1] http://current.cs.ucsb.edu/socialnets/

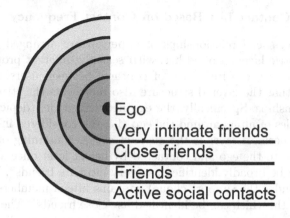

Fig. 2. Ego network model

In this work we use the contact frequency between users in Facebook as a proxy for the level of trust between them. This is supported by results in the literature that identified a strong relation between the contact frequency and the tie strength or emotional closeness between people, both in offline and on-line environments [4,11,13]. The complementary cumulative distribution function (CCDF) of the contact frequency for the links in the graph obtained from the data set is depicted in Fig. 1. The figure indicates that the distribution has a power law trend, thus implying that most of the links in the network have a very low level of trust, whereas only few links have very high trust. For this reason, we expect that restricting the network to trusted links only could have a strong impact upon the structural properties of the resulting graph.

3   Social Networks for Content Diffusion

Since in our analysis we are interested in users who actively communicate with others, we select from the Facebook graph only the users with at least one active link (i.e. with contact frequency > 0) and we discard all the other users, that indeed are inactive. Moreover, we further restrict the analysis to the set of users that have communicated with other users at least 6 months before the time the data set was downloaded. This ensures that our analysis is restricted to sufficiently stable users. In fact, the contact frequency of new users in OSN is generally higher that that of older (and more stable) users [2] and could bias the analysis. The resulting graph, after this pre-process, consists of $1,083,209$ nodes and $7,709,309$ links.

To simulate the restriction of communication to a list of trusted contacts for each user in DOSN we apply a series of filters to the Facebook social graph previously described, eliminating the links with contact frequency below the chosen threshold, that defines the boundary of the trusted contact list.

3.1   Trusted Contact List Based on Contact Frequency

In the literature, social relationships of a person are arranged in a series of inclusive concentric layers around her, with sensibly different properties. These layers are defined by the frequency of contacts between users, and therefore we can assume that the layered structure also represents the structure of trust of social relationships. Specifically, the ego network model (depicted in Fig. 2) defines four circles of alters around the ego (i.e. the considered individual) [14]. The first and innermost layer is the *support clique*, containing on average five people very close to the ego and contacted by her at least once a week. People in this layer can be broadly identified as "very intimate friends". The *sympathy group* (that includes the support clique) contains fifteen members contacted at least once a month, which can be identified as "close friends". The *affinity group* contains fifty members contacted at least ~ eight times a year [3]. People in this layer can be defined as "friends". Lastly, the *active network* contains 150 people contacted at least once a year. These people are those for whom the ego invests a non negligible amount of cognitive resources and can be defined as "active social contacts". Beyond the active network, alters are mere acquaintances, and their social relationships are not actively maintained by the ego.

Based on the definition of the ego network layers we can identify possible trusted contacts lists definitions that could be adopted in DOSN. For example, to simulate the presence of lists containing "friends" we can fix the minimum contact frequency to be considered in the analysis to eight messages a year. In the analysis we use all the values of contact frequency that define the ego network layers previously presented to identify four different possible definitions of trusted contacts list and we discuss the implications of using these filtering strategies in DOSN. Specifically, in the rest of the paper we indicate the values of the thresholds in number of messages per month, so "1/12" represents one message a year, "8/12" eight messages a year, "1" one message per month, and "4" four messages per month.

3.2   Network Connectivity

Having defined the values of the threshold to generate the network graphs at different levels of trust, we proceed the analysis of connectivity of these graphs to find out if they are suited for information diffusion. Specifically, for each graph we study the size of the largest component of connected nodes and we compare it to the number of nodes in the original graph (the one obtained after the pre-processing phase). In addition, we study the distribution of the size of the remaining components of connected nodes (not considering the largest one). This is useful for identifying the number of components that must be reached by information to cover a sufficiently large portion of the network.

As will be clear from the results in Sect. 4, for some threshold on the trust level we obtain quite small largest connected components, and a big number of extremely small additional disconnected components. To improve content spreadability of the network we tried, as a possible alternative to lowering the trust

Table 1. Percentage of nodes of the original graph covered by the largest component for the different thresholds. Thresholds are expressed in msg/month.

Threshold	Percentage of nodes in the largest component					
	No insert	High freq	Low freq	Prob	Inv. prob	Rand
1/12	0.966	0.994	0.994	0.994	0.994	0.994
8/12	0.297	0.714	0.705	0.726	0.722	0.725
1	0.191	0.642	0.634	0.661	0.657	0.661
4	0.028	0.386	0.385	0.453	0.444	0.456

value of the system, the re-insertion of one social contact for each user in the graph obtained at each level of trust. We tested several possible strategies to select this social contact for each user. Specifically, the strategies that we use are the following: (i) selection of the contact with the highest contact frequency; (ii) selection of the contact with lowest contact frequency; (iii) extraction with probability proportional to the contact frequency; (iv) extraction with probability inversely proportional to the contact frequency; (v) random uniform extraction. We assess the impact of the re-insertion of the social contacts on the global connectivity of the resulting graph (i.e. the largest component of the graph) and we evaluate the pros and cons of the adoption of the different strategies.

4 Results

The proportion of nodes of the original graph (i.e. the one obtained after the pre-processing phase described in Sect. 3) covered by the largest component for each threshold is reported in Tab. 1 in the column "No insert", which indicates that we have not applied any re-insertion strategy on these results. The first largest component obtained with the threshold coinciding with the contact frequency of "active social contacts" (as defined in Sect. 3.1) guarantees a very high node coverage, particularly favourable condition for information diffusion. With the second threshold, related to "friends", the number of nodes covered by the largest component drops to $\sim 30\%$. This could still be enough to diffuse information to a sufficiently high number of nodes. Nevertheless, for the other values of the threshold the node coverage is too low.

If we look at the distribution depicted in Fig. 3, representing the size of the components of connected nodes in the network excluded the largest one, we can notice that for all the thresholds, and especially in case of no re-insertion, these components are always really small, especially when compared to the largest one. In fact, the distributions show power-law trends with a maximum component size of 95 nodes. This indicates that if we want to reach a high number of nodes in the network and the largest component is not sufficient to do so, it is necessary to place information on a big number of additional components, without relying on automatic spread of information over trusted social links. This is further confirmed by the results in Tab. 2, 3, 4 and 5 under the row "No insert", that indicates the number of components that must be infected by

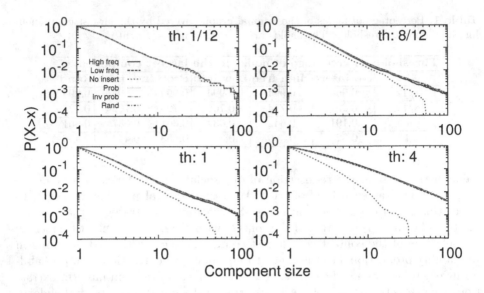

Fig. 3. CCDF of the size of the components for each threshold and strategy, excluded the largest component

information to reach the desired level of coverage, expressed in percentage with respect to the number of nodes in the original network. Also from these tables a sufficient coverage is obtained only with the first threshold (one message a year in Tab. 2), whereas for the other thresholds the number of components needed to reach a reasonable coverage (e.g. above 50% of the network) is very high and would result in a very expensive process. Moreover, whilst it could be relatively easy to identify the largest component in the network, it is not easy to identify all the remaining components, especially in decentralised systems like DOSN. This fact could further limit the diffusion process.

In case the level of trust needed in DOSN were too restrictive to reach a sufficient coverage for the dissemination of information, We evaluate a possible alternative to the mere decrease of the trust level, that would result in a less

Table 2. Number of components needed to cover the specified percentage of nodes in the original network using a threshold equal to 1/12 msg/month

Strategy	Coverage						
	40%	50%	60%	70%	80%	90%	100%
No insert	1	1	1	1	1	1	31,987
High freq	1	1	1	1	1	1	1,784
Low freq	1	1	1	1	1	1	1,784
Prob	1	1	1	1	1	1	1,784
Inv prob	1	1	1	1	1	1	1,784
Rand	1	1	1	1	1	1	1,784

Table 3. Number of components needed to cover the specified percentage of nodes in the original network using a threshold equal to 8/12 msg/month

Strategy	Coverage						
	40%	50%	60%	70%	80%	90%	100%
No insert	94, 218	202, 539	310, 860	419, 181	527, 502	635, 823	744, 143
High freq	1	1	1	1	43, 045	151.366	259, 686
Low freq	1	1	1	1	61, 369	169, 690	278, 010
Prob	1	1	1	1	37, 623	145, 944	254, 264
Inv prob	1	1	1	1	45, 197	153, 518	261, 838
Rand	1	1	1	1	40, 343	148, 664	256, 984

trusted system. Specifically, we add, for each user, a single additional social contact to the list of contacts trusted by the user. We apply the latter solution on the Facebook graph at each threshold, testing the different re-insertion strategies described in Sect. 3. In Tab. 1, from the third to the last column, we report the size of the largest component of connected nodes for each combination of threshold and re-insertion strategy. As can be noted, the impact of the re-insertion is substantial for thresholds $> 1/12$. For the threshold of $1/12$ the re-insertion is not needed, since most of the nodes of the original network are already present in the resulting graph. Even for the most restrictive threshold (4 messages per month) the gain due to the re-insertion brings the node coverage to $\sim 40\%$.

The results of the different strategies vary significantly, with the probabilistic and the random strategies ("Prob" and "Rand" in the tables) giving the highest improvement in terms of number of nodes covered, as reported in Tab. 1. In addition, as reported in Tab. 2, 3, 4 and 5, these two strategies are the most convenient also when all the other components, in addition to the largest one, are considered. This result is perhaps not surprising since the two fixed strategies related to the selection of the node with highest/lowest contact frequency with the considered user ("High freq" and "Low freq" in the table) often lead to a node too close to the user and with too many social contacts in common, that do not help to improve the number of covered nodes, or that, on average, has very low contact frequency also with other nodes, and thus introduces few

Table 4. Number of components needed to cover the specified percentage of nodes in the original network using a threshold equal to 1 msg/month

Strategy	Coverage						
	40%	50%	60%	70%	80%	90%	100%
No insert	208, 769	317, 090	425, 411	533, 732	642, 053	750, 374	858, 694
High freq	1	1	1	8, 801	87, 540	195, 861	304, 181
Low freq	1	1	1	13, 147	106, 719	215, 040	323, 360
Prob	1	1	1	4, 271	79, 561	187, 882	296, 202
Inv prob	1	1	1	5, 470	87, 379	195, 700	304, 020
Rand	1	1	1	4, 343	81, 852	190, 173	298, 493

Table 5. Number of components needed to cover the specified percentage of nodes in the original network using a threshold equal to 4 msg/month

Strategy	Coverage						
	40%	50%	60%	70%	80%	90%	100%
No insert	$391,174$	$499,495$	$607,816$	$716,137$	$824,458$	$932,779$	$1,041,099$
High freq	45	$2,332$	$12,660$	$47,708$	$144,729$	$253,050$	$361,370$
Low freq	68	$3,022$	$15,938$	$59,169$	$167,490$	$275,811$	$384,131$
Prob	1	431	$6,717$	$36,881$	$132,106$	$240,426$	$348,746$
Inv prob	1	608	$7,708$	$40,266$	$140,250$	$248,571$	$356,891$
Rand	1	396	$6,538$	$36,785$	$133,350$	$241,672$	$349,992$

nodes to the giant component. The inverse probabilistic strategy ("Inv prob" in the tables) favours contacts with too low contact frequency and, for the same reason of the "Low freq" strategy, introduces fewer other nodes connected to the largest component in the network. Therefore, the probabilistic and the uniform random choice seem the best strategies to adopt. However, the uniform random strategy, although being the easiest to implement, could lead more frequently to the selection of complete strangers to the users, and this could be a non desirable solution, as it maximises the probability for users to receive irrelevant content, due to the homophily argument. The probabilistic strategy prefers those contacts that are close to the user. Consequently, this strategy seems more reasonable compared to a pure uniform random choice.

We finally look at how the different re-insertion strategies impact on the distributions of the sizes of network components other than the largest one (see Fig. 3). All strategies, for each threshold, produce a similar distribution of the size of the components, excluded the largest one. Nevertheless, the distributions vary from the case in which no re-insertion is applied, especially for restrictive thresholds (1 message per month and 4 messages per month). This can be explained by the fact that for these thresholds the largest component is sensibly smaller than for the other thresholds, and the probability of re-inserting a node connected to this component is lower. Thus, there is the presence of a higher number of larger components disconnected from the largest one.

5   Related Work

DOSN were born in recent years to address privacy concerns over OSN. Diaspora*[2] is probably the most famous DOSN nowadays. Diaspora* supports the possibility of either creating a server (called *pod*) where the user can host her personal data or using an already existing one. Social interactions are carried out through a P2P system that makes users communicate directly with each other, without passing through a single centralised server. The authors of [6] propose a similar solution, that has been also extended to be used in case of absence of

---

[2] https://diasporafoundation.org/

stable Internet connectivity [5], a scenario particularly suited for mobile devices. In [9], the authors propose a DOSN based on the automatic identification, for each user, of her ego network layers (previously defined in 3.1), using the contact frequency between the user and her social contacts. The differences in terms of trust between the different layers are used to automatically adjust the privacy policies towards the people in the layers. Moreover, the personal social network of each user is limited to her "active network", and people beyond it are excluded from the main features of the system. The solutions proposed in [10] and [8] further exploit trust relationships arranged in concentric layers around the users to replicate the data of the user on her friend's devices, guaranteeing the access to her data even though her device were inaccessible due to a temporary disconnection or turnoffs.

6   Conclusions

In this paper we investigate the possible impact of the restriction of communications in DOSN to trusted social relationships only. This restriction is essential in DOSN, since the users are willing to distribute information coming only from trusted peers to limit the resources they dedicate to communications, that are generally limited. To perform the analysis we study the topological properties of the social graph generated by DOSN with such restrictions, looking for the presence of a large component of connected nodes (at a certain threshold of trust), within which information can spread and possibly reach all its nodes. On the other hand, disconnected small components and isolated nodes represent portions of the network that are difficult to reach and that will limit the diffusion of information.

Since the collection of a social graph representing DOSN is not easy, for the distributed nature of the system, we perform our analysis on a large-scale Facebook graph and, assuming that no central control exists upon it, we limit it selecting only links above a certain level of trust, estimated through the contact frequency between users. Hence, by applying four different thresholds, used in the literature as a natural classification for human social relationships, as the minimum level of trust in the network, we study the connectivity of the resulting graph. The results indicate that for the threshold representing "active social contacts" for the users, the resulting graph is highly connected and contains a large component covering more than 96% of the original network. On the other hand, for more restrictive thresholds, the node coverage drops significantly.

To overcome a situation, where diffusing information could be problematic due to the selected threshold on trust, we propose, in addition to a mere reduction of the global level of trust in the system, a different approach based on the addition to the list of trusted nodes of each user a single social contact, that was outside the list. We investigate different strategies to select this social contact, from a pure uniform random selection to the selection of the one with highest/lowest contact frequency with the considered user. The most effective strategies are a probabilistic selection of the contact based on its contact frequency and a uniform random selection. Nevertheless, the former is preferable since the latter could add more people that are unknown to the user, a non desirable situation.

Acknowledgements. This work is supported by the European Commission under the EINS (FP7-FIRE 288021) project.

References

1. Arnaboldi, V., Conti, M., La Gala, M., Passarella, A., Pezzoni, F.: Information Diffusion in OSNs: the Impact of Nodes' Sociality. In: SAC 2014, pp. 1–6 (2014)
2. Arnaboldi, V., Conti, M., Passarella, A., Dunbar, R.I.M.: Dynamics of Personal Social Relationships in Online Social Networks: a Study on Twitter. In: COSN 2013, pp. 15–26 (2013)
3. Arnaboldi, V., Conti, M., Passarella, A., Pezzoni, F.: Analysis of Ego Network Structure in Online Social Networks. In: SocialCom 2012, pp. 31–40 (2012)
4. Arnaboldi, V., Guazzini, A., Passarella, A.: Egocentric Online Social Networks: Analysis of Key Features and Prediction of Tie Strength in Facebook. Computer Communications 36(10-11), 1130–1144 (2013)
5. Buchegger, S.: Delay-Tolerant Social Networking. In: Extreme Workshop on Communication, pp. 1–2 (2009)
6. Buchegger, S., Schioberg, D., Vu, L.H., Datta, A.: PeerSoN: P2P Social Networking Early Experiences and Insights. In: SocialNets, pp. 46–52 (2009)
7. Curry, O., Dunbar, R.I.M.: Do birds of a feather flock together? The relationship between similarity and altruism in social networks.. Human Nature 24(3), 336–347 (2013)
8. Cutillo, L.A., Molva, R., Strufe, T.: Safebook: A Privacy-Preserving Online Social Network Leveraging on Real-Life Trust. IEEE Communications Magazine, 94–101 (December 2009)
9. Guidi, B., Conti, M., Ricci, L.: P2P architectures for distributed online social networks. In: International Conference on High Performance Computing & Simulation (HPCS), pp. 678–681 (2013)
10. Han, L., Nath, B., Iftode, L., Muthukrishnan, S.: Social Butterfly: Social Caches for Distributed Social Networks. In: SocialCom 2011, pp. 81–86 (2011)
11. Hill, R.A., Dunbar, R.I.M.: Social network size in humans. Human Nature 14(1), 53–72 (2003)
12. Lanier, J.: Who Owns the Future? (2013)
13. Marsden, P.V., Campbell, K.E.: Measuring Tie Strength. Social Forces 63(2), 482–501 (1984)
14. Sutcliffe, A., Dunbar, R., Binder, J., Arrow, H.: Relationships and the Social Brain: Integrating Psychological and Evolutionary Perspectives. British Journal of Psychology 103(2), 68–149 (2012)
15. Wilson, C., Sala, A., Puttaswamy, K.P.N., Zhao, B.Y.: Beyond Social Graphs: User Interactions in Online Social Networks and Their Implications. ACM Transactions on the Web 6(4), 1–31 (2012)

Comparison of Static and Dynamic Resource Allocations for Massively Multiplayer Online Games on Unreliable Resources

Radu Prodan[1], Alexandru Iosup[2], and Cristian Bologa[3]

[1] Institute of Computer Science, University of Innsbruck, Austria
[2] Parallel and Distributed Systems, Delft University of Technology, Netherlands
[3] Babeş-Bolyai University, Cluj-Napoca, Romania

Abstract. We investigate the use of a new Massively Multiplayer On-line Gaming (MMOG) ecosystem consisting of end-users, game providers, game operators, and Cloud resource providers, for autonomous, self-adaptive hosting and operation of MMOGs on unreliable resources. For this purpose, we developed an MMOG simulator compliant with our MMOG ecosystem in which we inject traces collected from a real-world MMOG and resource characteristics from 16 Cloud providers. Using our simulator, we study the impact on the involved actors by considering different resource availability levels, and highlight the advantages of dynamic resource allocation over the static overprovisioning with respect to two types of metrics: QoS offered to the clients and financial profit of game providers and operators.

1 Introduction

Massively Multiplayer Online Games (MMOGs) are a new type of large-scale distributed applications characterised by a real-time virtual world entertaining millions of players spread across the globe. MMOG are designed as a collection of networked game servers, concurrently accessed by a large number of players (or end-users). The players connect directly to one game server and are mapped to one avatar in the game world to whom they send their play actions and receive appropriate responses. Based on the actions sent, the avatar dynamically interacts with other avatars within a game session, influencing each others' state. The state update responses must be delivered within a given time frequency to ensure an adequate *Quality of Service (QoS)* for a smooth and responsive experience. The load of the game server is proportional to the number of inter-actions between entities. An overloaded game server delivers state updates to its clients at a lower frequency than required which makes the overall environment fragmented and unplayable.

To concurrently support millions of active players and many other server-driven entities (non-playing characters and other game objects) generating variable computational and latency-sensitive resource demands, the MMOG operators purchase and overprovision a multi-server infrastructure with sufficient

L. Lopes et al. (Eds.): Euro-Par 2014 Workshops, Part I, LNCS 8805, pp. 299–310, 2014.

computational, network and storage capabilities for guaranteeing the QoS requirements and a smooth gameplay at all times. This statically provisioned infrastructure has two major drawbacks: it has high operational costs and is vulnerable to capacity shortages in case of unexpected increases in demand.

To address these gaps, we investigated in previous research [3,7,8] the use of Cloud computing technology for on-demand provisioning of virtualised resources to MMOGs based on their actual variable load. For this purpose, we designed a new ecosystem for MMOG operation and provisioning [8] consisting of four actors with smaller and better focused roles that facilitate their market penetration and chances of business success: clients, game providers, game operators, and resource (Cloud) providers. The interaction between them is negotiated and regulated through bipartite Service Level Agreements (SLA), representing wrappers around QoS parameters which they agree to deliver (see Figure 1).

End-users join MMOG sessions offered by game providers on the basis of MMOG subscriptions, representing contracts between the two parties comprising terms such as the price to be paid by the end-users and the QoS gameplay guarantees (i.e. state update rate) to be delivered by the provider.

Game providers offer a selection of MMOGs by contracting new games from development companies. Based on clients' requests, game providers assign clients to game zones delegated to game operators for QoS-based execution. The quality of gameplay is monitored and in case of *SLA faults* (e.g. state update rate below minimum threshold), the client is compensated.

Game operators receive requests from game providers for operating different MMOG session zones with guaranteed QoS. Based on resource utilisation estimations (covered in [7]), the game operators construct *operation SLA* offers negotiated with game providers [8], and allocate resources accordingly (i.e. start new zones, allow client connections). To fulfill these agreements, game operators acquire resources by establishing *resource SLAs* with Cloud providers [3]. At predefined *measurement timesteps* during the gameplay, the operators analyse the QoS information from the MMOG servers and, whenever SLA faults are detected, they compensate the game providers.

Resource providers are Cloud data centres from which game operators lease computing resources for running game servers with guaranteed QoS. Whenever the resource SLA terms (mostly limited to resource availability) are breached, resource providers compensate the operators. We studied the opportunity of employing Cloud infrastructures for MMOG hosting in [3].

In this work, we investigate the use of our proposed Cloud-based middleware for autonomous, self-adaptive hosting and operation of MMOGs on unreliable resources. For this purpose, we developed an MMOG simulator compliant with our ecosystem capable of emulating the behaviour of the four actors using traces collected from a real-life MMOG and resource characteristics from real-world commercial Cloud providers. Using our simulator, we study the impact of MMOG operation and provisioning on the involved actors by considering different resource availability levels, and highlight the advantages of dynamic resource

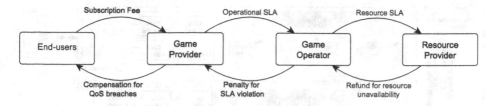

Fig. 1. Overview of MMOG ecosystem and SLA relationships

allocation over the static overprovisioning with respect to two metrics types: QoS offered to the clients and financial profit of the game provider and operator.

The paper is organised as follows. Section 2 introduces the failures that can occur during the MMOG operation considered in our model. Section 3 presents our MMOG simulation tool used for evaluation in Section 4 using traces collected from a real-life MMOG on commercial Cloud resources. Section 5 reviews the related work and Section 6 concludes the paper.

2 Failure Model

We identify in our MMOG operational model two principal types of failures that disturb the users' gameplay with a negative impact on the offered QoS, but from which the system is capable of recovering with no human intervention: *resource failures* and *management failures*.

Resource failure. In our scenario, the game operator runs the MMOG sessions on distributed heterogeneous resources provisioned from Cloud providers which are subject to a multitude of unexpected events that can lead to failures. If a machine crashes, hangs or becomes unreachable through the network, the running MMOG server is compromised disrupting the normal operation of the distributed MMOG session. In existing commercial deployments, such a severe unexpected event typically requires human intervention and can lead to hours of partial service unavailability, or even total unavailability in case of correlated failures. In our proposed architecture, the detection of this type of failure at the game operator level triggers a self-healing process consisting of two actions:

1. provisioning of a new resource or set of resources with the same (or better) characteristics as the failing one;
2. starting a new MMOG server part of the session and to which the clients are instructed to reconnect.

Thus, the MMOG session is salvaged but, regardless of these actions, the clients connected to the failing MMOG server will experience a *total interruption* in gameplay for a certain amount of time.

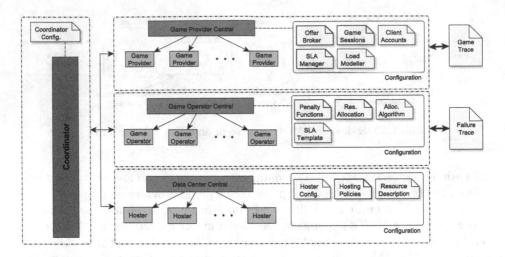

Fig. 2. Schematic MMOG simulation tool architecture

Management failure. The game operator automatically adapts the amount of provisioned resources in a dynamic fashion to achieve a proper MMOG session operation with reduced allocation costs while reaching the targeted QoS. In case of erroneous load estimations or sudden increases in the number of accessing users, the provisioned resources are not sufficient to handle the generated load leading to the degradation of the QoS. The players connected to the overloaded servers will experience in this case a fragmented, unrealistic gameplay. In this situation, the game operator compensates either by redistributing the users to other MMOG servers within the same session aiming a better load distribution and a more efficient utilisation of the already provisioned resources, or by provisioning more resources for the affected session. We call this type of disturbance, where the users are not disconnected from the MMOG session but their gameplay experience is degraded, as *partial interruption.*

3   MMOG Simulator

To ensure a flexible and complete validation of our MMOG research, we developed a trace-based MMOG simulation tool displayed in Figure 2 that implements our MMOG architecture and failure model.

Coordinator is the central part in charge of initialising the simulation according to the input configuration and managing the whole execution of the simulation through the following tasks: (1) calculation of the current game load and resources required; (2) checking of the current simulation state; (3) negotiation of new SLAs; (4) generation of resource requests and offers; (5) resource allocation; (6) creation output files needed for the evaluation of the experiment.

Game traces are the central element of every MMOG simulation, consisting of a data file for every active game zone, and containing the number of currently active clients and the corresponding timestamps. Based on these data, we simulate the same amount of game zones distributed over the world together with their related number of players using a configurable simulation time step. The overall duration of the simulation can be reduced by truncating the trace files.

User information is extracted from the trace files by a special service of the simulator based on the connected user accounts, necessary for the calculation of the subscription fees. To create a correct geographic mapping of the captured game, the simulator also uses the location of each individual client.

Game providers are in charge of managing the MMOG load models, connections to the user accounts, and provisioning of offers from the game operator to the customers. Based on the number of user access requests and their geographical origin, the game providers estimate the demand for each geographical area and construct operational SLA templates negotiated with the game operators. The SLA negotiation strategy and other fine-tuning provisioning variables can be altered in special configuration files. Additionally, the game providers manage the simulated game sessions by mapping the input traces to game zones.

Game operators are in charge of predicting and balancing of the load of the game sessions and zones, controlled by changing the properties for the respective services and algorithms. An essential part of the setup is the configuration of the *SLA templates* that manage the business transactions between the game operators and the game providers with variables such as the base price, the duration, and the number of serviced players. Based on historical data and the currently assigned users, the operator predicts the load for predetermined time intervals (shorter for dynamic MMOGs and longer otherwise) using the method presented in [7]. The prediction consists of the user distribution in the MMOG world and a load model for translating it into resource requirements. At each prediction interval, the operator evaluates the provisioned resources and makes adjustments by allocating or releasing resources and redistributing the load. Other configuration files allow controlling the penalties for QoS violations, resource unavailability, as well as sorting and ranking resource offers or the desired allocation time.

Data centre emulates a configurable network of Cloud providers with resources and services spread across the globe. To configure the resource providers, each setup configuration has a folder for every simulated data center containing information such as location, network bandwidth, and machines defined by their number of cores, processing speed and memory or disk size.

Failure traces are files containing the resource failures occurring during the simulated MMOG sessions. The format of the traces is inspired from the Failure Trace Archive (FTA), with a simplified format consisting of only three columns: the host name of the failing resource and the associated start and end (UNIX epoch) timestamps. Our resource availability model is based on three important parameters: (1) *inter-arrival time (IAT)* describing time between two consecutive failures, (2) *duration* of each individual failure, and (3) *size* described by the number of affected resources. Other parameters required for the failure generation are the number of available resources in the MMOG environment, the total duration of one simulation period, and the percentage of resource availability.

4   Experiments

For evaluating the impact of the resource and of the management failures, we use our MMOG simulator and six months of trace data collected from a real-world MMOG called RuneScape (http://www.runescape.com/).

4.1   Setup

We collected traces from 150 RuneScape servers with a sampling rate of two minutes, containing the number of players over time for each server group, aggregating approximately 40 million metric samples per simulation. Based on the number of concurrently active accounts from the RuneScape traces, we approximate the actual number of connected clients using the concurrent active account ratio metric approximated at around 15% for RuneScape. We use a prediction interval and a simulation step of two minutes, which proves to be adequate for this type of games and the collected traces. Since we also study the financial impact of resource unavailability on the MMOG actors, we modelled the client accounts with different monthly, bimonthly, trimestrial and semestrial subscription types based on the real subscription and payment methods of Jagex Ltd. (the developer and publisher of RuneScape) as of August 2010 (see Table 1). We employ a setup with one game operator and one game provider since their number does not impact the QoS metrics for the clients targeted by our experiments.

Table 1. RuneScape subscription plans for monthly, bimonthly, trimestrial, and semestrial payments

Plan	Payment	Subscription price [USD]			
		Monthly	Bimonthly	Trimestrial	Semestrial
SCC	Credit card	5.95	11.9	17.85	35.7
SPP	PayPal	7.5	12.99	18.15	36.1
SBT	Bank transfer	7.99	14.59	19.99	37.99

The traces contain the maximum load of approximately 150 concurrent game zones spread all across the globe, where every zone needs one virtual machine (VM) instance to be properly executed. For this purpose, we model a distributed heterogeneous environment with 16 commercial Cloud providers aggregating 70 different VM types (see Table 2) and providing a large enough resource pool for the game operator of approximately 3500 concurrent VM instances for running all game zone instances. The parameters that model each VM type include the number of cores (1 to 12), CPU speed, RAM size (1 to 48 GB), and in- and outbound network bandwidth. While most of the parameters are clearly defined

Table 2. Summary of Cloud providers

Provider	VM types	Location	Allocation time [hours]
Amazon	6	4 (Asia, UK, USA (E, W))	1
CloudCentral	5	1 (AUS)	1
ElasticHosts	4	1 (UK)	1
FlexiScale	4	1 (UK)	1
GoGrid	4	1 (USA (E))	1
Linode	5	1 (USA (E))	24
NewServers	5	1 (USA (E))	1
OpSource	6	1 (USA (E))	1
RackSpace	4	2 (USA (E, C))	1
ReliaCloud	3	1 (USA (C))	1
SoftLayer	4	3 (USA (E, C, W))	1
SpeedyRails	3	1 (CAN W)	24
Storm	6	2 (USA (E, W))	1
Terremark	5	1 (USA E)	1
Voxel	4	3 (USA (E), NED, AUS)	1
Zerigo	2	1 (USA (C))	1

Table 3. Number of machines for a given utilisation

Utilisation [%]	Number of machines
5	2120
20	520
40	280
60	190
80	150
95	140

in the specifications of the commercial Cloud providers, the processing power of the VMs is not concretely quantified. Thus, we express it using an appropriate metric called *RS unit* representing the equivalent computational requirements of one RuneScape server servicing 2000 concurrent clients. We compute this metric based on existing benchmarks[1,2] and our previous performance investigations [4].

Since one of our goals is to also show the impact of resource unavailability in a sparse resource environment, we derive six additional synthetic setups by gradually removing machines from the original VM instance pool to increase the resource utilisation, as illustrated in Table 3. In this table, the utilisation describes the percentage of machines to be allocated for a proper execution of all game zones at maximum load. In addition to the sparse resource environment, we introduce a controlled resource unavailability to our environment by associating to Cloud providers failure traces with tunable availability. We employ the resource availability model proposed in [2] and generate failure traces with average availabilities ranging from 99.5% to 99.9%. The traces are characterised through their failures' duration, size and IAT, each modelled through a statistical distribution. The distributions' parameters are presented in Table 4, along with the statistical properties of the resulting traces, where $Q1$, $Q2$ and $Q3$ represent the lower, the median, and the upper quartiles. For all traces we employ the same distribution for the failure duration and size, but we vary the resource availability by adjusting the failure IAT. Both independent and correlated failures are generated, the ratio between the two being 3 : 2.

We evaluate the advantage of dynamic resource allocation over a static approach with respect to two metric: QoS and financial impacts. In case of static allocation, resource provisioning is performed once the zone is registered for

---

[1] http://blog.cloudharmony.com/2010/05/what-is-ecu-cpu-benchmarking-in-cloud.html

[2] http://www.chadkeck.com/2010/05/cloud-hosting-provider-hardware-benchmarks/

Table 4. Resource availability parameters and statistical characterisation

Failure metric	Distribution	Scale	Shape	Statistical properties						Avail-ability
				Min	Max	Average	Q1	Q2	Q3	
Duration [min.]	Log-Normal	2.12	0.306	1	37	8	6	8	10	–
Size [machines]	Weibull	4	5	0	6	3	3	3	4	–
IAT [sec.]	Weibull	13600	7	2073	19668	12722	11381	12906	14254	99.5%
IAT [sec.]	Weibull	7000	7	888	10123	6548	5860	6645	7336	99.6%
IAT [sec.]	Weibull	4750	7	535	6988	4443	3976	4509	4977	99.7%
IAT [sec.]	Weibull	3550	7	476	5146	3320	2971	3370	3720	99.8%
IAT [sec.]	Weibull	2830	7	341	4119	2647	2369	2686	2965	99.9%

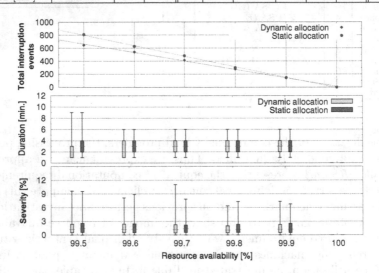

Fig. 3. Total interruption analysis for static and dynamic resource allocations for different resource availabilities

operation, and the session does not get additional resources after a failure event, but waits for the failure to end when the machine becomes operational again.

4.2   QoS Impact

Figure 3 compares the number, duration and severity of all total interruption events for varying resource availabilities for dynamic and static resource allocation approaches. In the top graph, it is visible that the number of total interruptions is increasing with higher resource unavailability for static allocation, leading to an average of 30% increase for a resource availability of 99.5%. We further observe stable, constant values for the severity and the duration of total interruptions (the two bottom graphs) across all resource availability values, which validates the automated process for recovery from resource failures of our MMOG architecture. The dynamic resource allocation reduces the medial duration of the total interruptions to two minutes (the duration of one simulation cycle) for the simulations with the lowest (99.5% − 99.6%) resource availability, and is below four minutes for more than 75% of the events. Despite the

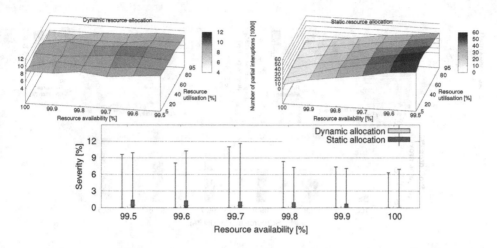

Fig. 4. Partial interruption analysis dynamic and static resource allocations for different resource availabilities

higher count of events and their prolonged duration, the median percentage of affected players (i.e. the severity) remains almost constant below 2% across all availability values, and is only slightly higher in case of the static allocations.

The impact of the different allocation strategies can be best noticed in the analysis of the partial interruption events displayed in Figure 4. While the number of partial interruptions increases with the decreasing resource availability for static allocations, they remain relatively constant for the dynamic allocation strategy for all availabilities and utilisations. On average, the number of partial interruptions for an availability of 99.5% is 4.5 times lower using dynamic allocations. With the dynamic allocation of resources, the partial interruption events have little to no impact on the QoS offered to the end-users (i.e. the severity) since our system can mitigates the effects by allocating additional resources or balancing the load. With static resource allocations, the partial interruption events affect on average about 1% of the connected players.

4.3   Financial Impact

Following the hierarchical architecture presented in Section 1, the first actors to analyse are the end-users who pay a subscription fee that allows them to enter gaming sessions provided by the game providers. Employing the static resource allocation approach not only leads to a degradation of the offered QoS, but also introduces a linear increase in the amount of QoS compensations paid to the users for lower availability and higher utilisation, as displayed in Figure 5. While the compensation payments lower the monthly costs for most of the clients, their overall play satisfaction will suffer.

The impact of the static allocation on the QoS can also be noticed in the financial situation of the game provider who earns money from penalties paid

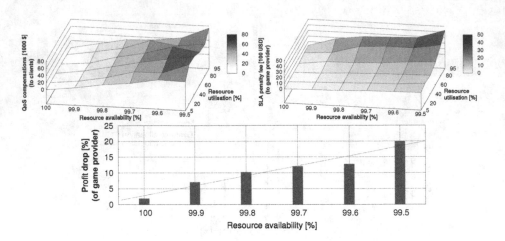

Fig. 5. Analysis of financial impact on involved actors for static resource allocations

by the game operator for SLA violations (part of which it transfers to the client as QoS compensations). The bottom chart Figure 5 shows the drop of the game providers' profit for using the static allocation approach in the different resource availabilities, averaged across all resource utilisation scenarios.

In the lowest tier, the game operator is directly affected by machine failures that occur in the data centres of the resource provider, where static allocation has a strong negative impact on the QoS. In case of a resource failure, the dynamic allocation mechanism provisions additional machines to ensure that no SLAs with the game provider are violated. Since it is not possible to allocate additional resources with the static allocation, almost every resource failure leads to a violation of an SLA, accompanied penalty fees. The top-right chart in Figure 5 shows increasing compensation fees to be paid by the game operator to the provider with increasing unavailability and utilisation of resources.

The financial situation of the resource providers is generally not affected by the static allocation since the negative impacts of this approach are mostly restricted to the three higher tiers of the architecture.

5   Related Work

Much recent work focuses on (soft) QoS guarantees for MMOG operation [5,6,15]. Wong [15] proposes a resource provisioning algorithm with QoS guarantees, but considers only networking aspects, whereas we focus on maintaining QoS even during total resource failures. Complementary to our study, Lee and Chen [5] investigate MMOG server consolidation techniques, focusing on energy consumption. There have been a number of research activities in assessing the performance of virtualised resources in Cloud computing environments [11] and in general [12], some also considering the availability of Cloud resources [9]. In contrast to these studies, ours targets realistic Cloud resources with limited availability for a new application class (MMOG). Regarding the resource and MMOG deployment models, one study [13] comes close to our approach by proposing virtual machines for multi-player game operation. However, our work focuses on MMOGs which, in contrast to classic multi-player games, are distributed applications (multiple MMOG servers interconnected in a single session) serving a several orders of magnitude higher number of clients. Additionally, we also consider the virtualised resources as part of commercial Cloud computing platforms. In the area of reliability, there are studies which investigate the characteristics of resource and workload failures, but do not assess their effects on the underlying systems' performance [10,14]. Other efforts consider uncorrelated failures in distributed systems [1] and evaluate the resulting performance of the affected systems [2], but only for high-performance computing applications. In contrast, we employ the failure model introduced by [2], but apply it to Cloud resources and evaluate the consequences of utilising such resources on the QoS of MMOGs.

6 Conclusions

We presented a simulator that implements a new ecosystem for operating MMOGs on Cloud infrastructures which effectively splits the traditional monolithic MMOG companies into three smaller and better focused actors whose interaction is regulated through bipartite SLAs: game providers, game operators, and resource providers. In our model, game operators dynamically provision resources from Cloud resource providers based on the MMOG load so that the QoS to the end-users is guaranteed at all times. Game providers lease operation SLAs from the game operators to satisfy all client requests and manage multiple distributed MMOG sessions. These three self-standing, smaller, more agile service providers enable access to the MMOG market for the small and medium enterprises, and to the current commercial Cloud providers. We evaluated in this paper using traces collected from a real-life MMOG the impact of resource availability and utilisation on the QoS and financial situation of the involved actors by comparing our novel dynamic resource allocation method with the traditional static allocation strategy. We found out that our MMOG ecosystem successfully mitigates the performance degradation of running MMOGs on real commercial Cloud resources with limited availability to gameplay disruptions of less than four minutes, independently of the duration of the underlying resource failure. The majority of resource failures affect less than 2% of the users participating in autonomously operated MMOG sessions. A low resource availability increases the number of gameplay disruptions, while a high resource contention results in longer disruptions affecting more clients. Finally, static resource allocation has a negative impact on the financial situation of the involved actors due to high compensation and penalty fees for QoS and SLA breaches upon low resource availability and high utilisation.

References

1. Bhagwan, R., Savage, S., Voelker, G.: Understanding availability. In: Kaashoek, M.F., Stoica, I. (eds.) IPTPS 2003. LNCS, vol. 2735, pp. 256–267. Springer, Heidelberg (2003)
2. Iosup, A., Mathieu, J., Sonmez, O., Epema, D.H.J.: On the dynamic resource availability in grids. In: 8th IEEE/ACM International Conference on Grid Computing. pp. 26–33. IEEE Computer Society (September 2007)
3. Iosup, A., Nae, V., Prodan, R.: The impact of virtualization on the performance and operational costs of massively multiplayer online games. International Journal of Advanced Media and Communication 4(4), 364–386 (2011)
4. Iosup, A., Ostermann, S., Yigitbasi, N., Prodan, R., Fahringer, T., Epema, D.: Performance analysis of Cloud computing services for many-tasks scientific computing. IEEE Transactions on Parallel and Distributed Systems 22(6), 931–945 (2011)
5. Lee, Y.-T., Chen, K.-T.: Is server consolidation beneficial to MMORPG? A case study of World of Warcraft. In: 3rd International Conference on Cloud Computing, pp. 435–442. IEEE Computer Society (July 2010)
6. Briceño, L.D., et al.: Robust resource allocation in a massive multiplayer online gaming environment. In: 4th International Conference on Foundations of Digital Games, pp. 232–239. ACM (2009)
7. Nae, V., Iosup, A., Prodan, R.: Dynamic resource provisioning in massively multiplayer online games. IEEE Transactions on Parallel and Distributed Systems 22(3), 380–395 (2011)
8. Nae, V., Prodan, R., Iosup, A.: SLA-based operation of massively multiplayer online games in competition-based environments. In: Proceedings of the International C* Conference on Computer Science & Software Engineering, pp. 104–112. ACM (July 2013)
9. Nagarajan, A.B., Mueller, F., Engelmann, C., Scott, S.L.: Proactive fault tolerance for hpc with xen virtualization. In: 21st Annual International Conference on Supercomputing, pp. 23–32. ACM (2007)
10. Nurmi, D., Brevik, J., Wolski, R.: Modeling machine availability in enterprise and wide-area distributed computing environments. In: Cunha, J.C., Medeiros, P.D. (eds.) Euro-Par 2005. LNCS, vol. 3648, pp. 432–441. Springer, Heidelberg (2005)
11. Palankar, M.R., Iamnitchi, A., Ripeanu, M., Garfinkel, S.: Amazon S3 for science grids: a viable solution? In: International Workshop on Data-aware Distributed Computing, pp. 55–64. ACM (2008)
12. Quétier, B., Neri, V., Cappello, F.: Scalability comparison of four host virtualization tools. Journal of Grid Computing 5, 83–98 (2007)
13. Reed, D., Pratt, I., Menage, P., Early, S., Stratford, N.: Xenoservers: Accountable execution of untrusted programs. In: Seventh Workshop on Hot Topics in Operating Systems, pp. 136–141 (1999)
14. Schroeder, B., Gibson, G.A.: A large-scale study of failures in high-performance computing systems. IEEE Transactions on Dependable and Secure Computing 7(4), 337 (2010)
15. Wong, K.W.: Resource allocation for massively multiplayer online games using fuzzy linear assignment technique. In: Consumer Communications and Networking Conference, pp. 1035–1039. IEEE (2008)

Epidemic Diffusion of Social Updates in Dunbar-Based DOSN

Marco Conti[2], Andrea De Salve[1], Barbara Guidi[1,2], and Laura Ricci[1]

[1] University of Pisa - Department of Computer Science,
Largo B. Pontecorvo, 56127, Pisa, Italy
[2] IIT-CNR, via G. Moruzzi, 1 56124 Pisa, Italy
{desalve,guidi,ricci}@di.unipi.it
m.conti@iit.cnr.it

Abstract. Distributed Online Social Networks (DOSNs) do not rely on a central repository for storing social data so that the users can keep control of their private data and do not depend on the social network provider. The ego network, i.e. the network made up of an individual, the ego, along with all the social ties she has with other people, the alters, may be exploited to define distributed social overlays and dissemination protocols. In this paper we propose a new epidemic protocol able to spread social updates in Dunbar-based DOSN overlays where the links between nodes are defined by considering the social interactions between users. Our approach is based on the notion of Weighted Ego Betweenness Centrality (WEBC) which is an egocentric social measure approximating the Betweenness Centrality. The computation of the WEBC exploits a weighted graph where the weights correspond to the tie strengths between the users so that nodes having a higher number of interactions are characterized by a higher value of the WEBC. A set of experimental results proving the effectiveness of our approach is presented.

Keywords: DOSN, P2P, Information Diffusion, Dunbar.

1 Introduction

In the last few years, Online Social Networks (OSNs) have become one of the most popular Internet services and they have changed the way of how people interact with each other. Currently popular OSNs are based on centralized servers which store all the user's information. In this way, users give up the control of their own data and their data is scattered over the Internet in different OSN providers. Centralized social networking services present several problems that include both technical and social issues that emerge as a consequence of the centralized management of the services.

A current trend for developing OSN services is towards the decentralization of the OSN infrastructure. A Distributed Online Social Network (DOSN) [6] is an Online Social Network implemented over a distributed information management

L. Lopes et al. (Eds.): Euro-Par 2014 Workshops, Part I, LNCS 8805, pp. 311–322, 2014.

platform, such as a network of trusted servers or P2P systems. The decentralization of the existing functionalities of Online Social Networks requires specific approaches for providing robustness against churn, distributing storage of data, propagating updates, defining an overlay topology and a protocol enabling searching and addressing, etc.

The inherent nature of how people connect with each other in a OSN makes P2P architectures suitable for building DOSNs. Our proposal takes into account the friendship relations and the interactions between users to model the system according to a simple social structure called ego network [16]. Ego networks are social networks made up of an individual (called *ego*) along with all the social ties she has with other people (called *alters*). The key property of this model is the *tie strength*, represented as the social distance between the ego and the alter involved in a relationship.

It has been shown that in (offline) ego networks there are a series of *circles* of alters arranged in a hierarchical inclusive sequence based on an increasing level of intimacy [18]. Dunbar et al. identify four layers [18]: "*support clique*", "*sympathy group*", "*affinity group*" and "*active network*" with the average size of 5, 12, 35, 150 respectively (Fig. 1). Each subset includes all the relationships of the previous circles along with an additional set of social links with a weaker level of intimacy. The last set contains simple acquaintances, with a relatively weak relationship with the ego while the first set contains only alters with a very strong relationship with the ego.

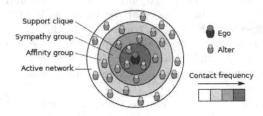

Fig. 1. Structuring ego networks: the Dunbar Approach

This paper presents an epidemic algorithm for the diffusion of social updates on DOSNs. A social update is defined as any social content that users share with their friends (profile information, wall postings, pictures, etc.). Users generate a huge amount of social update inside a social network which should be disseminated to their direct friends or to a larger extent, depending on the kind of the social update. Any social update should be disseminated with a low cost in term of time and messages. Even if the definition of the P2P social overlay is not the main focus of this paper, it is important to describe the model of the overlay which must support the spreading of the contents. In our proposal, the P2P overlay is defined by a one-to-one mapping between the social links connecting the ego to its Dunbar alters and the P2P overlay links. In this way, each node of the P2P network needs to support only active overlay connections (on average, at most 150 active relations per user [2]). In the following, this overlay will be referred as Dunbar-based overlay. The diffusion of the social updates on the Dunbar based overlay is performed by an epidemic algorithm.

Most existing DOSNs flood the social updates on the social overlay and this may result in several duplicate notifications. We introduce a novel centrality index, the Weighted Ego Betweenness Centrality (WEBC), which extends the classical notion of Ego Betweenness Centrality (EBC) [7] by considering the weights paired with the edges of the social overlay. The knowledge of the WEBC of the nodes in the ego network, enables the definition of a heuristics for guiding the epidemic spreading which reduces the number of duplicate messages and enables the diffusion of social updates on paths corresponding to higher tie strengths.

The rest of the paper is structured as follows. We discuss the related work in Section 2. Section 3 introduces some basic concepts of the OSN and define the social overlay of the DOSN. The WEBC is defined in Section 4 and the epidemic algorithm based on it is shown in Section 5. In Section 6 we present the evaluation of our proposal. Finally, Section 7 reports the conclusions and discusses future works.

2   Related Work

Several DOSNs are designed to address privacy in OSNs either through cryptography, architectural modifications and decentralization. Diaspora [1] is a really used social network in which users' profiles are hosted on servers that are administrated by individual users, without support for encryption. LifeSocial.KOM [8] is a P2P platform for secure online social networks which provides the functionality of common online social networks in a totally distributed and secure manner. LifeSocial.KOM is designed to create a modular plugin-architecture to assure extensibility and the plugins are hosted on a general platform for P2P application. PeerSoN [4] is a distributed infrastructure for social networks that provides encryption and direct data exchange. PeerSoN has a two-tier architecture, where one tier serves as a look-up service and the second tier consists of the peers that contains user data, such as user profiles. This approach pays attention to security and privacy concerns. Safebook [5] is a decentralized and privacy preserving DOSN which is composed of three major different components, the TIS (Trusted Identification Service), Matryoshkas which are specialized overlays encompassing each user, and a P2P location substrate based on Kademlia. In [17], a recent approach based on a Super-Peer architecture is shown. The system uses Super-Peers, which are nodes with a higher degree of bandwidth, storage space and higher availability, to manage DOSNs.

The social update diffusion problem has been studied in Social Butterfly [12] and in SocialCDN [13], which achieve the social update dissemination utilizing social caching techniques.

Another approach similar to ours is proposed in [14]. The authors propose a gossip protocol for data dissemination in DOSN in which each node requires knowledge of its set of friends and friends of friends. They utilize a vertex anticentrality selection heuristics to assign to each neighbour of the producer a selection probability which is inversely proportional to the number of their common neighbours. In addition, they improve the diffusion process with histories and a fragmentation heuristics that exploits the number of connected components to select where to send the gossip messages. However, our approach differs from theirs for several reasons: *i)* we use a different selection heuristics that takes into account the centrality of the node and the strength of the relationship; *ii)* we leverage a distributed algorithm for community detection; *iii)* we propose a different dissemination method in which nodes leverage only on the knowledge of the nodes directly connected to them.

3   Defining Distributed Social Overlays

An Online Social Network (OSN) may be formally described by an undirected social graph $G = (V, E)$, where V represents the set of users and E the friendship relations between them. The *ego network* of a user represents a structure built around the ego which contains her direct friends, known as *alters* and may also include information about the direct connections between the alters. Formally, each vertex $u \in V$ can be seen as an *ego* and $EN(u) = (V_u, E_u)$ is the ego network of u where $V_u = \{u\} \cup \{v \in V | (u, v) \in E\}$, and $E_u = \{(a, b) \in E | a = u \vee b = u \vee \{a, b\} \subseteq V_u\}$. $N(u) = V_u - \{u\}$ is the set of adjacent nodes of u. The alters in an ego network may be organized according to the *tie strength* between the ego and each alter. The tie strength defines the distance between them by exploiting factors of the OSN and may be represented by a weight paired with each edge of the ego network. As suggested by Dunbar, we include in the resulting ego network at most 150 active contacts and we will refer to it as Dunbar based ego network. We believe that this definition could be easily extended to consider the maximum number of active contacts an input parameter of our model.

The definition of the tie strength is currently an open problem and several alternatives have been presented in the literature. In [3] the tie strength is computed by considering a set of relational variables, like the number of likes, posts, comments, tags on the same picture and so on in a temporal window. Sala et al.[19] exploit an indirected weighted graph to describe the social relations, because they observe that most interactions on Facebook are reciprocated so that the notion of tie strength is symmetric. In other proposals (such as [10]) the notion of tie strength is asymmetric and a directed graph is exploited to describe social relations. In the following we will focus on undirected graph and we will suppose that the tie strength is computed as a function of the users' interactions occurred in both directions.

Let us now briefly discuss the issue of defining a distributed overlay for DOSN. In a DOSN, each user is mapped to a node of the distributed system and a social overlay connecting the nodes is defined. A direct mapping of the social graph onto the distributed social overlay is feasible, but this solution presents several drawbacks. As of September 2013 the average number of Facebook friends reached 338 among adults aged between 18-29, while it is about 200 for older adults. This implies that each node of the distributed system should maintain a large amount of connections with nodes paired with friends even if a large subset of them may be under-used.

We exploit the Dunbar's approach to limit the number of connections of each node. A link between a node A and a node B is defined in the social overlay iff B is in the Dunbar-based ego network of A. Each node n maintains a view which contains the descriptors of all the nodes which are directly connected to it. The number of nodes contained in a view is limited by the Dunbar number (150), and each node can directly communicate only with nodes in its view. Each link is weighted and the weight is the tie strength between two nodes. Note that not all the social relations are mapped onto the social overlay. The social relations characterized by low tie strengths are not supported by direct connections on the social overlay, since a few interactions occur on them. These interactions may be supported by on-demand communications.

4   Weighted Ego Betweenness Centrality

Ego Betweenness Centrality (EBC) is defined as the Betweenness Centrality (BC) of a node restricted to the nodes and the links in its ego network. The computation of the EBC for an undirected graph has been proposed in [7]. [9] shows a distributed approach to compute the EBC on undirected and directed graph exploiting two alternative distributed protocols, a broadcast and a gossip-based protocol, for disseminating the ego networks updates to the neighbours of a node.

BC and EBC are topology-based metrics, so that value for a node n depends on the position and on the connections of n in the graph. Consider, for instance, Fig. 2(a), representing the ego network of node E and let us neglect, for the moment, the weights paired with the links of the graph. The value of the EBC for nodes E, D and B is exactly the same, $\frac{1}{3}$, since a single shortest path out of 3 different shortest paths between A and C passes through each of them. Therefore, the value of the EBC does not permit us to decide, for instance, which node between them is the best choice for propagating a social update from A to C. This is due to the fact that the EBC considers only structural properties of the graph.

We introduce a new notion of EBC for weighted graphs, the *Weighted Ego Betweenness Centrality (WEBC)*, which discriminates the shortest paths crossing the ego according to the weights of the edges on those paths. The computation of the WEBC requires the adjacency matrix $A_{i,j}^n$ associated with the ego network of node n, $ego(n)$, and the weights matrix $W_{i,j}^n$ which contains the weights paired with the edges of $ego(n)$, (note that a weight may also be equal to 0). The elements of the matrices are accessed through the nodes' identifiers i and j. Given two nodes i and j belonging to $ego(n)$ such that $A_{i,j}^n = 0$, let

$$Path_{i,j}(n) = \sum_{k \in ego(n), k \neq i,j} A_{i,k}^n * A_{k,j}^n * W_{i,k}^n * W_{k,j}^n$$

be the sum of the weights of all the 2-hops paths between nodes i and j including only edges in $ego(n)$. The WEBC of a node n for an undirected graph is defined as follows:

$$WEBC(n) = \sum_{i,j \in ego(n), A_{i,j}^n = 0, j > i} \frac{W_{i,n}^n * W_{n,j}^n}{Path_{i,j}(n)} \qquad (1)$$

where all the nodes i e j such that there is not a directed link between them ($A_{i,j}^n = 0$) in the ego network of n are considered in the summation. The path between the nodes i e j crossing n has weight $W_{i,n}^n * W_{n,j}^n$.

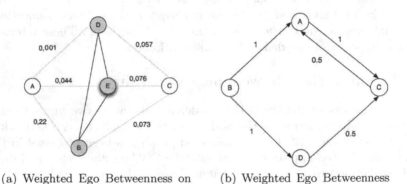

(a) Weighted Ego Betweenness on Undirected Graphs

(b) Weighted Ego Betweenness on Directed Graphs

Fig. 2. Weighted Ego Betweenness on Undirected/Directed Graphs

We have previously seen that nodes E, D and B in Fig. 2(a) are indistinguishable in term of EBC. The values of the WEBC for nodes E, D, and B obtained by applying Eq. (1) are the following ones: $WEBC(D)=0.0029$, $WEBC(E)=0.17$ and $WEBC(B)=0.82$. The WEBC highlights that the path connecting A and C and crossing B has a higher weight with respect the other ones.

In a Dunbar-based overlay, where the weights paired with the links of the overlay represent the tie strength between two users, we can exploit WEBC to distinguish among different paths the most important one in term of the number of the interactions between the nodes on that path.

In some scenarios, it is useful to evaluate $WEBC(n,a)$, the WEBC of a node n with respect to a particular alter a. We define the $WEBC(n,a)$ as follows:

$$WEBC(n,a) = \sum_{j \in ego(n), A_{a,j}^n = 0} \frac{W_{a,n}^n * W_{n,j}^n}{Path_{a,j}(n)} \qquad (2)$$

In the next section, we will see that $WEBC(n,a)$ can be exploited to evaluate the capability of node n to connect the alter a to nodes in the ego network of n which are not directly connected to a. An epidemic algorithm can exploit this information to define a heuristics for the neighbour selection when propagating a social update.

Even if in the next section we will apply WEBC on undirected graphs, it is important to notice that the computation of the WEBC on a directed graph requires some modifications to the previous definition. As a matter of fact, when we consider a direct graph, a node n may belong to the ego network of a node m, while the other way round may be not true. When computing the WEBC of a node n on a directed graph, a possible solution is to consider all the *shortest oriented paths* passing through n. In the graph shown in Fig. 2(b), the WEBC of A considers the *weighted oriented path* between B, and C crossing A with respect to all the weighted oriented paths linking B to C, resulting in *WEBC(A)=0.6*.

5   WEBC Based Information Diffusion in DOSN

In a OSN, like Facebook, a social update produced by user u should be sent to users which are k-hops distant from u in the social graph. The extent of the diffusion depends on the kind of the social update and on the privacy settings of the users. For instance, in Facebook, each post published by a user on her own wall should be sent to her 1-hop friends, i.e. to all the users in her ego network. In other scenarios, like the comment to a post or a photo of a friend the information may be transmitted to 2-hops distant users *FriendOfFriend(FoF)*. Some particular scenarios require to trasmit the update even to 3-hops-away friends *FriendOfFriendOfFriend (FoFoF)*.

In a DOSN, the social updates are transmitted to the k-hops neighbours through the links of the social overlay. We consider a Dunbar-based overlay, where each edge is paired with a weight representing the tie strength between the nodes it connects. The diffusion of the social update is done by an *epidemic algorithm* that exploits the WEBC selection heuristics and the community structures in order to guide spread of the social update towards more favoured regions. When a node v receives a social update it passes it to the neighbour n in its ego network maximizing $WEBC(n,v)$. This heuristic allows both to choose the neighbours able to connect v to nodes not belonging to its ego network and to speed up the spreading on highly weighted paths. Note that this heuristic can be implemented by exploiting only local information.

The differentiation of paths based on their weights implies that nodes belonging to highly weighted paths will receive the update earlier. This agrees with the recent design choice of current social networks, where the importance of social updates is classified according to the tie strength with the node generating the update (for instance each node in Facebook classifies the updates it receives according to this politics in order to present the updates on different news feeds, on the basis of their importance).

5.1   Our Algorithm

Let us suppose that a node X generates a social update. We focus on the case where the update has to be spread 2-hops away with respect to X (to its FoF), but our approach is valid also for in the general case of k-hops diffusion.

Our algorithm is organized into two phases: *i)* Communities discovery phase and *ii)* Diffusion of social content into each community phase.

The phase of community discovery allows to partition the i-hops, $i \in 1..2$, neighbours of X into a set of communities such that, if we exclude X from the graph, each pair of nodes within a community are connected by a path, while nodes belonging to different communities are not connected. Our community discovery algorithm is based on that proposed in [11]. Fig. 3(a) shows the node X together with its two hops social contacts. These nodes are shown into two concentric circles, according to their social distance from X. The different communities detected by the algorithm are shown with different colours.

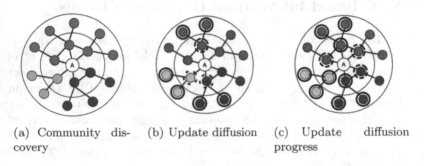

(a) Community dis-   (b) Update diffusion   (c) Update   diffusion
covery   progress

Fig. 3. Phases of the epidemic algorithm

The WEBC-based epidemic algorithm is executed in the second phase. Let $N_1(X)$, respectively $N_2(X)$, be the set of nodes which are 1-hop, respectively, 2-hops from X. The information diffusion distributed algorithm works as follows:

- the producer X of the update o starts the information diffusion by choosing a node for each community (i.e. nodes sorrounded by dotted line in Fig. 3(b)) and sending o to it. These nodes are selected on the basis of their WEBC computed with respect to X.
- if a node Y in $N_1(X)$ receives the update o from another node K in $N_1(X)$, it checks its ego network to see if it contains neighbours in $N_2(X)$ which are not also neighbours of K (recall that the ego network of Y includes also the links connecting neighbours of the ego). If the set of these neighbours is not empty, it sends the update to each node in this set (i.e. nodes sorrounded by solid line in Fig. 3(b)). Then Y chooses one neighbour belonging to $N_1(X)$ according to the WEBC-based heuristics (i.e.one of the nodes sorrounded by dotted line in Fig. 3(c)) and propagates the update to it.
- nodes in $N_2(X)$ do not propagate the update.

- each node n maintains the list of updated nodes *UpdatedNodes*, which is initially empty. n records in this list the nodes which are known to have received the update. Whenever n sends an update to one of its neighbours, it adds this neighbour to this list.
- if a node receives a social update, but all the neighbours in its ego network belongs to *UpdatedNodes*, it stops the diffusion of the information.

Note that the previous algorithm may be refined in several directions. For instance, in the second step, the check related to the common neighbours in the ego networks of the sender and of the receiver does not guarantee that the message will be propagated only to nodes which has not received it previously. As a matter of fact, each node has only a local and partial view of the nodes of the community, restricted to its ego network. To face this problem, it is possible to pair each update with an *history* recording the nodes which have already received the update, as proposed in [14]. This allows to reduce the number of duplicate updates at the expense of a larger usage of the network bandwidth.

6 Experimental Results

We have developed a set of simulations of our system using the P2P Peersim simulator [15], a highly scalable simulator written in java. We have used a Facebook Regional Network[1] dataset to build the Dunbar-based social overlay. The dataset is composed by:

- A *Social Graph*: an undirected graph which defines the whole network structure. An edge corresponds to a social relation between two Facebook users.
- Four *Interaction Graphs*: directed graphs which define the interactions between users within different time windows: *last month, last 6 months, last year, 2004-2008*. The Interaction graphs contain an edge for each interaction (Post or Photo Comment) between two users happened in the considered time window. If a user j has had an interaction with a user i, a link from j to i is created in the Interaction Graph.

Table 1 shows some characteristics of the Social Graph computed in [2].

Table 1. Social Graph

# Nodes	3,097,165
# Edges	23,667,394
Average Degree	15.283
Average Clustering Coefficient	0.098
Assortativity	0.048

---

[1] Referred as Anonymous regional network A on
http://current.cs.ucsb.edu/facebook/.

We have evaluated the EBC and WEBC centrality indexes for several networks randomly extracted from the real dataset. The contact frequencies of the social relations extracted from the Interaction Graphs are used to compute the weights associated with each relation. The nodes are ranked on the basis of the value of their EBC/WEBC. Figure 4(a) reports on the x-axis the rank of the nodes and on the y-axis the value of the centrality indexes on a logarithmic scale for one of the selected networks. We can observe that the WEBC provides a better differentiation of nodes, i.e. it allows to evaluate nodes not only from the point of view of their structural properties, but also from a qualitative point of view. We can observe that nodes with a similar EBC are redistributed by the WEBC on the basis of the contact frequency of the paths.

We have evaluated the epidemic diffusion algorithm on a subset of nodes extracted from the original dataset. The dimension of the extracted networks is, respectively, of 4000 and 10000 nodes. Table 2 shows the structural properties of the two extracted networks.

Table 2. Network properties

Network Properties	4000 Nodes	10000 Nodes
Min. Nodes Degree	1	1
Max. Nodes Degree	150	150
Mean Nodes Degree	6.692	7.674
StdDev Nodes Degree	10.788	11.84
Min. Dim. *FriendOfFriend*	1	1
Max. Dim. *FriendOfFriend*	861	2542
Mean Dim. *FriendOfFriend*	105.734	160.41
StdDev Dim. *FriendOfFriend*	74.77	139.318

We have evaluated our protocol with the WEBC and EBC selection heuristic which selects the neighbours on the basis of the WEBC and EBC. Our protocols are compared with respect to a baseline flooding method in which source messages are trasmitted to all attached network nodes. Fig. 4(b) shows the CDF of the percentage of FoF (Friend Of Friend) which have received at least a replica on each of two networks, with respect to the different solutions. The results show that our algorithm actually permits to obtain a lower number of replicas with respect to flooding, while the two heuristics are very close in term of replicated updates.

Fig. 5 show the number of replicated updates as a function of the size of the communities by using the two heuristics and by considering the network of 10000 nodes. The figures shows that the percentage of replica is similar for the two heuristics and is proportional to the size of the communities. We can conclude that the heuristics based on the WEBC outperforms the other one, because it is able both to return a similar number of replicas and to select the most important paths in terms of tie strength of the nodes.

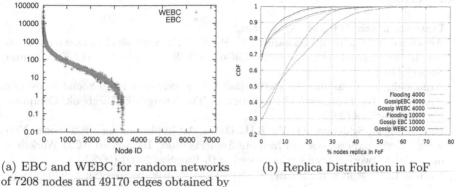

(a) EBC and WEBC for random networks   (b) Replica Distribution in FoF
of 7208 nodes and 49170 edges obtained by
the dataset

Fig. 4. Results of the simulation

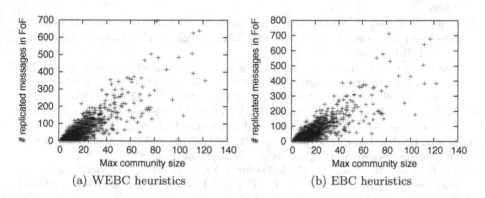

(a) WEBC heuristics   (b) EBC heuristics

Fig. 5. Number of replica according to the community dimension in a network of 10000 nodes

7   Conclusion and Future Works

This paper has presented how the Dunbar based approach can be exploited to define a Distributed Social Network. The introduction of a novel centrality index, the Weighted Betweenness Centrality, enables the definition of an efficient epidemic algorithm able to select the paths for the propagation of the social updates on the basis of the weights paired with them.

We plan to extend our work in several directions. The epidemic algorithm may be refined by pairing a history with each update in order to further reduce the number of duplicated updates. We plan to integrate with our system a strategy to guarantee the availability of the social content for peers offline. Finally, we will investigate the application of the WEBC in other contexts, for instance for the link prediction problem.

References

1. Diaspora, https://joindiaspora.com/
2. Arnaboldi, V., Conti, M., Passarella, A., Pezzoni, F.: Analysis of ego network structure in online social networks. In: SocialCom/PASSAT, pp. 31–40. IEEE Computer Society (2012)
3. Arnaboldi, V., Guazzini, A., Passarella, A.: Egocentric Online Social Networks: Analysis of Key Features and Prediction of Tie Strength in Facebook. Computer Communications (2013)
4. Buchegger, S., Schioberg, D., Vu, L.H., Datta, A.: Implementing a P2P Social Network - Early Experiences and Insights from PeerSoN. In: Second ACM Workshop on Social Network Systems (Co-located with EuroSys 2009) (2009)
5. Cutillo, L.A., Molva, R., Strufe, T.: Safebook: A privacy-preserving online social network leveraging on real-life trust. Comm. Mag. 47(12) (December 2009)
6. Datta, A., Buchegger, S., Vu, L., Strufe, T., Rzadca, K.: Decentralized online social networks. In: Furht, B. (ed.) Handbook of Social Network Technologies, pp. 349–378. Springer (2010)
7. Everett, M.G., Borgatti, S.P.: Ego network betweenness. Social Networks 27, 31–38 (2005)
8. Graffi, K., Gross, C., Mukherjee, P., Kovacevic, A., Steinmetz, R.: Lifesocial.kom: A p2p-based platform for secure online social networks. In: Peer-to-Peer Computing, pp. 1–2. IEEE (2010)
9. Guidi, B., Conti, M., Passarella, A., Ricci, L.: Distributed protocols for ego betweenness centrality computation in DOSNs. In: The Fifth IEEE Workshop on Pervasive Collaboration and Social Networking 2014 (PerCol 2014) (March 2014)
10. La Gala, M., Arnaboldi, V., Passarella, A., Conti, M.: Ego-net Digger: a New Way to Study Ego Networks in Online Social Networks. Tech. rep., IIT-CNR (2012)
11. Leung, I.X.Y., Hui, P., Liò, P., Crowcroft, J.: Towards real-time community detection in large networks. Physical Review E 79(6), 66107 (2009)
12. Lu, H., Nath, B., Iftode, L., Muthukrishnan, S.: Social Butterfly: Social Caches for Distributed Social Networks. In: IEEE Third International Conference on Social Computing (Socialcom), pp. 81–86 (2011)
13. Lu, H., Punceva, M., Nath, B., Muthukrishnan, S., Iftode, L.: SocialCDN: Caching techniques for distributed social networks. In: IEEE 12th International Conference on Peer-to-Peer Computing (P2P), pp. 191–202 (2012)
14. Mega, G., Montresor, A., Picco, G.P.: Efficient dissemination in decentralized social networks.. In: Peer-to-Peer Computing, pp. 338–347 (2011)
15. Montresor, A., Jelasity, M.: Peersim: A scalable p2p simulator. In: Schulzrinne, H., Aberer, K., Datta, A. (eds.) Peer-to-Peer Computing, pp. 99–100 (2009)
16. Roberts, S.G., Dunbar, R.I.M., Pollet, T.V., Kuppens, T.: Exploring variation in active network size: Constraints and ego characteristics. Social Networks 31 (February 2009)
17. Sharma, R., Datta, A.: Supernova: Super-peers based architecture for decentralized online social networks. In: COMSNETS, pp. 1–10 (2012)
18. Sutcliffe, A., Dunbar, R.I.M., Binder, J., Arrow, H.: Relationships and the social brain: integrating psychological and evolutionary perspectives. British Journal of Psychology 103, 149–168 (2011)
19. Wilson, C., Sala, C., Puttaswamy, K.P.N., Zhao, B.Y.: Beyond social graphs: User interactions in online social networks and their implications. TWEB 6(4), 17 (2012)

Hierarchical Approach for Green Workload Management in Distributed Data Centers

Agostino Forestiero[1], Carlo Mastroianni[1], Michela Meo[2],
Giuseppe Papuzzo[1], and Mehdi Sheikhalishahi[3]

[1] ICAR-CNR and Eco4Cloud srl, Rende (CS), Italy
[2] Politecnico di Torino, Italy
[3] University of Calabria, Rende (CS), Italy

Abstract. The efficient management of geographically distributed data centers has become an important issue not only for big companies that own several sites, but also due to the emerging of inter-Cloud infrastructures that allow heterogeneous data centers to cooperate. These environments open unprecedented avenues for the support of a huge amount of workload, but they need the definition of novel algorithms and procedures for their management, where scalability is a priority. The complexity derives by the size of the system and by the need for accomplishing several and sometimes conflicting goals, among which: load balancing among multiple sites, prevention of risks, workload consolidation, and reduction of costs, consumed energy and carbon emissions. In this paper a hierarchical approach is presented, which preserves the autonomy of single data centers and at the same time allows for an integrated management of heterogeneous platforms. The framework is purposely generic but can be tailored to the specific requirements of single environments. Performances are analyzed for a specific Cloud infrastructure composed of four data centers.

Keywords: Cloud Computing, Distributed Data Center, Energy Saving.

1 Introduction

The ever increasing demand for computing resources has led companies and resource providers to build private warehouse-sized data centers, or to offload applications to the data centers owned by a Cloud company. Overall, data centers require a significant amount of power to be operated. The total electricity demand of data centers increased by about 56% from 2005 to 2010, and the electricity usage accounted for about 1.5% of the worldwide electricity usage in 2010 [6], which is comparable to the aviation industry. The financial impact for the data center management is also huge, since a data center spends between 30% to 50% of its operational expense toward electricity. The efficient utilization of resources in these data centers is therefore essential to reduce costs, energy consumption, carbon emissions and also to ensure a high quality of service to users.

The virtualization technology allows multiple Virtual Machines (VMs) to be run on the same physical server. Although this helps to increase the efficiency of data centers,

L. Lopes et al. (Eds.): Euro-Par 2014 Workshops, Part I, LNCS 8805, pp. 323–334, 2014.

the optimal distribution of the applications to servers [1] is still an open problem, especially in large and dynamic systems. The problem is even more complex in geographically distributed data centers, whose adoption is rapidly increasing. They are deployed by major cloud service providers, such as Amazon, Google, and Microsoft, to match the increasing demand for resilient and low-latency cloud services, or to interconnect heterogenous data centers owned by different companies, in the so-called "Inter-Cloud" scenario. In such environments, data centers offer different and time-varying energy prices, and workload variability is experienced both within single sites and across the whole infrastructure.

The dynamic migration of workload among data centers has become an opportunity to improve several aspects: better resiliency and failover management, improved load balancing, and exploitation of the the "follow the moon" paradigm, i.e., move the workload where the energy is cheaper/cleaner and/or cooling costs are lower. Intersite migration is enabled by the availability of a much higher network capacity, thanks to both physical improvements (e.g., through techniques such as wavelength division multiplexing) and logical/functional enhancements (e.g., the adoption of Software Defined Networks). Reliable and low-latency connections can be used to shift significant amount of workload from one site to another through dedicated networks or even via regular Internet connections.

Nonetheless, these advancements do not reduce the complexity of the involved issues, among which: determine whether the benefits of workload migrations may overcome the drawbacks, from which site and to which site to migrate, what specific portion of the workload should be migrated, how to reassign the migrating workload in the target site, etc. Some significant efforts have been done in this area. The electricity price variation, both across time and location, is exploited to reduce overall costs using different strategies, among which: the Stratus approach [2] exploits Voronoi partitions to determine to which data center requests should be routed; the algorithm proposed by Mehta et al. [9] assigns virtual machines to servers using a constraint programming approach; Ren at al. [10] use an online scheduling algorithm based on Lyapunov optimization techniques. The algorithms presented in [7] and [4] tackle the problem considering the user's point of view, and aim to choose the most convenient data center to which the user should consign a service or VM.

However, the cited approaches, as well as many others, aim to solve the optimization problem as a whole, in a centralized fashion, undergoing the risk of originating two main issues: (i) algorithms of this kind may be poorly scalable, both for the number of parameters that they must consider and for the huge size of the problem, as it may involve tens of thousand of servers; (ii) they generally assume that all sites share the same strategy and algorithms, which may hamper their autonomy. The need for autonomous management is self-explanatory in multi-owned data centers, and is crucial even within a single-owner infrastructure, for example in the case that one or several sites are the former asset of an acquired company, or are hosted by co-located multi-tenant facilities.

A self-organizing hierarchical architecture is proposed in [3], but it is limited to the management of a single data center. This paper presents EcoMultiCloud, a hierarchical framework for the distribution and consolidation of the workload on a multi-site platform. The framework allows for an integrated and homogeneous management of heterogeneous platforms but at the same time preserves the autonomy of single sites. It is composed of two layers: at the lower layer, each site adopts its own strategy to distribute and consolidate the workload internally. At the upper layer, a set of algorithms – shared by all the sites – are used to evaluate the behavior of single sites and distribute the workload among them, both at the time that new applications/VMs are assigned and when some workload migration from one site to another is deemed appropriate. At each site one server is elected as point of contact (PoC) and periodically sends to other sites' PoCs a number of parameters that summarize the state of the site, possibly including the overall utilization of resources, the efficiency of computation, the energy costs, the amount of CO_2 emissions, etc. Upon reception of such data from the other sites, the PoC executes the upper layer algorithms to: (i) determine the target data center to which a new application should be assigned; (ii) check if the workload is well balanced among the different sites, and (iii) trigger migration of applications when needed. This strategy resembles the one used to cope with traffic routing in the Internet, where a single protocol – Border Gateway Protocol – is used to interconnect different Autonomous Systems (ASs), while every AS is free to choose its own protocol – e.g., RIP or OSPF – for internal traffic management.

The reminder of the paper is organized as follows: Section 2 describes the EcoMultiCloud architecture and illustrates the roles and objectives of two layers; Section 3 describes the algorithm used by the upper layer for the assignment of Virtual Machines; Section 4 analyzes the performance of the assignment algorithm in terms of carbon emissions and load balancing and compares EcoMultiCloud with a reference algorithm; Finally, Section 5 concludes the paper.

2   Architecture for Inter-DC Workload Distribution

This section describes the hierarchical architecture of EcoMultiCloud for the efficient management of the workload in a multi-site scenario. The architecture is composed of two layers: (i) the *upper layer* is used to exchange information among the different sites and drive the distribution of Virtual Machines among the data centers and (ii) the *lower layer* is used to allocate the workload within single data centers.

EcoMultiCloud extends the decentralized/self-organizing approach, recently presented in [8], for the consolidation of the workload in a single data center. The single data center solution, referred to as EcoCloud, dynamically consolidates Virtual Machines (VMs) to the minimum number of servers, and allows the remaining servers to enter low consuming sleep modes. With EcoCloud key decisions regarding the local data center are delegated to single servers, which autonomously decide whether or not to accommodate a VM or trigger a VM migration. The data center manager has only a co-ordination role. In a similar fashion, at the upper level of the multi-site EcoMultiCloud architecture, most of the intelligence is left to single data centers which, for example, decide which information is relevant and should be delivered to other data centers, which portion of the local workload should be migrated elsewhere, etc. Coordinating decisions, for example about the necessity of migrating an amount of workload from one site to another, are taken combining the information related to single data centers. Beyond decentralization, a key feature of EcoMultiCloud is its modularity: provided

that the interface between the lower and the upper layer is preserved, each layer is free
to modify the respective algorithms and their implementation. At the lower layer, each
data center is fully autonomous, and can manage the internal workload using either
EcoCloud or any other consolidation algorithm. So different data centers can adopt different internal algorithms. On the other hand, the upper layer algorithms may be tuned
or modified without causing any impact on the operation of single sites.

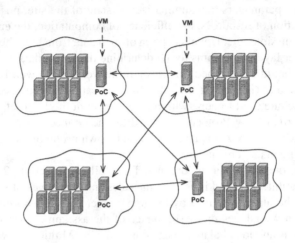

Fig. 1. EcoMultiCloud scenario: the PoCs of the different data centers exchange high level information about the state of local data centers. Such information is used, for example, to decide
which site should accommodate a new VM.

The reference scenario is depicted in Figure 1, which shows four interconnected data
centers. Each data center elects a single Point of Contact (PoC), a software that in the
most typical case may be deployed on the same host as the manager of the local virtualization infrastructure, e.g., the vCenter in the case of VMware. The PoC integrates the
information coming from the lower layer and uses it to implement the functionalities
of the upper layer. The PoC is required to: (i) communicate with the local data center manager in order to acquire detailed knowledge about the current state of the local
data center, for example regarding the usage of host resources and the state of running
VMs; (ii) extract relevant high level information about the state of the data center; (iii)
transmit/receive such high level information to/from all the other PoCs; (iv) execute the
algorithms of the upper layer to combine the collected information and take decisions
about the distribution of the workload among the data centers. For example, the assignment algorithm is used to decide to which data center a new VM should be assigned.
Once the VM is delivered to the target site, this will use the lower layer algorithms to
assign the VM to a specific host.

The framework is designed so that all the PoCs are able to execute the upper layer
algorithms and, for example, choose the target DC for a VM originated locally. This
requires an all-to-all data transmission among the PoCs, but this is not an issue due to
the relatively low number of interconnected sites and the tiny amount of transmitted

data. Indeed, in a multi-site scenario the choice of a single coordination point would be unappropriate for both technical and administrative reasons.

Since the single data centers are autonomous regarding the choice of the internal algorithms for workload management, this paper focuses on the algorithms of the upper layer. At least three algorithms must be executed at each PoC: (i) an assignment algorithm that determines the appropriate target data center for each new VM; (ii) a redistribution algorithm that periodically evaluates whether the current load balance is appropriate and, if necessary, decides whether an amount of workload should be migrated to/from another site; (iii) a migration algorithm that determines to which target site or from which source site the workload should be migrated.

The assignment algorithm is the core one: it has the primary role of distributing the workload of new VMs on the basis of a set of objectives decided by the management and pertaining to costs, consumed energy, carbon emissions, load balancing, etc. The other two algorithms are tailored to the dynamic redistribution of the workload. They share the same objectives of the assignment algorithm, but may take into account additional considerations, among which: the tolerance admitted on the achievement of the objectives, the limits on the frequency of migrations and on the amount of migrated data, the balance between benefits and costs related to migrations etc. This work focuses on the assignment algorithm and leaves the analysis of workload migration to future research.

3   Multi-site Assignment Algorithm

As mentioned in the previous section, a key responsibility of the PoC is to analyze detailed data about the local data center and summarize relevant information that is then transmitted to remote PoCs and used for the assignment and redistribution of workload. The nature of the high level information depends on the objectives that must be achieved. Some important goals are:

1. Reduction of costs. The cost associated to the execution of a given workload depends on many factors, among which the cost of power needed for computation, for cooling and for power distribution, the costs related to staff, servers maintenance, etc. An important element to consider is that the cost of electricity is generally different from site to site and also varies with time, even on a hour-to-hour basis, therefore the overall cost may be reduced by shifting portions of the workload to more convenient sites;
2. Reduction of consumed energy. The amount of consumed energy is generally easier to evaluate than the costs, as moderns data centers are equipped with sensors that monitor the power usage in computational resources. The total power may be obtained by multiplying the power consumed for computation by the PUE (Power Usage Efficiency) index;
3. Reduction of carbon emissions. Companies are today strongly encouraged to reduce the amount of carbon emissions, not only to compel to laws and rules, but also to advertise their green effort and attract customers that are increasingly careful about sustainability issues;
4. Quality of service. The workload must be distributed without overloading any single site, as this may affect the quality of the service perceived by users. Moreover,

quality of service may be improved by properly combining and assigning applications having different characteristics, for example, CPU-bound and RAM-bound applications;

5. Load balancing. In a multi-DC environment, especially if managed by the same organization, it may be important to balance the load distributed to the different sites. Among the rationales are: a better balance may help improve the responsiveness of the sites, decrease the impact on physical infrastructure – e.g., in terms of cooling and power distribution – help to prevent overload situations.

6. Inter-DC data transmission. In some cases it is more efficient to assign a VM to the local data center, instead of delivering it to a more convenient remote data center, depending on many factors, among which the amount of data used by the VM, the available inter-DC bandwidth and the type of applications hosted by the VMs. For example, choosing a local data center is more convenient in the case that the VM hosts a database server, much less if it runs a Web service, especially in the frequent case that Web services are replicated on several data centers.

The goals are not independent from each other: for example, overall costs depend on the consumed power, while a good load balance may help improve the quality of service. All the mentioned goals are important, yet different data centers may focus on different aspects, depending on the specific operating conditions and on the priorities prescribed by the management. The assignment algorithm described in the following is specifically devised for the case in which the two primary objectives are the reduction of overall carbon emissions and the load balancing. These two goals are chosen because they are representative of two opposite needs, the need for optimizing the overall efficiency and the need for guaranteeing the fairness among data centers. However, the assignment algorithm can be easily adapted to a different choice of the objectives.

For the described scenario, the PoC of each data center collects two kinds of information: the overall utilization of the data center resources, separately computed for each resource type (CPU, RAM, disk memory etc.) and the carbon footprint rate of the servers. The overall utilization of CPU is computed as the total amount of CPU utilized by servers divided by the CPU capacity of the entire data center. The same type of computation is done for the other hardware resources. The bottleneck resource for a data center is the one with the largest utilization. The carbon footprint rate of a server s, c_s, is measured in Tons/MWh [5]. The contribution of a server to carbon emissions is computed by multiplying the carbon footprint rate by the energy it consumes. The overall carbon footprint of a data center can then be approximated by summing the contributions of the servers and then multiplying the obtained quantity by the data center PUE, which allows the contribution of the physical infrastructure to be considered. When assigning a VM, the target data center should be chosen so as to minimize the incremental increase of the carbon footprint and at the same time keep/improve the load balance among the data centers. To this aim, a PoC does not need to know the carbon footprint rate of all the servers of remote sites: it only needs to know, per each site, the *best available carbon footprint rate*, i.e., the minimum rate among the servers that are available to host the VM. In fact, if the assignment algorithms of local sites share the same goals, the VM will be assigned to a server with that value of the carbon footprint rate.

Following these considerations, the assignment algorithm requires that the PoC of a server i transmits to the others three very simple pieces of data: (i) the utilization of the bottleneck resource – denoted as U_i, (ii) the best available carbon footprint rate of a local server, c_s, and (iii) the data center PUE. The last two parameters may be combined, and the carbon parameter C_i of a data center i is defined as:

$$C_i = PUE_i \cdot min\{c_s|\ server\ s\ is\ available\} \tag{1}$$

In a data center many servers have the same characteristics, for example the servers included in the same rack/cluster. Therefore, the computation of C_i can be simplified by considering the carbon emission rate of each cluster instead of each server, and by evaluating the "*is available*" condition for entire clusters as well. Knowing the values of C_i and U_i for each remote data center, the PoC can now choose the best target data center for a VM. For each data center i, the function f^i_{assign} is computed as follows:

$$f^i_{assign} = \beta \cdot \frac{C_i}{C_{max}} + (1 - \beta) \cdot \frac{U_i}{U_{max}} \tag{2}$$

In the expression, values of C_i are normalized with respect to the maximum value communicated by the data centers, and the same is done with U_i. The two mentioned goals – reduction of carbon emissions and load balancing – are weighted through a parameter β, having value between 0 and 1. After computing the values of f_{assign} for each data center, the VM is assigned to the data center having the lowest value. Depending on the value of β this may correspond to giving higher priority to the reduction of carbon emissions (values of β closer to 1) or to the fair balance of load (values of β closer to 0). Expression (2) can be easily generalized to the cases that more or different objectives are chosen.

```
function EcoMultiCloud-AssignmentAlgorithm(β)
    while VM arrives
        for each remote datacenter DCᵢ
            Request Cᵢ, Uᵢ parameters
        end for
        Cmax = Max{Cᵢ| i = 1···N_DC}
        Umax = Max{Uᵢ| i = 1···N_DC}
        for each DCᵢ : DCᵢ is not full, that is, Uᵢ < U_Tᵢ
            f^i_assign = β · Cᵢ/Cmax + (1 − β) · Uᵢ/Umax
        end for
        DCtarget = DCⱼ such that f^j_assign = min{f^i_assign| i = 1···N_DC}
        Assign VM to DCtarget
    end while
end function
```

Fig. 2. The EcoMultiCloud assignment algorithm

Figure 2 reports the pseudo-code used by a data center PoC to choose the target data center, among the N_{DC} data centers of the system, for a VM originated locally. First, the PoC requests the values of U_i and C_i to all the remote data centers[1]. Then, it computes the maximum values of both parameters, for the normalization, and computes the expression (2) for any data center that has some spare capacity, i.e., for which the utilization of the bottleneck resource does not exceed a given threshold U_{T_i}. Finally, the VM is assigned to the data center that has the lowest value of expression (2). Once consigned to the target data center, the VM will be allocated to a physical host using the local assignment algorithm. This paper does not focus specifically on the inter-DC migration of VMs. However the same algorithm, or a variant, may be used to determine the target data center of a VM that is being migrated.

4   Performance Evaluation of the Assignment Algorithm

To correctly evaluate the performance of the EcoMultiCloud assignment algorithm, it is necessary to prove that the hierarchical approach – according to which the VM is assigned in two steps, first to a target data center, then to a physical host – does not cause a performance degradation with respect to a single layer algorithm that has full visibility about all VMs and servers. Such a confirmation would suggest the choice of the hierarchical approach, which offers notable advantages in terms of scalability, autonomy of sites, overall administration, information management.

To this aim, we take as a reference a single level/centralized assignment algorithm presented and evaluated in [5]. The reference algorithm, called ECE (Energy and Carbon-Efficient VM Placement Algorithm) considers all the clusters of the distributed architecture and sorts them with respect to the value of (PUE x carbon footprint rate). Each VM is assigned to the available cluster with the minimum value and then, within that cluster, is assigned to the most power-efficient server. In [5] it is shown that this algorithm performs better than a number of other common heuristics based on the First Fit approach. Comparison is made to the hierarchical EcoMultiCloud approach, where the upper layer assignment algorithm is the one described in Section 3, while the lower layer algorithm is ECE, applied not the whole system but to single data centers.

For a fair comparison we consider the same scenario as [5], with four interconnected data centers having values of PUE and carbon footprint rate as reported in Table 1. Each data center includes two "rooms", a room A with newer and more efficient servers and a room B with older and less efficient servers. A data center has a single value of PUE, but two different values of carbon footprint rate for the two rooms.

Data about VMs and physical hosts was taken from the logs of a real Proof of Concept performed by the company Eco4Cloud srl (www.eco4cloud.com), spin-off from the National Research Council of Italy, on the data center of a telecommunications operator. The data center contains 56 servers virtualized with the platform VMware vSphere 5.0. Among the servers, 38 are equipped with processor Xeon 24 cores and 100-GB RAM, and 18 with processor Xeon 16 cores and 64-GB RAM. All the servers have network adapters with bandwidth of 10 Gbps. The servers hosted 992 VMs which

---

[1] As an alternative, values can be transmitted periodically in a push fashion. In both cases the amount of transmitted information is tiny.

Table 1. PUE and carbon footprint rate of the four data centers in the considered scenario

Data center	PUE	Carbon footprint rate (Tons/MWh)	
		Room A	Room B
DC 1	1.56	0.124	0.147
DC 2	1.7	0.350	0.658
DC 3	1.9	0.466	0.782
DC 4	2.1	0.678	0.730

were assigned a number of virtual cores varying between 1 and 8 and an amount of RAM varying between 1 GB and 16 GB. Servers and VMs were replicated for all the rooms of the considered scenario, and only the values of PUE and carbon footprint rate were differentiated as described in Table 1. The most utilized resource in this scenario is the RAM, therefore the RAM utilization of data centers is considered when computing expression (2). A constraint imposed by the data center administrators was that the utilization of server resources cannot exceed 80%. The *overall load* of the entire system, used as a parameter in the evaluation, is defined as ratio between the total amount of RAM utilized by the VMs and the RAM capacity of the system.

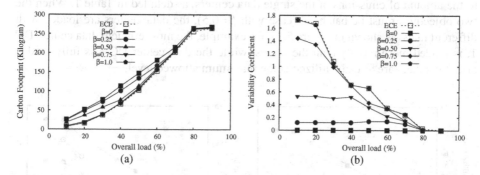

Fig. 3. Total carbon footprint (a) and variability coefficient (b) vs. the overall load with different values of the parameter β

The performances have been analyzed with an event-based Java simulator that has been previously validated with respect to real data for the case of a single data center [8]. The VMs are assigned one by one executing the described assignment algorithm at the data center where each VM is located. Figure 3 shows the performance of the assignment algorithm versus the overall load of the system, when using values of β equal to 0 (such a value means that the load balance is the only goal), 0.25, 0.50, 0.75 and 1 (the only goal is the reduction of carbon footprint). The two plots report two indices: the total carbon footprint (a) and the variability coefficient (b). The latter is used as an index for the load balance and is computed by considering the RAM utilization of the four data centers and dividing the standard deviation by the average. We prefer the variability coefficient rather then the standard deviation because this helps to highlight relative rather than absolute deviations with respect to the average.

The performance of the single level ECE algorithm is also reported for comparison. As the two objectives are contrasting, a higher value of β allows the carbon footprint to be decreased, but at the expense of a greater load imbalance. It is interesting to notice that the values obtained with $\beta=1$ are almost equal to those obtained with the single level algorithm. This is consistent with the fact that the ECE algorithm does not consider the load balance as an objective. More importantly, this means that the hierarchical approach does not cause any performance degradation regarding the two considered metrics, which corresponds to the desired behavior, as said at the beginning of this section.

Depending on the management requirements, a proper value of β can be set accordingly. For example, if a constraint is given either on the admitted degree of load imbalance or on the overall carbon emissions, the value of β can be set so as to respect the constraint while optimizing the value of the other goal. This optimization analysis is left to future work. In the following, we analyze the behavior observed with specific values of β. Figures 4, 5 and 6 show the values of RAM utilization and carbon footprint rate for the single data centers, with values of β equal to 0, 0.5 and 1, respectively. From Figure 4 we can analyze the case where the only goal to be achieved is a fair load balance. Indeed, the servers are all utilized at the same level, whatever is the overall load, as seen in Figure 4(a), while Figure 4(b) shows that the carbon footprint is proportional to the amount of emissions of the single data centers, as detailed in Table 1. When the two objectives must be balanced (case with $\beta=0.5$), the data centers are loaded with different rates, as shown in Figure 5(a): for example, the most efficient data center, DC 1, is loaded more rapidly than the others, while the data center DC 4 is fully loaded after the others are already utilized at the maximum allowed level.

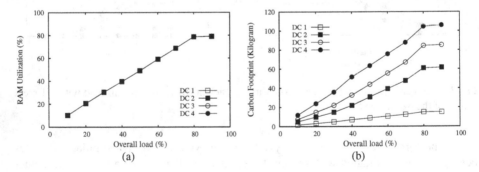

Fig. 4. RAM utilization (a) and carbon footprint (b) of the four data centers vs. the overall load with $\beta=0$

Figure 6 focuses on the case in which we are only interested is the reduction of carbon emissions. The two plots show that the data centers are loaded in an order that corresponds to their efficiency. Even more, we can notice that the order is respected also with reference to single data center rooms. For example, after DC 1 is fully loaded, the VMs are first assigned to Room A of DC 2, than to Room A of DC 3, then to Room B of DC 2, and so on. It may be easily verified that this order follows the values of (PUE x carbon footprint rates) of the different rooms, as reported in Table 1. It is noticed

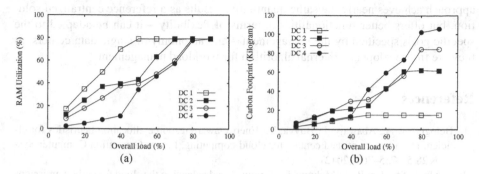

Fig. 5. RAM utilization (a) and carbon footprint (b) of the four data centers vs. the overall load with β=0.5

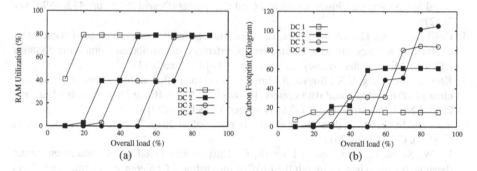

Fig. 6. RAM utilization (a) and carbon footprint (b) of the four data centers vs. the overall load with β=1

that the curves of carbon footprint, in Figure 6(b), intersect among each other: with a low overall load, carbon footprint emissions are larger in more efficient data centers, because these are the first to be loaded; with a high overall load, all the data centers are highly utilized and the least efficient are those that cause the highest carbon emissions.

5   Conclusions

This paper has presented EcoMultiCloud, a hierarchical approach that aims to improve the workload management of a multi-site data center. The related architecture comprises two layers, the upper layer for the assignment/migration of workload among remote sites, and the lower layer that assigns Virtual Machines to physical hosts within every local site. The approach is flexible and can be utilized to achieve and balance different goals, among which reductions of costs/consumed energy/carbon emissions, load balancing, etc. The paper has focused on the analysis of a four-site system in the case that the goals to be achieved are the reduction of carbon emissions and the load balancing among data centers. Performance analysis has proven that the hierarchical approach achieves nearly the same quantitative results as a reference centralized solution, but offers better functionalities in terms of flexibility – it can be adapted to the specific goals specified by the management – and autonomy of single data centers, as they are free to adopt any internal algorithm for workload management.

References

1. Beloglazov, A., Abawajy, J., Buyya, R.: Energy-aware resource allocation heuristics for efficient management of data centers for cloud computing. Future Generation Computer Systems 28(5), 755–768 (2012)
2. Doyle, J., Shorten, R., O'Mahony, D.: Stratus: Load balancing the cloud for carbon emissions control. IEEE Transactions on Cloud Computing 1(1), 116–128 (2013)
3. Feller, E., Rilling, L., Morin, C.: Snooze: A scalable and autonomic virtual machine management framework for private clouds. In: Proceedings of the 2012 12th IEEE/ACM International Symposium on Cluster, Cloud and Grid Computing (Ccgrid 2012), pp. 482–489 (May 2012)
4. Goiri, I., Le, K., Guitart, J., Torres, J., Bianchini, R.: Intelligent placement of datacenters for internet services. In: 31st International Conference onDistributed Computing Systems (ICDCS), Minneapolis, Minnesota, USA, pp. 131–142 (June 2011)
5. Khosravi, A., Garg, S.K., Buyya, R.: Energy and carbon-efficient placement of virtual machines in distributed cloud data centers. In: Wolf, F., Mohr, B., an Mey, D. (eds.) Euro-Par 2013. LNCS, vol. 8097, pp. 317–328. Springer, Heidelberg (2013)
6. Koomey, J.: Growth in data center electricity use 2005 to 2010. Tech. rep., Analytics Press, Oakland, CA (August 2011)
7. Li, W., Svärd, P., Tordsson, J., Elmroth, E.: Cost-optimal cloud service placement under dynamic pricing schemes. In: 6th IEEE/ACM International Conference on Utility and Cloud Computing, Dresden, Germany, pp. 187–194 (2013)
8. Mastroianni, C., Meo, M., Papuzzo, G.: Probabilistic consolidation of virtual machines in self-organizing cloud data centers. IEEE Transactions on Cloud Computing 1(2), 215–228 (2013)
9. Mehta, D., OSullivan, B., Simonis, H.: Energy cost management for geographically distributed data centres under time-variable demands and energy prices. In: 6th IEEE/ACM International Conference on Utility and Cloud Computing, Dresden, Germany, pp. 26–33 (December 2013)
10. Ren, S., He, Y., Xu, F.: Provably-efficient job scheduling for energy and fairness in geographically distributed data centers. In: 2012 IEEE 32nd International Conference on Distributed Computing Systems (ICDCS), pp. 22–31 (June 2012)

Network Based Malware Detection within Virtualised Environments

Pushpinder Kaur Chouhan, Matthew Hagan,
Gavin McWilliams, and Sakir Sezer

Centre for Secure Information Technologies,
Queens University of Belfast, Northern Ireland, UK

Abstract. While virtualisation can provide many benefits to a networks infrastructure, securing the virtualised environment is a big challenge. The security of a fully virtualised solution is dependent on the security of each of its underlying components, such as the hypervisor, guest operating systems and storage.

This paper presents a single security service running on the hypervisor that could potentially work to provide security service to all virtual machines running on the system. This paper presents a hypervisor hosted framework which performs specialised security tasks for all underlying virtual machines to protect against any malicious attacks by passively analysing the network traffic of VMs. This framework has been implemented using Xen Server and has been evaluated by detecting a Zeus Server setup and infected clients, distributed over a number of virtual machines. This framework is capable of detecting and identifying all infected VMs with no false positive or false negative detection.

1 Introduction

Cloud Computing is a technology which allows consumers access to a broad range of computing resources, products and stored information whenever they need them, where ever they need them, using a variety of devices. Cloud Computing services are marketed as a utility in a similar manner to traditional electricity, gas, water and telephony provision. The simplicity and scalability that cloud computing offers has attracted the attention of both private citizens and enterprises. Virtualisation is the fundamental technology that enables cloud computing and differentiates it from traditional IT deployments by dramatically improving machine utilisation and reducing overall total cost of ownership.

Virtualisation is the emulation of the software and/or hardware platforms upon which other software and operating systems run. Ideally, virtualisation allows us to build an environment that enables one computer to perform the tasks of multiple diverse computing platforms, by sharing the resources of a single hardware platform across multiple virtual systems. An emulated system is called a virtual machine. The operating system installed in a virtual machine is called a guest operating system.

The guest operating systems on a host are managed by either a hypervisor or a Virtual Machine Monitor. This additional software layer controls the flow

L. Lopes et al. (Eds.): Euro-Par 2014 Workshops, Part I, LNCS 8805, pp. 335–346, 2014.

of instructions between the guest operating systems and the physical hardware e.g. the CPU, disk storage, memory, and network interface cards. A Virtual Machine Monitor (VMM) is a software solution that implements virtualisation in conjunction with or on top of the physical machine's host operating system. In contrast, a hypervisor runs directly on the physical hardware without any intervention from the host operating system. Fig. 1 shows the different level of virtualisation.

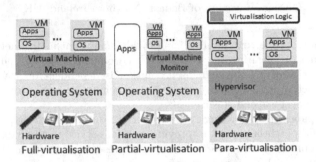

Fig. 1. Level of Virtualisation

In full virtualisation, complete simulation of the actual underlying hardware allows guest operating systems to run unmodified. In partial virtualisation, the virtual machine simulates multiple instances of much of an underlying environment particularly address spaces. In para-virtualisation, the guest operating system needs to be modified to run on top of the hypervisor to access the underlying hardware inside a virtual machine. In hardware assisted virtualisation, the hardware provides architectural support that facilitates building a hypervisor. Hardware-assisted virtualisation enables efficient virtualisation through the use of advanced microprocessors such as Intel VT-x features or AMD-V processor series.

A great advantage of virtualisation is the increase in operational efficiency made by sharing the load of multiple physical systems on a single computer. This provides a potential security benefit by offering a single, centralised platform on which security applications can run. In theory, a single security service running on the hypervisor could potentially work to provide security to all virtual machines running on the system, so long as the virtual machine data is accessible to the hypervisor.

This paper will describe the design and implementation of a hypervisor based framework, which performs specialised security tasks for all underlying guest virtual machines. The aim of this paper is to introduce the following contributions: (1) a new framework for dynamic behaviour-based malware detection in the virtualised environment; (2) a working prototype of this framework; and (3) an evaluation of the proposed framework, validating the feasibility, efficiency and accuracy of its operation.

The rest of the paper is organised as follows. Section 2 describes how the proposed framework relates to and complements the related work in this area. Section 3 explains the framework, its components and mentions the tools and technique used to implemented the framework. Section 4 presents the framework validation results and finally, Section 5 presents the conclusion.

2   Related Work

Malware (malicious software) is a class of software used to disrupt computer operation, gather sensitive information (data and identity theft), or manipulate data within the system (system and data corruption). Malware is any program or file that is harmful to a computer or end-user which is installed without proper consent of the owner. Malware includes computer viruses, worms, Trojan horses, and also spyware, programs that profiles user behaviour.

Researchers are providing new techniques to counter the malware attacks [10,14,4]. One of these approaches is through the use of host based applications to scan the hard disk and memory for known malicious applications or malware traits within executable files. However, malware developers have refined their techniques, with the introduction sophisticated methods such as polymorphism (different encryptions of the same binary) and metamorphism (different code for the same functionality).

Another malware detection technique is to identify the symptoms of malicious behaviour. [10] presented a method that looks for the malware symptoms by using Forensic Virtual Machines (FVMs). FVMs report to a Command & Control module that collects and correlates information so as to take remedial actions in real-time. This method shows effective detection of malware but the main drawback is that an FVM is required for each malicious symptom.

In traditional host based antivirus software, suspicious programs are run in a protected sandbox. If malicious activity is detected then the file can be blacklisted immediately. The sandbox will not operate in a completely isolated network environment and hence there is a small residual risk associated with this technique. Scalability may also cause problems in that it is not possible to provide a sandbox for every device/environment present within an enterprise. To overcome these problems, AV vendors have started to leverage the cloud to track the reputation of individual files.

CloudAV [14] is a program that provides antivirus protection as a cloud service. CloudAV allows the user to take advantage of multiple antivirus programs without running them locally so the user's computer performance is not affected. The program uses a technique called N-version protection to identify malicious software by using multiple, heterogeneous antivirus detection engines in parallel. However, file hashes and byte (or intrusion) signatures can be obfuscated through the use of polymorphism. In addition, the CloudAV is reliant on signature based antivirus products which may not detect new malware quickly enough. The latency window of exposure (when attack occurs and when specific malware files are known) has to be taken into account.

Some researchers have proposed a twin track solution to protecting the privacy of Cloud Service user data. By separating trusted computing on to one cloud service and passing all other data to a second cloud service. More generally they propose clouds for separate computation of arbitrary functions according to different security and performance criteria. TwinClouds [4], by using two clouds, raises redundancy and privacy issues relating to the use of shared storage mechanisms.

Terra [7] is a VM-based architecture for supporting various security models on a single physical machine by combining the good aspects of closed and open box platforms. In closed box platform service provider has control over applications, content, and media, and restricts convenient access to non-approved applications or content. Where as in open platform consumers have unrestricted access to applications, content, and much more. Terra considers the implementation of a trusted virtual machine monitor on top of trusted platform module. The Trusted Virtual Machine Monitor verifies that hosts are trusted by the cloud service user. Terra prevents the owner (Cloud service provider) of a physical host from inspecting and interfering with the computation of a running VM in a trusted host.

Trusted Cloud Computing Platform (TCCP) provides a closed box execution environment which makes the computation taking place in a virtual machine confidential to privileged users. Thus, if TCCP [16] is deployed by a service provider such as Amazon EC2, cloud service users can verify that computation is confidential. Even a privileged user with access to the VM state cannot obtain user data. The main limitation of TCCP is that every virtual machine has to be launched on a trusted VMM which may reduce the elasticity feature of cloud computing.

Although frameworks such as Terra [7], TCP [17], TCCP [16], and improved-TCCP [9], allow users to attest whether the service is secure and/or running on a secure host before the launch of virtual machine, however, after the launch of a virtual machine an attack by an external bot has to be determined by other means. Thus, our proposed framework is complementary to existing trusted cloud computing frameworks.

ReVirt [5] is a virtual machine based logging and replay system that attempts to address the lack of completeness provided by traditional system loggers. Re-Virt logs instruction level detail for each virtual machine and then carries out analysis looking for malicious activity. However, the main drawback of this system is that it too may leak sensitive information if the logs are not well protected. Our framework overcomes this drawback, as all the sensitive and malware related information is stored on a separate secure system.

Many other VMM based security systems (LiveWire [8], Siren [3], SubVirt [12], VM-based IDS [19,1]) have been developed based on VM-isolation, VMM-inspection and VMM-interposition capabilities. However, to construct a truly effective and efficient virtual machine monitor based security system the functionality of the previously mentioned detect malicious activities in real-time. Our proposed framework features network (VM communication) based malware detection in real time. The network traffic analysis is useful in malware detection in virtualised environments as it allows us to observe a wide range of behaviour e.g. browser requests, sending an email or a file transfer. The attacker may use the victims network connection to perform malicious activities, such as participate in DDoS attacks, connect to a malicious command and control server, or other attacks. The network activity may also consist of data exfiltration, whereby confidential information may be extracted from the machine, through various automated or manual methods, and transmitted to the attacker.

In virtualised environments all virtual machine network traffic must pass through the hypervisor. Hence there is an opportunity for the hypervisor to passively observe this network activity to perform malware detection. It is envisaged that upon the detection of malware activity, the hypervisor can log activity or interact with the infected virtual machine by shutting it down or providing a warning message to the user. The concept of network based analysis to detect malware behaviour through network analysis is complementary to host-based malware detection techniques (signature-based, symptoms-based, etc.) used for Virtual Environment protection.

3   Malware Detection System for Virtual Environments

The Malware Detection System for Virtual Environments (MDSVE) observes network traffic and identifies any patterns and trends that indicate activities which can potentially have malicious effects on the virtualised environment. The overall functionality of MDSVE is to capture the network traffic of each virtual machine and build useful contextual information to aide traffic analysis. Detected threats will precipitate security alerts or direct action on the VMs involved. Tasks performed by MDSVE are:

1. Track virtual machine lifecycle
2. Monitor virtual machine communications i.e. internal communications between VMs in the same physical host, and external communications traversing a network interface card on the physical host
3. Capture malware activities
4. Match any suspicious activities with the corresponding virtual machine.
5. Inform management console about suspicious virtual machine instances.

3.1   Components of MDSVE

The MDSVE is made up of four basic functional blocks: network sniffer, malware trait detector, virtual machine information collector, and virtualisation security manager, as shown in Fig. 2.

Network Sniffer- (NS) captures all of the network packets in real-time and performs flow classification. That is, all packets relating to a logical session are linked together and offered up for further analysis as a contiguous flow of traffic.

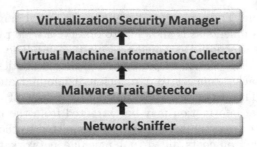

Fig. 2. Architecture of Malware Detection System for Virtual Environment

A PCAP library based platform called ITACA (Internet Content and Traffic analysis) [11] is used for this purpose.

Malware Trait Detector- (MTD), analyses the complete flow looking for series of events and features which indicate the presence of specific malware. Some malware detection techniques and tools make use of network analysis; for example, Bothunter [15] attempts to identify generic traits within network traffic, such as malware downloaded.

Virtual Machine Information Collector- (VMIC) monitors the virtual machine life cycle and captures the virtual machine status along with basic parameters so as to match the virtual machine with the suspicious bot as analysed by the malware analyser and alerts the virtualisation security manager.

Virtualisation Security Manager- (VSM) acts as a security console displaying the alerts and information provided by the VMIC. If malware is detected on any of the virtual machines, then according to the severity of the threat VSM can take action accordingly. For example, inform host based anti-virus system, sinkhole traffic destined to the virtual machine, or even suspend the virtual machine.

3.2   Setup Malware Detection System for Virtual Environment

Based on our framework, a prototype of MDSVE was implemented using some pre-existing software and tools: Xen is used for the virtual environment setup, ITACA [11] is used to capture the network traffic, the Zeus [6] botnet server is used as the primary source of malware infection, and a Zeus malware detection plugin for ITACA [6] provides a malware trait detector. A new software component implements the VMIC functionality.

Xen Virtualised Environment- Xen [2] is used to build virtualised environment because virtualisation over head remain under 3% for virtualising Linux, FreeBSD and Windows XP. Xen [13] is an open-source native, type-1 or bare-metal hypervisor. A Xen guest typically has access to one or more paravirtualised (PV) network interfaces. These PV interfaces enable fast and efficient network communications for domains without the overhead of emulating a real network device.

A paravirtualised network device consists of a pair of network devices. The frontend will reside in the guest domain while the backend will reside in the backend domain (typically Dom0). A similar pair of devices is created for each virtual network interface. The front and backend devices are linked by a virtual communication channel. Frontend devices generate the traffic that has to be transported. Guest networking is achieved by arranging for traffic to pass from the backend device onto the wider network, using bridging, Network Address Translation or routing.

Network Sniffer- Internet Traffic And Content Analysis (ITACA) [11] is a network packet sniffer that monitors network traffic in real-time, scrutinizing each packet closely to detect a dangerous payload or suspicious anomalies, developed at CSIT, Queen's University of Belfast. ITACA is based on libpcap, a tool that is widely used in TCP/IP traffic sniffers and analysers. ITACA captures packet traffic and builds derived sets of data, from which the correctness of protocol formats are established. The ITACA platform enables the creation of sophisticated security analysis systems using modular plugin functions implemented in software and/or hardware.

ITACA has a three layer architecture; the network layer, the ITACA core and the plugin layer. The network layer interfaces with the network to extract the raw bytes of packet data using PCAP library. These captured bytes are passed to the ITACA core to extract and process all available information such as the 5-tuple (Source and Destination IP Address, Source and Destination Port Number and Protocol ID) which characterises a flow or logical session. The plugin layer is used to support multiple customised traffic treatments that operate independently and efficiently.

Plugins are created using a well-defined C++ API and make use of an event driven architecture optimised for multi-threaded operation.

ITACA is used to perform the task of two components in the MDSVE architecture; the network sniffer and the malware trait detector. The network layer and the ITACA core layer provide network sniffer functionality whereas the plugin layer provides the malware trait detector.

Malware Trait Detector- (MTD) is implemented by a malware detection plugin in ITACA. The Plugin layer of ITACA allows the implementation of specialist network analysis methods. During registration with ITACA, plugins specify the types of traffic that are of interest to them. Plugins operate in parallel to the ITACA core (and each other), allowing the running of additional plugins with limited effect on system performance.

For the prototype implementation of our framework, a Zeus detection plugin was deployed. Zeus was selected for testing because of its predominance it is the most popular botnet amongst online criminals, with a prevalence rate against other botnet software of 57.9% according to a recent McAfee study [18] which analysed half a million malware samples from January to March 2013.

The function of the Zeus botnet plugin is to analyse traffic and detect the periodic communication which takes place between an infected machine and the Zeus command and control servers. Rather than detecting the infection mechanism employed, which may include methods like browser exploitation or social engineering, the plugin only aims to detect malware network traffic activity, subsequent to infection.

Virtual Machine Information Collector- (VMIC) detects if any of the running VMs on a host are infected with malware. The function of VMIC is to correlate reports of malicious network activity (from the Zeus detector plugin) with the VM status tables i.e. to match the network activity with a running VM. The VMIC then inform the management console (VSM).

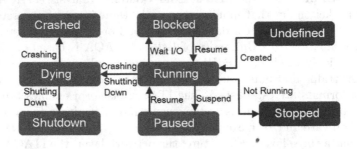

Fig. 3. Xen VM Lifecycle-flows from one state to another

Xen domain can be in one of the six states (shown in Fig. 3). A virtual machines state can be displayed in VMM or by viewing the results of the xm list command, which abbreviates the state using a single character.

r - running - The virtual machine is currently running and consuming allocated resources.

b - blocked - The virtual machines processor is not running and not able to run. It is either waiting for I/O or has stopped working.

p - paused - The virtual machine is paused. It does not interact with the hypervisor but still maintains its allocated resources, such as memory and semaphores.

s - shutdown - The guest operating system is in the process of being shutdown, rebooted, or suspended, and the virtual machine is being stopped.

c - crashed - The virtual machine has crashed and is not running.

d - dying - The virtual machine is in the process of shutting down or crashing.

Detailed information of each VM is collected and stored as a table of records which include the VMID, VMName, VM MAC address, installed OS on the VM, state and start time of the VM.

To find the malware infected virtual machine, the VMIC matches the MAC address of the virtual machine with the source or destination MAC address of the malicious network packet.

The virtual machine information table is updated dynamically as and when VM status changes occur. Reported Zeus botnet features are collected and evaluated for each VM instance. A threat index is calculated and when this exceeds a high-water mark the virtual machine is deemed to be malicious and the VSM is informed immediately.

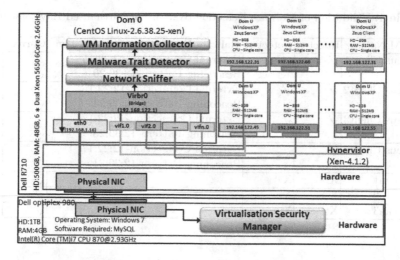

Fig. 4. Network Based Malware Detection System for Virtualised Environment

4   Validation of the Malware Detection System within a Virtualised Environment

The objective of this experiment is to validate that the proposed network-based malware detection framework is a viable solution for future cloud and application security. The validation requires that a small subset of virtual machines are infected with known malware creating a realistic scenario. It is also assumed that the virtual machines produce traffic patterns typical to virtualised environments. This section presents the experimental design, procedure and results to validate the proposed framework.

4.1   Experimental Setup

To evaluate the proposed framework, a prototype implementation was deployed within the hypervisor. The implementation consisted of the three essential components of the architecture: the network traffic analyser, the malware trait detector and the virtual machine information collector. A fourth component, the virtualisation security manager, was deployed on a separate machine acting as a security console. All four components run as independent processes. An SQLite database was used by the VMIC to store the VM information. The test-bed is shown in Fig. 4 with connectivity between a few VMs depicted.

Xens default network configuration was used, bridging within the backend domain (Dom-0). This allows all domains to appear on the network as individual systems. ITACA analyses all traffic traversing the default gateway (e.g. eth0) and any intra-VM communications on the virtual bridge.

Table 1. Validation of Malware Detection System For Virtualised Environment

VM Name	Infected	Detected	Malware Feature detected- at Time	Correct
Zeus Client1	√	√	External Connection-12:22:15 Beaconing Pattern-12:39:20	√
Zeus Client2	√	√	External Connection-12:22:15 Beaconing Pattern-12:39:24	√
Zeus Client3	√	√	External Connection-12:22:17 Beaconing Pattern-12:39:28	√
Zeus Client4	√	√	External Connection-12:22:17 Beaconing Pattern-12:39:31	√
Clean1	X	X		√
Clean2	X	X		√
Clean3	X	X		√

4.2   Network Traffic Capturing

To validate the proposed framework two types of virtual machines were launched in the testbed environment. 5 VMs are used to form a Zeus botnet (1 Zeus Server and 4 Zeus Clients) and 3 VMs are benign, which generate random traffic by running the web access applications (email, Dropbox, Facebook and Skype).

The network packets captured from traffic between VMs (VM-VM communication) and between VM and outside Virtual environment (VM-external machine communication) are analysed by the framework.

4.3   Experimental Result

Under default settings, firm detection of Zeus takes one hour, usually with a short additional time period to account for network connection latency. The default Zeus configuration beaconing period is 60 minutes with the shorter exfiltration event running every 20 minutes. The result of Zeus network traffic detection experiment is shown in Table 1. Infected VMs were detected by the proposed framework based on the Zeus detection features. The time delta between infection and Zeus feature detection demonstrates malware detection within reasonable time, assuming use of the default Zeus configuration. All infected VMs are detected, without false positives reported. These experiment results demonstrate correctness of the proposed framework.

4.4   Privacy and Security Issues

One area of concern is the fact that all network traffic captured is observed by software for the purposes of detecting malicious activity. This may raise privacy concerns with network operators and users, as network monitoring may be used for gaining information about network users. However, within this framework, network monitoring software will be run with the sole aim of detecting malicious activity, with only the VMID and IP addresses being reported during a suspicious event. While a false positive result may inadvertently disclose a connected IP address, the program will reveal no further information to an administrator. In terms of information observed, the detection system is no more intrusive than other commonly used IDS.

In terms of security, having a powerful monitoring entity on the hypervisor is potentially a concern, should the hypervisor be compromised. However, in order to attack users on the network, the attacker would need to install and utilise their own detection utility. The presence of the malware detection utility would have little relevance within this attack, since the attacker would merely be able to use the application as intended by the administrator or disable it, rather than use it maliciously.

5 Conclusion

In this paper, a new network based malware detection framework for virtualised environments has been proposed and experimentally proven. The proposed framework is advantageous in a number of ways. For example, the proposed system is scalable in that it can function with a high number of users and traffic while remaining functional. In terms of performance, under normal conditions, the overhead of deploying the system is negligible as only one additional application is needed on the hypervisor to detect malicious activity across all Virtual Machines. The framework is accurate, in that it divises a method of uniquely identifying a virtual machine based on its MAC address.

The proposed framework detected all the malware infected VMs without false positive or false negative detection of Zeus bot. This paper has shown that the work done by the forensic community in malware detection through network analysis is directly applicable to Virtual Environment malware detection. By providing interfaces between the two worlds, the difficulty of developing new virtual security solutions can be significantly reduced. It is envisaged that this work can be used as a basis for virtual machine security, in that a centralised hypervisor process can perform security related detection and scanning functions for all the virtual machines it is hosting. Such processes would enable greater convenience and security for the end user of the virtual machine, as well as decreasing security based application and management overhead.

References

1. Azmandian, F., Moffie, M., Alshawabkeh, M., Dy, J., Aslam, J., Kaeli, D.: Virtual machine monitor-based lightweight intrusion detection. SIGOPS Oper. Syst. Rev. 45(2), 38–53 (2011)
2. Barham, P., Dragovic, B., Fraser, K., Hand, S., Harris, T., Ho, A., Neugebauer, R., Pratt, I., Warfield, A.: Xen and the art of virtualization. SIGOPS Oper. Syst. Rev. 37(5), 164–177 (2003)

3. Borders, K., Zhao, X., Prakash, A.: Siren: Catching evasive malware (short paper). In: Proceedings of the 2006 IEEE Symposium on Security and Privacy, SP 2006, pp. 78–85. IEEE Computer Society, Washington, DC (2006)

4. Bugiel, S., Nürnberger, S., Sadeghi, A.-R., Schneider, T.: Twin clouds: Secure cloud computing with low latency. In: De Decker, B., Lapon, J., Naessens, V., Uhl, A. (eds.) CMS 2011. LNCS, vol. 7025, pp. 32–44. Springer, Heidelberg (2011)

5. Dunlap, G.W., King, S.T., Cinar, S., Basrai, M.A., Chen, P.M.: Revirt: Enabling intrusion analysis through virtual-machine logging and replay. SIGOPS Oper. Syst. Rev. 36(SI), 211–224 (2002)

6. Falliere, N., Chien, E.: Zeus: King of the bots (2009)

7. Garfinkel, T., Pfaff, B., Chow, J., Rosenblum, M., Boneh, D.: Terra: A virtual machine-based platform for trusted computing. In: 9th ACM Symposium on Operating Systems Principles, SOSP 2003, pp. 193–206. ACM, New York (2003)

8. Garfinkel, T., Rosenblum, M.: A virtual machine introspection based architecture for intrusion detection. In: Proc. Network and Distributed Systems Security Symposium, pp. 191–206 (2003)

9. Han-zhang, W., Liu-sheng, H.: An improved trusted cloud computing platform model based on daa and privacy ca scheme. In: 2010 International Conference on Computer Application and System Modeling (ICCASM), Oct 2010, vol. 13 (2010)

10. Harrison, K., Bordbar, B., Ali, S.T.T., Dalton, C.I., Norman, A.: A Framework for Detecting Malware in Cloud by Identifying Symptoms, pp. 164–172. IEEE (2012)

11. Hurley, J., Munoz, A., Sezer, S.: Itaca: Flexible, scalable network analysis. In: ICC, pp. 1069–1073. IEEE (2012)

12. King, S.T., Chen, P.M., Wang, Y.-M., Verbowski, C., Wang, H.J., Lorch, J.R.: Subvirt: Implementing malware with virtual machines. In: IEEE Symposium on Security and Privacy, SP 2006, pp. 314–327. IEEE Computer Society (2006)

13. Nguyen, A.-Q., Takefuji, Y.: A novel approach for a file-system integrity monitor tool of xen virtual machine. In: Bao, F., Miller, S. (eds.) ASIACCS, ACM (2007)

14. Oberhcide, J., Veeraraghavan, K., Cooke, E., Flinn, J., Jahanian, F.: Virtualized in-cloud security services for mobile devices. In: 1st Workshop on Virtualization in Mobile Computing, MobiVirt 2008, pp. 31–35. ACM, New York (2008)

15. Porras, P.A.: Directions in network-based security monitoring. IEEE Security & Privacy 7(1), 82–85 (2009)

16. Santos, N., Gummadi, K.P., Rodrigues, R.: Towards trusted cloud computing. In: Proceedings of the 2009 Conference on Hot Topics in Cloud Computing, HotCloud 2009. USENIX Association, Berkeley (2009)

17. Shen, Z., Li, L., Yan, F., Wu, X.: Cloud computing system based on trusted computing platform. In: International Conference on Intelligent Computation Technology and Automation, ICICTA 2010, vol. 01. IEEE Computer Society (2010)

18. Thakar, N.: Botnets remain a leading threat (2013), https://blogs.mcafee.com/business/security-connected/ tackling-the-botnet-threat

19. Wang, H., Zhou, H., Wang, C.: Virtual machine-based intrusion detection system framework in cloud computing environment. JCP 7(10), 2397–2403 (2012)

The Impact of Routing Attacks on Pastry-Based P2P Online Social Networks

Felix A. Eichert[1], Markus Monhof[1], and Kalman Graffi[2]

[1] University of Paderborn, Germany
[2] Technology of Social Networks, Heinrich Heine University Düsseldorf, Germany
graffi@cs.uni-duesseldorf.de
http://tsn.hhu.de

Abstract. Peer-to-Peer (p2p) networks are common in several areas by now. Besides the well-known file sharing platforms, p2p overlays also emerge as a basis for decentralized social networks. In these, the overlay is used as robust storage for several kinds of social information. With gaining relevance, attackers might have an interest in tampering the functionality of the overlay. In this paper we investigate the routing attacks on the distributed hash table Pastry that we use as basis in our p2p social network LifeSocial. We determine through simulations the impact of routing attacks on the performance of the overlay.

1 Introduction

Online social networks (OSNs) are popular nowadays due to the ease of connecting billions of users and allowing them to interact through a set of communication options. Facebook, as most prominent example, connects around 1 billion users worldwide. A limitation of the current centralized approaches is given by the single operator running the social networking site. This operator is able to censor content and opinions, read private and confidential messages, market user data or be shut off in oppressive countries that want to reduce communication on specific topics, like during the Arab spring. Although the majority of the users remain unaware of the risks of using centralized OSNs and ignore the possibility of the communication being overheard, for some users in the world it is crucial or even vital to have the opportunity to communicate and organize with friends in a secure and anonymous way.

Peer-to-Peer (p2p)-based networks [21] can be made indestructible, as no component is considered crucial. Structured p2p overlays, especially distributed hash tables (DHTs) like Chord [27] or Pastry [24] offer a key-based routing [4] interface that allows to implement an efficient and fully retrievable simple storage. Using replication approaches like PAST [6] allow to keep content stored in the DHT remaining, even in the (expected) failure of the initial content hosting node. Distributed social networks propose to alleviate the security and censorship risk of centralized OSN sites.

In previous work, we have presented [16], [11] and [12], which builds a plugin-based p2p framework for hosting online social networks. LifeSocial aims at solving the main challenges in p2p based social networking: reliable and flexible data

L. Lopes et al. (Eds.): Euro-Par 2014 Workshops, Part I, LNCS 8805, pp. 347–358, 2014.

storage, security and controlled quality. Pastry [24] is used as basic substrate, PAST [6] is used for replication, SCRIBE [25] for an integrated publish / subscribe approach. For LifeSocial, we presented a practical access control approach in [15], which introduces a root of trust, deploys a secure key infrastructure and allows to cryptographically provide access control for single data elements. For the control of the quality of the overlay, we created a tree-based monitoring approach in [13] which is used to capture the current state of the running network. A further extension to a large-scale distributed control loop has been sketched in [17] and [18].

Security and especially the proper functionality of the overlay is vital for a p2p based online social network. As routing is solely performed by participating peers, routing might be tampered by these due to several reasons, such as free riding [26] or malicious aims. In this paper, we focus on routing attacks in Pastry [24] that are relevant in the context of social network. For that we introduce in Section 2 briefly in the underlying structure of the p2p overlay that we examine as well as the potential attacks in this overlay. We discuss approaches presented in literature that address routing attacks in Pastry in Section 3. We then present the evaluation setup and our simulation results on the impact of malicious nodes in Pastry in Section 4. Finally we conclude with an summary of our results and a look-out for future work in Section 5.

2 Background

In this section introduce shortly in Pastry, which has been implemented in FreePastry. FreePastry is popular in the academic community and has been used for several prototypes. After that we present attacks that can be conducted on a p2p network using the Pastry overlay. As stated in Section 1, we will limit the selection to routing attacks.

2.1 Pastry Overlay

P2P networks typically consist of an immense number of participants which often are referred to as nodes or peers. Those nodes have no hierarchical order and each have the same role in the network, so there is no centralized organization like in common client-server architectures. Such networks need certain algorithms to locate nodes or respectively nodes that are responsible for desired data and for routing messages to those nodes. Today most p2p networks are implemented as so called *overlay networks* which are using some sort of IP based network for communication

Pastry is an overlay for p2p networks with good performance and high reliability according to [24]. Each node in the Pastry overlay is assigned a unique identifier, the so-called "nodeId", that is uniformly distributed over a 128bit range. The state of a single node contains a *Leaf set*, a *Routing table* and a *Neighborhood set*. The *Routing table* contains a selection of nodes, and its corresponding IP addresses, which pose alternatives for routing of messages. For the

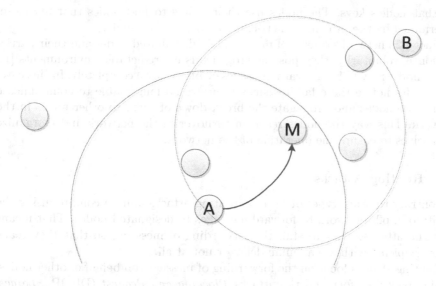

Fig. 1. Sample trajectory of a lookup-message initiated by the node A with the encounter of a malicious node using the *DROP* strategy. This malicious node M drops the message that comes from A instead of forwarding it to another node so the message will eventually reach the destination B.

purpose of routing the nodes in this table are ordered by the length of the shared prefix of their identifier with the identifier of node that owns this *Routing table*. The *Leaf set* contains nodes, whose identifier are closest to the owning node's identifier while the *Neighborhood set* contains nodes that are closest measured by a proximity metric. This proximity metric might for example be the number of IP routing hops or geographic distance. These sets allow the nodes to organize their connection between each other and to route messages throughout the network.

There are a few parameters that can be defined by the originator of the network which affect its overall performance and reliability of the network. One parameter is b defines the basis of how many bits are considered as one character in the nodeId. b is typically 4 or 16. The nodeId is represented as a String of characters and the prefixes are calculated based on characters.

The Pastry overlay implements a DHT. Therefore each node is responsible for holding a certain range of keys denoted by the distance of the nodes identifier to the next smaller one. To lookup a value of a certain key that is not hold by the requesting node, this node sends a request message to a node which has an identifier closer to the target node. This message is forwarded from one node to another until it reaches the node that holds the requested key. For a normal operating network, when N is the number of node in the network, the destination is reached in $\lceil \log_{2^b} N \rceil$ steps. In the case a certain node denies service, the node with the next higher identifier takes over the responsibility for that node's keys. The nodes use their states to find nodes that are close, determined by the proximity metric, to the destination node.

Since p2p networks consist of many widely distributed nodes and their participation is voluntarily, they pose heterogeneous unpredictable environments [1]. Single nodes may fail to forward messages or break down completely. In this case, near nodes notice these failures since they are no longer able to communicate with those nodes and propagate the break-down of them to other nodes in the network. This way the nodes react on turnover in the network and reorganize themselves to ensure the operation of the network.

2.2   Routing Attacks

In contrary to other types of attacks, routing attacks aim on compromising the ability of a p2p network to forward messages to designated nodes. That means that the attacker tries to stall the forwarding of messages so that they reach their recipients with a maximum delay or not at all.

Routing attacks focus on the forwarding of messages on behalf of other nodes. In this paper we focus on the attacks *Blocking any Request* (DROP), *Largest Distance First* (LDF) and *Approach at Minimum Pace* (AMP). The *DROP* strategy simply drops all messages to forward, but answers those directed at the current node. Thus we focus on forwarding routing attacks. In the case of a node joining, the node picks bootstrapping nodes until it is served. This strategy can easily be transferred to the Pastry overlay. It is illustrated in Figure 1. When it comes to countermeasures, this strategy, while it is easy to implement, might easily be detected and then be ignored. Detected nodes are not able to harm the network anymore.

The second attack strategy is termed *Largest Distance First* strategy (LDF). This strategy is illustrated in Figure 2. Here a malicious node forwards incoming lookup messages. The malicious approach is that the node does not forward the message in the direction of the targeted node like a ordinary node would do. This node estimates the node of those he knows whose identifier has the largest distance to the targeted node. This has the effect that the message moves away from instead of moving towards its destination. An implication of this attack is an increase of the routing hops a message needs to reach its destination. That increases the number of nodes that are involved in the processing of one message and therefore increases the load of those nodes. The increase of routing hops might additionally lead to longer physical distances that the message has to travel what results in longer transmission delays. While the message is not dropped and might eventually reach its destination, its processing is being stalled. This lowers the efficiency of the network.

The last attack strategy that we consider is the *Approach at Minimum Pace* strategy (AMP). As shown by Figure 3, a malicious node following this strategy, also forwards lookup messages. In contrary to *LDF*, in this strategy as next hop for a message to be forwarded a node is chosen which is closer to the destination of the message, such as the neighboring node of forwarding node. While the distance to the destination does not increase, it decreases at a minimal pace.

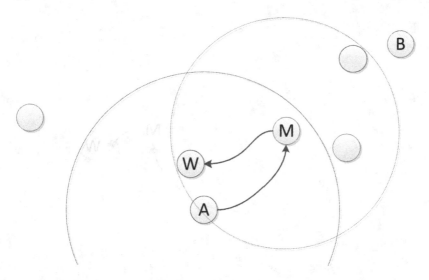

Fig. 2. Sample trajectory of a lookup message with the encounter of a malicious node using the *LDF* strategy. The message from *A* is being forwarded by the malicious node *M*. Instead of forwarding the message into the direction of the destination *B*, *M* forwards it to node *W*, which is the node with the largest distance to *B* that *M* knows.

This means that the direct effect of this strategy is not as striking as the *LDF*s. Waiving this part of significance might circumvent certain types of countermeasures. The node still forwards messages in the correct direction. Therefore, we suspect the detection of those malicious nodes to be much harder than e.g. those following the *LDF* strategy.

In both the *LDF*- and the *AMP* strategy we use the distance of the nodeIds. Pastry however with the Neighborhood set provides another term of distance, which relies on arbitrary proximity metrics. Because a node can not necessarily know the distance in terms of the Neighborhood set between to other nodes, it can not decide if a node has a higher or lower distance to the destination node of a message than itself. So it is not a reliable basis for the behavior of a malicious routing strategy.

3   Related Work

Security is a crucial issue of p2p networks and is in focus of several scientific publications. [5] indicates some open problems including security problems of today's p2p networks. They state that the p2p networks suffer from the unreliable nature of single peers. Secure Routing in organic networks has been addressed in [22], [23] and [14]. In these papers, networks are considered with multi-hop routing, in which the forwarding actions of the nodes cannot be directly observed. The authors propose to maintain a compressed history about the forwarded data by each peer, which might be occasionally verified publicly.

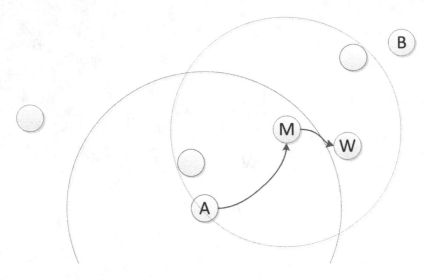

Fig. 3. Sample trajectory of a lookup message initiated by the node A. The message is being sent to the malicious node M that uses the AMP strategy in this example. M forwards the message into the direction of the destination node B. M chooses the node W, which is a bit closer to B, but as close to M as possible.

[3] proposes an approach for a reputation-based selection of peers that are used for routing operations. This enhances the reliability of the network by avoiding unreliable or faulty nodes. This countermeasure could dampen the effect of the routing attacks proposed in this paper. Mechanisms that ensure cooperation of peers in a p2p network are developed by [7]. These prevent peers from taking advantage of services of a network without contributing into the infrastructure. Some attacks are being presented by [2] which aim to prevent the attacked p2p network to fail to route messages properly. The paper also presents countermeasures against those attacks. An overview on further countermeasures is given in [28]. The authors provide a taxonomy on possible solutions, but do not give an evaluation on their effectiveness in various DHTs, such as Pastry.

A different approach of harming a p2p network, called Index Poisoning, is presented by [20]. It is stated that p2p file sharing systems are very vulnerable to this kind of attack. Index Poisoning harms the network by flooding it with wrong data that makes it difficult to retrieve correct data from it.

In [9], the authors researched the effect of one type of a routing attack on p2p networks. The paper defines a certain testbed for a simulation and gives the results of it. The scenario of the simulation is limited to a attack where malicious peers in a network do not forward any messages which equates to the $DROP$ strategy that we simulate. Since this simulation is similar to ours, we will take the experimentation results from this paper in comparison with our results for the specific kind of attack.

Table 1. Malicious strategies and corresponding measurements of network performance/reliability

Strategy	Measurement
DROP	ratio of failed lookups
LDF	average number of hops per lookup
AMP	average number of hops per lookup

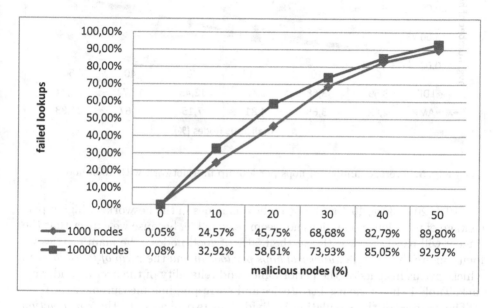

	0	10	20	30	40	50
1000 nodes	0,05%	24,57%	45,75%	68,68%	82,79%	89,80%
10000 nodes	0,08%	32,92%	58,61%	73,93%	85,05%	92,97%

malicious nodes (%)

Fig. 4. Failed lookups in addiction to malicious nodes

4   Evaluation

For the evaluation of impact of the various attack strategies we used the the event based p2p network simulator PeerfactSim.KOM[1] [19], whose layered architecture allows easy implementation of different simulation scenarios. An introduction into the structure and functionality of PeerfactSim.KOM is given in [10] and [8]. PeerfactSim.KOM offers the advantage that it simulates multiple layers of a communication system, e.g. the transport layer, the network layer and the application layer. For each layer it contains multiple standard implementations, which can be interchanged, when needed.

For each network size we examine the influence of the three different kinds of attack strategies stated in Section 2.2 on the performance and robustness of the overlay. For the experiments we use the following scenario: We have Pastry of either 1000 or 10000 nodes and for both numbers of nodes we evaluate the effect of

---

[1] http://www.peerfact.org

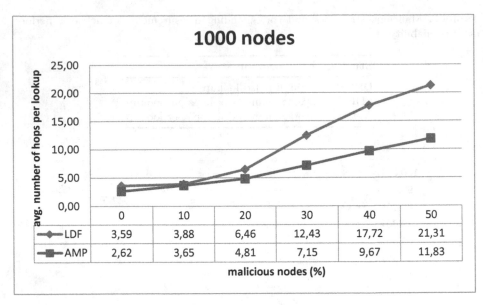

Fig. 5. Average number of hops per lookup in a network with 1000 nodes

0%, 10%, 20%, 30%, 40% and 50% malicious nodes in the network. A higher percentage of malicious nodes does not seem reasonable, because we expect that the Pastry will barely work with less than 50% of good nodes. The main metrics we focus on are the *average number of hops per lookup* and the *ratio of failed lookups* which give us insights on the performance and reliability of the overlay under attack. Table 1 shows the used strategies and corresponding measurements.

The process of the simulation is divided in two phases. In the *construction phase*, whose duration of 40 simulation minutes, all nodes act normally and build up the network. The second phase is the *operation phase* in which the nodes start lookup operations for keys in the DHT. We set its duration to 80 minutes in simulation time. For all three strategies we used a preferably realistic Net-Layer, which is capable of empirical determined latency, bandwidth and packet loss. The value of b, which is in a way the step size per hop, for the Pastry overlay is set to 4, as it is proposed in [24].

4.1   Experimental Results

First we present the results of the simulations with the *DROP* strategy. Figure 4 shows the failed lookups according to the percentage of malicious nodes. As we can see even a small percentage of malicious nodes leads to a alarming ratio of failed lookups. For larger networks the impact of this strategy is higher. Especially this is noticeable for a malicious node ratio between 10% and 30%. This is as with a larger amount of peers the average number of hops per lookups has to increase, so there is a higher chance that a node on the route is behaving maliciously. With 50% malicious nodes nearly all lookups fail.

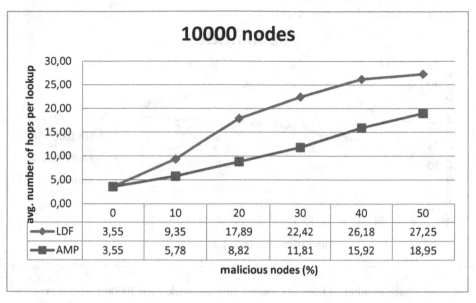

Fig. 6. Average number of hops per lookup in a network with 10000 nodes

In contrast to this, the impact of the *Approach at Minimum Pace-* and the *Largest Distance First* strategy on the failed lookups is negligible. Even for 10000 nodes and 50% malicious nodes the percentage of failed lookups lays around 1% for the *AMP* strategy, for the *LDF* strategy it is even less. This is due to the fact that these strategies only prolong the delivery of the messages in order to be harder to detect.

For these strategies we have a look at the *average number of hops per lookup*. The results for a network with 1000 nodes are illustrated in Figure 5. As we can see, the red line, which shows the impact of malicious nodes with the *AMP* strategy, has a nearly linear growth, the *LDF* strategy has a much higher influence on the average number of hops. This is due to the *AMP* strategy at least routes the lookup message in the right direction towards its destination, the *LDF* strategy however sends the message to that node (which is known by the current node) that has the largest distance, in terms of the node identifier, to the destination node. So with higher probability of malicious nodes, the probability that the next hop behaves badly is increased. In the worst case for the *LDF* strategy the lookup message can get stuck in an infinite loop, while the *AMP* strategy always routes the message to its destination. The results for 10000 nodes are shown in Figure 6 and they are conform to that for 1000 nodes. For both strategies the impact is just slightly higher.

Another result is, that the *average hops per lookup* are increasing in time, at least for the beginning of the *construction phase*. A graphical representation of this is given in Figure 7 for a network with 10000 from which 50% are malicious. The normal development is showed as a reference, too. Why that is the case might be interesting for future work.

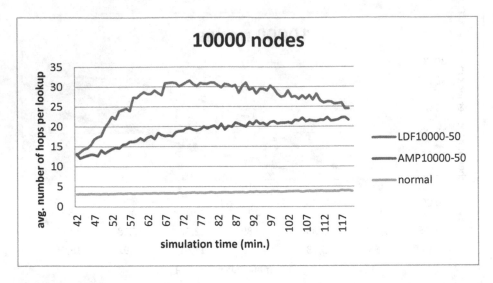

Fig. 7. Average number of hops per lookup in a network with 10000 nodes over simulation time

5   Conclusion

We simulated malicious nodes with three different strategies in Pastry overlay networks with 1000 and 10000 nodes. As a result we can state that Pastry is vulnerable for routing attacks. Nodes that simply drop all messages to forward effect large damage on the network. Solution are to be found to detect and isolate these nodes. Assuming that solutions for detecting misbehavior are found, malicious nodes might still try to modify the route length by sending the message only a bit forward or as far from the target away as they can. Through our simulations we show, that especially for big networks a small ratio of malicious nodes is sufficient to highly decrease the performance of the network. One aspect that could be interesting to be examined in the future could be why the number of hops is increasing over time or first in- and then decreasing. Also for these attacks, solutions need to be found and implemented. On the long term, secure p2p overlays, such as Pastry, are suitable to implement novel applications on top, such as online social networks.

References

1. Buragohain, C., Agrawal, D., Suri, S.: A Game Theoretic Framework for Incentives in P2P Systems. In: IEEE P2P 2003: Proc of the Int. Conf. on Peer-to-Peer Computing, pp. 48–56 (September 2003)
2. Castro, M., Druschel, P., Ganesh, A., Rowstron, A., Wallach, D.S.: Secure routing for structured peer-to-peer overlay networks. SIGOPS Oper. Syst. Rev. 36(SI), 299–314 (2002)

3. Cornelli, F., Damiani, E., di Vimercati, S., Paraboschi, S., Samarati, P.: Choosing reputable servents in a p2p network. In: ACM WWW 2002: Proc. of the Int. Conf. on World Wide Web, pp. 376–386 (2002)
4. Dabek, F., Zhao, B.Y., Druschel, P., Kubiatowicz, J., Stoica, I.: Towards a Common API for Structured Peer-to-Peer Overlays. In: Kaashoek, M.F., Stoica, I. (eds.) IPTPS 2003. LNCS, vol. 2735, Springer, Heidelberg (2003)
5. Daswani, N., Garcia-Molina, H., Yang, B.: Open problems in data-sharing peer-to-peer systems. In: Calvanese, D., Lenzerini, M., Motwani, R. (eds.) ICDT 2003. LNCS, vol. 2572, pp. 1–15. Springer, Heidelberg (2002)
6. Rowstron, A.I.T., Druschel, P.: Storage Management and Caching in PAST, A Large-scale, Persistent Peer-to-peer Storage Utility. In: IEEE HotOS 2001: Proc. of the Workshop on Hot Topics in Operating Systems (2001)
7. Feldman, M., Lai, K., Stoica, I., Chuang, J.: Robust Incentive Techniques for Peer-to-Peer Networks. In: ACM EC 2004: Proc. of the ACM Conf. on Electronic Commerce, pp. 102–111 (2004)
8. Feldotto, M., Graffi, K.: Comparative Evaluation of Peer-to-Peer Systems Using PeerfactSim.KOM. In: IEEE HPCS 2013: Proc. of the Int. Conf. on High Performance Computing and Simulation (2013)
9. Gottron, C., König, A., Steinmetz, R.: A Survey on Security in Mobile Peer-to-Peer Architectures - Overlay-Based vs. Underlay-Based Approaches. Future Internet 2(4), 505–532 (2010)
10. Graffi, K.: PeerfactSim.KOM: A P2P System Simulator Experiences and Lessons Learned. In: IEEE P2P 2011: Proc. of the Int. Conf. on Peer-to-Peer Computing (2011)
11. Graffi, K., Groß, C., Mukherjee, P., Kovacevic, A., Steinmetz, R.: LifeSocial.KOM: A P2P-based Platform for Secure Online Social Networks. In: IEEE P2P 2010: Proceedings of the International Conference on Peer-to-Peer Computing (2010)
12. Graffi, K., Groß, C., Stingl, D., Hartung, D., Kovacevic, A., Steinmetz, R.: LifeSocial.KOM: A Secure and P2P-based Solution for Online Social Networks. In: Proc. of IEEE CCNC (2011)
13. Graffi, K., Kovacevic, A., Xiao, S., Steinmetz, R.: SkyEye.KOM: An Information Management Over-Overlay for Getting the Oracle View on Structured P2P Systems. In: IEEE ICPADS 2008: Proc. of the Int. Conf. on Parallel and Distributed Systems, IEEE (2008)
14. Graffi, K., Mogre, P.S., Hollick, M., Steinmetz, R.: Detection of Colluding Misbehaving Nodes in Mobile Ad Hoc and Wireless Mesh Networks. In: IEEE Global Telecommunications Conference (GLOBECOM). IEEE (2007)
15. Graffi, K., Mukherjee, P., Menges, B., Hartung, D., Kovacevic, A., Steinmetz, R.: Practical Security in P2P-based Social Networks. In: IEEE LCN 2009: Proceedings of the International Conference on Local Computer Networks (2009)
16. Graffi, K., Podrajanski, S., Mukherjee, P., Kovacevic, A., Steinmetz, R.: A Distributed Platform for Multimedia Communities. In: IEEE ISM 2008: Proceedings of the International Symposium on Multimedia (2008)
17. Graffi, K., Stingl, D., Rückert, J., others: Monitoring and Management of Structured Peer-to-Peer Systems. In: IEEE P2P 2009: Proceedings of the International Conference on Peer-to-Peer Computing (2009)
18. Klerx, T., Graffi, K.: Bootstrapping Skynet: Calibration and Autonomic Self-Control of Structured Peer-to-Peer Networks. In: IEEE P2P 2013: Proceedings of the International Conference on Peer-to-Peer Computing (2013)

19. Kovacevic, A., Kaune, S., Heckel, H., Mink, A., Graffi, K., Heckmann, O., Steinmetz, R.: PeerfactSim.KOM - A Simulator for Large-Scale Peer-to-Peer Networks. Tech. Rep. Tr-2006-06, Technische Universität Darmstadt, Germany (2006)

20. Liang, J., Naoumov, N., Ross, K.W.: The Index Poisoning Attack in P2P File Sharing Systems. In: IEEE INFOCOM 2006: Proceedings of the International Conference on Computer Communications, vol. 6 (2006)

21. Liebau, N., Pussep, K., Graffi, K., Kaune, S., Jahn, E., Beyer, A., Steinmetz, R.: The Impact Of The P2P Paradigm. In: AMCIS 2007: Proceedings of Americas Conference on Information Systems (2007)

22. Mogre, P., Graffi, K., Hollick, M., Steinmetz, R.: A Security Framework for Wireless Mesh Networks. Wireless Communications and Mobile Computing Special Issue: Architectures and Protocols for Wireless Mesh, Ad Hoc, and Sensor Networks (2010)

23. Mogre, P.S., Graffi, K., Hollick, M., Steinmetz, R.: AntSec, WatchAnt, and AntRep: Innovative Security Mechanisms for Wireless Mesh Networks. In: IEEE LCN 2007: Proc. of the Annual Conf. on Local Computer Networks. IEEE (2007)

24. Rowstron, A., Druschel, P.: Pastry: Scalable, Decentralized Object Location, and Routing for Large-Scale Peer-to-Peer Systems. In: Guerraoui, R. (ed.) Middleware 2001. LNCS, vol. 2218, p. 329. Springer, Heidelberg (2001)

25. Rowstron, A., Kermarrec, A.-M., Druschel, P.: SCRIBE: The Design of a Large-Scale Event Notification Infrastructure. In: Crowcroft, J., Hofmann, M. (eds.) NGC 2001. LNCS, vol. 2233, p. 30. Springer, Heidelberg (2001)

26. Schoder, D., Fischbach, K.: Peer-to-Peer Prospects. Communications of the ACM 46(2), 27–29 (2003)

27. Stoica, I., Morris, R., Karger, D., Kaashoek, M.F., Balakrishnan, H.: Chord: A Scalable Peer-to-Peer Lookup Service for Internet Applications. In: SIGCOMM 2001: Proceedings of the International Conference on Applications, Technologies, Architectures, and Protocols for Computer Communications, ACM (2001)

28. Villanueva, R., Villamil, M.-D.-P., Arnedo, M.: Secure routing strategies in dht-based systems. In: Globe 2010: Int. Conf. on Data Management in Grid and Peer-to-Peer Systmes (Globe), pp. 62–74 (2010)

SLA-Based Cloud Security Monitoring: Challenges, Barriers, Models and Methods

Dana Petcu

West University of Timişoara, Romania
petcu@info.uvt.ro
http://web.info.uvt.ro/~petcu/

Abstract. Despite the tremendous efforts in cloud computing to overcome its main adoption barriers, like security concerns or quality of service guarantees, there is currently no commercial product or research prototype of a SLA-based cloud security monitoring system. This paper investigates the main challenges and barriers in designing a SLA-based cloud security monitoring system and the models and methods that can be used in its development.

Keywords: cloud computing, monitoring, service level, security.

1 Introduction

A monitoring process aims to observe and track applications and resources at run-time. In particular, cloud monitoring is a very important task for both cloud service provider (CSP in this paper) and consumer (CSC) as it involves dynamically tracking the Quality of Service (QoS) parameters related to virtualized resources (e.g., VM, storage, network, appliances), the physical resources they share, the applications running, and data hosted on them. Moreover, cloud monitoring is the basis of control operations and corrective actions for running systems on clouds [2]. Therefore, cloud monitoring is a key tool for managing software and hardware resources and providing continuous information on these resources as well as for consumer's applications hosted on the cloud. However, the monitoring is used in various other contexts, like performance, SLA management, security, billing and troubleshooting [1].

Service provisioning in the cloud relies on Service Level Agreements (SLAs) representing a contract signed between CSC and CSP which includes the requirements of the service specified as QoS and penalties in case of violations. Flexible and reliable management of resources and SLA agreements are of paramount importance to both CSP and CSC. On the one hand, CSP have to prevent SLA violations to avoid penalties, and, on the other hand, they have to ensure high resource utilization to prevent costly maintenance of unused resources. The continuous monitoring of the cloud and of its SLAs (e.g. in terms of availability, delay) supplies both CSP and CSC with such information as the workload generated by the CSC and the performance and QoS by the CSP, also allowing to implement mechanisms to prevent or recover violations.

L. Lopes et al. (Eds.): Euro-Par 2014 Workshops, Part I, LNCS 8805, pp. 359–370, 2014.

Cloud monitoring tools can assist a CSP or CSC in: (1) keeping their resources and applications operating at peak efficiency; (2) detecting variations in resource and application performance; (3) tracking the leave and join operations of cloud resources due to failures and other dynamic configuration changes; (4) accounting the SLA violations of given QoS parameters. Therefore the monitoring process is the key element that has to be studied further and enhanced to upgrade the QoS level. Cloud monitoring and SLAs are correlated in the sense that one has an impact on the other [1,2]: (a) enhancing monitoring functionalities can help to meet SLAs; (b) SLA has to be met by the CSP in order to reach the required reliability level required by consumers; (c) monitoring may allow CSP to formulate more realistic and dynamic SLAs and better pricing models by exploiting the knowledge of user-perceived performance.

Security monitoring is of high importance in a cloud environment. An extensive monitoring capability is essential if the operational security of a CSP platform has to be assessed [11]. To sustain information security in operation, it is necessary to plan the handling of attacks and security incidents in advance, and the service behaviour should be monitored. If regulated in the SLA – e.g., when there is a high availability requirement for the cloud services –, the CSC should also be able to contact the CSP' security incident handling and troubleshooting team. For administration to be auditable, all administrative activities should be logged. In this way, the CSP can provide their customers with evidence of when and which changes have been made to the service, and by whom. To identify attacks, log files (showing system statuses, failed authentication attempts, etc.) and other data sources related to security – e.g., analyses by system monitoring tools (like intrusion detection system or integrity checker) – should be used and correlated. Where a CSC has a requirement for protecting the confidentiality of his information (e.g., for data leakage protection), special tools need be deployed to control the data flow. These should detect or even intervene, if confidential data is sent via insecure routes or falls into the wrong hands.

An analysis of the available Cloud monitoring systems, SLA management systems, and Cloud security systems shows that no SLA-based cloud security monitoring system is currently available. We have reported this fact in the recent paper [20]. Moreover, that paper includes a review of various systems or tools for monitoring or SLA management or security in clouds (not to be repeated in this paper). More recently, we introduced in [19] a taxonomy that is necessary for the design of a SLA-based cloud security monitor. In this paper we discuss the main challenges that are faced in the design of such a system (Section 2) and the models and methods that can be followed or extended in its development (Section 3). This preliminary study is meant to support the development in the next year of the monitoring system of the SPECS project [22].

2   Challenges and Barriers

The main challenges and barriers related to the design of a SLA-based cloud security monitoring system are stated in what follows.

2.1   Security Related Challenges and Barriers

The ability to monitor what goes on in the cloud has become the most critical part of information security in the cloud. However, security monitoring lags behind other security features made available by CSP, and is typically less developed than operational performance monitoring.

A first barrier is the fact that security SLAs are not in place. A security SLA is an SLA that specifies the security obligations associated with a service. In contrast to traditional SLAs, a security SLA includes a set of security requirements [3]. According to [26], CSP contracts will not provide detailed and substantive security SLAs before 2016. The absence of security aspects in SLAs, combined with the lack of methods for making objective comparisons between different service offerings, makes it virtually impossible for CSP to offer trustworthy services to CSC when third party providers are involved [3]. Security SLAs can not only increase the trust in CSP, but also facilitate objective comparisons between different CSP on the basis of their security features. Such an approach will also form a basis for composing services from different CSPs, based on a set of pre-defined security requirements.

A second barrier is related to privacy. Privacy laws are restricting today CSP from instant monitoring, as considered an intrusion into the customer processes and data. Which data are allowed to be collected need to be well defined, and specific frameworks or SLAs are not available.

A high challenge is related to the data security monitoring. Guarantees and penalty clauses in the SLA are the best ways to ensure that the data are protected. However, data security is the most difficult problem in information security right now and data security-related risks have been greatly magnified by cloud computing. The processing of big data on clouds is introducing a new dimension to the problem as the control of large data sets is time consuming and instant reaction of the monitoring system is difficult to be achieved. The continuous monitoring of the data is coming with a potential penalty on the performance of the data processing.

2.2   SLA Related Challenges and Barriers

The fact that nowadays monitoring infrastructures lack appropriate solutions for SLA monitoring [9] is currently the main barrier.

A first challenge is the mapping between low-level metrics and application-based SLA parameters. Application level monitoring is a difficult task, as the infrastructure and platform layer metrics need to be mapped to the required metrics at the application to support SLA management. The performance of the application is described as a high-level SLA parameter, as, for example, the availability. But, applications run on physical or virtual resources, which are characterized with low-level metrics such as CPU, memory, uptime, downtime, etc. So, there is a gap between the low-level resource metrics and the high-level SLA parameters and a mapping between them is not obvious. Another related topic is how to determine appropriate monitoring intervals at the application level, keeping the balance between the early detection of possible SLA violations and the intrusiveness of the monitoring tools on the whole system. Through monitoring of the cloud infrastructure resources, the CSP gains information about the usage of the resources and the current resource availability status. The rate of acquisition of this information is an important factor, impacting the overall performance of the system and the profit of the CSP. On the one hand, monitoring at a high rate delivers fast updates about the resource status to the CSP but it can cause high overhead, which possibly degrades the performance of the system. On the other hand, monitoring at a low rate causes the miss of information such as failing to detect SLA violations, which leads to SLA penalties for the CSP. To address this issue, techniques to determine the optimal measurement intervals to efficiently monitor to detect SLA violations are required [9]. Moreover, there is still lack of adequate monitoring infrastructures able to predict possible SLA violations: most of the available monitoring systems rely either on Grid or service-oriented infrastructures, which are not directly compatible with clouds, due to the differences in resource usage models.

A second challenge is related to the need of layer agnosticism. Application components (streaming servers, web servers, indexing servers, compute services, storage services, and network) can be distributed across cloud layers (e.g. PaaS and IaaS). Therefore it is critical to be able to monitor SLA parameters to multiple cloud layers. Hence, the challenge here is to develop monitoring tools that can capture and react to the parameters associated with different layers. Monitoring tools are originally oriented to perform monitoring tasks over services only in one of the layers. Moreover, most of current commercial tools are designed to keep track of the performance of resources provisioned at the IaaS layer [2].

A third challenge is related to the fact that the definition of the term security metric is still vague. Being quantifiable and measurable are essential metric attributes. However, the definition of a security that can be quantifiable and can be expressed in a service level is still a hurdle to be overcome [4].

2.3   Cloud Related Challenges and Barriers

A first barrier is related to the uncertainty associated with the cloud environments: due to the very high complexity of cloud systems, it not always possible to be sure that all events can be actually observed. For example, if we put a probe in an application that runs in the cloud to collect information on the rate at which it exchanges information with other applications running in the same cloud, we do not necessarily know if the measured rate is affected by the transfer rate of the network. The rate depends on where the two applications are running (on the same physical host or not) and this information is not always exposed by CSP. Similar issues arise for evaluating the performance of computation: the time required for a task completion can depend on the current hardware that is executing the instructions (can be a different hardware to the next deployment in the cloud, while the available information from CSP is only in terms of ranges of CPU model, not the concrete values) and on the workload due to other virtualized environments running on the same physical server (which are not exposed to the CSC by the CSP) [1].

A second barrier is related to the fact that virtualization makes monitoring harder than in other environments. Most of existing monitoring tools (including security ones) have not yet grown to understand virtual and cloud environments. Notions like hypervisor security or cloud stack introspection are essentially not dealt with. Moreover, it is challenging (if not impossible) for a CSP to de-multiplex security monitoring data from shared environments.

A high challenge is the cloud agnosticism. Many public CSPs enable their CSCs to monitor their applications using monitoring tools. Often these tools are tightly integrated in their cloud and do not allow to monitor cloud services of other providers. For example, Amazon's CloudWatch enables consumers to manage and monitor their applications, but it is not possible to extend it to monitor an application component that may reside on other CSP infrastructure [2]. Engineering provider-agnostic monitoring tools is challenging, primarily due to fact that there is no common unified application programming interface for calling runtime statistics of cloud services. Agnostic monitoring tools are also required if one wants to realize a hybrid cloud architecture involving services from private and public clouds.

Only if the cloud agnosticism is achieved, the monitoring of large scale distributed virtual environments on Clouds can be enabled. Obtaining a comprehensive cross-domain monitoring solution represents a task that has not yet been properly addressed. Among different cloud monitoring infrastructures there is a high heterogeneity of systems, tools, and exchanged information. Moreover, a recent research [1] on cross-domain data leakage and its prevention pointed that the ability to monitor services performance is considered as a security risk.

3   Models and Methods

In this section we discuss the main models and methods that are the basic building blocks for a potential SLA-based cloud security monitoring system.

3.1   Cloud Security Models

Multi-layer Model for Cloud Security. According to [6], cloud security is a multi-layered approach. Clouds can be modeled in seven layers: facility, network, hardware, operating system, middleware, application, and the user. In more details, security monitoring is handled, according to [18,25], as follows.

At facility layer, security is mainly handled at physical level, involving the implementation of access control through authentication systems (e.g. using the access control model based on UCON [8]), alarm systems and sensors, and so on. The main objective is to prevent malicious intrusion and data manipulation, ensuring the integrity of facilities and components.

At hardware level, security metrics are in line with those adopted in the premises. The CSP is responsible for monitoring the hardware, and can use specfic software to monitor the connection topology, memory use, bus speeds, processor loads, disk storage, temperature, voltage, and so on. The CSP measure such quantities to effectively load-balance its resources.

At network level, mechanisms such as firewalls, intrusion detection systems, intrusion prevention systems can be adopted. The network defense devices are collecting information about security events on the network. The CSP can log this information; these logs are used in auditing the network's security.

The security of virtual infrastructure resources can be associated with operating systems. In this case, the metrics should be extracted from monitoring operating system events and system calls between VMs and hardware. The purpose is mainly to prevent copy and data violations. The host operating system monitors and arranges all system calls between the VMs and the hardware, so it can access any data passing to or from the VM.

At middleware layer, the metrics are related to monitoring of virtualization and safety systems in heterogeneous cloud architectures. The middleware monitor ensure the secure communication between various system components as it mediates between the applications and the OS. Assurance concerns fall in three categories: software architecture flaws, e.g. as result from human misconfiguration of resources or policies; coding vulnerabilities, e.g. due to common software defects; security services, including monitoring, access control, data validation.

At application level the number of security vulnerabilities is a relevant metric, since it is necessary to monitor behavior to detect possible violations. Other components to be monitored are mostly digital certificates, private keys, etc.

If the cloud just provides services for distributing public information, such as a web page, the user's consumption has little security impact. However, if the users are members of the CSC organization, they are integral to the security policy. Access patterns can be monitored for malicious behavior. In addition, the CSC might need to make an addendum proscribing access to sensitive data.

Cloud Security Control Domains. These were defined recently in the Cloud Control Matrix [6]. The list of domains includes: application and interface security, interoperability and portability, identity and access management, governance and risk management, legal and standards compliance, data security and information lifecycle management, datacenter security, change control and configuration management, infrastructure and virtualization security, e-discovery and cloud forensics, encryption and key management, supply chain management, transparency and accountability, mobile security, threat and vulnerability management, business continuity management and operational resilience, human resources security.

3.2   Metrics and Security Parameters

Cloud Metrics. A conceptual metrics model, Cloud Service Measure and Metric (CSMM) (not focused on security metrics), was presented in [17]. The intent of the model is to capture the necessary information needed to describe and interpret metrics focused on cloud services. The concept model entities are:

(a) scenario: the user side of a metric (application, SLA definition); (b) measure definition: data and meta-data constitutive of a measure definition; (c) metric: data, meta-data and rules constitutive of a metric definition; (d) measurement: run-time data or dynamically generated data, resulting from applying a metric.

Service Measurement Index. It is a set of business-relevant key performance indicators that provide a standardized method for measuring and comparing a business service regardless of whether that service is internally provided or sourced from an outside company [24]. It is designed to become a standard method to help organizations measure cloud-based business services based on their specific business and technology requirements. However, it is not focused on security metrics. The category of 'Security and Privacy' includes attributes that indicate the effectiveness of a service provider's controls on access to services, service data, and the physical facilities from which services are provided: access control and privilege management; data geographic/political; data integrity; data privacy and data loss; physical and environmental security; proactive threat and vulnerability management mechanisms; retention/disposition.

Security Metrics. We can use the definitions from [23] for security indicators, measures and metrics.

A security indicator is any observable characteristic that correlates (or is assumed to correlate) with a desired security property. The set of feasible indicator values is assumed to form (at least) a nominal scale. For many proposed indicators, the required correlation with security has not been formally established, but is only postulated based on informal reasoning. An example of an indicator is the rate of compliance with a given catalogue of security criteria or security best practices (i.e., the relative number of requirements met).

A security measure assigns to each measured object a security indicator value from an ordinal scale according to a well-defined measurement protocol. In many cases, the measured values are numbers, but measures may also assign non-numeric designators such as low, medium, high.

A security metric is a security measure with an associated set of rules for the interpretation of the measured data values.

Cloud Security Properties. The CUMULUS project has established recently the principles for the construction of a generic attribute-based security property vocabulary [7], where each property has a unique identifier. A top-down approach was used to build a vocabulary starting with control domain borrowed from an industry cloud security control framework [6]. For each property in the vocabulary, three core elements are defined: a unique identifier, a definition, and a set of attributes, with a further distinction between performance and parametric attributes. Performance attributes are attributes of the property for which the CSP provide guarantees, such as the percentage of uptime or the level of confidentiality. Parametric attributes are attributes that contribute to the definition of the property itself, such as the length of a measurement period which allows to distinguish several flavors of the same property, such as weekly or hourly uptime.

The attributes included in security properties only describe the parameters that are strictly needed to describe a security property unambiguously.

Security Parameters for Monitoring. According to [10], the security parameters for a security monitoring framework can be classified in the following categories: incident response, data life-cycle management, change management, log management and forensics, service availability, service elasticity and load tolerance, technical compliance and vulnerability management, and data isolation. These parameters need to be considered according to the use-case: e.g. IaaS, PaaS and SaaS have different monitoring requirements and/or division of responsibilities.

3.3 Monitors

Monitoring Types. Two basic types of cloud monitoring can be considered, according [15]: CSC-oriented monitoring or CSP-side monitoring (either virtual system monitoring or physical system monitoring).

The approach undertaken in CSC-oriented monitoring is depending on the Cloud service delivery model. In SaaS model, service costs, usage of resources, status of the application and access history are monitored. In PaaS model, the impact of resource usage on costs and the usage of resources (development tools, network traffic and hosting space) are monitored. In IaaS model, the cost per instance, the consumed time, and the VM status are monitored.

CSP-side monitoring is done either on physical systems or on virtual systems. In the first case the evolution and the performance are monitored. In the second case the approach is depending again on the delivery model. In SaaS model, the resources sharing among applications and application usage patterns are tracked. In PaaS model, simultaneous connections and used hosting space are observed. In IaaS model, the status of internal resources and of each VM is monitored.

In particular, the security monitoring is currently done: on-premises, on monitored IaaS or via SaaS/other third party. In the first case, usually a Security Information and Event Management (SIEM) is able to make use of specific software-as-a-service APIs as well to collect logs from public cloud services. In the second case, the SIEM system is loaded directly into an IaaS. The advantages are that the tools are familiar and there is no high bandwidth requirement. However, high storage costs in the cloud can occur. Unfortunately, there is a lack of a unified view on on-premises and on-IaaS monitoring. In the third case, specific data from the cloud service are obtained (if available) and handed to a managed security service provider (e.g., Splunk Storm).

Monitoring the behavior of VMs is a critical requirement for CSP and CSC. There are two monitoring mechanisms on virtualized platforms [27]: (a) take a complete VM as the monitoring granularity, so that they cannot capture the malicious behaviors within individual VMs, or (b) focus on specific monitoring functions that cannot be used for heterogeneous VMs concurrently running on a single cloud node.

For monitoring software assets, two types of approaches have been proposed to provide an assurance of the behaviors of software elements [16]: static or dynamic. Static approaches – e.g., code inspection and automated analysis, formal methods, testing and so on – are based on checking the security of the software before it is actually executed by the users. The static verification activities must be carried out in simulated environments. Dynamic approaches – e.g., monitoring, surveillance and other form of runtime analyses – are based on the observation of the actual behavior of the software and are carried out in the environment where the software is actually used.

High and Low Level Monitoring. According to [1], the monitoring can be of high-level or low-level. High-level monitoring is related to information on the status of the virtual platform. This information is collected at the middleware, application and user layers by CSP or CSC through platforms and services operated by themselves or by third parties. In the case of SaaS, high-level monitoring information is generally of more interest for the CSC than for the CSP (being closely related to the QoS experienced by the former). Low-level monitoring is related to information collected by the CSP and usually not exposed to the CSC, and it is more concerned with the status of the physical infrastructure of the whole cloud (e.g. servers and storage areas).

Low-level monitoring tests can be divided into two main categories: computation-based or network-based. Computation-based tests are related to monitoring activities aimed at gaining knowledge about and at inferring the status of real or virtualized platforms running cloud applications. The tests can be related, for example, to the following metrics: CPU speed or utilization, CPU time per execution, memory page exchanges per execution, throughput/delay of message passing or of disk/memory, server throughput, response time, access time, VM acquisition/release/startup time, up-time. Network-based tests are related to the monitoring of network-layer metrics; the monitored data are, for example: traffic volume, available bandwidth, throughput, round-trip time, packet/data loss, capacity.

Security monitoring falls mostly in the category of high-level monitoring. For low-level monitoring, specific utilities for collecting information about security refer to the followings: to the hardware layer, workload, voltage, temperature, memory, CPU; to the operating system and middleware layers, software vulnerabilities and bugs; to the facility layer, authentication data; to the network layer, firewall, intrusion detection systems, intrusion prevention systems.

Monitor Architecture, Models and Properties. According to [2], there are two types of architectures: centralized and decentralized. In the first case the PaaS and IaaS resources send status update queries to the centralized monitoring server; the monitoring techniques continuously pull the information from the components via periodic probing messages. Decentralized cloud monitoring tools have recently gained momentum. A monitoring tool is considered as decentralized if none of the components in the system is more important than others; in case one of the components fails, it does not influence the operations of any other component in the system. Following [21], other design criteria for the monitor architecture, are the followings: event notification (asynchronous or synchronous), network transport (like UDP or TCP), historical data (with or without), measurement update strategy (like periodic, event or no update), communication model (pull or push), distributed architecture (like publish-subscribe, service-client, server-agent or client-server), QoS support (with or without), notification strategy (on change or event or periodic), metadata (out-band or in-band), exchange format (proprietary, XDR-XML, XDR, plain text or CDR), filtering (time-based, content-based or no filtering), discovery (with or without, only sensors, registration, or cluster level), communication cardinality (1:N or N:M), transport protocol (standard or proprietary).

Moreover, the models of monitoring frameworks are needed to assess their performance and verify results obtained from measurement. An analytic model of the behaviour of a monitoring framework that is usefull in the context of Cloud services is the one provided in [12].

According to [1,5], a monitoring system is required to have several properties: scalability, elasticity, adaptability, timeliness, autonomicity, comprehensiveness, extensibility, non-instrusiveness, accuracy. If the system is working with multiple clouds, a supplementary requirement is interoperability. If the system is dealing with security, than the following supplementary properties should be fulfilled, according to [13,14]: effectiveness, precision, transparency, non-subvertability, deployability, dynamic reaction, accountability and multi-tenancy.

Input Data for Security Monitoring. In terms of security requirements, the monitoring tests are quite complex. One of the reasons is the restricted access to the monitoring data. Here we mention shortly only the parameters categories. The data available are depending on the delivery model. In SaaS model, the available data are: if the CSP allows, application logs; if applicable, the access data like browser based or client-based monitoring data, proxy/gateway data. In PaaS model, the available data are: application logs; if the CSP allows, error or platform logs; if a proxy/gateway is used, the access data. In IaaS model, the available data are: logs of databases, applications or operating systems; local host traffic for network monitoring; antimalware or other agents logs for host/endpoint activity; if the CSP allows, change and hypervisor logs; if a proxy/gateway is used, access data.

4   Conclusions

The lack of a SLA-based cloud security monitoring system in the current market is reflecting the complexity of its design and implementation. This paper intended to reveal the main challenges and barriers (like the definition of security SLAs or big data monitoring), encountered in an initiative that intends to build a such system. Moreover, it has point towards the building blocks that make possible the development at this moment in time, following the recent definition of the cloud security parameters. The development of the prototype is an on-going work in the SPECS project (www.specs-project.eu).

Acknowledgment. This research is partially supported by the Romanian grant PN-II-ID-PCE-2011-3-0260 (AMICAS), as preliminary study for the grant FP7-ICT-2013-10-610795 (SPECS).

References

1. Aceto, G., Botta, A., De Donato, W., Pescapè, A.: Survey cloud monitoring: A survey. Computer Networks 57(9), 2093–2115 (2013), http://dx.doi.org/10.1016/j.comnet.2013.04.001
2. Alhamazani, K., Ranjan, R., Mitra, K., Rabhi, F.A., Khan, S.U., Guabtni, A., Bhatnagar, V.: An overview of the commercial cloud monitoring tools: Research dimensions, design issues, and state-of-the-art. CoRR abs/1312.6170 (2013), http://arxiv.org/abs/1312.6170
3. Bernsmed, K., Jaatun, M.G., Meland, P.H., Undheim, A.: Security slas for federated cloud services. In: 2011 Sixth International Conference on Availability, Reliability and Security (ARES), pp. 202–209 (August 2011), http://dx.doi.org/10.1109/ARES.2011.34
4. de Chaves, S.A., Westphall, C.B., Lamin, F.R.: Sla perspective in security management for cloud computing. In: 2010 Sixth International Conference on Networking and Services (ICNS), pp. 212–217 (March 2010), http://dx.doi.org/10.1109/ICNS.2010.36
5. Clayman, S., Galis, A., Chapman, C., Toffetti, G., Rodero-Merino, L., Vaquero, L.M., Nagin, K., Rochwerger, B.: Monitoring service clouds in the future internet. In: Towards the Future Internet, pp. 115–126. IOS Press (March 2010), http://dx.doi.org/10.3233/978-1-60750-539-6-115
6. Cloud Security Alliance: Cloud controls matrix. Tech. Rep. Version 3, CSA (September 2013), https://cloudsecurityalliance.org/download/cloud-controls-matrix-v3/
7. CUMULUS Consortium: Security-aware sla specification language and cloud security dependency model. Tech. Rep. Deliverable D2.1, CUMULUS (September 2013), http://cumulus-project.eu/index.php/public-deliverables
8. Danwei, C., Xiuli, H., Xunyi, R.: Access control of cloud service based on ucon. In: Jaatun, M.G., Zhao, G., Rong, C. (eds.) Cloud Computing. LNCS, vol. 5931, pp. 559–564. Springer, Heidelberg (2009), http://dx.doi.org/10.1007/978-3-642-10665-1_52
9. Emeakaroha, V.C.: Managing Cloud Service Provisioning and SLA Enforcement via Holistic Monitoring Techniques. Ph.D. thesis, Vienna University of Technology (2012), http://www.infosys.tuwien.ac.at/staff/vincent/pub/Emeakaroha_thesis.pdf
10. European Union Agency for Network and Information Security: Procure secure: A guide to monitoring of security service levels in cloud contracts. Tech. rep., ENISA (April 2012), http://www.enisa.europa.eu/activities/Resilience-and-CIIP/cloud-computing/procure-secure-a-guide-to-monitoring-of-security-service-levels-in-cloud-contracts
11. Federal Office for Information Security: Security recommendations for cloud computing providers. Tech. rep., BSI (June 2011), https://www.bsi.bund.de/SharedDocs/Downloads/EN/BSI/Publications/Minimum_information/SecurityRecommendationsCloudComputingProviders.html
12. Lahmadi, A., Andrey, L., Festor, O.: Design and validation of an analytical model to evaluate monitoring frameworks limits. In: Eighth International Conference on Networks, ICN 2009, pp. 397–402 (March 2009)

13. Laniepce, S., Lacoste, M., Kassi-Lahlou, M., Bignon, F., Lazri, K., Wailly, A.: Engineering intrusion prevention services for iaas clouds: The way of the hypervisor. In: 2013 IEEE 7th International Symposium on Service Oriented System Engineering (SOSE), pp. 25–36 (March 2013), http://dx.doi.org/10.1109/SOSE.2013.27
14. Manavi, S., Mohammadalian, S., Udzir, N.I., Abdullah, A.: Secure model for virtualization layer in cloud infrastructure. International Journal of Cyber-Security and Digital Forensics 1(1), 32–40 (2012)
15. Montes, J., Sánchez, A., Memishi, B., Pérez, M.S., Antoniu, G.: Gmone: A complete approach to cloud monitoring. Future Generation Computing Systems 29(8), 2026–2040 (2013), http://dx.doi.org/10.1016/j.future.2013.02.011
16. Muñoz, A., Gonzalez, J., Maña, A.: A performance-oriented monitoring system for security properties in cloud computing applications. The Computer Journal 55(8), 979–994 (2012), http://dx.doi.org/10.1093/comjnl/bxs042
17. NIST Cloud Computing Standards Roadmap Working Group: Nist cloud computing reference architecture cloud service metrics description. Tech. rep., NIST (September 2013), http://www.nist.gov/itl/cloud/
18. Palhares, N., Lima, S.R., Carvalho, P.: A multidimensional model for monitoring cloud services. In: Rocha, Á., Correia, A.M., Wilson, T., Stroetmann, K.A. (eds.) Advances in Information Systems and Technologies. AISC, vol. 206, pp. 931–938. Springer, Heidelberg (2013), http://dx.doi.org/10.1007/978-3-642-36981-087
19. Petcu, D.: A taxonomy for sla-based monitoring of cloud security. In: 2014 IEEE 38th Annual Computer Software and Applications Conference (COMPSAC) (in print July, 2014)
20. Petcu, D., Crăciun, C.: Towards a security sla-based cloud monitoring service. In: 2014 4th International Conference on Cloud Computing and Services Science (CLOSER), pp. 598–603 (April 2014), http://dx.doi.org/10.5220/0004957305980603
21. Povedano-Molina, J., Lopez-Vega, J.M., Lopez-Soler, J.M., Corradi, A., Foschini, L.: Dargos: A highly adaptable and scalable monitoring architecture for multi-tenant clouds. Future Generation Computer Systems 29(8), 2041–2056 (2013), http://dx.doi.org/10.1016/j.future.2013.04.022
22. Rak, M., Suri, N., Luna, J., Petcu, D., Casola, V., Villano, U.: Security as a service using an sla-based approach via specs. In: 2013 IEEE 5th International Conference on Cloud Computing Technology and Science (CloudCom), vol. 2, pp. 1–6 (December 2013), http://dx.doi.org/10.1109/CloudCom.2013.165
23. Rudolph, M., Schwarz, R.: A critical survey of security indicator approaches. In: 2012 Seventh International Conference on Availability, Reliability and Security (ARES), pp. 291–300 (August 2012), http://dx.doi.org/10.1109/ARES.2012.10
24. Siegel, J., Perdue, J.: Cloud services measures for global use: The service measurement index (smi). In: Annual SRII Global Conference, pp. 411–415 (2012)
25. Spring, J.: Monitoring cloud computing by layer, part 1. IEEE Security and Privacy 9(2), 66–68 (2011), http://dx.doi.org/10.1109/MSP.2011.33
26. Wagner, R., Heiser, J., Perkins, E., Nicolett, M., Kavanagh, K.M., Chuvakin, A., Young, G.: Predicts 2013: Cloud and services security. Tech. Rep. G00245775, Gartner (Nov 2012), https://www.gartner.com/doc/2254916/predicts--cloud-services-security
27. Zou, D., Zhang, W., Qiang, W., Xiang, G., Yang, L.T., Jin, H., Hu, K.: Design and implementation of a trusted monitoring framework for cloud platforms. Future Generation Computer Systems 29(8), 2092–2102 (2013), http://dx.doi.org/10.1016/j.future.2012.12.020

A Survey on Parallel and Distributed Multi-Agent Systems

Alban Rousset, Bénédicte Herrmann, Christophe Lang, and Laurent Philippe

Femto-ST Institute
University of Franche-Comté
16 Route de Gray 25030 Besançon cedex - France
{alban.rousset,bherrman,clang,lphilipp}@femto-st.fr

Abstract. Simulation has become an indispensable tool for researchers to explore systems without having recourse to real experiments. Depending on the characteristics of the modeled system, methods used to represent the system may vary. Multi-agent systems are, thus, often used to model and simulate complex systems. Whatever modeling type used, increasing the size and the precision of the model increases the amount of computation, requiring the use of parallel systems when it becomes too large. In this paper, we focus on parallel platforms that support multi-agent simulations. Our contribution is a survey on existing platforms and their evaluation in the context of high performance computing. We present a qualitative analysis, mainly based on platform properties, then a performance comparison using the same agent model implemented on each platform.

Keywords: multi-agent simulation, parallelism, MAS.

1 Introduction

In the field of simulation, we often seek to exceed limits, that is to say analyse larger and more precise models to be closer to the reality of a problem. Increasing the size of a model has however a direct impact on the amount of needed computing resources and centralised systems are often no longer sufficient to run these simulations. The use of parallel resources allows us to overcome the resource limits of centralised systems and also to increase the size of the simulated models.

There are several ways to model a system. For example, the time behavior of a large number of physical systems is based on differential equations. In this case the discretization of a model allows its representation as a linear system. It is then possible to use existing parallel libraries to take advantage of many computing nodes and run large simulations. On the other hand it is not always possible to model any time dependent system with differential equations. This is for instance the case of complex systems. A complex system is defined in [25] as "*A system that can be analyzed into many components having relatively many relations among them, so that the behavior of each component depends on*

L. Lopes et al. (Eds.): Euro-Par 2014 Workshops, Part I, LNCS 8805, pp. 371–382, 2014.

the behavior of others". Thus the complexity of the dependencies between the phenomena that drive the entities behavior makes it difficult to define a global law that models the entire system. For this reason multi-agent systems are often used to model complex systems because they rely on an algorithmic description of agents that interact and simulate the expected behavior. From the viewpoint of increasing the size of simulations, multi-agent systems are constrained to the same rules as other modelling techniques but there exists less support for parallel execution of the models.

In this article, we focus on multi-agent platforms that provide parallel distributed programming environments for multi-agent systems. Recently, the interest for parallel multi-agent platforms has increased. This is because parallel platforms offer more resources to run larger agent simulations and thus allows to obtain results or behavior that was not possible to obtain with smaller number of agents (eg. simulation of individual motions in a city/urban mobility).

The contribution of this article is a survey on parallel distributed multi-agent platforms. This survey is based on an extensive bibliographical work done to identify the existing platforms, a qualitative analysis of these platforms in terms of ease of development, distribution management or proposed agent model, and a performance evaluation based on a representative model run on a HPC cluster.

The article is organised as follows. First, we give the context of multi-agent system (MAS) in general and parallel distributed multi-agent systems (PDMAS) in particular. We then introduce the different multi-agent platforms found in our bibliographical research. In the third section, we describe the method used to classify platforms and we describe the model implemented in each platform to evaluate its performance. In the fourth section, we present the qualitative comparison of the different PDMAS followed by the benchmark based on the implemented model. We finish the paper with conclusion and future work.

2   Related Works

The concept of agent has been studied extensively for several years and in different domains. It is not only used in robotics and other fields of artificial intelligence, but also in fields such as psychology [6] or biology [23]. One of the first definitions of the agent concept is due to Ferber [13] :

> "An agent is a real or virtual autonomous entity, operating in a environment, able to perceive and act on it, which can communicate with other agents, which exhibits an independent behavior, which can be seen as the consequence of his knowledge, its interactions with other agents and goals it need to achieved".

A multi-agent system, or MAS, is a platform that provides the mandatory support to run simulations based on several autonomous agents. These platforms implement functions that provide services such as agent life cycle management, communication between agents, agent perception or environment management. Among well known platforms we can cite Repast Simphony [21], Mason [19],

NetLogo [28] and Gama [1]. These platforms however do not natively implement a support to run models in parallel and it is necessary to develop a wrapper from scratch, in order to distribute or parallelize a simulation. There exists several papers that propose survey on these multi-agent platforms [29,5,4,16].

Some platforms like RepastHPC [10], D-Mason [12], Pandora [2], Flame [8] or JADE [3] provide a native support for parallel execution of models. This support usually includes the collaboration between executions on several physical nodes, the distribution of agents between nodes and so on. During our analysis of the literature, we did not find any survey about parallel multi-agent platforms except the paper written by Coakley and al. [8]. This comparison is based on qualitative criteria such as the implementation language but the paper does not provide any performance comparison of the studied platforms.

After an extensive bibliographical work, we identified 10 implementations or projects of parallel multi-agent platforms. For each platform we tried to download the source or executable code and we tried to compile it and test it with the provided examples and templates. Some of the platforms cannot be included in our study because there is no available source code or downloadable executable (MACE3J [15], JAMES[17], SWAGES [24]), or because only a demonstration version is available (PDES-MAS [22,27]), or because there is a real lack of documentation (Ecolab [26]). It was thus not possible to build a new model in these platforms and thus to assess their parallel characteristics and performance. These platforms have subjected to a qualitative analysis which is not included in this paper.

For the 5 remaining platforms, on which we were able to implement our model, we can consider that they truly offer a functioning parallel multi-agent support. We succinctly present each of these platforms in the following.

D-Mason (Distributed Mason) [12] is developed by the University of Salerno. D-Mason is the distributed version of the Mason multi-agent platform. The authors choose to develop a distributed version of Mason to provide a solution that does not require users to rewrite their already developed simulations and also to overcome the limitations on maximum number of agents. D-Mason uses ActiveMQ JMS as a base to implement communications. D-Mason uses the Java language to implement the agent model.

Flame [8] is developed by the University of Sheffield. Flame was designed to allow a wide range of agent models. Flame provides specifications in the form of a formal framework that can be used by developers to create models and tools. Flame allows parallelization using MPI. Implementing a Flame simulation is based on the definition of X-Machines [9] which are defined as finite state automata with memory. In addition, agents can send and receive messages at the input and the output of each state.

Jade [3] is developed by the Telecom laboratory of Italia. The aims of Jade are to simplify the implementation of distributed multi-agent models across a FIPA compliant [3] middleware and to provide a set of tools that support the debugging and the deployment phases. The platform can be distributed across multiple computers and its configuration can be controlled from a remote GUI.

Agents are implemented in Java while the communications relay on the RMI library.

Pandora [2] is developed by the Supercomputing center of Barcelona. It is explicitly programmed to allow the execution of scalable multi-agent simulations. According to the literature, Pandora is able to treat thousands of agents with complex actions. Pandora also provides a support for a geographic information system (GIS) in order to run simulations where spatial coordinates are used. Pandora uses the $C++$ language to define and to implement the agent models. For the communications, Pandora automatically generates MPI code from the Pandora library.

RepastHPC [10] is developed by the Argone institute of USA. It is a part of a series of multi-agent simulation platforms: RepastJ and Repast Simphony. RepastHPC is specially designed for high performance environments. RepastHPC use the same concepts as the core of RepastSimphony, that is to say it uses also the concept of projections (grid, network) but this concept is adapted to parallel environments. The $C++$ language is used to implement an agent simulation but the ReLogo language, a derivative of the NetLogo language, can also be used. For the communications, the RepastHPC platform relays on MPI using the Boost library [11].

From these descriptions we can note that some platforms have already been designed to target high performance computing systems such as clusters whereas others are more focused on distribution on less coupled nodes such as a network of workstations.

3 Survey Methodology

In this section we explain the methodology used to make this survey. As already stated we started by a bibliographical search (using keywords on search engines and following links cited in the studied articles). This bibliographical search allowed us to establish a first list of existing platforms. By testing the available platforms we established a second list of functioning platforms. To our knowledge this list is complete and their is no other available and functional platform that provide a support for parallel distributed MAS. Note we only concentrate on distributed platforms and that the list excludes shared memory parallel platforms and many-cores (as GPU or Intel Xeon Phi) platforms. After we defined different criteria to compare and analyse each platform. We finished by implementing a reference model on each platform and executing it in order to compare the platform performance. These evaluation steps are detailed in the following.

This survey mainly focuses on the implementation, more precisely the development, of models and their execution efficiency. To classify the platforms we defined two sets of criteria: first, implementation and execution based criteria and, second, criteria about classical properties of parallel systems. We briefly explain in which correspond each criteria.

For the implementation and execution criteria, all platforms have their own constraints that impact on the ease of the model implementation. The chosen criteria are:

1. Programming language,
2. Agent representation
3. Simulation type, time-driven or event-driven
4. Reproductibility, do several executions of a simulation give the same results?

For the classical properties of parallel systems, we focus on:

1. Scalability of platform, in terms of agents and nodes,
2. Load balancing, agent distribution,
3. MultiThread execution, to take benefit of multicore processors,
4. Communication library.

To further compare the platforms, we have defined a reference agent model that we implemented on each platform. The reference model is based on three important behaviors for each agent: the agent perception, the communications between agents and/or with the environment and agent mobility. The reference model simulates each of these behaviors.

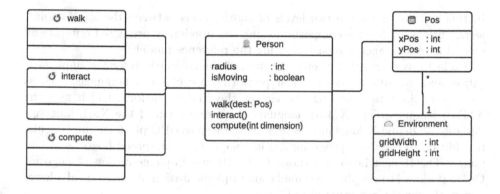

Fig. 1. AML representation of the reference agent model

Figure 1 gives an AML [7] (Agent Modeling Language) representation of our reference model. The *Environment* is represented by a square grid. *Agents* are mobile and move randomly on the grid. A *vision* characterised by the "radius" property is also associated with each agent. It represents the limited perception of the agent on the environment.

Each agent is composed of 3 sub-behaviors :

1. The walk behavior allows agents to move in a random direction on the environment. This behavior is used to test the mobility and the perception of the agents. As the agents walk through their environment to discover other agents and other parts of the environment, interactions and communications with the environment are also tested with this behavior.

2. The interact behavior allows agents to interact and send messages to other agents in their perception fields. This behavior intends to simulate communications between agents and to evaluate the communication support of the platforms.
3. The compute behavior allows agents to compute a "Fast Fourier Transform (FFT)" [14] in order to represent a workload. This behavior intends to simulate the load generated by the execution of the agent inner algorithms.

The global agent behavior consists in performing each of this three behaviors at each time step. The reference model has several parameters that determine the agent behavior and also the global model properties. For instance, the model allows to vary the workload using different sizes of input for the FFT calculus. It is also possible to generate more or less communications between agents by setting the number of contacted agents in the interact behavior or to assess the agent mobility by setting the agent speed in the walk behavior.

4   Qualitative Analysis

In this section we expose two levels of comparisons between the studied platforms: first a qualitative comparison using the previously presented criteria and second a performance comparison using the reference model.

Table 1 gives a synthetic representation of the comparison for the implementation and execution criteria. Most platforms use classical languages such as C-C++ or Java to define agents, except the Flame platform which uses the XMML language. The XMML language is an extension of the XML language designed to define X-Machines. Note that the RepastHPC platform implements, in addition to the C++ programming language, the widespread Logo agent language. The Repast-Logo or R-Logo is the Repast implementation of Logo for C++. It allows to simplify the simulation implementation at the price of a lower power of expression compared to C++.

Table 1. Comparison of implementation and execution properties

	RepastHPC	D-Mason	Flame	Pandora	Jade
Prog. lang.	C++/R-Logo	Java	XMML/C	C/C++	Java
Agent represent.	Object	Object	X-Machine	Object	Object
Simu. type	event-driven	time-driven	time-driven	time-driven	time-driven
Reproductibility	Yes	Yes	No	Yes	No

Agents are usually defined as objects with methods representing behaviors. An agent container gathers all the agents. This container is cut and distributed in the case of parallel execution. The agent implementation is different for the Flame platform that does not use the object concept to define a agent but rather uses automatas called X-Machines. In a X-Machine, a behavior is represented by a state in the automata and the order of execution between behaviors are represented by transitions. This difference changes the programming logic of a model but induces no limitation compared with other platforms because agents are in fact encoded in C language.

For the simulation type, event or time driven, all platforms use the time-driven approach except RepastHPC which is based on the event-driven approach. RepastHPC however allows to fix a periodicity to each scheduled event, so that we can reproduce the behavior of time-driven simulations.

Finally all platforms allow agents to communicate. This communication can be performed either *internally* with agents that are on the same node, or *externally*, with agents that are on different nodes. The D-Mason and Pandora platforms propose remote method invocations to communicate with other agents while the other platforms use messages to communicate between agents.

Table 2 summarises the criteria of the platforms about classical properties of parallel systems. Globally we can note that all studied platforms meet the demands for the development of parallel simulations. Note that we did not find any information on the scalability property of the Pandora and Jade platforms, so they are marked as Not Available (NA) for this property. To efficiency exploit the power of several nodes the computing load must be balanced among them. There is different ways to balance the computing load . The load can be balanced at the beginning of the simulation (Static) or adapted during the execution (Dynamic). A dynamic load balancing is usually better as it provides a better adaptation in case of load variation during the model execution, but it can also be subject to instability. Most platforms use dynamic load balancing except the Jade and Flame platforms. In [20] the authors propose a way to use dynamic load balancing with the Flame platform.

Table 2. Comparison classical properties of parallel systems

	RepastHPC	D-Mason	Flame	Pandora	Jade
Scalability	1028 proc. [18]	36 nodes [8]	432 proc. [8]	NA	NA
Load Balancing	Dynamic	Dynamic	Static [8]	Dynamic	Static [3]
Multithread exec	Yes [8]	Yes [12,8]	No [8]	Yes	Yes
Com. library	MPI [11,10]	JMS [12]	MPI [18]	MPI [2]	RMI

Note that only Flame does not support multi-threaded executions. The platform however relays on the MPI messaging library. As most MPI libraries provide optimised implementations of message passing functions when the communicating processes are on the same node, using processes located on the same node instead of threads does not lead to large overhead. In the implementation of a multi-agent system this probably leads to equivalent performance as the simplification of synchronisation issues may compensate the cost of using communication functions.

Last, the communication support for most platforms is MPI. This is not surprising for platforms targeting HPC systems as this library is mainly used on these computers. Note that the D-Mason platform relays on the JMS communication service despite it is not the most scalable solution for distributed environments. An MPI version of D-MASON is in development. Finally, the Jade platform is based on the java Remote Method Invocation (RMI) library which is not very adapted to parallel applications as it is based on synchronous calls. During the model implementation we also noted that the Jade platform seems to be more oriented for equipment monitoring and cannot be run on HPC computers due to internal limitations. Jade is thus not included in the rest of the comparisons.

5   Performance Evaluation

For the performance evaluation we have implemented the reference model defined in section 3 on the four functional platforms: RepastHPC, D-MASON, Flame, Pandora. During this model implementation, we did not encounter noticeable difficulties expect with the RepastHPC platform for which we have not been able to implement external communications, communications between agents running on different nodes. RepastHPC does not have the native mechanisms to make it whereas it is possible to implement it on the other platforms. RepastHPC actually offers the possibility to interact with an agent on an other node but not to report the modifications.

Although we have been able to run the four platforms, D-Mason, Flame, Pandora, RepastHPC, on a standard workstation, only two of them (RpastHPC, Flame) have successfully run on our HPC system. The D-Mason platform uses a graphical interface that cannot be disconnected. We are thus not able to run D-MASON on our cluster, only accessible through its batch manager. The Pandora simulations have deadlock problems even if we use examples provided with the platform. For these reasons the presented results only consider the Flame and RepastHPC platforms.

We have realised several executions in order to exhibit the platform behaviors concerning scalability (Figures 2 and 3) and workload (Figure 4). To assess scalability we vary the number of nodes used to execute the simulations while we fix the number of agents. We then compute the obtained speedup. For workload we fix the number of nodes to 8 and we vary the number of agents in the simulation. Each execution is realised several times to assess the standard variation and the presented results are the mean of the different execution durations. Due to a low variation in the simulation runtime, the number of executions for a result is set to 10.

About the HPC experimental settings, we have run the reference model on a 764 cores cluster using the SGE batch system. Each node of the cluster is a bi-processors, with Xeon E5 (8*2 cores) processors running at 2.6 Ghz frequency and with 32 Go of memory. The nodes are connected through a non blocking DDR infinyBand network organised in a fat tree. The system is shared with other users but the batch system garanties that the processes are run without sharing their cores.

Execution results for scalability for a model with 10 000 agents are given on Figure 2 and 3, with the ideal speedup reference. Note that the reference time

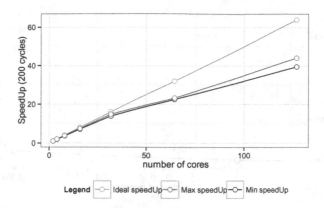

Fig. 2. Scalability of FLAME simulations using 10 000 agents, FFT 100 and 200 cycles

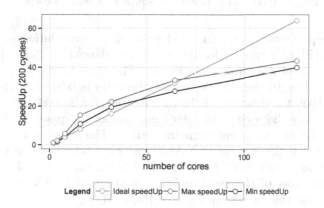

Fig. 3. Scalability of RepastHPC simulations using 10 000 agents, FFT 100 and 200 cycles

used to compute the speedup is based on a two core run of the simulations. This is due to RepastHPC which cannot run on just one core so that its reference time must be based on two core runs. The speedup is therefore limited to half the number of nodes. We can note that both platforms scale well up to 32 cores but the performance does not progress so well after, becoming 2/3 of the theoretical speedup for 128 cores. In addition on Figure 3 we can see that RepastHPC results are above the theorical speedup for simulations with less than 50 cores. As we suspected that these better results come from cache optimizations in the system, we did more tests to confirm this hypothesis. The realized tests increase the number of agents and the load on each agent to saturate the cache and force memory accesses. As the results for these new tests are under the theorical speedup the hypothesis is validated.

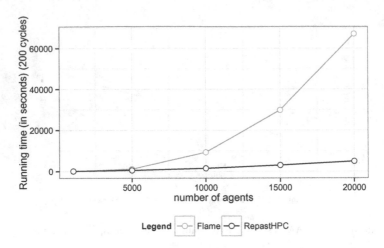

Fig. 4. Workload behavior for simulation using 8 cores

Figures 4 represents the workload behavior of the two platforms. The inner load of agents (FFT) is here set to 100. The figure shows that RepastHPC really better reacts to load increasing than Flame. The same behavior has also been noted for a load of 10 (for 20 000 agents the ratio is 0.92). On the opposite for a load of 1000 the difference is less noticeable (for 20 000 agents the ratio is 0.81). Obviously the used model does not use all the power of Flame as it is limited in term of inter-agent communications. The question to answer is: is it due to the use of the concept of X-Machines or synchronisation mechanisms in the underlying parallelism? Another possible reason that could justify this difference is the cost of the synchronisations provided by Flame when using remote agents and that is not managed in RepastHPC.

6   Conclusion

In this article we have presented a comparison of different parallel multi-agent platforms. This comparison is performed at two levels, first at a qualitative level using criteria on the provided support, and second at a quantitative level, using a reference agent model implementation. The qualitative comparison shows the properties of all the studied platforms. The quantitative part shows an equivalent scalability for both platforms but better performance results for the RepasHPC platform.

When implementing our reference model we have noticed that the synchronisation support of the platforms does not provide the same level of service: the RepastHPC platform does not provide communication support for remote agents while Flame do it. This support seems to be a key point in the platform performance.

For this reason, in our future work, we intend to better examine the efficiency of synchronisation mechanisms in parallel platforms. For example how are the synchronizations made during an execution and is there a way to improve synchronization mechanisms in parallel multi-agent systems?

Acknowledgement. Computations have been performed on the supercomputer facilities of the Mésocentre de calcul de Franche-Comté.

References

1. Amouroux, E., Chu, T.-Q., Boucher, A., Drogoul, A.: GAMA: An environment for implementing and running spatially explicit multi-agent simulations. In: Ghose, A., Governatori, G., Sadananda, R. (eds.) PRIMA 2007. LNCS, vol. 5044, pp. 359–371. Springer, Heidelberg (2009)
2. Angelotti, E.S., Scalabrin, E.E., Ávila, B.C.: Pandora: a multi-agent system using paraconsistent logic. In: Computational Intelligence and Multimedia Applications, ICCIMA 2001, pp. 352–356. IEEE (2001)
3. Bellifemine, F., Poggi, A., Rimassa, G.: Jade–a fipa-compliant agent framework. In: Proceedings of PAAM, London, vol. 99, p. 33 (1999)
4. Berryman, M.: Review of software platforms for agent based models. Technical report, DTIC Document (2008)
5. Bordini, R.H., Braubach, L., Dastani, M., El Fallah-Seghrouchni, A., Gomez-Sanz, J.J., Leite, J., O'Hare, G.M., Pokahr, A., Ricci, A.: A survey of programming languages and platforms for multi-agent systems. Informatica (Slovenia) 30(1), 33–44 (2006)
6. Carslaw, G.: Agent based modelling in social psychology. PhD thesis, University of Birmingham (2013)
7. Červenka, R., Trenčanský, I., Calisti, M., Greenwood, D.P.A.: AML: Agent modeling language toward industry-grade agent-based modeling. In: Odell, J.J., Giorgini, P., Müller, J.P. (eds.) AOSE 2004. LNCS, vol. 3382, pp. 31–46. Springer, Heidelberg (2005)
8. Coakley, S., Gheorghe, M., Holcombe, M., Chin, S., Worth, D., Greenough, C.: Exploitation of hpc in the flame agent-based simulation framework. In: Proceedings of the 2012 IEEE 14th Int. Conf. on HPC and Communication & 2012 IEEE 9th Int. Conf. on Embedded Software and Systemsm, HPCC 2012, pp. 538–545. IEEE Computer Society, Washington, DC (2012)
9. Coakley, S., Smallwood, R., Holcombe, M.: Simon Coakley, Rod Smallwood, and Mike Holcombe. Using x-machines as a formal basis for describing agents in agent-based modelling. Simulation Series 38(2), 33 (2006)
10. Collier, N., North, M.: Repast HPC: A platform for large-scale agentbased modeling. Wiley (2011)
11. Collier, N.: Repast hpc manual (2010)
12. Cordasco, G., De Chiara, R., Mancuso, A., Mazzeo, D., Scarano, V., Spagnuolo, C.: A Framework for Distributing Agent-Based Simulations. In: Alexander, M., et al. (eds.) Euro-Par 2011, Part I. LNCS, vol. 7155, pp. 460–470. Springer, Heidelberg (2012)
13. Ferber, J., Perrot, J.-F.: Les systèmes multi-agents: vers une intelligence collective, InterEditions Paris (1995)
14. Frigo, M., Johnson, S.G.: The design and implementation of fftw3. Proceedings of the IEEE 93(2), 216–231 (2005)

15. Gasser, L., Kakugawa, K.: Mace3j: fast flexible distributed simulation of large, large-grain multi-agent systems. In: Proceedings of the First Inter. Joint Conf. on Autonomous Agents and Multiagent Systems: part 2, pp. 745–752. ACM (2002)

16. Heath, B., Hill, R., Ciarallo, F.: A survey of agent-based modeling practices (january 1998 to july 2008). JASSS 12(4), 9 (2009)

17. Himmelspach, J., Uhrmacher, A.M.: Plug'n simulate. In: Proceedings of the 40th Annual Simulation Symposium, ANSS 2007, pp. 137–143. IEEE Computer Society, Washington, DC (2007)

18. Holcombe, M., Coakley, S., Smallwood, R.: A general framework for agent-based modelling of complex systems. In: Proceedings of the 2006 European Conf. on Complex Systems (2006)

19. Luke, S., Cioffi-Revilla, C., Panait, L., Sullivan, K.: MASON: A New Multi-Agent Simulation Toolkit. Simulation 81(7), 517–527 (2005)

20. Márquez, C., César, E., Sorribes, J.: A load balancing schema for agent-based spmd applications. In: International Conf. on Parallel and Distributed Processing Techniques and Applications, PDPTA (accepted 2013)

21. North, M.J., Collier, N.T., Ozik, J., Tatara, E.R., Macal, C.M., Bragen, M., Sydelko, P.: Complex adaptive systems modeling with repast simphony. Complex Adaptive Systems Modeling 1(1), 1–26 (2013)

22. Oguara, T., Theodoropoulos, G., Logan, B., Lees, M., Dan, C.: Pdes-mas: A unifying framework for the distributed simulation of multi-agent systems. School of computer science research - University of Birmingham 6 (2007)

23. Rodin, V., Benzinou, A., Guillaud, A., Ballet, P., Harrouet, F., Tisseau, J., Le Bihan, J.: An immune oriented multi-agent system for biological image processing. Pattern Recognition 37(4), 631–645 (2004)

24. Scheutz, M., Schermerhorn, P., Connaughton, R., Dingler, A.: Swages-an extendable distributed experimentation system for large-scale agent-based alife simulations. Proceedings of Artificial Life X, 412–419 (2006)

25. Simon, H.A.: The architecture of complexity. Springer (1991)

26. Standish, R.K., Leow, R.: Ecolab: Agent based modeling for c++ programmers. arXiv preprint cs/0401026 (2004)

27. Suryanarayanan, V., Theodoropoulos, G., Lees, M.: Pdes-mas: Distributed simulation of multi-agent systems. Procedia Comp. Sc. 18, 671–681 (2013)

28. Tisue, S., Wilensky, U.: Netlogo: Design and implementation of a multi-agent modeling environment. In: Proceedings of Agent, vol. 2004, pp. 7–9 (2004)

29. Tobias, R., Hofmann, C.: Evaluation of free java-libraries for social-scientific agent based simulation. JASS 7(1) (2004)

Resolving Conflicts between Multiple Competing Agents in Parallel Simulations

Paul Richmond

Department of Computer Science, The University of Sheffield, UK
p.richmond@sheffield.ac.uk
http://www.paulrichmond.staff.shef.ac.uk.

Abstract. Agents within multi-agent simulation environments frequently compete for limited resources, requiring negotiation to resolve 'conflict'. The negotiation process for resolving conflict often relies on a transactional or serial processes that complicates implementation within a parallel simulation framework. This paper demonstrates how transactional events to resolve competition can be implemented within a parallel simulation framework (FLAME GPU) as a series of iterative parallel agent functions. A sugarscape model where agents compete for space and a model requiring optimal assignment between two populations, the stable marriage problem, are demonstrated. The two case studies act as a building block for more general conflict resolution behaviours requiring negotiation between agents in a parallel simulation environment. Extensions to the FLAME GPU framework are described and performance results are provided to show scalability of the case studies on recent GPU hardware.

Keywords: Agent-Based Simulations, FLAME GPU, Graphics Hardware, CUDA, Conflict Resolution, Multi-Agent Competition.

1 Introduction

Agent based modelling provides a natural mechanism for describing complex systems where agents are represented as a set of individuals with behavioural rules. By simulating agents and their interactions over a period of time, emergent behaviour can be observed, giving insight into processes of the system which the model represents. Agent based simulations are typically more computationally expensive than traditional top down equation based models as each individual and their interactions must be simulated. Previous work has shown that agent based simulations can be accelerated and scaled to increasing levels through the use of parallel [5,10,1,7] and distributed methods [11]. In some cases [5,10,11] such methods are implemented as part of a simulator providing a high level interface for describing agents with a level of abstraction hiding the complexity of the parallel or distributed architecture from end users (modellers).

A common behaviour within agent based models is for agents to compete for some resource. A simple example of this is reflected by any agent based model

L. Lopes et al. (Eds.): Euro-Par 2014 Workshops, Part I, LNCS 8805, pp. 383–394, 2014.

consisting of a regular lattice based (grid) environment in which a sequential simulator moves agents between grid cells. To determine a movement strategy, each agent is free to examine the environment to locate free space (unoccupied by any other agent) and decide upon an optimal movement often driven by the availability of some finite resource. Reproducing this same model with a parallel simulation environment is less straightforward. If each agent simultaneously makes a decision to move there is a potential risk that multiple agents will move to the same grid space (especially if it is highly desirable). Translating models built upon serial abstractions in parallel simulators therefore requires that conflicts in movement can be resolved robustly.

Agent movement in lattice environments represents a special case where competition is introduced indirectly via the migration of a serial algorithm to a parallel environment. Agent competition is not however limited to examples involving movement. For example, any form of assignment may result in agents competing against one another. This paper presents a general method for implementing conflict resolution, demonstrated through two case studies implemented within the Flexible Large-scale Agent Modelling Environment for the Graphics Processing Unit (FLAME GPU) simulation framework. The first example is an implementation of the sugarscape model [3] demonstrating how movement collision avoidance can be implemented in parallel. The second case study demonstrates how an iterative approach to conflict resolution can be applied to an agent based implementation of a classic assignment task 'the stable marriage problem' [4]. The paper provides FLAME GPU background and shows how both case studies can be implemented through a series of iterative stages (or rounds) providing results which demonstrate performance characteristics.

2   FLAME GPU

The FLAME framework is an agent based simulation platform with implementations targeting parallel agent simulation on both distributed (FLAME) [5] and GPU architectures (FLAME GPU)[10]. Both implementations use the same underlying mode of an agent, a communicating stream X-machines (a form of extended state machine containing an internal memory). Agents are expressed as a set of states performing some 'behaviour' that updates an agents internal memory when transitioning from one state to another. Agents are able to communicate indirectly through messages stored in globally accessible message lists. After a message is sent it is persistent within the message list as read only data for a single simulation iteration. Ensuring agents never write and read from the same message list during a single agent function gives a natural synchronisation barrier which enforces a stream like paradigm, preventing race conditions and providing a robust format for mapping to parallel architectures.

FLAME for the GPU (or the FLAME GPU) is an implementation of FLAME which utilises graphics card hardware to accelerate FLAME agent models by automatically translating the model to optimised GPU code. Rather than using a custom model parser, FLAME GPU uses XSLT templates to generate a complete simulation in NVIDIA CUDA C code. The advantage of a code generation process is that performance overheads of having a programming API are avoided lending to extremely high performance. Whilst based on the same principles as FLAME, FLAME GPU has a number of key differences which are important to understand the features and limitations with respect to parallel simulation.

From a simulation perspective, FLAME GPU utilises the Single Program Multiple Data (SPMD) architecture of GPUs to map agent functions as individual GPU kernels operating over agent (and message) memory, stored as arrays of linearly offset data. FLAME GPU makes a distinction between mobile and non mobile agents (Cellular Automaton) so that performance can be optimised in each case. In order to optimise performance for common communication strategies a distinction is made between three common types of message communication, discrete (for cellular automaton), brute-force (for all to all communication) and spatial partitioning (for limited range interactions). In each case, message data is cached using an efficient algorithm to reduce the number of global memory accesses and improve performance.

In certain cases, FLAME GPU provides a massive performance increase over FLAME however it is best suited to large populations of relatively simple (in terms of agent memory requirements) agents. When large number of agents are simulated many GPU threads can be spawned providing an effective mechanism for hiding memory latencies through context switching. If low numbers of threads are used then hiding memory latency becomes more difficult. Similarly if large (complex) agents are used performance is impacted due to the the limited availability of registers. As such methods for solving conflicts and assignments within FLAME GPU must be highly parallel and not for example rely on a single 'large' agent that resolves conflict by having a global overview of the entire population.

3   Competition between Agents on a Lattice

Lattice based agent simulations are a common abstraction within serial agent based simulation software. In such simulation software the serial order of processing agents is either randomised to ensure fairness or based on a priority scheme which gives preference to agents according to some trait. In translating the movement of agents into a parallel architecture it is important that many agents can perform movement simultaneously creating the potential for conflict through competition at highly desirable locations. If the model is built upon the principle that a discrete spatial cell of the environment may be occupied by only a single agent [EA96] then this conflict must be resolved. Within a parallel simulator such as FLAME GPU there are a number of ways to address this competition in parallel. The simplest is to simply to relax the rule preventing grid cells from being occupied by multiple agents. Whilst computationally inexpensive this simplification ultimately changes the nature of the model and will produce significantly different results to the model which relies on sequential processing to avoid conflict. If the rule to relax cells from containing multiple agents is not appropriate then the alternative approach is to serialise some parts of the movement processes where conflicts are observed.

To demonstrate how to address the serialisation of movement conflicts between agents, this paper considers a model of an artificial society (the sugarscape model) proposed by Epstein and Axtell [3]. The sugarscape model in its simplest form it consists of a population of agents (a society) distributed across an environment with a renewable resource (i.e. sugar). Agents require sugar to survive and sequentially move to empty cells within the lattice environment (without breaking the constraint of a single agent per cell) to consume sugar. Each agent has a sugar store which is incremented by accumulating sugar from the environment. During each simulation step an agent is required to use up part of its sugar store to survive at a rate determined by its randomly assigned metabolism. Epstein and Axtell describe a number of more advanced rules including pollution, reproduction, seasonal environments, cultural connections and combat. For the purposes of this paper these additional rules are omitted as the purpose of this model is to demonstrate the use of transactional movement techniques in FLAME GPU agent simulations.

3.1   Implementing Sugarscape in FLAME GPU

It has already been shown by Lynsenko and D'Souza [6] that the sugarscape model is suitable for simulation on a GPU by scattering agents to collision map to resolve movement collisions. Within Lynsenkos work the use of atomic operations ensures that only the highest priority agent is able to occupy a single space. Agents which are superseded by higher priority agents attempt to move in a subsequent step which is repeated until all collisions are resolved. The implementation for the sugarscape agent model within FLAME GPU uses this same principle of iterative rounds of agent movement to resolve conflicts. The FLAME GPU implementation differs however in that atomic operations are replaced with a series of transactional bids (negotiation) placed through messages between agents. This approach of agent negotiation makes the processes applicable to any parallel simulator or to parallel architectures where atomic operations are not supported. More specifically the process to allow agent movement uses the following sequence of events which are defined within FLAME GPU as individual agent functions (an agent in this case represents a spatial cell which may or may not contain an agent);

1. Cells containing agents read in messages from the environment to determine the best place to move to. Once a target location is identified, they output a request to move as a message containing the targets location identifier and the agents identifier information.
2. Unoccupied cells read all request messages to determine if any neighbouring sugarscape agents would like to move to the location. If multiple agents request to move to the same cell then the cell uses the agents priority to determine which agent should move. After all requests have been considered the cell becomes occupied by the agent with the highest priority. It then sends a confirmation response with the agents identifier to notify the old cell that the agent has moved.

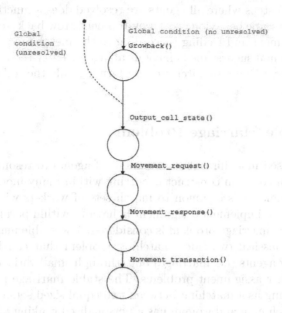

```
          Global              Global condition (no unresolved)
          condition
          (unresolved)        Growback()



                              Output_cell_state()



                              Movement_request()



                              Movement_response()



                              Movement_transaction()
```

Fig. 1. The sugarscape model consists of a *Growback* agent function which performs the 'normal' agent behaviour e.g. consumption of sugar, etc. This function is only triggered if all agents are in a resolved state indicating that all agents have moved. If any agents are unresolved then a simulation step consists of agents performing an iterative round of bidding where only the highest priority agent is allowed to move should conflict occur.

3. Cells containing agents which previously requested to move, check the confirmation response messages. If a confirmation is found the agent knows it has been relocated and updates the cell to an unoccupied state. If no confirmation is found then the agent remains at the same location.

The above steps represent a single iteration of agent movement and do not guarantee that all agents with the desire to relocate will actually do so. To overcome this problem, it is essential that the process is repeated until every agent has moved. To guarantee movement of all agents potentially requires the process to be repeated for every possible location that an agent could move into. With a simple vision radius of 1, 8 potential repetitions represent the worst case scenario. In many cases all agent movement can be resolved in far fewer iterations so a FLAME GPU global function condition is used to determine the global state of agent movement. A global function condition allows agents to perform a state transition (and perform the necessary agent function in doing so) only when a conditional statement is met by all agents (for which the function is applied). In this case agents are assigned two states, resolved and unresolved (with respect to their movement) and the global function condition only allows the population of agents to move to a resolved state when all agent movements are resolved. Only within simulation steps where all agents are resolved does a function performing the 'normal sugarscape behaviour', e.g. environment grow back, removal of sugar from the environment and feeding (according to the metabolic rate) take place. Following the normal sugarscape behaviour all agents enter the unresolved state resulting in the next simulation iteration performing only the collision resolution steps (Figure 1).

4   The Stable Marriage Problem

Within agent based modelling the assignment of agents to resources (including other agents) is a common construct occurring within many models. For example within economics it is common to match sets of workers with firms [2]. To demonstrate how to implement assignment behaviour within parallel agent based models, the stable marriage problem is considered. The stable marriage problem is a example a classical two sided matching problem that can be applied not only to matching agents (i.e. marriage) but (through small variations) is equally applicable to other assignment problems. The stable marriage problem defines two sided matching as a matching between two equal sized sets of n men and n woman where each man and woman has a personalised ranking of all member of the opposite sex. The goal is to find a stable solution of matches where stability is defined as a set of matches where there are no two couples that would prefer to swap with each others partners.

The Gale-Shapley algorithm [4] is an iterative algorithm which guarantees to find a solution where everyone is married and marriages are stable. It does not guarantee optimality from the perspective of both sides but is in fact optimal from the perspective of the proposer. The algorithm works by iterating through a number of rounds of proposals. During each round, single men (men who are not engaged) propose to the woman that they have highest preference for and which they have not previously proposed. Each woman then considers all proposals and accepts the proposal of highest preference rejecting all others. At this stage a provisional engagement between a couple is formed. This can only be broken if the woman receives a a proposal from a man which she prefers in subsequent rounds.

4.1   Implementing the Gale-Shapley Algorithm in FLAME GPU

In order to handle the storage requirements of the stable marriage problem within FLAME GPU an extension to the existing framework has been made to allow agents to hold fixed length arrays within the internal memory of an agent. This effectively allows both a man and woman agent to hold a list of length n (the number of men and woman) corresponding to the rank of their preferred partners. Fixed length array agent memory variables have been implemented in such as way as to preserve the coherence of memory accesses for a group of agents simultaneously access the ith value from the array. In order to ensure coherent memory accesses array items are organised as a Structure of Arrays

(SoA) rather than an Array of Structures(AoS). Figure 2 demonstrates how agent variables including (newly supported) arrays are assembled in memory. Array items for each agent are separated in memory by a stride of n and as such agent memory array access functions have been incorporated into the FLAME GPU code generation templates to handle accessing variables with the appropriate strides.

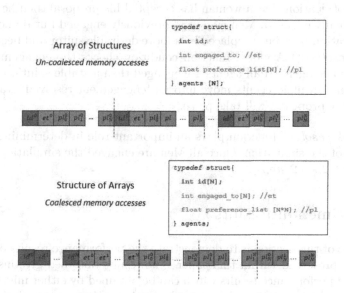

Fig. 2. Figure shows the memory layout differences of agent memory variables and agent memory variable arrays when using an Array of Structures (AoS) vs a Structure of Arrays (SoA) for data storage. Superscript indicates agent index, subscript indicates array index. When using a SoA agent variables and indices of arrays are grouped sequentially for each agent, allowing coalesced memory access.

The Gale-Shapley algorithm has been implemented within FLAME GPU as two agents (men and woman) with the following five agent functions which represent the behaviour of a single round of the algorithm;

1. *make_proposals*(): Only men who are not engaged propose to their highest ranked woman who they have not already proposed to. To select the next highest ranking woman, men select from an ordered list of indices representing the rank of woman they prefer. Proposal messages contain the index of the woman who is being proposed to and the index of the man who is proposing.
2. *check_proposals*(): All woman iterate all proposals to check if any are directed towards them (by considering the indices stored in the proposal messages). If they have received a proposal from any men in which they have a higher preference for than their current provisional partner (or if they do

not have partner) then the details of this 'suitor' are saved and the woman becomes provisionally engaged.

3. *notify_suitors*(): An agent function filter determines woman who are provisionally engaged and allows these woman to notify suitors by sending a notification message containing her unique index and the index of the suitor that she has chosen.

4. *check_notifications*(): All men check all notification messages. If a man sees a notification that a woman has accepted his proposal then he becomes provisionally engaged. Men who were previously engaged but do not receive a notification have been replaced by a more desirable suitor and become free.

5. *check_resolved*() A global function condition checks the engagement state of each male agent. If all agents are engaged then a stable solution has been found and all male agents move into an 'engagement resolved' state where no further proposals will take place.

The *check_resolved* function plays an important role in determining the terminal state of the simulation. Once all Men are engaged the simulation ends (in at worst $n^2 + 2n - 2$ steps).

5   Experimental Results

The purpose of this section is to demonstrate the performance results of the two case studies presented within this paper. The results obtained give insight into the expected performance results which can be obtained by either migrating lattice based serial movement models or implementing assignment resolution within a FLAME GPU model. The two case studies have been implemented in FLAME GPU 1.3 for CUDA 6.0 (available online for free at http://www.flamegpu.com) which contains the new functionality to support array value agent memory variables. Both models are available within the updated framework to ensure results to be producible. Results have been obtained from an Intel Core i7-2600K Machine using an NVIDIA K40 GPU with CUDA 6.0. A fixed number of 64 threads per block is applied to all FLAME GPU kernels. FLAME GPU has a one to one mapping of agent functions and GPU kernals, additional GPU kernels provide background management of agent and message data for additional information readers are directed to previous publications on these methods [8,9].

The sugarscape model is configured by randomly selecting 50 percent of available cells to contain sugarscape agents. The environment is also initialised with a random sugar distribution. Figure 3 (**A**) shows that over a million FLAME GPU agent cells are able to perform a single simulation step in just over 5ms, a single simulation step with over 16 million cells takes on average 76 ms. Each simulation step represents a single iteration of the movement conflict resolution processes described in section 3.1 and as such agent behaviour such as consumption (of sugar) and environmental grow-back is only performed within simulation steps where movement conflicts are fully resolved. Figure 3 (**B**) shows simultaneously; a breakdown of simulation step performance of 1048576 cells over the

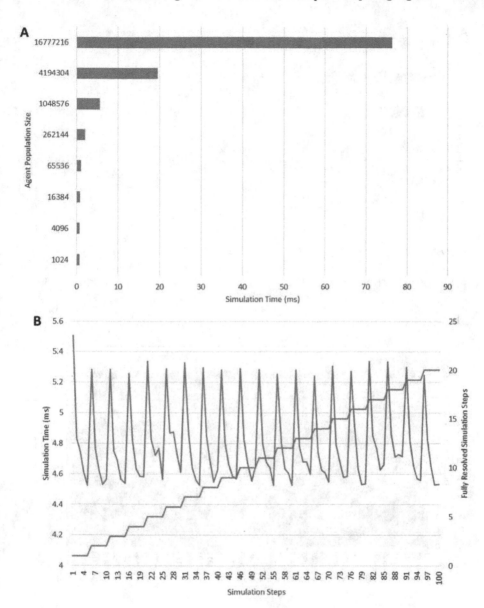

Fig. 3. Performance results of the sugarscape simulation showing; **A**: The performance scaling of the simulation by increasing the agent population size. Timings (in milliseconds) are measured over 100 simulation steps and then averaged. **B**: A breakdown of simulation performance over the first 100 steps of simulation. Primary (left hand) axis corresponds with the blue simulation timings (in milliseconds), the secondary (right hand) axis shows the number of fully resolved resolution steps (where all agents have resolved movement collision conflicts).

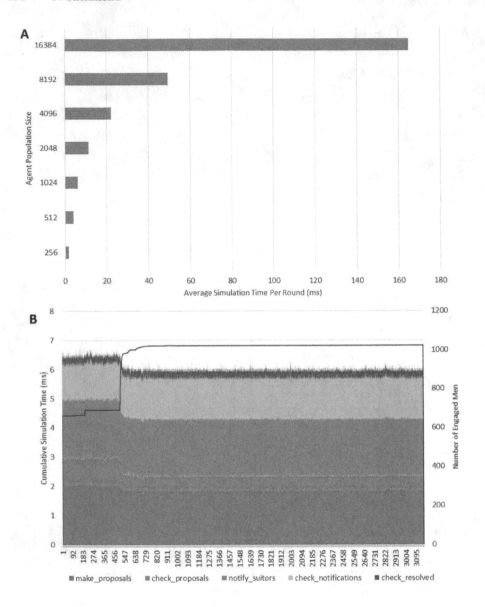

Fig. 4. Performance results of the Gale-Shapely simulation showing; **A**: The performance scaling of the simulation where the agent population size represents half the total number of agents (i.e. the population size of either the men or woman). Timings show the time required to simulate an average round of the Gale-Shapely algorithm. **B**: A breakdown of the cumulative timings (primary left hand axis) for each of the agent functions. The total number of engaged men is shown on the secondary (right hand) axis.

first 100 simulation steps and the total number of complete (fully resolved) simulation steps. The performance fluctuates between simulation steps in a fairly repeatable pattern as a simulation step where movement is resolved takes longer to process than a simulation step performing only movement resolution. Performance is also shown to improve as agents trend towards a fully resolved state as subsequent resolution steps are required to perform less work (e.g. simulation steps 2-5 in the figure). On average it can be observed that it takes roughly 5 iterations of the simulation to resolve all movement conflicts.

The stable marriage model has been initialised by assigning each man and woman with a randomly ordered preference for agents of the opposite sex. Within Figure 4 (**A**) performance has been measured by averaging simulation time over the total number of rounds required to reach a stable solution. Given the random preference of agents the average number of rounds to reach a stable solution is roughly 3.2 times the population size of a single sex. For example 1024 agents (of each sex) are resolved in 3166 rounds in a total of 19 seconds and 16384 agents are resolved in 49168 steps taking just over 2 hours. Figure 4 (**B**) shows simultaneously; the cumulative timing performance of each of the agent functions and the total number of engaged men for a population size of 1024 (men and woman). As the number of engaged men increases the performance of a simulation step improves. This is mainly a result of performance improvements in the Woman agents *check_proposals* function which has fewer proposal messages to iterate per round. It should be noted that as the number of engaged men increases the number of agents performing the *make_proposals* agent function decreases to the point that the level of parallelism is lower than the amount required to fully utilise the GPU. To avoid underutilising the GPU a potential solution would be to transfer the execution of this agent function to the CPU. The disadvantage of using the CPU for simulation would be that in this case the transfer cost would outweigh the underutilisation of the hardware until very small agent population sizes were observed. To provide optimal GPU and CPU sharing of agent functions for general cases would require dynamic load balancing, an area being explored for FLAME and FLAME GPU in future work.

6   Conclusion

Two cases studies have been demonstrated in which 'conflict' resolution is required in order to manage competition between agents. The first case study demonstrated a common problem which arises from the translation of a lattice based agent system from a serial to a parallel simulation framework. The second demonstrates a classic assignment problem. In each case the FLAME GPU framework has been shown to be a suitable parallel simulator to demonstrate implementation of an iterative method to resolve conflicts, allowing high performance agent interactions to be exploited to provide negotiation for a conflict resolution process. The case studies provide a building block for more complex models to be implemented using FLAME GPU, allowing improved scaling and performance. Further more they act as a guide in the translation of serial models to parallel simulators where negotiation can be used to resolve movement or assignment conflicts. In future work the process of resolving competitive assignment will be applied to economic and biological models.

References

1. Aaby, B.G., Perumalla, K.S., Seal, S.K.: Efficient simulation of agent-based models on multi-gpu and multi-core clusters. In: Proceedings of the 3rd International ICST Conference on Simulation Tools and Techniques. ICST, p. 29 (2010)
2. Crawford, V.P., Knoer, E.M.: Job matching with heterogeneous firms and workers. Econometrica 49(2), 437–450 (1981)
3. Epstein, J.M.: Growing artificial societies: social science from the bottom up. Brookings Institution Press (1996)
4. Gale, D., Shapley, L.S.: College admissions and the stability of marriage. American Mathematical Monthly, 9–15 (1962)
5. Kiran, M., Richmond, P., Holcombe, M., Chin, L.S., Worth, D., Greenough, C.: Flame: Simulating large populations of agents on parallel hardware architectures. In: Proceedings of the 9th International Conference on Autonomous Agents and Multiagent Systems, AAMAS 2010, International Foundation for Autonomous Agents and Multiagent Systems, Richland, SC, vol. 1, pp. 1633–1636 (2010), http://dl.acm.org/citation.cfm?id=1838206.1838517
6. Lynsenko, M., D'Souza, R.M.: A framework for megascale agent based model simulations on graphics processing units. Journal of Artificial Societies & Social Simulation 11(4) (2008)
7. Moser, D., Riener, A., Zia, K., Ferscha, A.: Comparing parallel simulation of social agents using cilk and opencl. In: IEEE/ACM 15th International Symposium on Distributed Simulation and Real Time Applications (DS-RT), pp. 88–97. IEEE (2011)
8. Richmond, P.: FLAME GPU Technical Report and User Guide (CS-11-03). Tech. rep., Department of Computer Science, University of Sheffield (2011)
9. Richmond, P., Romano, D.: Template-driven agent-based modeling and simulation with cu da. GPU Computing Gems Emerald Edition, p. 313 (2011)
10. Richmond, P., Walker, D., Coakley, S., Romano, D.: High performance cellular level agent-based simulation with flame for the gpu. Briefings in Bioinformatics (2010), http://bib.oxfordjournals.org/content/early/2010/02/01/bib.bbp073.abstract
11. Scarano, V., Cordasco, G., De Chiara, R., Vicidomini, L.: D-MASON: A short tutorial. In: an Mey, D., et al. (eds.) Euro-Par 2013. LNCS, vol. 8374, pp. 490–500. Springer, Heidelberg (2014), http://dx.doi.org/10.1007/978-3-642-54420-0_48

Programmability and Performance of Parallel ECS-Based Simulation of Multi-agent Exploration Models

Alessandro Pellegrini and Francesco Quaglia

DIAG, Sapienza, University of Rome

Abstract. While the traditional objective of parallel/distributed simulation techniques has been mainly in improving performance and making very large models tractable, more recent research trends targeted complementary aspects, such as the "ease of programming". Along this line, a recent proposal called Event and Cross State (ECS) synchronization, stands as a solution allowing to break the traditional programming rules proper of Parallel Discrete Event Simulation (PDES) systems, where the application code processing a specific event is only allowed to access the state (namely the memory image) of the target simulation object. In fact with ECS, the programmer is allowed to write ANSI-C event-handlers capable of accessing (in either read or write mode) the state of whichever simulation object included in the simulation model. Correct concurrent execution of events, e.g., on top of multi-core machines, is guaranteed by ECS with no intervention by the programmer, who is in practice exposed to a sequential-style programming model where events are processed one at a time, and have the ability to access the current memory image of the whole simulation model, namely the collection of the states of any involved object. This can strongly simplify the development of specific models, e.g., by avoiding the need for passing state information across concurrent objects in the form of events. In this article we investigate on both programmability and performance aspects related to developing/-supporting a multi-agent exploration model on top of the ROOT-Sim PDES platform, which supports ECS.

1 Introduction

Timeliness in the delivery of simulation output is an increasingly relevant issue to cope with, especially in contexts where simulation is exploited as a tool for time-critical decision making. This happens in many fields, ranging from agent based simulation of rescue scenarios [1] to simulation of on-line rescaling/reconfiguration policies of systems deployed in, e.g., Cloud Computing environments [2]. For the case of Discrete Event Simulation (DES) models, performance issues have been traditionally targeted via the Parallel-DES (PDES) paradigm [3], which has been based on the partitioning of the simulation model into distinct simulation objects (also known as Logical Processes - LPs) to be executed concurrently, so as to allow the exploitation of (large scale) parallel platforms to speedup model execution.

L. Lopes et al. (Eds.): Euro-Par 2014 Workshops, Part I, LNCS 8805, pp. 395–406, 2014.

The PDES paradigm laid its foundation on a programming model where the states of the involved simulation objects are disjoint, and where memory access operations (upon event processing) are confined within the state of the simulation object dispatched for processing the event. This approach implicitly requires the application programmers to shift from a sequential programming model where the application is designed and coded to run serially (namely to process one event at a time) and has the possibility to access any valid memory location upon the execution of whichever event. In other words, parallelism is achieved by a-priori, namely at code design/development time, forcing separation of the accesses to slices of the simulation model state, each one representing an individual object.

In order to recover from the scenario where parallelism in the execution is forced to be bound (in the programming model) to memory disjoint accesses to an a-priori partitioned simulation model state, recent design/development trends in PDES systems gave rise to the possibility of sharing state information across the concurrent simulation objects (see, e.g., [4,5,6]). A very recent result in this area is the Event and Cross State (ECS) synchronization protocol presented in [7], which is based on a proper x86_64/Linux memory management architecture and on user-transparent system-level events whose processing rules allow to "transactify" the execution of any individual simulation event, even in case it accesses (in either read or write mode) the state of multiple simulation objects. ECS is suited for simulations carried out on machines relying on multi-core technology, which is a mainstream architectural support for parallelism. With ECS we are exposed to a sequential-style programming/execution model based on ANSI-C event-handlers, where any code block of a handler can access any valid memory location within the simulation model state, and events are processed by providing the illusion of a traditional sequential (timestamp ordered) execution, where nothing can happen in memory except for read/write actions related to a single event at a time. On the other hand, simulation events are actually processed concurrently as in traditional PDES systems, thus allowing the possibility to still exploit parallelism in the underlying architecture for performance reasons. ECS has been integrated within the open source ROOT-Sim simulation environment [8], in combination with the native ROOT-Sim support for speculative (optimistic) processing.

In this article we investigate on the effects of ECS on programmability of a multi-agent exploration scenario, as well as on the finally delivered performance while executing the simulation model. We will show how ECS permits coding the model very easily by allowing the combination of kind of active (agents) and passive (regions) simulation objects. The region information can be directly accessed in read/write mode by the agents simulation objects while processing their events (e.g., an access-to-region event) which allows for avoiding (A) the need for marshalling/unmarshalling region information and exchanging it in the form of query/reply events and (B) the need for scheduling region update events (e.g. command events) destined to be processed by passive region-objects. Further, being the regions distinct (although passive) objects, they still allow for concurrency in their accesses by the different agent objects. Overall, thanks to

ECS we can get both a reduction of the complexity of the coding process (e.g. via the avoidance of query/reply events) and a transparent support for efficient parallelization. To the best of our knowledge, this is the first study aimed at assessing the effectiveness of techniques for transparent parallelization of multi-agent models on multi-core machines via the provisioning of support for a truly sequential-style programming model based on ANSI-C. Hence, as a matter of fact, we also implicitly provide indications on how to exploit ECS as the support for coding different kinds of models entailing the need for representing both spatial regions and active entities operating within the regions.

The remainder of this paper is organized as follows. Related work is discussed in Section 2. In Section 3 we provide an overview of ECS. In Section 4 we discuss how to exploit ECS facilities for coding the multi-agent exploration model. Experimental results are provided in Section 5.

2   Related Work

A few studies exist in the area of porting sequential agent-based simulators to parallel platforms (see, e.g., [9]). However, the approach there taken is mostly based on the aforementioned query/reply or command events, which are in some cases handled via wrappers encapsulating the actual application code and intercepting the attempt to access to a remote object state (as in classical RPC architectures). Also, these proposals target object oriented programming languages, while ECS is aimed at transparent parallelizing simulation programs based on ANSI-C. Additionally, as far as we know, the proposal in [9] relies on time-stepped (conservative) synchronization as implemented on top of the facilities offered by the Mozart framework [10], while we target transparent parallelization in the context of asynchronous optimistic discrete event simulation.

Other literature studies (see, e.g., [11,12,13,14]) provide techniques and environments for parallel execution of agent-based simulation models. However, their primary focus is not on parallelism transparency (in the form of allowing a sequential style code to be directly processed concurrently). Hence, these proposals stand as orthogonal to what we present in this paper.

3   ECS Overview

The ECS synchronization protocol [7] is based on managing the virtual memory destined for usage to any simulation object according to *stocks*. More in detail, when the object requests new memory buffers for installing and/or updating its state layout, which is supported via the traditional `malloc` service, redirected to a proper memory allocator integrated with ECS, the memory management architecture reserves an interval of page-aligned virtual memory addresses, namely the stock, via the standard `mmap` POSIX API.

To understand how ECS manages the stocks, let us consider the actual paging scheme supported by Linux on top of x86_64 architectures, namely the target platform for the ECS protocol. Virtual addresses are used as access keys for

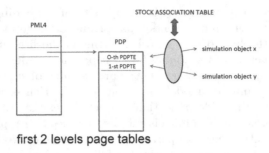

Fig. 1. Example association between stocks of virtual memory and simulation objects

a 4-level paging scheme, ultimately managing pages of 4KB in size. The top level page table is called PML4 (or PGD—Page General Directory) and keeps 512 entries. All the other page tables, operating at lower levels, also have 512 entries each. In ECS, the stock of virtual memory pages destined to allocate memory buffers for a given simulation object corresponds to the set of contiguous virtual-pages whose virtual-to-physical memory translation is associated with a single entry of the second-level page table, which is called PDP—Page Directory Pointer (its entries are therefore referred to as PDPTE). Note that a single stock corresponds to 512^2 pages, for a total of 1GB of virtual memory. Hence, a single stock allows managing an object-state requesting up to 1GB of (dynamic) memory. On the other hand, reserving multiple stocks for a same simulation object will lead to managing object states reaching multiple gigabytes in size. In Figure 1 we show an example where a given PDP table has its 0-th entry—and hence the corresponding stock of virtual memory pages—reserved for object x, and its 1-st entry reserved for object y.

The above scheme is complemented by having different worker threads within the simulation process (run on the multi-core machine) associated with multiple *sibling* page tables, which is achieve by augmenting the Linux paging scheme with the facilities offered by a special device file, as designed in [7] (installed via an external module). When a simulation object x is dispatched to be run by worker thread T_i for processing its next event e, then the access rule to the stock associated with x is changed in the corresponding PDP entry of the sibling page tables associated with T_i from NULL to a value allowing read/write access by the thread (which is done via an `ioctl` command issued towards the special device file). Instead, the memory stocks associated with the other simulation objects are left unaccessible, in terms of read/write permission. If during the processing of the event e at object x, the event handler run by thread T_i performs an access to a virtual memory region currently in use for the stock associated with object y, ECS captures the access via a lightweight trap-handler (not requiring to pass through the full memory-fault handling chain of Linux) and "transactifies" the execution of the event by allowing the handler run by thread T_i to access the target stock (opening the access permission on the sibling page tables of T_i) in mutual exclusion. Also, the transaction associated with the event e needs to observe the snapshot of the target object y exactly at the timestamp of e. To achieve this, ECS relies on special system-level rendez-vous events, which support a temporary block of the source/target object along virtual time (at the rendez-vous point). In particular, the source object x remains blocked until the correct snapshot of the target one is available, while the target object y remains blocked in the rendez-vous until the event e is completely processed by object x.

The actual synchronization protocol instantiated in ECS is optimistic, with the meaning that the local simulation clock of the target object y might be beyond the value of the timestamp of the event e at the time when the corresponding transaction (namely rendez-vous) needs to be processed. This is addressed by having rendez-vous events marked with the correct timestamp for their occurrence (namely, the timestamp of e in our example discussion), and by forcing a rollback of the state snapshot of the target object y to a simulation time equal to the timestamp of the rendez-vous in case of out of timestamp order occurrence of the rendez-vous.

As also discussed in [7], the ECS synchronization protocol is deadlock free, thanks to a priority scheme adopted to process events whose timestamp falls in the past of the current logical clock of the target object. In particular, anytime an event in the past needs to be processed by an object which is currently blocked due to a rendez-vous it issued (which still needs to be finalized since the state image of the target object, hit by the rendez-vous, is still unavailable), the block phase is squashed, thus avoiding indefinite block scenarios. On the other hand, in case the event to be processed is scheduled at the same time of the blocking rendez-vous, then classical tie-break mechanisms can be adopted to prioritize event processing and to avoid permanent blocking situations.

Further, the guarantee of freedom from the domino effect within the rollback scheme can be provided in ECS by integrating classical sparse state saving strategies (see, e.g., [15,16,17,18,19,20,21]), aimed at (infrequently) logging the state image of the simulation objects (either for recoverability purposes within the synchronization scheme or for on-the-fly/a-posteriori inspection of the state trajectory of the simulation objects) with forced logs taken so to avoid any rendez-vous event to be reprocessed as an artifact of the reconstruction phase of non-logged state images. Essentially this implies forcing additional logs on both source and destination objects right after the rendez-vous is processed.

We note that in case each simulation object only accesses its own state (namely the data structure logically associated with such a state), which is the only scenario valid for classical PDES programming approaches, then the performance penalty incurred by ECS compared to classical optimistic PDES synchronization is exclusively related to opening the access into the sibling page tables upon dispatching some object along a given worker thread. However, thanks to the current support offered by modern processors for fast system-call paths, the corresponding `ioctl` operation imposes negligible overhead except for simulation models with very fine event-granularity. On the other hand, the management of rendez-vous events induces a cost to be necessarily paid to allow the parallel run to mimic a classical sequential one where the simulation events are processed in non-decreasing timestamp order, while jointly being allowed to access any valid memory location belonging to the state of the simulation model (namely any memory location logically belonging to the state of some object included in the simulation model). But, as we will show in the next section, this has the potential for extremely simplifying the application programmer job.

4   Programming the Multi-agent Exploration Model

To assess the programmability and performance of ECS, we have implemented a distributed multi-robot exploration and mapping simulation model, according to the results in [22]. Specifically, a group of robots is set out into an unknown space, with the goal of fully exploring it, while acquiring data from sensors (e.g., cameras, lasers, ...) which are used to map the environment. The robots are equipped with enough processing power to elaborate the sensors data online (thus, the map is constructed during the exploration), so as to allow them to rely on the acquired knowledge to drive the exploration in a more efficient way. Specifically, whenever a robot has to make a decision about which direction should be taken to carry on the exploration, it is done by relying on the notion of *exploration frontier*. By keeping a representation of the explored world, the robot is able to detect which is the closest unexplored area it can reach, computes the fastest way to reach it and continues the exploration.

The robots explore independently of each other until one coincidentally detects another robot. Whenever two robots enter a proximity region, they perform three different actions: i) they use their sensors to estimate their mutual physical position—recall that they are just in *proximity*; ii) they verify the goodness of their position hypothesis by creating a rendez-vous point in the explored part of the region, and trying to meet again there; iii) if the hypothesis is verified, they exchange the data acquired during the exploration, thus reducing the exploration time and allowing for a more accurate decision of the actions to be taken. Additionally, in case step ii) succeeds (i.e., the robots actually meet in the rendez-vous point), it means that the estimation of their respective position is correct. Therefore, they can form a *cluster*, i.e. they can start exploring the environment in a collaborative way. Specifically, this collaborative exploration can take place in two different ways. On the one hand, they jointly define (by relying on *cost* and *utility* functions, as defined in [22]) their next exploration targets, so that they can minimize the time required for a complete environment exploration. On the other hand, they might decide to make a *guess* about the position of other robots (the total number of which is known) which are not part of the cluster yet. In the latter case, one of the robots (the one for which the utility/cost ratio is convenient) targets the hypothesized position. If a robot is found there, the aforementioned steps are carried out, so as to increase the knowledge of the environment.

When implementing a PDES simulation model for this scenario, three main hindrances are found. First, discovering the presence of a nearby robot can be difficult. In fact, either the robots must communicate to each other their current position (thus exponentially increasing the number of exchanged messages, which in turn can limit the performance of the simulation), or they have to notify it to specific simulation objects (i.e., the regions), again increasing the number of messages exchanged. Second, to estimate the respective position of the agents, many simulation events could be required. In this specific case, these events should be marked with the same timestamp, thus requiring efficient (but non-negligible in cost) tie-breaking approaches, like the one in [23]. Third, exchanging map information could entail a data transfer non-negligible in size, posing a huge burden on the communication subsystem. Additionally, all these programmatic steps are not straightforward, as they force the modeler to reason according to the state-separation paradigm proper of PDES.

On the other hand, as mentioned, relying on ECS allows for a completely transparent synchronization of the simulation objects involved in any mutual state update, which therefore simplifies the development process of the simulation model. In our implementation[1], we rely on two different types of simulation objects, namely active ones (implementing the robots) and passive ones (implementing regions of the exploration environment). More specifically, the environment is represented as a square region, divided into hexagonal cells. This choice allows us to define a meaningful mobility model for the agents, and at the same time allows us to define proximity regions which are used by the agents to detect the presence of other robots in the nearby. Also, in our model, periodic events occurring into any cell are envisaged as the basis for modeling the evolution (inside the cell) of any phenomenon characterizing the dynamic change in the state of the explored region.

At simulation startup, each passive simulation object creates random obstacles (which prevent the agents from reaching any neighbour cell), mimicking a rescue scenario where an open space is modified by an accident and the robots are used to explore it for rescue activities. At the same time, each passive object instantiates in its private simulation state (by relying on a traditional `malloc` call) a *presence bitmap*. Each bit is associated with a specific robot, and its value is associated with the robot being in the cell or not. By relying on a fast bitmap scan, each robot (thus each active simulation object) is able to discover which ones are present in the cell. Finally, the passive object registers its simulation state by storing a pointer in a global array called `states[]`, thus allowing any other simulation object to directly access (and/or modify) it. This is done by relying on standard (sequential) code, where the modeler is not required to rely on any platform-specific API, as illustrated in the following code snippet which is executed upon initializing the simulation model.

```
1  // Allocated state
2  state = malloc(sizeof(agent_state_type));
3
4  for(i = 0; i < 6; i++) {
5      if(isValidNeighbour(me, i)) {
6          // With a random probability, an obstacle prevents from getting there
7          if(Random() < OBSTACLE_PROB) {
```

---

[1] The full source code of our model implementation can be found at http://svn.dis.uniroma1.it/svn/hpdcs/root_sim/trunk/examples/robot_explore/

```
 8            state->neighbours[i] = -1;
 9          } else {
10            state->neighbours[i] = GetNeighbourId(me, i);
11          }
12        } else {
13          state->neighbours[i] = -1;
14        }
15 }
16 // Allocate the presence bitmap
17 state->agents = malloc(BITMAP_SIZE(n_prc_tot - num_cells));
18 bzero(state->agents, BITMAP_SIZE(n_prc_tot - num_cells));
19 // Register the state
20 states[me] = state;
```

isValidNeighbour() is a model-specified function determining whether a cell
is placed on the boundary of the square region, GetNeighbourId() is a model-
defined function which performs hexagonal-to-linear coordinates conversion for
detecting a neighbour id, num_cells is a variable defined by the model (and
initialized at simulation startup by the user) which tells how many cells must
be used to represent the square region, BITMAP_SIZE is a model-defined macro
which converts the number of agents to be represented into the bitmap to a
number of sequential bytes providing the relative number of bits, n_prc_tot is
a variable initialized at simulation startup which tells the total number of simulation objects in the current run, and me is a unique integer used to identify
a specific simulation object, passed as input to callbacks giving control to the
application for event processing (as in most traditional simulation frameworks).
At this point, when an active agent executes the event associated with the en-
trance within a specific hexagonal cell (the id of the cell is piggy-backed on the
event), registering its presence in the cell is as simple as:

```
21 state->current_cell = event_content->cell;
22
23 // Register the position of the robot in the cell
24 cell = (cell_state_type *)states[state->current_cell];
25 cell->present_agents++;
26 SET_BIT(cell->agents, me - num_cells);
```

Then, the agent has to acquire information about the environment (which in
our model is represented by the obstacles in the current cell) and has to detect
the presence of additional robots. Since we have direct access to the cell's state
thanks to ECS, this can be easily done by reading this information from it:

```
27 // Mark the cell as explored and "discover" the surroundings
28 state->visit_map[state->current_cell].visited = true;
29 memcpy(&state->visit_map[state->current_cell].neighbours, cell->neighbours, sizeof(
        unsigned int) * 6);
30
31 // Is there any other robot in the cell?
32 if(cell->present_agents > 1) {
33     <scan the bitmap>
34 }
```

In case one robot is found in the cell, then the agent simply "merges" its view
of the environment. This can be easily done by relying again on the states[]
array, provided that each robot registers a pointer to its private state in it at
simulation startup:

```
35  robot = (agent_state_type *)states[robot_index];
36  for(j = 0; j < num_cells; j++) {
37      if(robot->visit_map[j].visited) {
38          memcpy(&state->visit_map[j], &robot->visit_map[j], sizeof(map_t));
39      } else if (state->visit_map[j].visited) {
40          memcpy(&robot->visit_map[j], &state->visit_map[j], sizeof(map_t));
41      }
42  }
```

No notion of parallelism is present in the shown code snippets from the simulation model, yet (by relying on ECS) ROOT-Sim is able to run the simulation model in parallel, exploiting the computing power offered by multi/many-core architectures. We emphasize that the simulation model is written in a pure sequential style, without the need for respecting any programming model constraint, except for the signature of the event handlers, which is compliant with the one adopted by ROOT-Sim. Therefore, by relying on ECS, any sequential model developed for the traditional DES paradigm can be easily run concurrently, by making extremely minor modifications to it.

As a final note, ECS is triggered in different lines of the above code snippets. In particular, lines 25 and 32 trigger the synchronization with a cell (i.e., the current cell hosting the robot), while lines 37, 38, and 40 synchronize with another robot, namely one of the (possibly multiple) robots found to be in the cell. It is interesting to note that lines 25 and 32 access the state in different ways, the former being a read/write operation, the latter being simply a read operation. Similarly, line 37 accesses the state in read mode, while lines 38 and 40 entail writing multiple bytes of memory. Nevertheless, despite the multiple accesses, ECS requires executing the synchronization protocol only once per each other simulation object the state of which is being accessed while processing the current event. It is interesting to note that, if the same model were implemented using traditional message passing, multiple messages should have been exchanged to support the execution of a single event.

5   Performance Data

In this section we report performance results related to the execution of the previously described simulation model. The hardware architecture used for running the experiments is a 64-bit NUMA machine, namely an HP ProLiant server, equipped with four 2GHz AMD Opteron 6128 processors and 64GB of RAM. Each processor has 8 cores (for a total of 32 cores) that share a 12MB L3 cache (6 MB per each 4-cores set), and each core has a 512KB private L2 cache. The operating system is 64-bit Debian 6, with Linux Kernel version 2.6.32.5 (with supports for ECS [7]). The compiling and linking tools used are gcc 4.3.4 and binutils (as and ld) 2.20.0.

We simulated a region with 4096 cells, and we varied the number of agent (robot) units moving around between 100 and 1000, passing though the intermediate value of 500. The higher values (say 500 and 1000 agents) give rise to average agent density into the explored space on the order of 0.12 and 0.24

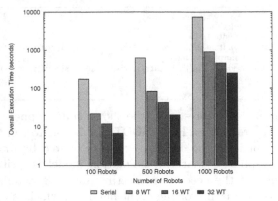

Fig. 2. Sequential vs parallel ECS-based execution times

per cell, respectively. Although these values might be above realistic settings, especially for cells modeling regions with non-minimal size, they help anyway assessing how the performance of the ECS support for easy of programming and transparent parallelization scales vs variations of the ratio between the number of passive simulation objects (the cells) and the number of active ones (the agents). On the other hand, the configuration with 100 agents gives rise to an average density of per-cell agents of 0.02, realistically representing cases where, e.g., a reduced number of highly specialized agents is employed for the exploration of a non-minimally sized region.

In Figure 2 we report the execution time of the simulation model for the three different cases, and for different amounts of ROOT-Sim worker threads (say 8, 16, and 32) deployed on top of the multi-core computing system. We also report the execution time for running the very same application code sequentially, on top of a classical calendar-queue scheduler. By the data we see how the parallel runs provide speedup that ranges between 30 and 35, which also linearly scales while varying the number of worker threads in the parallel simulation platform. This demonstrates the effectiveness of ECS in delivering adequate performance, beyond providing support for easy of programming. Also, the implementation patterns used in our model can constitute a reference for different scenarios entailing both passive (region) and active (agent) simulation objects.

6   Conclusions

In this article we have discussed how to exploit the innovative ECS (Event and Cross State) synchronization protocol for discrete event simulation in order to easily implement a multi-agent exploration model. The objective of ECS is to provide the illusion of a sequential style execution mode for models based on multiple simulation objects that develop (mutual) cross-state dependencies via direct cross-references on their states, while actually running the model in parallel. With ECS, the programmer is exposed to a classical and easy sequential style approach for coding the state transitions associated with the occurrence of simulation events (e.g. the application code is allowed to reference any valid memory location while performing whichever state transition, under the programmer's illusion that all the transitions are sequentialized). On the other hand, the ECS-based run-time environment, which has been integrated within the ROOT-Sim open source simulation platform, allows for executing the objects (namely, the simulation events destined to them) concurrently, while correctly maintaining causality across state transitions. We have discussed the relation between ECS and multi-agent exploration models from a twofold perspective: on one side we have shown code snippets illustrating the simplicity according to which the programmer can code his model; on the other side we have provided data related to speedup results achieved via ECS-based runs (which are able to transparently support parallel execution of the sequentially conceived code) on top of a 32-core commodity machine.

References

1. Takahashi, T., Tadokoro, S., Ohta, M., Ito, N.: Agent based approach in disaster rescue simulation - from test-bed of multiagent system to practical application. In: Birk, A., Coradeschi, S., Tadokoro, S. (eds.) RoboCup 2001. LNCS (LNAI), vol. 2377, pp. 102–111. Springer, Heidelberg (2002)
2. Di Sanzo, P., Antonacci, F., Ciciani, B., Palmieri, R., Pellegrini, A., Peluso, S., Quaglia, F., Rughetti, D., Vitali, R.: A framework for high performance simulation of transactional data grid platforms. In: Proceedings of the 6th International ICST Conference on Simulation Tools and Techniques, SimuTools 2013. ICST, pp. 63–72 (2013)
3. Fujimoto, R.M.: Parallel discrete event simulation. Communications of the ACM 33(10), 30–53 (1990)
4. Low, M.Y.H., Gan, B.P., Wei, J., Wang, X., Turner, S.J., Cai, W.: Shared state synchronization for HLA-based distributed simulation. Simulation 82(8), 511–521 (2006)
5. Gan, B.P., Low, M., Wei, J., Wang, X., Turner, S., Cai, W.: Synchronization and management of shared state in HLA-based distributed simulation. In: Proceedings of the Winter Simulation Conference, pp. 847–854 (December 2003)
6. Pellegrini, A., Vitali, R., Peluso, S., Quaglia, F.: Transparent and efficient shared-state management for optimistic simulations on multi-core machines. In: Proceedings 20th International Symposium on Modeling, Analysis and Simulation of Computer and Telecommunication Systems, pp. 134–141. IEEE Computer Society (August 2012)
7. Pellegrini, A., Quaglia, F.: Transparent multi-core speculative parallelization of DES models with event and cross-state dependencies. In: Proceedings of the 2014 ACM SIGSIM Conference on Principles of Advanced Discrete Simulation. PADS, pp. 105–116. ACM (May 2014)
8. Quaglia, F., Pellegrini, A., Vitali, R., Peluso, S., Didona, D., Castellari, G., Gheri, V., Cucuzzo, D., D'Alessio, S., Santoro, T.: ROOT-Sim: The ROme OpTimistic Simulator - v 0.99 RC-1 (October 2011), http://www.dis.uniroma1.it/~hpdcs/ROOT-Sim/

9. Popov, K., Vlassov, V., Rafea, M., Holmgren, F., Brand, P., Haridi, S.: Parallel agent-based simulation on a cluster of workstations. In: Kosch, H., Böszörményi, L., Hellwagner, H. (eds.) Euro-Par 2003. LNCS, vol. 2790, pp. 470–480. Springer, Heidelberg (2003)

10. The Mozart Programming System, http://mozart.github.io/

11. Cordasco, G., De Chiara, R., Mancuso, A., Mazzeo, D., Scarano, V., Spagnuolo, C.: A framework for distributing agent-based simulations. In: Alexander, M., et al. (eds.) Euro-Par 2011, Part I. LNCS, vol. 7155, pp. 460–470. Springer, Heidelberg (2012)

12. Hybinette, M., Kraemer, E., Xiong, Y., Matthews, G., Ahmed, J.: Sassy: A design for a scalable agent-based simulation system using a distributed discrete event infrastructure. In: Proceedings of the 2006 Winter Simulation Conference, WSC, pp. 926–933. Society for Computer Simulation (2006)

13. Richmond, P., Walker, D.C., Coakley, S., Romano, D.M.: High performance cellular level agent-based simulation with FLAME for the GPU. Briefings in Bioinformatics 11(3), 334–347 (2010)

14. Marurngsith, W., Mongkolsin, Y.: Creating GPU-enabled agent-based simulations using a PDES tool. In: Omatu, S., Neves, J., Rodriguez, J.M.C., Paz Santana, J.F., Gonzalez, S.R. (eds.) Distrib. Computing & Artificial Intelligence. AISC, vol. 217, pp. 227–234. Springer, Heidelberg (2013)

15. Fleischmann, J., Wilsey, P.A.: Comparative analysis of periodic state saving techniques in time warp simulators. In: Proceedings of the 9th Workshop on Parallel and Distributed Simulation, pp. 50–58. IEEE Computer Society (June 1995)

16. Preiss, B.R., Loucks, W.M., MacIntyre, D.: Effects of the checkpoint interval on time and space in Time Warp. ACM Transactions on Modeling and Computer Simulation 4(3), 223–253 (1994)

17. Quaglia, F.: Combining periodic and probabilistic checkpointing in optimistic simulation. In: Proceedings of the 13th workshop on Parallel and distributed simulation, pp. 109–116. IEEE Computer Society Press (1999)

18. Quaglia, F.: Event history based sparse state saving in time warp. In: Proceedings of the 12th Workshop on Parallel and Distributed Simulation, pp. 72–79. IEEE Computer Society Press (1998)

19. Quaglia, F.: A cost model for selecting checkpoint positions in Time Warp parallel simulation. IEEE Transactions on Parallel and Distributed Systems 12(4), 346–362 (2001)

20. Rönngren, R., Ayani, R.: Adaptive checkpointing in Time Warp. In: Proceedings of the Workshop on Parallel and Distributed Simulation, Society for Computer Simulation, pp. 110–117 (July 1994)

21. Cucuzzo, D., D'Alessio, S., Quaglia, F., Romano, P.: A lightweight heuristic-based mechanism for collecting committed consistent global states in optimistic simulation. In: Proceedings of the IEEE/ACM International Symposium on Distributed Simulation and Real Time Applications, pp. 227–234. IEEE Computer Society, Los Alamitos (2007)

22. Fox, D., Ko, J., Konolige, K., Limketkai, B., Schulz, D., Stewart, B.: Distributed multirobot exploration and mapping. Proceedings of the IEEE 94(7), 1325–1339 (2006)

23. Mehl, H.: A deterministic tie-breaking scheme for sequential and distributed simulation. In: Proceedings of the Workshop on Parallel and Distributed Simulation. ACM (1992)

Exploiting D-Mason on Parallel Platforms: A Novel Communication Strategy

Gennaro Cordasco[1], Francesco Milone[2],
Carmine Spagnuolo[2], and Luca Vicidomini[2]

[1] Dipartimento di Psicologia, Seconda Università degli Studi di Napoli, Italy
gennaro.cordasco@unina2.it
[2] Dipartimento di Informatica, Università degli Studi di Salerno, Italy
milone.francesco1988@gmail.com, {cspagnuolo,lvicidomini}@unisa.it

Abstract. Agent-based simulation models are a powerful experimental tool for research and management in many scientific and technological fields.

D-MASON is a parallel version of MASON, a library for writing and running Agent-based simulations.

In this paper, we present a novel development of D-MASON, a decentralized communication strategy which realizes a *Publish/Subscribe* paradigm through a layer based on the MPI standard. We show that our communication mechanism is much more scalable and efficient than the previous centralized one.

Keywords: Publish/Subscribe, MPI, Agent-based simulation models, MASON, D-MASON, Parallel Computing, Distributed Systems, High Performance Computing.

1 Introduction

Agent-Based Model (ABM) denotes a class of models which, simulating the behavior of multiple agents (i.e., independent actions, interactions and adaptation), aims to emulate and/or predict complex phenomena.

Successes in Computational Sciences over the past ten years have caused increased demand for supercomputing resources, in order to improve the performance of ABMs in terms of both number of agents and complexity of interactions.

Parallel computing has becoming the dominant paradigm for computational scientist (indeed, serial-processing speed is reaching a physical limit [15]). Unfortunately, exploiting parallel systems is not an easy task: performance has to be realized through concurrency, with applications designed to scale as the number of resources increases.

Computer science community has responded to the need for tools and platforms that can help the development and testing of new models in each specific field by providing tools, libraries and frameworks that speed up and make easier the task of developing and running parallel ABMs for complex phenomena.

L. Lopes et al. (Eds.): Euro-Par 2014 Workshops, Part I, LNCS 8805, pp. 407–417, 2014.
© Springer International Publishing Switzerland 2014

D-MASON [6,16] is a parallel version of the MASON [3,10,11] library for running ABMs on distributed systems. D-MASON adopts a framework-level parallelization mechanism approach, which allows to harness the computational power of a parallel environment and, at the same time, hides the details of the architecture so that users, even with limited knowledge of parallel computer programming, can easily develop and run simulation models.

In [7] a preliminary discussion about the use of MPI primitives for the development of a Publish/Subscribe (PS) service has been showed. This paper makes a step forward in that direction; we present a novel communication strategy, based on the PS paradigm, which uses the MPI Standard [17] as an example of distributed communication on D-MASON.

After a brief review and a critical analysis of the state of the art of D-MASON (Section 2), we report, in Section 3, the details of the novel MPI Publish/Subscribe layer which: (i) improves the preliminary version (cf. [7]); (ii) provides also a hybrid approach exploiting the advantages of both the centralized and decentralized communication strategies. Finally, in Section 4 we report an extensive set of experiments showing that the novel MPI-based Publish/Subscribe mechanism is extremely advantageous when the number of computing machines is large. In this case, in fact, a single communication server is unable to handle all the communication that the system requires and thus it represents a bottleneck for the whole system.

2   Mason and D-Mason

MASON toolkit is a discrete-event simulation core and visualization library written in Java, designed to be used for a wide range of ABMs. MASON is based on a standard Model-View-Controller (MVC) paradigm and three layers compose it: the *simulation* layer, the *visualization* layer and the *utility* layer.

D-MASON adds a new layer named D-Simulation, which extends the MASON simulation layer. The new layer adds some features to the simulation layer that allow the distribution of the simulation workload on multiple, even heterogeneous, machines. The intent of D-MASON is to provide an effective and efficient way of parallelizing MASON simulations: effective because with D-MASON you can do more than what you can do with MASON, efficient because the porting of an application from MASON to D-MASON happens with some incremental modifications to the MASON application without the need of re-designing it.

D-MASON is based on a Master-Worker paradigm: some workers, henceforth logical processors (LPs), perform the simulation while a master application is in charge of: discovering the LPs, bootstrapping the system, managing and interacting with the simulation. D-MASON adopts a space partitioning approach where the space to be simulated (D-MASON's field) is partitioned into regions. Each region, together with the agents contained in it, is assigned to a LP. Since usually the area of interest (AOI) of an agent is small compared with the size of a region, the communication between workers, required to synchronize the simulation step by step, is limited to local messages (messages between LPs, managing neighboring spaces, etc.).

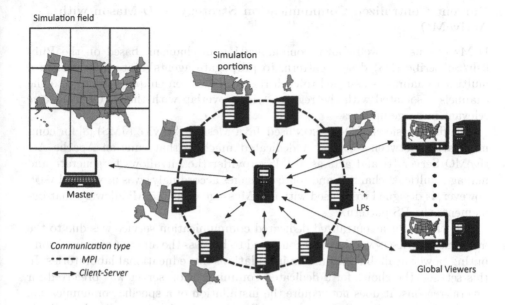

Fig. 1. D-MASON scheme

In a discrete-event simulation, events need to be processed in a non-decreasing timestamp order, because an event with a smaller timestamp can potentially modify the state of the system and thereby affect events that happen later. We call this phenomenon *causality constraint*. On a sequential simulation, the causality constraint is easily satisfied by using a queue of events ordered by timestamp. On parallel simulation, the problem is much tougher and two main approaches have been introduced to deal with it: *Optimistic approach,* which allows events to be processed out of order. Once a causality error is detected, the offending LP has to rollback and recover from such an error. This kind of approach requires state saving and recovery mechanisms [9]; *Conservative approach* which guarantee that events are always processed in the right order. D-MASON adopts a conservative approach: each simulation step is divided in two phases: *communication/synchronization* and *simulation*. Each simulation step is associated with a fixed state of the simulation. Regions are simulated step by step: the step i of a region r is computed according to the states $i - 1$ of r's neighboring regions, so the step i of a region cannot be executed until the states $i - 1$ of its neighbors have been computed and delivered. This approach does not need any rollback strategies but each simulation step represents a barrier; the system advances with the same speed provided by the slower LP in the system. For this reason, it is necessary to balance the load among workers.

Figure 1 depicts the architecture of D-MASON.

Current Centralized Communication Strategy in D-Mason with ActiveMQ

D-MASON uses a well-known communication mechanism, based on the Publish/Subscribe (PS) design pattern, to propagate agents' state information: a multicast channel is assigned to each region; LPs then simply subscribe to the channels associated with the regions, which overlap with their AOI to receive relevant message updates.

The first versions of D-MASON used Java Message Service (JMS) [8] for communication between workers. A dedicated machine that runs an Apache ActiveMQ Server [1] and acts as a JMS provider (i.e., it allows to generate and manage multicast channels and route messages accordingly) was used. D-MASON however, is designed to be used with any Message Oriented Middleware that implements the PS pattern.

The choice for a centralized dedicated communication service was due to the fact that D-MASON was initially conceived to harness the amount of unused computing power available in common installations like educational laboratories. In this setting, the choice for a dedicated communication server was preferred for several reasons. It does not require the installation of a specific communication middleware on each logical processor. All communication is handled by a single machine, consequently all the computational power provided by LPs is dedicated to simulation phase. The number of machines (LPs) available in common laboratory is limited, therefore the centralized communication does not represent a bottleneck for the system, as confirmed by the experiments in [6].

The More You Get, the More You Want

Considering the good results obtained by D-MASON we wondered if the approach used by D-MASON (a framework-level parallelization mechanism) could also be exploited for dedicated installation, such as massively parallel machines and clusters of workstations. If so, what changes are needed in order to adapt D-MASON for dedicated installation? These platforms usually offer a large number of homogeneous machines that, on one hand, simplify the issue of balancing the load among LPs [4], but, on the other hand, the considerable computational power provided by the system weakens the efficiency of the communication server. Indeed, centralized solutions cannot scale with the growth of the computational power (which affects the amount of communication) and especially in the number of LPs (number of communication).

The main goal of our paper is to check whether the communication strategy in D-MASON architecture can be improved using a distributed MPI layer.

3 Decentralized Communication Strategy in D-Mason with MPI

MPI is a library specification for message-passing, designed for high performance on both massively parallel machines and on workstation clusters. MPI has emerged as one of the primary programming paradigms for writing efficient parallel applications; it provides point-to-point and collective communications and guarantees portability with all platforms compliant with the MPI Standard. MPI provides several collective operations, which are very important because they sustain very high parallel speed-ups for parallel applications [17]. Our implementation is based on *mpiJava*, a Java binding of MPI-1.1 Standard [2,5].

A Distributed MPI Publish/Subscribe Layer

The communication model in D-MASON is potentially n-to-n, which means that each LP of the network may need to communicate with all others. D-MASON is based on the Publish/Subscribe paradigm to meet the requirements of flexibility and scalability of the system. In more details, the Communication Layer of D-MASON exploits the flexibility of the Publish/Subscribe paradigm to virtualize groups of communication between the agents. In the distributed simulation, these groups communicate at the end of each simulation step.

MPI does not provide Publish/Subscribe functionalities so we had to develop a different layer, according to the communication interface of D-MASON, which exposes some routines to publish and receive messages on specific topics. This layer is based on MPI collective communications (i.e., MPI_Bcast and MPI_Gather) which allows making a series of point-to-point communications in one single call. MPI processes can be grouped and managed by an object called *Communicator* [13].

The JMS Strategy and the MPI one handle the synchronization in a different way. In the JMS strategy the synchronization is implemented at the framework level using a data structure that indexes, for each step, the updates and acts as barrier, so that each cell remains locked until it receives all updates. In the MPI strategy, we take advantage of the intrinsic synchronization of MPI, because the collective communication primitives are blocking.

In [7] the details of three different implementations have been presented: *MPI_Bcast, MPI_Gather* and *MPI_Parallel*. The first two strategies are based on the MPI group communication primitives of the same name and are almost equivalent in terms of performances in real scenarios, while *MPI_Parallel* allows us to increase the degree of parallelism during the synchronization phase, resulting in increased performances.

The parallel strategy is based on the following considerations. Each synchronization phase requires a certain set C of communication where each communication is identified by a pair ⟨sender, receiver⟩. Using MPI a set of communication can be executed in parallel provided that each process appears at most once (either as sender or as receiver). Hence, we need to partition C in such a way that each set obtained can be executed in parallel and the number of sets is as small as possible. This problem is a well-known NP-Hard problem: *Edge coloring* [12]. An edge coloring of a graph is a minimum assignment of colors to the edges of the graph so that no adjacent edges have the same color. In [7] a simple randomized heuristic was presented to find a good partition in a reasonable time.

Implementation

A preliminary implementation of MPI Publish/Subscribe pattern was provided in a previous work [7]. In this work, we updated the implementation according to the latest Java binding available in OpenMPI V. 1.7.5.

This required, in fact, a major rewrite of our implementation. Briefly, the previous Java binding relied upon the `MPI.Object` class in order to automatically perform (de-)serializing of arbitrary Java objects. This feature was removed in OpenMPI V. 1.7.5 so we had to manually perform (de-)serializing in order to send arrays of `MPI.Byte` objects.

The package `dmason.util.connection` provides the interface `Connection`, which defines the Publish/Subscribe functionalities. In this new version, D-MASON's communication layer offers three implementations: one is based on *Apache ActiveMQ*, one on *MPI* and one, named *hybrid*, uses both ActiveMQ and MPI. Specifically, the hybrid implementation uses MPI for 1-to-n communications between the system management and the LPs and for n-to-1 communications between the LPs and the visualization component, while it uses MPI for the simulation updates between LPs (synchronization). Both the implementations that exploit MPI have been implemented using two out of the tree strategies described above: MPI_Bcast and MPI_Parallel. The latter strategy is highly recommended when running simulations with a large number of LPs.

In Section 4 we show a performance analysis of the new D-MASON's decentralized communication layer.

4   Results

We analyzed the performance of the novel D-MASON communication layer against the centralized ActiveMQ approach performing a number of tests on large simulations. Experiments have been carried on several configurations obtained varying several parameters: number of agents, fields dimension, AOI radius and number of regions. Such parameters determine a ratio between the communication and computation requirements. We expected that the benefits of the new strategy are proportional to the ratio communication / computation. Indeed using the centralized approach, the synchronization is handled by the ActiveMQ server, whereas using the decentralized approach the synchronization represents a computational cost for each LP. Hence, only when the ratio communication / computation is sufficiently large, that cost is paid off in terms of efficiency of communication.

We also evaluated the scalability and the effectiveness of latest implementation of D-MASON's communication layer in exploiting homogeneous hardware.

Setting and Goals of the Experiments

We have used a cluster of eight nodes, each equipped as follows:

- CPUs: 2 x Intel(R) Xeon(R) CPU E5-2680 @ 2.70GHz (#core 16, #threads 32)

– RAM: 256 GB
– Network: adapters Intel Corporation I350 Gigabit

Considering the high computational power of each node we were able to run several (up to 90) LPs on each node. Simulations have been conducted on a scenario consisting of seven machines for computation and one for managing the simulations and running the ActiveMQ server when needed.

We have tested the simulation *Flockers* available in MASON, an implementation of the well–known *"Boids"* model by Craig Reynolds [14], stated in 1986. We chose this simulation due to the embarrassingly parallelizable nature of the problem. Concisely, the *Flockers* model simulates the flocking behavior of birds and its relevant aspect is that the interactions are purely local between each agent and its neighbors; for such reason the simulation fits very well to the execution in a distributed environment.

We performed three categories of experiments:

1. *Communication scalability*: this test aims to evaluate the scalability of the communication layer in terms of the number of LPs. As the number of LPs increases, the communication requirements become crucial in the efficiency. On the other hand, on very large simulations the ability to run a large number of LPs is essential in order to partition the overall computation without exceeding the physical limits of each LP in the system;
2. *Computation scalability*: this test aims to evaluate the scalability of the communication layer in terms of the number of simulated agents. In this case an increase of the number of agents corresponds to an increase of the computational power required, and consequently to a reduction of the ratio communication / computation.
3. *Robustness*: this test aims to assess the effectiveness of the proposed solution on different scenarios.

Communication Scalability Test

For this experiment, we fixed both the field size $(10,000 \times 10,000)$, the number of agents (1 million) and the AOI (10). We employ 16 test settings, each characterized by: the field partitioning configuration (number of rows and columns), which determines also the number of Logical Processes (Number of LPs = $[R]ows \times [C]olums$) and the communication scheme (MPI or ActiveMQ). A couple (P, S) identifies each test setting where

– $P \in \{2 \times 2, 3 \times 3, 4 \times 4, 5 \times 5, 10 \times 10, 15 \times 15, 20 \times 20, 25 \times 25\}$ is the field partitioning configuration.
– $S \in \{ActiveMQ, MPI\}$ is the communication scheme.

We compared the two communication schemes by running the simulation *Flockers* for 3,000 simulation steps. Each simulation has been executed several times in order to check for any fluctuations in the results but we observed no significant changes.

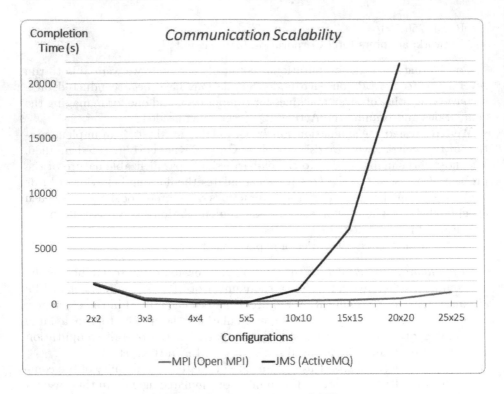

Fig. 2. Communication scalability

Figure 2 presents the results. The X−axis indicates the value of P (left to right the number of LPs is increasing), while the Y−axis indicates the overall execution time in seconds. Notice that there is a point missing because the test setting (25×25, $ActiveMQ$) crashes after few steps (the ActiveMQ server is not able to manage the communication generated by 625 LPs.)

When the number of LPs is small, the advantage of the decentralized communication does not appear because the message broker is much efficient comparing to the coarse grain synchronization requirement of the decentralized one. By increasing the number of LPs, the efficiency of the centralized message broker gets down dramatically and the simulation performance does exhibit the benefits of using the decentralized communication. This trend is due to the fact that by increasing the LPs number there are much more messages in the system and the effort needed to have a synchronizing mechanism in the decentralized communication approach is hidden by the time taken by the message broker to deliver all the messages.

Computation Scalability Test

For this experiment, we fixed the density of the field (i.e., field area divided by number of agents) and the AOI (10). We employ 72 test settings, each characterized

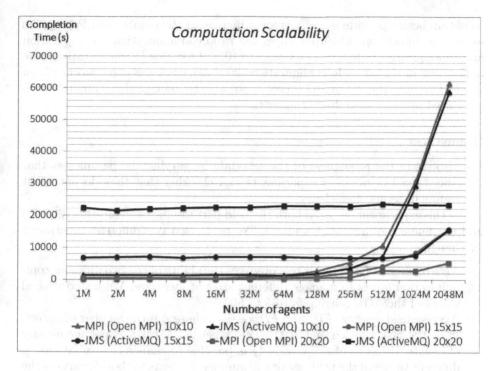

Fig. 3. Computation scalability

by: the field partitioning configuration, the communication scheme and the number of agents. Each test setting is identified by a triple (P, S, A) where

- $P \in \{10 \times 10, 15 \times 15, 20 \times 20\}$ is the field partitioning configuration.
- $S \in \{ActiveMQ, MPI\}$ is the communication scheme.
- $A \in \{1, 2, 4, 8, 16, 32, 64, 128, 256, 512, 1024, 2048\} \times 1,000,000$ (M) is the number of agents.

We compared six configurations, each one characterized by a field partitioning configuration and a communication scheme, by running the simulation *Flockers* for 3,000 simulation steps.

Figure 3 presents the results. The $X-$axis indicates the number of agents A, while the $Y-$axis indicates the overall execution time in seconds. The test starts with a field size of $10,000 \times 10,000$ and one million of agents, these values are scaled up proportionally in such a way to keep a fixed density along the overall test.

The figure shows that for each field configuration the MPI approach performs better than ActiveMQ up to a certain number of agents (i.e., $64M$ for 10×10 configuration) that is when the computational requirement are significantly higher than the communication one. However, the figure shows also that if this is the case then the system deserves a finer field partitioning. Indeed, by increasing the number of LPs (i.e., moving from 10×10 to 15×15) we are able to obtain better performances. Moreover increasing the number of LPs requires more communication, which increases the ratio communication / computation and consequently shifts the *"cross-point"* ($1024M$ for 15×15 configuration). We notice that in the last field configuration (20×20), the cross point has not been reached because the ActiveMQ server is not able to manage the communication generated by more than $2048M$ agents.

Robustness

We also study the robustness of the schedule by varying the parameters that have been fixed in previous experiments and checking that they do not affect the results in terms of efficiency.

For this experiment, we fixed both the field partitioning configuration (20×20) and the number of agents (1 million). We performed two different experiment by changing:

- Area of interest (AOI), this test observes the ability of the two different communication layers to manage different sizes of messages. We tested several values of the AOI, ranging from 5 to 80;
- Average field density (FD), the $FD = \frac{A}{W \times H}$, where A is the number of agents, W is the field's width and H the field's height. FD is the average density of agents within the field, obviously is possible to change this value setting different values of the field size or the number of agents (or both); varying the value of FD affect both the messages size and the computation requirements. We tested different FDs, changing the field size in a range from $5,000 \times 5,000$ ($FD = 1/25$) to $20,000 \times 20,000$ ($FD = 1/400$).

Both the experiments show the same trend in which the MPI solution clearly beats the centralized one. The improvement is always more than 95%. Because the new results are so close to the ones we have presented, there would be no value in exhibiting new plots.

5   Conclusions and Future Works

The performance results described in the previous Section show that the novel communication strategy allows taking advantage from using homogeneous hardware when the simulation requires a sensible amount of communication. As a future work, it would be interesting to devise a specific test in order to characterizing the communication / computation trade-off, that is to determine the minimum ratio communication / computation, beyond which the MPI approach is more efficient than the centralized one.

The *MPI* communication layer uses the Java binding of *MPI*, available in *OpenMPI*; during our work, we discovered some limits of this kind of solution as described in [7]. Moreover, the current stable binding is not tread safe.

The bindings is in continuous development following a JNI approach; mpiJava [2] was taken as a starting point for *OpenMPI* Java binding, but it was later totally rewritten.

The novel MPI approach provides also several by-products: First of all the synchronization among LPs is easier because MPI calls are blocking. Moreover, MPI provides also several features, such as *dynamic process creation and management*, which simplifies the management of the system, especially using heterogeneous hardware.

Finally, we are still working to enhance the efficiency of the MPI communication layer on either the communication strategy or the *mpiJava* implementation.

References

1. Apache ActiveMQ Server, http://activemq.apache.org/
2. Baker, M., Carpenter, B., Fox, G., Ko, S.H., Lim, S.: mpiJava: An object-oriented Java interface to MPI. In: Rolim, J., et al. (eds.) Parallel and Distributed Processing. LNCS, vol. 1586, pp. 748–762. Springer, Heidelberg (1999)
3. Balan, G.C., Cioffi-Revilla, C., Luke, S., Panait, L., Paus, S.: MASON: A Java Multi-Agent Simulation Library. In: Proceedings of the Agent 2003 Conference (2003)
4. Carillo, M., Cordasco, G., Chiara, R.D., Raia, F., Scarano, V., Serrapica, F.: Enhancing the Performances of D-MASON - A Motivating Example. In: SIMULTECH, pp. 137–143 (2012)
5. Carpenter, B., Fox, G.C., Ko, S.-H., Lim, S.: mpijava 1.2: API Specification (1999)
6. Cordasco, G., De Chiara, R., Mancuso, A., Mazzeo, D., Scarano, V., Spagnuolo, C.: Bringing together efficiency and effectiveness in distributed simulations: The experience with D-MASON. SIMULATION: Transactions of The Society for Modeling and Simulation International 89(10), 1236–1253 (2013)
7. Cordasco, G., Mancuso, A., Milone, F., Spagnuolo, C.: Communication Strategies in Distributed Agent-Based Simulations: The Experience with D-MASON. In: an Mey, D., et al. (eds.) Euro-Par 2013. LNCS, vol. 8374, pp. 533–543. Springer, Heidelberg (2014)
8. Java Message Service Concepts, http://docs.oracle.com/javaee/6/tutorial/doc/bncdq.html
9. Liu, J.: Parallel Discrete-Event Simulation. Wiley Encyclopedia of Operations Research and Management Science (2009)
10. Luke, S., Cioffi-revilla, C., Panait, L., Sullivan, K.: MASON: A New Multi-Agent Simulation Toolkit. In: Proceedings of the 2004 SwarmFest Workshop (2004)
11. Luke, S., Cioffi-Revilla, C., Panait, L., Sullivan, K., Balan, G.: MASON: A Multi-agent Simulation Environment. Simulation 81(7), 517–527 (2005)
12. Misra, J., Gries, D.: A Constructive Proof of Vizing's Theorem. Inf. Process. Lett. 41(3), 131–133 (1992)
13. MPI-2: Extensions to the Message-Passing Interface. Technical report, University of Tennessee, Knoxville, TN, USA (July 1997)
14. Reynolds, C.W.: Flocks, Herds and Schools: A Distributed Behavioral Model. SIGGRAPH Comput. Graph. 21(4), 25–34 (1987)
15. Sutter, H.: The Free Lunch Is Over: A Fundamental Turn Toward Concurrency in Software. Dobb's Journal 30(3) (2005)
16. D-MASON Official Website, http://www.dmason.org (accessed May 2014)
17. MPI Standard Official Website, http://www.mcs.anl.gov/research/projects/mpi/index.htm (accessed: April 25, 2013)

Adaptive Simulation with Repast Simphony and Swift

Jonathan Ozik[1,3], Michael Wilde[2,3], Nicholson Collier[1,3], and Charles M. Macal[1,3]

[1] Argonne National Laboratory, Global Security Sciences, Argonne, IL, U.S.A
[2] Argonne National Laboratory, Mathematics and Computer Science, Argonne, IL, U.S.A
[3] Computation Institute, University of Chicago, Chicago, IL, U.S.A
{jozik,wilde,ncollier,macal}@anl.gov

Abstract. We present a general approach for adaptive ABMS, which integrates Repast Simphony's distributed batch components and the Swift parallel scripting language. Swift is used to launch Repast Simphony simulations on parallel resources, collect the results from those simulations, and generate further simulations based on an analysis of the results. In order to demonstrate the benefits and capabilities of this approach, we developed a simulated annealing reference workflow and applied it to a modified Repast Simphony "JZombies" demonstration model. The workflow was able to successfully and efficiently find areas of the model parameter space that yielded the desired outcomes, as specified by an objective function. The workflow was run on a high-performance cluster, launching 16 concurrent simulated annealing optimization processes, each executing 100 simulated annealing loops over 16 stochastic model variations – a total of 25,856 adaptive simulation runs, accounting for a 96.3% reduction in the number of simulations that were required compared to a complete enumeration of parameter space. The materials used in the workflow are included as linked external resources to allow replication.

Keywords: agent-based modeling, ABMS, Repast Simphony, Swift, parallel scripting, adaptive simulation, workflow software.

1   Introduction

Agent-based modeling and simulation (ABMS) is being applied in a variety of domains to model ever-larger and complicated systems. For such models to be useful, they require extensive calibration and validation via large-scale ensemble modeling to explore their often high-dimensional parameter spaces. Some current ABMS toolkits have the ability to distribute large numbers of simulations on ad hoc computer networks and high-performance computing clusters. However, current capabilities for adaptive parameter space exploration at these scales are very limited.

In this paper we present a general approach for adaptive ABMS, which integrates Repast Simphony's [1] (http://repast.sourceforge.net) distributed batch components and the Swift [2] (http://swift-lang.org) parallel scripting language. Swift is used to launch Repast Simphony simulations on parallel resources, collect the results from those simulations, and generate further simulations based on

L. Lopes et al. (Eds.): Euro-Par 2014 Workshops, Part I, LNCS 8805, pp. 418–429, 2014.

an analysis of the results. In order to demonstrate the benefits and capabilities of this approach, we developed a simulated annealing reference workflow and applied it to a modified Repast Simphony "JZombies" demonstration model. The workflow was able to successfully and efficiently find areas of the model parameter space that yielded the desired outcomes, as specified by an objective function. The workflow was run on a high-performance cluster, launching 16 concurrent simulated annealing optimization processes, each executing 100 simulated annealing loops over 16 stochastic model variations – a total of 25,856 adaptive simulation runs, which was completed in 17 minutes, and accounted for a 96.3% reduction in the number of simulations that were required compared to a complete enumeration of parameter space. The materials used in the workflow are presented as a set of Github Gists [3] to allow replication.

The rest of the paper is structured as follows. Section 2 provides relevant background on adaptive simulation, the Swift parallel scripting language, related work in workflow software, and agent-based modeling toolkits with batch capabilities. Section 3 describes the Repast Simphony distributed batch components. Section 4 presents a case study of the integrated Repast Simphony/Swift system for large-scale adaptive simulation via simulated annealing. We conclude in Section 5.

2   Background

2.1   Adaptive Simulation

ABMS studies typically require the execution of many model runs to account for stochastic variation in model outputs as well as to explore the possible range of model outcomes under alternative parameter settings and decision policies. More generally, Kleijnen et al. [4] identify reasons for conducting series of simulation model experiments that include: developing a basic understanding of a particular simulation model or system through exploration of the parameter space, finding robust decisions or policies rather than optimal solutions that may be prone to being unstable under small perturbations, or comparing and ranking the merits of various decisions or policies. In each of these cases, it is often necessary to run repeated simulation runs in which the results of one simulation inform the setup for the next simulation run. The need for adapting such simulation experiments over time comes up in several situations, including: design of simulation experiments [5,6], simulation exploration in which the simulation is used to explore the parameter space either locally or globally, and in simulation optimization in which the goal is to find a set of parameter values that maximize an objective or achieve satisfactory levels [7]. In addition, any adaptive simulation exploration is made more complex by the stochastic nature of the underlying simulations [8].

2.2   The Swift Parallel Scripting Language

Swift [2] is a task-parallel scripting language that enables users to specify and run workflows that execute large numbers of ordinary application programs in parallel, on parallel and distributed computing systems. Swift lets you define functions to "wrap" application programs, and to cleanly structure more complex scripts built up from calling these lowest-level functions. Swift app functions take files and numeric or string parameters as inputs and return files as outputs.

The simplest of Swift workflows typically run a large set of independent application invocations in parallel, often to implement a parameter sweep or to process all the files of a dataset in parallel. These are expressed with 10-20 lines of code, the heart of which is a single Swift "foreach" statement that sweeps over a set of data files and/or parameter variations. More complex parameter sweeps are expressed as a nested set of such loops. Reduction functions can be coded which reduce the output of a parallel foreach to a single result. The Swift data model and functional programming paradigm make such "sweep and reduce" patterns (which are very much like map-reduce in nature) easy to express. The Swift language has the typical scalar data types found in other scripting languages like Python (boolean, int, string, float) as well as a "file" type which allows it to automatically pass files to and from remotely executed applications. Collections of these types are dynamic, sparse arrays of arbitrary dimension, and structures of scalars and/or arrays. Swift variables are "single assignment". This makes Swift a natural parallel data flow language. Swift's foreach statement is the main parallel workhorse of the language, and executes all iterations of the loop concurrently. The actual number of parallel tasks executed is based on available resources and settable throttling parameters. In fact, Swift conceptually executes all the statements, expressions and function calls in your program in parallel, based on data flow. These are similarly throttled based on available resources and settings.

2.3   Related Work in Workflow Software

Numerous approaches, languages, and tools exist to express and execute workflows in parallel and on distributed resources. Often these have tradeoffs in terms of the flexibility vs. familiarity of the expression model; the complexity and scalability of the parallelism; and the difficulty of execution on distributed and/or heterogeneous parallel resources. We briefly survey here several representative approaches.

Language-neutral scripting tools. MyCluster [9] comprised extensions to the UNIX shell that allow a user to define a dataflow graph, including the concepts of fork, join, cycles, and key-value aggregation, but which execute on single parallel systems or clusters. These mechanisms, however, do not generalize to highly parallel and distributed environments.

Library-based approaches. Map-reduce [10] is a programming model and a runtime system to support the processing of large-scale datasets. Unlike Swift, which is tailored for composing workflows from application programs, like Repast Simphony, the map-reduce programming model is more oriented to using key-value pairs as input or output datasets.

Static DAG tools. DAGMan [11] is a workflow engine that manages Condor jobs organized as directed acyclic graphs (DAGs) of explicit task precedence. It has no knowledge of data flow, and in a distributed environment it requires a higher-level, data-cognizant layer. It is based on static workflow graphs and lacks dynamic features such as iteration or conditional execution. Pegasus [12] translates a workflow graph into location-specific DAGMan input, adding data staging, inter-site transfer, and data registration. These approaches lack the expressiveness of Swift's functional programming model for the composition of adaptive agent-based modeling work-flows.

Language-based approaches. Dryad [13] is an infrastructure for running data-parallel programs on a parallel or distributed system. Dryad graphs are explicitly developed by the programmer; Dryad appears to be used primarily for clusters and well-connected groups of clusters in single administrative domains and in Microsoft's cloud. Dryad lacks the flexibility that Swift provides for multi-site and multi-platform execution.

Visual workflow management environments. Many workflow systems (e.g., Taverna [14], Kepler [15], and Galaxy [16]) are based on comparable data-driven computing models but lack Swift's scalability, its simple generality for supporting arbitrary applications, and its provider-based architecture for broad platform support. Recent work is integrating Swift's execution model into the Galaxy user interface model, to provide the best benefits of both workflow models [17].

2.4 Batch Capabilities in Agent-Based Modeling Toolkits

ABMS studies typically require the execution of many model runs to account for stochastic variation in model outputs as well as to explore the possible range of outcomes. These ensembles of runs can be organized into parameter sweeps, known as batch runs. A batch run consists of multiple individual model runs each using their own combination of parameters. The independence of the individual model runs allows them to be distributed over numbers of processes on both multi-core desktop and high-performance computing platforms. A user defines a parameter space and uses the batch run capability to iterate through the parameter combinations in that space. Some level of batch run capability is built into virtually all ABMS toolkits. A mixture of external frameworks together with ABMS toolkit APIs has also been used to create custom batch capabilities [18].

ABMS toolkits typically allow the user to define the parameter space, and the toolkit then automates the iteration through that space. The parameter space is defined in some toolkit-specific format specifying each parameter in terms of a range, and a step value, or as a list of elements. The toolkit takes this formatted parameter space as input and executes the required runs.

3 Repast Simphony Distributed Batch Components

Given a user-defined parameter space, Repast Simphony [1] divides that space into discrete sets of parameter values and executes in-parallel runs iterating over these sets. These runs can be performed in parallel on a local machine (e.g., a laptop or desktop), on remote machines (secure shell [ssh] accessible resources), in the cloud (e.g., Amazon EC2), or on a combination of the three. Runs can also be done on a dedicated high-performance computing cluster. Once completed the individual results of the runs are aggregated for analysis. In Repast Simphony's default configuration, the actual runs themselves are executed using a master-client type architecture. A master process spawns child processes that perform the actual runs. The master process periodically polls these client processes to see if they have finished. Once they are finished the master process gathers the output from each client process and concatenates it together to form the total model output for all the runs. Each client works concurrently on its own subset of the parameter space, performing individual runs for each parameter combination in the subset.

This master client architecture is composed of three components: SessionsDriver, LocalDriver and InstanceRunner. The SessionsDriver distributes parameter sets and the required executable code to local and remote machines as specified by the user. It then launches a LocalDriver on each local and remote machine. The LocalDriver in turn launches a specified number of concurrent InstanceRunners that process a set of parameter combinations. Each InstanceRunner receives a set of parameters from the LocalDriver and runs the model once for each of the parameter combinations in the set. Each InstanceRunner iterates through its parameter set sequentially. However, all the InstanceRunners execute in parallel. The LocalDriver monitors the InstanceRunners for completion and the SessionsDriver monitors the LocalDriver. Once all the runs have been completed the SessionsDriver gathers the output from the local and remote machines and copies it to the master machine. If appropriate, these various outputs are then concatenated into a single file or files.

In the default workflow, these components are invisible to the user. In the batch run GUI, the user defines the parameter space, and specifies the local and remote machines on which to execute the runs. Launching the parameter sweep from the GUI creates a "model archive" jar file that contains all the code necessary to run the model and then starts a SessionsDriver. The SessionsDriver subsequently distributes the parameters and model archive and launches the LocalDrivers.

Alternate workflows can easily be created however. InstanceRunners are independent of LocalDrivers, expecting only some set of parameter combinations as input. Consequently, they can be launched by other control structures such as a bash, PBS, or Swift script on a high-performance computing cluster. The following section describes how the InstanceRunner component was used in conjunction with a Swift script to perform an adaptive parameter sweep using simulated annealing.

4   Case Study: Simulated Annealing

Here we present an example of an adaptive simulation workflow developed with Swift (version 0.95) and driving Repast Simphony (version 2.2) batch runs. The particular adaptive method used is simulated annealing (SA)[19]. The intent here is to show the ease of use and capabilities that are made possible by combining Swift and Repast Simphony, for any number of adaptive simulation methods, e.g., evolutionary algorithms, rather than to promote SA as the adaptive method of choice.

SA is a widely used stochastic global optimization approach. It mimics the physical process of annealing, whereby a metal is cooled slowly to relieve internal stresses by allowing the material to have time to find more favorable internal arrangements. In the case of SA a parameter space is stochastically explored while keeping track of the best results so far while allowing exploration of less than optimal solutions. To determine the viability of a result an objective function is used. In the case of an adaptive exploration of an ABMS parameter space, the objective function takes the result of a simulation and returns some derived value to be minimized. In SA, a global "temperature" is used to determine how far from optimality the algorithm is allowed to venture while looking for better results. As the algorithm proceeds and the temperature is reduced the allowed sub-optimality is reduced.

For this case study, we adapted the JZombies demonstration model, which is distributed with Repast Simphony [20]. The JZombies model involves two agent types, Zombies and Humans, where the Zombies chase after Humans, seeking to infect the Humans. Once a Human agent is infected it is transformed into a Zombie agent. A typical simulation run will eventually see all agents become Zombies, with the time until there are no remaining Humans varying by particular choices of parameters. The standard parameters in the JZombies model are the integer type parameters *zombie_count* and *human_count*, the initial number of Zombies and Humans, respectively. To this base model we introduced a varying step size for each of the agent types. The original model had Zombies move in steps of length 1 (in units of the model space) and Humans in steps of length 2. The present model encapsulates these two values into two float type parameters *zombieStep* and *humanStep*, respectively.

We used the Repast Simphony Batch GUI to create a model archive (see Section 8 in [21]) of the modified JZombies model. The model archive contains all of the Repast Simphony components, including the model code. This archive can be copied to a remote machine (e.g., a cluster login node) and unarchived into an appropriate directory. The rest of the components that we describe below were placed within the unarchived model archive.

Fig. 1 shows the overall flow of the Swift script (sa.swift) that was developed. The contents of sa.swift are available at the link provided in [3]. Every SA process begins with an initial point in a parameter space and explores the rest of the space from that point. We provide an input file (input.txt [3]) that specifies the various starting points. Each line in the input file represents a starting point for the simulated annealing process, along with a label of the experiment (e.g., 'exp0001'). The script reads all of the lines from the input file (sa.swift: line 260) and for each of the lines initiates a separate concurrent SA process by calling the *main* compound procedure (sa.swift: lines 270-272).

In *main*, the float and integer parameters are separated into arrays *a* and *b*, respectively. Swift relies on a write once data model to determine the procedure workflow. Thus, *a* and *b*, are both two dimensional arrays, which track arrays of parameter values over each SA loop. The one dimensional array *y* stores the objective function results, holding a floating point scalar value for each SA loop. We use the *aa*, *bb*, *a_best*, and *b_best* array variables to store the latest accepted set of a's and b's, and the best set of a's and b's, respectively (sa.swift: lines 163-175).

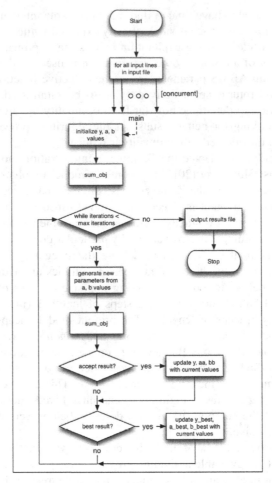

Fig. 1. Overall workflow of the sa.swift [3] simulated annealing Swift script

Once the data arrays are initialized, the "summarizing objective" compound procedure *sum_obj* is called (sa.swift: line 181). Fig. 2 describes the workflow within each *sum_obj* procedure, which plays a central role in the SA algorithm. Any individual simulation run of an ABMS with stochastic components yields a particular simulated trajectory and associated outputs. If one varies the random seed of a simulation, the outputs can change, sometimes dramatically. To account for the stochastic variations between model runs we execute *sv* stochastic variations for each parameter combination. Given a set of parameters, the *createUpfs* app procedure (sa.swift: line 40) invokes the *createUpfs.sh* script [3], generating the *sv* individual stochastic variation parameter files in a form that can be understood by the Repast Simphony distributed batch InstanceRunner class. The generated files, the upf_xxxx.txt files in Fig. 2, each contain a single set of parameters and are identical except for the different random seeds.

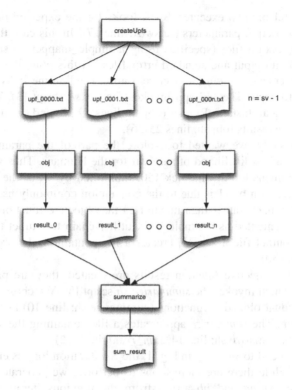

Fig. 2. Workflow within each *sum_obj* compound Swift procedure. The value *sv* is the number of stochastic variations to run for each parameter combination.

The external executable invoked by createUpfs.sh is a Java class (see UPFCreator [3]). This was a choice of convenience as there are extensive utilities built into the Repast Simphony distribution for reading and generating parameter files. The model archive contains Repast Simphony components in the form of Java Archives, or jars, in a *lib* folder. The compiled UPFCreator.class file was added as a jar into the lib folder. Since the Java classpath is defined to be the contents of the lib folder (createUpfs.sh: lines 8,11), this process can be repeated for any other external executable that is developed in Java, or other Java Virtual Machine language (e.g., Groovy).

Swift stages files into sandboxed working directories as needed by app procedures. The necessary files are specified as input parameters to an app. In lines 17-19 of sa.swift *_cUpfsScript* (the createUpfs.sh file), *_scenario* (the scenario.rs folder contents) and *_libs* (the lib folder contents) parameters are passed to the createUpfs app. The createUpfs.sh file is staged so that its name (@_cUpfsScript) can be passed to the shell command *sh*. The scenario.rs directory contents are needed to read in the model's parameters. For those parameters that are not explicitly specified to be varied by the SA procedure, the values in the model's parameters.xml file (within the scenario.rs folder) are used. The contents of the lib directory are needed for the classpath setting described above.

After the createUpfs app executes, Swift looks for the expected output, indicated by the files in the output parameters (sa.swift: line 17). In this case the outputs are a file array of upf_xxx.txt files (specified using a simple_mapper on sa.swift: line 34) along with standard output and standard error files. At this point the *sum_obj* procedure launches *sv* concurrent *obj* ("objective") apps, sending the individual generated parameter files to each. The *obj* app invokes the *obj.sh* script [3]. The script is in charge of launching an InstanceRunner (obj.sh: lines 19-23) and calculating an objective function on the results (obj.sh: lines 25-26).

For this case study, we wanted to explore the part of the parameter space that would yield the highest likelihood of survival for the Humans. Thus we chose to use the number of Humans left at time tick 150, multiplied by -1, as the objective function. The multiplication by -1 is due to the convention commonly used in SA where the goal is to minimize (rather than maximize) the objective function. The objective function was implemented as a simple Unix utility chain to extract this information from the model output file. Each *obj* creates a file containing the objective function result (obj.sh: line 30).

Once all of the objective function results are created, they are passed on to the *summarize* app, which invokes the *summarize.sh* script [3]. We chose to use the average of the individual objective functions (summarize.sh: line 10) as the summarized objective function. The *summarize* app creates a file containing the summarized objective function (summarize.sh: line 14, *sum_result* in Fig. 2).

After the initial call to *sum_obj* in Fig. 1, the SA iteration loop is entered (sa.swift: lines 192-226). While there are more loops to perform, we generate new parameter values based on the *aa* and *bb* arrays from the previous iteration with calls to *newx_float* and *newx_int* (sa.swift: lines 194-195). The two *newx* procedures accept the original scalar value (*x*), an increment (*dx*), a minimum value (*_min*), and a maximum value (*_max*). The values that are provided to the individual *newx* calls effectively split up the 4-dimensional parameter space into 20 x 20 x 10 x 11 = 44,000 parameter combinations and make the SA implementation a constrained optimization problem.

The newly generated parameters are used to call *sum_obj* again (sa.swift: line 200). Once *sum_obj* completes, the returned summarized objective function variable *ny* is compared to the *y* variable from the previous iteration for acceptance with a call to *accept*. The *accept* procedure implements the SA accept algorithm directly in Swift (sa.swift: lines 94-113). If *ny* is accepted the values for *aa*, *bb*, and *y* are updated based on the current values of *a*, *b* and *ny*. Otherwise, *aa*, *bb*, and *y* carry over their previous values. Next, the current value of *y* is compared with the *y_best* variable (the best value of *y* so far) and if it is an improved objective function, *y_best*, *a_best* and *b_best* are updated based on the current values of *a*, *b* and *y*.

Finally, when the predefined number of SA loops are completed, each *main* procedure creates an output file based on the defined *Output* type (sa.swift: lines 252-258), which includes the *y_best*, *a_best* and *b_best* tracked over each SA loop.

For this case study we made use of high performance computing resources available at the University of Chicago, specifically the Midway cluster at the University of Chicago Research Computing Center [22]. The cluster scheduling is managed by the

SLURM resource manager [23]. However, since Swift is responsible for most of the direct interactions with resource managers, the specific type of resource manager only minimally affects the configuration specified in the swift.properties file [3] that is provided to Swift when launching a job.

The sa.swift script was launched with the command:

```
swift sa.swift -i=input.txt -sv=16 -al=100
```

This set the input file as input.txt, the number of stochastic variations as 16, and the number of annealing loops as 100. Thus, for each SA procedure we ran 16 stochastically varied simulations in parallel, repeating the process 100 times. Furthermore, the input.txt file contained 16 separate SA experiments (labeled 'exp0000'- 'exp1111'), which launched 16 concurrent SA procedures. This resulted in a theoretical maximum of 256 simulations running concurrently, with results from each simulation run feeding into and directing the next set of concurrent runs. In order to utilize the necessary number of computing units on the Midway cluster, we defined the swift.properties file's *midway* section (swift.properties: lines 20-33) to submit 16 separate jobs (*maxJobs*=16), where each job utilized exactly one node (*jobGranularity*=1, *maxNodesPerJob*=1), and each node could launch 16 workers (*tasksPerWorker*=16). To ensure that no job throttling took place we specified *taskThrottle*=512, double our expected concurrent tasks. Finally, we conservatively estimated the total length of each job, a complete SA procedure, to take 1 hour (*jobWalltime*=01:00:00) and each individual task (e.g., createUpfs, obj, summarize) to take 2 minutes (*taskWalltime*=00:02:00).

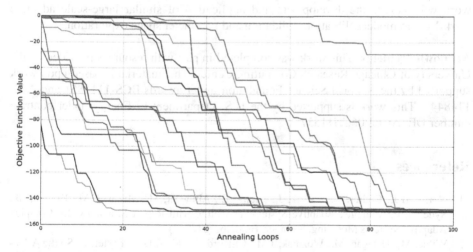

Fig. 3. Paths showing the evolution of the best objective function, *y_best*, for the 16 parallel simulated annealing processes over the course of 100 annealing loops

The sa.swift script took 17 minutes to complete, including job submission, execution and collecting of the output data, running a total of 25,856 simulation runs. Fig. 3 shows the paths of the *y_best* variables for each of the 16 experiments over the course of the 100 annealing loops. All but one of the experiments were able to reach a state where almost 150 Humans were left after 150 simulation ticks. That is, almost all of the experiments found parameter combinations where all of the maximum allowable number of Humans were able to elude the Zombies at least until tick 150. The general characteristics of the "solutions" that were found involved setting *zombieStep* to its smallest value, *humanStep* to a large value, *zombie_count* to it's smallest value, and *human_count* to its largest value. This confirmed that almost all of the SA processes were able to recover this intuitively expected results for achieving the highest likelihood of survival for Human agents. These results were found with a total of 25,856 simulation runs, compared to 704,000 simulation runs for a complete enumeration of the 44,000 element parameter space, and including 16 stochastic variations for each element (a reduction of 96.3% of the total simulation runs required).

5   Conclusion

As ABMS is applied to ever-larger and complex systems, ABMS capabilities will need to continue to evolve. Here we have presented a general approach for large-scale adaptive simulation, which integrates Repast Simphony's distributed batch components and the Swift parallel scripting language. We have provided a reference simulated annealing workflow, along with annotated materials, to make these capabilities accessible to the agent-modeling community. We have shown in the example presented that adaptive simulation enables strategic exploration of a model's parameter space, potentially offering vast improvements in computational efficiency. Future work will include the development and application of similar large-scale adaptive workflows to model calibration, validation and parameter space exploration.

Acknowledgements. This work was completed in part with resources provided by the University of Chicago Research Computing Center. This material is based upon work supported by the National Science Foundation under awards BCS-1114851 and ACI-1148443. This work is supported by the U.S. Department of Energy under contract number DE- AC02-06CH11357.

References

1. North, M.J., Collier, N.T., Ozik, J., Tatara, E., Altaweel, M., Macal, C.M., Bragen, M., Sydelko, P.: Complex Adaptive Systems Modeling with Repast Simphony. In: Complex Adaptive Systems Modeling. Springer, Heidelberg (2013)
2. Wilde, M., Hategan, M., Wozniak, J.M., Clifford, B., Katz, D.S., Foster, I.: Swift: A language for distributed parallel scripting. Parallel Computing 37(9), 633–652 (2011)
3. Adaptive Simulation with Repast Simphony and Swiftsupplemental materials, https://gist.github.com/jozik/74b7f40a7ed8bd4c37a9
4. Kleijnen, J.P.C., Sanchez, S.M., Lucas, T.W., Cioppa, T.M.: A user's guide to the brave new world of simulation experiments. INFORMS Journal on Computing 17(3), 263–289 (2005)

5. Sanchez, S.M.: Work Smarter, Not Harder: Guidelines For Designing Simulation Experiments. In: Perrone, L.F., Wieland, F.P., Liu, J., Lawson, B.G., Nicol, D.M., Fujimoto, R.M. (eds.) Proc. 2006 Winter Simulation Conf., pp. 47–57 (2006)
6. Barton, R.R.: Designing Simulation Experiments. In: Pasupathy, R., Kim, S.-H., Tolk, A., Hill, R., Kuhl, M.E. (eds.) Proc. 2013 Winter Simulation Conf., pp. 342–353 (2013)
7. Fu, M.C.: Optimization for simulation: Theory vs. practice. INFORMS J. Comput. 14, 192–215 (2002)
8. Spall, J.C.: Introduction to Stochastic Search and Optimization: Estimation, Simulation, and Control. Wiley, New York (2003)
9. Walker, E., Xu, W., Chandar, V.: Composing and executing parallel data-flow graphs with shell pipes. In: Workshop on Workflows in Support of Large-Scale Science at SC 2009 (2009)
10. Dean, J., Ghemawat, S.: MapReduce: Simplified data processing on large clusters. In: Proc. Operating Systems Design and Implementation (2004)
11. Thain, T., Tannenbaum, T., Livny, M.: Distributed computing in practice: The Condor Experience. Concurrency and Computation: Practice and Experience 17(2-4), 323–356 (2005)
12. Deelman, E., Singh, G., Su, M., Blythe, J., Gil, Y., Kesselman, K., Mehta, G., Vahi, K., Berriman, G.B., Good, J., Laity, A., Jacob, J.C., Katz, D.S.: Pegasus: A framework for mapping complex scientific workflows onto distributed systems. Scientific Programming 13, 219–237 (2005)
13. Isard, M., Budiu, M., Yu, Y., Birrell, A., Fetterly, D.: Dryad: Distributed data parallel programs from sequential building blocks. In: Proc. EuroSys (2007)
14. Oinn, T., Addis, M., Ferris, J., Marvin, D., Senger, M., Greenwood, M., Carver, T., Glover, K., Pocock, M.R., Wipat, A., Li, P.: Taverna: a tool for the composition and enactment of bioinformatics workflows. Bioinformatics 20, 3045–3054 (2004)
15. Ludscher, B., Altintas, I., Berkley, C., Higgins, D., Jaeger-Frank, E., Jones, M., Lee, E., Tao, J., Zhao, Y.: Scientific workflow management and the Kepler system. Concurrency and Computation: Practice & Experience 18, 1039–1065 (2006)
16. Goecks, J., Nekrutenko, A., Taylor, J.: The Galaxy Team: Galaxy: a comprehensive approach for supporting accessible, reproducible, and transparent computational research in the life sciences. Genome Biol 11(8), R86 (2010)
17. Maheshwari, K., Rodriguez, A., Kelly, D., Madduri, R., Wozniak, J., Wilde, M., Foster, I.: Enabling multi-task computation on Galaxy-based gateways using Swift. In: 2013 IEEE International Conference on Cluster Computing (CLUSTER), pp. 23–27 (2013)
18. Koehler, M.T., Tivnan, B.F.: Clustered computing with NetLogo and Repast J: beyond chewing gum and duct tape. In: Proceedings of the Agent 2005 Conference on Generative Social Processes, Models, and Mechanisms, pp. 43–54 (2005)
19. Kirkpatrick, S.: Optimization by Simulated Annealing: Quantitative Studies. Journal of Statistical Physics 34(5–6), 975–986 (1984), doi:10.1007/BF0100945
20. Repast Java Getting Started Guide, http://repast.sf.net/docs/RepastJavaGettingStarted.pdf
21. Repast Simphony Batch Runs Getting Started, http://repast.sf.net/docs/RepastBatchRunsGettingStarted.pdf
22. University of Chicago Research Computing Center, http://rcc.uchicago.edu/resources/midway_specs.html
23. SLURM Resource Manager, https://computing.llnl.gov/linux/slurm/

Towards a Framework for Adaptive Resource Provisioning in Large-Scale Distributed Agent-Based Simulation

Masatoshi Hanai[1,2], Toyotaro Suzumura[2,4],
Anthony Ventresque[2,3,4], and Kazuyuki Shudo[1]

[1] Tokyo Institute of Technology,
Dept. of Mathematical and Computing Sciences
2-12-1 Ookayama, Meguro, Tokyo, 152-8552 Japan
{hanai.aa,shudo}@{m,is}.titech.ac.jp
[2] School of Computer Science and Informatics,
University College Dublin, Ireland
anthony.ventresque@ucd.ie
[3] Lero, the Irish Software Engineering Research Centre
[4] Smarter Cities Technology Centre, IBM Research,
Damastown Industrial Estate, Mulhuddart, Dublin 15, Ireland
suzumura@acm.org

Abstract. Large scale distributed agent-based simulations run on several computing units (e.g., virtual machines in the Cloud, nodes in a supercomputer). Classically, these systems try to (re-)load-balance the nodes as overloaded nodes slow down the process. However another challenge in large scale distributed simulations is that the *overall load evolves*. In this paper we leverage on commodity computing to adapt resource provisioning (number of computing units) to the load during the execution of the simulation. We also propose an asynchronous migration mechanism that migrate workload between computing nodes efficiently when nodes wait for synchronisation barriers to happen. We validate our implementation on a scenario simulating one day of vehicular traffic in Tokyo, running on 2 to 8 machines depending on the demand. Our evaluation shows a 26% reduction in data migration time compared to a naive migration approach between computing units.

1 Introduction

Agent-based simulation is an important field of research that has led to important and promising findings in areas such as transportation, environmental protection and economy [17]. Bringing agent-based simulations up to the scale required by large systems (e.g., large urban areas, social systems) is a challenging problem and several methods and simulators have been proposed [10,20]. In short, large scale simulations need to run on several computing nodes in parallel to speed-up their processing, and the challenges are usually load-balancing and minimisation of communication between nodes.

L. Lopes et al. (Eds.): Euro-Par 2014 Workshops, Part I, LNCS 8805, pp. 430–439, 2014.

In this paper we are interested in a different problem: *how can we efficiently adapt the number of computing resources to the load?* Our idea comes from two simple observations: (i) overall simulation load evolves over time [19], e.g., for a urban traffic simulation, there are less vehicles to process during the night than during peak commuting hours; and (ii) the number of computing nodes required during low and peak demands should vary accordingly. Figure 1 shows the traffic pattern (number of cars) of a day in Tokyo; in the system we describe below (Megaffic) 100,000 vehicles per computing node is a good number and it is clear from the figure that while we sometimes need 8 machines to run the simulation, there are other moments when less are required.

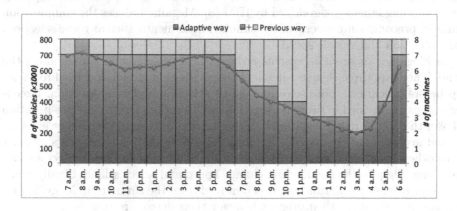

Fig. 1. Typical day of traffic (number of vehicles) in Tokyo and number of machines required to simulate it with our adaptive system

This provisioning and releasing of resources according to demand is challenging in a high-performance computing setting, i.e., the classical context for large scale simulations. However the situation is different nowadays, with the advent of pay-as-you-go mechanisms in both Cloud computing and supercomputers (see Section 2 for details). This is why we propose in this paper a new method to adapt resource provisioning, which enables to increase and decrease the number of machines during execution and achieves an efficient utilization of computational resources. Our main contribution are:

1. The description of a framework which can control the number of machines during execution.
2. An asynchronous migration mechanism for simulated objects, keeping the simulation consistent when the number of executing machines is changing.

The rest of paper is organized as follows: Section 2 describes the context of our research; Section 3 gives a description of our framework, Section 4 details our efficient object migration technique and Section 5 summarizes our implementation decisions; we evaluate the performance of our system in Section 6; Section 7 compares our work to related efforts; we finally conclude in Section 8.

2   Background

This section gives a description of two of the main elements of our work: the traffic simulator and the Cloud computing infrastructure.

2.1   IBM Mega Traffic Simulator

IBM Mega Traffic simulator, or *Megaffic* [15,20,16], is a large-scale distributed traffic flows simulator. Megaffic is built on top of the platform XAXIS (*X10-based Agent eXecutive Infrastructure for Simulation*), a highly scalable multi-agent simulation distributed middleware based on X10, the parallel computing programming language developed by IBM [9]. Megaffic reduces the computation time by precomputing several of the simulation elements, such as route selection, lane selection and vehicle speed.

In Megaffic, an agent represents a driver of a vehicle, who travels along the road. There are three elements defining the simulation model that need to be set up before execution: route selection, speed selection and lane selection. Execution steps are divided in two: pre-iteration and iteration. During the pre-iteration phase, the origin, the destination and the departure time of each agent are generated according to the model. The iteration phase then starts, agents interact with other agents according to the defined behavior model. Agents select a route from the origin to the destination, change speed and select a lane. Finally when an agent reaches its destination, it is removed from the simulation. Megaffic also creates new agents at their origin whenever their departure time is reached.

In our research, the computation model and the agent behavior are based on Megaffic. Thus each agent has a tentative path, driver preference and origin-destination data in advance.

Other than Megaffic, some large-scale traffic simulators have been proposed in recent years. For instance Bragard et al. recently proposed dSUMO [8], which is a distributed version of SUMO, an open source microscopic traffic simulation system including the simulation application and supporting tools for network imports and demand modeling. Another example is Matsim [4], which achieves a large-scale microscopic traffic simulation on a single computer. For example, the traffic in all of Switzerland was simulated using Matsim, but some of the details were omitted from their simulation models for scalability [18].

2.2   Pay-as-you-go Cost Model for Computing Resources

Pay-as-you-go is a new model for renting computational resources, where users can decide how much and for how long they want to use specific resources. This model is fine-grained: e.g., renting can be done in the order of seconds [7] or minutes [2,5,6], and it is also flexible, allowing users to define exactly what infrastructure they need, in terms of memory, network or CPU [1]. While pay-as-you-go is often associated with the Cloud computing environment, it is also popular in the area of supercomputers: see for instance the examples of Tsubame [7] and K computer [3].

3   Framework for Adaptive Resource Provisioning

This section describes in details the simulation model used in Megaffic and our system. In particular, we give a presentation of the three main modules of our framework: workload predictor, resource provisioning optimizer, resource controller.

3.1   Simulation Model of Megaffic Simulation

As mentioned in the previous section, we assume the same computational model and the same agent behavior as Megaffic. The simulator gets data such as road definition and vehicle trip description (origin, destination, exact path and departing time). After giving this data to the system, roads and vehicles are distributed to each worker according to the precomputed road map partitions. The roads have as many queues as they have lanes, and each vehicle is inserted in the queues. The system starts iterating then, each iteration representing 1 second of real world time. During each iteration the vehicles are processed to determine where they are at the next iteration. After finishing to process all its vehicles, each worker start communicating with the roads of its neighboring workers. And so on until the end of the simulation.

3.2   Overview of the System

To achieve an efficient resource utilization on a pay-as-you-go system that is fine-grained (in terms of renting time) and flexible, we have mainly three problems to address:

- How do we predict the workload in the next steps to provision exactly the required resource?
- How do we optimize cost given some user's objectives, such as, "as fast as possible simulation (whatever cost)", "as fast as possible but for a cost less than 20 dollars", "as cheap as possible but not lasting more than 1 hour"?
- How do we increase and decrease the number of machines during the simulation according to the objectives we want to optimize?

To solve these problems, our system consists of mainly three components in addition to the traffic simulator itself: the workload predictor, the resource arrangement optimizer and the resource controller. Figure 2 shows an overview our system. The system is built on top of a master-worker architecture where the master controls utilization of the resources and manages the synchronization of the simulation and the meta-data such as the cross points and roads arrangement given to the workers. The workers process the simulation scenario itself.

Workload predictor The workload predictor predicts the workload for next iterations based on its analysis of the input data and some feedback from all workers. It returns the predicted next the workload information for next steps such as CPU usage, memory usage, network I/O usage, number of outgoing vehicles and incoming vehicles.

Resource provisioning optimizer The resource provisioning optimizer optimizes the cost of running the simulation according to some user-defined requirements. The optimizer gets the result of predicted workload and returns the most efficient arrangement of the simulation state to the workers.

Resource controller The resource controller controls the physical and/or virtual machines environment of the simulation. According to the optimized arrangement, the controller launches new machines via the proper IaaS API if it requires extra machines. After finishing an iteration, the controller also releases the possible unused machine.

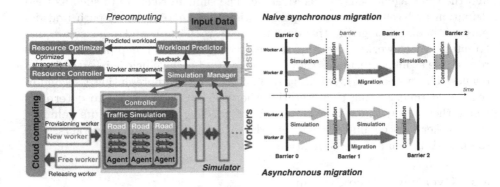

Fig. 2. System overview   **Fig. 3.** Asynchronous migration

4   Efficient Migration for Agent-Based Simulation

In order to change the number of workers during the simulation while keeping consistency of the simulating result, we need to migrate part of the simulation state between workers. But migration cost is high as it requires a lot of communication between workers and serialization and deserialization of simulation objects, which increases execution time and CPU cost. Suppose C_a is cost to migrate 1 agent, C_r is cost to migrate 1 road, $N_a(i)$ is the number of migrating agents in $road_i$, and N_r is the number of migrating roads. The total cost of migration C_{total} is:

$$C_{total} = C_r \times Nr + \sum_{i=0,1,2,,..Nr} \{C_a \times N_a(i)\} \tag{1}$$

Each road migration is independent, thus you can easily parallelize it and if there are enough processes and enough network bandwidth, the execution time is:

$$T_{paraTotal} = \max_{i \in \{0,1,2,\cdots,N_r\}} \{Time(C_r + N_a(i) \times C_a),\} \tag{2}$$

where $Time(x)$ gives the time required to process the corresponding cost.

The key idea of our proposed solution is to include the migration in the simulation execution itself: the load imbalance between nodes leaving time when workers can exchange workload. To do so, we make the migration *asynchronous*. The problem that needs to be considered carefully is how to keep consistency of simulating results. If migration occurs at arbitrary points during the simulation, the meta data of the simulation state (roads and cross points) may change incorrectly, which could result in inconsistent simulation results. In our system, for appropriate asynchronous migration, the migration occurs only at the beginning of the iteration.

In Megaffic, the whole simulation flow consists of a series of iterations of parallel processing of individual roads and communications alternatively. Between the processing of roads and the communication, the synchronization barrier occurs in all roads. Thus for a consistent asynchronous simulation it is sufficient to synchronise the simulation state metadata at the start of the communication. Figure 3 shows the comparison between a naive way of synchronising and our proposed solution. In the naive synchronous way to migrate, workers with no migration are idle until all migrations are finished. In contrast, in our asynchronous solution, the migrations overlap with the simulation execution and we reduce the total execution time.

5   Implementation

As we already mentioned, we use a master-worker architecture, meaning that a master process controls the resource management and the synchronization of the traffic simulation while workers execute each a part of the traffic simulation. We use ZooKeeper, an open source software for distributed systems configuration, to manage the coordination of the system. ZooKeeper is in charge of naming registry, synchronization mechanism, addressing of machines, role of each machine, and to maintain the status of each machine.

In our traffic simulation, which is mainly implemented in Java, the heaviest process is communication between workers, especially the sending and reception of Java objects. Regarding the communication between objects, we use Messagepack serialization format to serialize simulation object and Netty, nonblocking networking framework, for sending and receiving such serialized simulation objects. As for the predictor, the evolution in the number of departing vehicles at each iteration step is analyzed statically before executing the simulation. Then the predictor returns the sum of the departing vehicles and vehicles to process by each worker. In the optimizer, the worker resource arrangement is optimized based on precomputed partitioned road map data and the number of vehicles at the next step as predicted by the predictor. The road map data is partitioned by a k-ways graph partitioning algorithm [12] using METIS [13] before execution. Other solutions could be used among the various space/graph/road network partitioning algorithms, such as SParTSim [21]. The resource controller uses physical machines instead of the flexible resource provider, just for evaluation purposes. This does not include the shutdown or start up of machines, and the provisioning occurs instantly.

6   Evaluation

In this section, we evaluate our proposed cost reduction method for traffic simulation. We use eight worker machines in total and one master machine, all
running Linux 3.8.0. Each machine has two 2.40 GHz Xeon E5620 CPUs and
32GB RAM. We execute the simulation on Java SE 7 update 4 with option
-Xmx16g. We use the road network of the bay area in Tokyo, which includes
161,364 crosspoints (junctions) and 20,2976 roads. There are a total of 250,000
vehicle trips over a 24 hour period (82,800 steps). The evolution of the number
of vehicles during 24 hours are based on the ratio of some traffic data in All of
Tokyo collected by the MLIT (Ministry of Land, Infrastructure, Transport and
Tourism) in 2011 (see Figure 1 in section 1).

We first conduct evaluations of the scalability and the roads migration time.
Figure 4 shows the execution time of simulating 24 hours in Tokyo according to
the number of machines. The execution time decreases to as low as 52 % of a
single machine's execution time, but plateaus in 6 or 7 machines. This is because
the communications cost increases with the number of workers. Figure 5 shows
the migration time of roads between two machines. The migration cost increases
according to the number of roads and the number of vehicles on the roads.

We then evaluate our proposed asynchronous migration of roads and vehicles
for distributed traffic simulation. We adapt the number of workers to the number
of new departing vehicles (given before the simulation by the predictor). The
optimizer optimizes the roads arrangement every hour (3,600 steps) to keep
the number of new vehicles to 2,000. Figure 6 shows the average time for one
iteration in synchronous or asynchronous migrations. Note that the migration
can be included in the simulation itself (not the communication though) and the
time for the asynchronous migration could decrease even more. However, in our
traffic simulation scenario, the simulation time is very short compared to the
migration time, and the effect of the asynchronous migration does not appear as
important as it should be. The asynchronous migration technique could be more
effective if the simulation time is large compared to the migration time. Figure

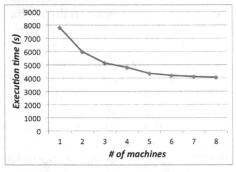

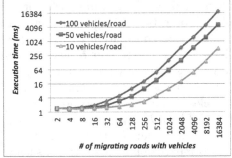

Fig. 4. Scalability of the traffic simulation   **Fig. 5.** Migration time for roads

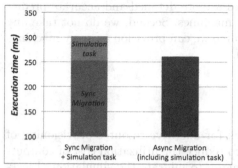 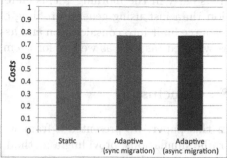

Fig. 6. Overall execution time   **Fig. 7.** Cost of migration

7 shows the comparison of costs (i.e., sum of the CPU times including idle time in all machines) between static and adaptive migrations. Adaptive techniques reduce the cost of migration by 26% compared to the static solution.

7   Related Work

Shengming Li, et al. [14] proposed a workload prediction-based multi-VM provisioning mechanism, which contains a multi-VM provisioning technique based on time-based billing aware multi-VM provisioning algorithm (TBAMP) and a workload prediction technique based on ARIMA (autoregressive integrated moving average). This technique achieves effective rental cost saving in the Cloud and consists of a prediction module and an optimizing module, like our work. However, unlike our approach, this technique does not take machine communication into consideration. This is ok for applications without any machine communication, like web servers or cache servers, which can be linearly faster with more machines and do not require to keep consistency. However this is not the case in the agent-based simulation domain. We then need to take network topology (e.g., communication) into consideration to keep or even improve the performance, and we need a migration solution of the simulation states for consistency.

Efficient resource allocation of computer resources is a challenging research topic. There are a lot of work on efficient resource allocation using resource provider. For example, Gandhi et al. [11] proposed a method to reduce the energy cost while meeting SLAs by using a workload prediction and a reactive allocations modules. This approach is similar to ours but from a different perspective: we are interested in users of computational resources while they focus on resource providers. Thus, we do not share the same assumptions. First, we can use some application specific and some semantic information for prediction. For instance, we can get some input about the number of vehicles and the road map data, and we can predict based on traffic semantics such as "it is noon" or "it is early in the morning". This enables a more detailed and accurate prediction than just using general profiling of machines. Second, we do not take any resource limit into consideration and assume we can provision as many machines as we need (as long as we pay for them).

8   Conclusion

In this paper, we presented a framework for adaptive resource provisioning of traffic simulations, providing a method to reduce the utilization cost of computing resources. We also proposed a technique to migrate the simulation objects efficiently by overlapping the simulating processes. We simulated the traffic of Tokyo with 8 commodity servers and we confirmed that our method can save up to 26 % of the simulation costs without impacting the simulation results.

We would like to improve some of the components of our framework as future work. The prediction could be more accurate by using some mathematical or machine learning techniques. For example, we can predict traffic flows more precisely using ARIMA. The optimizer could benefit from a dynamic graph partitioning and would certainly optimize the resource assignment for next steps. For example, by using incremental graph partitioning technique, we can adapt the resource assignment more effectively to the information given by moving vehicles. Finally we need to implement and evaluate fully the Cloud computing environment in the resource controller module.

Acknowledgment. This work was supported, in part, by JST CREST and JSPS KAKENHI Grant Numbers 25700008 and 26540161, by Science Foundation Ireland grant 10/CE/I1855 to Lero and by Science Foundation Ireland Industry Fellowship grant 13/IF/12789.

References

1. Amazon EC2, https://aws.amazon.com/ec2/
2. Google Compute Engine, https://cloud.google.com/products/compute-engine/
3. K computer, http://www.kcomputer.jp/en/
4. Matsim, http://www.matsim.org/
5. Microsft Asure, http://azure.microsoft.com/
6. Rackspace Cloud, http://www.rackspace.com/
7. Tsubame 2.5, http://www.gsic.titech.ac.jp/en/tsubame/
8. Bragard, Q., Ventresque, A., Murphy, L.: dSUMO: towards a distributed SUMO. In: SUMO Conference (2013)
9. Charles, P., Grothoff, C., Saraswat, V., Donawa, C., Kielstra, A., Ebcioglu, K., Von Praun, C., Sarkar, V.: X10: an object-oriented approach to non-uniform cluster computing. ACM SIGPLAN Notices 40(10), 519–538 (2005)
10. Collier, N., North, M.: Repast HPC: A platform for large-scale agent-based modeling. Wiley (2011)

11. Gandhi, A., Chen, Y., Gmach, D., Arlitt, M., Marwah, M.: Minimizing data center sla violations and power consumption via hybrid resource provisioning. In: Green Computing Conference and Workshops, pp. 1–8. IEEE (2011)
12. Karypis, G., Kumar, V.: Multilevel k-way partitioning scheme for irregular graphs. Journal of Parallel and Distributed Computing 48(1), 96–129 (1998)
13. Karypis, G., Kumar, V.: METIS - a software package for partitioning unstructured graphs, meshes, and computing fill-reducing orderings of sparse matrices-version 5.0. University of Minnesota (2011)
14. Li, S., Wang, Y., Qiu, X., Wang, D., Wang, L.: A workload prediction-based multi-vm provisioning mechanism in cloud computing. In: Asia-Pacific Network Operations and Management Symposium, pp. 1–6. IEEE (2013)
15. Osogami, T., Imamichi, T., Mizuta, H., Morimura, T., Raymond, R., Suzumura, T., Takahashi, R., Ide, T.: IBM Mega Traffic Simulator. Technical report, Technical Report RT0896, IBM Research–Tokyo (2012)
16. Osogami, T., Imamichi, T., Mizuta, H., Suzumura, T., Ide, T.: Toward simulating entire cities with behavioral models of traffic. IBM Journal of Research and Development 57(5), 1–6 (2013)
17. Paolucci, M., et al.: Towards a living earth simulator. The European Physical Journal Special Topics 214(1), 77–108 (2012)
18. Raney, B., Cetin, N., Völlmy, A., Vrtic, M., Axhausen, K., Nagel, K.: An agent-based microsimulation model of swiss travel: First results. Networks and Spatial Economics 3(1), 23–41 (2003)
19. Suzumura, T., Kanezashi, H.: Accelerating large-scale distributed traffic simulation with adaptive synchronization method. In: ITS World Congress (2013)
20. Suzumura, T., Kato, S., Imamichi, T., Takeuchi, M., Kanezashi, H., Ide, T., Onodera, T.: X10-based massive parallel large-scale traffic flow simulation. In: ACM SIGPLAN X10 Workshop, p. 3. ACM (2012)
21. Ventresque, A., Bragard, Q., Liu, E.S., Nowak, D., Murphy, L., Theodoropoulos, G., Liu, J.Q.: SParTSim: A space partitioning guided by road network for distributed traffic simulations. In: DS-RT, pp. 202–209. IEEE (2012)

Theoretical Nabladot Analysis of Amdahl's Law for Agent-Based Simulations

Claudio Cioffi-Revilla

Center for Social Complexity and Department of Computational Social Science,
George Mason University, Fairfax, Virginia 22314, USA
ccioffi@gmu.edu
http://krasnow.gmu.edu/socialcomplexity/faculty/csc-faculty-dr-cioffi/

Abstract. Amdahl's Law states that execution speedup S is nonlinearly proportional to the percentage of parallelizable code P and the number N of processors. Additional terms must be added to Amdahl's Law when applied to agent-based simulations, depending on how synchronization is implemented. Since P is continuous but N is discrete, traditional multivariate operators based on nabla or del ∇ are applicable only for P, not for N, regardless of synchronization architecture (linear, logarithmic, constant, among other). Moreover, relatively low values of N (bound by Miller's number 7 ± 2) are common in some cases. Here I apply a novel and exact operator, called "nabladot" and denoted by the symbol $\dot{\nabla}$, that is defined for hybrid function such as Amdahl's Law. The main results show how exact solutions using nabladot differ from traditional approximations, particularly in the logarithmic case that is characteristic of hierarchical synchronization. Improvements in precision are inversely proportional to P and N, converging to 0.8 as $N \to 2$.

Keywords: Amdahl's Law, nabladot, multivariate vector analysis, distributed systems, concrete mathematics, hybrid functions.

1 Introduction

Agent-based simulations represent an emergent field of computational science, including the convergence of natural, social, and engineering sciences to advance our understanding of complex systems (Cioffi 2014a). This section provides basic motivation and background for the theoretical analysis that follows, focusing on Amdahl's Law for distributed systems and its application to a set of important cases in agent-based simulations.

1.1 Amdahl's Law

Consider a computer program operating as a distributed system over a number N of processors and let P denote the relative proportion of code that can be parallelized, where $N \geq 2$ and $0 \leq P < 1$. Accordingly, $1 - P$ is the proportion of code that remains serialized.

L. Lopes et al. (Eds.): Euro-Par 2014 Workshops, Part I, LNCS 8805, pp. 440–451, 2014.
© Springer International Publishing Switzerland 2014

The following question is of enduring interest in the theory of computing, especially with regard to time and space (or spatio-temporal) complexity: What is the speedup S resulting from different values of N and P? Amdahl's Law (1967) states that S, the amount of time that can be gained by parallelization, is given by the following formula:

$$S = \frac{1}{(1 - P) + \frac{P}{N}} \tag{1}$$

$$= \frac{N}{N + P - NP} . \tag{2}$$

Several improvements to Amdahl's Law have advanced the field during the past decades (Eyerman and Eeckhout 2010; Gustafson 1988; Hill and Marty 2008), so formal analysis of laws of parallel and distributed systems remains significant in the theory of computation.

Equation 1 is the most common form of Amdahl's Law found in the literature, including most formal interpretations of Amdahl's statement in his original historic paper.[1] This equation for Amdahl's Law also provides a nice interpretation in terms of sequential and parallel components, corresponding to the denominator terms $(1 - P)$ and P/N, respectively. By contrast, Eq. 2 is a simpler formula obtained through easily verifiable algebraic manipulation.

The advantage of Eq. 2 over Eq. 1 is that the latter is simpler and highlights the multiple dependencies of the mapping between speedup and P and N, or the multivariate function $f : (P, N) \rightarrow S$. With respect to P, S shows an inverse additive dependency ($S \propto 1/N$, based on the first term in the denominator) as well as an inverse multiplicative or inverse interactive dependency ($S \propto 1/NP$, the last term in the denominator). The same is also true with respect to N but, *in addition*, S has a linear dependency ($S \propto N$, based on the numerator), which is lacking with respect to P. Therefore, speedup has three different dependencies on N versus two for P—a feature that is missed when viewing Amdahl's Law simply as a function of two variables.

The retrospective implication of these multiple and concurrent dependencies is that Amdahl's Law is deceptively simple in its algebraic form. In fact, speedup is anything but intuitive as a multivariate function of P and N except in trivial cases, such as $P = N = 1$ or 0. Figure 1 shows the graph of Amdahl's Law for values of P and a range of low values of N. The general intuition that S should increase with both P and N is correct—as shown by the graph—but details matter greatly, given the nonlinear structure of Amdahl's Law.

Given these properties of Amdahl's Law, additional questions arise. Arguably, the following is fundamental: What is speedup more sensitive to, code parallelization P or processor parallelization N? Alternatively, viewed as an optimal allocation problem: in terms of speedup and given finite resources available, is it better to invest resources in P or in N? The complex functional dependencies

---

[1] Amdahl's 1967 paper contains the original statement of his law of speedup, but did not state a specific mathematical function.

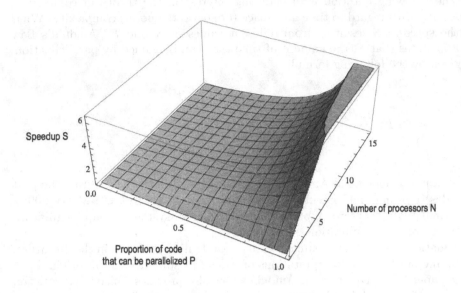

Speedup S

Number of processors N

Proportion of code
that can be parallelized P

Fig. 1. Graph of Amdahl's Law for up to sixteen processors in the domain of N

of speedup on P and N prevent straightforward answers to these and related questions. This is a problem in multivariate calculus for functions of the form $g(x_1, x_2, x_3, \cdots)$, one that should be tractable with traditional methods from vector analysis for computing gradient fields, norm values, and the like (i.e., gradient, divergence, curl, and related functions).

Before attempting to answer this problem, however, Amdahl's Law needs to be understood at a more fundamental level as a function of two different *kinds* of variables with interesting properties. As a relative proportion, P is continuous over the $[0,1.0)$ interval, assuming the program (or process) is sufficiently long that portions of it can be approximated as a continuous variable. By contrast, N is strictly discrete and assumes values on the interval $[1, n]$, where n is finite. Therefore, in terms of the optimal allocation problem just stated, traditional multivariate methods from vector analysis are not applicable, except as approximations for high values of N.

A hybrid function consisting of a mix of continuous and discrete variables—such as Amdahl's Law—may be called a "concrete function," paraphrasing Graham, Knuth, and Patashnik (1994). A combined differential-difference multivariate calculus operator for analyzing and better understanding such hybrid or concrete functions has not been available, until recently (Cioffi 2013, 2014).

Definition 1 (Hybrid concrete function). *Let* $\varphi(X_1, X_2, X_3, \cdots, X_N;$ $Y_1, Y_2, Y_3, \cdots, Y_M) = \varphi(X_i, Y_j)$ *denote a multivariate function in* $N + M$ *variables. The function* $\varphi(\cdot)$ *is called a concrete function if and only if its* N

independent variables (X_i) are continuous with real values, and its M independent variables (Y_j) are discrete with integer values.

1.2   Amdahl's Law for Agent-Based Simulations

Amdahl's Law is highly relevant in the context of agent-based simulations, because such models have additional requirements for executing in "lockstep" to update the state of agents. Accordingly, Amdahl's Law can be modified by adding a third term in the denominator, a function $\psi(N)$, representing synchronization across N processors:

$$S = \frac{1}{(1-P) + \frac{P}{N} + \psi(N)}. \tag{3}$$

The following three cases are significant in agent-based simulation:

Case 1: Linear synchronization function Let $\psi(N) \propto N$. Then

$$S_\lambda = \frac{1}{(1-P) + \frac{P}{N} + \lambda N}, \tag{4}$$

where $\lambda > 0$ is a constant (scale parameter).

Case 2: Logarithmic synchronization function Let $\psi(N) \propto N$. When synchronization is hierarchical, then

$$S_{log} = \frac{1}{(1-P) + \frac{P}{N} + \log N}. \tag{5}$$

Case 3: Constant synchronization function When synchronization is insensitive to N, then

$$S_k = \frac{1}{(1-P) + \frac{P}{N} + k}, \tag{6}$$

where $k > 0$ is a constant.

The three cases are illustrated in Figures 2–4. Surprising, the linear case shows that speedup is not significant, in clear contrast with the basic Amdahl Law (Fig. 1). The logarithmic case (Fig. 3) shows gains in speedup, with a more complex surface that includes a saddle-point for null baseline of single processing ($N = 1$). Speedup remains significant for high parallelizable programs, but decreases with increasing values of N. The constant case shows no significant gains in speedup. Therefore, only case 2 (logarithmic synchronization) seems interesting.

Remark The equations in each case, as well as in subsequent extensions of Amdahl's law (e.g., Eyerman and Eeckhout 2010; Gustafson 1988; Hill and Marty 2008), retain the hybrid combination of discrete and continuous variables and parameters that is the defining feature of concrete equations.

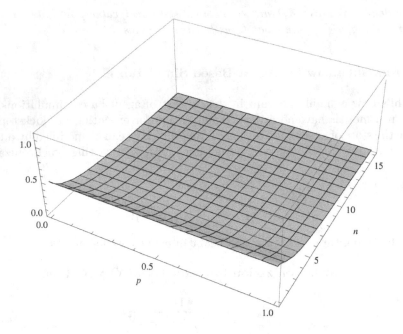

Fig. 2. Graph of Amdahl's Law for linear synchronization (Case 1)

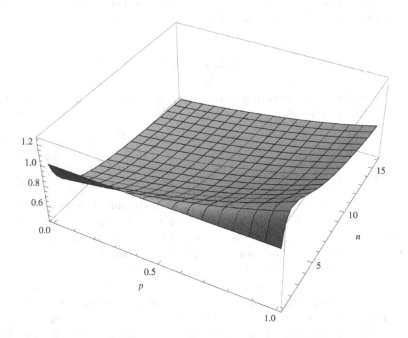

Fig. 3. Graph of Amdahl's Law for logarithmic synchronization (Case 2)

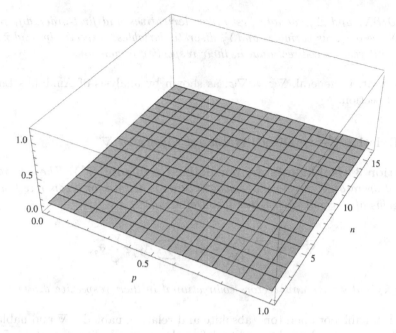

Fig. 4. Graph of Amdahl's Law for constant synchronization (Case 3)

2 The Nabladot Operator

The "nabladot" operator is strictly defined for a concrete function $\varphi(\cdot)$. Further, this operator is defined in both absolute and relative (i.e., normalized) terms, corresponding to unit-based and dimensionless scales, respectively.

2.1 Absolute Nabladot Operator ∇

Definition 2 (Nabladot; absolute nabladot operator ∇). *The nabladot operator ∇ is a vector associated with a concrete function φ and defined as*

$$\vec{\nabla}\varphi \equiv \frac{\partial\varphi}{\partial X_1}\hat{\mathbf{x}}_1 + \frac{\partial\varphi}{\partial X_2}\hat{\mathbf{x}}_2 + \cdots + \frac{\partial\varphi}{\partial X_N}\hat{\mathbf{x}}_N + \Delta_{y_1}\varphi\hat{\mathbf{y}}_1 + + \Delta_{y_2}\varphi\hat{\mathbf{y}}_2 + \cdots + \Delta_{y_M}\varphi\hat{\mathbf{y}}_M \tag{7}$$

$$= \sum_{i=1}^{N} \frac{\partial\varphi}{\partial X_i}\hat{\mathbf{x}}_i + \sum_{j=1}^{M} \Delta_{Y_j}\varphi\hat{\mathbf{y}}_j, \tag{8}$$

where $\partial/\partial X_i$ and Δ_{y_j} denote first-order derivatives and first-order differences w.r.t. X_i continuous variables and Y_j discrete variables, respectively; and $\hat{\mathbf{x}}_i$ and $\hat{\mathbf{y}}_j$ are unit vectors codirectional in their respective dimensions.[2]

Note that, in general, $\nabla\varphi \neq \nabla\varphi$, as shown by analysis of Amdahl's Law in the next section.

2.2   Relative (Normalized) Nabladot Operator ∇^*

Definition 3 (Nabladot-star; normalized nabladot ∇^*). *The normalized nabladot operator ∇^*, also called nabladot-star, is defined for a concrete function φ in terms of normalized sensitivities (Definition 1), as*

$$\vec{\nabla}^*\varphi \equiv \sum_{i=1}^{N} \frac{\partial\varphi}{\partial X_i}\frac{X_i}{\varphi}\hat{\mathbf{x}}_i + \sum_{j=1}^{M} \Delta_{Y_j}\varphi\frac{Y_j}{\varphi}\hat{\mathbf{y}}_j, \qquad (9)$$

where $\hat{\mathbf{x}}_i$ and $\hat{\mathbf{y}}_j$ are unit vectors codirectional in their respective dimensions.

In turn, nabladot operators (absolute and relative, nabladot ∇ and nabladot-star ∇^*, respectively) can be used to define the corresponding operators (Laplacian $\nabla^2\varphi$, divergence $\nabla\cdot\varphi$, curl $\nabla\times\varphi$) analogous to those in the standard vector calculus for continuous multivariate fields. The advantage is that nabladot operators are well-defined for hybrid functions such as Amdahl's Law and, therefore, the resulting vectors and fields are exact, whereas traditional methods yield approximations with varying degrees of error.

3   Nabladot Analysis of Amdahl's Law

This section provides an analysis of the Amdahl Law equations 2 and 4–6, based on nabladot's exact solutions, rather than through traditional approximations that would treat the number of processors N as if it were a continuous variable. Given that all Amdahl Law equations are nonlinear multivariate functions of two independent variables, its first-order rates of change with respect to each variable is of basic interest. This is possible using the nabladot operator for hybrid functions such as Amdahl's.

3.1   General Parallelization

The objective is twofold, based on Def. 2 and Eqs. 8–9: (i) to obtain the first-order derivative of speedup S with respect to continuous variable P and, similarly, (ii)

---

[2] By convention (Grady & Polimeni 2010; Hamrick 2011), the first-order finite difference is defined as $\Delta_y\varphi = \Delta\varphi/\Delta y \equiv \varphi(y+1) - \varphi(y)$, which is the `DifferenceDelta` operator in Mathematica.

to obtain the first-order difference with respect to N (discrete). The first part yields

$$\frac{\partial S}{\partial P} = \frac{N(N-1)}{(N+P-NP)^2},\tag{10}$$

while the second part yields

$$\Delta_N S = \frac{P}{(NP-N-1)(NP-P-N)}.\tag{11}$$

These two equations are exact results, not approximations. The gradient of speedup with respect to its two independent variables is obtained by simply substituting Eqs. 10 and 11 into continuous and discrete components of Eq. 8, respectively, we obtain the following new expression for the vector field of $S = f(P, N)$:

$$\nabla S = \frac{\partial S}{\partial P}\hat{\mathbf{x}}_p + \Delta_N S\hat{\mathbf{y}}_n\tag{12}$$

$$= \frac{N(N-1)}{(N+P-NP)^2}\hat{\mathbf{x}}_p + \frac{P}{(NP-N-1)(NP-P-N)}\hat{\mathbf{y}}_n.\tag{13}$$

Equation 13 brings us a significant step closer to answering the question concerning which variable has the greater effect on speedup. Finally, nabladot-star provides the normalized gradient field. This is obtained by applying Eq. 9 containing dimensionless elasticities.

By contrast, the continuous approximation used by traditional methods that ignore the discreteness of N would have resulted in the following (erroneous) vector component in Eq. 11:

$$\frac{\partial S}{\partial N} = \frac{N(N-1)}{(N+P-NP)^2},\tag{14}$$

rather than the correct component.

How does the exact solution given by Eq. 13 compare with the approximation in Eq. 14? This is shown in Figure 5. The graph on the left was drawn by the traditional approach using Eq. 14 (ignoring discreteness), while the graph on the right was drawn by the exact method provided by Eq. 11 based on the new nabladot operator (respecting discreteness). The visual similarity between the two gradient fields seems unquestionably close, but appears misleading once greater precision is used to compare the two.

Let ϵ denote the difference between the two functions plotted in Fig. 5. Arguably the simplest viable way to specify ϵ is by subtracting one graph from the other, as in a difference map. This is shown in Fig. 6, which shows the result of subtracting the difference from the derivative of Amdahl's Law in both cases with respect to N to see if they are in fact the same.

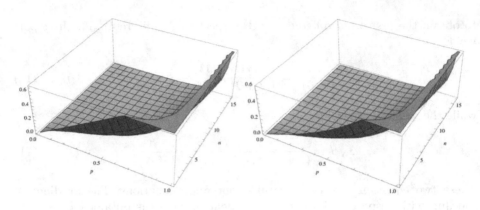

Fig. 5. Multivariate analysis of Amdahl's Law. First-order derivative function (left - incorrect approximate solution) and first-order difference function (right - correct exact solution) shown practically identical results. However, see next figure.

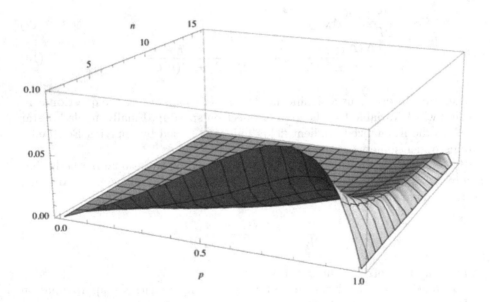

Fig. 6. Difference graph of the first-order derivative function minus the first-order difference function in Fig. 5

Clearly the two graphs in Fig. 5 are not the same, although they are similar. Several features observed in Fig. 6 merit highlighting:

1. The error surface $\epsilon(P, N)$ is not flat (which would indicate a low or constant error of the derivative approximation Eq. 14). Instead, the graph shows significant curvature.
2. The size of the largest error is approximately 7 percent.

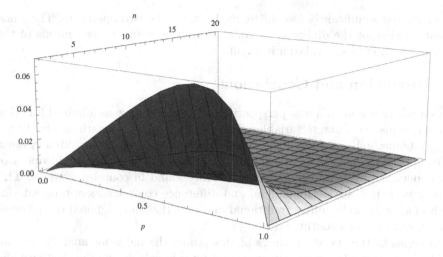

Fig. 7. Difference error graph of the standardized nabla-norm $\| \nabla^* S \|$ minus the standardized nabladot-norm $\| \nabla^* S \|$ of Amdahl's Law.

3. This occurs for $N = 2$, which is clearly where the error is maximal.
4. The error decreases as N increases, but in a non-uniform way.
5. Error increases with increasing values of P, as can be seen by the ridge extending toward the distance as N increases.

Another way to assess the difference between nabla and nabladot gradients of Amdahl's Law is to compare their respective standardized norms:

$$\| \nabla^* S \| = \sqrt{\left(\frac{\partial S}{\partial P}\frac{P}{S}\right)^2 + \left(\frac{\partial S}{\partial N}\frac{N}{S}\right)^2} = \sqrt{\frac{P^2(2 - 2N + N^2)}{(N + P - NP)^2}} \quad (15)$$

$$\| \nabla^* S \| = \sqrt{\left(\frac{\partial S}{\partial P}\frac{P}{S}\right)^2 + \left(\Delta_N S\frac{N}{S}\right)^2} \quad (16)$$

$$= \sqrt{P^2\left(\frac{1}{(1 + N - NP)^2} + \frac{(N - 1)^2}{N + P - NP}\right)} \quad (17)$$

The difference (error) function between these two functions (Eqs. 15 and 17) is shown in Figure 6. The topology of this function is the same as the previous error function for gradients, but the geometry differs in terms of the smaller scale of the range (< 0.07) and less pronounced ridge for high values of parallelization P.

3.2 Parallelization in Agent-Based Simulations

The case of Amdahl's Law under logarithmic synchronization (Eq. 5, Fig. 3) is interesting, as was shown earlier (Sec. 1.2). By contrast, linear and constant cases showed significantly less difference between the two operators. The same result obtains for the difference (error) function between the two norms of the synchronization case, as shown in Figure 3.

4   Discussion and Conclusions

This analysis proposed a new perspective on Amdahl's Law as a hybrid function of continuous and discrete variables. This requires applying mathematically appropriate methods for deepening scientific understanding of distributed systems of computation. The nabladot operator is an improved gradient field operator for understanding hybrid functions commonly found in complex systems. This is because it is based on differential and difference components appropriate for each kind of variable, unlike traditional methods that have ignored discreteness and simply assumed continuity.

In terms of the specific findings of this study, the nabladot analysis of Amdahl's Law revealed a previously unnoticed error in calculating the elasticity and related gradient fields of speedup with respect to parallelization and number of processors. Whereas traditional methods based on continuous operators (nabla) provide approximate results, the newly proposed hybrid operator for concrete functions such as Amdahl's Law provides exact solutions. The distribution of error with respect to the domain of speedup (i.e., the space of $P \times N$) is not uniform, which is explained by the nonlinearities involved in Amdahl's Law and others like it. This is true for the original Amdahl's Law as well as for the logarithmic variant applicable to parallelized ABMs with hierarchical synchronization.

All cases have the same topology, but their geometry differs, depending on each case. The main differences in geometry occur with Miller's number 7 ± 2. For agent-based simulations, the logarithmic case associated with hierarchical synchronization seems most interesting in terms of showing significant difference between approximate nabla-based results and exact nabladot-based results, while results are similar for linear and constant cases.

Error distributions between nabla-based and nabladot-based results (Figs. 6 and 7) seem confined to systems with low number of processors and weakens further with increased potential for parallelization.

All in all, this analysis has brought to light aspects of Amdahl's Law that seem intriguing and potentially worth further exploration. Whereas the mathematical nature of the analysis highlights theoretical features, it may also be the case that computer scientists and engineers may uncover practical aspects through experimental analysis.

With respect to broader issues related to Amdahl's Law, one of the most salient is the fact that computing is only one instance among many others classes of distributed systems. Bureaucracies, investigations, negotiations, and infrastructure systems, are among other systems where the architecture of complexity hinges critically on parallel or distributed systems. Thus, Amdahl's Law and its more recent sucessors—and concepts, features, or principles such as those analyzed here—holds much promise for advancing our understanding of complex systems.

Acknowledgments. Presented at the 2nd Workshop on Parallel and Distributed Agent-Based Simulations (PADABS 2014), Porto, Portugal, August 25, 2014. Thanks to six anonymous referees and workshop participants for helpful comments and discussions, especially Sean Luke, Mark Coletti, and Vittorio Scarano for discussions on Amdahl's Law and distributed systems, and to Keith Sullivan for recommending readings. Funding for this study is provided by CDI grant no. 1125171 from the US National Science Foundation, MURI grant no. N000140810921 from the Office of Naval Research, and by the Center for Social Complexity at George Mason University.

References

Amdahl, G.: Validity of the Single Processor Approach to Achieving Large-Scale Computing Capabilities. AFIPS Conference Proceedings 30, 483–485 (1967)

Cioffi-Revilla, C.: The Nabladot Operator for Hybrid Concrete Functions in Complex Systems. Presented at the Monday Seminar, Krasnow Institute for Advanced Study, George Mason University, Fairfax (2013)

Cioffi-Revilla, C.: Introduction to Computational Social Science: Principles and Applications. Heidelberg, Springer (2014a)

Cioffi-Revilla, C.: The Nabladot Operator for Hybrid Concrete Functions in Complex Systems. In: Proceedings of the Second World Conference on Complex Systems (WCCS 2014), Agadir, Morocco (2014b)

Eyerman, S., Eeckhout, L.: Modeling Critical Sections in Amdahls Law and its Implications for Multicore Design. In: ISCA 2010, Saint-Malo, France, June 19–23 (2010)

Grady, L.J., Polimeni, J.R.: Discrete Calculus: Applied Analysis on Graphs for Computational Science. Heidelberg, Springer (2010)

Graham, R.L., Knuth, D.E., Patashnik, O.: Concrete Mathematics: A Foundation for Computer Science, 2nd edn. Addison-Wesley, Reading (1994)

Gustafson, J.L.: Reevaluating Amdahl's Law. Comm. ACM, 532–533 (May 1988)

Hill, M.D., Marty, M.R.: Amdahl's Law in the Multicore Era, pp. 33–38. Computer - IEEE Computer Society (July 2008)

A Semantic-Based Approach to Attain Reproducibility of Computational Environments in Scientific Workflows: A Case Study

Idafen Santana-Perez[1], Rafael Ferreira da Silva[2], Mats Rynge[2], Ewa Deelman[2], María S. Pérez-Hernández[1], and Oscar Corcho[1]

[1] Ontology Engineering Group, Universidad Politécnica de Madrid, Madrid, Spain
{isantana,mperez,ocorcho}@fi.upm.es
[2] USC Information Sciences Institute, Marina Del Rey, CA, USA
{rafsilva,rynge,deelman}@isi.edu

Abstract. Reproducible research in scientific workflows is often addressed by tracking the provenance of the produced results. While this approach allows inspecting intermediate and final results, improves understanding, and permits replaying a workflow execution, it does not ensure that the computational environment is available for subsequent executions to reproduce the experiment. In this work, we propose describing the resources involved in the execution of an experiment using a set of semantic vocabularies, so as to conserve the computational environment. We define a process for documenting the workflow application, management system, and their dependencies based on 4 domain ontologies. We then conduct an experimental evaluation using a real workflow application on an academic and a public Cloud platform. Results show that our approach can reproduce an equivalent execution environment of a predefined virtual machine image on both computing platforms.

1 Introduction

Reproducibility of results of published scientific experiments is a cornerstone in science. Therefore, the scientific community has been encouraging researchers to publish their contributions in a verifiable and understandable way [18]. In computational science, or *in-silico* science, reproducibility often requires that researchers make code and data publicly available so that the data can be analyzed in a similar manner as in the original work described in the publication. Code must be available to be distributed, and data must be accessible in a readable format [20].

In the context of scientific experiments, terms such as reproducibility, replicability, and repeatability are sometimes used as synonymous. Even though there is no clear consensus on how to define both (definitions may vary over different scientific areas), in this work we understand them as separated concepts [9]. In this work, we address the reproducibility of the execution environment for a scientific workflow, as we do not aim to obtain an exact incarnation of the original one, but rather an environment that is able to support the required capabilities exposed by the former environment.

L. Lopes et al. (Eds.): Euro-Par 2014 Workshops, Part I, LNCS 8805, pp. 452–463, 2014.

Scientific workflows are a useful representation for managing the execution of large-scale computations. Many scientists now formulate their computational problems as scientific workflows running on distributed computing infrastructures such as campus Clusters, Clouds, and Grids [22]. This representation not only facilitates the creation and management of the computation but also builds a foundation upon which results can be validated and shared. Since workflows formally describe the sequence of computational and data management tasks, it is easy to trace the origin of the data produced. Many workflow systems capture provenance at runtime, which provides the lineage of data products and as such underpins the whole of scientific data reuse by providing the basis on which trust and understanding are built. A scientist would be able to look at the workflow and provenance data, retrace the steps, and arrive at the same data products. However, this information is not sufficient for achieving full reproducibility.

Currently, most of the approaches in computational science conservation, in particular for scientific workflow executions, have been focused on data, code, and the workflow description, but not on the underlying infrastructure—which is composed of a set of computational resources (e.g. execution nodes, storage devices, and networking) and software components. We identify two approaches for conserving the environment of an experiment: *physical conservation*, where the real object is conserved due to its relevance and the difficulty in obtaining a counterpart; and *logical conservation*, where objects are described in such a way that an equivalent one can be obtained in a future experiment.

The computational environment is often conserved by using the physical approach, where computational resources are made available to scientists over a sustained period of time. As a result, scientists are able to reproduce their experiments in the same environment. However, such infrastructures demand huge maintenance efforts, and there is no guarantee that it will not change or suffer from a natural decay process [12]. Furthermore, the infrastructure may be subjected to organization policies, which restricts its access to a selective group of scientists, thus limiting reproducibility to this restricted group. On the other hand, data, code, and workflow description can be conserved by using a logical approach that is not subjected to natural decay processes.

Accordingly, we propose a logical-oriented approach to conserve computational environments, where the capabilities of the resources (virtual machines (VM)) are described. From this description, any scientist, interested in reproducing an experiment, will be able to reconstruct the former infrastructure (or an equivalent one) in any Cloud computing infrastructure (either private or public). One may argue that it would be easier to keep and share VM images with the community research through a common repository, however the high storage demand of VM images remains a challenging problem [15,25].

Our approach uses semantic-annotated workflow descriptions to generate lightweight scripts for an experiment management API that can reconstruct the required infrastructure. We propose to describe the resources involved in the execution of the experiment, using a set of semantic vocabularies, and use those descriptions to define the infrastructure specification. This specification can then be used to derive the set of instructions that can be executed to obtain a new equivalent infrastructure. We conduct a practical evaluation for a real scientific workflow application in which we describe the application and its environment using a set of semantic models, and use an experiment management tool to reproduce a workflow execution in two different Cloud platforms.

In this work we entail reproducibility from the execution environment point of view. For the sake of showing how our approach works, we provide an example in which we have also include the data and the workflow execution of the experiment.

The paper is organized as follows. Section 2 describes our semantic approach for documenting computational infrastructures. Section 3 presents the practical evaluation and the description of the tools used to implement the semantic models and manage the experiment. Section 4 presents the related work, and Section 5 summarizes our results and identifies future works.

2   Semantic Modeling of Computational Resources

Scientific workflows are also used for preserving and sharing scientific experiments in science. Research efforts focused on describing the workflow structure and the experimental data, both input data and results. In this work, we argue that the information about the computational resources should be also provided for achieving full reproducibility. These descriptions allow the target audience, usually another scientist in the same domain, to understand the underlying components involved in a workflow execution.

We propose the definition of semantic models for describing the main domains of a computational infrastructure, and for defining the taxonomy of concepts and the relationships between them. These models describe the software components, hardware specifications, and the available computational resources (in the form of VMs). They also capture infrastructure dependencies of the workflows. As a result, this process facilitates experiment's reusability since a new experiment, which may reuse parts of the workflow previously modeled, or a reproduction of a workflow, would benefit from the infrastructure dependencies already described.

We have identified four main domains of interest for documenting computational scientific infrastructures. We have developed a set of models, one for each domain, and an ontology network that defines the inter-domain relations between these models (Fig. 1):

- *Hardware domain*: identifies the most common hardware information, including CPU, Storage and RAM memory, and their capacities.
- *Software domain*: defines the software components involved on the execution. It includes the pieces of executable software (e.g. scripts, binaries, and libraries) used in the experiment. In addition, dependencies between those components and configuration information are also defined, as well as the required steps for deploying them.

- *Workflow domain*: describes and relates workflow fragments (a.k.a transformations) to their dependencies. Therefore, scientists can understand what are the relevant infrastructure components for each part of the workflow.
- *Computing Resources domain*: expresses the information about the available computing resources. In this domain, only virtualized resources are currently considered (i.e. VMs). It includes the description of the VM image, its provider, and specifications.

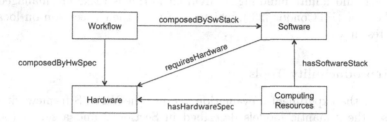

Fig. 1. Overview of the ontology network (→ denotes inter-domain relation)

3 Reproducibility in Scientific Workflows

In this section, we conduct a practical evaluation through experimentation in which we instantiate the semantic models aforementioned for a real scientific workflow application. We study and document the Montage [4] workflow and its execution environment, which includes the application software components and the workflow management system. Montage is and astronomy workflow application that is widely used by many astronomers to construct large image mosaics of the sky.

3.1 Scientific Workflow Execution

Scientific workflows allow users to easily express multi-step computational tasks, for example retrieve data from an instrument or a database, reformat the data, and run an analysis. Scientific workflows are described as high-level abstraction languages which conceal the complexity of execution infrastructures to the user. In most cases workflows are described as directed acyclic graphs (DAGs), where the nodes represent individual computational tasks and the edges represent data and control dependencies between tasks. Workflow interpretation and execution are handled by a workflow management system (WMS) that manages the execution of the application on the distributed computing infrastructure.

In this work, we use the Pegasus WMS [8] as our workflow engine. The Pegasus WMS can manage workflows comprised of millions of tasks, recording data about the execution and intermediate results. In Pegasus, workflows are described an abstract workflows, which do not contain resource information, or the physical locations of data and executables. The abstract workflow description is represented as a DAX (DAG in XML), capturing all the tasks that perform computation, the execution order of these tasks, and for each task the required inputs, expected outputs, and the arguments with which the task should be invoked. During a workflow execution, the Pegasus WMS translates an abstract workflow into an executable workflow, determining the executables, data, and computational resources required for the execution. Pegasus maps executables to their installation paths or to a repository of stageable binaries defined in a Transformation Catalog (TC). A workflow execution includes data management, monitoring, and failure handling. Individual workflow tasks are managed by a task scheduler (HTCondor [23]), which supervises their execution on local and remote resources.

3.2   Reproducibility Tools

To conduct the experimental evaluation, we use the WICUS framework, which comprises the semantic models described in Section 2 and a set of tools for annotating and consuming data, and the PRECIP [2] experiment management tool to manage the experiment. Below, we describe each of these tools in detail.

WICUS. We introduce here the Workflow Infrastructure Conservation Using Semantics ontology (WICUS), an OWL2 [17] (Web Ontology Language) ontology network that implements the semantic models introduced in Section 2. This ontology network is available online[1] and it is a continuous effort to discover and define the relevant and required properties for describing scientific computational infrastructures.

Besides the ontology network, WICUS has a set of modules that facilitates the annotation of the resources involved on the execution of a scientific workflow. These tools are not fully automated yet, but represent a first step on helping users to define the requirements of their experiments. Fig. 2 shows the main modules, their flow and intermediate results involved in the process for achieving reproducibility, and describes the process of data generation and consumption.

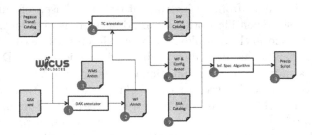

Fig. 2. WICUS annotation modules and flow

---

[1] http://purl.org/net/wicus

1. DAX Annotator. This tool parses a DAX (Pegasus' workflow description) and generates a set of annotations, using the terms of the WICUS vocabulary, representing workflow transformations and the workflow infrastructure requirements.

2. Workflow annotations. An RDF file containing the description of the workflow and its infrastructure requirements.

3. WMS annotations. An RDF file containing the information of the WMS component and its dependencies. This information will be added to the Software Components Catalog.

4. Transformation Catalog Annotator. This tool parses the Pegasus Transformation Catalog (which describes the binaries involved on the workflow execution and their locations) and the WMS annotations file, to generate two set of annotations: the *Software Components Catalog* and the *Workflow & Configuration Annotation* files.

5. Software Components Catalog. An RDF file containing the set of annotations about the binaries, dependencies, deployment plans and scripts, and configuration information of the software involved in the experiment.

6. Workflow & Configuration Annotation File. An RDF file containing the same information as in 2, but enriched with the configuration information for each workflow execution step, as specified in the transformation catalog.

7. Scientific Virtual Appliances Catalog. An RDF file describing available VM appliances. Information about the related infrastructure providers and the VM images that compose an appliance are included in this dataset.

8. Infrastructure Specification Algorithm. This process reads files 5, 6, and 7, and generates a configuration file (e.g. a PRECIP script), which describes VMs and software components to be created and deployed.

9. PRECIP script. This script creates a PRECIP experiment, which runs a VM, copies the required binaries, and executes deployment scripts to set the environment for the workflow execution. It also contains the PRECIP commands from the original experiment in order to re-execute it.

PRECIP. The Pegasus Repeatable Experiments for the Cloud in Python (PRECIP) [2] is a flexible experiment management control API for running experiments on all types of Clouds, including academic Clouds such as FutureGrid [11], and commercial Clouds such as Amazon EC2 [1]. In PRECIP, interactions with the provisioned instances are done by tagging. When an instance is provisioned, the scientist can add arbitrary tags to that instance in order to identify and group the instances in the experiment. API methods such as running remote commands, or copying files, all use tags to specify which instances to target. PRECIP does not force the scientist to use a special VM image, and no PRECIP components need to be pre-installed in the image. Scientists can use any basic Linux image and PRECIP will bootstrap instances using SCP and SSH commands. PRECIP provides functionality to run user-defined scripts on the instances to install/configure software and run experiments, and also manages SSH keys and security groups automatically.

In this work, PRECIP usage is twofold. First, the tool is used to describe and perform a workflow execution using the Pegasus WMS on a predefined VM image. Second, the WICUS annotation modules use PRECIP to generate a script able to reproduce the execution environment of the former experiment, and run it on different Cloud platforms.

3.3   Experimental Evaluation

The goal of this experiment is to reproduce an original workflow execution in two different Cloud infrastructures: FutureGrid [11] and Amazon EC2 [1]. Future-Grid is an academic Cloud test-bed facility that includes a number of computational resources at distributed locations. Amazon Web Services EC2 is a public infrastructure provider and the *de facto* standard for IaaS Cloud platforms.

Generating Semantic Annotations. Fig. 3 shows a simplified overview of the annotations generated for the Montage workflow using the WICUS ontology network.

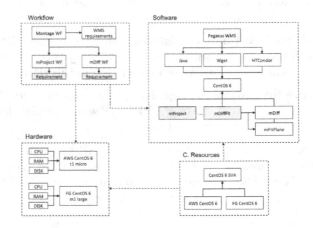

Fig. 3. Annotations for the Montage workflow using the WICUS ontology network

As shown in Fig. 2, the first step in the process of documenting a workflow is the annotation of the workflow DAX file. We use the `Workflow` domain ontology to describe the Montage workflow as 1) an individual that represents the top level workflow, and 2) another 9 individuals representing its sub-workflows, one for each transformation. We also generate 10 requirements, one for the top level workflow, which specifies the WMS requirements, and the remaining for defining the software components required by each transformation. At this point, these requirements are empty, as they are not yet related to their software components.

In this experiment, we address two types of components: the WMS and the application related components. The WMS components include the workflow engine, in our case the Pegasus WMS, and its dependencies. Pegasus uses HT-Condor as task manager, and also depends on Java. We use the Software domain ontology to describe these components as individuals, and to represent their dependencies. The 3 components also depend on the operating system, which in our case is CentOS.

To describe the deployment of the WMS components, we studied their installation processes according to their documentation. We then defined a set of installation bash scripts for each of them. These scripts are included on the deployment plans of the components along with their configuration information.

Application components are described from the Montage workflow's Transformation Catalog, where the binary file, version, and destination path are defined. These components are also described as individuals using the Software domain ontology. We use this information to generate the configuration parameters of the deployment script, which in this case is the same for all components. The script downloads the binary files from an online repository and copies them to the specified destination path. This process identified 59 software components for the Montage workflow that are annotated and included in the Software Components Catalog. Then, the Transformation Catalog Annotator module relates each transformation requirement, defined using the Workflow domain ontology, to the application component, and therefore to the deployment information. In this experiment, we define 9 Montage components that are linked to the requirements, and another two sub-components that are defined as dependencies in the software catalog (*mDiffFit* depends on the *mDiff* and *mFitPlane* components).

To describe computational resources we use the Computing Resources and Hardware domain ontologies. The Scientific Virtual Appliances Catalog includes the description of two virtual machine images, one for FutureGrid and another for Amazon EC2. These two images are conceptually equivalent, as they both provide CentOS 6 operating system. Therefore, we generate two Image Appliances (FG CentOS 6 and AWS CentOS 6) that are grouped into one single Scientific Virtual Appliance (CentOS 6 SVA). Depending on which providers are available, one or the other will be selected.

Reproducing Workflow Executions. The last step on the process for achieving reproducibility in scientific workflows (Fig. 2) is to execute the Infrastructure Specification Algorithm (ISA). The ISA combines the annotated data based on the 4 domain ontologies in order to find a suitable infrastructure specification that is able to run the workflow. The algorithm retrieves and propagates the WMS requirements of the top-level workflow (Workflow domain ontology) to its related sub-workflows. Requirements and software components are matched, and a dependency graph is built based on the relation between the requirements and the component dependencies. This graph is then used to compute the intersection between the set of software components from the SVA and the dependency graph of each sub workflow. ISA selects the intersection where the value is maximized for each sub-workflow. Software components already available in the SVA are then removed from the chosen graph. To reduce the number of SVAs, the algorithm attempts to merge sub-workflows requirements into a single SVA. Requirements can be merged if all their software components are compatible. Finally, ISA generates a PRECIP script with the set of required instructions to instantiate, configure, and deploy the computational resources and software components.

In this experiment, we execute ISA over the annotated data in a scenario where FutureGrid is the only available platform for resource provisioning, and in a scenario where the available platform is Amazon EC2. In both cases, the algorithm is able to obtain a PRECIP script for each infrastructure. Each generated script is composed by the following main sections:

- *Experiment Creation*: generates a new experiment using the given VM image ID and the user credentials for the selected infrastructure provider;
- *Software Deployment*: executes the set of instructions defined on the deployment plan of each software component to install and configure the required software to execute the workflow. In this section, both the workflow management system and the application are deployed with their dependencies;
- *User Setup*: creates a user account on the VM (if it does not exist) and configures the necessary SSH keys to enable file transfers and execution. This account will be used to run the workflow;
- *Data Stage and Workflow Execution*: stages all the input data of the Montage workflow on the VM, and launches the workflow execution. Since our work is focused on infrastructure reproducibility, data and workflow management are not covered in our approach.

Note that all the configuration and deployment commands (first 3 sections) require superuser privileges on the VM. The workflow execution, however, is performed under the user account created in the third section.

We executed the scripts on their corresponding platforms. Both executions succeeded on deploying and running the Montage workflow, the Pegasus WMS, and their dependencies. We also performed the same execution of the Montage workflow in a predefined VM image, where the execution environment is already in place. Results show that the VM execution environments deployed by both scripts are equivalent to the former one. In addition, we used a perceptual hash tool[2] to compare the resulting image (0.1 degree image of the sky) generated by both executions against the one generated by the baseline execution. We obtained a similarity factor of 1.0 (over 1.0) with a threshold of 0.85, which means the images are identical. Therefore we are obtaining the same results as the original workflow. In this work we do not aim to reproduce either the performance or the execution time of the original experiment.

All the original and generated scripts are available as part of the experimental material included in the Research Object (RO) [3] associated with this paper[3]. This RO also contains pointers to the software and resources used in this experiment.

---

[2] pHash - http://www.phash.org
[3] http://pegasus.isi.edu/publications/reppar

4 Related Work

A computational experiment involves several elements that must be conserved to ensure reproducibility. Most of the works addresses the conservation of data and the workflow description, however the computational environment is often neglected. An study to evaluate reproducibility in scientific workflows is conducted in [24]. The study evaluates a set of domain-specific workflows, available in the myExperiment [19] collaborative environment, to identify causes of workflow decays. The study shows that nearly 80% of the workflows cannot be reproduced, and that about 12% are due to the lack of information about the execution environment, and that 50% are due to the use of third-party resources such as web services and databases. Note that some of those third-party resource issues could be also considered as execution environment problems.

The Executable Paper Grand Challenge [10] and the SIGMOD conference in 2011 [5] highlighted the importance of allowing the scientific community to reexamine an experiment execution. The conservation of virtual machine (VM) images emerges as a way of preserving the execution environment [6,13]. However, the high storage demand of VM images remains a challenging problem [15,25]. Moreover, the cost of storing and managing data in the Cloud is still high, and the execution of high-interactivity experiments through a network connection to remote virtual machines is also challenging. A list of advantages and challenges of using VMs for achieving reproducibility is exposed in [14]. ReproZip [7] is a provenance-based tool that tracks operating system calls to identify the libraries and data dependencies, as well as the configuration parameters involved in an experiment. The tool combines all these dependencies into a single package that can be used to reproduce an experiment. Although this approach avoids storing VM images, it still requires storing the application binaries and their dependencies. Instead, our work uses semantic annotations to describe these dependencies.

Software components cannot be preserved just by maintaining their binary executable code, but by guaranteeing the performance of their features. In [16], the concept of adequacy is introduced to measure how a software component behaves relatively to a certain set of features. Our work is based on this same concept, where we build a conceptual model to semantically annotate the relevant properties of each software component. Then, we use scripting to reconstruct an equivalent computational environment using these annotations.

A recent and relevant contribution to the state of the art of workflow preservation is being developed within the context of the TIMBUS project [21]. The project aims to preserve and ensure the availability of business processes and their computational infrastructure, aligned with the enterprise risk and the business continuity managements. They also propose a semantic approach for describing the execution environment of a process. Even though TIMBUS has studied the applicability of their approach to the eScience domain, their approach is mainly focused on business processes.

5   Conclusion and Future Work

In this work, we proposed a semantic modeling approach to conserve computational environments in scientific workflow executions, where the resources involved in the execution of the experiment are described using a set of semantic vocabularies. We defined and implemented 4 domain ontologies, aggregated in the the WICUS ontology network. From these models, we defined a process for documenting a workflow application (Montage), a workflow management system (the Pegasus WMS), and their dependencies. We then used the PRECIP experiment management tool to describe and execute the experiment. Experimental results show that our approach can reproduce an equivalent execution environment of a predefined VM image on an academic and a public Cloud platforms.

The semantic annotations of the computational environment combined with the scripting functionality provided by PRECIP is a powerful approach for achieving reproducibility of computational environments in future experiments, and at the same time addresses the challenges of high storage demand of VM images. The drawback of our approach is that it assumes the application and the workflow management system binaries are publicly available.

In the future we plan to apply our approach in a larger set of scientific workflows and involve users from different scientific areas, aiming to automate the generation process of the semantic annotations to describe both the workflow application and the workflow management system. We also plan to extend the WICUS ontology network to include new concepts and relations such as software variants, incompatibilities, and user policies for resource consumption.

Acknowledgements. This material is based upon work supported in part by the National Science Foundation under Grant No. 0910812 to Indiana University for "FutureGrid: An Experimental, High-Performance Grid Test-bed", the FPU grant from the Spanish Science and Innovation Ministry (MICINN), and the Ministerio de Economía y Competitividad (Spain) project "4V: Volumen, Velocidad, Variedad y Validez en la Gestión Innovadora de Datos" (TIN2013-46238-C4-2-R). We also thank Gideon Juve and Karan Vahi for their valuable help.

References

1. Amazon Elastic Compute Cloud: Amazon EC2, http://aws.amazon.com/ec2
2. Azarnoosh, S., Mats, Rynge, o.: Introducing precip: an api for managing repeatable experiments in the cloud. In: 2013 IEEE 5th International Conference on Cloud Computing Technology and Science. CloudCom, vol. 2, pp. 19–26 (2013)
3. Belhajjame, K., Corcho, O., et al.: Workflow-centric research objects: First class citizens in scholarly discourse. In: Proc. Workshop on the Semantic Publishing (SePublica), Crete, Greece (2012)
4. Berriman, G.B., Deelman, E., et al.: Montage: a grid-enabled engine for delivering custom science-grade mosaics on demand. In: SPIE Conference on Astronomical Telescopes and Instrumentation, vol. 5493, pp. 221–232 (2004)

5. Bonnet, P., Manegold, S., et al.: Repeatability and workability evaluation of sigmod. SIGMOD Rec. 40(2), 45–48 (2011)

6. Brammer, G.R., Crosby, R.W., et al.: Paper mache: Creating dynamic reproducible science. Procedia Computer Science 4(0), 658–667 (2011); Proceedings of the International Conference on Computational Science

7. Chirigati, F., Shasha, D., Freire, J.: Reprozip: Using provenance to support computational reproducibility (2013)

8. Deelman, E., Gurmeet, Singh, o.: Pegasus: A framework for mapping complex scientific workflows onto distributed systems. Scientific Programming 13(3) (2005)

9. Drummond, C.: Replicability is not reproducibility: Nor is it good science. In: Proceedings of the Evaluation Methods for Machine Learning Workshop at the 26th ICML (2009)

10. Executable paper grand challenge (2011), http://www.executablepapers.com/

11. Futuregrid, http://portal.futuregrid.org

12. Gavish, M., Donoho, D.: A universal identifier for computational results. Procedia Computer Science 4, 637–647 (2011); Proceedings of the ICCS 2011

13. Van Gorp, P., Mazanek, S.: Share: a web portal for creating and sharing executable research papers. Procedia Computer Science 4, 589–597 (2011); Proceedings of the International Conference on Computational Science, ICCS 2011

14. Howe, B.: Virtual appliances, cloud computing, and reproducible research. Computing in Science Engineering 14(4), 36–41 (2012)

15. Mao, B., Hong, Jiang, o.: Read-performance optimization for deduplication-based storage systems in the cloud. Trans. Storage 10(2) (2014)

16. Matthews, B., Shaon, A., et al.: Towards a methodology for software preservation (2009)

17. Owl 2 web ontology language, http://www.w3.org/TR/owl2-overview/

18. Reproducible research: Addressing the need for data and code sharing in computational science (2009), http://www.stanford.edu/~vcs/Conferences/RoundtableNov212009/RoundtableOutputDeclaration.pdf

19. De Roure, D., Goble, C., Stevens, R.: Designing the myexperiment virtual research environment for the social sharing of workflows. In: Proceedings of the Third IEEE International Conference on e-Science and Grid Computing, pp. 603–610 (2007)

20. Stodden, V., Leisch, F., Peng, R.D.: Implementing Reproducible Research. Chapman and Hall (2014)

21. Strodl, S., Mayer, R., Antunes, G., Draws, D., Rauber, A.: Digital preservation of a process and its application to e-science experiments (2013)

22. Taylor, I., Deelman, E., et al.: Workflows for e-Science. Springer (2007)

23. Thain, D., Tannenbaum, T., Livny, M.: Distributed computing in practice: The condor experience: Research articles. Concurr. Comput. Pract. Exper. 17(2-4), 323–356 (2005)

24. Zhao, J., Gomez-Perez, J.M., et al.: Why workflows break - understanding and combating decay in taverna workflows. In: 2012 IEEE 8th International Conference on E-Science, pp. 1–9 (2012)

25. Zhao, X., Zhang, Y., et al.: Liquid: A scalable deduplication file system for virtual machine images. IEEE Trans. on Paral. and Distr. Syst. (99) (2013)

Reproducible Experiments in Parallel Computing: Concepts and Stencil Compiler Benchmark Study

Danilo Guerrera, Helmar Burkhart, and Antonio Maffia

University of Basel, Switzerland
{danilo.guerrera,helmar.burkhart,antonio.maffia}@unibas.ch

Abstract. For decades, the majority of the experiments on parallel computers have been reported at conferences and in journals usually without the possibility to verify the results presented. Thus, one of the major principles of science, reproducible results as a kind of correctness proof, has been neglected in the field of experimental high-performance computing. While this is still the state-of-the-art, current research targets for solutions to this problem. We discuss early results regarding reproducibility from a benchmark case study we did. In our experiments we explore the class of stencil calculations that are part of many scientific kernels and compare the performance results of four stencil compilers. In order to make these experiments reproducible from remote, a first prototype of an replication engine has been developed that can be accessed via the internet.

1 Introduction

Whenever you read a paper that reports on computational experiments, immediate questions such as the following arise:

- If we could rerun the experiment: will we get the same, similar or different results? What if we run the experiment on a different compute environment?
- Results are often for a specific problem only. What if we define a slightly different test case?
- Libraries and software components influence measurements. For instance, have compilation flags been properly set?

One would reach another level of trust in scientific results if we could somehow reproduce experiments. Such trust problems have already been reported in the pharmaceutical industry, in finance, and other fields. "It is impossible to believe most of the computational results presented at conferences and in published papers today. Even mature branches of science, despite all their efforts, suffer severely from the problem of errors in final published conclusions" [1]. It is therefore crucial to be able to test results for science to be self-correcting. "The ability to reuse and extend the results enable science to move forward" [2].

The difficulty in reproducing computational research is in large part caused by the difficulty in capturing every last detail of the software and computing

L. Lopes et al. (Eds.): Euro-Par 2014 Workshops, Part I, LNCS 8805, pp. 464–474, 2014.

environment, which is what is needed to achieve reliable replication [3]. As can be found, articles often do not have a sufficiently detailed description of their experiments, and do not make available the software used to obtain the results claimed. As a consequence, parallel computational results are most often impossible to reproduce, often questionable, and therefore of little or no scientific value [4].

The problem has been detected and early results have been reported. Dolfi et al. [5] propose a model for reproducible papers such that "the current manuscript already contains sufficient details, codes, and scripts to reproduce all the presented numerical results and figures". A constellation of tools and prototypes is available in order not only to document the workflow of an application but also make it reproducible. Taverna [6] and Vistrails [7] integrate data acquisition, derivation, analysis, and visualization as executable components throughout the scientific exploration process. Repeatability is facilitated by ensuring that the evolution of the software components used in the workflow is controlled by the organizations that design the workflows. This "controlled services" approach is shared by other WFMS such as Kepler [8] and Knime [9], an open-source workflow-based integration platform for data analytics.

In this paper, we explore the reproducibility of benchmark experiments and demonstrate early results of a project with the goal of building an ecosystem for reproducible computational experiments. In Section 2 we define a taxonomy which is the basis for the design of our system. Section 3 describes the functionality of our system envisaged and an early prototype of a workflow engine. In Section 4 we present a case study by introducing the stencil motif and the performance results of different compilers. Conclusions and sketches of further work are given in Section 5.

2 Taxonomy for Reproducible Benchmark Experiments

2.1 Space of Computational Experiments

Computational problem solving in general can be described as follows: A computational **problem** is solved by an algorithmic **method** on a compute **system**. We call the triple (Problem / Method / System) a *micro-experiment*, which can be considered as being one point in the space of experiments (see Figure 1).

- **Problem**: Solve a (random) dense system of linear equations in IEEE double precision arithmetic.
- **Method**: Two-dimensional block-cyclic data distribution. Right-looking variant of the LU factorization with row partial pivoting (see [10]).
- **System**: Distributed-memory computer with Message Passing Interface (MPI 1.1 compliant) and Basic Linear Algebra Subprograms (BLAS) installed.

What we usually want is a comparison between data resulting from more than a single micro-experiment. Keeping two out of the three dimensions fixed, we get an experiment which is a function of the third one: the red line shown in Figure

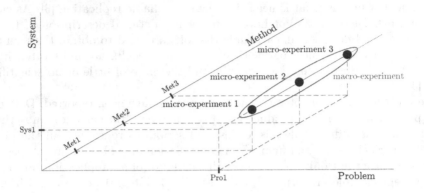

Fig. 1. Space of Computational Experiments

1 identifies such a *macro-experiment*, which is a collection of micro-experiments (e.g. the black dots in Figure 1). Macro-experiments can be categorised as being either system-oriented, method-oriented, or problem-oriented.

2.2   Replication, Recomputation, and Reproduction

Given the taxonomy of above, we obtain different levels of repeatability:

- **Replication**: *Basic replication* means re-running the original micro- or macro-experiment with all values in the experiment space kept fixed. As a result, execution properties that have been claimed become verifiable, which guarantees a high-level of credibility. *Advanced replication* mechanisms even support the changing of certain problem parameters while keeping method and system dimensions fixed. One of the major difficulties for providing replication support are security concerns because the system needs to be accessible from outside. In addition, the workload in high-performance computing scenarios is often significant, which forces the setting of limits for the number of replication calls.
- **Recomputation**: Portable methods are usually considered as being a good quality criterion for computational experiments. Therefore, methods used to solve a particular problem should not be bound to a specific compute environment. In the context of high-performance computing where parallel systems are used, this movement is however restricted to related machine models.
- **Reproduction**: Computational experiments are only an aid for getting actual scientific results. If different methods end up with the same scientific results in terms of computed output, some kind of experimental proof of the scientific insight is given.

3 Towards BETSc: Basel Ecosystem for Trusted Scientific Computing

3.1 Design Issues

In addition to the taxonomy described in the previous section, we identified some features we would like to achieve. The major problem when talking about reproducibility of experiments is that people other than the original researcher have to deal with the configuration of their own environment, which likely differs from the one used in the original test: we therefore target for **dependency check** (which must represent the first step of an experiment) and **portability**. A scientific discovery process may require the application of several steps and activities and it is necessary to trace and collect sufficient provenance information over this process, thus achieving **provenance support**. Allowing to **automatically run** tests, makes it possible to generate **documentation** regarding the environment in which the experiment was executed and store it as a unique identifier. What scientists aim for are results: since they are so important, it is necessary to be sure about their correctness, therefore introducing a **correctness check** at the end of the experiment's execution, and only at this point **visualize** the outputs.

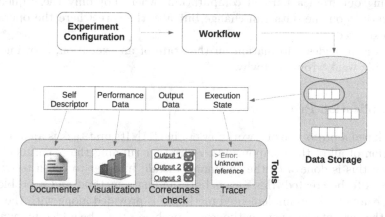

Fig. 2. Experiment flow

The key idea is that, once an experiment is characterized (i.e. the problem to be explored is stated), a user can define the macro-experiments to be executed, and pass such information to the workflow engine. The workflow sets up the environment and produces a structured output. Such an output was designed in order to allow flexibility in treating the data. As shown in Figure 2, it is composed of:

- **self-descriptor**: this field stores the information which uniquely defines an experiment. An environment stamp with libraries and dependencies is created, then all of the experiment-dependent parameters are added, together with information about hardware and threads used.

- **performance data**: each micro-experiment generates data, which are used to set up a comparison based on different performance metrics (e.g. GFlop-s/s, speedup, etc.).
- **output data**: these are simply the numerical results produced by each micro-experiment. Later on, they can be used to verify the correctness of the execution.
- **execution state**: at the end of a micro-experiment, potential fails can be detected thanks to log data generated at run time and stored in this field.

In order to analyze or visualize the information stored in the data structure described above, BETSc will provide a tool suite:

- **Documenter:** provides information about the experiments, in particular the settings as defined in the configuration phase;
- **Visualizer:** provides graphs regarding the performance output of a macro-experiment (stored in the field Performance Data of the structured output);
- **Correctness Checker:** verifies the correctness of an execution. Numerical simulation outputs are not suitable for checking bit-wise correctness due to their nature, and this is even worse when talking about numerical results coming out from a parallel computation, where not only the sequence of operations on the data can change but also the core where the operations are executed;
- **Tracer:** provides information on the state of an execution, showing what possibly went wrong and why.

3.2   Replication Prototype

We developed a prototype of a workflow engine [11]. Its first task is an automatic installation of all of the components required for running the experiments (see Figure 3): this is done with the command *install*. In order to run a test, a test suite needs to be created: this means both adding a method and a problem. A working example (fully implemented methods) is provided along with the workflow: at the current stage new methods and problems must be added manually by the user. Under development are the commands to do it automatically: adding a new method will be done by the command *add_method*, which generates a directory structure for the method passed as argument to it. A skeleton of *Makefile* will be provided in the newly created directory structure: it has to be modified by the user according to the peculiarity of the method. The same has to be done for new problems: after a problem has been added, the user has to provide the implementations for it, according to the methods he is intending to test.

After this configuration, it is possible to automatically execute all of the specified micro-experiments using the command *run* followed by a specification of the methods you want to use. Problem specific parameters as well as particular system settings (e.g. number of threads to be used) are passed through the *SetEnv* file. The workflow manages the execution of such experiments, setting the parameters, actually running the test, gathering the results, and sending

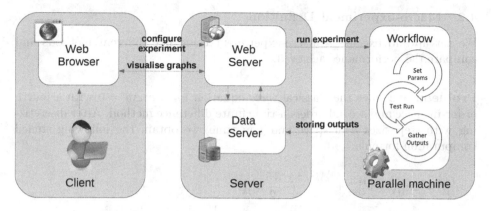

Fig. 3. Workflow architecture

them to the data server for storing. It is then possible to visualize different kinds of graphs regarding the executed experiments, starting from the fields of the structured data stored (as defined above, see Figure 2).

4   Case Study: Stencil Compiler Comparisons

4.1   Stencil Motif Background

In his 2004 lecture titled *Defining Software Requirements for Scientific Computing*, Phillip Colella identified *seven so-called dwarfs*, which are defined as algorithmic methods that capture a reusable pattern of computation and communication. The dwarf idea was later taken up by scientists at Berkeley and the list of dwarfs (renamed to motifs) was extended [12]. In this list, stencil computations are present as motif *Structured Grid*. It defines operations on a multi-dimensional grid, which are repeatedly applied such that the value of a grid point depends on the value of the point itself and the values of neighbours in a previous time step. The stencil motif has manyfold applications in science and engineering such as weather forecast, geophysics, computational fluid dynamics, and image processing.

Stencil computations expose a high degree of parallelism, however performance is not for free. They are memory-bound as typically only a limited amount of computation is performed per grid point (i.e. low arithmetic intensity). Because of this memory bandwidth limitation, different optimization strategies are possible. For example, if the application requires that the stencil has to be applied multiple times, there is potential to exploit temporal data locality, i.e. reuse cache data across iterations. A fair amount of research has addressed the question how temporal and spatial optimization can be done and what algorithmic changes and code transformations are needed. It is the purpose of our case study to experimentally explore different compilation methods.

4.2   Macro-experiment Definition

We set up and execute a macro-experiment using five different methods and compare the performance achieved.

Problem: We solve the classical wave equation $u_{tt} - c^2 \Delta u = 0$ with a fourth order-in-space and second order-in-time finite difference method. After discretizing with step sizes h in space and t in time, we obtain the following stencil computation formula:

$$u_{ijk}^{t+1} = 2u_{ijk}^t + u_{ijk}^{t-1} + \frac{\Delta t^2 c^2}{h^2}(-\frac{15}{2}u_{ijk}^t +$$

$$\frac{4}{3}(u_{i\pm1,j,k}^t + u_{i,j\pm1,k}^t + u_{i,j,k\pm1}^t) - \frac{1}{12}(u_{i\pm2,j,k}^t + u_{i,j\pm2,k}^t + u_{i,j,k\pm2}^t)).$$

We use a 3-dimensional grid of 200^3 points and calculate 100 timesteps.

Method: The following five methods are used in micro-experiments:

- **Directive-based approach** exploits a set of compiler directives that influence run-time behaviour. OpenMP uses a portable, scalable model that gives programmers a simple and flexible interface for developing parallel applications for platforms ranging from the standard desktop computer to the supercomputer.
- **Cache-oblivious algorithm** for stencil computations of Frigo and Strumpen [13]. An algorithm is cache-oblivious when it does not contain parameters (set at either compile-time or runtime) that can be tuned to optimize the cache complexity for the particular cache size and line length. POCHOIR[14], extends the cache-oblivious algorithm by using hyperspace cuts which improve parallelism. The compiler translates the embedded stencil code into Cilk code.
- **Auto-tuning** is the use of search to select the best performing code variant and parameter configuration from a set of possible versions. A compiler following this approach is HALIDE[15], which is specialized for image processing pipelines. It separates the algorithm from the scheduling task which uses an auto-tuning approach. LLVM is used for just-in-time compilation and parallelization is realized with pthreads.
- **Polyhedral model** [16] is a framework for automatic optimization and parallelization. It is applicable to loops with affine index functions and affine loop bounds, interprets the iteration space as a polyhedron, and loop transformations correspond to operations on or affine transformations of that polyhedron. PLUTO [17], is a source to source compiler that uses the polyhedral model approach for compiler optimization. The compiler uses C code as input and provides as output an OpenMP parallelized C code.
- **DSL + Auto-tuning** approach. Domain Specific Languages allow the programmer to express a stencil computation in a concise way independently of hardware architecture-specific details. PATUS [18], developed at University

of Basel, separates the specification of the stencil operation from strategy specifications (i.e. optimization and parallelization methods such as cache-blocking). Auto-tuning is used to find the best strategy and code generation-specific parameters.

Source code for all variants is available at [11].

System: We ran the benchmarks on an AMD Opteron 6274 CPU with a total number of 16 cores which has a 16 KB L1 cache, a 2 MB shared exclusive L2 cache and a 6MB shared L3 cache, with 2.2 GHz clock rate, running Ubuntu 12.04.4 LTS (kernel 3.8.0-38-generic).

The following C/C++ compiler were used: GNU gcc 4.6.3 and Intel icc 13.1.2.

4.3   Results

Stated system configuration and parameter setting, we want to obtain a comparison between the GFlops (calculated as product of *number of timestep * grid size * stencil floating point operations*, out of five executions) produced by the methods presented above. The result of such a comparison is shown in Figure 4. It is a visualization mash-up of 6 macro-experiments using different number of cores (1, 2, 4, 8, 16 and 32).

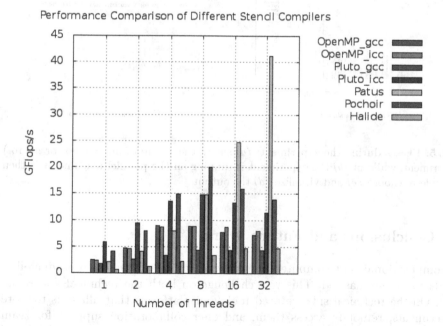

Fig. 4. Benchmark results with 100 timesteps

4.4   Replication Proof via Internet

The question which now arises is: can external people verify these measurements? In order to allow it, we set up a web interface (see Figure 5): you can configure the micro- or macro-experiments and submit them to our parallel machine. The experiment can be called, in principle, from outside, but at this stage it is only possible from our internal network, due to security and load problems.

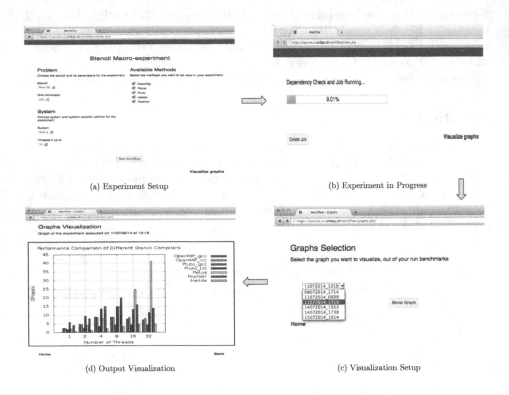

(a) Experiment Setup

(b) Experiment in Progress

(d) Output Visualization

(c) Visualization Setup

Fig. 5. Phases during the experiment: *(a)* shows the set-up of an (macro- or micro-) experiment, while in *(b)* the experiment is running on the parallel machine; it is then possible to choose *(c)* and visualize *(d)* the output

5   Conclusions and Future Work

If computational and computer science want to be a science, reproducibility needs to be emphasized. This is a challenge on both the technical and social side. On the technical side we need tools and platforms that allow us to store experiments, remotely access them, and offer collaboration support for team efforts but also security and protection guarantees from misuse. On the social side we have to think about incentives for those who spend time in making their experiments reproducible.

We so far achieved a replication prototype for stencil experiments that can be remotely recalled via the Internet. Taking this as a starting point, our taxonomy defines the roadmap for future work. We will extend the distributed architecture, develop security layers and load attack fences, and formalize data and workflow descriptions at the micro- and macro-experiment level. Future system versions should thus support not only replication but also recomputation and reproduction, as well as more generalized experiment settings in computational science.

Acknowledgement. We thank Severin Gsponer for his early contributions to the workflow engine [19].

References

1. Victoria, S.: Trust your science? Open your data and code. Amstat News (2011)
2. Freire, J., Silva, C.T.: Making computations and publications reproducible with VisTrails. Computing in Science Engineering 14(4), 18–25 (2012)
3. Davison, A.P.: Automated capture of experiment context for easier reproducibility in computational research. Computing in Science Engineering 14(4), 48–56 (2012)
4. Hunold, S., Träff, J.L.: On the state and importance of reproducible experimental research in parallel computing. CoRR abs/1308.3648 (2013)
5. Dolfi, M., Gukelberger, J., Hehn, A., Imriska, J., Pakrouski, K., Rønnow, T.F., Troyer, M., Zintchenko, I., Chirigati, F.S., Freire, J., Shasha, D.: A model project for reproducible papers: critical temperature for the Ising model on a square lattice. CoRR abs/1401.2000 (2014)
6. Missier, P., Soiland-Reyes, S., Owen, S., Tan, W., Nenadic, A., Dunlop, I., Williams, A., Oinn, T., Goble, C.: Taverna, Reloaded. In: Gertz, M., Ludäscher, B. (eds.) SSDBM 2010. LNCS, vol. 6187, pp. 471–481. Springer, Heidelberg (2010)
7. Scheidegger, C.E., Vo, H.T., Koop, D., Freire, J., Silva, C.T.: Querying and re-using workflows with VisTrails. In: Proceedings of the 2008 ACM SIGMOD International Conference on Management of Data, SIGMOD 2008, pp. 1251–1254. ACM, New York (2008)
8. Ludäscher, B., Altintas, I., Berkley, C., Higgins, D., Jaeger, E., Jones, M., Lee, E.A., Tao, J., Zhao, Y.: Scientific workflow management and the Kepler system. Concurrency and Computation: Practice and Experience 18(10), 1039–1065 (2006)
9. https://www.knime.org/knime
10. HPL - A portable implementation of the high-performance Linpack Benchmark for distributed-memory computers (2008), http://www.netlib.org/benchmark/hpl/
11. Danilo Guerrera and Antonio Maffia. Workflow for reproducibility (2014), https://github.com/sguera/workflow_repro
12. Asanovic, K., Bodik, R., Catanzaro, B.C., Gebis, J.J., Husbands, P., Keutzer, K., Patterson, D.A., Plishker, W.L., Shalf, J., Williams, S.W., Yelick, K.A.: The landscape of parallel computing research: A view from Berkeley. Technical Report UCB/EECS-2006-183, EECS Department, University of California, Berkeley (December 2006)
13. Frigo, M., Strumpen, V.: Cache oblivious stencil computations. In: Proceedings of the 19th Annual International Conference on Supercomputing, ICS 2005, pp. 361–366. ACM (2005)

14. Tang, Y., Chowdhury, R.A., Kuszmaul, B.C., Luk, C.-K., Leiserson, C.E.: The Pochoir stencil compiler. In: Proceedings of the Twenty-Third Annual ACM Symposium on Parallelism in Algorithms and Architectures, SPAA 2011, pp. 117–128. ACM, New York (2011)
15. Kelley, J.R., Barnes, C., Adams, A., Paris, S., Durand, F., Amarasinghe, S.: Halide: a language and compiler for optimizing parallelism, locality, and recomputation in image processing pipelines. SIGPLAN Not. 48(6), 519–530 (2013)
16. Benabderrahmane, M.-W., Pouchet, L.-N., Cohen, A., Bastoul, C.: The Polyhedral Model Is More Widely Applicable Than You Think. In: Gupta, R. (ed.) CC 2010. LNCS, vol. 6011, pp. 283–303. Springer, Heidelberg (2010)
17. Bondhugula, U., Ramanujam, J., Sadayappan, P.: PLuTo: A practical and fully automatic polyhedral parallelizer and locality optimizer. Technical Report OSU-CISRC-10/07-TR70, The Ohio State University (October 2007)
18. Christen, M., Schenk, O., Burkhart, H.: PATUS: A code generation and autotuning framework for parallel iterative stencil computations on modern microarchitectures. In: 2011 IEEE International Parallel Distributed Processing Symposium (IPDPS), pp. 676–687 (2011)
19. Gsponer, S.: Stencil compilers in practice: Workflow engine and code generation issues. Master's thesis, University of Basel (2014)

Effective Reproducible Research with Org-Mode and Git

Luka Stanisic and Arnaud Legrand

CNRS/Inria/Univ. of Grenoble, Grenoble, France
{firstname.lastname}@imag.fr

Abstract. In this article we address the question of developing a lightweight and effective workflow for conducting experimental research on modern parallel computer systems in a reproducible way. Our workflow simply builds on two well-known tools (Org-mode and Git) and enables to address issues such as provenance tracking, experimental setup reconstruction, replicable analysis. Although this workflow is perfectible and cannot be seen as a final solution, we have been using it for two years now and we have recently published a fully reproducible article [3], which demonstrates the effectiveness of our proposal.

1 Introduction

In the last decades, both hardware and software of modern computers became so complex that even experts have troubles fully understanding their behavior. Therefore, it could be argued that these machines are no longer deterministic, especially when measuring execution times of programs running on a large distributed computer systems or hybrid platforms. Controlling every relevant sophisticated component during such measurements is almost impossible, making the full reproduction of the experiments extremely difficult. Consequently, studying computers has become very similar to studying a natural phenomena and it should thus use the same principles as other scientific fields that had them defined centuries ago. Although many conclusions are based on experimental results in this domain of computer science, surprisingly articles generally poorly detail the experimental protocol. Left with insufficient information, readers have generally trouble to reproduce the study and possibly build upon it. Yet, as reminded by Drummond [1], *reproducibility* of experimental results is the hallmark of science and there is no reason why this should not be applied to computer science as well.

Hence, a new movement promoting the development of reproducible research tools and practices has emerged, especially for computational sciences. Such tools generally focus on *replicability* of data analysis [5]. Although high performance computing or distributed computing experiments involve running complex codes, they do not focus on execution results but rather on the time taken to run a program and on how the machine resources were used. These requirements call for different workflows and tools, since such experiments are not replicable by essence. Nevertheless in such cases, researchers should still at least aim at full reproducibility of their work.

L. Lopes et al. (Eds.): Euro-Par 2014 Workshops, Part I, LNCS 8805, pp. 475–486, 2014.

There are many existing solutions partially addressing these issues, but none of them was completely satisfying our needs and therefore we developed an alternative approach that is based on two well-known and widely-used tools: Org-mode and Git. We present our contributions in Section 3, where we first describe a specific use of Org-mode for doing the provenance tracking of the entire projects. Then, we propose a unique way to use Git for keeping synchronized experiment results and code that generated them. Finally, it will be demonstrated in Section 4 how the proposed methodology helped us conducting two very different studies in the High Performance Computing (HPC) domain. We will also state limits of our approach, together with some open questions.

2   Related Work

In the past few years, the field of reproducibility research tools has been very active, various alternatives emerging to address diverse problematic. However, in the HPC domain most of them are concentrated on platform accessibility, setting up environments and running the experiments on large clusters. Even though such tools are very useful in general, we could not benefit from them due to the specific nature of our research projects. The machines we needed to study are recent prototypes, with ever-changing libraries, set up by expert administrators and we do not have neither the permission nor the interest to do any modifications to the environment.

However, when conducting experiments and analysis, there are more aspects that need to be considered. We detail the ones related to software, methodology and provenance tracking, which are often neglected by researchers in our community.

Accessibility. It is widely accepted that tools like Git or svn are indispensable in everyday work on software development. Additionally, they help at sharing the code and letting other people contribute. Making data accessible, file hosting services, such as Dropbox, Google Drive and many others, became very popular among all scientists that want to collaborate. There is another group of services that is more oriented on making data publicly available and easily understandable to everyone, e.g., figshare[1].

Provenance tracking. Knowing how data was obtained is a complex problem. The first part involves collecting meta-data, such as system information, experimental conditions, etc., and it is often managed by experimental engines. The second, frequently forgotten in our domain, part is to track any applied transformation to the data, i.e., moving the objects from one state to another. Moreover, there is a question of storing both data and meta-data. Classical approach to solve these issues involves using a database. However, this solution has its limits, as managing source codes or comments in a database is not convenient and is handled in much better way by using version control systems and literate programming.

---

[1] http://figshare.com

Documenting. While provenance tracking is focused on how data was obtained, it is not concerned with why the experiments were run and what the observations on the results are. These things have to be thoroughly documented, since even the experimenters tend to quickly forget all the details. One way is to encourage users to keep notes when running experiment (e.g., in Sumatra [5, chap. 3]), while the other one consists in writing a laboratory notebook (e.g., with IPython[2]).

Extendability. It is hard to define good formats for all project components in the starting phase of the research. Some of the initial decisions are likely to change during the study, so system has to be flexible. In such a volatile context, integrated tools with databases, such as Sumatra, are too cumbersome for everyday extentions and modifications.

Replicable analysis. Researchers should only trust figures and tables that can be regenerated from raw data. Therefore, ensuring replicable analysis is essential to any study. Popular solution nowadays for this problem is to rely on open-source statistical software like R and knitr that simplify figure generation and embedding in final documents [5, chap. 1].

To address the previous problems, we propose to rely on a minimalist set of simple, lightweight, and well-known tools. We use **Org-mode** [2], initially an Emacs mode for editing and organizing notes, that is based on highly hierarchical plain text files which are easy to explore and exploit. Org-mode has also been extended to allow combining plain text with small chunks of executable code (Org-babel snippets). Such features follow the literate programming principles introduced by Donald Knuth three decades ago, and for which there is a renewed interest in the last years. In addition, for version control system we decided to rely on **Git**, a distributed revision control tool that has an incredibly powerful branch management system.

3   Tips and Tricks for Reproducible Research

In this section, we provide guidelines on best practices and hints on pragmatic ways to implement them. First, we illustrate how to handle provenance tracking issues with literate programming, in particular with Org-mode. The approach we propose is lightweight, to make sure the experiments are performed in a clean, coherent and hopefully reproducible manner without being slowed down by a rigid framework. However, it is tempting to sometimes break one of these rules, which hinders reproducibility in the end. This is why we harden these guidelines with a particular usage of Git that forces the user to keep data and code synchronized.

3.1   Provenance Tracking through Literate Programming

As described in Section 2, there are many tools that can help to automatically capture environment parameters, to keep track of experimentation process, to

----

[2] http://ipython.org

organize code and data, etc. However, it is not easy to understand how they work exactly, and additionally each of them creates new dependencies on specific libraries and technologies. Instead, we propose a solution based on plain text files, written in the spirit of literate programming, that are self-explanatory, comprehensive and portable. We do not rely on a huge cumbersome framework, but rather on a set of simple, flexible scripts, that address the following challenges.

Environment Capture. Environment capture consists in getting all the details about the code, used libraries and system configuration. It is necessary to gather as much useful meta-data as possible, to allow to compare experiment results with the previous ones and inspect if there were any changes to the experimental environment. This process should not be burdensome, but automatic and transparent to the researcher. Additionally, it should be easy to extend or modify, since it is generally difficult to anticipate relevant parameters before performing numerous initial experiments.

Once meta-data is captured, it can be stored either individually or accompanying results data. Some prefer keeping these two separated, making their primary results unpolluted and easier to exploit, but they soon run into difficulties when they need to retrieve information from meta-data. Therefore, we strongly believe that the experiment results should stay together with the information about the system they were obtained on. Moreover, keeping them in the same file makes the access straightforward and simplifies the project organization, as there are less objects to handle. Consequently, even if data sustains numerous movements and reorganizations, one would never doubt which environment setup corresponds to which results.

In order to permit users to easily examine any of their information, these files have to be well structured. The Org-mode format is a perfect match for such requirements as its hierarchical organization is simple and can be easily explored. A good alternative might be to use the yaml format, which is typed and easy to parse but we decided to stay with Org-mode (which served all our needs) to keep our framework minimalist.

A potential issue of this approach is raised by large files, typically containing several hundreds of MB and more. Opening such files can temporary freeze a text editor and finding a particular information can then be tedious. We haven't yet met with such kind of scenario, but obviously it would require some adaptations to the approach.

Note that all the data and meta-data are gathered automatically using scripts, finally producing a read-only Org-mode document. Why the experiments were performed and what are the observations on its results is stored elsewhere, more precisely in a laboratory notebook of the project.

Laboratory Notebook. A paramount asset of our methodology is the laboratory notebook (labbook), similar to the ones biologist, chemists and scientist from other fields use on a daily basis to document the progress of their work. For us, this notebook is a single file inside the project repository, shared between all collaborators. The main motivation for keeping a labbook is that anyone, from original researchers to external reviewers, can later use it to understand all the steps of the study and potentially reproduce and improve it. This self-contained unique file has multiple purposes. Indeed, the labbook should not only serve as journal but also play the following software development roles to ensure that it can be exploited by others:

1. README: The labbook should explain ideas behind the whole project purpose and methodology, i.e., what the workflow for doing experiments is and how the code and data are organized in folders. It should state the conventions on how the labbook should be used. This part serves as a starting point for newcomers and is also a good reminder for experienced users.
2. Documentation: The labbook should detail what are the different programs and scripts, and what is their purpose. This documentation concerns source code for the experimentation as well as tools for manipulating data and analysis code for producing plots and reports. Additionally, there should be explanations on the revision control usage and conventions.
3. Examples: The labbook should contain example usages of how to run scripts, displaying the most common arguments and format. Although such information might seem redundant with the previous documentation part, in practice such examples are indispensable even for everyday users, since some scripts require lots of environment variables, arguments and options.
4. Log: It is important to keep track of big changes to the source code and the project in general inside a log section. Since all modifications are already captured and commented in Git commits, the log section should offer a much more coarse grain view of the code development history. There should also be a list with descriptions of every Git tag in the repository as it helps finding the latest stable, or any other specific, version of the code.
5. Experiment results: Every set of experiment should be carefully noted here, together with the key input parameters, the motivation for running such experiment and finally observations on the results. Inside the descriptive conclusions, Org-mode allows to use both links and git-links connecting the text to the actual files in the Git repository. These hyperlinks point to the crucial data and the analysis reports that illustrate a newly discovered phenomena.

Managing efficiently all these different information in a single file requires a solid hierarchical structure, which once again motivated our use of Org-mode. We also took advantage of the Org-mode tagging mechanism, which allows to easily extract information, improving labbook's structure even further. Org tags can be used to distinguish which collaborator conducted a given set of experiments or to list expertise requests. Although many of these information may already be present in the experiment files, having it at the journal level revealed very convenient. Experiments can also be tagged to indicate on which machine they were performed and whether the results were important or not. Again, although such tagging is not required it is very handy in practice and make the labbook much easier to understand and exploit.

Several alternatives exist for taking care of experiment results and progress on a daily basis. We think that a major advantage of Org-mode compared to many other tools is that it is just a plain text file that can thus be read and modified on any remote machine without requiring to install any particular library. Using a plain text file is also the most portable format across different architectures and operating systems.

Data File Organization. Having a clear, coherent and hierarchical organization of all the files is a good practice for a proper scientific work, especially when external collaborators are involved. Once again, the approach we propose is lightweight and flexible but is motivated by the three following important points:

1. There should never be any critical information in file organization. Important information should be in the files themselves. Indeed, we could as well have blobs rather than files but managing data and extracting important information would probably not be very convenient. Thus, we do not recommend to impose much on file organization so that users can organize their data in a way that is natural to them. We think this lack of rules is not an issue as long as this organization is explained in the labbook.
2. The file organization should be flexible enough to be changed and adapted as the experimental data set grows. Such reorganization could seemingly break the labbook hyperlinks. However, as we briefly mentioned, we recommend to use git-links in the labbook, which are Org-mode hyperlinks that store links to specific revisions of files (typically when they were created). So reorganizing the data files will not break the labbook information.
3. The naming convention should not impede the activity of the researcher, so here we used almost no convention at all. According to our experience, all experiment results could simply be saved in folders, each of them representing one set of measurements and having a unique characteristic name, e.g., the name of the machine on which it was performed. Inside a folder, file names could be prefixed by additional key characteristics of the experiment set, followed by an ordinal number indicating in which order experiments were run. This idea seemed the most natural one to adopt, but we are reconsidering alternatives for the future projects.

Conclusion. The approach we described implicates a partial redundancy of some data and meta-data, typically saved in both experiment result files and in the laboratory notebook. However, such information are never entered twice manually. Most data should always be automatically tracked, although when some data convey key information, they should be manually added to other places as well, since it provides a better overview of the whole project.

We think that following the proposed guidelines is sufficient to conduct a clean, comprehensible and reproducible research while having a very fluid workflow. However, not all scientists are rigorous enough to always follow such conventions and even those who are, occasionally have the need to bend the rules in order to quickly get some results in a dirty way. This sometimes pollutes the whole project organization, often breaking the chains of the workflow processes and making some parts incoherent.

In order to force researchers to be more disciplined and help them doing their work in a reproducible manner, we propose to combine the previous approach with a particular usage of Git.

3.2   Using Git for Improving Reproducible Research

Even when the project is well organized, meta-data tracked, all the collaborators follow the conventions and take notes in the laboratory notebook, several practical issues may still arise:

1. Although a svn revision or a Git sha1 of the source code is captured, this does not guarantee that the experiment was run correctly and that the results can easily be reproduced. There could exist some uncommitted differences between the tracked and the current version of the code or the compilation could be out-of-date, i.e., code was compiled with an old revision.
A solution proposed for example by Davison [5, chap. 3] and which we applied as well, is to force recompilation and systematically verify that everything is fully committed before running any experiment. The only exception to this rule are the tests performed to validate the workflow.
2. Even with the complete and correct meta-data and code revisions, it is not always easy to reconstruct the experimental setup, especially if it consists of the code from numerous external repositories. Multiplying repositories hinders provenance tracking, coherency and experimental reproduction. The solution we propose is to increase the reproducibility confidence level by using only revision control and a collection of simple scripts that automatically track information. Additionally, we suggest to store both code and experimental data in the same Git repository, so that they are always perfectly synchronized, which eases the obtainment of the code that produced a particular data set. Nevertheless, this introduced the following new challenges.
3. Unlike source code, data files can be large, thus keeping them together in the same repository can rapidly increase its size. Moreover, doing code modifications, analysis and experiments in the same Git branch complicates its history and makes experimental setup reproduction slightly ambiguous.
4. Another difficulty comes from managing several external beta source codes that should now coexist in the same repository. Since these codes are also under development, they are regularly upgraded by their developers and these changes need to be propagated to local project as well. Additionally, these codes typically have their own revision control, which rises many issues with potential local code modifications and commits that concern now both local and external projects.

Proposal. To solve aforementioned problems we propose an approach that uses Git with two parallel interconnected branches, displayed in Figure 1. The first

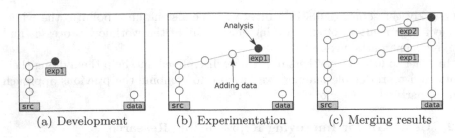

(a) Development   (b) Experimentation   (c) Merging results

Fig. 1. Different phases in git workflow

branch, named *src*, includes only the source code, i.e., code and scripts for running the experiments and the analysis. The second, *data*, branch consists of all the source code as well as all the data and analysis reports (statistical analysis results, figures, etc.). These two branches live in parallel and are interconnected through a third type of branches, the *exp#* branches, where the experimentation is performed. All these together form a "ladder like" Git repository, depicted in Figure 1(c).

We now explain the typical workflow usage of such branching scheme:

1. **Development phase**: Researchers work on a code development inside the *src* branch, committing the changes, as shown on Figure 1(a). These modifications can impact local or external code, analysis or even the scripts for running the experiments. Later, such modifications should be tested and the correctness of the whole workflow should be validated. Only then can one start doing real useful experiments.

2. **Experimentation phase**: Researcher creates a new branch from the *src* branch containing and a new folder to store the results. We used the convention that these two (branch and directory) should always have equal names, which eases the usage of both Git and labbook. In the example of Figure 1(a), this new branch for doing the measurements is called *exp1*. Next, new experiments are executed running the scripts and generate results. The resulting data, together with the captured environment meta-data, are then committed to the Git. After that, one might want to do some basic analysis of the data, investigating the results, which may later trigger another round of experimentation and so on, as it is showed on the Figure 1(b). Finally, only when all desired measurements are finished, *exp1* will be merged with the *data* branch.

3. **Merging and reports phase**: All experimental *exp#* branches are in the end merged with *data*, as it can be seen on Figure 1(c). In addition, result observations for each *exp#* branch are written to the labbook. Afterwards, comparison of different experiments can be performed by generating figures, tables and clear explanations, to describe the newly discovered phenomena. Since the changes to the source code from *src* branch are also propagated through *exp#*, the head of the *data* branch will always contain the latest code together with all the data. Nevertheless, the older version of code responsible for producing a particular data or analysis can always be found in the Git history.

A peculiar situation occurs when there are source modifications inside the experimental branches. They have to be committed (as measurements are never done with an uncommitted code), even though in most cases they represent an ad hoc change, specific to an individual machine and its installation. These minor, local hacks would pollute the *data* branch and thus it has to be ensured that they are not propagated. It is done by using a special script for merging the branches instead of classical Git merge command. At the end of the *exp#* branch, all source code changes (not the data) have to be invalidated by using `git revert`, i.e., the "anti-commit" of all the previously committed modifications inside that branch. This way modifications remain local for that *exp#* branch and the experimental setup can still be reproduced by pulling the revision before the revert operation, i.e., the one used to generate the data.

If the researcher eventually realizes that some of the source code modifications done inside *exp#* branch could be useful for the whole project, there are two ways to inserted them in the *src* branch. The first one involves rewriting Git history and it is not advised as it leads to incoherences between Git repositories. The second option is to cherry-pick the desired commits. Although this approach produces some redundancy, it is very easy and safe and keeps the Git history clear and coherent.

External software. One more challenge arises when there are external software repositories imported inside a local project. For example, one could have external source code B that is a part of a bigger local project A. Since B is also under development, one occasionally needs to pull the updates from its server, which can cause conflicts with local modifications to the code. Resolving these conflicts manually can sometimes be very tedious.

Even bigger problem occurs if one wants to push such local changes, as they can be committed to either our project A, or external project B, or even to both of them together. We decided to propagate, by default, these modifications only to the project A, keeping the Git sha1 of A always valid and up-to-date. Later if necessary, they can be pushed to B as well, but this has to be done by explicitly calling the necessary commands.

Dealing with described challenges is error-prone, thus we started using `git-subrepo` tool for cleaner and semi-automated management of external Git projects inside our local one. However, we still have to do everything manually when working with codes that are using other version control systems, notably svn.

Analysis. We now analyze the proposed solution and investigate how it addresses the stated problematic.

First, a complete synchronisation of code, data and analysis is ensured. The convention to use the same name for Git experiment branches and folders containing experiment results, additionally carefully noting it in the labbook, makes exploration of project history very smooth. This way one can easily find when a particular data or a figure was created, pull the revision used to generate it, inspect the code, reconstruct the environment and finally reproduce the object.

Using experimental branches also allows some local source modifications, that are specific for the remote machine or some other part of the experimentation setup. These changes stay local for that *exp#* branch avoiding to pollute main *src* and *data* branches, elegantly making the project easier to read while still keeping it coherent. Additionally, Git permits to put tags on certain commits, which can be used to annotate an important revision, such as the ones with the stable source code or the ones with some specific adjustments. With the evolution of the study, Git history becomes large and harder to explore, thus these tags can help to quickly find a desired state of the project.

By using Git as proposed, it is extremely easy to set up an experimental platform on a remote machine by pulling only the head of the *src* branch. This solves the problem of long and memory consuming retrieving of the entire data and Git history, as the *src* branch is typically very small.

On the other hand, one might want to gather all the experimental data at once, which can be easily done by pulling only the *data* branch. This is the case for the researchers that are not interested in the experimentation process, but only at the analysis of the whole set of results. For them, *src* and *exp#* branches are completely transparent, as they will retrieve only the latest version of the source code (including needed analysis scripts) and the entire data.

Another use case is when someone wants to write an article or a report based on the experiment results. A completely new branch can be created from *data*, selecting from the repository only the data and analysis code needed for the publication and deleting the rest. This way complete history of the study behind the article is preserved for the reviewers.

Holding external projects inside a local one allows to do `git pull` or `svn checkout` in sub-directories, keeping them up-to-date. Small problems arise when some modifications to the external code are done. These changes *de facto* influence both external and local repository but our solution ensures that they are committed only to the local revision control. Therefore in the meta-data part of the experiment files, tracked revision of the external code corresponds to the version pulled before any of the local changes, which is not strictly legitimate. Nevertheless, this small issue is not critical, since the revision in local project is stored in meta-data as well, and this value is always perfectly correct. Pulling this version will bring the right code, keeping the research reproducible.

4   Evaluation

We used the described methodology in two very different use cases. The first one is a part of the study of CPU cache performance on various Intel and ARM micro-architectures [4]. The developed source code was very simple, containing only a few files, but there were numerous input parameters to be taken into account. Probably the critical part of this study is about the environment setup, which proved to be unstable, and thus, responsible for many unexpected phenomena. Therefore, it was essential to capture, understand and easily compare as much meta-data as possible. Although it did not lead to a reproducible article as we were only discovering such tools, we used this workflow and can still track the whole history of these experiments. The second use case [3] aims at providing accurate performance predictions for dense linear algebra kernels, using the StarPU runtime on top of the SimGrid simulator. By contrast, input parameters and environment here are fixed, but the source code is very complex and in constant evolution. Moreover, we had to manage code from two external repositories as well many of our own scripts.

The proposed solution proved generally successful in both use cases. We have determined several good and bad sides, while for some aspects still remain rather uncertain.

Pros. Our approach is fast and efficient for a daily usage. It provides reasonable boundaries without taking away too much flexibility from the users. It offers good code modification isolation, which is important for *ad hoc* changes. Perfect provenance tracking, which was painless to extend and explore, was crucial for the cache measurement study. Although these two use cases are very different, most of the captured environment meta-data is the same for both projects: date and time, hostname, Linux and gcc version, users logged on the machine, environment variables, used external libraries, code revisions, memory hierarchy of the machine, CPU governor and frequency, compilation outputs, etc. Since all the source code and data is in Git repository, reconstructing experimentation setup is straightforward. One could argue that not all elements are completely captured, since operating system and external libraries can only be reviewed but not reconstructed. To handle this, researchers would have to use virtual machines to run the experiments, which would introduce many new performance issues. Finally, after applying such a methodology throughout the whole research process, it was extremely easy to write an article [3] in Org-mode that was completely reproducible as well. Along with the text, this Org-mode document contains all the analysis scripts and the raw data is provided as the article companion [6] and can be inspected by reviewers.

Cons. The biggest disadvantage of our approach is that it has many not so common conventions along with a steep learning curve workflow, hence it is difficult for new users. Moreover, it requires an expertise in Org-mode, preferably using Emacs text editor, together with a good understanding of Git. However, we believe that these tools provide benefits that are worth investing time.

Additionally, we find current way of managing external source repositories slightly cumbersome, and we are searching for a better solution. One path could be to use recipes or experiment engines, that would do the checkout of external sources for us and would only apply the right modifications before compiling.

The problem of storing large data files in repositories is well-known to the community. It has been already solved for the Mercurial revision control tool, but even after an thorough research we could not find a satisfactory solution for Git. Git repositories can quickly reach a few Gigabytes, which does not hinder daily committing but significantly slows down rebase operations to move back to previous experimental conditions of a specific dataset.

Open Questions. It is still unclear how this approach would scale for multiple users working simultaneously, doing code modifications and experiments in parallel. In theory it should work if everyone has sufficient experience of the tools and workflow, but we have never tried it with more than two persons.

Another interesting feature that we haven't yet experienced is collaboration with external users. These researchers could clone our project, work on it on their own, try to reproduce the results and build upon our work, potentially improving the code and contribute data sets back. Even though such utilization should work smoothly, there could be some pitfalls that we haven't anticipated.

These are only few of the unknown, and as there are certainly many more, we are hoping for the audience suggestions and remarks.

5 Conclusion

In this paper, we did not intend to propose new tools for reproducible research, but rather investigate whether a minimal combination of existing ones can prove useful. The approach we described is a good example of using well-known, lightweight, open-source technologies to properly perform a very complex process like computer science experimentation. Although our methodology is undoubtedly improvable and similar results could be obtained with other frameworks, we nonetheless find it very smooth for a daily usage and extremely beneficial to our work. We can only encourage people to build on such simple workflows to conduct their own studies, as it is clearly a very effective way to produce a reproducible research.

References

1. Drummond, C.: Replicability is not reproducibility: Nor is it good science. In: Proceedings of the Evaluation Methods for Machine Learning Workshop at the 26th ICML (2009)
2. Schulte, E., Davison, D., Dye, T., Dominik, C.: A multi-language computing environment for literate programming and reproducible research. Journal of Statistical Software 46(3), 1–24 (2012), http://www.jstatsoft.org/v46/i03
3. Stanisic, L., Thibault, S., Legrand, A., Videau, B., Méhaut, J.-F.: Modeling and simulation of a dynamic task-based runtime system for heterogeneous multi-core architectures. In: Silva, F., Dutra, I., Santos Costa, V. (eds.) Euro-Par 2014 Parallel Processing. LNCS, vol. 8632, pp. 50–62. Springer, Heidelberg (2014)
4. Stanisic, L., Videau, B., Cronsioe, J., Degomme, A., Marangozova-Martin, V., Legrand, A., Méhaut, J.F.: Performance analysis of hpc applications on low-power embedded platforms. In: Proceedings of the Conference on Design, Automation and Test in Europe, DATE 2013, EDA Consortium, pp. 475–480 (2013), http://dl.acm.org/citation.cfm?id=2485288.2485403
5. Stodden, V., Leisch, F., Peng, R.D. (eds.): Implementing Reproducible Research. The R Series. Chapman and Hall (2014), https://osf.io/s9tya/wiki/home/
6. Companion of the StarPU+SimGrid article. Hosted on Figshare online version of this article with access to the experimental data and scripts (in the org source, 2014), http://dx.doi.org/10.6084/m9.figshare.928338

Statistical Validation Methodology of CPU Power Probes

Abdelhafid Mazouz, Benoît Pradelle, and William Jalby

University of Versailles St-Quentin en Yvelines, France
{first.last}@uvsq.fr

Abstract. Achieving or proving energy efficiency necessarily relies on the ability to perform power measurements at some point. In order to simplify power measurements at the CPU level, recent processors support model-based energy accounting interfaces such as Intel RAPL or AMD APM. Though such interfaces are an attractive option for energy characterization, their accuracy and reliability has to be verified before using them.

We propose a new statistical validation methodology for CPU power estimators that does not require any complex hardware system instrumentation. The methodology only relies on a single full-system AC power meter and is able to make statistically relevant decisions about the probes reliability. We also present an experimental evaluation using two Intel machines equipped with a RAPL interface and investigate the impact of multiple parameters such as the CPU frequency or the number of active cores on the probe accuracy.

Keywords: Statistical performance evaluation, Power measurement, RAPL.

1 Introduction

Reducing energy consumption is now a major concern for computing systems. Indeed, application power accounting, power modeling, power capping, and Dynamic Voltage and Frequency Scaling (DVFS) are now common tasks performed in data centers. All of them share a common requirement: they are all based on physical power measurements, including device-specific measurements. However, device-specific power measurements often require physical access to the device and expensive measurement probes.

In order to ease power measurements on processors, new CPU devices integrate model-based interfaces for energy consumption estimation like Intel *Running Average Power Limit* (RAPL) [16] or AMD *Application Power Management* (APM) [1]. In both systems, power or energy can be read directly by userspace software using *Model Specific Registers* (MSR). The spreading of such model-based interfaces provokes a considerable attraction for power measurement at the CPU package or at CPU core level. However, the accuracy and reliability of such interfaces has to be considered and validated before using them.

L. Lopes et al. (Eds.): Euro-Par 2014 Workshops, Part I, LNCS 8805, pp. 487–498, 2014.

Obviously, the most precise approach to validate power estimation interfaces is to add a power probe directly on the CPU. However, setting up an additional probe on the CPU is complex and requires a physical access to an experimental machine. To simplify the validation, we propose a statistical validation methodology that does not require precise instrumentation of the processor. Instead, we only use a full-system digital power measurement (DPM) device. A statistical quantification approach is then employed to overcome the limits of system-level instrumentation. Thus, the presented method simplifies and reduces the cost of CPU power probe validation while maintaining a high accuracy thanks to statistics. It is then possible to easily expose some of the limits of the power probes without having to void the hardware warranty because of the instrumentation process. Moreover, it allows anyone with a calibrated full system power meter to check the power probes before using them in a production mode.

The paper is organized as follows. Section 2 defines our protocol for statistical validation of the RAPL power estimation. Section 3 describes our experimental setup (software and hardware) and our measurement methodology. Section 4 shows experimental results on two Intel machines. Finally, we present some related work in Section 5, and conclude in the last section.

2   Validation Methodology

To mitigate the low precision of system-level instrumentation, the presented methodology is based on the execution of a large number of micro-benchmarks stressing only the CPU. Power consumption is measured for the whole execution of each micro-benchmark with various experimental configurations, no sampling is performed. The RAPL power estimation is compared against whole system power measurements obtained by a digital power meter (DPM). The intuition behind the experimental methodology is the following: the DPM measures power consumption for the whole system, including processors, then, if the RAPL interface indicates an increased power consumption, the DPM must report at least an equivalent increase.

2.1   Experimental Configuration and Validity Test

We define an experimental configuration as a set of experimental parameters, each one being either a hardware setting such as the CPU frequency, a software parameter such as the number of cores on which the benchmark is replicated on, or an environmental factor such as the system temperature. An experimental configuration could consist for instance in having a benchmark replicated on all the cores, the highest frequency set, the CPU temperature left to the ambient one. Such configuration is not related to any benchmark and can be used for many of them.

Let us consider that we have two experimental configurations $C1$ and $C2$ that differ only by a single parameter. $C2$ is such that it implies a higher CPU power consumption than $C1$. For instance, $C2$ could be a configuration similar to $C1$ except that more CPU cores are used. We then expect that the power consumption measured when running a benchmark b under $C2$ is higher than that of $C1$, both at the CPU and system level. Let $Pcpu(C, b)$ be the power measured at the CPU level using the RAPL interface when running b with an experimental configuration C, and $Psys(C, b)$ be the power consumption reported by the DPM. $Pcpu(C, b)$ and $Psys(C, b)$ are the median of multiple measurements. Depending on the power increase observed at each level, we may encounter two different situations.

First, $Psys(C2, b) - Psys(C1, b) \geq Pcpu(C2, b) - Pcpu(C1, b)$. The power consumption increased more on the system than on the CPU. Consequently, we cannot conclude that the model-based CPU power estimation is inaccurate. Note that the CPU probes are however not proven accurate.

Second, $Psys(C2, b) - Psys(C1, b) < Pcpu(C2, b) - Pcpu(C1, b)$. Either the rest of the system power consumption decreased, or the DPM is wrong, or the RAPL interface is wrong. However, $C2$ is chosen to generate a higher CPU power consumption than $C1$, the benchmarks are built so that they only stress the CPU, and the rest of the system is kept idle by stopping all the non-essential processes. Thus, some components may increase their consumption (think about fans for instance) but cannot possibly consume less power. Moreover, the DPM is assumed to be working and correctly calibrated. Thus, there is a strong evidence that the CPU power estimation is inaccurate. Moreover, $C1$ and $C2$ differ only by a single parameter, which provides hints on the cause of the inaccuracy.

The test does not allow us to find all the potential flaws of the probe. Indeed, it only detects situations where the RAPL interface reports excessive power increase. When the power increase is under estimated, it cannot be detected because the extra power consumption measured at the system level can also be due to other components activity. Thus, the test may report false positives. However, it exposes all the situations where the power increase is over-approximated by the RAPL interface without having to perform complex hardware instrumentation.

The described test is the core of our methodology. The complete probe validation methodology is described hereafter along with the statistical tools required to decide whether the probe can be considered as accurate or not.

2.2 Statistical Significance

Let us define $\mathcal{B}$ be the set of micro-benchmarks. For each pair of experimental configurations $C1$ and $C2$, where $C2$ implies a higher CPU power consumption than $C1$, computing the set of power differences is done as follows:

1. For each micro-benchmark $b \in \mathcal{B}$, compute $\Delta Psys(b) = Psys(C2, b) - Psys(C1, b)$ and $\Delta Pcpu(b) = Pcpu(C2, b) - Pcpu(C1, b)$
2. Compute the set $\Delta P = \{\Delta Psys(b) - \Delta Pcpu(b) | \forall b \in \mathcal{B}\}$ of power increase differences between DPM measurements and model-based CPU power estimations.

The set ΔP contains the power increase differences between those reported by the DPM and the RAPL interface. Thus, checking for negative values in ΔP

is the simplest way to determine if there are cases where the RAPL interface miss-estimate power consumption. However, because the system-level measurements are often not precise enough, such simple test frequently reports irrelevant RAPL errors. Consequently, we use a more robust statistical method to check for positive values in ΔP.

Statistical hypothesis testing is a widely used technique in the process of decision making based on empirical or observed data. The idea behind hypothesis testing is to make a choice (accept or reject) between two hypotheses: the null hypothesis called H_0, and the alternative hypothesis called H_a. H_0 represents our general belief about a particular data set. For example, a medicine A is not more efficient than an another medicine B. On the other hand, H_a represents an another belief about the data set. Then, having a fixed risk level α, a hypothesis test evaluates whether H_0 can be proven false. If H_0 is rejected with a risk level α, then the alternative hypothesis H_a is usually considered to be true with a confidence level $1 - \alpha$, although it only approximates the exact confidence level $1 - \beta$ [20]. Such statistical hypothesis tests are useful to determine if a particular belief on a data-set can be considered true or not, which is exactly what needs to be done in our case.

We rely on the *Wilcoxon Signed-Rank Test* [14], a one-sample statistical test. It imposes that H_0 is formulated as the median of a sample is equal to an arbitrarily chosen value. Then, the test computes a p-value, which is a probability that quantifies the strength of evidence to not reject H_0. If the p-value is very small, then H_0 is unlikely to be true, and the alternative hypothesis is likely to be true. In practice, if p-value $\leq \alpha$, where α is a specified risk level, then H_0 is rejected and H_a is usually accepted with a confidence level $1 - \alpha$. Unlike other statistical hypothesis tests, the Wilcoxon test does not assume any specific distribution of the data set. Indeed, most of the statistical tests in the literature impose that the data distribution follows the normal distribution. However none of our experimental results follow the normal distribution. The Wilcoxon Signed-Rank test is then perfectly suited to our case. Moreover, we fulfill the two conditions that are required to correctly use the test: 1) all the values in ΔP are mutually independent, and 2) each value in ΔP comes from a continuous population (not necessarily the same).

Let us now show how we can use the test in our context. The test imposes that H_0 is formulated as $med(\Delta P) = 0$, and H_a is formulated as $med(\Delta P) > 0$ or $med(\Delta P) < 0$ or $med(\Delta P) \neq 0$. We also know that to prove that RAPL correctly estimates power, we must prove $med(\Delta P) \geq 0$. However, there is nothing in the forms of H_0 and H_a that allow us to express $med(\Delta P) \geq 0$. Consequently, instead of proving that RAPL is accurate, we try to prove that RAPL is inaccurate. Thus, we express H_a as $med(\Delta P) < 0$. If we succeed to reject H_0, then we can prove with an approximated confidence level $1 - \alpha$ that RAPL is inaccurate. Otherwise, we assume that RAPL is accurate.

The Wilcoxon test allows us to verify a binary knowledge on a data-set. However, rather than providing a yes/no answer about the accuracy of the measurements with a fixed confidence level, it would be more useful to determine the probability for the RAPL interface to incorrectly estimate power. In fact, the p-value resulting from the test can be used for that purpose. Indeed, accepting H_a, requires p-value $\leq \alpha$, then $1 - p$-value $\geq 1 - \alpha$, where $1 - \alpha$ represents the confidence level one desires in order to accept H_a. Thus, $1 - p$-value is the maximal confidence level one can have when considering H_a as true. Thus, rather than comparing the p-value with a risk level α as it is classically done in the Wilcoxon test, we consider $1 - p$-value as the confidence one can have when considering the RAPL interface as inaccurate.

2.3   Comparison to Simple Metrics

Let us show the benefits of a rigorous statistical protocol for probe validation over simple metrics like proportions or sample median. A sample proportion ρ represents the fraction N^- out of N benchmarks, where the power increase difference between that reported by the DPM and the RAPL interface is negative. One may consider that the higher this proportion is, the better is our confidence on the inaccuracy of CPU power probe. The sample median and ρ are both simple tests that could typically be used to distinguish between a failure of the RAPL interface or a success.

Figure 1 reports an observed distribution of power increase differences when the benchmarks are run on 1 or 2 cores on the SandyBridge machine while the idle cores remain in the level C2 C-state. In addition to the histogram, the figure reports the 1-p-value, the sample proportion ρ, and the sample median. In the presented case, $\rho = 51\%$, i.e. there are slightly more negative values than positive ones in ΔP. Moreover the median is close to 0. Thus, the conclusion about the RAPL interface precision in this case is uncertain, especially with regard to the dispersion in the set. On the other hand, the Wilcoxon test indicates that in order to declare that the RAPL interface overestimates power consumption, we should accept at most a confidence level $1 - p$-value of 47.46%. Such low confidence level clearly states that the RAPL interface can hardly be said incorrect, whereas the other metrics are unclear. In fact, the p-value resulting from the Wilcoxon test takes into account the data distribution and is then more robust than the other considered metrics. Thus, not only the Wilcoxon test provides a clearer answer in the presented case, but it is also more reliable than classical metrics one could think of.

2.4   Discussion

The methodology detects when RAPL estimations are incorrect either because power consumption in the low power configuration $C1$ is under-estimated or because it is over-estimated in the high power configuration $C2$. However, the methodology cannot distinguish which one of the two cases happened. Moreover, the methodology is also not sensitive to over-estimations of power in $C1$ nor under-estimations in $C2$. Although the two limitations restrict the precision of the diagnostic, the methodology is already sufficient to uncover many issues with the power probes, as shown in the experiments.

The methodology allows one to detect incorrect power estimations with only whole system instrumentation. If one is also interested in estimating the importance of the detected flaws in ΔP, other metrics such as confidence intervals or probability density functions can be used. Such tools are then useful to quantify the errors detected by the test.

Table 1. Going from the minimal to the maximal frequency on the `IvyBridge` machine

Cores used	1	2	3	4
$1 - p$-value (%)	100	0	0	0
ρ (N^-/N in %)	99.8	0	0	0

Table 2. Going from the minimal to the maximal frequency on the `SandyBridge` machine

Cores used	1	2	3	4
$1 - p$-value (%)	0	0	0	0
ρ (N^-/N in %)	0	0	3	4.6

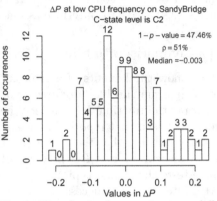

Fig. 1. The observed power increase difference when comparing a 1 core configuration to a 2 cores one on `SandyBridge`

3   Experimental Setup and Methodology

We performed measurements on two distinct Intel machines highlighting different use cases. First, a `SandyBridge` machine consisting in a Intel Xeon E3-1240 processor with 4 cores, where Hyper-Threading is disabled. On that machine, the minimal CPU frequency is 1.6 GHz and the maximal one is 3.3 GHz. Second, a `IvyBridge` machine consisting in a Intel Core i7-3770 processor of 4 cores with Hyper-Threading enabled. There are 8 hardware threads available in the machine and frequencies range from 1.6 GHz to 3.4 GHz. All the test machines run a x86_64 Linux kernel version higher than 3.2.

Each processor has a RAPL interface to estimate energy consumption. The modeled energy values are obtained by combining the status of a set of architectural performance events and energy weight across the set of cores on the chip. The RAPL interface works at the granularity of power planes that enclose the various CPU parts. Usually, three power planes are provided: one for the whole package, one for the cores, and one for the uncore part, sometimes replaced by DRAM power consumption on some server chips [5]. During our experiments, we considered the package power plane and accessed it through MSRs. Our testing processors do not provide any DRAM power plane.

In this study, RAPL power estimation is compared against a digital power meter (DPM). The RAPL and the DPM were configured to measure energy consumption instead of power. Power consumption is then computed using energy and measurement duration. We use a *Yokogawa* WT210 measurement device located between the power supply of the computer and the electrical plug, integrating the overall energy consumption of the system from power measurements performed every 0.1 s.

The accuracy of RAPL power estimation is studied in various experimental configurations. The goal of the experiments is to determine if each parameter affects the accuracy of RAPL. We consider the following parameters: First, CPU frequency: minimal and maximal frequency. Second, number of cores: the micro-benchmark is replicated over 1 to the maximal number of cores available. Third, temperature: cold or warm CPU. Finally, idleness: idle or active CPU. Though the `IvyBridge` machine has Hyper-Threading, we did not study its accuracy. In fact, it is not obvious whether using all the hardware threads (8 in our case) may lead to a higher power consumption than using only 4 hardware threads (1 hardware thread per core). With an 8 threads execution, the result is an interleaved execution of the 8 threads. Consequently, due to context switching, we may observe a lower power consumption for some micro-benchmarks.

Knowing that RAPL power estimation accounts only for processor power consumption, our experimental methodology considers only workloads that stress the processor components. Indeed, workloads accessing memory create off-chip activity that is not accounted by the RAPL interface but that is measured by the DPM. Moreover, it is often unclear how memory power consumption evolves when an experimental parameter varies. For instance, although we can safely expect the CPU power consumption to increase when more cores are used, it is not certain that using more cores will increase memory consumption. Indeed, resource contention and the increased number of opportunities for batching memory accesses may in fact lead to a slightly lower memory power consumption. Consequently, to ensure the predictability of our experimental results, we consider compute-intensive workloads with negligible memory traffic.

For our evaluation, we automatically generated 500 distinct random compute-bound micro-benchmark. The average LLC miss rate is around $1.6e^{-6}$ indicating a negligible memory activity. Each micro-benchmark exhibits a distinct mix of scalar and vector instructions. The instructions are randomly taken from the most represented instructions in the binary programs available in our `/bin` directory and are expressed as inline assembly. The benchmarks are compiled using the `gcc-4.6` compiler with flag `-O3`. While the execution of our micro-benchmarks is repeated 5 times, each of them was sized to run for at least 10 s (shorter runs lead to unstable results). Considering long measurements allows us to ensure the reproducibility of the results. Measurement probes (time and energy) are inserted before and after the execution of the micro-benchmarks, limiting the introduction of noise or overhead in our measurements.

To achieve high precision in our measurements, we use thread affinity for better performance stability and the time stamp counter (TSC) for precise time measurements. To access TSC, we follow the measurement technique proposed by Intel [15]. For our test machines, the time stamp counter increments at a fixed rate [16] and is not affected by CPU frequency change. Furthermore, it ensures accurate time measurements regardless of the used CPU frequency. We use the userspace Linux governor to select a particular CPU frequency. The test machines were entirely dedicated during the experiments to a single user. The experiments were done on a minimally-loaded machine (disable all inessential OS services), minimizing I/O and memory activity.

Raw data, including the micro-benchmark source code, results, and the scripts used to process them are also provided at http://github.com/BenoitP/eprobe_validation. As can be seen on the repository, we used the R software to process the data.

4   Experimental Results and Analysis

4.1   CPU Frequency

The goal of the first set of experiments is to study the impact of CPU frequency on the accuracy of the RAPL interface. We analyze the power differences between the DPM and RAPL interface when setting the minimal and maximal CPU frequencies. All the other experimental parameters remain fixed during the measurements in order to isolate the impact of frequencies on the RAPL interface accuracy. Then, we have to check whether the power increase between the minimal and maximal CPU frequencies estimated by RAPL is at least the same as the one reported by the DPM.

The statistical protocol leads to the results presented in Tables 1 and 2 that report the maximal accepted confidence level $1 - p$-value to declare if RAPL is inaccurate for different number of cores. They also report the sample proportion ρ of benchmarks having negative power increase difference between DPM and RAPL. As far as CPU frequency is considered, and except for the case of single thread executions on the IvyBridge machine, the methodology reveals no errors in the RAPL interface. Indeed, regardless of the test machine, all the computed confidence levels are equal or close to $0\,\%$, where the p-values are close to 1. We can also observe that all the reported proportions are very small.

However, when using a single core on the IvyBridge machine, all the values in ΔP but one are negative. We then conclude that the RAPL interface estimation is inaccurate. The methodology however does not determine if it is due to under-estimations with the minimal frequency, over-estimation with the maximal frequency, or both. As a conclusion, it is clear that the RAPL interface is inaccurate when a single core is used on that machine and care must be taken when considering the RAPL interface power information in such situation.

4.2   Number of Active Cores

Let us now analyze the RAPL power estimation accuracy while the benchmarks are replicated over an increasing number of cores. For a fixed CPU frequency, we analyze power differences between the DPM and RAPL interface for each pair of increasing number of cores. For example, with a quad-core CPU, our protocol will test the pairs (1,2), (1,3), (1,4), (2,3), (2,4) and (3,4). Using more processor cores should always translate into a higher power consumption.

Table 3. Impact of the number of cores used on the IvyBridge machine

Cores used	Minimal frequency		Maximal frequency	
	$1 - p$-value (%)	ρ (%)	$1 - p$-value (%)	ρ (%)
$1 \Rightarrow 2$	100	100	0	0
$1 \Rightarrow 3$	100	100	0	0
$1 \Rightarrow 4$	0	0	0	0
$2 \Rightarrow 3$	100	84.4	0	0
$2 \Rightarrow 4$	0	0	0	0
$3 \Rightarrow 4$	0	0	0	0

Table 4. Impact of the number of cores used on the SandyBridge machine

Cores used	Minimal frequency		Maximal frequency	
	$1 - p$-value (%)	ρ (%)	$1 - p$-value (%)	ρ (%)
$1 \Rightarrow 2$	100	86.8	100	86.2
$1 \Rightarrow 3$	0	0	100	89.2
$1 \Rightarrow 4$	0	0	100	79.2
$2 \Rightarrow 3$	0	0	100	89.2
$2 \Rightarrow 4$	0	0	100	68.6
$3 \Rightarrow 4$	100	66.8	0	14.2

Table 3 reports $1 - p$-value resulting from the Wilcoxon test and the proportion ρ of benchmarks which have negative power increase difference between DPM and RAPL on the IvyBridge machine. All the metrics agree on the absence of power miss-estimation from the RAPL interface for any number of active cores when the maximal frequency is used. On the other hand, this observation does not hold when the minimal CPU frequency is used. Indeed, while half of the tested configurations exhibits significant confidence level (100%), the remaining half exhibits negligible ones (0%). Among the configurations where the RAPL power estimation accuracy is low, two of them involve the case of using 1 core. The results can be correlated to the data from Table 1: both tables indicate that the RAPL interface tends to report incorrect power consumption when the frequency is low and when a small number of cores is used on that machine.

Similarly, Table 4 reports the same power metrics for the SandyBridge machine. Unlike IvyBridge, the maximal frequency seems to be a problematic case for the RAPL interface as it nearly always reports inconsistent values when increasing the number of cores. Note that, in the presented case, the statistical methodology is not only more robust but it also provides a clearer decision on the RAPL interface accuracy compared to simple proportions. On the other hand, setting the minimal CPU frequency shows that only 2 out 6 configurations exhibit important confidence on the inaccuracy of the RAPL interface. As shown in Table 2, while changing the CPU frequency on the SandyBridge platform does not lead to incorrect power estimation, changing the number of cores, may lead to inaccurate power estimation with RAPL interface on that machine.

The methodology reveals flaws in both platforms. The measurements performed under the problematic conditions should then be considered with care and, ideally, validated with another measurement tool. However, the exact solution to handle such inaccuracy depends on the ultimate goal of the measurements and is then out of the scope of the methodology.

4.3 Other Parameters

Along the frequency and the number of active cores, we also evaluated two other parameters that may have an impact of the RAPL interface accuracy. First, we varied the CPU temperature by running a long and intense workload before performing the measurements. Second, we also evaluated the RAPL interface accuracy when the CPU is idle compared to having one or several active cores. Both parameters were evaluated but our methodology did not expose any issue with such configurations.

5 Related Work

Many energy-related work in the past exploited power measurement for various purposes. Some research efforts focused on power efficiency of large scale HPC systems [18,9]. In the context of power monitoring tools, the Power Pack framework [8] aims at isolating power consumption of devices like disks, memory, inter-connect networks and processors in HPC clusters. Georgiou et al. [11] propose a framework integrated to SLURM [21] allowing energy accounting for distinct jobs at the cluster node level. Power measurements are also widely used for performance-profile based estimations. In [2,19,17] total energy consumption measurements are combined to hardware performance counters to estimate energy usage of either hardware or software components. Obviously, precise power measurements can only be performed if the probes themselves are accurate. Thus, it is of primary importance for the work based on measurements to be able to assess the probes accuracy. The presented methodology can then help improving the correctness of any results based on power measurements.

Despite its large usage, only a few research efforts focused on the accuracy of on-chip model-based power estimation for x86 architectures. In [6,7] the accuracy of RAPL interface is studied using linear algebra kernels and algorithms. For the tested algorithms, they concluded that RAPL power estimation represents a viable alternative to physical power meters. Hackenberg et al. [12] performed a quantitative comparison of various power measurement techniques on compute nodes. They showed that the RAPL interface is accurate in most of the cases. However, the RAPL interface was showed to be inadequate to measure energy for short codes [13,3]. All previous studies validate the accuracy of the RAPL interface either by simply comparing RAPL estimation to full system power meter measurements or to dedicated CPU power devices. On the other hand, we propose a more rigorous statistical validation approach of CPU power probes.

Statistical analysis has recently gained more focus in the computer science community. However, the majority of the proposed analysis techniques address only temporal performance. Georges et al. [10] proposed statistical measurement methodologies based on the analysis of variance to compare the performance of Java programs. Touati et al. [20] proposed a performance analysis protocol that computes statistically significant speedups. The proposed protocol relies on well-known parametric and non-parametric hypothesis tests. Similarly, to compare the performance of computers, Chen et al. [4] proposed a statistical protocol that relies on non-parametric tests. We extend previous works to check the accuracy of power measurement probes by means of statistical techniques.

6   Conclusion

We propose a rigorous statistical approach to validate the accuracy of model-based CPU power estimation. The main advantages are twofold: portability and low cost. First, the statistical protocol can be extended to support the validation of any kind of power measurement probe. Second, the approach does not require complex hardware instrumentation as only full-system instrumentation such as a DPM or an IPMI-based probe is needed. Statistical validation is also more robust than simple metrics such as the sample median or proportions. With this regard, the proposed method outperforms the techniques commonly used.

The proposed methodology is able to pinpoint the couple of experimental parameters that influence the most the accuracy of power probes, although it does not exactly indicate which parameter is the source of the observed flaws. As an illustration, we applied our methodology on two Intel based machines and report the incorrect estimations detected and the associated parameters that seem to cause them. We also observed that in overall, RAPL power estimation is more accurate on `IvyBridge` than on `SandyBridge`, reflecting an increased accuracy in newer processors.

References

1. AMD: Amd opteron 6200 series processors, linux tuning guide (2012),
   http://developer.amd.com/wordpress/media/2012/10/
   51803A_OpteronLinuxTuningGuide_SCREEN.pdf
2. Bellosa, F.: The benefits of event: Driven energy accounting in power-sensitive systems. In: Proceedings of the 9th Workshop on ACM SIGOPS European Workshop: Beyond the PC: New Challenges for the Operating System, EW 9, pp. 37–42. ACM, New York (2000)
3. Cao, T., Blackburn, S.M., Gao, T., McKinley, K.S.: The yin and yang of power and performance for asymmetric hardware and managed software. In: 39th International Symposium on Computer Architecture (ISCA), pp. 225–236. IEEE (2012)
4. Chen, T., Chen, Y., Guo, Q., Temam, O., Wu, Y., Hu, W.: Statistical performance comparisons of computers. In: Proceedings of the 18th IEEE International Symposium on High-Performance Computer Architecture, HPCA 2012, pp. 1–12. IEEE Computer Society, Washington, DC (2012)
5. David, H., Gorbatov, E., Hanebutte, U.R., Khanna, R., Le, C.: Rapl: Memory power estimation and capping. In: ACM/IEEE International Symposium on Low-Power Electronics and Design (ISLPED), pp. 189–194 (2010)
6. Demmel, J., Gearhart, A.: Instrumenting linear algebra energy consumption via on-chip energy counters. Tech. Rep. UCB/EECS-2012-168, EECS Department, University of California, Berkeley (June 2012), http://www.eecs.berkeley.edu/Pubs/TechRpts/2012/EECS-2012-168.html

7. Dongarra, J., Ltaief, H., Luszczek, P., Weaver, V.M.: Energy footprint of advanced dense numerical linear algebra using tile algorithms on multicore architectures. In: Second International Conference on Cloud and Green Computing (CGC), pp. 274–281. IEEE (2012)

8. Ge, R., Feng, X., Song, S., Chang, H.-C., Li, D., Cameron, K.W.: Powerpack: Energy profiling and analysis of high-performance systems and applications. IEEE Trans. Parallel Distrib. Syst. 21(5), 658–671 (2010)

9. Ge, R., Feng, X., Subramanya, S., Sun, X.-H.: Characterizing energy efficiency of i/o intensive parallel applications on power-aware clusters. In: IEEE International Symposium on Parallel & Distributed Processing, Workshops and Phd Forum (IPDPSW), pp. 1–8. IEEE (2010)

10. Georges, A., Buytaert, D., Eeckhout, L.: Statistically rigorous java performance evaluation. In: Proceedings of the 22nd Annual ACM SIGPLAN Conference on Object-Oriented Programming Systems and Applications (OOPSLA 2007), pp. 57–76. ACM, New York (2007)

11. Georgiou, Y., Cadeau, T., Glesser, D., Auble, D., Jette, M., Hautreux, M.: Energy accounting and control with SLURM resource and job management system. In: Chatterjee, M., Cao, J.-n., Kothapalli, K., Rajsbaum, S. (eds.) ICDCN 2014. LNCS, vol. 8314, pp. 96–118. Springer, Heidelberg (2014)

12. Hackenberg, D., Ilsche, T., Schone, R., Molka, D., Schmidt, M., Nagel, W.E.: Power measurement techniques on standard compute nodes: A quantitative comparison. In: 2013 IEEE International Symposium on Performance Analysis of Systems and Software (ISPASS), pp. 194–204 (2013)

13. Hähnel, M., Döbel, B., Völp, M., Härtig, H.: Measuring energy consumption for short code paths using rapl. SIGMETRICS Perform. Eval. Rev. 40(3), 13–17 (2012)

14. Hollander, M., Wolfe, D.A.: Nonparametric Statistical Methods, 2nd edn. Wiley Interscience (January 1999)

15. Intel Corporation: How to benchmark code execution times on Intel IA-32 and IA-64 instruction set architectures (2000), http://download.intel.com/embedded/software/IA/324264.pdf

16. Intel Corporation: Intel 64 and IA-32 architectures software developer's manual: System programming guide (2013), http://www.intel.com/content/www/us/en/processors/architectures-software-developer-manuals.html

17. Isci, C., Martonosi, M.: Runtime power monitoring in high-end processors: Methodology and empirical data. In: Proceedings of the 36th Annual IEEE/ACM International Symposium on Microarchitecture, MICRO 36, p. 93. IEEE Computer Society, Washington, DC (2003)

18. Kamil, S., Shalf, J., Strohmaier, E.: Power efficiency in high performance computing. In: IEEE International Symposium on Parallel and Distributed Processing (IPDPS), pp. 1–8. IEEE (2008)

19. Kansal, A., Zhao, F.: Fine-grained energy profiling for power-aware application design. SIGMETRICS Perform. Eval. Rev. 36(2), 26–31 (2008)

20. Touati, S.-A.-A., Worms, J., Briais, S.: The speedup-test: a statistical methodology for programme speedup analysis and computation. Concurrency and Computation: Practice and Experience, 22 (2012)

21. Yoo, A., Jette, M., Grondona, M.: Slurm: Simple linux utility for resource management. In: Feitelson, D.G., Rudolph, L., Schwiegelshohn, U. (eds.) JSSPP 2003. LNCS, vol. 2862, pp. 44–60. Springer, Heidelberg (2003)

Stepping Stones to Reproducible Research: A Study of Current Practices in Parallel Computing

Alexandra Carpen-Amarie, Antoine Rougier, and Felix D. Lübbe

Vienna University of Technology, Austria,
Faculty of Informatics, Institute of Information Systems
Research Group Parallel Computing
Favoritenstrasse 16/184-5, 1040 Vienna, Austria
{carpenamarie,rougier,luebbe}@par.tuwien.ac.at

Abstract. Experimental research plays an important role in parallel computing, as in this field scientific discovery often relies on experimental findings, which complement and validate theoretical models. However, parallel hardware and applications have become extremely complex to study, due to their diversity and rapid evolution. Furthermore, applications are designed to run on thousands of nodes, often spanning across several programming models and generating large amounts of data. In this context, reproducibility is essential to foster reliable scientific results. In this paper we aim at studying the requirements and pitfalls of each stage of experimental research, from data acquisition to data analysis, with respect to achieving reproducible results. We investigate state-of-the-art experimental practices in parallel computing by conducting a survey on the papers published in EuroMPI 2013, a major conference targeting the MPI community. Our findings show that while there is a clear concern for reproducibility in the parallel computing community, a better understanding of the criteria for achieving it is necessary.

1 Introduction

Researchers across a wide spectrum of computer science disciplines have been calling for reproducibility, as a means to assess the reliability, correctness and trustworthiness of published experimental results. This is especially the case in the area of parallel computing, where novel systems or algorithms are often backed up by computational experiments. Existing systems, tools and applications are becoming increasingly diverse and complex, typically targeting thousands of nodes, spanning across several programming models and generating large amounts of data.

A large set of papers in this domain investigate novel techniques to improve specific metrics, such as performance, and validate their approaches by performing experiments in customized environments. As a consequence, providing in-depth technical details regarding the implementation and experimental process to allow other researchers to reproduce their findings is of utmost importance.

The problem of experimental reproducibility is not a new one, and the scientific community has put a lot of effort into understanding the requirements of

L. Lopes et al. (Eds.): Euro-Par 2014 Workshops, Part I, LNCS 8805, pp. 499–510, 2014.

reproducible research across a variety of domains. When discussing the means to attain reproducibility in computational sciences, Peng introduces the concept of *reproducibility spectrum* to classify papers according to their degree of replicability [6]. Thus, the full replication of a study would require the availability of both source code of the proposed contribution and data originally collected by the authors to substantiate their claims. In this paper, our goal is to understand the criteria allowing us to position papers across this broad reproducibility spectrum and to examine the (often subtle) requirements for achieving reproducibility in each stage of experimental research. We target *scientific replicability*, as defined in the work of Hunold and Träff [4], that is, reproducibility of the experimental outcome, as opposed to numerical replicability, which implies bitwise reproducibility of results.

The contribution of this paper is twofold. First, we look at state-of-the-art reproducibility criteria adopted in various areas of computational research and we propose a more in-depth classification of the factors that impact the reproducibility of experimental evaluations. We argue that clearly delimitating the stages of experimental work and identifying reproducibility criteria for each of them will further facilitate both sounder research and more efficient means to review and build upon existing scientific papers. Second, we conduct a small-scale study on a series of parallel computing papers published in the 2013 EuroMPI proceedings, in order to evaluate their reproducibility potential according to our previously defined criteria.

The remainder of the paper is structured as follows. Section 2 discusses existing initiatives for reproducible research. In Section 3, we highlight the experimental stages we identified for achieving reproducible studies. We continue in Section 4 by surveying a set of published parallel computing papers to assess the weight such papers allot to each reproducibility criterion. Our experiences in attempting to replicate two of the studied papers are detailed in Section 5 and we finally point out the lessons learned in Section 6.

2   Related Work

Reproducibility is a fundamental concern in many areas of computational science, as shown by a wide range of papers addressing various facets of the subject. A set of guidelines for conducting reproducible research are stated in the work of Sandve et al. [8], who argue that reproducibility is tightly connected to the availability of all experimental details. The paper advocates for keeping track of all versions of the produced experiments, along with collected data and scripts to generate it. Vitek and Kalibera [10] investigate the root causes of non-reproducible papers in computational science, contending they can be mitigated by a careful selection of benchmarks, workloads and methodologies to document and make the experimental process available. The work of Peng and Eckel [6], despite coming from the field of biostatistics, reinforces the case for reproducibility, stating that it should be considered a "gold standard" of rigorous scientific research.

In 2012, Freire et al. [3] reviewed existing tools for computational reproducibility, proposing a three-dimensional approach for evaluating it. They argue that the level of reproducibility of an experimental paper depends on its portability to different environments, as well as on the availability of all the details related to the experimental workflow, from the source code, to the description of parameters and workload. In this paper, we focus on the same direction and we attempt to better define the criteria that characterize a fully reproducible experiment. We build on the work of Hunold and Träff [4], who first explored the state and the importance of reproducibility in parallel computing.

Several survey papers have attempted to quantify the state of reproducible research in various fields of computer science. Thus, Vandewalle et al. [9] conducted a study on a number of papers in the area of signal processing, discussing each step of their scientific methodology. With respect to the experimental workflow, the paper contends that only a small fraction of the examined papers are reproducible, although the impact of a paper seems to increase with the degree of reproducibility. Starting in 2008, the SIGMOD conference initiated an experimental reproducibility effort aiming at exploring the repeatability of experiments presented in the accepted papers [1,5]. A large reproducibility survey in systems research has also been conducted by Collberg et al. [2], where the authors study 613 papers published in several top conferences and journals. They attempt to obtain and run the code of all experimental papers surveyed, proposing a specification system to classify papers according to the availability of their code and/or data. We take a step further and look in more detail into the methodology of reproducing experiments, as the cited studies rely on code availability as being the main factor determining reproducibility. Our study focuses on a smaller sample, that is, the proceedings of the 2013 EuroMPI conference, as a first step to investigating the reproducibility of research papers in parallel computing.

3   Criteria for Reproducible Research

This section discusses the requirements of achieving reproducible experiments in parallel computing. The scientific methodology roughly relies on four fundamental stages: (1) formulating a research question, (2) devising a hypothesis, (3) designing an experiment to test for its correctness and finally (4) analysing the results in order to draw appropriate conclusions. As experimental findings represent a huge drive of scientific discovery in parallel computing, the quality and usefulness of experimental practices is essential to understanding published contributions or extending previous research. From the standpoint of an experimenter whose goal is to verify the scientific results, providing repeatable and reproducible experiments revolves around the last two elements of the scientific method. Thus, we base our reproducibility analysis on two main steps: we will refer to experiment execution as the (1) *data acquisition* step, in which all the necessary data to evaluate the studied hypothesis are generated, and to the data processing approaches that lead to the presented conclusions as the (2) *data analysis* step. The reason for partitioning reproducibility criteria into two steps

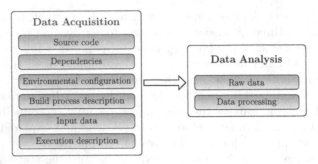

Fig. 1. Criteria for reproducible research

lies in the fact that each of them builds on specific prerequisites, namely the availability of the source code for *data acquisition* and the the availability of the raw measured data for *analysis*.

Vandewalle et al. [9] emphasize the need for code availability, along with data and algorithm description. However, code availability is often not enough to guarantee experiment reproducibility by other researchers, as many experiments require the deployment of customized and complex software stacks. Another perspective on reproducibility criteria is provided by Peng [7], whose work focuses only on processing already measured data. Whereas he identifies several steps necessary to obtain the final results presented in scientific papers, we contend they all belong to what we call the *data analysis* step, as they depend on the availability of experimental data. Other attempts assimilate reproducibility to code availability and its successful compilation and execution [2], or focus on the same two high-level steps [1]. We propose a more nuanced look at the requirements for reproducible experiments, taking into account the impact of various fine-grained factors on reproducibility. For instance, let us consider a paper proposing a new algorithm and comparing it to state-of-the-art implementations. Even when the source code is made available in the paper, replicating the obtained results and, furthermore, extending or improving the work can be a tedious task. The readers are often forced to make their own decisions regarding compilation details, environment setup, or runtime application parameters. Such partial descriptions of the experiment may hinder the entire *data acquisition* process and result in misleading conclusions. Furthermore, the *data analysis* methodology is very often overlooked, as most papers only provide the final graphs reflecting their results and skip a detailed description allowing the reader to assess the statistical relevance of the claimed conclusions.

To investigate such issues, we propose a faceted approach to estimating the reproducibility of a given experimental workflow, by looking into several aspects for each of its stages, summarized in Figure 1.

3.1   Reproducibility Criteria for Data Acquisition

At the *data acquisition* level, we identify a set of criteria necessary for an accurate understanding and replication of an experiment:

Source code / implementation of algorithm. The availability of the source code is essential for the reproducibility of the entire experimental workflow. While papers might provide links to a source code repository, the claim for availability is not fulfilled unless the precise code version employed in the experiments is reported, and the implementation is complemented by a comprehensive documentation.

Dependent software. The majority of experimental papers rely on synthetic benchmarks or real-life applications to validate their claims, or make use of additional frameworks and libraries in order to run correctly. A key factor to verify and improve on the results is the availability of such programs. Furthermore, employed benchmarks and applications are frequently modified to highlight only specific test cases or to emphasize particular findings. Without an in-depth description of such modifications backed by the corresponding source code, other researchers and reviewers have little chance of objectively assessing the meaningfulness of experimental results.

Environmental configuration. While access to the proposed implementation is required for repeating experiments, it needs to be complemented by a rigorous description of the environment used for the study. We analyze the environment configuration by looking at three layers that can impact the experimental outcome. First, we contend that a minimal description of the employed *hardware configuration* is the key to objectively evaluate the paper conclusions. Second, the *software environment* may shape the results and provide valuable hints for a researcher attempting to reproduce the results. In particular, information concerning the operating system, the versions of installed compilers and libraries should not be overlooked. Finally, many papers disregard the need to provide *platform configuration* information along with the source code. System parameters such as process pinning, CPU frequency, or Turbo capabilities may significantly distort results and should be carefully recorded and presented.

Description of the build process. Space limitations is one of the main reasons cited for omitting code compilation details within experimental research papers. However, this is an essential step towards reproducing an experiment, and deficient descriptions may prevent researchers from being able to use the source code and associated applications. In addition, employed compilation options should be commented on, as they may have a huge impact on subsequent measurements, such as in the case of performance evaluations. Ideally, documentation should be accompanied by scripts to enable automatic parameter setup and compilation.

Description of input data. Most applications and frameworks require tuning through runtime parameters, as well as a means to initialize the processed data. Such parameters need to be documented in order to render the experiment repeatable under the same conditions. Input data sets play an equally important role as the implementation. While in some cases their investigation alone can lead to conclusions about the applicability and generality of the proposed solution, papers usually fail to thoroughly explain their workload choice.

Execution description. The manner in which the execution workflow is reported in the paper plays a key role in understanding the proposed solutions and makes it easier for other researchers to build upon them. Ideally, each scientific experiment should be complemented by an accurate depiction of the evaluation protocol. Even when the implementation of a given algorithm is available, the workflow required to test it might be complex. Thus, reproducibility calls not only for a list of employed software tools, but also for the accurate description of the means to interconnect them. Additionally, making execution scripts accessible along with the implementation facilitates the task of reproducing the experiment in a different environment.

3.2   Reproducibility Criteria for Data Analysis

Data analysis has received a lot of interest in the context of reproducible research. However, whereas in other science areas the community has imposed strict publication rules with respect to statistical significance of results, in our domain the presentation of results often lacks a detailed description of the performed underlying data processing. In this context, reproducing the data analysis phase of an experiment depends on two main criteria.

Raw data. To promote results replicability, experimental studies could make the obtained data available for other researchers interested in analysing it. Typically, it is assumed that the raw data can be generated, provided that the *data acquisition* phase is reproducible. However, this is not always the case. For instance, when the experimental settings rely on specific hardware that is not commonly accessible, a study may enable reproducibility only for the *data analysis* part by promoting publicly available data sets.

Information on data processing. A data processing step is almost always required to study raw data and to generate the final plots and tables included in the paper. It is usually an iterative process generating intermediate data sets and it consists of scripts designed to curate data, e.g., by removing outliers, to summarize, highlight particular findings and visualize them by applying statistical analysis techniques. Such scripts should be provided along with the data to substantiate the statistical significance of presented results. In their absence, reproducible *data analysis* calls for an exhaustive description of all the processing steps required to support the paper's claims. Moreover, the data processing phase often includes a qualitative analysis stage, which might be a complex process of understanding and interpreting the data, possibly requiring additional tools, such as interactive profilers or visualization tools.

4   Reproducibility Survey

To assess the state of reproducible research in parallel computing, we conducted a study on the papers published in the EuroMPI 2013 proceedings. This survey involved the 22 accepted papers, which constitute a very small and possibly not representative sample of the total number of papers published in this area. However, this survey is intended as a first attempt to study current reproducibility practices. We hope to understand the various degrees of reproducibility, as well as to better estimate the requirements of reproducible research reporting and how to improve the quality of our own research in this respect.

4.1 Overview of the Survey Process

Our survey aims at evaluating each paper against the reproducibility criteria identified in the previous section. First, for each of the 21 non-theoretical papers, we verified whether the presented experimental results are complemented with available source code. To this end, we manually scanned the papers for links to the implementation of the proposed contribution, and we additionally checked the authors' websites for further details. Furthermore, we contacted the authors to obtain access to the source code and additional information related to the other reproducibility criteria.

Next, we conducted a careful investigation for details concerning each key component of both *data acquisition* and *data analysis* phases, gathering all our findings in Table 1, which also includes the information we obtained by exchanging emails with the authors. We anonymized the collected data about the papers by listing them in random order in Table 1 We marked each reproducibility criterion with a "+", when the corresponding information was present in the paper or sent us by the authors. Papers that failed to provide any kind of information for a particular step were marked with a "o". In particular, the *Source code* and *Raw data* criteria received a "+" only if the the code/data were specifically made available in the paper. The table also comprises an estimation of the degree of reproducibility of each paper, computed as the percentage of "+" symbols that each paper has earned out of the total number of experimental stages. Moreover, the last row presents our overall results, indicating the number and the percentage of papers that include at least minimal information for each specific criterion. Some of the papers depicted experiments that did not require information related to all the previously presented criteria. In such cases, we marked the appropriate stages with a "." and we excluded them from the computation of the overall results.

Although we anonymized the collected data, our analysis is reproducible in the sense that anyone who has access to the investigated papers is able to evaluate them with respect to the proposed reproducibility criteria. Furthermore, the data processing scripts we employed can be made available upon request.

4.2 Findings

The results in Table 1 show that a link to the source code was provided by the authors in only 30% of the papers, while information about the benchmark applications used to validate findings and input data was present in over 85% of the papers. On the other hand, the survey confirms our intuition that several steps of the experimental process are often neglected. Thus, only 40% of the papers mention the compilation process, while only 50% include a description of how the actual execution and measurements were performed. It is worth mentioning,

Table 1. Results of the reproducibility study on the 21 papers relying on experimental evaluations, which were published in the EuroMPI 2013 proceedings. Each reproducibility criterion is marked with a "+" if the corresponding information is included in the paper, with a "o" if the paper does not mention that particular stage, or with a "." if such information is not needed for reproducing the paper's results.

Paper	Data acquisition					Data analysis			Repr.%
	Source code	Dep. soft- ware	Env. config.	Build process	Input data	Exec. de- scrip- tion	Raw data	Data Pro- cessing info	
1	o	+	+	o	+	o	o	o	37%
2	+	+	.	.	+	.	o	.	75%
3	o	+	+	+	+	o	o	o	50%
4	+	+	+	+	+	+	o	+	87%
5	o	+	+	o	+	o	o	o	37%
6	+	+	+	+	+	o	o	+	75%
7	+	+	+	+	+	+	+	+	100%
8	o	+	+	o	+	+	o	+	62%
9	o	o	+	o	o	+	o	o	25%
10	o	.	+	o	o	o	o	.	16%
11	.	+	+	o	+	o	o	+	57%
12	o	+	+	o	+	+	o	o	50%
13	o	o	+	o	+	+	o	+	50%
14	o	+	+	o	+	o	o	o	37%
15	+	o	+	+	.	o	o	o	42%
16	o	+	+	+	+	o	o	o	50%
17	o	o	+	o	+	+	o	o	37%
18	o	+	+	+	+	+	o	o	62%
19	+	+	+	+	+	+	+	o	87%
20	o	o	+	o	+	o	o	o	25%
21	o	+	+	o	o	+	o	o	37%
Total	6/20 30%	15/20 75%	20/20 100%	8/20 40%	17/20 85%	10/20 50%	2/21 9%	6/19 31%	

however, that such low percentages are correlated to some extent with code availability. Thus, making the implementation accessible for readers would also imply devising compilation and possibly execution scripts, as well as a comprehensive documentation of these steps.

Since most papers heavily rely on the experimental section, all of them provide at least a minimal description of the employed experimental environment. Each paper exhibited a hardware description of the clusters or machines used for conducting their respective studies, including informations about the architecture,

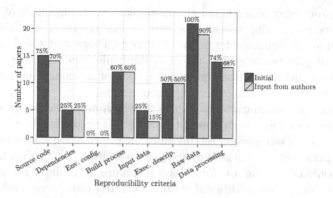

Fig. 2. Survey results: number of papers that fail to comply with each reproducibility criterion before and after contacting the authors

processors and network interconnect. Additionally, some studies also mention the memory hierarchy and the available storage space, especially when this information is needed for further understanding and assessing the impact of the results. The software stack installed is surprisingly described in only a fraction of the considered papers, with a special focus on the employed libraries (such as MPI) and/or compilers (e.g., GCC). As the installed versions are not systematically pointed out, one could conclude that the burden of attempting to reproduce the results might be significant even for an experienced researcher. Furthermore, the information regarding specific platform configurations is even scarcer, as less than half of the papers include such details as process pinning or hyper-threading usage.

Most examined papers relied on publicly available benchmarks. Despite this fact, the high percentage corresponding to the availability of input data does not accurately account for reproducible executions, as in many cases the authors employed customized versions of the classic benchmarks and include only a brief description of the changes in the paper. Regarding the execution description, only half of the papers mention the measurement procedure or the number of repetitions and provide an insight into their workload generation approach.

Our survey unveils even more dramatic findings concerning the *data analysis* component. None of the inspected papers included a pointer to the raw data generated by their experiments, thus minimizing the possibility of further analysis by external researchers. However, in some cases we were able to obtain access to all collected data by directly contacting the authors. We contend nevertheless that the ratio of papers providing access to the raw results should be much higher. On the one hand, it would allow for a swift validation of the claimed results, provided that the data processing step is also explained. On the other hand, given the diversity and cost of today's high-performance machines, not all researchers will have access to the hardware used for the evaluation, relying only on the availability of the raw data for at least a limited reproducibility.

The data processing phase is mostly overlooked, with only 31% of the experimental papers mentioning the steps taken to analyze the data. Most papers directly provide performance figures and disregard any statistical analysis. A small subset of papers state they resort to multiple repetitions of the experiment and draw conclusions based on some method of summarizing data, such as choosing the mean or median of the obtained results.

Our findings are summarized in Figure 2, which emphasizes the number of papers that do not meet each specific criterion. The dark-colored bars show the initial results of our survey, relying only on information gathered from the published papers and the authors or projects websites, prior to contacting the authors. In contrast, the light-colored bars in Figure 2 highlight the slightly improved final values, when additional source code and data were made available for our study directly by the authors. Whereas no paper obtained a reproducibility score of 100% in our initial evaluation, the interaction with the authors led to a slightly increased value for these scores, as presented in Table 1. Nevertheless, a majority of papers do not include any information related to at least 5 of the total of 8 criteria, that is, they achieve a reproducibility score of less than 60%.

5   Case Studies: Reproducing Experiments in Practice

We selected the two papers that achieved the highest reproducibility score according to our classification and we attempted to reproduce a subset of the presented experiments. We only targeted the experiments for which we had the suitable hardware to match the setup employed by the original papers and we relied on the source code advertized within the paper as a link to the project's website or obtained by directly contacting the authors.

The findings of other reproducibility surveys [1,2] suggest that very often compiling and running the code out-of-the-box is a time-consuming or even impossible task. In our case, we were able to obtain and compile the code, as well as to run several examples provided along with the implementation. However, code availability was not a guarantee for an effortless build process, mainly because of mismatching code versions and insufficient documentation. While this is an essential step towards reproducibility, being able to fully reproduce experiments is not limited to compiling and executing the code. The next challenge was to repeat the experiment in an environment setup similar to the one employed by the paper authors. To this end, we attempted to follow the configuration steps provided in each of the two papers.

In the first case, despite the fact that the paper details a broad range of platform and configuration data, we were unable to recreate the execution process. At this point we contacted the authors, who provided us with full access to the evaluation scripts they had been using. Thus, they supplied us with benchmarking source code, which we would have otherwise needed to re-implement based on a brief description included in the paper. We also obtained the raw data employed for the evaluation section, as well as the analysis scripts allowing us to directly generate the graphs. For the second case study, the authors provided us with both the source code and execution scripts to configure and run the experiments. Similarly to the first attempt, we also obtained the benchmarks needed for the experiments. However, conducting a similar experiment was not possible without first understanding and customizing the scripts to suit our software stack.

Interestingly, the raw data proved to be a valuable asset in our attempt to reproduce the *data acquisition* step of the experiments. While we assumed we would be able to generate our own results upon executing the experiment, having access to the original data provided by the authors helped us better understand what kind of data we needed for the next phase and what was the most appropriate format for collecting such data. Equipped with the adapted execution scripts and configuration parameters, we managed to perform the experiments on our machines effortlessly. One of the evaluated papers included the processing scripts used to generate the presented graphs. Thus, replicating the *data analysis* step was in this case equivalent to a straightforward execution of the analysis scripts on our data to obtain the corresponding figures. In the second scenario, the data processing scripts were missing, and we relied on the details reported in the paper to interpret raw data and generate figures. However, the experiments under consideration did not require complex processing steps and thus we managed to plot similar graphs to the ones depicted in the paper.

These specific examples led us to learn several important lessons. First, even though we had full access to the source code repository, we experienced compatibility problems caused by the different versions of the code we selected for our reproducibility tests. Moreover, the format of the raw data collected from our experiment did not exactly match the requirements of the processing scripts or the format of the original raw data. Consequently, we needed to manually adjust the scripts in order to generate an error-free output. It is thus essential to fully document the versions of both customized code and libraries (either within the papers or in the corresponding code/data repositories), an aspect that is often ignored in experimental descriptions. Additionally, the complexity of the software stack required for the experiments may pose problems even if all the individual details of each tool and benchmark employed are carefully presented. This was the case for one of our reproducibility tests, where the lack of execution scripts providing the correct combination of interrelated tools and benchmarks would have hindered the entire experiment replication process.

Finally, a surprising finding of our reproducing the experiments on our hardware was the fact that we obtained slightly different results from the ones depicted in the paper. We will further attempt to investigate this aspect and to identify the means to assess whether the provided results hold for the specific environment they were tested on, or they are generalizable across a wider range of platforms.

6   Conclusions

In this paper we addressed the requirements of reproducible research in terms of sound experimental practices and reporting. We discussed the impact of each of the two experimental steps, i.e., *data acquisition* and *data analysis*, on achieving reproducible results and we identified a set of reproducibility criteria matching each of them. We presented our experiences with assessing reproducibility for a selection of parallel computing papers, which helped us obtain a better understanding of the inherent difficulties of rigorous experimentation in this field. Our findings suggest that, whereas a majority of papers reflect a significant concern for reproducibility, much further work is required to attain full experimental reproducibility.

We intend to extend this survey with a wider range of papers published in this field, as well as to better understand the mechanisms for improving the state of research reproducibility at the level of each experimental stage. In our study, the compliance with a given reproducibility criterion is a binary decision. As a result, the reproducibility score we computed can only be interpreted as a measure of the minimal requirements a paper has to meet to achieve reproducibility. We plan to explore the means to fine-tune the decision for successful fulfillment of each criterion and possibly to quantify the weight of each criterion within a specific experimental scenario. Our future work will target the design of a framework for rigorously evaluating reproducibility, which can provide an objective assessment of papers in the context of reproducible research.

Acknowledgements. We would like to thank Sascha Hunold (Vienna University of Technology) for many helpful discussions and suggestions.

References

1. Bonnet, P., Manegold, S., Bjørling, M., et al.: Repeatability and workability evaluation of SIGMOD 2011. SIGMOD Record 40(45), 48 (2011)
2. Collberg, C., Proebsting, T., et al.: Measuring Reproducibility in Computer Systems Research (2014), http://reproducibility.cs.arizona.edu/tr.pdf
3. Freire, J., Bonnet, P., Shasha, D.: Computational reproducibility: State-of-the-art, challenges, and database research opportunities. In: Proceedings of the 2012 ACM SIGMOD International Conference on Management of Data, SIGMOD 2012, pp. 593–596. ACM, New York (2012)
4. Hunold, S., Träff, J.L.: On the state and importance of reproducible experimental research in parallel computing. CoRR abs/1308.3648 (2013)
5. Manolescu, I., Afanasiev, L., Arion, A., et al.: The repeatability experiment of SIGMOD 2008. SIGMOD Record 37(39), 45 (2008)
6. Peng, R.D.: Reproducible research in computational science. Science 334(6060), 1226–1227 (2011)
7. Peng, R.D., Eckel, S.P.: Distributed reproducible research using cached computations. Computing in Science and Engineering 11(1), 28–34 (2009)
8. Sandve, G.K., Nekrutenko, A., J., Taylor, O.: Ten simple rules for reproducible computational research. PLoS Computational Biology 9(10), e1003285 (2013)
9. Vandewalle, P., Kovacevic, J., Vetterli, M.: Reproducible research in signal processing. IEEE Signal Processing Magazine 26(3), 37–47 (2009)
10. Vitek, J., Kalibera, T.: R3: Repeatability, reproducibility and rigor. SIGPLAN Notices 47(4a), 30–36 (2012)

On Undecidability Aspects of Resilient Computations and Implications to Exascale

Nageswara S.V. Rao

Computer Science and Mathematics Division,
Oak Ridge National Laboratory, Oak Ridge, TN 37831
raons@ornl.gov
http://www.csm.ornl.gov/~nrao

Abstract. Future Exascale computing systems with a large number of
processors, memory elements and interconnection links, are expected
to experience multiple, complex faults, which affect both applications
and operating-runtime systems. A variety of algorithms, frameworks and
tools are being proposed to realize and/or verify the resilience properties of computations that guarantee correct results on failure-prone
computing systems. We analytically show that certain resilient computation problems in presence of general classes of faults are undecidable,
that is, no algorithms exist for solving them. We first show that the
membership verification in a generic set of resilient computations is undecidable. We describe classes of faults that can create infinite loops
or non-halting computations, whose detection in general is undecidable.
We then show certain resilient computation problems to be undecidable
by using reductions from the loop detection and halting problems under two formulations, namely, an abstract programming language and
Turing machines, respectively. These two reductions highlight different
failure effects: the former represents program and data corruption, and
the latter illustrates incorrect program execution. These results call for
broad-based, well-characterized resilience approaches that complement
purely computational solutions using methods such as hardware monitors, co-designs, and system- and application-specific diagnosis codes.

Keywords: Exascale systems, resilient computations, undecidability,
uncomputability.

1 Introduction

Exascale computing systems are expected to be built using a large number of
multi-core processors and accelerators with computing elements totaling a million or more [1,11]; in addition, they consist of interconnects, switches and hierarchies of memory units, and are supported by specialized software stacks
[25]. Typical life-span of the commercial off-the-shelf components used in these
systems is about 5-10 years, particularly for processors. Thus, as a rough approximation, computations running for hours may experience multiple failures,
and they in turn may result in errors in applications as well as in operating and

L. Lopes et al. (Eds.): Euro-Par 2014 Workshops, Part I, LNCS 8805, pp. 511–522, 2014.
© Springer International Publishing Switzerland 2014

runtime systems that execute the applications [20]. Furthermore, the sheer size and complexity of these systems may lead to complex faults, not all of which can be known precisely or anticipated accurately. Indeed, they range from manufacturing and device fatigue faults in components, to dynamic hot-spots created in computer racks due to interactions between device placement and cooling systems, to interactions of software modules with degraded hardware components. These faults may manifest in a variety of ways: memory faults may cause the executables to be corrupted and the variables to assume out-of-bound values; circuit faults may cause incorrect loading of the program counters and errors in arithmetic and logic operations; and, bus and interconnect faults may corrupt the data in transit between the processing units.

A broad spectrum of algorithms, frameworks and tools are being actively developed to support resilient computations on failure-prone computing systems. They include hardware monitors, HPL codes [15], application-specific detection methods [16,17,5,9], verification systems [3], Algorithm-Based Fault Tolerance (ABFT) methods [10], resilience ecosystems [18], software-based fault detection [12,19], and likely invariants for detecting hardware faults [22] (to name a few). It is generally expected that the development and proliferation of such methods will continue as we gain a deeper understanding of the design space of Exascale systems and make progress towards building them.

In this paper, we explore the boundaries of resilient computations that produce correct results on computing systems that are subject to broad classes of failures. We address both the algorithms for resilient computations as well as the provability of assertions about their outputs, particularly, involving arithmetic and logic computations. In a nutshell, we show that the resilient computation problems present significant computational challenges if the underlying failures are not precisely characterized and anticipated. We show a broad class of resilience computation problems to be undecidable in the sense of Turing [23], that is, no algorithms exist for solving them. These results, although based on broad failure models, provide motivation for targeting a smaller and more precisely characterized failure classes that may render these problems decidable.

We first show that verifying if a given program has the property defined by a set of resilient computations is an undecidable problem. We then show that resilient computations under data and program corruption and execution errors are undecidable by using reductions from the classical loop-detection and halting problems. We present the proofs under two formulations, namely, the abstract programming language $\mathcal{L}$ [8] and Turing machines [6], that highlight different aspects of the underlying failures; the former represents program and data corruption, and the latter illustrates incorrect program execution. We outline relativization results that indicate that even if halting problems due to these errors are decidable, it is still possible for undecidable problems to persist. We briefly describe an example failure class based on arithmetic systems that could lead to algorithms for which performance guarantees are hard to prove. The literature in the areas of resilient computations, Exascale systems and undecidable problems is extensive and deep. In this paper, we only refer to a small (perhaps, unevenly represented) set of works that illustrate the main concepts, and recast some of the results from the theory of computation within the context of resilient computations.

These undecidability results indicate that unless the class of faults is limited, these problems cannot be solved by purely computational and analytical means. Hence, they call for broad-based approaches that complement computational solutions, which integrate methods such as hardware monitors, co-design of hardware and software solutions, system-specific diagnosis methods, and application-specific resilience methods. Furthermore, algorithms, frameworks and ecosystems used in such approaches must clearly identify their target failures, and establish that the underlying computational problems are indeed not undecidable. However, severely limiting the class of faults does not necessarily lead to tractable solutions, as indicated by the NP-completeness of stuck-at faults [13] (where the underlying problems are decidable).

We briefly describe undecidable problems and their relationship to resilient computations in Section 2. We describe some examples of failures in computing systems that can could lead to challenges in realizing resilient computations in Section 3. We present undecidability results in Section 4 using language $\mathcal{L}$ in Section 4.1 and Turing machines in Section 4.2. We discuss some implications of these results for Exascale systems and conclusions in Section 5.

2   Context of Undecidable Problems

The notion of undecidability plays two roles in resilient computations, namely, non-existence of algorithms in the framework of Turing [23] and unprovability of assertions about their outputs in the framework of Godel [14] [1]. As pointed out by Chaitin [4], these two results are closely related: informally, they both capture the "finiteness" of algorithms and proofs, which is insufficient to address certain "infinite" requirements of computations and assertions, respectively. The undecidability results are formally proved within the frameworks of recursive functions expressed in $\mathcal{L}$ [8], Turing machines [6], lambda calculus [4], and others [24]. For concreteness, we follow the first two in this paper.

Several of the well-known undecidable problems belong to the decision problems about Turing machines such as the halting problem, empty-set detection and equivalence of Turing machines [6]. These problems might appear somewhat abstract, but there are a number of more "practical" undecidable problems, including virus detection problems [7], programs to test randomness of a string [4], testing the equivalence of context-free grammars, smallest program capable of generating a given string, and computing the Kolmogorov complexity of strings. And, the resilient computations for Exascale systems represent another class of such challenging problems.

Among the existing undecidable problems, closely related to resilient computations are the virus detection problems, wherein the disruptive effects on code

---

[1] Godel's incompleteness results on provable assertions about arithmetic systems were published in 1931 [14] years before Turing's results on computations in 1936 [23].

executions are to be detected and accounted for. In some sense, the effects of viruses on computer codes are similar to those of complex failures in computing systems. However, the latter are fundamentally different from viruses which are generated by computable or recursive functions. The effects due to failures are not similarly restricted, and as a result the intractability results of virus do not simply carryover to resilient computations. Nevertheless, they both are capable of introducing non-halting computations into otherwise terminating computations, which is one (but not all) of the sources of undecidability in these problems.

3   Complex Faults In Exascale Systems

Complex failures or faults may arise due to a variety of factors in Exascale systems [2,20]. In addition to individual component faults (due to statistics of larger numbers), multi-component faults can occur as a result of the sheer complexity of Exascale systems, for example, multi-core processor errors due to hot spots in server shelves. We are particularly interested in faults that lead to non-halting computations in codes that are guaranteed to terminate and produce correct results on failure-free computing systems. In particular, infinite loops that lead to non-halting computations can be created by several fault mechanisms including the following:

(a) *Code Corruption:* Program executables may be corrupted and lead to non-terminating loops, for example, the condition $i < N$ may be changed to $i > 0$. Another example would be go to statements changed to be self-referential. Third example could be the corruption of base conditions on recursive calls.

(b) *Parameter and Variable Errors:* Infinite loops can be created without modifications to codes by errors in the contents of certain memory locations, for example, loop control variables.

(c) *ALU Circuit Errors:* Failures in Arithmetic and Logic Unit (ALU) circuits can create loops by incorrect execution of terminating conditions of loops and base conditions of recursive calls.

(d) *Program Counter Errors:* Program counters hold the next instructions to be executed, and loading errors in their contents can lead to infinite loops, for example, by repeatedly loading the same instruction.

Within the framework of language $\mathcal{L}$ and Turing machines, both programs and their inputs are treated essentially the same way, namely, as strings. In that sense, there is not much difference between the faults of type (a) and (b), since both can be caused by memory errors; together, they represent program and data corruption, and may be abstracted as string errors in language $\mathcal{L}$. However, failures in (c) and (d) are different in that they occur during the program execution, and may be abstracted as incorrect state transitions of Turing machines. Given the diversity of failure sources of non-halting computations and the complexity of Exascale systems, it not clear if all of them can be adequately known or even if that set is bounded. Furthermore, some of these errors may occur simultaneously, for example, high shelf temperatures might lead to the failures in memory elements and ALU circuits at the same time. Computer viruses modify codes and their executions, and several virus detection problems are known to be undecidable [7]. But, code modifications by viruses do not reflect the entire diversity of faults in Exascale systems due to their possible "non-computational" origins.

4   Resilient Computation Problems

In this section, we present undecidability results within the formal frameworks of abstract programming language $\mathcal{L}$ described in Davis and Weyuker [8] and Turing Machines (TM) [6]. These two frameworks are equivalent for undecidable problems, but the former shows the effects of infinite loops at an algorithm level, whereas the failure effects on memory and circuits are more apparent in the latter. We only present an outline of results from a resilient computations perspective, and details of these formulations and their relationships can be found in [8,6] (or in introductory books on theoretical computer science).

One of the key notions behind the undecidability is the concept of a universal programming language or equivalently the Universal Turing Machine (UTM) wherein each program can be specified as a string. Both the program P and its input w are specified as strings, and P is "interpreted" in $\mathcal{L}$ and "executed" by a TM with w as the input. That is, these are abstract models of computers wherein the code P is stored as an executable in the memory along with its input w. While these abstract models are much more primitive than complex computing systems, they both are equivalent in terms of the underlying computability as per the Church-Turing thesis [6,4]. We consider that the programs are coded as integers under a scheme such as Godel numbering in the former [8], and Boolean strings for TMs [6]; in both cases, they can be enumerated like the natural numbers with the caveat that not every natural number represents a valid program P in either scheme.

4.1   Predicates about Programs in $\mathcal{L}$

We follow the programming language abstraction $\mathcal{L}$ described in [8], wherein each program is described as a set of instructions. The programs in $\mathcal{L}$ are converted into numbers using schemes such as the Godel numbers, which are sufficient to describe all computable functions [8] so that a program P is represented by its numerical code $y=\#(P)$. Under fault-free conditions, the output of program y with input x is denoted by $\Phi_y(x) = o(x)$, which is also specified by a partially computable function $\Phi(x,y)$ by the Universality Theorem [8]; here, $\Phi(.)$ is universal in that it "executes" any program y with x as its input. Under fault-free conditions, both y are x specified initially, and neither is altered at any point during the execution of y. Under faulty conditions, however, both can be altered any time during the execution in two ways: contents of y and x can be altered through data corruption, and instructions of y can be erroneously executed due to hardware faults. Then, under faulty conditions, the output of y with input x is denoted by $\Phi_y^F(x) = g(x)$ such that $o(x_0) \neq g(x_0)$ for some x_0.

Undecidability of Membership in Resilient Computation Classes. Let y_R denote a *resilient version* of the original program y such that under faulty conditions it produces the same output as y under fault-free conditions. For a given input x, let $g(x)$ and $g_R(x) = o(x)$ denote the outputs of functions computed by programs y and y_R under faulty conditions, respectively. Thus, y_R accounts for faults in y and x, and yet produces the correct output. For example, consider a hypothetical single-fault case of y producing a Boolean output which is complemented; then, y_R can simply execute y and complement its output to produce the correct answer.

We now show that there is no algorithm for verifying if a given program y possesses the resilience property implemented by a set of resilient codes of type y_R, by showing the underlying decision problem to be undecidable. Let $\mathcal{A}$ be a set of original programs that halt under fault-free conditions, but run erroneously under faulty conditions, namely, they either do not halt or produce incorrect or undefined output; $\mathcal{A}$ is assumed to be *non-trivial* [8] which implies it is non-empty and does not span all codes. Then, the corresponding non-trivial set of all $\mathcal{A}$-resilient programs is denoted by $\mathcal{R} = \{y_R | y \in \mathcal{A}\}$, which is assumed to exist and may be custom designed to overcome the faults that are specific to programs in $\mathcal{A}$. For example, $\mathcal{R}$ could consist of all resilient versions of a set of non-linear solvers $\mathcal{A}$ that are designed to correct for ALU faults. We assume that errors are such that $y \in \mathcal{A}$ by itself is not a resilient version of any other original program $y_1 \in \mathcal{A}$. Then, the index set of these $\mathcal{A}$-resilient programs $\mathcal{R}$ is

$$R_{\mathcal{R}} = \{t \in N | \Phi_t^F \in \mathcal{R}\},$$

which we show to be a non-computable set.

Theorem 1. *The index set of $\mathcal{A}$-resilient programs $R_{\mathcal{R}}$ is not computable, that is, the problem of verifying if a given program belongs to $\mathcal{R}$ under faulty conditions is undecidable for any non-trivial set of original programs $\mathcal{A}$.*

Proof: The proof is through contradiction. Consider that $R_{\mathcal{R}}$ is computable, and consider $g_R \in \mathcal{R}$ is a resilient version of the original (non-resilient) $g \in \mathcal{A}$. Let us define a function

$$h(t, x) = \begin{cases} g(x) & \text{if } t \in R_{\mathcal{R}} \\ g_R(x) & \text{if } t \notin R_{\mathcal{R}}. \end{cases}$$

Then, the following function is partially computable [8]

$$h(t, x) = 1_{R_{\mathcal{R}}}(t).g(x) + [1 - 1_{R_{\mathcal{R}}}(t)].g_R(x),$$

under faulty conditions, where $1_S(.)$ is the indicator function for set S: $1_S(t) = 1$ if and only if $t \in S$ and $1_S(t) = 0$ otherwise. In particular, a program to compute $h(t, x)$ is composed by using that for $1_{R_{\mathcal{R}}}(.)$ as a sub-routine. Then, by the Recursion Theorem, there is a program e such that

$$\Phi_e^F(x) = h(e, x) = \begin{cases} g(x) & \text{if } \Phi_e^F \in \mathcal{R} \\ g_R(x) = o(x) & \text{if } \Phi_e^F \notin \mathcal{R}, \end{cases}$$

where $\Phi_e^F(x) = \Phi^F(x, e)$ for a universal partially computable function Φ^F specified by the Universality Theorem applied under faulty conditions. Now consider that $e \in R_{\mathcal{R}}$ that is, it is $\mathcal{A}$-resilient and can be executed under faulty conditions such that $\Phi_e^F(x) = o(x)$; but, by definition of $h(e, x)$, we have $\Phi_e^F(x) = g(x)$ and in particular $\Phi_e^F(x_0) = g(x_0) \neq o(x_0) = \Phi_e^F(x_0)$. On the other hand, consider that $e \notin R_{\mathcal{R}}$, that is, it is not $\mathcal{A}$-resilient, namely $\Phi_e^F(x_0) \neq o(x_0)$; then, by above definition of $h(e, x)$, we have $\Phi_e^F(x) = g_R(x) = f(x)$, and in particular, $\Phi_e^F(x_0) = o(x_0) \neq \Phi_e^F(x_0)$. Thus, in both cases we have a contradiction, which proves the theorem. $\square$

This result is a particular application of the well-known Rice's Theorem to resilience computations. Informally, it implies that it is not possible to verify if a given program possesses the resilience property embodied by $R_{\mathcal{R}}$. While establishing the undecidability with respect to classes of resilient computations, this result does not pinpoint the sources of undecidability in individual programs. We next show that the dynamic loops created by the faults are sufficient to lead to undecidability of verifying the resilience of individual codes.

Infinite Loops. The halting problem is specified by the predicate $\text{HALT}(x, y)$ which is true if and only if the program y with input x halts. This problem is *undecidable* in that there does not exit a program written in $\mathcal{L}$ that can decide if this proposition is true or false (Theorem 2.1, Chapter 4, [8]). We consider a class of failures that can be captured by the *failure function*, $f(x, y) = (x_f, y_f)$ that replaces x by x_f and y by y_f just before the execution of y is initiated, and no other failures occur. We note that this characterization is limited to deterministic failures since such functions are not sufficient to characterize random errors, which indeed can occur in Exascale systems. We consider that the execution of y with input x produces yes/no answer in a finite time on a failure-free machine.

Consider the predicate $\text{RESILIFY}(x, y, f)$ which is true if and only if there exists a program P_f that "executes" y_f with input x_f and produces the output identical to that produced by y with input x. Now, we further restrict $f(.)$ to functions $\mathcal{F}_L$ that create infinite loops due to *data and program corruption* that modify one or both y and x, for example, by using (but not limited to) mechanisms listed in Section 3.

We next show that $\text{RESILIFY}(x, y, f)$, $f \in \mathcal{F}_L$ is not a computable predicate, by reducing the following simpler problem to it. Let $\text{NO-LOOP}(x, y)$ denote the predicate that the program y with input x does not loop forever, that is, it will produce yes/no output in a finite number of steps.

Theorem 2. *RESILIFY(x, y, f), $f \in \mathcal{F}_L$ is not a computable predicate under program and data corruption.*

Proof: We prove this theorem in three steps. First, $\text{RESILYFY}(x_f, y_f, I)$ true if and only if $\text{RESILYFY}(x, y, f)$ true, where f changes y to y_f, for $y_f \in \mathcal{F}_L$, x to x_f, and I is the identity function. Next, we note that $\text{NO-LOOP}(x_f, y_f)$ is true if and only if $\text{RESILIFY}(x_f, y_f, I)$ is true, thereby showing that the undecidability of the former implies that of the latter by restriction. We now show that NO-LOOP(x, y) is an undecidable predicate by contradiction using the well-known proof method used in [8]; we present the details here for completeness. Let us assume NO-LOOP(x, y) is computable, and hence can be inserted into the following program P:

> [P]: **if** NO-LOOP(x, x) **go to** P
> **else return** NO

This program takes a single input x and uses NO-LOOP(x, x) as a subroutine. Based on the above code, P keeps looping while NO-LOOP(x, x) is true, that is it halts if and if only if the predicate NO-LOOP(x, x) is not true, that is $\sim$NO-LOOP(x, x). Now let $y_0 = \#(P)$ denote the code of the above program P expressed under Godel's numbering. By using $y = y_0$ in the definition we have: NO-LOOP(x, y_0) if and only if $y_0 = \#(P)$ does not loop forever, that is $\sim$NO-LOOP(x, x) is true by the definition of P. Since the above statement is valid for any value of x, we choose $x = y_0$ which leads to the contradiction: NO-LOOP(y_0, y_0) if and only if $\sim$NO-LOOP(y_0, y_0).   □

Informally, this theorem shows that there is no algorithm to determine if the failures cause the code execution to be stuck in an infinite loop. But, for very restricted cases in which infinite loops can be created by known mechanisms, this problem could be decidable. More generally, there might be other complex failures, such as purely random errors or introduction of non-compressible strings [4], that could potentially lead to undecidable resilient computation problems. Also, under certain strictly component-level failures, one can develop targeted component diagnosis codes [21] that can verify that no stuck-at failures have occurred during the code execution.

4.2   Turing Machines for Resilient Computations

We now repeat the result of Theorem 2 within the formulation of UTM that "executes" a given TM M on input w. This formulation abstracts a general purpose computer by UTM that executes a program specified by M using w as its input. A Turing machine M is composed of a tape of cells that holds w, and is also used for holding intermediate results; the operation of M is specified by a finite set of transitions such that in each the tape head reads a cell and moves left or right by possibly writing a symbol in the cell. Details of Turing machines can be found in introductory computing theory books, and we use the specific formulation from [6] and details of the dynamic states from [7]. In this formulation, TM M plays the role of program y in the previous section, and UTM plays the role of Φ in "executing" M by emulating its transitions.

While the overall undecidabilty result is same as in the previous section, this formulation is based on using reduction from the haltinng problem and illustrates additional aspects of complex errors. The TM M and its input w are both represented as strings on the tape, and hence they can be corrupted by "memory" faults either at the start of computation (as in the previous section) or dynamically at any time during UTM operation that executes M (similar to the case of a virus [7]). Another source of faults is in the execution of transitions of M by UTM, wherein the contents on the tape, namely the instructions, may be read incorrectly, or may be written incorrectly onto the tape; these abstract data transfer errors, for example, between memory and ALU. Also, the transition operations of UTM may be incorrect, for example, tape head being stuck or moving to an incorrect tape cell, and these faults abstract errors in CPU control units. Thus in this model, the failures in string M are analogous to corruption in program codes, and failures in w or in other tape cells are analogous to data corruption errors. Also, UTM transition and state errors are analogous to the errors in ALU and control units.

A *Resilient TM* M_R takes as input TM M and its w under the failure function f, and halts and produces the same output as M with input w under no failures. As in the previous section the fault function f, changes M_R's input to M_f and w_f dynamically as the input is being read as a result of executional and data corruption.

Theorem 3. *The resilient Turing machine M_R that produces under the failure function f the same output as M with input w under no failures, does not exist under executional errors and data corruption.*

Proof: Consider that M_R exits, which requires that there is a program that detects when M_f does not halt, and intervenes and reproduces the output of M, that is, it solves the halting problem of M_f. We now present the undecidability proof of this halting problem for completeness, and also illustrate some details specific to resilient computations. Let M_R be a TM that produces output yes if M_f produces yes with input M_f, and produces no otherwise. Then, we construct another Turing machine $\bar{M}_R$ that simply flips the output of M_R, namely, it outputs yes if M_f outputs no or does not halt with input M_f, and outputs no if M_f outputs yes with input M_f. Now consider the behavior of $\bar{M}_R$ with input $\bar{M}_R$. If $\bar{M}_R$ outputs yes means M_R outputs no with input $\bar{M}_R$, which is a contradiction. On the other hand, if $\bar{M}_R$ outputs yes it means that M_R outputs no or does not halt on input $\bar{M}_R$, which is again a contradiction. Hence M_R does not exist. □

Notice that in the above proof, to establish the non-existence of M_R it is not necessary to require that it produces the same result as M; instead, it is sufficient to require that it detects non-halting execution of M_f. We note that non-halting computations may be created during the execution of M_f due to errors in UTM transitions, even if M_f does not initially contain infinite loops; this scenario is analogous to the errors due to certain viruses [7], and typically these undecidability proofs require more detailed dynamic versions of TMs. Furthermore, it is possible that they are other complex failures that could lead to undecidable resilient computation problems beyond the halting problem as described next.

Beyond Halting Problems. In the relativization framework, a computing task G is abstracted to be carried out by an oracle to gain insights into the residual underlying complexity. In particular, by using H-oracle that solves the halting problem, a hierarchy of problems is shown to exist, each of which "more unsolvable" than the preceding one (through the so-called the jump process of G, Theorem 4.10 [8]). Let $\mathcal{A}_\mathcal{F}$ denote the original programs that are not resilient under a class of faults $\mathcal{F}$, and let $\mathcal{R}_{\mathcal{A}_\mathcal{F}}$ denote their resilient versions. Let $\mathcal{B}_\mathcal{F}$ denote the original programs that remain non-resilient under H-oracle relativization, and let $\mathcal{R}_{\mathcal{B}_\mathcal{F}}$ denote their resilient versions; it is, however, an open question if faults exit that lead to such non-resilient programs. A set of programs $\mathcal{A}$ is called *non-trivial*, if it is non-empty and there is at least one program that is not contained in it. Based on a relativised version of the Rice theorem (Theorem 8.1, Chapter 16, [8]), the halting problem is one-one reducible to that of checking the membership in a non-trivial class of programs $\mathcal{A}$; this result means that the halting problem is no harder than checking the membership in $\mathcal{A}$. Within the context of resilient computations, if there are programs that belongs to $\mathcal{B}_\mathcal{F}$ and resilient versions of them exist, then $\mathcal{R}_{\mathcal{B}_F}$ is a non-trivial class. Then by Theorem 1, the problem of checking the resilience property of programs in $\mathcal{R}_{\mathcal{B}_\mathcal{F}}$ is undecidable under H-oracle, and is harder than the halting problem. Considering the broad spectrum of potential faults in Exascale systems, $\mathcal{B}_\mathcal{F}$ would be non-empty unless all possible faults are shown to lead to problems no harder than the halting problem; without such proof, undecidable problems persist beyond the halting problem in resilient computations.

4.3   Assertions on Error Corrections

Several computations on Exascale systems involve arithmetic operations, and it would be of interest to prove certain assertions about their outputs when executed on a failure-prone system, such as, a statement that errors will always be corrected. We now show a formulation wherein such assertions may turn out to be very difficult to prove or disprove. Consider a program to compute an integer function $G(x, a) = x^a$ on a failure-prone system wherein x is corrupted at the beginning to a smaller value x_f. Consider a class of error correcting algorithms that only compute integer functions of the form $G(y, a) = y^a$, $y < x$ and make an additive correction to make up the difference such that the correct answer $G(x, a) = G(x_f, a) + G(y, a)$ is produced. However, such guarantee for arbitrary values of $a > 2$ contradicts the Fermat's last theorem that states that the correction term does not exist; furthermore, the proof of this theorem itself remained open for more than 300 years (until resolved by Andrew Wiles in 1995). In particular, assertions that broad classes of errors will be corrected by a proposed method should rule out their dependence on assertions such as the existence of resilient TMs described in Theorem 3.

5   Conclusions

We addressed certain limits on algorithmic solutions to resilient computation problems under a broad class of failures in large computing systems, and showed that no general algorithms exist to achieve resilient computations if the classes of faults are unrestricted. However, effective solutions may be found for certain smaller classes of errors, provided it is established that those are a complete set of faults for the given system. In another direction, the algorithmic solutions may be combined with other co-design methods to overcome the limitations of these purely algorithmic methods. For example, individual components may be monitored using hardware monitors to ensure their proper operation during the execution of codes. Also, hardware replication methods may be used to mask component errors. Software replication and checkpoint methods may be utilized to correct certain faults. Moreover, such methods may be combined to generate ecosystems [18] to support resilient computations using both hardware and software methods. However, it is very critical that such solutions clearly specify their target class of faults. When faults are limited to individual components and are non-sporadic, targeted fault detection algorithms may be designed and executed along with the codes. And, if no faults are detected, confidence measures may be assigned to indicate fault-free execution of codes. However, even under a simple failure model of circuit-level faults, the underlying computational problems, while decidable, can be computationally intractable [13].

This work explores only a very small fraction of the complex problem space of computations that produce correct results on failure-prone computing systems, in particular Exascale systems with complex failures. However, these general undecidability results motivate a deeper study and understanding of various types of faults that can occur in Exascale systems and their taxonomy so that solutions may be appropriately targeted. It would be of future interest to investigate similar computational limits of probabilistic computations that guarantee correct results with a specified probability, or deterministic computations that provide confidence measures for computations under probabilistic faults.

Acknowledgments. This work is funded by the Mathematics of Complex, Distributed, Interconnected Systems Program, Office of Advanced Computing Research, U.S. Department of Energy at Oak Ridge National Laboratory managed by UT-Battelle, LLC for U.S. Department of Energy under Contract No. DE-AC05-00OR22725.

References

1. Cappello, F.: Fault tolerance in petascale/exascale systems: Current knowledge, challenges and research opportunities. Journal of High Performance Computing Applications 23(3), 212–226 (2009)
2. Cappello, F., Geist, A., Gropp, B., Kale, S., Kramer, B., Snir, M.: Towards exascale resilience. Journal of High Performance Computing Applications 23(4), 374–388 (2011)
3. Carbin, M., Misailovic, S., Rinard, M.C.: Verifying quantitaive realiability for programs that execute on unreliable hardware. In: Conference on Object-Oriented Programming Systems, Languages, and Applications, OOPSLA (2013)
4. Chaitin, G.J.: Information, Randomness and Incompleteness, 2nd edn. World Scientific Pub. (1990)
5. Chen, Z.: Online-abft: An online algorithm based fault tolerance scheme for soft error detection in iterative methods. In: ACM SIGPLAN Symp. on Principles and Practice of Parallel Programming (2013)

6. Cohen, D.I.A.: Inroduction to Computer Theory. John Wiley and Sons, Inc (1986)
7. Cohen, F.B.: Computational aspects of computer virus. Computer & Security 8, 325–344 (1989)
8. Davies, M.D., Weyuker, E.J.: Computability, Complexity, and Languages. Academic Press, Inc. (1983)
9. Davies, T., Chen, X.: Correcting soft errors online in lu factorization. In: Symposium on High-Performance Parallel and Distributed Computing (2013)
10. de Kruijif, M., Nomura, S., Sankaralingam, K.: Relax: An architectural framework for software recovery of hardware faults. In: International Symposium on Computer Architecture, ISCA (2010)
11. Dongarra, J.: P Beckman, and et al. The international exascale software roadmap. International Journal of High Performance Computer Applications 25(1) (2011)
12. Erez, M., Jayasena, N., Knight, T.J., Dally, W.J.: Fault tolerance techniques for the merrimac streaming supercomputer. In: International Conference for High Performance Computing, Networking, Storage and Analysis, SC (2005)
13. Fujiwara, H., Toida, S.: The complexity of fault detection problems for combinational logic circuits. IEEE Trans. on Computers C-31(6), 553–560 (1982)
14. Godel, K.: On formally undecidable propositions of principia mathematica and related systems i. Monatshefte fur Math. und Physik 38, 173–198 (1992); Englishe translation by Meltzer, B., published by Dover Publications, Inc. (1992)
15. HPL - a portable implementation of the high-performance linpack benchmark for distributed-memory computers, http://www.netlib.org/benchmark/hpl
16. Huang, Y., Kintala, C.: Software fault tolerance of the application layer. In: Lyu, M.R. (ed.) Software Fault Tolerance, pp. 231–248 (1995)
17. Jia, Y., Luszczek, P., Bosilca, G., Dongarra, J.: Cpu-gpu hybrid bidiagonal reduction with soft error resilience. In: Workshop on Latest Advances in Scalable Algorithms for Large-Scale Systems, ScalA (2013)
18. Li, D., Chen, Z., Wu, P., Vetter, J.S.: Rethinking algorithm-based fault tolerance with a cooperative software-hardware approach. In: ACM/IEEE International Conference for High Performance Computing, Networking, Storage and Analysis (2013)
19. Li, M., Ramachandran, P., Sahoo, S.K., Adve, S.V., Adve, V.S., Zhou, Y.: Understanding the propagation of hard errors to software and implications for resilient system design. In: Architectural Support for Programming Languages and Operating Systems, ASPLOS (2008)
20. Lu, C., Reed, D.A.: Assessing fault sensitivity in mpi applications. In: Proceedings of the 2004 ACM/IEEE Conference on Supercomputing (2004)
21. Rao, N.S.V.: Fault detection in multi-core processors using chaotic maps. In: 3rd Workshop on Fault-Tolerance for HPC at Extreme Scale, FTXS 2013 (2013)
22. Sahoo, S.K., Li, M.-L., Ramachandran, P., Adve, S.V., Adve, V.S., Zhou, Y.: Using likely program invariants to detect hardware errors. In: International Conf. on Dependable Systems and Networks (2008)
23. Turing, A.N.: On computable numbers, with an application to the Entscheidungsproblem. Proc. London Math. Society 42(3,4), 230–265 (1936)
24. Uspensky, V.A.: Godel's Incompleteness Theorem. Mir Publsihers, English translation (1987)
25. Vetter, J.S. (ed.): Contemporary High Performance Computing: From Petascale toward Exascale. Chapman and Hall (2013)

An Automated Performance-Aware Approach to Reliability Transformations

Jacob Lidman[1], Sally A. McKee[1], Daniel J. Quinlan[2], and Chunhua Liao[2]

[1] Department of Computer Science and Engineering
Chalmers University of Technology
Gothenburg, Sweden
{lidman,mckee}@chalmers
[2] Lawrence Livermore National Laboratory
Livermore, CA, USA
{dquinlan,liao6}@llnl.gov

Abstract. Soft errors are expected to increase as feature sizes shrink and the number of cores increases. Redundant execution can be used to cope with such errors. This paper deals with the problem of automatically finding the number of redundant executions needed to achieve a preset reliability threshold. Our method uses geometric programming to calculate the minimal reliability for each instruction while still ensuring that the reliability of the program satisfies a given threshold. We use this to approximate an upper bound on the number of redundant instructions. Using this, we perform a limit study to find the implications of different redundant execution schemes. In particular we notice that the overhead of higher redundancy has serious implications to reliability. We therefore create a scheme where we only perform more executions if needed. Applying the results from our optimization improves reliability by up to 58.25%. We show that it is possible to achieve up to 8% better performance than Triple Modular Redundancy (TMR). We also show cases where our approach is insufficient.

Keywords: High Performance Computing, Fault Tolerance, N-Modular Redundancy, Reliability Optimization.

1 Introduction

Technology trends like shrinking feature sizes and increasing numbers of processor cores on chip make transient faults in hardware increasingly common. These transient faults manifest themselves as bit-flips, and they can originate from external sources (e.g., radiation events) or internal sources (e.g., voltage drops, power supply noise, or leakage). Such faults are termed *soft errors* because they cause no permanent device damage.

As hardware increases in complexity, so does the software that runs on it. Increased complexity results in increased error vulnerability at all levels of the software stack. These problems affect all segments of computing, but they are of particular concern for High Performance Computing (HPC) platforms that

L. Lopes et al. (Eds.): Euro-Par 2014 Workshops, Part I, LNCS 8805, pp. 523–534, 2014.

must continue to perform correctly in the presence of such faults. Architects have long proposed hardware enhancements [1] to improve fault tolerance, but implementing dedicated hardware solutions requires design and verification effort, consumes chip real estate, and increases hardware complexity: at some point the proposed solution itself becomes part of the problem. Furthermore, large-scale supercomputers have historically been built from commodity parts not designed for use at such scales; as such, they lack dedicated hardware support, and adding it "after the fact" is difficult and impractical, if not impossible.

Scalable software solutions could become attractive alternatives, but software approaches can incur high performance overheads. As with dedicated fault-tolerant hardware solutions, the fault-tolerant software itself can potentially introduce new errors, since it adds to the (growing) complexity of the application software. To balance these tradeoffs, we study the problem of automatically introducing fault tolerance in software to correct for hardware-induced faults.

Software-implemented hardware fault tolerance (SIHFT) typically relies on adding some form of redundancy. This could entail re-executing instructions when faults are detected (temporal redundancy) or executing multiple independent instructions and adjudicating on their results (spatial redundancy) [15]. The former approach is typically called checkpointing or replay, and HPC systems have traditionally employed it at multiple levels (e.g., in both the OS and the application). Engelmann et. al [2] argue that as the number of nodes increases, system availability will decrease due to single node failures. Increasing the number of nodes also increases the time it takes to save and restore the state when faults occur. The latter approach is termed N-modular redundancy, or NMR (where N signifies the number of independent instructions). In both cases, the amount of work a processing element needs to perform increases, which increases the opportunities for incurring soft errors. An understanding of the tradeoffs between reliability and performance is necessary to make efficient use of hardware resources while delivering a desired level of resilience.

To understand the motivation for automatically deducing N, consider a program in which an instruction I_X consumes the results produced by an instruction I_Y. The probability that I_X produces the correct result can be increased by either hardening I_X or I_Y. In particular, if executing I_X comes at a lower performance cost than executing I_Y, we may prefer to harden the former. In extending to even more instructions, we need to consider how results propagate: producers with more consumers need more protection. The typical approach to applying NMR using a fixed number of redundant executions for all instructions neglects this issue. If I_X and I_Y are redundantly executed different numbers of times, then we also need a means by which to decide how to propagate results when there are fewer consumers than producers (or vice versa). Here we develop an automated approach to determining an appropriate level of redundancy for each instruction and leave the second problem of deciding the interconnection between producers and consumers for future work. We therefore combine producer results before consumer instructions need them.

2 Related Work

Checkpointing has long been the standard approach to hardening HPC applications. Application and system state are periodically saved at dedicated nodes. In the event of a crash, the application is rolled back to a committed state. Lu et. al. [7] highlight the need to keep multiple checkpoint versions to deal with latent errors: this lets them restart in a stable state from before an error was generated, even if the time between occurrence and detection exceeds a single checkpoint interval. The overheads of checkpoint/restart are expected to cause system utilization to decrease rapidly as systems grow to exascale [3]. Researchers are thus investigating a limited amount of modular redundancy, as it allows some soft errors to be handled by a local node cluster, rather than invoking a global restart [3,4,5]. These approaches use a static number of redundant executions.

Minimizing the performance impact of resilient code is naturally important to the HPC community. Shamsunder et. al. [6] consider the problem of minimizing the number of assertion checks in a multiprocessor environment. They use a CFG-like graph model to represent computation and find an efficient algorithm for the case in which the number of faults is fixed. In contrast, our approach uses a probabilistic description of whether an operation suffers a fault. Misailovic et. al. [8] present an algorithm for replacing operations with less reliable versions while minimizing power consumption and maintaining a preset reliability. Their approach uses a formulation of the optimization problem similar to ours, but they use Integer Linear Programming (ILP) to solve it.

3 Approach

We want to generate code delivering a specified level of reliability while minimizing the performance costs of redundant execution. Our approach is based on the duality between a program's data flow and the probabilistic flow, or how the probability of a state's being correct increases/decreases as it is altered by operations. All data-flow operations increase execution time. Similarly, in the probabilistic interpretation, all non-ideal operations degrade the reliability of producing a correct output. We restrict ourselves to cases where reliability and performance are linearly related. By viewing the operations as constraints on the probabilistic flow, we can find a solution that satisfies a reliability threshold while minimizing performance overheads.

Let a program be represented by a control-flow graph (CFG) $G = \langle V, E \rangle$. Each block $v \in V$ is a sequence of binary ($r_D = I_{op}(r_S, r_T)$) or unary ($r_D = I_{op}(r_S)$) operations over a finite state-space of non-overlapping symbols from a set R. Informally, the semantics of a unary (binary) data-flow operation is that r_D is the destination symbol of an operation I_{op} on symbols r_S (and r_T). We use functions f^V to map a symbol r_x to a variable that symbolically represents the probability that r_x is correct.

Associated with all unary (binary) data-flow operations is a probability $P_{I_{op}}$ that I_{op} computes correctly given correct operands. Although one would generally expect this probability to change with the operand values, it is common to assume that the failure of the operation and its operands are independent [10]. We denote the probability of successful execution prior to optimization as $P_{I_{op}}^{init}$, which we refer to as the *initial execution probability* of I_{op}. Similarly, we refer to the value of $P_{I_{op}}$ following optimization as the *optimal execution probability* of I_{op}. The probability that a binary operation I_{op} produces the correct result (for some f^V) is then given by $P_{I_{op}} f^V(r_S) f^V(r_T)$.

3.1   Optimization Problem

Algorithm 1 translates a program into a set of constraints that reflect the probability that the data flow is correct. The function $newVar()$ returns a fresh variable, and *Constraint(op, v_{Id}, f^V, r_D, S, C)* adds a constraint[1] of the form $1 = v_{Id}^{-1} P_{I_{op}} \prod_{s \in S} f^V(s)$ to C and maps r_D to v_{Id} in f^V. The $P_{I_{op}}$ variables differ from the v_x variables in that we associate a weight w_{op} with the former. The goal of the optimization process is to minimize $\sum_i w_i P_{I_i}$ subject to the constraints generated by the algorithm, namely that each variable $\in [0,1]$, and that the reliability of *important symbols* reach a predefined level $\hat{P}$. Such an optimization problem is called a *geometric programming problem*. The resulting (optimal) P_{I_i} is later used to find an appropriate N for each instruction.

Algorithm 1. OptGen — Constraint Generator

Input: $G = \langle V, E \rangle$ CFG
Input: f_{In}^V — Total map from symbol to variable
Output: C — Set of constraints
; $f_{Map}^V = \{v \mapsto f_{In}^V | v \in V\}$;
foreach $v \in V$ **do**
   $f^V = f_{Map}^V(v)$;
   foreach $I \in v$ **do**
      $v_{Id} = newVar()$;
      case I **is**
         $I_{op}(r_D, r_{S1}, r_{S2})_l \Rightarrow Constrain(op, v_{Id}, f^V, r_D, \{r_{S1}, r_{S2}\}, C)$
         $I_{op}(r_D, r_S) \Rightarrow Constrain(op, v_{Id}, f^V, r_D, \{r_S\}, C)$
      $f^V(r_D) = v_{Id}$;

Let $c > 0, x_i \in \mathbb{R}^+$ and $a_i \in \mathbb{R}$. Then $g_k(\boldsymbol{x}) = c \prod_i x_i^{a_i}$ is a *mononomial* function. Similarly $f_j(\boldsymbol{x}) = \sum_i g_i(\boldsymbol{x})$ is a *posynomial* function. A geometric programming (GP) problem in standard form is given by:

$$\min f_0(x) \text{s.t.} (\forall j \in [1, m] : f_j(x) \leq 1) \wedge (\forall k \in [1, p] : g_k(x) = 1)$$

GP problems can be transformed into a convex equivalent form by taking the logarithm of all posynomials. The resulting functions are called log-sum-exp

---

[1] These constraints impose restrictions on the probabilistic flow of an instruction with destination symbol r_D and source symbols $s \in S$.

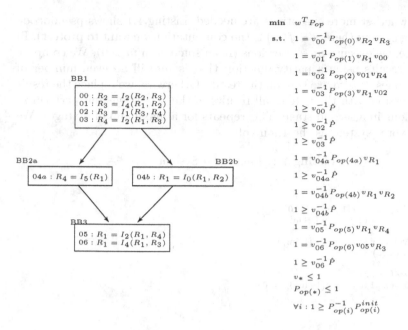

The corresponding equations shown in the figure:

$$\textbf{min} \quad w^T P_{op}$$

$$\textbf{s.t.} \quad 1 = v_{00}^{-1} P_{op(0)}{}^v R_2{}^v R_3$$

$$1 = v_{01}^{-1} P_{op(1)}{}^v R_1{}^v 00$$

$$1 = v_{02}^{-1} P_{op(2)}{}^v 01{}^v R4$$

$$1 = v_{03}^{-1} P_{op(3)}{}^v R_1{}^v 02$$

$$1 \geq v_{00}^{-1} \hat{P}$$

$$1 \geq v_{02}^{-1} \hat{P}$$

$$1 \geq v_{03}^{-1} \hat{P}$$

$$1 = v_{04a}^{-1} P_{op(4a)}{}^v R_1$$

$$1 \geq v_{04a}^{-1} \hat{P}$$

$$1 = v_{04b}^{-1} P_{op(4b)}{}^v R_1{}^v R_2$$

$$1 \geq v_{04b}^{-1} \hat{P}$$

$$1 = v_{05}^{-1} P_{op(5)}{}^v R_1{}^v R4$$

$$1 = v_{06}^{-1} P_{op(6)}{}^v 05{}^v R3$$

$$1 \geq v_{06}^{-1} \hat{P}$$

$$v_* \leq 1$$

$$P_{op(*)} \leq 1$$

$$\forall i : 1 \geq P_{op(i)}^{-1} P_{op(i)}^{init}$$

BB1

00 : $R_2 = I_2(R_2, R_3)$
01 : $R_3 = I_4(R_1, R_2)$
02 : $R_3 = I_1(R_3, R_4)$
03 : $R_4 = I_2(R_1, R_3)$

BB2a

04a : $R_4 = I_5(R_1)$

BB2b

04b : $R_1 = I_0(R_1, R_2)$

BB3

05 : $R_1 = I_2(R_1, R_4)$
06 : $R_1 = I_4(R_1, R_3)$

Fig. 1. Example CFG and Corresponding GP Optimization Problem

functions (i.e., $y = log(\sum_i e_i^x)$). Off-the-shelf solvers [9] can find the minimum of a GP problem in convex form efficiently even for large numbers of variables. Note that the convex form of a GP problem of only monomial functions, as in our case, is a linear programming problem.

As an example, consider the CFG in Figure 3.1. Variables $\{v_{R_0}, v_{R_1}, v_{R_2}, v_{R_3}, v_{R_4}\}$ denote the probability that symbols R_0, R_1, R_2, R_3 and R_4, respectively, are correct at the entry of a block. The corresponding GP problem is given to the right. We add constraints (for symbols that have been updated in the block) to enforce the requirement that the probability of correctness reaches at least $\hat{P}$. The reliability of an NMR system with majority voting as the adjudication mechanism and a component reliability of p is given by $\sum_{j=n+1}^{N} \binom{N}{j} p^j (1-p)^{N-j}$ (where $N = 2n + 1$). Using this we calculate the necessary number of redundant instructions (with initial and optimal execution probabilities p_i and p_o, respectively) by finding the lowest N such that $p_o \leq \sum_{j=n+1}^{N} \binom{N}{j} p_i^j (1-p_i)^{N-j}$.

3.2   1.mn Voter

The number of redundant executions our approach recommends can be quite high if $\hat{P}$ is high and/or P_{op} is low. As these numbers may represent pessimistic estimates of the number of situations in which faults occur, we introduce a voter system that adds redundant executions only as needed.

The voting system consists of n stages (for some $n \in \mathbb{N} - \{0\}$). Each stage includes a sequence of redundant executions followed by an assertion that tries to establish whether more executions are needed. Listing 1.1 shows pseudocode for the voting system (here $x = f(...)$ is the computation we want to protect). In the first stage, we execute $m + 1$ versions (from some even $m > 0$). We compare these $m + 1$ results using a parity function that is zero iff an even number of operands are ones. If zero, we vote on the result. Otherwise, we replace the result of the first version with the vote of all results in the first stage and perform m more executions in a second stage. This repeats for a maximum of n stages. We refer to this voter system as the 1.mn voter.

Listing 1.1. 1.mn Voter System

```
x[1] = f (...)
...
x[1+m] = f (...)
IF (PARITY(x[1],...,x[1+m]) = 0)
    res = VOTE(x[1],...,x[1+m])
ELSE {
    x[1] = VOTE(x[1],...,x[1+m])
    x[2] = f (...)
    ...
    x[1+m] = f (...)
    IF (PARITY(x[1],...,x[1+m]) = 0)
        ...
    ELSE
        ...
}
```

4   Evaluation

To compare our approach to assigning a fixed number of redundant executions, we use the matrix kernels listed in Table 1. We choose these kernels to show benefits and weaknesses of our approach rather than based on application domain.

Table 1. Evaluation Kernels

Name	Description	Matrix Size
Approx-log	Approximates the logarithm of fix-point numbers in the range [0,1]	5×5
Determinant	Computes the determinant by Laplace expansion recursively	5×5
Gaussian	Implements convolution with a 9×9 Gaussian smoothing kernel	10×10
Bubblesort	Implements Median filtering using 3×3 bubblesort sorting network	10×10
Mincomp	Implements Median filtering using 3×3 minimum comparison sorting network	10×10
Mintime	Implements Median filtering using 3×3 minimum time sorting network	10×10

4.1   Experimental Setup

In our experiments we use the gem5 simulator [14] to model an in-order 32-bit MIPS processor. We modify the simulator to include a pseudo-random number generator for flipping bits in the inputs of the integer ALU in the execution stage. Faults are only injected into instructions that belong to the application. Instructions that do not involve ALU units (e.g., memory loads/stores or moving data between registers) are considered ideal, since effective hardware fault-tolerance methods exist for these cases (e.g., redundant buses or error-correcting codes).

The random variable controlling which ALU unit to zap is exponentially distributed with the unit's normalized area and a constant λ_k (i.e., $1 - e^{-\lambda_k \frac{Area_{unit}}{Area_{ALU}}}$). The flip probability of each unit is given in Table 3. The initial successful execution probabilities, $P_{I_{op}}^{init}$, similarly use these probabilities. We vary the constant λ_k across experiments to conduct a limit study. Which input bit to flip (of an ALU unit) is uniformly distributed. To obtain area numbers we synthesize an in-house MIPS implementation with the Synopsys Design Compiler using a commercial 65 nm low-power process technology. This implementation models a five-stage MIPS R3000-like processor.

Accessing pages that have not been allocated makes the OS terminate the process. This is a common case when injecting faults [15]. To avoid such terminations, we change the gem5 virtual memory system so that pages are allocated before we read/write memory. Reading from an invalid memory address then returns a non-deterministic value. This concept has been called *failure-oblivious computing* [16]. With these changes, an invalid memory access can be handled with error-correction logic, as opposed to terminating the execution.

4.2 Methodology

We compile our kernels with GCC 4.0.0[2] and optimization level 0 (-O0) to include DWARF debugging information (-g). We analyze the binaries with ROSE [11] to produce a GP problem, as described in Section 3. We require that the probability of correctness of each 32-bit register assigned in the block reaches at least $\hat{P} = 0.99^3$. For the sake of demonstration, we use unit weights for all ALU instructions except div/mul, for which we use 10 (since they are typically about an order of magnitude higher in performance cost). We use CVX 2.0 beta [12,13] in MATLAB R2012 to solve the GP problem and return the resulting optimal execution probabilities to ROSE. For each pair of initial and optimal execution probabilities we approximate an upper bound on the number of redundant executions, N, for each instruction. Since ROSE::FTTransform [15] operates on source code, we use the DWARF sourceline-instruction address mapping to transfer this number back to the source level. Since source lines map to multiple instructions, we use the maximum N of all instructions mapping to a particular source line. We use a $1.2N_i$ voter for each source line, where N_i versions were recommended if $N_i > 1$. For $N_i = 1$ we do not apply any transformation. Table 2 shows the values of N for each kernel.

For each kernel we use ROSE::FTTransform to produce two sets of versions. The first set contains the results of applying each kernel to a transformer in which we use 3MR, 5MR, and 7MR versions with majority voting. The second set uses a $1.2n$ voter, where n is set to $\{2,3,4\}$ to produce versions called 1.2-2, 1.2-3, and 1.2-4. These two sets and the set of versions produced by our

---

[2] This particular toolchain is supported by gem5's MIPS simulator in system-call emulation mode.

[3] We arbitrarily choose this value for the purposes of our limit study.

Table 2. Distributions of N for All Source Lines of Each Kernel

	λ_k					
	1.0		**0.1**		**0.01**	
Name	$\tilde{N}$	**N Values**	$\tilde{N}$	**N Values**	$\tilde{N}$	**N Values**
Approx-Log	3	{1,3,7}	3	{1,3}	3	{1,3}
Determinant	3	{1,3,7,9,23}	3	{1,3,5,9}	3	{1,3}
Gaussian	31	{1,3,19,23,27,31}	13	{1,3,9,11,13}	9	{1,3,5,7,9}
Bubblesort	3	{1,3,5}	3	{1,3}	3	{1,3}
Mincomp	7	{1,3,7,9}	5	{1,3,5,7}	3	{1,3,5}
Mintime	7	{1,3,7,9,11}	5	{1,3,5,7}	3	{1,3,5}

Table 3. Flip probabilities for ALU units

ALU Unit	P(flip)
Add/Sub	1-0.998766
Mul/Div	1-0.953567
Comparator	1-0.999705
And	1-0.999799
Or	1-0.999778
Xor	1-0.999685
Nor	1-0.999852
Shift	1-0.998343

optimizer (called OPT) and the original kernel (called Orig), collectively make up the kernel versions considered in this work.

For each kernel version we then perform an experiment consisting of 2000 runs with $\lambda_k \in \{1, 0.1, 0.01\}$. We choose the values of λ_k s.t. reliability results of the evaluations of the original kernel versions map to the range [0%, 100%]. Each run is classified as correct or incorrect. The incorrect class includes runs that time out (meaning the kernel did not complete within one minute[4]), encounter miscellaneous errors (e.g., control-flow errors or invalid syscall requests), and terminate with incorrect results (i.e., silent data corruptions). For each experiment we use the percentage of runs that are classified as correct to measure reliability. Similarly, we compute the median of the number of executed CPU cycles (as reported by gem5) of all correct runs, which we use to represent performance.

Table 4. Reliability Results for Each Kernel Version at Each λ_k (1, 0.1, 0.01)

Version	Kernel								
	Approx-Log			**Determinant**			**Gaussian**		
	λ_k=1.0	λ_k=0.1	λ_k=0.01	λ_k=1.0	λ_k=0.1	λ_k=0.01	λ_k=1.0	λ_k=0.1	λ_k=0.01
Orig	0.00%	29.85%	80.60%	0.20%	39.50%	84.40%	0.00%	0.60%	44.65%
3MR	4.20%	69.30%	92.05%	0.80%	56.40%	87.45%	2.20%	72.15%	92.00%
5MR	0.15%	34.70%	67.60%	0.35%	49.30%	82.40%	0.00%	36.15%	66.80%
7MR	0.00%	1.50%	21.80%	0.05%	23.10%	61.90%	0.00%	1.60%	20.15%
OPT	5.30%	69.90%	91.05%	1.10%	59.00%	90.75%	0.00%	0.00%	0.00%
1.2-2	3.40%	66.90%	90.25%	0.95%	55.90%	88.70%	4.40%	73.10%	91.95%
1.2-3	3.50%	67.40%	90.40%	1.20%	56.90%	89.25%	3.55%	74.95%	92.15%
1.2-4	3.70%	67.55%	90.50%	0.90%	59.20%	90.85%	4.90%	72.85%	91.30%

Version	Kernel								
	Mincomp			**Mintime**			**Bubblesort**		
	λ_k=1.0	λ_k=0.1	λ_k=0.01	λ_k=1.0	λ_k=0.1	λ_k=0.01	λ_k=1.0	λ_k=0.1	λ_k=0.01
Orig	0.00%	21.65%	76.30%	0.00%	25.25%	76.65%	0.00%	19.60%	73.20%
3MR	9.95%	79.95%	94.30%	11.45%	79.95%	94.40%	8.65%	77.45%	93.15%
5MR	1.45%	58.75%	83.60%	1.65%	58.25%	82.85%	0.45%	48.65%	77.45%
7MR	0.00%	18.45%	51.10%	0.00%	7.65%	38.75%	0.00%	8.30%	36.80%
OPT	12.95%	79.90%	94.35%	12.30%	79.45%	95.10%	9.90%	76.75%	92.60%
1.2-2	11.60%	81.50%	95.25%	11.45%	79.95%	95.20%	11.15%	75.15%	93.25%
1.2-3	12.95%	80.10%	94.15%	12.20%	80.45%	95.40%	10.85%	77.00%	92.85%
1.2-4	11.75%	78.20%	94.90%	12.20%	79.35%	95.30%	7.70%	75.40%	92.30%

---

[4] Normal program execution takes less then ten seconds for all kernels.

4.3   Results

Table 4 shows the reliability results for each version (rows) and each kernel/λ_k (columns). As expected, results improve with decreasing λ_k. At $\lambda_k = 0.01$, 44.65-84.4% of all runs using the original version complete with correct results. For the NMR versions, increasing N does not improve reliability in our evaluations. This is due to the increased fault probability of the majority voter as N increases. The number of clauses for $N = 3, 5$, and 7 is 3, 10, and 35, respectively. The 1.2n versions and the 3MR version achieve similar reliabilities. With the exception of the Gaussian kernel, the versions produced by our approach achieve among the best reliabilities for all experiments. We discuss the results of the Gaussian kernel more in Section 5.

Table 5 shows the performance results. An "-" entry indicates that no execution terminated with correct results. Performance stays somewhat constant over all λ_k for all versions except OPT. This is expected for the original and NMR versions but surprising for the 1.2n versions. These results indicate that we tend to end up in the same stage independent of λ_k. The fact that performance cost decreases for OPT can be understood by looking at Table 2: the number of executions used decreases for decreasing λ_k. These numbers should not be used to assess general performance overhead of redundant execution. Our earlier work [15] shows that we need to hide memory latencies to keep the overhead low. This requires optimizations such as SIMDization and versioning to make use of parallel resources.

Figure 2 shows the geometric means of the reliability and performance results for all runs, excluding those of the Gaussian kernel. For each version, OPT achieves marginally better reliability than the other resilient versions. At the same time, if λ_k is sufficiently low, its performance can be even better then 3MR (which indiscriminately adds redundancy in cases where our approach does not). For high λ_k the execution overhead is quite high.

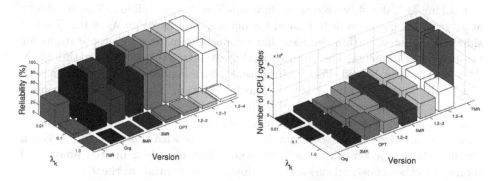

Fig. 2. Geometric Mean of Reliability (left) and Performance (right) Results

Table 5. Median CPU Cycles for Each Kernel Version at Each λ_k

Version	Kernel								
	Approx-Log			Determinant			Gaussian		
	$\lambda_k=1.0$	$\lambda_k=0.1$	$\lambda_k=0.01$	$\lambda_k=1.0$	$\lambda_k=0.1$	$\lambda_k=0.01$	$\lambda_k=1.0$	$\lambda_k=0.1$	$\lambda_k=0.01$
Orig	-	89380	89380	64198	63986	63986	-	107258	107192
3MR	226534	225818	225738	107406	106966	106900	313871	308869	308337
5MR	479330	478074	477918	200758	200898	200832	-	1913594	1912978
7MR	-	2031302	2031017	421331	520667	520535	-	6223762	6223072
OPT	358369	219939	219859	419488	197007	101368	-	-	-
1.2-2	399996	398956	398862	159122	158592	158496	1304283	1297262	1296546
1.2-3	576538	575591	575501	207896	207761	207671	3158828	3153470	3152882
1.2-4	750603	750004	749956	255271	256290	256298	4197134	4194096	4193656

Version	Kernel								
	Mincomp			Mintime			Bubblesort		
	$\lambda_k=1.0$	$\lambda_k=0.1$	$\lambda_k=0.01$	$\lambda_k=1.0$	$\lambda_k=0.1$	$\lambda_k=0.01$	$\lambda_k=1.0$	$\lambda_k=0.1$	$\lambda_k=0.01$
Orig	-	124310	124310	-	135194	135194	-	178702	178702
3MR	2250657	2249985	2249901	2250653	2249989	2249901	3689882	3689220	3689136
5MR	6855928	6854958	6854864	6855988	6854958	6854866	9523724	9522746	9522652
7MR	-	21741416	21741266	-	30197146	30197008	-	30197151	30197008
OPT	6959278	4671986	2078021	8224106	5503566	2890332	3727170	3266087	3266005
1.2-2	5231408	5233664	5233950	5247188	5249624	5249954	7188489	7190031	7190215
1.2-3	7674798	7686217	7687520	7714317	7726648	7728076	10515264	10525612	10526772
1.2-4	10053976	10080261	10082966	10131521	10157786	10160536	13786320	13811295	13813971

5   Discussion

We have introduced an algorithm to minimize the number of redundant executions for instructions in a CFG. This algorithm considers both the reliability of the instruction and its performance cost, and the surrounding framework represents a promising first cut at an automated solution. Nonetheless, we find that our current algorithm can be overly conservative in that it calculates the maximum number of redundant executions, which may, in turn, degrade reliability. For instance, in Section 4, the OPT version of the Gaussian kernel achieves a 0% reliability. This kernel makes heavy use of multiplication, which is our most unreliable operation due to the area of the multiplier.

Looking at Table 4, we see that Gaussian is not very resilient. The reliability at $\lambda_k = 0.01$ is comparable to that of the determinant kernel at $\lambda_k = 0.1$. Table 2 shows that our algorithm deduces that we need as many as 31 replications for most of the statements. The 1.mn voter that we introduced to cope with high N does not have the desired effect in this case. Performing redundant execution with just NMR, on the other hand, is not a feasible solution. The overhead of majority voting as N increases becomes very high (for both performance and reliability). This example highlights the need to consider not just the probability of correct execution but also the uncertainty that we associate with this probability. When the uncertainty becomes too high, we could then include a limited amount of replay (or other construction) to bring down the potential overhead.

We have not considered the case of optimizing performance/reliability over the entire acyclic CFG (but rather over each basic block individually). For this we would need to combine contributions from mutually exclusive control-flow paths. An affine join function could be used for this, but then we would need to include posynomial equality constraints, and geometric programming does not allow such constraints, in general. Allowing these makes it a *signomial programming* [9] problem, for which no efficient optimization algorithm is known to exist.

Although we show benefits over 3MR, the improvements are marginal with our current approach. Nonetheless, the fact that our approach considers more variables makes it applicable to more complex environments (for instance, where only a subset of the instructions are faulty). We have not investigated such scenarios because the current study has highlighted the importance of considering how the uncertainty of our probabilistic flow calculations increases with the number of instructions in the section of the CFG we target. In particular, we have shown that schemes that only add redundant executions as needed can outperform NMR schemes.

6   Conclusion

One problem in using a redundant execution scheme is how to find the number of executions to use for each instruction. We show an algorithm for approximating this number while taking into account performance costs. Our evaluations show that it is possible to achieve good reliability while still minimizing performance overheads. We improve reliability by up to 58% compared to the original versions of our benchmarks. The median performance cost is up to 8% lower then triple modular redundancy.

Our results vary considerably with the assumed probability of an instruction's successful execution. If this probability is low, we conservatively recommend a high number of redundant versions. Adding more redundancy may be harmful, since it gives the faulty environment more changes to alter the semantics of the execution. Determining this probability is of course a big problem in itself. Although our $1.mn$ voter relieves some of these problems, it does not represent a general solution. Our results however show that reliability/performance improve if we only execute versions as needed to cope with this uncertainty. We believe a better optimization algorithm would factor this uncertainty into decisions.

Acknowledgments. The authors thank Alen Bardizbanyan and Kasyab Subramaniyan for helping to synthesize the MIPS processor.

References

1. Cappello, F., Geist, A., Gropp, B., Kale, L., Kramer, B., Snir, M.: Toward Exascale Resilience. International Journal of High Performance Computing Applications 23(4), 374–388 (2009)
2. Engelmann, C., Ong, H.H., Scott, S.L.: The Case for Modular Redundancy in Large-Scale High Performance Computing Systems. In: Proc. IASTED International Conference on Parallel and Distributed Computing and Networks (PDCN), pp. 189–194 (February 2009), Related work

3. Li, D., Lee, S., Vetter, J.S.: Evaluating the viability of application-driven cooperative CPU/GPU fault detection. In: an Mey, D., et al. (eds.) Euro-Par 2013. LNCS,
vol. 8374, pp. 670–679. Springer, Heidelberg (2014)
4. Fiala, D., Mueller, F., Engelmann, C., Riesen, R., Ferreira, K., Brightwell, R.: Detection and Correction of Silent Data Corruption for Large-scale High-performance
Computing. In: Proceedings of the International Conference on High Performance
Computing, Networking, Storage and Analysis, pp. 78:1–78:12 (2012)
5. Elliott, J., Kharbas, K., Fiala, D., Mueller, F., Ferreira, K., Engelmann, C.: Combining Partial Redundancy and Checkpointing for HPC. In: Proceedings of the
International Conference on Distributed Computing Systems (ICDCS 2012), pp.
615–626 (2012)
6. Shamsunder, R., Rosenkrantz, D.J., Ravi, S.S.: Exploiting Data Flow Information
in Algorithm-Based Fault Tolerance. In: Proc. International Symposium on Fault-
Tolerant Computing (FTCS), pp. 280–289 (June 1993)
7. Lu, G., Zheng, Z., Chien, A.A.: When is Multi-version Checkpointing Needed? In:
Proc. 3rd Workshop on Fault-Tolerance for HPC at Extreme Scale (FTXS), pp.
49–56 (June 2013)
8. Misailovic, S., Carbin, M., Achour, S., Zichao, Q., Rinard, M.: Reliability-Aware
Optimization of Approximate Computational Kernels with Rely. MIT-CSAIL-TR-
2014-001 (January 2014)
9. Boyd, S., Kim, S.-J., Vandenberghe, L., Hassibi, A.: A tutorial on geometric programming. Optimization and Engineering 8(1), 67–127 (2007)
10. Carbin, M., Misailovic, S., Rinard, M.C.: Verifying Quantitative Reliability for
Programs That Execute on Unreliable Hardware. In: Proc. SIGPLAN International
Conference on Object Oriented Programming Systems Languages & Applications
(OOPSLA), pp. 33–52 (October 2013)
11. Quinlan, D., Liao, C.: The ROSE Source-to-Source Compiler Infrastructure. In:
Cetus Users and Compiler Infrastructure Workshop, with the International Conference on Parallel Architectures and Compilation Techniques, PACT (October
2011)
12. Grant, M., Boyd, S.: CVX: Matlab Software for Disciplined Convex Programming,
version 2.0 beta (June 2014), http://cvxr.com/cvx
13. Grant, M.C., Boyd, S.P.: Graph Implementations for Nonsmooth Convex Programs. In: Blondel, V., Boyd, S., Kimura, H. (eds.) Recent Advances in Learning
and Control. LNCIS, vol. 371, pp. 95–110. Springer, Heidelberg (2008)
14. Binkert, N., Beckmann, B., Black, G., Reinhardt, S.K., Saidi, A., Basu, A., Hest-
ness, J., Hower, D.R., Krishna, T., Sardashti, S., Sen, R., Sewell, K., Shoaib, M.,
Vaish, N., Hill, M.D., Wood, D.A.: The Gem5 Simulator. Computer Architecture
News 39(2), 1–7 (2011)
15. Lidman, J., Quinlan, D.J., Liao, C., McKee, S.A.: ROSE:FTTransform – A Source-
to-Source Translation Framework for Exascale Fault-Tolerance Research. In: Proc.
2nd Workshop on Fault-Tolerance for HPC at Extreme Scale (FTXS), pp. 1–6
(June 2012)
16. Rinard, M., Cadar, C., Dumitran, D., Roy, D.M., Leu, T., Beebee Jr., W.S.: Enhancing Server Availability and Security Through Failure-Oblivious Computing.
In: Proc. 6th Symposium on Operating Systems Design & Implementation (OSDI),
p. 21 (Decedmber 2004)

The External Recovery Problem*

Arkadiusz Danilecki, Mateusz Hołenko, Anna Kobusińska, and Piotr Zierhoffer

Institute of Computing Science
Poznań University of Technology, Poland
{adanilecki,akobusinska,mholenko}@cs.put.poznan.pl

Abstract. We consider an external recovery problem, where a system is divided into autonomous subsystems which can be recovered only by the means of logging the messages exchanged between the subsystems. The question follows: what restrictions to the subsystem's autonomy are required to make the external recovery possible? We present example solutions affecting different aspects of system's independence.

Keywords: Message logging, fault tolerance, checkpointing, distributed system.

1 Introduction

The probability of a node crash in a modern, large-scale computing systems, consisting of hundreds of thousands of nodes, comes near certainty. One approach is to divide the system into subsystems, and to isolate the crash effects within a subsystem where the crash occurred. Then, a coordinated checkpointing can be used within a subsystem [13], while to prevent crash effects from spreading, the messages exchanged with processes from different subsystems could be logged in a pessimistic manner. An interesting theoretical question arises: under which conditions a subsystem could be recovered *only* by logging the messages exchanged with other subsystems – by what we call an *external recovery*.

There is an unspoken assumption that all parts of the system are under control of one organization, that they cooperate freely and that they expose all information necessary for the recovery. These assumptions may not hold in the future, when subsystems may be more independent. Future cooperating components involved in distributed computation may be unwilling to restrict their independence by e.g. revealing the information commonly assumed to be available for the message logging protocols. Nevertheless, if the subsystem is to be recovered using external message logging, it can't completely retain its independence. This observation spurred the question: *What must be minimally known about a system and what minimal restrictions must be imposed on a system behavior, in order to make the external recovery possible?*

This paper is a first step in the direction of solving this puzzle, by identifying the problem, the possible trade-offs, and by presenting two example approaches

---

* This work was supported by the Polish National Science Center under Grant No. DEC-2011/03/D/ST6/01331.

L. Lopes et al. (Eds.): Euro-Par 2014 Workshops, Part I, LNCS 8805, pp. 535–546, 2014.

to restricting system independence. While we find the problem interesting from purely theoretical reasons, we are convinced that it will have practical applications, for example in creation of recovery protocols for federated clusters [16].

Our paper is organized as follows. Section 2 introduces the system model. Sections 3 and 4 present solutions restricting different aspects of a subsystem's independence. Section 5 discusses related work. Section 6 concludes the paper.

2 System Model

We consider a distributed system $\mathcal{S} = \mathcal{P} \cup \mathcal{W} \cup \mathcal{I}$, where $\mathcal{P} = \{P_1, P_2, \ldots P_n\}$ is a set of n processes, $\mathcal{W}$ denotes external world, and $\mathcal{I}$ is an *interceptor*. Intuitively, if $\mathcal{S}$ would be a set of clusters, then $\mathcal{P}$ would denote processes in a particular cluster under a consideration and $\mathcal{W}$ would consist from processes from all other clusters (for simplicity treated as singular entity). Interceptor $\mathcal{I}$ is a layer responsible for logging the messages exchanged between $\mathcal{P}$ and $\mathcal{W}$. The processes in $\mathcal{P}$ communicate via message passing using asynchronous reliable FIFO links. In addition, $\mathcal{W}$ may send messages to any $P_i \in \mathcal{P}$ (hereafter denoted as *inputs*) and any $P_i \in \mathcal{P}$ may send messages to $\mathcal{W}$ (*outputs*). The inputs and outputs always pass through $\mathcal{I}$ where they may be inspected, delayed, discarded, or stored in a stable storage. We stress that the interceptor is just a theoretical construct. $\mathcal{I}$ may be implemented as a single node, many independent nodes, or even as logging mechanism atop processes in $\mathcal{P}$.

Processes have states. At any given time t, a sum of states of all processes in $\mathcal{P}$ forms a global state of $\mathcal{P}$. We understand the consistent state of $\mathcal{P}$ in a usual way [7]. Processes execute programs, generating *events*. Each event changes the process state. Of special interest are *send* and *receive events*, produced when process sends or receives a message. For brevity, a receive event of an input will be called an *input event*. Processes in $\mathcal{P}$ are initially passive; they become active only as an effect of receive event. It follows that absent inputs, processes in $\mathcal{P}$ are continuously passive. Each time a process P_i becomes active, it produces a finite sequence of events. Each event changes P_i's state and may involve sending messages to some $P_j \in \mathcal{P}$ or to $\mathcal{W}$.

History $H(t)$ at a global time t is a set of events produced by all processes in $\mathcal{P}$ until t, partially ordered by Lamport's happened-before $\mapsto$ relation [12]. It follows that the global state of $\mathcal{P}$ at t is a result of $H(t)$. In addition, there is a relation of *true dependency* $\xrightarrow{true}$ between the events [24][1], and we say that if $e^j \xrightarrow{true} e^k$, then e^k was *truly caused* by e^j. A *session* S of an input M is a set of all events truly caused by the receipt of M, ordered by $\mapsto$ relation. Each event in a history H belongs to some session. We assume sessions do not overlap and are of finite size. A *reaction* to an input M is a set of outputs forwarded by the $\mathcal{I}$ to $\mathcal{W}$, whose send events belong to session of M.

---

[1] Lamport's relation reflects system point of view; that is, if $e \mapsto e'$, system must assume that indeed e' was caused by e, and without e, e' would not happen. True dependency reflects real, logical dependencies resulting from application logic. See also always-happened-before relation in [21].

For any $P_i \in \mathcal{P}$, given the P_i state, only some events are possible. If only one event is possible, then this event is deterministic. Otherwise, it is non-deterministic. In a piecewise-deterministic (PWD) model, all the non-deterministic events (usually, only the receive events) can be identified, and their *determinants* (the information needed to replay the event) can be stored [23]. Given some initial state of P_i, always the same state of P_i is produced when a sequence of events is generated from a given set of determinants. In a send-deterministic [6] model, informally, the order of receive events does not influence the send events.

The processes in $\mathcal{P}$ may crash, losing their state. In that case we assume all processes within $\mathcal{P}$ restart from an initial, consistent state, but the algorithms may be extended to $\mathcal{P}$ periodically taking consistent checkpoints (e.g. by finding out which messages do not have to be replayed during the recovery). A perfect failure detector is available, notifying $\mathcal{I}$ when all processes in $\mathcal{P}$ are restarted. We assume $\mathcal{I}$ and $\mathcal{W}$ do not crash, crashes are rare and no crash happens during a recovery; this is a reasonable assumption, if the size of a $\mathcal{P}$ is small enough (e.g. within a range of hundreds, rather than thousands of processes). The recovery is correct if the reaction to any input in a history with the crash and recovery events would be possible in some history without crash events.

There exists a mechanism discarding messages sent before, but received after the crash, including inputs sent to $\mathcal{P}$ by interceptor, e.g. by using epoch numbers. Let all processes in $\mathcal{P}$ and $\mathcal{I}$ maintain epoch number e incremented after each restart (note $\mathcal{I}$ and $\mathcal{P}$ will have always identical epoch numbers). Each message (including inputs) is assigned a current epoch number. Processes ignore all messages with epoch smaller than e.

3 Restricting the Behavior Only

The following constraints may be imposed on $\mathcal{P}$'s autonomy: its behavior (set of possible histories) may be restricted a priori; the information about the behavior (the history of the computation) and about the $\mathcal{P}$'s structure (e.g. how many processes are in $\mathcal{P}$) may be exposed to $\mathcal{I}$; finally, processes in $\mathcal{P}$ may have to cooperate with $\mathcal{I}$ during the recovery (e.g. exchanging control messages with $\mathcal{I}$).

Intuitively, the external recovery is possible if $\mathcal{P}$ can be treated (from the point of view of $\mathcal{I}$) as a single, piecewise-deterministic (PWD) process. If processes in $\mathcal{P}$ are piecewise-deterministic, then from the definition of PWD we conclude that unless the determinants of non-deterministic events are exposed to $\mathcal{I}$, and unless $\mathcal{P}$ cooperates with $\mathcal{I}$ during the recovery, $\mathcal{P}$ cannot be externally recovered. From this we can see that either the system behavior must be restricted (e.g. it have to follow more restrictions than piecewise-determinism), and/or it must expose more information about its behavior and the structure. Algorithms which do not follow either of those methods, must be incorrect.

Remark 1. If $\mathcal{P}$ does not expose internal information and does not cooperate with $\mathcal{I}$, and if processes in $\mathcal{P}$ work under a PWD model, then external recovery of $\mathcal{P}$ is impossible.

Variables used in a description:
   queue<messages> Q :: *Queue of input messages*
   queue<messages> L :: *Queue of messages sent to* $\mathcal{P}$
   queue<messages> Out :: *Queue of output messages*
   enum<ready,busy> *state* $\leftarrow$ **ready**   :: *State of the interceptor*
   integer *count*   :: *Number of outputs for last input*

Upon receiving message M **Upon receiving message** M^o **from** $\mathcal{P}$ **at** $\mathcal{I}$
      from $\mathcal{W}$ **at** $\mathcal{I}$
1: $Q \leftarrow Q \cup M$ :: M *is appended at*   8: **if** $M \notin Out$ **then**
   the end of Q 9: $Out \leftarrow Out \cup M^o$
                                                    10:     **forward** M^o **to** $\mathcal{W}$
When $Q \neq \emptyset \wedge state = $ **ready**   11: **else**
2: *state* $\leftarrow$ **busy**   12:   **discard** M^o :: *discarding*
3: $M \leftarrow Q.front$ *duplicates*
4: *count* $\leftarrow 0$ 13: **end if**
5: **send** M **to** $\mathcal{P}$ 14: **increment** *count*
                                                    15: **if** *count* $= k_M$ **then**
Upon detecting a restart in $\mathcal{P}$ **at** $\mathcal{I}$ 16: $M \leftarrow Q.front$
                                                    17:     $Q \leftarrow Q \setminus M$
   :: *Event is fired when restart of*   18:   *state* $\leftarrow$ **ready**
   $\mathcal{P}$ *is finished*   19:   **if** $M \notin L$ **then**
6: $Q \leftarrow L \cup Q$ :: *The* $\cup$ *operator* 20: $L \leftarrow L \cup M$
   prepends L *to* Q 21:   **end if**
7: *state* $\leftarrow$ **ready**   22: **end if**

Fig. 1. Algorithm 1, requiring no cooperation with $\mathcal{P}$, restricting $\mathcal{P}$'s behavior only

We will now demonstrate the possibility of external recovery with restricting only one aspect of $\mathcal{P}$'s independence, with no cooperation between $\mathcal{I}$ and $\mathcal{P}$ during the recovery and without requiring $\mathcal{P}$ to expose any information to $\mathcal{I}$. As a reminder, we require that after a single crash in $\mathcal{P}$, all processes restart and $\mathcal{I}$ is notified by failure detector restart is completed.

We impose the following restrictions on the $\mathcal{P}$'s behavior: (R1) Within each session, processes in $\mathcal{P}$ are send-deterministic. Note (R1) applies only to receive events within each session, not to input events. (R2) After k_M-th message in a reaction to input M is sent to $\mathcal{I}$, no events truly caused by M may occur in $\mathcal{P}$, where $k_M > 0$ is known a priori and may differ for every M.

The interceptor $\mathcal{I}$ maintains three FIFO message queues Q, L and Out, and a variable *state*, set initially to *ready* (fig. 1). Arriving inputs are appended at the end of Q. While in *ready* state, $\mathcal{I}$ continuously checks a condition $Q \neq \emptyset$. If $Q \neq \emptyset$, *state* is set to *busy* and $\mathcal{I}$ sends the message M in front of Q to $\mathcal{P}$. When an output M^o arrives at $\mathcal{I}$, it is discarded if it is already in an output queue Out, otherwise $\mathcal{I}$ stores M^o in Out before forwarding it to $\mathcal{W}$. If this is k_M-th output in reaction to M, M is removed from Q and appended to L queue. Finally, $\mathcal{I}$ sets *state* to *ready*. When a crash and restart of $\mathcal{P}$ is detected, interceptor prepends all messages in L at the beginning of Q and sets *state* to *ready*. Processes in $\mathcal{P}$ do not distinguish between messages sent during normal operation or recovery.

Theorem 1. *For any history H with a crash, the recovery of $\mathcal{P}$ is correct*

Proof. From R1), the send events are determined only by the ordering of the input events in H and the initial state. The algorithm ensures that after receiving an input M, new input may arrive to $\mathcal{P}$ only when $\mathcal{I}$ receives k_M outputs. From R2), at that point the session of M has ended and the processes in $\mathcal{P}$ have already sent all messages forming a reaction to M, so new inputs cannot impact a reaction to M. It follows that a reaction to M is determined solely by the order in which $\mathcal{I}$ sends inputs. In case of crash all processes restart from the initial state and $\mathcal{I}$ resends inputs in an exactly the same order as before the crash, so after the recovery $\mathcal{P}$ produces the reactions possible if the crash would not occur in H. Some of the messages forming reaction to M produced by $P_i \in \mathcal{P}$ (outputs) may be duplicates of the messages sent before the crash – due to our assumptions, those are the only duplicates which our algorithm must handle. Those duplicated outputs are discarded by $\mathcal{I}$. We conclude that the reactions observed by $\mathcal{W}$ would be possible if a crash would not occur in H.

Constraints on the $\mathcal{P}$'s behavior could be understood both as expressing which histories are possible, and which possible histories with different event ordering lead to the same $\mathcal{P}$'s global state (i.e. which histories are equivalent with respect to $\mathcal{P}$'s state). For example, ordering of receive events matters in PWD, but not in the send-deterministic model. If a constraint C allows for all histories allowed by C' and in addition at least one history not allowed by C', then C' is more strict than C. Similarly, if under C histories H and H' are equivalent (despite having different ordering of the events), while under C' they are not, C is more strict than C' with respect to event ordering. Full determinism is more strict (in both senses) than PWD, PWD is more strict than send-determinism and so on.

We will now prove that the constraints on $\mathcal{P}$'s behavior are minimal in the sense that a deterministic external recovery (producing the same outputs in the same order) is possible without requiring cooperation and/or more information from $\mathcal{P}$, only when a constraint w.r.t. event ordering is at least as strict as R1)[2], and R1) is not enough unless a constraint at least as strict as R2) is imposed.

Theorem 2. *The restrictions imposed on a $\mathcal{P}$'s behavior are minimal.*

Proof. Minimality of R1). Assume that send events may be impacted not just by the ordering of the input events, but in addition there is a non-deterministic event e and depending on whether a history H contains e, or depending on ordering of e with respect to other events, it is possible that H will produce different outputs, say either M^o or $M^{o\prime}$ (not necessarily a reaction to the same M). Assume that e occurred before a crash, producing M^o. After the recovery e may not happen or may be ordered differently, producing $M^{o\prime}$. Since M^o

---

[2] Channel-determinism[21] would produce the same outputs, but possibly in different order, which may or might not matter from the point of $\mathcal{W}$.

and $M^{o\prime}$ are different, $\mathcal{I}$ would not discard one of them as a duplicate, causing $\mathcal{W}$ to observe both – impossible in a history without a crash. That could be prevented only by replaying e, which would require preserving its determinants. Since processes have no stable storage, determinants could be preserved only by sending them to $\mathcal{I}$ (exposing information) and during the recovery the processes would have to know how to use that information (requiring cooperation).

Minimality of R2). Assume that R1) holds and while there still may occur the events truly caused by M, a new input M' arrives. Depending on the ordering of the event of receiving M' with respect to the events truly caused by M, a history may contain an event of sending either M^o or $M^{o\prime}$, but not both. By reasoning analogous as with the discussion of R1) we conclude that the correct recovery requires exposing information to $\mathcal{I}$ and a cooperation with $\mathcal{I}$. Therefore, new input must arrive into $\mathcal{P}$ only when no events truly caused by the previous input will occur. Interceptor cannot determine this if $\mathcal{I}$ does not not know a priori the number of outputs, unless processes in $\mathcal{P}$ expose information to $\mathcal{I}$ (e.g. by attaching tags to outputs, to notify $\mathcal{I}$ whether the output is the last one).

4   Restricting the Behavior, Exposing the Information

The solution analysed in previous section is mostly of theoretical value. Obviously it would severely limit the performance of most applications, as it forces $\mathcal{P}$ to process all inputs serially. If $\mathcal{P}$ could process n inputs in parallel, both recovery and normal processing would be at least n times slower. This would be acceptable for applications where processing is done in request-reply manner, requiring cooperation of all processes in $\mathcal{P}$, or with applications where size of $\mathcal{P}$ is limited. Allowing inputs to be processing in parallel would both increase the performance, the potential size of $\mathcal{P}$, and the number of cases where external recovery would be applicable. The approach presented below, based on our previous work[5], demonstrates trade-offs inherent in the external recovery: to achieve higher performance, we must put more constraints on $\mathcal{P}$'s independence.

Let $\mathcal{S}$ be a set of all sessions in $H(t)$, and let $\forall e \in H(t), \exists S \in \mathcal{S} : e \in S$. Set of sessions $\mathcal{S} \subset H(t)$ is serializable if there exists a total order relation $\xrightarrow{s}$ in $\mathcal{S}$, preserving $\mapsto$ relation ($\forall e \in S, \forall e' \in S' : e \mapsto e' \Rightarrow S \xrightarrow{s} S'$). Each session $S \in \mathcal{S}$ has a unique session identifier $S.id$. Slightly abusing the notation, we will say that a message m belongs to a session S if the event of sending m belongs to S.

We restrict the $\mathcal{P}$'s behavior as follows: (R1) processes in $\mathcal{P}$ are send-deterministic within each session. (R3) The sessions are serializable. (R4) For each input M, number of outputs $k_M > 0$ in a reaction to M is known a priori (note R4 is less strict version of R2). (R5) $\forall P_i \in \mathcal{P}$, when P_i receives a message from session S, it must eventually send at least one message (possibly, an output) within S.

$\mathcal{P}$ expose the information about how the sessions were serialized: each message m (including each output) has the session identifier $m.sId$ and the ordered set of all the preceding sessions $m.prec$. We assume sessions are serializable.

The interceptor $\mathcal{I}$ maintains sets $\mathcal{M}^{in}$ and $\mathcal{F}$ (fig. 2). Each element $x \in \mathcal{M}^{in}$ represents a session and has five fields: an input msg, an input's session identifier

sId, a set of preceding session identifiers $prec$, a set of outputs out (a reaction to msg), and a boolean fwd. When an input M arrives at $\mathcal{I}$, $\mathcal{I}$ creates an element x with $x.msg \leftarrow M$, sets $M.sId$ and $x.sId$ to a new unique session identifier sId, $x.prec \leftarrow \mathcal{F}$, $x.out \leftarrow \emptyset$ and $x.fwd \leftarrow false$. The x is then added to $\mathcal{M}^{in}$, and M is send to $\mathcal{P}$.

When an output M^o arrives at $\mathcal{I}$, $\mathcal{I}$ finds an element x in $\mathcal{M}^{in}$ with $x.sId = M^o.sId$. M^o is discarded if $M^o \in x.out$. Otherwise $\mathcal{I}$ appends $M^o.prec$ to a $x.prec$ field, M^o is stripped from $prec$ and sId fields and added to $x.out$. If cardinality of $x.out$ is k_M, then $x.sId$ is added to $\mathcal{F}$. For each $x \in \mathcal{M}^{in}$, the interceptor $\mathcal{I}$ periodically checks a condition $x.sId \in \mathcal{F} \wedge \forall y \in \mathcal{M}^{in} : y.sId \notin \mathcal{F} \Rightarrow x.sId \in y.prec \vee y.sId \in x.prec$. If the condition is true, $\mathcal{I}$ sets $x.fwd \leftarrow true$ and forwards messages in $x.out$ to $\mathcal{W}$.

When $\mathcal{P}$ crashes, $\mathcal{I}$ stops passing messages into $\mathcal{P}$ and creates two sets: $\mathcal{M}'$ contains a copy of all elements $x \in \mathcal{M}^{in}$ such that $x.fwd = true$, while $\mathcal{M}^{oth} = \mathcal{M}^{in} \setminus \mathcal{M}'$ (fig. 3). Then, $\forall x \in \mathcal{M}^{in} : \neg x.fwd \Rightarrow x.out \leftarrow \emptyset$. Next, an element $x \in \mathcal{M}' : x.prec = \emptyset$ is chosen and a message $x.msg$ is sent to $\mathcal{P}$. Interceptor $\mathcal{I}$ then waits until it receives k_M outputs, discarding each of them. When this happens, x is removed from $\mathcal{M}'$ and $\forall y \in \mathcal{M}', y \neq x$, $x.sId$ is removed from $y.prec$. Finally, another element with an empty $prec$ set is chosen. If $\mathcal{M}'$ is empty, $\mathcal{I}$ sends all messages from $\mathcal{M}^{oth}$ set to $\mathcal{P}$ (in any order, sequentially or in parallel). Normal execution then resumes.

The information about session serialization is gathered as follows: each process P_i maintains set of session identifiers $prec_i$ and current session identifier sId_i. When P_i receives m such that $m.sId \neq sId_i$, $prec_i \leftarrow prec_i \cup m.prec \cup sId_i$ and $sId_i \leftarrow m.sId$. When P_i sends a message m, the $prec_i$ is added to m as $m.prec$. The set $prec_i$ can be prevented from growing indefinitely with the use of garbage collecting, or by putting stricter constraints on $\mathcal{P}$'s behavior.

Lemma 1. *For every session $S' \neq S$ such that S' has started before S has ended, and for any event $e \in S$ at P_i, e can be replayed during recovery if and only if either no event from S' occurs at P_i, or information of precedence between S' and S with respect to $\mapsto_i$ is preserved at $\mathcal{I}$.*

Proof. From R3), we know that if a process P_i receives message first from a session S and then from a session $S' \neq S$, P_i will receive no further messages from S (P_i sees that locally S precedes S'). Let $\mapsto_i$ denote the session ordering as seen by P_i. Obviously, $S \mapsto_i S' \Rightarrow S \xrightarrow{s} S'$. From R1), a send event e at P_i from S can be impacted only by the previous receive events at P_i, belonging to different sessions, i.e. by the sessions preceding S w.r.t. $\mapsto_i$ relation. To replicate e, we must 1) replay all sessions preceding S before S and 2) make sure that all the sessions preceded by S will be executed after S. If S has ended before S' has started, S' cannot precede S w.r.t. $\mapsto_i$. So, to be sure we can replay e, for every session $S' \neq S$ such that S' has started before S has ended, we must be able to tell that either no event from S' occurs at P_i, or whether $S' \mapsto_i S$ or $S \mapsto_i S'$. This information must be then preserved at $\mathcal{I}$.

Message type Packet ⟨⟩ **is:**

    integer sId
    set<integer> prec
    message data

Structure Session is:

    message msg   :: *Input starting the session*
    integer sId   :: *Session identifier*
    set<integer> prec   :: *preceding sessions*
    set<message> out   :: *Outputs to the session*
    boolean fwd   :: *Were outputs forwarded to* $\mathcal{W}$

Variables used in a description:

    set<Session> $\mathcal{M}^{in}$ :: *Sessions*
    set<integer> $\mathcal{F}$ :: *Finished sessions*
    set<Session> $\mathcal{M}/$ :: *Part of* $\mathcal{M}^{in}$
    set<Session> $\mathcal{M}^{oth}$ :: *Part of* $\mathcal{M}^{in}$
    Session x :: *Single session element*
    Packet pkt :: *Packets used within* $\mathcal{P}$
    enum<ready,busy> mode ← **ready**

Upon receiving message M
    from $\mathcal{W}$ **at** $\mathcal{I}$

1: $x.msg \leftarrow M$
2: $x.sId \leftarrow$ **new unique session**
    identifier
3: $x.prec \leftarrow \emptyset, x.out \leftarrow \emptyset$
4: $x.fwd \leftarrow$ **false**
5: $\mathcal{M}^{in} \leftarrow \mathcal{M}^{in} \cup x$
6: $pkt.data \leftarrow M$
7: $pkt.sId \leftarrow x.sId$
8: $pkt.prec \leftarrow \emptyset$
9: **wait until** $mode =$ **ready**
10: **send** pkt **to** $\mathcal{P}$

Upon receiving message M^o **of type**
    Packet from $\mathcal{P}$ **at** $\mathcal{I}$

11: $x \leftarrow \{x : x \in \mathcal{M}^{in} \wedge x.sId = M^o.sId\}$
12: $\mathcal{M}^{in} \leftarrow \mathcal{M}^{in} \setminus x$
13: **if** $M^o.data \notin x.out$ **then**
14:    $x.prec \leftarrow x.prec \cup M^o.prec$
15:    $x.out \leftarrow x.out \cup (M^o.data)$
16:    $\mathcal{M}^{in} \leftarrow \mathcal{M}^{in} \cup x$
17:    **if** $|x.out| = k_M$ **then**
18:        $\mathcal{F} \leftarrow \mathcal{F} \cup x.sId$
19:    **end if**
20: **else**
21:    discard M^o
22: **end if**

When $\exists x \in \mathcal{M}^{in} : x.sId \in \mathcal{F} \wedge x.fwd =$ **false** $\wedge \forall y \in \mathcal{M}^{in}, y.sId \notin \mathcal{F} \Rightarrow x.sId \in y.prec \vee y.sId \in x.prec$

23: $x.fwd \leftarrow$ **true**
24: **foreach** $msg \in x.out$ **do**
25:    **send** msg **to** $\mathcal{W}$
26: **end for**

Fig. 2. Algorithm 2, part 1: failure-free execution

Upon detecting a restart in $\mathcal{P}$ at $\mathcal{I}$
:: *Event is fired when restart of $\mathcal{P}$ is finished*

```
 1: mode ← busy
 2: M/ ← {x ∈ M^in : x.fwd = true}
        :: Copy of elements in M^in
 3: M^oth ← M^in \ M/
 4: foreach x ∈ M^in do
 5:     if x.fwd = true then
 6:         x.out ← ∅
 7:     end if
 8: end for
 9: while M/ ≠ ∅ do
10:     foreach x ∈ M/ do
11:         if x.prec = ∅ then
            :: At least one element with
            :: empty prec field must be in
            :: M/ due to (R4)
            :: restriction on P's behavior
12:             break
13:         end if
14:     end for
```

```
15:         pkt.msg ← x.msg
16:         pkt.prec ← ∅
17:         pkt.sId ← x.sId
18:         send pkt to P
19:         for i ∈ {1..k_M} do
20:             receive pkt from P
21:             discard pkt
22:         end for
23:         M/ ← M/ \ x
24:         foreach y ∈ M/ do
25:             y.prec ← y.prec \ x.sId
26:         end for
27:     end while
28:     foreach x ∈ M^oth do
29:         pkt.msg ← x.msg
30:         pkt.prec ← ∅
31:         pkt.sId ← x.sId
32:         send pkt to P
33:     end for
34:     mode ← ready
```

Fig. 3. Algorithm 2, part 2: recovery

Lemma 2. *For some $x \in \mathcal{M}^{in}$ and $S \in \mathcal{S}$, let S.prec be x.prec where $x.sId = S.id$. When a k_M-th output M^o from S arrives to $\mathcal{I}$, for each $S' \in \mathcal{S}$ such that S' has not started after S has ended, $S'.id \in S.prec \iff \exists P_i \in \mathcal{P} : S' \mapsto_i S$.*

Proof. When P_i receives a message from a session S', $sId_i \leftarrow S'.id$. Later, when P_i receives a message from a session S, S' is added to the $prec_i$ ($S' \mapsto_i S \wedge sId_i = S.id \Rightarrow S'.id \in prec_i$). Before sending a message m within S, P_i sets $m.prec \leftarrow prec_i$, so $S' \mapsto_i S \wedge m.sId = S.id \Rightarrow S'.id \in m.prec$. When P_j receives a message m from P_i it adds $m.prec$ to $prec_j$. By recursion, it follows that for every m (including every output) $m.sId = S.id \wedge S'.id \in m.prec \Rightarrow \exists P_i \in \mathcal{P} : S' \mapsto_i S$. Since $S.prec$ is a sum of all outputs' $prec$ fields, this concludes the if part. From R5), at least one message is sent by P_i within a session S, containing $prec_i$, either to $\mathcal{W}$ or to some P_j. Since our system models assumes all sessions are finite, and by R4) number of outputs is finite, eventually there must be an output (at most k_M-th) including ordering of S' and S w.r.t. $\mapsto_i$ (only if part).

Theorem 3. *For any history H with a crash, the recovery of $\mathcal{P}$ is correct*

Proof. Let $x \in \mathcal{M}'$, and let $S.prec$ be $x.prec$ where $x.id = S.id$. Let $\xrightarrow{p}$ will be a relation on $\mathcal{S}$, such that if $S' \in S.prec \Rightarrow S' \xrightarrow{p} S$. Algorithm ensures that no output M^o from session S (reaction to S) is send to $\mathcal{W}$ until for all other session

S', $S' \in \mathcal{F} \vee S' \xrightarrow{p} S \vee S \xrightarrow{p} S'$. Assume $S' \in \mathcal{F}$ and $\neg(S' \xrightarrow{p} S \vee S \xrightarrow{p} S')$. From R4) and R5), no new events within S' will happen. If any event in S' would occur at P_i, then by R5) and lemma 2), $S' \xrightarrow{p} S \vee S \xrightarrow{p} S'$, so we conclude that no event from S' occurred at P_i.

Assume $S' \xrightarrow{p} S \vee S \xrightarrow{p} S'$. From lemma 2) we conclude that $S' \xrightarrow{p} S \iff \exists P_i \in \mathcal{P} : S' \mapsto_i S$ (resp. $S \xrightarrow{p} S' \iff \exists P_i \in \mathcal{P} : S \mapsto_i S'$), or S started after S' has ended. From that and from lemma 1) we conclude that to replicate reaction to S, it is enough to replay all the sessions preceding S with respect to $\xrightarrow{p}$. It is easy to see that algorithm does exactly that during the recovery. After that, inputs for which no output was forwarded to $\mathcal{W}$ may be send to $\mathcal{P}$ in any order; from lemma 1) it is clear that any such input couldn't impact any output forwarded to $\mathcal{W}$ before the crash, and reaction to any such input could be impacted by sessions from $\mathcal{M}'$ in a history without a crash.

After the recovery all sessions which produced outputs forwarded to $\mathcal{W}$ before a crash will be replayed while outputs which could not be replicated and duplicates will be discarded. Any additional output forwarded to $\mathcal{W}$ could also appear if a crash would not occur in H. We conclude that a reaction to any input M in H could occur in a history without a crash.

5   Related Work

In the context of message-passing systems, there are two general techniques for system recovery: checkpointing and message logging (See [15] for survey). Checkpointing may be done in a coordinated manner [13] or independently. In the latter case a domino effect may appear [19], leading researchers to propose many communication-induced protocols: index-based [25] or model-based [22,17].

Message logging may be pessimistic, optimistic or causal. With pessimistic logging event determinants are saved immediately into the stable storage [3]. The performance penalty of this approach is avoided by optimistic logging where determinants may be stored in volatile memory before being written to the stable storage [11]. Optimistic approach complicates recovery. Causal logging tries to combine advantages of both approaches [1]. Send-determinism is a promising model of system behavior, allowing new, efficient protocols [8,9]. Message logging was also studied in the context of the SOA systems [2] and Distributed Shared Memory [18].

The independent recovery of large system's sub-components was analyzed in the context of cluster federations, in which processes/nodes could be statically assigned to the independent, non-overlapping groups [16,10], may be divided into groups using either the code analysis or based on their behavior [20,14], or by residing on single, multi-core machine [4]. Usually coordinated checkpoint is used within a group, while only messages exchanged between the groups are logged [9].

6   Conclusions

This paper is a first step in an exploration of the external recovery problem. We presented two algorithms allowing the system to be recovered using the messages logged by an intercepting layer. The algorithms differ in the kind of restrictions imposed on a system, serving as an illustration of the tradeoffs involved when a system is to be recovered by external message logging: one must either expose more system information and agree to cooperate more with intercepting layer, or impose a stricter constraints on possible system behaviors.

Our work could be extended in several ways. First, the externally recoverable systems offer a possibility of building large-scale systems where each subsystem could be dynamically modified or replaced, with different internal fault-handling logic. Second, it would be interesting to investigate other ways in which system's behavior could be restricted, especially if there exists other set minimal restrictions allowing system's external recovery. Third, a similar work could be carried on the questions of minimal information needed by external recovery mechanism given particular restriction on system's behavior. Finally, important part of future work is experimental analysis of performance of presented solutions, and of their scaling characteristics.

References

1. Alvisi, L., Marzullo, K.: Message logging: Pessimistic, optimistic, causal, and optimal. Software Engineering 24(2), 149–159 (1998)
2. Barga, R.S., Lomet, D.B., Shegalov, G., Weikum, G.: Recovery guarantees for internet applications. ACM Trans. Internet Techn. 4(3), 289–328 (2004)
3. Bouteiller, A., Cappello, F., Hérault, T., Krawezik, G., Lemarinier, P., Magniette, F.: MPICH-V2: a fault tolerant MPI for volatile nodes based on pessimistic sender based message logging. In: SC, p. 25. ACM (2003)
4. Bouteiller, A., Hérault, T., Bosilca, G., Dongarra, J.J.: Correlated set coordination in fault tolerant message logging protocols for many-core clusters. Concurrency and Computation: Practice and Experience 25(4), 572–585 (2013)
5. Brzeziński, J., Danilecki, A., Hołenko, M., Kobusińska, A., Kobusiński, J., Zierhoffer, P.: D-ReServE: Distributed reliable service environment. In: Morzy, T., Härder, T., Wrembel, R. (eds.) ADBIS 2012. LNCS, vol. 7503, pp. 71–84. Springer, Heidelberg (2012)
6. Cappello, F., Guermouche, A., Snir, M.: On communication determinism in parallel HPC applications. In: 2010 Proceedings of 19th International Conference on Computer Communications and Networks (ICCCN), pp. 1–8 (2010)
7. Elnozahy, E.N., Alvisi, L., Wang, Y.-M., Johnson, D.B.: A survey of rollback-recovery protocols in message-passing systems. ACM Comput. Surv. 34(3), 375–408 (2002)
8. Guermouche, A., Ropars, T., Brunet, E., Snir, M., Cappello, F.: Uncoordinated checkpointing without domino effect for send-deterministic message passing applications. In: Accepted to the 25th IEEE International Parallel and Distributed Processing Symposium, IPDPS (May 2011)

9. Guermouche, A., Ropars, T., Snir, M., Cappello, F.: HydEE: Failure containment without event logging for large scale send-deterministic mpi applications. In: 2012 IEEE 26th International Parallel Distributed Processing Symposium (IPDPS), pp. 1216–1227 (2012)

10. Gupta, B., Rahimi, S., Allam, V., Jupally, V.: Domino-effect free crash recovery for concurrent failures in cluster federation. In: Wu, S., Yang, L.T., Xu, T.L. (eds.) GPC 2008. LNCS, vol. 5036, pp. 4–17. Springer, Heidelberg (2008)

11. Johnson, D., Zwaenepoel, W.: Recovery in distributed systems using optimistic message logging and checkpointing. J Algorithms 11, 462–491 (1990)

12. Lamport, L.: Time, clocks, and the ordering of events in a distributed system. Communications of the ACM 21(7), 558–565 (1978)

13. Lemarinier, P., Bouteiller, A., Herault, T., Krawezik, G., Cappello, F.: Improved message logging versus improved coordinated checkpointing for fault tolerant MPI. In: CLUSTER 2004: Proceedings of the 2004 IEEE International Conference on Cluster Computing, Washington, DC, USA, pp. 115–124 (2004)

14. Luo, Y., Manivannan, D.: Hope: A hybrid optimistic checkpointing and selective pessimistic message logging protocol for large scale distributed systems. Future Generation Comp. Syst. 28(8), 1217–1235 (2012)

15. Maloney, A., Goscinski, A.: A survey and review of the current state of rollback-recovery for cluster systems. Concurrency and Computation: Practice and Experience 21(12), 1632–1666 (2009)

16. Monnet, S., Morin, C., Badrinath, R.: A hierarchical checkpointing protocol for parallel applications in cluster federations. In: IPDPS (2004)

17. Netzer, R.H.B., Xu, J.: Necessary and sufficient conditions for consistent global snapshots. IEEE Transactions on Parallel and Distributed Systems 6(2), 165–169 (1995)

18. Park, T., Lee, I., Yeom, H.Y.: An efficient causal logging scheme for recoverable distributed shared memory systems. Parallel Computing 28(11), 1549–1572 (2002)

19. Randell, B.: System structure for software fault tolerance. IEEE Transactions on Software Engineering 1(2), 221–232 (1975)

20. Ropars, T., Guermouche, A., Uçar, B., Meneses, E., Kalé, L.V., Cappello, F.: On the use of cluster-based partial message logging to improve fault tolerance for MPI HPC applications. In: Jeannot, E., Namyst, R., Roman, J. (eds.) Euro-Par 2011, Part I. LNCS, vol. 6852, pp. 567–578. Springer, Heidelberg (2011)

21. Ropars, T., Martsinkevich, T.V., Guermouche, A., Schiper, A., Cappello, F.: Spbc: Leveraging the characteristics of mpi hpc applications for scalable checkpointing. In: Proceedings of the International Conference on High Performance Computing, Networking, Storage and Analysis, SC 2013, pp. 8:1–8:12. ACM, New York (2013)

22. Russell, D.L.: State restoration in systems of communicating processes. IEEE Trans. Software Eng. 6(2), 183–194 (1980)

23. Storm, R., Yemini, S.: Optimistic recovery in distributed systems. ACM Trans. Comput. Syst. 3(3), 204–226 (1985)

24. Tarafdar, A., Garg, V.K.: Addressing false causality while detecting predicates in distributed programs. In: Proceedings of the 18th IEEE International Conference on Distributed Computing Systems (ICDCS 1998), pp. 94–101 (1998)

25. Tsai, J.: An efficient index-based checkpointing protocol with constant-size control information on messages. IEEE Trans. Dependable Sec. Comput. 2(4), 287–296 (2005)

FlipIt: An LLVM Based Fault Injector for HPC

Jon Calhoun, Luke Olson, and Marc Snir

University of Illinois at Urbana-Champaign, Urbana, IL 61801, USA
{jccalho2,luko,snir}@illinois.edu

Abstract. High performance computing (HPC) is increasingly subjected to faulty computations. The frequency of silent data corruptions (SDCs) in particular is expected to increase in emerging machines requiring HPC applications to handle SDCs. In this paper we, propose a robust fault injector structured through an LLVM compiler pass that allows simulation of SDCs in various applications. Although fault injection locations are enumerated at compile time, their activation is purely at runtime and based on a user-provided fault distribution. The robustness of our fault injector is in the ability to augment the runtime injection logic on a per application basis. This allows tighter control on the spacial, temporal, and probability of injected faults. The usability, scalability, and robustness of our fault injection is demonstrated with injecting faults into an algebraic multigird solver.

1 Introduction

Driven by a need to solve ever larger problems, high performance computing (HPC) has become a fundamental part of scientific investigation and discovery. This dependence is evident in the push for increased performance of supercomputers over the past few decades. The petascale barrier was broken almost six years ago , and while the exascale barrier is expected to be broken within the next decade, it is not expected to be met without overcoming a host of challenges [10] [3]. One key challenge facing HPC as we march toward exascale is the need to deal with faults. Faults afflicting HPC systems are classified as either hard or soft, and are the cause of errors in the system. Hard faults are faults that are reproducible — e.g. the inability to communicate with a node that is offline. Soft faults are faults where activation is not systematically reproducible [1] — e.g. a bit-flip caused by a charged particle.

Traditionally failures due to hard faults are handled by checkpoint-restart [9]. Issues with scalability [14] [15] are prompting the development of hierarchical approaches [2], while alternatives to checkpoint-restart focus on replication [7]. Although these solutions provide safeguards against faults present in the system, they provide little if any insight about the application's ability to handle faults.

Soft errors are common on DRAM chips, and all DRAMs in modern HPC include error correcting codes (ECC). The addition of ECC and more advanced features such as chipkill dramatically reduce the errors in DRAM [17]. Processors are more difficult to protect, but recent designs add protection to memories, data

L. Lopes et al. (Eds.): Euro-Par 2014 Workshops, Part I, LNCS 8805, pp. 547–558, 2014.

paths, and register files. Even so, with increased core count and continued use of commodity parts, soft errors are likely to be common encounters in emerging architectures [3].

Consequently, we are motivated to determine the impact of soft errors on HPC applications and the effectiveness of resiliency schemes to safeguard against them. Because soft errors are rare and do not normally exhibit during testing, their manifestation must be simulated by a fault injector.

This paper makes the following contributions:

- The development of a robust LLVM based fault injector that targets HPC applications.
- An overview in its utility as a general purpose fault injection framework.
- A demonstration of its usability, scalability, robustness on production level HPC code.

The remainder of this paper is structured as follows. In the next section, we discuss related background in the area of fault injection. Section 3 details the design, use, and adaptation to individual applications. Results from its usability, scalability, and robustness are shown in Section 4.

2   Background

There are many forms of fault injectors. The more accurate the fault injector the closer to physical hardware the faults are injected. At the lowest level, injections come in two forms real and simulated.

In real injections, the hardware is bombarded with a concentration of neutrons. While this method is highly accurate, it has significant drawbacks mainly its cost and availability to a limited number of researchers, which limits its applicability to HPC.

Simulated injections comprise many techniques at both the hardware and software level. At the hardware level, gate-accurate models are constructed, and fault injection occurs systematically with gate level granularity. With gate-accurate simulations, execution of a full application is possible, but a large scale machine is prohibitive due to execution overhead. A fault injection framework that operates with low overhead on current hardware is needed to inject faults in HPC applications.

Many fault injectors have been created that operate in real time and on real hardware. DOCTOR [8] injects faults into memory, the CPU, and network communications by using time-outs and traps to overwrite memory locations and modify the binary. XCEPTION [4] is an exception handler that injects faults when triggered by accesses to specific memory addresses, and simulates stuck-at-zero, stuck-at-one, and bit-blips. NFTAPE [18] uses a driver based fault injection scheme to inject fault inside the user or kernel space, but requires OS modification.

In compiler based fault injection, hard errors are simulated by adding extra instructions that always inject in the same location. To address the static nature of these injections, the injection is made dynamic by addition of code that corrupts data at runtime based on programmatic and environmental factors.

Fault injection for MPI applications is often focused on *message* injection [7]. Yet other works consider soft errors that manifest in register modifications [5] or that arise in the memory image of the running application [13,12]. The approach in [12] allows user identification of stack and heap items to target for injection. This is similar to our approach where we allow the user to select functions that are faulty.

Since DRAMs have a higher level of protection from silent errors than processors thanks to being easier to protect by ECC and chipkill, our focus is on faults that arise in the processor. In the following section, we detail the design of our fault injector that simulates the presence of silent errors as the manifestation of bit-flips in register values.

Relax [6], an LLVM based fault injector, is similar to our approach; however, it is not publicly available, is designed from an old version of LLVM, and does not target HPC applications. KULFI [16] is a publicly available fault injector similar to Relax. Because KULFI is still currently maintained and is easily modifiable, its structure provides a basis for our fault injector. In particular, we utilize the framework of their compiler pass. We provide a fault injector that is more expansive, extensible, and provides more user control than KULFI.

3   Fault Injector

3.1   Overview

Our fault injector is structured as an LLVM compiler pass [11] and is based on KULFI [16]. Notable extensions have been added to increase its robustness and efficacy. Such extensions include:

- Support for complex pointer types.
- Ability to work with multiple source files simultaneously.
- User customized fault distribution and event logger.
- Support for a larger subset of the LLVM instructions.
- MPI rank aware.

We chose to use an LLVM compiler pass to simulate transient errors instead of randomly flipping bits inside the binary in order to provide more control over what section of the code is faulty and when faults arise. The compiler pass proceeds by iterating over all modules in a source file. Upon discovery a module marked for injection, the included instructions are surrounded by instructions that probabilistically inject a fault. Here we say a fault is a single bit-flip in a source operand or the result of an LLVM instruction. Figure 1 illustrates this transformation for a single **add** instruction in which the result is corrupted.

All subsequent use of the variable that is possibly corrupted is replaced with the value returned from the corrupt function. The locations where faults can occur are enumerated at compile time, but their activation occurs randomly at runtime based upon a user provided fault distribution.

```
define i32 @add(i32 %a, i32 %b) #0 {
entry:
    %add = add nsw i32 %a, %b
    %data = sext i32 %add i64
    %tmp = call i32 @crptInt(i32 0, i32 0,
                  double 0.01, i32 2, i64 %data)
    %crptAdd = trunc i64 %tmp to i32
    ret i32 %crptAdd
}
```

```
define i32 @add(i32 %a, i32 %b) #0 {
entry:
    %add = add nsw i32 %a, %b
    ret i32 %add
}
```

(a) Original LLVM IR.   (b) Transformed LLVM IR.

Fig. 1. Code Transformation to Inject Faults

3.2 Design

As shown in Figure 1, a function call to `crptInt` is used to determine if a bit should be flipped and performs the flip. Algorithm 1 provides generic logic for the injection. In every corrupting function, the argument list is the same except for the data type of the value being corrupted. Table 1 details the argument list of the corrupt functions from left to right. The byte where a bit-flip is to occur is either determined at compile time (0-7) or is calculated randomly at runtime, negative value. If the byte specified is outside the range of the data type, we use the modulus operator to wrap the bytes to the correct range. For both the dynamic and static byte selection, the bit that is flipped is determined at random. We fix a byte before selecting a bit to flip in order to provide the ability to look at bit flips in certain bit positions.

Algorithm 1. Generic corrupt logic

Input: $siteProb$: Probability that this site is faulty.

$\quad\quad\quad$ $siteIndex$: Unique index of this fault site.

$\quad\quad\quad$ $data$: Value eligible for corruption.

Result: Data unmodified(no injection), or data with a single bit-flip(injection).

1 **if** $\neg\, shouldInject(injectorOn,\ siteProb)$ **then**

2 $\quad\mid\quad$ **return** $data$;

3 **else**

4 $\quad\mid\quad$ $bitPosition \leftarrow$ random bit position in targeted byte;

5 $\quad\mid\quad$ logInjection($siteIndex,\ bitPosition$);

6 $\quad\mid\quad$ $data_{corrupt} \leftarrow data \oplus (0x1 \ll bitPosition)$;

7 $\quad\mid\quad$ **return** $data_{corrupt}$;

In our basic model and the experiments in Section IV, we make the simplifying assumption that all LLVM instructions have an equal probability for a fault to be injected. Each LLVM instruction should have differing probabilities and is a function of the underline hardware. Therefore, if one knew this information for a processor *a priori*, the scaled probabilities should be incorporated into to the configuration file of the fault injector.

Advance pointer types, multiple levels of indirection, are not considered for injection in KULFI. Pointers are represented using a finite number of bits;

Table 1. Corrupt function's arguments (left to right)

Arg	Description
1	Unique fault site index.
2	Boolean: one injection per active rank.
3	Probability that instruction is faulty.
4	Byte location targeted for bit-flip.
5	Data to be corrupted by a bit-flip.

```
#include "/path/to/fault/lib/corrupt.h"
#include <mpi.h>
int main(int argc, char** argv) {
  MPI_Init(&argc, &argv);
  int id; int seed = 71;
  MPI_Comm_rank(MPI_COMM_WORLD, &id);
  FLIPIT_Init(id, argc, argv, seed);
  foo();
  FLIPIT_Finalize(NULL);
  MPI_Finalize();
}
```

Fig. 2. Source modifications to use fault injector

Table 2. User callable functions

Function name	Description
FLIPIT_Init	Initializes fault injector. Turns on injector.
FLIPIT_Finalize	Cleans up injector. Turns off injector.
FLIPIT_SetInjector	Zero: turns off injector. Non-zero: turns on injector.
FLIPIT_SetFaultProbability	Sets the probability function with a user defined function.
FLIPIT_SetCustomLogger	Sets user defined logging function. Called on all injections.

therefore, in our solution, we inject into pointers by first casting the variable to a 64-bit integer. Next, a call to corrupt this 64-bit integer is inserted, and the value returned from this call is cast back to the appropriate data type. As with all corruptions, all subsequent uses are replaced.

Since a function targeted for corruption may include additional function calls, corrupting these function calls is critical to properly modeling a fault function. There are two options to handle propper corruption, depending on the type of function. First, proper corruption may be issued by recompiling the source of the corrupting function. Second, if recompilation is not an option — e.g. due to unavailable source — then we scale the probability of injecting a fault into return value or argument of the `call` instruction. The probably is not specified until compile time, either by using the function's execution time or by the amount of hardware active during its execution.

In order to support HPC injections, our fault injector is aware of the processes' current MPI rank inside `MPI_COMM_WORLD`. This allows fault injections on a subset of ranks specified at runtime via command line arguments. Large scale machines have custom MPI distributions that are tuned for performance. Because a substantial portion of time in MPI applications is spent in MPI routines, we must consider MPI calls as faulty. The source code for the machine optimal MPI is not available. This implies that we must utilize the mechanism outlined above to modify probabilities of function call injections based upon the execution characteristics of the function.

3.3   Usability and Extensibility

Source Modification. Our fault injector is designed to require minimal modification to existing codes while at the same time providing a high degree of robustness and flexibility. Figure 2 shows the minimum required changes to `main` in order to use the fault injector. The call to `FLIPIT_Init` should dominate all usage of code compiled with our fault injector, and no such code should be executed after the call to `FLIPIT_Finalize`. We elect to have the user to insert calls to `FLIPIT_Init` because it is possible that we never see the file containing `MPI_Init`. To provide the user with a more fine grain control over fault injection, the functions in Table 2 are provided.

Compiling. The use of our fault injector requires little modification to current building practices. Once functions have been identified by the programmer, the source files containing the functions is recompiled using our compiler pass. Figure 3 shows this process with a change in the Makefile.

```
                        INJPASS = /path/to/compiler/pass
                        INJLIB = -L/path/to/injeciton/lib -lcorrupt.a
                        FIPARMS = -prob 0.01 -funcList "foo1 foo2"
                        HEADER =/path/to/bitcode/header
                        clang -g -emit-llvm bob.c -c -o bob.bc
                        llvm-link -o bob_c.bc bob.bc $(HEADER)
                        opt -load $(INJPASS) $(FIPARMS) < bob_c.bc > bob_F.bc 2> bob.log
                        clang -c bob_F.bc -o bob.o
   $(CC) -c bob.c       $(CC) [...] bob.o [...] $(INJLIB)

   (a)   Original                    (b)  Modified Makefile line.
   Makefile line.
```

Fig. 3. Compilation steps

Step 1 in the compilation process has the original source being compiled with clang into LLVM bitcode. We compile with `-g` to relate fault sites indexed by our injector to the source code lines. If this flag is omitted we can relate the injection to the location it the bit-code which doesn't always have a clear translation back to the source code due to a provided optimization level. The bitcode generated is transformed in Step 2 via our compiler pass to enable fault injections. Here we add code to inject faults into the functions `foo1` and `foo2` with a fault probability of 1×10^{-2}, each instruction has a 1 in 100 chance of producing an incorrect result. Table 3 details all possible arguments to our compiler pass and their default values. Step 3 compiles this transformed bit-code into object code. Finally we compile the application linking with a static library that contains the functions used by our injector. To simplify we provide a wrapper script that replaces the selected compiler in the Makefile.

For MPI applications, `mpicc` is a wrapper around a native compiler. The compiler flags `-show` and `-showme` for MPICH and OpenMPI, respectfully, provides the exact compiler command used to compile the source file. This command is subsequently modified in accordance to Figure 3, or this information can be provided to our wrapper script.

Table 3. Compiler pass arguments

Argument	Type	Req.	Default	Description
config	string	No	FlipIt.config	Path to configuration file.
funcList	string	Yes	—	Functions to corrupt.
prob	double	Yes	1e-8	Default per instruction fault probability.
byte	int	No	-1	Byte to flip bit in (0-7). (-1 random).
singleInj	bool	No	true	One injection per rank.
ptr	bool	No	true	Allow bit-flips in pointers.
ctrl	bool	No	true	Allow bit-flips in control variables.
arith	bool	No	true	Allow bit-flips in arithmetic.

Programmer Control. The choice to use a static library for the corruption routines is influenced by three key points: 1) the need to compile multiple source files for a single executable; 2) the ability to limit overhead of the fault injector; and 3) to allow for application specific behavior such as the collection of user defined statistics. Straightforward use of KULFI is restricted to one source file, which limits use by requiring the programmer to place all functions of interest into a single source file, or by requiring multiple recompilations to cover all functions of interest, but sacrificing the ability to look at complex function interactions.

Our approach to fault injection increases the static and dynamic instruction count for the application, which leads to increased execution time. The overhead depends on the additional computation performed by the corrupted functions apart from injecting the fault. Extra instructions are attributed to collecting statistics and the granularity of the spacial and temporal locality of a fault. Algorithm 1 shows the outline for a generic, corrupt function, and Algorithm 2 shows a basic `shouldInject` function. This function allows for fine-grained application specific selectivity for fault injection, but requires recompilation of the static library when modified. A simple modification of Algorithm 2 allows for fault injection on certain MPI modifications of the conditional in line 2; this introspection includes a check for a faulty rank.

Algorithm 2. Basic `shouldInject` logic.

Input: *siteProb*: Probability that this site is faulty.
      injectorOn: Boolean signifying if injector is on.
Result: Boolean indicating an injection.
1   $P \leftarrow$ probability();
2   **if** *injectorOn* **and** *siteProb* > P **then**
3     $\lfloor$ **return** $TRUE$;

4   **else**
5     $\lfloor$ **return** $FALSE$;

Injection at the finest granularity in an MPI application has only one active fault site, capable of generating a bit-flip, on a single MPI rank. To remove the need for recompilation, command line arguments are provided and passed to

Table 4. Command line arguments for fault injector

Argument	Description
--numFaulty	Number of faulty MPI ranks.
--faulty	List of faulty MPI ranks.
--numFaultyLoc	Number of active fault locations.
--faultyLoc	List of active fault locations.

FLIPIT_Init detailing which fault sites are active and which MPI ranks are candidates for injection. These command line arguments listed in Table 4.

The three classifications of injection types mentioned in Table 3 are *pointer*, *control*, and *arithmetic*. The classification *pointer* refers to all calculations directly related to use of a pointers (loads, stores, and address calculation), *control* refers to all calculations of branching and control flow (comparisons for branches and modification of loop control variables), *arithmetic* refers to pure mathematical operations. By default all of these are active, but each can be toggled to simulate different injection campaigns.

Analysis. As code is being compiled with our fault injector, a log file is generated that specifies all locations where faults can be injected. Each fault site is given a unique identifier and classified depending on which the fault is injected *pointer*, *control*, or *arithmetic*. In addition, a brief description of the fault site is listed to discern any ambiguities about the injection location along with the source line number if compiled with -g.

As the application is run, information about the faults being injected is logged per rank for later inspection. Two types of data are logged every time a fault is injected. The first kind is information about the faults themselves — i.e. the fault site numbers, bits flipped, and values from the fault distribution. This information is used in conjunction with the fault site log files to determine in what function and where in this function the fault is injected. The second type of information logged on each fault injection is accomplished through a user-defined function. This user defined function is set using FLIPIT_SetCustomLogger (Table 2).

Even if no faults are injected, some statistics are still collected. For every rank, a histogram is generated showing the frequency each fault site is looked at. To determine if the execution path of the application changes due to a fault, the histogram generated in the fault free case is compared with the histogram from an application run with faults. Any discrepancies in these histograms suggest differing paths of execution. Further insights are found by using the injection log and the fault site log along side the histograms to determine precisely what occurred due to the fault, as we see in the next section.

4   Experiments on Hypre

In order to show the scalability and flexibility of our fault injector, we compile sections of Hypre with our fault injector to look at SDCs that arise during the solving of a linear system. To solve the linear system we use Algebraic Multigrid (AMG) with one iteration of Jacobi relaxation for smoothing. The problem is a 2D Laplacian with zero on the boundaries. Profiling Hypre allows us to determine the call stack inside `HYPRE_BoomerAMGSolve`. We select all functions in this call stack for injection.

4.1 Scalability

To characterize the scalability of our fault injector, we run weak scaling experiments on Blue Waters with 16 processes per node, Figure 4, where each data point is the average of three runs. In this figure, the injector is turned on, but we inject no faults due to the probability of injecting a fault being zero.

Table 5. Increase in execution time due to fault injector

Processes	Increased Time	Processes	Increased Time
1	123.77x	128	44.41x
2	89.48x	256	38.06x
4	82.55x	512	37.89x
8	69.04x	1024	28.79x
16	62.58x	2048	26.59x
32	54.40x	4096	20.96x
64	48.05x	8192	17.21x

The number of unknowns per process is kept at approximately 16,384 throughout all weak scaling runs. From Figure 4 we see that our modified Hypre's execution time grows roughly linearly on a log scale just as the unmodified Hypre. From this we can conclude that the weak scaling results demonstrate that our fault injector is scalable. To determine how much our fault injector adversely effects performance we look at how much it increases execution time, Table 5. Our fault injector increases the dynamic instruction count, which produces a corresponding increase computation time. Yet, the overhead introduced by our injection is reduced as the the number of processes increases since communication becomes the bottleneck.

4.2 Selective Injection

To show the ease at which our fault injector can inject precise injections, we target the first element of the residual vector just before it is written to memory for injection. The fault occurs during the first cycle on the finest level as we are creating the residual vector before restriction. In order to have this precise injection, we need to first determine which fault site should be active. To determine the correct fault site index, we consult the fault site log. The index is passed to our fault injector via command line arguments along with the rank that is to experience the fault, rank 0. Because the residual is computed via a SpMV routine, that is also used during problem setup, two calls to `FLIPIT_SetInjector` are added, one to turn off the injector after initialization and the other to turn it on just before calculating the residual. Figure 5 shows what effect this injection

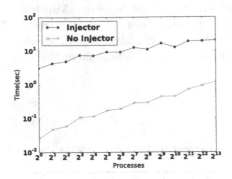

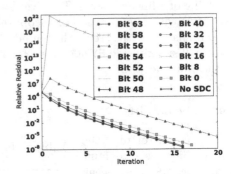

Fig. 4. Weak scaling of Hypre. Approximately 16,384 unknowns per process.

Fig. 5. Selective injection in residual calculation on rank 0. 8 processes with approximately 16,384 unknowns per process

has on the relative residual, the stopping criterion for AMG. The name of the trend indicates which bit is flipped in the 64-bit floating point number.

As we can see, a single SDC can either be masked by the application, or increase the number of iterations. Since this fault occurs in the mathematics of the problem, it wouldn't be detected until the application's results were analyzed. This suggests that work should be done to design SDC detectors to catch such SDCs early. In order to test the effectiveness of these SDC detectors, a fault injector such as the one presented here is required.

We now look at the result of injection into certain instruction types as outlined in Table 3. For this we inject a single fault into the aforementioned problem on rank 3.

Our fault injector allows us to target different classifications of instructions, and depending upon what classifications are active, the effects on the application vary. In Table 6, the average of 1000 trials, we see injection into pointers has a corresponding increase in the percent of tri-

Table 6. Results of injecting into certain types

	Pointer	Control	Arithmetic	All
Crash	41	29	21	29
More V-Cycles	6	0	6	4
Same V-Cycles	53	71	73	67

als that crash. Likewise injection in the mathematics of AMG, or accessing the wrong data with corrupted pointers, increases the percent of trials that require a higher number of iterations required to converge. We see a small increase in the percent of trials that crash with control injections due taking incorrect paths and incorrect indexing. By the use of these classifications, unique injection campaigns can be created allowing the study of an applications susceptibility to certain types of errors and the effectiveness of detection schemes.

5   Conclusion

As SDCs become more common in HPC, research needs conducted to investigate application resilience and the effectiveness of SDC detectors. This paper presents an LLVM based fault injector designed for HPC that can aid research in this area. Scalability of our fault injector is shown with weak scaling experiments with Hypre. Our fault injector's overhead diminishes as the application's communication begins to dominate computation. To support various application requirements, our fault injector is designed to be extensible. We provide the ability to turn injections on and off from inside the application and use custom probability distributions and logging information. Using the aforementioned features we inject a fault into Hypre at a specific location and time and show that it can significantly impact convergence.

Acknowledgments. This work is sponsored by the Air Force Office of Scientific Research under grant FA9550-12-1-0478. It is also supported by the Blue Waters sustained-petascale computing project, which is supported by the National Science Foundation (awards OCI-0725070 and ACI-1238993) and the state of Illinois. Blue Waters is a joint effort of the University of Illinois at Urbana-Champaign and its National Center for Supercomputing Applications.

References

1. Avizienis, A., Laprie, J.-C., Randell, B., Landwehr, C.: Basic concepts and taxonomy of dependable and secure computing. IEEE Transactions on Dependable and Secure Computing 1(1), 11–33 (2004)
2. Bautista-Gomez, L., Tsuboi, S., Komatitsch, D., Cappello, F., Maruyama, N., Matsuoka, S.: FTI: high performance fault tolerance interface for hybrid systems. In: Proceedings of 2011 International Conference for High Performance Computing, Networking, Storage and Analysis, SC 2011, pp. 32:1–32:32. ACM, New York (2011)
3. Cappello, F., Geist, A., Gropp, B., Kale, L., Kramer, B., Snir, M.: Toward exascale resilience. Int. J. High Perform. Comput. Appl. 23(4), 374–388 (2009)
4. Carreira, J., Madeira, H., Silva, J.G.: Xception: a technique for the experimental evaluation of dependability in modern computers. IEEE Transactions on Software Engineering 24(2), 36–125 (1998)
5. Casas, M., de Supinski, B.R., Bronevetsky, G., Schulz, M.: Fault resilience of the algebraic multi-grid solver. In: Proceedings of the 26th ACM International Conference on Supercomputing, ICS 2012, pp. 91–100. ACM, New York (2012)
6. de Kruijf, M., Nomura, S., Sankaralingam, K.: Relax: An architectural framework for software recovery of hardware faults. In: Proceedings of the 37th International Symposium on Computer Architecture (ISCA) (2010)
7. Fiala, D., Mueller, F., Engelmann, C., Riesen, R., Ferreira, K., Brightwell, R.: Detection and correction of silent data corruption for large-scale high-performance computing. In: Proceedings of the International Conference on High Performance Computing, Networking, Storage and Analysis, SC 2012, pp. 1–78. IEEE Computer Society Press, Los Alamitos (2012)

8. Han, S., Rosenberg, H.A., Shin, K.G.: Doctor: An integrated software fault injection environment (1995)
9. Hargrove, P.H., Duell, J.C.: Berkeley lab checkpoint/restart (BLCR) for linux clusters. Journal of Physics: Conference Series 46(1), 494 (2006)
10. Kogge, P.M., La Fratta, P., Vance, M.: [2010] facing the exascale energy wall. In: Proceedings of the 2010 International Workshop on Innovative Architecture for Future Generation High-Performance Processors and Systems, IWIA 2010, pp. 51–58. IEEE Computer Society, Washington, DC (2010)
11. Lattner, C., Adve, V.: LLVM: A Compilation Framework for Lifelong Program Analysis & Transformation. In: Proceedings of the 2004 International Symposium on Code Generation and Optimization (CGO2004), Palo Alto, California (March 2004)
12. Li, D., Vetter, J.S., Yu, W.: Classifying soft error vulnerabilities in extreme-scale scientific applications using a binary instrumentation tool. In: Proceedings of the International Conference on High Performance Computing, Networking, Storage and Analysis, SC 2012, pp. 57:1–57:11. IEEE Computer Society Press, Los Alamitos (2012)
13. Lu, C.-d., Reed, D.A.: Assessing fault sensitivity in MPI applications. In: Proceedings of the 2004 ACM/IEEE Conference on Supercomputing, SC 2004, p. 37. IEEE Computer Society, Washington, DC (2004)
14. Riesen, R., Ferreira, K., Da Silva, D., Lemarinier, P., Arnold, D., Bridges, P.G.: Alleviating scalability issues of checkpointing protocols. In: Proceedings of the International Conference on High Performance Computing, Networking, Storage and Analysis, SC 2012, pp. 1–18. IEEE Computer Society Press, Los Alamitos (2012)
15. Sato, K., Gamblin, T., Moody, A., de Supinski, B.R., Mohror, K., Maruyama, N.: Design and modeling of non-blocking checkpoint system. In: Proceedings of the ATIP/A*CRC Workshop on Accelerator Technologies for High-Performance Computing: Does Asia Lead the Way?, ATIP 2012, pp. 39:1–39:2. A*STAR Computational Resource Centre, Singapore (2012)
16. Sharma, V.C., Haran, A., Rakamarić, Z., Gopalakrishnan, G.: Towards formal approaches to system resilience. In: Proceedings of the 19th IEEE Pacific Rim International Symposium on Dependable Computing, PRDC (2013)
17. Sridharan, V., Liberty, D.: A study of DRAM failures in the field. In: Proceedings of the International Conference on High Performance Computing, Networking, Storage and Analysis, SC 2012, pp. 76:1–76:11. IEEE Computer Society Press, Los Alamitos (2012)
18. Stott, D.T., Floering, B., Burke, D., Kalbarczyk, Z., Iyer, R.K.: NFTAPE: A framework for assessing dependability in distributed systems with lightweight fault injectors. In: Proceedings of the IEEE International Computer Performance and Dependability Symposium, pp. 91–100 (2000)

Efficient Reliability in Volunteer Storage Systems with Random Linear Coding

Ádám Visegrádi and Péter Kacsuk

Computer and Automation Research Institute,
Hungarian Academy of Sciences, Hungary
{visegradi.adam,kacsuk.peter}@sztaki.mta.hu

Abstract. Volunteer systems pose difficult challenges for data storage. Because of the extremely low reliability of volunteer nodes, these systems require so high redundancy that replication is infeasible. Erasure coding has been proposed to cope with this problem as it needs much less redundancy to achieve the same reliability. Its downside is that the reparation of the system creates high overhead, as fully decoding the original data is required to generate new coded data.

Random linear coding has been proposed to be used as a data storage method, as it provides a better redundancy/reliability ratio, and less control overhead. We propose that it also helps in the reparation of the system, as decoding is not required; instead, coded data can be generated from already existing coded data. However, it may be possible that this iterative reparation leads to degradation of data over time; even more so, if sparse coding is used to increase compute efficiency.

This paper examines the effects of random linear coding and the iterative reparation of the system. It shows the reliability that can be achieved with random linear coding in a highly volatile distributed system. We conclude that random linear coding can achieve high reliability even in highly volatile systems.

1 Introduction

Volunteer and community compute systems use the donated compute capacity of people or organisations. This scheme provides immense computational power for extremely low cost. These volunteers can also contribute storage space to the system; however, this poses difficult architectural challenges.

The main problem is that the nodes of the system are highly unreliable, and that no policy can be enforced on these nodes (cf. grids or clusters). This is not a concern for computation, as any task can be restarted on another node if fails. In data storage however, this unreliability necessitates high redundancy and, therefore, high storage overhead.

More reliable systems, like Hadoop[9] and MapReduce[10] have proven that using cheap commodity hardware is a feasible alternative to expensive RAID storages, but even these systems may require high redundancy overhead to store data reliably. The BOINC[7] volunteer compute middleware is used widely to

L. Lopes et al. (Eds.): Euro-Par 2014 Workshops, Part I, LNCS 8805, pp. 559–569, 2014.

support compute intensive applications for the fraction of the cost of owning a cluster, and it would have ample resources for data intensive applications.[8] However, BOINC does not support data intensive applications well. Although it has support for raw block storage[6], and a data archival solution is being developed[5], it yet lacks a working distributed storage. In any case, the distributed storage system will require redundancy, which decreases the effective storage capacity.

1.1   Achieving Redundancy

The basic way to introduce redundancy is to *replicate* the blocks of the data. Although it is the simplest solution, this approach has major drawbacks. First, the raw storage space required to store some data is the (integer) multiple of the size of the data; and this factor of redundancy has to be very high if the nodes' reliability is low. Second, as failing nodes remove replicas of a block of the data from the system, that block may become rare, impairing locality.

Erasure coding (EC) is an alternative to replication that alleviates both problems of replication, at the cost of CPU time. Erasure coding algorithms—e.g. Reed–Solomon[18] or Fountain codes[17]—create $n > k$ coded blocks from the original data in a way that *any* $k' >= k$ coded blocks will be sufficient for reconstruction. That is, they are block codes with a coding rate (n, k). Because *any* k' block is sufficient for reconstruction, a much lower factor of redundancy is sufficient than in case of replication[21].

Furthermore, in erasure coding, the factor of redundancy does not have to be an integer. Although this seems to be a trifle, but, for instance, the difference between a theoretically required redundancy—given a set of QoS parameters—of 2.1 (erasure coding) and $\lceil 2.1 \rceil = 3$ (replication) can be substantial when there are peta-bytes of data.

The problem with erasure coding is the design complexity of the system, and the overhead required for its reparation[19]. In both cases (replication and EC), when blocks go missing, they have to be complemented. In case of replication, only rare blocks have to be further replicated. In case of erasure coding, to complement the missing blocks, the whole data has to be reconstructed, so new coded blocks can be generated from it[19][12]. Dimakis et al. propose regenerating codes[11] to remedy this problem. Regenerating codes use network coding[4] to communicate encoded packets, which enables the reparation of redundancy without reconstructing the original data. However, if the data is very dispersed and each node stores only one piece of a data object, this approach may not provide many benefits. This can happen in large volunteer systems, which are of particular interest to us. Furthermore, if a deterministic erasure coding scheme is used, then each block will have its own identity, and when a block goes missing, *that* particular block must be complemented. This requires each individual block to be identifiable, which imposes managment overhead on the system.

A promising approach is to use *random linear coding* (RLC) to store the data. Linear coding treats the blocks of data as vectors—and the data itself as a matrix—over a finite field $\mathbb{F}(2^w)$ ($w \geq 1$). Coding is performed by creating linear combinations of the original blocks, while decoding is done by solving the corresponding linear system. Linear coding has been well studied in the area of networking, as an alternative to routing[15, 13]; and random network coding has been proposed as a simple solution for finding suitable coefficients for linear combinations[14].

Random linear coding can be considered to be a *rateless* erasure coding method, as $n > k$ randomly encoded packets can be generated from the original file for any n (rateless), of which any $k' >= k$ will be sufficient for reconstruction (erasure coding). Furthermore, it is stochastically optimal, and it converges to optimal with increasing field size[14]; that is, $P[k' = k] \longrightarrow 1(q \longrightarrow \infty)$.

As a rateless erasure coding, RLC could solve the problems of replication; it would even perform better in terms of redundancy than traditional erasure coding schemes [3]. Also, the problem of reparation in a RLC system would become quite straight-forward: as stored blocks are random linear combinations (r.l.c.) of the original data blocks, a r.l.c. of the *coded* blocks will *also* be a r.l.c. of the *original* blocks. That is, reparation can be done by randomly selecting existing coded blocks from the system, and creating r.l.c.-s of them—we call this *iterative reparation*. With iterative reparation no reconstruction is needed to generate coded data. These properties make RLC a great candidate for coding data in distributed storage scenarios.

A drawback of RLC is that it's CPU intensive. The more blocks we cut the data into (as we increase n), the more reliable the RLC scheme becomes—but increasing n also increases decoding time (linearly). Intuitively, coding „trades" redundancy requirements for CPU requirements. Although this may be problematic in HPC, we have shown[2] that RLC can provide reasonable throughput with the right parameter set.

Furthermore, storage media have considerable delay, particularly when seeking. Therefore, it is but reasonable to perform coding and decoding solely in working memory, which limits the file size. The solution for this is to cut data into *segments* that are coded and encoded independently. This enables us to store arbitrarily large files using RLC.

While a given RLC scheme provides a predictable throughput, segmenting enables us to control the initial delay (decoding the first segment) when decoding successive segments in a stream. Seeking in the stream is also possible, but with the time cost of the initial delay.

In this paper, *file* and *data* refer to such a segment.

1.2   Reliability of a System Using Random Linear Coding

The most interesting question about RLC is what reliability/redundancy ratio can it achieve when the nodes of the underlying system are extremely unreliable; e.g. when 50-90% of the blocks fail between maintenance events.

This question is even more interesting when *sparse coding* is used. In sparse coding, the coefficients in the coding matrix will be set to 0 with a given probability. This alleviates the CPU overhead of RLC (as multiplications with 0 can be omitted), but decreases reliability (greater probability of singular coefficient matrices). Therefore, we hypothesize that the reliability of the system would decrease when the iterative reparation is used with sparse coding because of gradual information loss.

These questions has been addressed in network transfer scenarios[20, 16]. In this paper we present our simulational results showing how RLC performs under specific conditions we consider to represent volunteer storage scenarios.

2   Simulation Framework

2.1   Storage Scheme

We have conceived the following model of a RLC distributed storage system. The system itself is considered as a bag of coded blocks. When storing a file, it is loaded into memory, cut into N blocks, and R coded blocks are generated from it. The coded blocks are generated using linear combinations; each linear combination is a result of multiplying the set of original blocks with a randomly chosen vector of N elements. As sparse coding is used, each coefficient is set to 0 with probability $(1 - A)$; that is, about $A \cdot N$ coefficients will be non-zero.

The system has to be maintained, which means that the coded blocks are *replenished* from time to time. Between replenishing blocks, each block may fail with probability F. That is, our system is a simple iteration of replenishing blocks, where about $100 \cdot F\%$ percent of the blocks fail between iterations. Replenishing blocks takes place only when the number of blocks fall under a certain threshold T, and when it does, so many blocks are generated that the total number of blocks becomes again R. The special case is when $T = R$, that is, when a certain level of redundancy is maintained.

The iteration described is shown in Figure 1; the catalog of parameters is shown in Table 1.

Table 1. Parameters of the simulation

$N \in \{4, 8, ..., 128\}$	The number of blocks the file is cut into.
$A \in \{0.1, 0.2, ..., 1\}$	Probability of a coefficient is selected randomly from $\mathbb{F}\left(2^{16}\right)$. *Otherwise*, it is set to 0.
$F \in \{0, 0.1, ..., 0.9\}$	Probability of a block failing between maintenance events.
$T \in \left\{N, \frac{3}{2}N, 2N, 3N, 4N\right\}$	Threshold for replenishing blocks.
$R \in \left\{N, \frac{3}{2}N, 2N, 3N, 4N\right\}; R > T$	Target redundancy.

Reconstruction and replenishment requires at least N coded blocks to be gathered, as any less than that would produce an under-determined rectangular matrix, which cannot be inverted. On the other hand, RLC is stochastically optimal; that is, with high probability, N coded blocks will be sufficient. Depending on the parameters, it is more or less likely to gather N blocks whose coefficient matrix is singular. In this case, it is not necessary to gather another N blocks. If there is a single vector that is a linear combination of the others, it can be exchanged with a new, randomly selected block. However, finding the offending vector(s) is computationally demanding and is not necessary. The simplest solution is to drop either a randomly selected block, or the one where the Gaussian elimination has failed, and then complement it with one randomly selected from the system. After this change, the probability of the matrix being still singular is even lower.

Therefore, in the unfortunate case when a singular matrix is found, instead of trying every possible combination of vectors (which is infeasible in a distributed system), we try dropping a block from the gathered set and complement it with a random one from the system, never using a block twice. We repeat this process until either we have found a non-singular matrix or we have tried all blocks with no avail. This means an $\omega(N)$–$O(R)$ communication cost, but the upper bound may further be restricted in a particular implementation if necessary. It should also be noted that this overhead is very low, as these operations—that is, the matrix inversion—require transferring only the coefficient vectors, but not the corresponding data blocks.

This strategy is shown in Figure 2.

Input: file
Output: replenish_failed | ∅
1 file_blocks := load_file(file);
2 block_set := replenish(file_blocks, R);
3 **while not** *replenish_failed* **do**
4   block_set =
   remove_randomly(block_set, F);
5   **if** *length(block_set)* < T **then**
6   block_set =
      replenish(block_set, R);
7   **end**
8 **end**

Fig. 1. System maintenance cycle

Input: block_set
Output: working_set | failure
1 candidates := block_set;
2 **for** $i = 1$ **to** N **do**
3   move_random(
4   candidates → working_set);
5 **end**
6 **while** *singular(working_set)*
7   **and** *length(candidates)* ≠ *0* **do**
8   remove_random(working_set);
9   move_random(
10   candidates → working_set);
11 **end**
12 **if** *singular(working_set)*
13   **and** *length(candidates)* = *0* **then**
14   failure := **true**;
15 **end**

Fig. 2. Strategy for gathering a usable block set

2.2 Measurements

We have used our RLC library[1] to implement a simulation framework. This library can perform finite field operations over $\mathbb{F}(2^8)$ and $\mathbb{F}(2^{16})$ using discrete logarithm tables. We have used the finite field $\mathbb{F}\left(2^{16}\right)$ as it is faster and produces a more reliable RLC scheme than $\mathbb{F}\left(2^8\right)$ [2].

In our measurements, we have used one small file of 256 bytes (i.e. 128 finite field elements) with random content, which we cut into $N \in \{4, 8, ..., 128\}$ blocks. The reason to use a small file was that the actual size of the file does not affect its reliability whatsoever; it only affects the de/coding time.

We have performed two kinds of measurements. First, we have measured the reliability of RLC as a function of sparsity (A), without a time dimension (single step). And second, we have measured the reliability of a simulated system over time.

In the single step scenario, the following restrictions were applied to the model. As there is no time dimension, redundancy in the system does not fluctuate; therefore, the redundancy threshold (T) has no meaning, only the target redundancy (R). In this case, lines [3..8] in Figure 1 are not executed; instead, after the generating initial blocks, the data is immediately attempted to be reconstructed using the strategy shown in Figure 2. Also, the failure ratio (F) has no meaning in this case either.

In the simulational scenario, F is introduced in the system to model block failures. The case where $F = 0$ is not evaluated, as it would be identical to the single step scenario. When $F > 0$, the redundancy threshold *must* be greater than the number of blocks: if $N = T$ and $F > 0$, the system is bound to fail before the first maintenance event. Therefore, the $N = T$ case is not evaluated either.

In both cases, the goal was to measure the reliability of the system. Defining reliability as the general ability to reconstruct the original file is not feasible for either of these measurement—neither is in a real world scenario. Denoting the set of coded blocks available in the system with $BlkSet$, this general definition can be formulated as follows: $\exists S \subset BlkSet : |S| = N \wedge \det(\text{coeff\_matrix}(S)) \neq 0$; that is, there is *a* way to reconstruct the data. However, the size of $BlkSet$ can be huge, it is between T and R at any time, and trying all possible combinations $(\omega\binom{T}{N}$ and $O\binom{R}{N}))$ is not feasible. Thus, we define the feasibility of a system as the ability to reconstruct the file using the strategy shown in Figure 2. We measure reliability as the fraction of test cases in which a) the file could be reconstructed from coded data – single step scenario; and b) the file could be reconstructed after several maintenance iterations – simulation scenario. Thus, we define **reliability** as the estimated probability of a file being reconstructable in the system using the aforementioned algorithm. In these measurements, the total number of iterations were limited to 100, and a simulation for each parameter set was repeated 50 times.

As it is possible that this strategy needs to use more than N blocks to reconstruct the data, we also measured **wasted communication**, which we define as the number of *extra* blocks needed to reconstruct the data: total_blocks_needed $- N$.

3   Simulation Results

In this section we present the results of our measurements. Most of the figures presented show the reliability of a system, based on a two-dimensional parameter set, while the reliability (as defined in 2.2) is a value between 0 and 1. These figures present this function in the following way: the two axes of the diagrams pertain to the two dimensions of the parameter space, while the value of reliability is represented as a shade of gray. The black regions (reliability=0) mean that for that parameter set, all experiments have failed, the data could not be reconstructed; while white regions (reliability=1) mean that, in those cases, RLC have not failed at all. As we will show, gray areas are surprisingly narrow, and therefore, we believe that this form of presentation can convey all essential information to the reader.

3.1   Single Step Scenario

This scenario is intended to measure the reliability of RLC itself, without a time dimension. In this scenario, F and T are meaningless. The file is cut into N blocks, R blocks are generated, from which the file is attempted to be reconstructed.

The results of these measurements are shown in Figure 3. The three charts show the results with redundancy factors 1 (no redundancy), 1.5 and 2 respectively. The black area shows the parameter sets where the file could not be reconstructed at all (infeasible parameters). The white area shows the experiments where the file could always be reconstructed (reliable parameters). What immediately meets the eye is that there is little or no gradient between reliable and unfeasible parameter sets (feasible but unreliable parameters). This implicates that if a parameter set is feasible, it is very likely to be reliable too.

Another observation is that for higher values of N, even extremely sparse, $A = 0.1$ coding is feasible. This means that each coefficient is set to 0 with 90% probability, which can theoretically decrease coding time to 1/10th of the non-sparse case.

As stated before, it is possible, that reconstructing a file requires the transfer of more than N blocks. Figure 4 shows the wasted communication cost (as defined in 2.2). Using parameters outside the dashed line (lower left corner), in no experiment were we able to reconstruct the file (infeasible parameters). As these parameters are infeasible, wasted communication is undefined. Inside the dashed line, the lightness of a point represents the average number of extra blocks transferred to reconstruct the file (in this figure, darker is better). Again, the transient area is very narrow, which means that either a parameter set is not feasible (no reconstruction is possible), or it likely generates negligible wasted communication.

3.2   Simulational Scenario

In this scenario we measured the reliability of the system over time, with maintenance events in each interval. We did 100 iterations, and recorded the instant

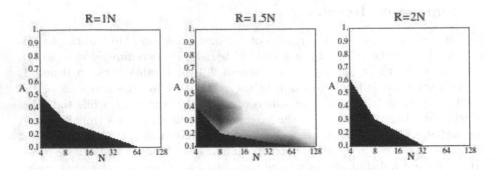

Fig. 3. Reliability as a function of sparsity (A) and the number of original blocks (N)

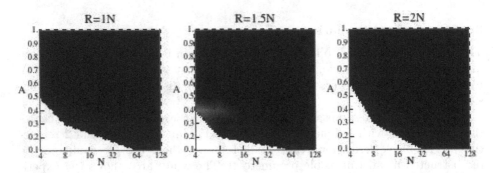

Fig. 4. Average number of wasted blocks as a function of sparsity (A) and the number of original blocks (N)

when the file became unavailable. We considered an experiment successful, if the data did not become unavailable in this time.

For experiments that were *not* successful, we have measured for how long the file was available; that is, we recorded the iteration in which the experiment has failed. In Figure 5, we show how many experiments have failed in that iteration overall. Each line corresponds to a specific value of F; the inner figure is a magnification of the outer one.

In the outer figure, we can see that almost all failed experiment have failed at the beginning. Of the failed experiments, 68% has failed in the first iteration, and more than 90% has failed in the first 15 iteration.

In the inner, magnified figure, we can see that for $F = 0.9$ and 0.8, failure is imminent at the beginning, while for lower values, failure is 1) less likely as time goes on, and 2) the actual value of F does not affect failure much (lines converge together).

In Figure 6 the reliability of the system is shown as a function of N and F, for different factors of redundancy and for two factors of sparsity. In these cases, we used the same values for maintenance threshold and target redundancy ($R = T$). The first row shows the results for $A = 1$, that is, when sparse coding is not used.

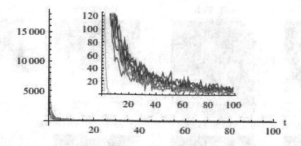

Fig. 5. Number of failed experiments in each iteration (t), for specific values of F

The second row corresponds to $A = 0.5$. From left to right in a row, redundancy increases.

It can be seen that the two rows look very much alike, the only considerable difference being at the "corners" of the reliable sets (white area). This matches the observation of the single step case, that RLC can be very reliable even with low values for A—especially when N is high.

In terms of N, reliability increases with N up to a point, where it plateaus. This peak is reached later if A is lower. This means that to achieve reliability, there is a lower bound on N depending on the reliability of the system (F) and the value we choose for A.

It is also clear—and expected—that using higher factors of redundancy increases the reliability of the system, in that higher values of F can be tolerated (see the increasing plateaus of the white areas). We would like to note here that, for example, Hadoop uses a replication factor of 3 in cluster environments, while our measurements show that, with the same level of redundancy, a failure rate of 50% ($F = 0.5$) can be tolerated by RLC even with sparse coding. Using three-fold *replication*, losing 50% of blocks would very likely make the data unrecoverable.

Also note that although F depends on the properties of the particular system, it is not entirely out of our control. By increasing the frequency of maintenance events, we can decrease the value of F, and therefore we can trade off maintenance network cost for redundancy; that is, network overhead for storage overhead.

We have also examined a scenario where the reparation threshold T was lower than the target redundancy R ($3N$ and $4N$ respectively). We have found that this system behaves the same way as when R and T were both chosen to be $4N$: it plateaus at the same point ($N = 32$), and at the same level ($F = 0.6$). The difference is so subtle, that we have omitted a figures about this case, as the reader could not distinguish them from the right side charts in Figure 6: the average reliability over all cases is slightly lower when $T < R$, the difference is 10^{-3} when $A = 1$ and $3 \cdot 10^{-2}$ when $A = 0.5$. Graphically, this means that gray points would be unnoticeably darker, but the "white area" would be essentially the same. Note that the similar case is the one with the higher redundancy; that is, although we allow the system to degrade to a block count of T, it essentially works like if it was repaired in every maintenance event.

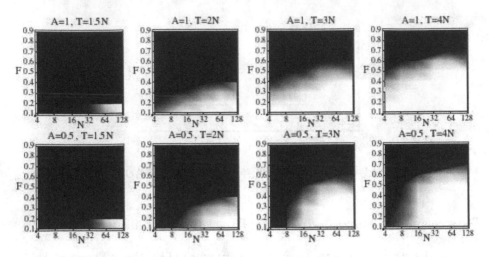

Fig. 6. Reliability as a function of N and F, for specific values of T and A. First row: $A = 1$, second row: $A = 0.5$.

4   Conclusion

In this paper, our goal was to determine the reliability of a distributed storage system employing random linear coding. With random linear coding we are trying to address the extreme challenges posed by volunteer storage systems, which stem from the nodes of a volunteer system being unreliable.

We have experimented with a model which, we believe, captures the main properties of a volunteer storage reasonably well; and used parameters that emulate the unreliability of such a system.

We have shown that random linear coding performs surprisingly well under such conditions, and can tolerate huge loss of data even when redundancy is relatively low. We have also shown that it achieves this reliability with virtually no wasted bandwidth. Furthermore, while using sparse coding is good solution for random linear coding being CPU intensive, its effects on the reliability are negligible.

Based on these results we conclude that random linear coding is a suitable solution for volunteer storage systems; therefore, we feel confident implementing such a storage system in the future on top of the BOINC middleware to support data intensive applications on volunteer computing platforms.

References

[1] Random Network Coding Library, https://github.com/avisegradi/rnc-lib (accessed: September 10, 2013)
[2] Efficient Random Network Coding for Distributed Storage Systems, Ádám Visegrádi and Péter Kacsuk. Euro-Par 2013, MHPC Workshop (2013) (in press)

[3] Acedanski, S., Deb, S., Médard, M., Koetter, R.: How good is random linear coding based distributed networked storage. In: Workshop on Network Coding, Theory and Applications (2005)

[4] Ahlswede, R., Cai, N., Li, S.Y.R., Yeung, R.W.: Network information flow. IEEE Transactions on Information Theory 46(4), 1204–1216 (2000)

[5] Anderson, D.: BOINC volunteer data archival, https://boinc.berkeley.edu/trac/wiki/VolunteerDataArchival (accessed January 2014)

[6] Anderson, D.: BOINC volunteer storage, https://boinc.berkeley.edu/trac/wiki/VolunteerStorage (accessed January 2014)

[7] Anderson, D.P.: BOINC: a system for public-resource computing and storage. In: Proceedings of the Fifth IEEE/ACM International Workshop on Grid Computing, pp. 4–10 (November 2004)

[8] Anderson, D.P., Fedak, G.: The computational and storage potential of volunteer computing. In: Sixth IEEE International Symposium on Cluster Computing and the Grid, CCGRID 2006, vol. 1, pp. 73–80. IEEE (2006)

[9] Borthakur, D.: The hadoop distributed file system: Architecture and design. Hadoop Project Website 11(21) (2007)

[10] Dean, J., Ghemawat, S.: MapReduce: simplified data processing on large clusters. Communications of the ACM 51(1), 107–113 (2008)

[11] Dimakis, A.G., Godfrey, P.B., Wu, Y., Wainwright, M.J., Ramchandran, K.: Network coding for distributed storage systems. IEEE Transactions on Information Theory 56(9), 4539–4551 (2010)

[12] Dimakis, A.G., Ramchandran, K., Wu, Y., Suh, C.: A survey on network codes for distributed storage. Proceedings of the IEEE 99(3), 476–489 (2011)

[13] Fragouli, C., Le Boudec, J.-Y., Widmer, J.: Network coding: an instant primer. ACM SIGCOMM Computer Communication Review 36(1), 63–68 (2006)

[14] Ho, T., Médard, M., Koetter, R., Karger, D., Effros, M., Shi, J., Leong, B.: A random linear network coding approach to multicast. IEEE Transactions on Information Theory 52(10), 4413–4430 (2006)

[15] Li, S.-Y.R., Yeung, R.W., Cai, N.: Linear network coding. IEEE Transactions on Information Theory 49(2), 371–381 (2003)

[16] Ma, G., Xu, Y., Lin, M., Xuan, Y.: A content distribution system based on sparse linear network coding. In: NetCod 2007 (2007)

[17] MacKay, D.J.C.: Fountain codes. IEEE Proceedings Communications 152, 1062–1068 (2005)

[18] Reed, I., Solomon, G.: Polynomial codes over certain finite fields. Journal of the Society for Industrial & Applied Mathematics 8(2), 300–304 (1960)

[19] Rodrigues, R., Zhou, T.H.: High availability in dHTs: Erasure coding vs. Replication. In: van Renesse, R. (ed.) IPTPS 2005. LNCS, vol. 3640, pp. 226–239. Springer, Heidelberg (2005)

[20] Wang, M., Li, B.: How practical is network coding? In: 14th IEEE International Workshop on Quality of Service, IWQoS 2006, pp. 274–278 (2006)

[21] Weatherspoon, H., Kubiatowicz, J.D.: Erasure coding vs. Replication: A quantitative comparison. In: Druschel, P., Kaashoek, M.F., Rowstron, A. (eds.) IPTPS 2002. LNCS, vol. 2429, p. 328. Springer, Heidelberg (2002)

What Is the Right Balance for Performance and Isolation with Virtualization in HPC?[*]

Thomas Naughton[1,2,**], Garry Smith[2], Christian Engelmann[1], Geoffroy Vallée[1], Ferrol Aderholdt[3], and Stephen L. Scott[1,3]

[1] Oak Ridge National Laboratory,
Computer Science and Mathematics Division,
Oak Ridge, TN 37831, USA
naughtont@ornl.gov
[2] The University of Reading
Reading, RG6 6AH, UK
[3] Tennessee Tech University
Computer Science
Cookville, TN, 38505, USA

Abstract. The use of virtualization in high-performance computing (HPC) has been suggested as a means to provide tailored services and added functionality that many users expect from full-featured Linux cluster environments. While the use of virtual machines in HPC can offer several benefits, maintaining performance is a crucial factor. In some instances performance criteria are placed above isolation properties and selective relaxation of isolation for performance is an important characteristic when considering resilience for HPC environments employing virtualization.

In this paper we consider some of the factors associated with balancing performance and isolation in configurations that employ virtual machines. In this context, we propose a classification of errors based on the concept of "error zones", as well as a detailed analysis of the trade-offs between resilience and performance based on the level of isolation provided by virtualization solutions. Finally, the results from a set of experiments are presented, that use different virtualization solutions, and in doing so allow further elucidation of the topic.

1 Introduction

As high-performance computing (HPC) systems increase in size and complexity, the associated system software faces new challenges to balance performance, usability and robustness. The use of virtualization in HPC has gained attention in recent years [4,9,13,15,20,21,23,24,6], mainly for enabling isolation, customization and resilience abilities. The benefit of having a user-customized execution environment is one advantage [5,21,23]. Also, the ability to provide increased functionality without having

---

[*] The submitted manuscript has been authored by a contractor of the U.S. Government under Contract No. DE-AC05-00OR22725. Accordingly, the U.S. Government retains a non-exclusive, royalty-free license to publish or reproduce the published form of this contribution, or allow others to do so, for U.S. Government purposes.

[**] Corresponding author.

L. Lopes et al. (Eds.): Euro-Par 2014 Workshops, Part I, LNCS 8805, pp. 570–581, 2014.
© Springer International Publishing Switzerland 2014

to require this in all instances is another use case [4,20]. For example, microkernels have been used on several supercomputers to achieve minimal system-level interference [20], i.e., *"the OS should stay out of the way"*. Adding the ability to load virtual machines (VMs) that run more feature rich operating system (OS) environments is one way to balance usability and performance, while maintaining the ability to run natively on the microkernel to achieve the full performance potential [20]. In the context of system resilience, virtualization enables both advanced reactive and pro-active policies by providing capabilities such as VM migration and checkpoint/restart [22]. Furthermore, virtualization has been leveraged for the design and implementation of fault injection techniques in order to study the impact of failures on the execution of scientific simulations [17,16]. These capabilities usually rely on isolation characteristics of virtualization solutions, i.e., isolation decouples the management of resources exposed within the VM from the physical resources, making the VMs independent from the host on which they run.

The HPC community recently introduced the concept of *enclave* as an operating and runtime system design characteristic for addressing current scalability, resilience and performance limitations at extreme scale. For instance, the Hobbes project, which aims at designing operating system/runtime (OS/R) interfaces for extreme-scale systems [4], defines an enclave as *"a partition of the system allocated to a single application or service"* and has proposed a design based on system-level virtualization. Figure 1 shows a diagram of the proposed Hobbes software architecture. The project is focused on techniques to support composition primitives to aid applications and leverages system-level virtualization to provide flexible support for additional OS/R functionality. Resilience is one of the cross-cutting concerns the Hobbes project is seeking to address. This includes work on developing resilience building blocks as well as work to experiment with error management in system software. As new OS/R interfaces are developed, the robustness of the overall system will be probed to identify areas for improvement.

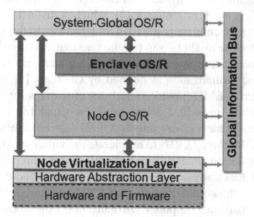

Fig. 1. Hobbes software components for Extreme-Scale OS/R [4]. The component API interactions are reflected by vertical arrows and data exchanges via horizontal arrows; research targets are shown in **bold**.

As HPC software stacks begin to leverage virtualization, questions emerge about what degree of isolation should be maintained to keep applications running efficiently without overly sacrificing fault management primitives (i.e., isolation mechanisms). Since virtualization is an important component of the OS/R research for next generation system software, we consider *the trade-offs and perspectives for balancing performance and isolation* in this context.

The primary contributions of this paper are to study the balance for performance and isolation in the context of HPC resilience. The examination contributes to the more general topic of error models in HPC. The paper discusses: (i) a classification of errors in the context of HPC resilience and HPC virtualization; (ii) an analysis of the trade-offs between performance and isolation for HPC workloads and its impact on system resilience, especially in the context of the Hobbes project; and (iii) experiments that demonstrate variations in the effects of synthetic errors in virtualized environments.

The remainder of the paper is organized as follows, in Section 2 we review related work and provide background information on the topic of virtualization in HPC. In Section 3 we analyze the problem of balancing performance and isolation with VM-based HPC environments, followed by an evaluation of an example error scenario using different virtualization solutions in Section 4. Finally we conclude in Section 5.

2   Background

The *Palacios* virtual machine monitor (VMM) was developed from scratch by Northwestern University (NU) and University of New Mexico (UNM), in cooperation with Sandia National Laboratories (SNL) [18,13]. The Palacios VMM can be run on the *Kitten* microkernel [11,13] and as a loadable kernel module on Linux based systems. The VMM requires the hardware to support virtualization extensions, e.g., AMD-V and Intel VT. Palacios runs on standard x86 commodity clusters and Cray XT 4/5 & XK6/7 supercomputers. Palacios guest VMs can run either 32-bit or 64-bit OS kernels.

The *QEMU* tool is a machine emulator [3], which is distinct from a type-II VMM proper [7] because it may emulate non-native architectures to the guest. For example, the native host architecture might be x86 but the guest virtual machine (VM) could see an ARM or MIPS architecture in the emulated environment. However, the distinction between emulator and virtualization as defined by Goldberg [7] is less important for the the current context. QEMU provides a rich set of features for interfacing with the machine monitor and an embedded debugger. These capabilities make it a common component in OS development environments. QEMU can be combined with the Linux *Kernel-based Virtual Machine (KVM)* to accelerate the virtual machine execution [14]. This removes the emulation capabilities of QEMU and requires the VM and host architectures match. It does however provide the rich frontend and debugger capabilities of QEMU for use with the kernel-implemented KVM backend. KVM runs on x86 machines and requires hardware supported virtualization extensions, e.g., AMD-V and Intel VT. The widespread use of Linux has led to KVM being widely used for type-II virtualization due to its seamless integration with the OS distributions.

The presence of virtualization in HPC be limited and virtual machines may not be supported on all systems. However, virtualization is becoming more widely available and is slowly becoming just another system software feature, especially for environments that use Linux as their base operating system. The Palacios VMM was specifically developed with HPC environments as a target and is under active development for use on Cray supercomputers, e.g., Cray XK7. The KVM VMM is a standard component in modern Linux distributions. Additionally, the QEMU environment can be run entirely in user-space without the need for advanced permissions (i.e., does not require `root` privileges), albeit at a lower performance level if acceleration like KVM or kqemu is not used.

3 Analysis

Virtualization. The management of unprivileged *user-space* and privileged *kernel-space* is a standard approach for OS protection. For example, on x86-based systems the hardware offers protection domains, or "rings" (Figure 2), that can be used to enforce this user/kernel separation [10]. System-level virtualization extends the protection layers by adjusting the protection domains to have the virtual machine monitor run at the highest protection level in order to marshal access to physical resources [19]. The result is a guest/host (virtual/native) separation, which places the standard OS user/kernel within a virtual region, i.e., a guest VM. The guest VM runs the OS and the VMM provides a software layer between the guest OS and the physical resources. While overly simplified, this description captures the divisions used to provide stronger isolation between the guest environment (virtual) from the host environment (native).

As mentioned previously, the OS/R marshals access to hardware resources, e.g., CPU, main memory, network interfaces and I/O (storage) devices. The overhead for providing protection is often governed by whether the isolation mechanism is hardware or software based. For example, the cost for unprivileged CPU instructions is equivalent for guest/user and host/user. When managing memory, if there is no hardware-level support (e.g., nested page tables), then shadow pages must be managed in software. The CPU and memory resources are fairly well supported at this stage with hardware level protection mechanisms. In contrast, the multiplexing of network and I/O devices for virtualized environment often requires software based methods. New technology

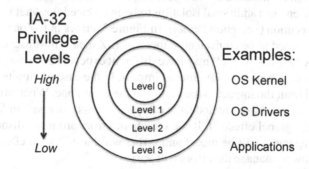

Fig. 2. Intel Architecture (IA-32) hardware supported protection mechanisms provide four privilege levels: high (Level 0) e.g., OS, low (Level 3) e.g., Applications [10]

like Single Root I/O Virtualization (SR-IOV) and IOMMU should help decrease this overhead as they become more widely available.

Resilience. Resilience is an important aspect for HPC systems and is a cross-cutting topic in the Hobbes project. To be clear, we begin by briefly reviewing a bit of resilience terminology from Laprie et al. [1]. A *fault* is a defect that exists and may be "active" or "dormant", and an "active fault" is an *error*. An error that is not contained, e.g., resulting in service interruption, creates a *failure*. There are numerous potential faults, which can originate at different phases: design, implementation, operation, etc. An error model provides an abstraction of the potential faults that may occur and offers structure to help understand and reason about erroneous behavior in a system [8].

Virtualization and Resilience. The kernel/user and guest/host structure described previously provides different *error zones* ("E-Zones") as shown in Figure 3. For example, in a non-virtualized setting, errors in E-Zone#1 (host/kernel) are often considered fatal, and can result in the entire system being compromised or crashing. In contrast, errors in E-Zone#2 (host/user) may be fatal but would (generally) only affect the victim process and should never crash the full system.

	Kernel	**User**
Host	E-Zone #1	E-Zone #2
Guest	E-Zone #3	E-Zone #4

Fig. 3. Error zones for standard and virtualized systems

Adding virtualization to the system offers additional error zones, where the kernel/user separation is enhanced by incorporating an additional layer for protection (i.e., guest/host). This enables additional isolation to be introduced for what would normally be privileged execution (i.e., guest kernel). In Figure 3, errors in E-Zone#4 (guest/user) are generally assumed to be equivalent to those of E-Zone#2 (host/user). However, the errors in E-Zone#3 (guest/kernel) may have different expected behavior. The effects of errors may have very broad or very limited impact. In the case of "limited effects", the isolation should limit the impact to the victim in the error zone. When errors may have a broader impact, e.g., the entire node, the effects of errors can result in failures for the full system (i.e., "global effects"). If the effects of errors are more disparate then the associated management will be mixed and errors will have "varied effects". Restated, the policy for how to manage the errors will vary.

In summary, the error model for this virtualization-enabled context (Figure 3) is:

E-Zone#1 – errors may crash full system (global effects)
E-Zone#2 – errors may crash individual victim (limited effects)
E-Zone#3 – errors may crash full system (global effects), *or*
          errors may be managed in mixed manner (varied effects), *or*
          errors may crash individual victim (limited effects)
E-Zone#4 – errors may crash individual victim (limited effects)

The reason for the variation in the error model for E-Zone#3 instances is mainly due to the balance between isolation and performance. Figure 4 illustrates this isolation/performance continuum. In some instances, strong isolation is the most critical criteria and may outweigh performance criteria. For example, if there are many virtual machines on a single host (i.e., web hosting platforms with direct user access) the protection against a user crashing a virtual machine and indirectly crashing the host (and all other users) is more critical than individual user performance. In contrast, more relaxed isolation may be appropriate if performance is important and reasonable protection mechanisms can be used that offer an acceptable level of control.

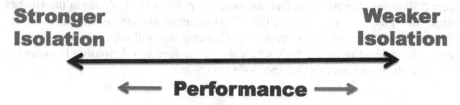

Fig. 4. Performance / Isolation continuum

Notice that in the case that strong isolation is the highest criteria, then E-Zone#3 is equivalent to E-Zone#4 in order to limit the effects of errors. Additionally, if performance is the most important criteria (even at the cost of isolation) then E-Zone#3 can devolve to being equivalent to E-Zone#1, where errors have a global effect. As such, a guest/kernel error could crash the full system and have an impact on the entire node (global effects).

The case where E-Zone#3 ≡ E-Zone#1 is still (potentially) a valid case in some HPC contexts. For example, one motivation mentioned previously for virtualization in HPC was to provide additional functionality beyond what is provided by the default microkernel case. In this scenario, virtualization enables users to run full-featured legacy OS instances in VMs on top of the native microkernel OS [20]. Therefore, this error model (E-Zone#3 ≡ E-Zone#1) may be appropriate as the objective is not added protection, but added functionality.

Hobbes Context. The Hobbes project is interested in system software for next-generation systems. This research includes work in designing OS/R interfaces for large-scale HPC systems. There are two key distinguishing elements to the project: (i) enclaves and (ii) composition. An enclave is a partitioned region given to a particular application or service [2,4]. Enclaves house applications and therefore will be composed to form more complex application instances [4]. Virtualization can be used to implement this partitioning and isolation between enclaves. Therefore, enclave composition will require selectively relaxing the isolation to accommodate the required interactions between the OS instances, which are shown in Figure 1 [4].

An important step in the resilience effort for the Hobbes project, and HPC in general, is to begin to refine the error models. As such, we begin by presenting our initial thoughts on an error model that takes into consideration the distinguishing elements of Hobbes, namely: enclaves and composition.

Based on this, an important question for the Hobbes project will be to identify instances where the E-Zone#3 model can employ mixed policies for error management. This is likely to be influenced by the performance cost for implementing the isolation. Additionally, in the Hobbes context the E-Zone#3 policies will be influenced by enclave composition. For example, consider the previously noted case where the objective is to offer increased functionality via virtualization, so E-Zone#3 $\equiv$ E-Zone#1 may be appropriate. When composing different enclaves, this may be less straightforward due to cross-enclave dependencies that should limit indirect effects. Restated, crashing a single enclave (VM) may be acceptable but if there are multiple enclaves (VMs) then the isolation may need to be increased to avoid indirectly affecting another instance. Figure 5 illustrates the two axes that influence the policies for E-Zones in the Hobbes context. In Figure 5(a), two Enclave OS (EOS) instances are shown and reflect the relationship during enclave composition. The other case that will influence the balance of isolation is depicted in Figure 5(b), which shows the vertical relationship between the Node Virtualization Layer (NVL) and Node OS (NOS).

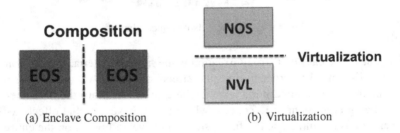

(a) Enclave Composition   (b) Virtualization

Fig. 5. Diagrams showing two key building blocks in the Hobbes design: (a) enclave composition, and (b) virtualization

4   Evaluation

We performed a set of tests to demonstrate the viability of leveraging VMs to improve protection during fault-injection experiments. The experiments presented in this section demonstrate the following: (i) host OS system log (syslog) monitor to notify when violations occur in a Palacios guest VM based on guest OS heartbeats; (ii) demonstration of VM isolation to avoid corruption of host context.

4.1 Setup

The host OS was Linux v3.5.0. KVM was version v1.0+noroms-0ubuntu13, which was installed from the Ubuntu 12.04 LTS packages. QEMU was v1.7.0, which was installed from source. Palacios was Git clone 619573f (11-mar-2014) with minor patches for compilation issues under Linux v3.5.0. The KVM and Palacios VMMs are implemented as loadable kernel modules and were loaded exclusively, i.e., only one module was active during the tests. The QEMU VMM was run without the acceleration support and ran entirely as a user-space application.

The guest OS used a Linux v2.6.33.7 kernel with Busybox v1.20 to create a very small system installation. In the Palacios case, the guest VM is configured to use shadow paging with a Linux virtio-based NIC that is bridged via the VMM to the host network interface. The KVM and QEMU cases did not have networking enabled during the tests.

All tests were performed on a Linux cluster (*SAL9000*) at ORNL. The machine was configured with a dual-bonded 1 Gbps Ethernet interconnect. The 40 compute nodes each have 2 AMD64 CPU (24 cores), a Nvidia Tesla S2050 GPU, 64 GB of memory, and run a Ubuntu Linux 12.04 LTS operating system. The guest OS startup script files were updated to automatically load a custom fault-injection (FI) kernel module (described below). The guest OS configuration was identical in all tests, as was the host OS configuration. The only differences between test runs were related to the virtualization solution being used. The experiments were all run on a single compute node (node40) of the SAL9000 cluster.

4.2 Guest OS Errors

The experiments use different virtualization solutions to demonstrate the isolation provided by VMs. The three virtualization implementations used during these tests were: QEMU [3], KVM [19,14], and Palacios [13,18].

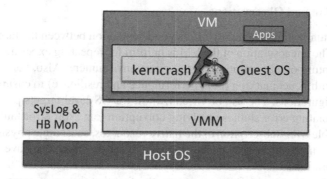

Fig. 6. Diagram showing the VM+FI harness with an OS Kernel crash running in the Guest VM, isolated from the host context managing the experiment

A custom kernel module (`kerncrash`) was written to intentionally cause a failure when a timer expired. The kernel module would perform a divide-by-zero error that forced a fatal exception that would crash the kernel. When the module is loaded into the kernel it sets a timer and after N seconds the error occurs. The tests used manual inspection to confirm that the kernel crashed based on console output, which could also have been obtained from system logs if the VM was forwarding the syslogs over the network or to the host via a virtual serial log. The integrity of the host was determined by whether or not the host was responsive after the crash for running further tests. Figure 6 depicts the self-injected error in the guest OS.

4.3 Testing

The experiments that introduced guest OS errors show the benefits of running with strong isolation. The fatal guest OS experiments were each run 5 times on a single node of the SAL9000 cluster. As expected, the `kerncrash` resulted in a fatal guest kernel error in all instances. The KVM and QEMU test cases offered a clear separation with no change in the host after the guest OS's kernel crash. In the Palacios case the results were mixed. When run on SAL9000, the host became unstable soon after the guest crashed and required a reboot to resolve the issue. At the time of writing, the root cause for this error has not been determined but additional testing on another development machine indicated that the problem might be due to some shared networking used by the Palacios guest. The preliminary investigation indicated that this might be related to the virtual network bridge that Palacios establishes between the host and guest to provide network access in the guest VM. Subsequent experiments on a different machine resulted in similar disruptions of the host environment and showed a Palacios-related kernel thread that was responsible for much of the load (a network related routine running as Linux kernel thread in host OS). This may be a host-level misconfiguration or more simply an implementation bug.

4.4 Discussion and Observations

The use of virtualization potentially offers good separation between the target and control harness. The encapsulation of the VM is helpful for repeating experiments, and can be used to capture output and monitor the guest environment. Also, the reproducibility is useful with benchmarking (both performance and resilience) to ensure consistent machine configurations. The use of virtualization for OS-level targets provides useful support for isolating error studies involving corruption (e.g., soft error fault injection). VMs also enable over-subscription of the native resources, so a single physical machine can be used to run multiple tests concurrently or in series, which can have entirely different configurations.

In the low-level system software use case, the fact that the exact same environment with the exact same OS and synthetic bug could be reproduced on the same hardware platform is a clear benefit of using VMs for resilience investigations. It also allows for repeatable research and low-level debugging capabilities, e.g., VMM embedded debugger in QEMU. The issues raised during testing with Palacios and host/guest sharing highlight a more fundamental point to consider when working with virtualization and

HPC. There are many instances where the isolation properties are intentionally relaxed to gain performance. For example, the host network interface might be directly mapped into the guest OS to provide near native performance from within the guest environment. This might also be due to the fact that the network device is not easily virtualizable, i.e., not able to multiplex between the host and guest OS. These are factors that must be considered when using VMs in a HPC context for performance reasons and they are factors that must be managed when used for resilience investigations.

5   Conclusion

This paper discussed details associated with resilience for virtualization-based HPC systems. In this context, we propose a new error model as well as an initial evaluation. Thus, our contributions are (i) a classification of the various errors, (ii) an analysis of the resilience/isolation trade-offs, and (iii) a set of experiments to elucidate the discussion.

The proposed classification is based on the distinctions between four "error zones" and different scenarios were outlined to illustrate the applicability of the concept to HPC. Experiments were performed that reflected three different data points along the isolation/performance continuum: QEMU, KVM, and Palacios. Finally, we presented an analysis of how the concept of error zones can be used in the context of the Hobbes project, which aims at developing OS/R interfaces for extreme-scale systems. More precisely, we analyzed the impact of failures on the overall Hobbes' architecture, especially on the composition capability. Ultimately, this study provides input to help respond to questions about errors in HPC environments, and more specifically in cases where virtualization is used.

The current focus has been to refine the error models to provide structure to guide the research into resilience, which can be beneficial for the Hobbes project. In future work, as the OS/R interfaces for the Hobbes software stack (Figure 1) are published, we plan to perform robustness testing [12] on the APIs. The intent is to identify any weakness in the interfaces and offer feedback for improvements in system-level resilience.

References

1. Avižienis, A., Laprie, J.C., Randell, B., Landwehr, C.: Basic concepts and taxonomy of dependable and secure computing. IEEE Transactions on Dependable and Secure Computing (TDSC) 1(1), 11–33 (2004), http://dx.doi.org/10.1109/TDSC.2004.2

2. Beckman, P., Brightwell, R., de Supinski, B.R., Gokhale, M., Hofmeyr, S., Krishnamoorthy, S., Lang, M., Maccabe, B., Shalf, J., Snir, M.: Exascale Operating Systems and Runtime Software Report. Tech. rep., U. S. Department of Energy (December 28, 2012)

3. Bellard, F.: QEMU, a fast and portable dynamic translator. In: USENIX 2005 Annual Technical Conference. Anaheim, CA, USA (April 2005)

4. Brightwell, R., Oldfield, R., Maccabe, A.B., Bernholdt, D.E.: Hobbes: Composition and virtualization as the foundations of an extreme-scale OS/R. In: Proceedings of the 3rd International Workshop on Runtime and Operating Systems for Supercomputers (ROSS 2013), pp. 2:1–2:8. ACM, New York, http://doi.acm.org/10.1145/2491661.2481427

5. Engelmann, C., Scott, S.L., Ong, H., Vallée, G., Naughton, T.: Configurable Virtualized System Environments for High Performance Computing. In: Proceedings of the 1st Workshop on System-level Virtualization for High Performance Computing (HPCVirt 2007), Held in Conjunction with the ACM EuroSys 2007, Lisbon, Portugal (March 20, 2007), http://www.csm.ornl.gov/srt/hpcvirt07
6. Gallard, J., Lèbre, A., Vallée, G., Morin, C., Gallard, P., Scott, S.L.: Refinement proposal of the goldberg's theory. In: Hua, A., Chang, S.-L. (eds.) ICA3PP 2009. LNCS, vol. 5574, pp. 853–865. Springer, Heidelberg (2009)
7. Goldberg, R.P.: Architecture of Virtual Machines. In: Proceedings of the Workshop on Virtual Computer Systems, pp. 74–112. ACM Press, New York (1973)
8. Goloubeva, O., Rebaudengo, M., Reorda, M.S., Violante, M.: Software-Implemented Hardware Fault Tolerance. Springer (August 2006)
9. Huang, W., Liu, J., Abali, B., Panda, D.K.: A case for high performance computing with virtual machines. In: ICS 2006: Proceedings of the 20th annual international conference on Supercomputing, pp. 125–134. ACM Press, New York (2006)
10. Intel® Corporation: Intel® 64 and IA-32 Architectures Software Developer's Manual – Volume 1: Basic Architecture (February 2014), http://www.intel.com/products/processor/manuals, Order Number: 253665-050US
11. Kitten lightweight kernel, https://software.sandia.gov/trac/kitten (last visited: August 29, 2009)
12. Koopman, P., DeVale, J.: The exception handling effectiveness of POSIX operating systems. IEEE Transactions on Software Engineering 26(9), 837–848 (2000)
13. Lange, J., Pedretti, K., Hudson, T., Dinda, P., Cui, Z., Xia, L., Bridges, P., Gocke, A., Jaconette, S., Levenhagen, M., Brightwell, R.: Palacios and Kitten: New high performance operating systems for scalable virtualized and native supercomputing. In: IEEE International Symposium on Parallel Distributed Processing (IPDPS), pp. 1–12 (April 2010)
14. Linux Kernel-based Virtual Machine (KVM), http://www.linux-kvm.org, http://www.linux-kvm.org (last visited: March 30, 2014)
15. Liu, J., Huang, W., Abali, B., Panda, D.K.: High performance VMM-Bypass I/O in virtual machines. In: Proceedings of the Annual USENIX Technical Conference (USENIX 2006), pp. 29–42. USENIX Association (2006), http://www.usenix.org/events/usenix06/tech/liu.html
16. Naughton, T., Bland, W., Vallée, G.R., Engelmann, C., Scott, S.L.: Fault Injection Framework for System Resilience Evaluation: Fake Faults for Finding Future Failures. In: Proceedings of the 2nd Workshop on Resiliency in High Performance Computing (Resilience 2009), ACM Press, New York (June 9, 2009); held in conjunction with HPDC 2009, Munich, Germany
17. Naughton, T., Vallée, G., Engelmann, C., Scott, S.L.: A case for virtual machine based fault injection in a high-performance computing environment. In: Alexander, M., et al. (eds.) Euro-Par 2011, Part I. LNCS, vol. 7155, pp. 234–243. Springer, Heidelberg (2012)
18. Palacios: An OS independent embeddable VMM, http://v3vee.org/palacios, Project URL: http://v3vee.org/palacios/ (Last visited: April 26, 2014).
19. RedHat: (Whitepaper) KVM - Kernel-based Virtual Machine (September 1, 2008), http://www.redhat.com/resourcelibrary/whitepapers/doc-kvm (last visited: April 1, 2014).
20. Riesen, R., Brightwell, R., Bridges, P.G., Hudson, T., Maccabe, A.B., Widener, P.M., Ferreira, K.: Designing and implementing lightweight kernels for capability computing. Concurrency and Computation: Practice and Experience 21(6), 793–817 (2009), http://dx.doi.org/10.1002/cpe.1361

21. Scott, S.L., Vallée, G., Naughton, T., Tikotekar, A., Engelmann, C., Ong, H.: Research on System-Level Virtualization at the Oak Ridge National Laboratory. Future Generation Computer Systems (2009)
22. Vallée, G., Naughton, T., Ong, H., Scott, S.L.: Checkpoint/restart of virtual machines based on xen. In: HAPCW 2006: High Availability and Performance Computing Workshop. Held in conjunction with LACSI 2006, Santa Fe, New Mexico, USA (October 2006)
23. Vallée, G.R., Naughton, T., Engelmann, C., Ong, H.H., Scott, S.L.: System-level virtualization for high performance computing. In: Proceedings of the 16th Euromicro International Conference on Parallel, Distributed, and network-based Processing (PDP), February 13-15, pp. 636–643. IEEE Computer Society, Los Alamitos (2008),
http://www.csm.ornl.gov/~engelman/
publications/vallee08system.pdf
24. Youseff, L., Seymour, K., You, H., Dongarra, J., Wolski, R.: The impact of paravirtualized memory hierarchy on linear algebra computational kernels and software. In: Proceedings of the 17th International Symposium on High Performance Distributed Computing (HPDC 2008), pp. 141–152. ACM, New York (2008)

Author Index